Read this book online today:

With SAP PRESS BooksOnline we offer you online access to knowledge from the leading SAP experts. Whether you use it as a beneficial supplement or as an alternative to the printed book, with SAP PRESS BooksOnline you can:

- Access your book anywhere, at any time. All you need is an Internet connection.
- Perform full text searches on your book and on the entire SAP PRESS library.
- Build your own personalized SAP library.

The SAP PRESS customer advantage:

Register this book today at *www.sap-press.com* and obtain exclusive free trial access to its online version. If you like it (and we think you will), you can choose to purchase permanent, unrestricted access to the online edition at a very special price!

Here's how to get started:

1. Visit *www.sap-press.com*.
2. Click on the link for SAP PRESS BooksOnline and login (or create an account).
3. Enter your free trial license key, shown below in the corner of the page.
4. Try out your online book with full, unrestricted access for a limited time!

Your personal free trial **license key** for this online book is:

93re-m8kq-24z5-uvis

Reporting and Analysis with SAP® BusinessObjects™

SAP PRESS is a joint initiative of SAP and Galileo Press. The know-how offered by SAP specialists combined with the expertise of the Galileo Press publishing house offers the reader expert books in the field. SAP PRESS features first-hand information and expert advice, and provides useful skills for professional decision-making.

SAP PRESS offers a variety of books on technical and business related topics for the SAP user. For further information, please visit our website: www.sap-press.com.

Loren Heilig et al.
SAP NetWeaver BW and SAP BusinessObjects: The Comprehensive Guide
2012, 795 pp., hardcover
978-1-59229-384-1

Coy Yonce
100 Things You Should Know About Reporting with SAP Crystal Reports
2012, 344 pp., hardcover
978-1-59229-390-2

Ingo Hilgefort
Inside SAP BusinessObjects Advanced Analysis
2011, 343 pp., hardcover
978-1-59229-371-1

Jim Brogden, Heather Sinkwitz, Mac Holden
SAP BusinessObjects Web Intelligence
2010, 583 pp., hardcover
978-1-59229-322-3

Ingo Hilgefort

Reporting and Analysis with SAP® BusinessObjects™

Bonn • Boston

Galileo Press is named after the Italian physicist, mathematician and philosopher Galileo Galilei (1564—1642). He is known as one of the founders of modern science and an advocate of our contemporary, heliocentric worldview. His words *Eppur si muove* (And yet it moves) have become legendary. The Galileo Press logo depicts Jupiter orbited by the four Galilean moons, which were discovered by Galileo in 1610.

Editor Kelly Grace Harris
Copyeditor Pamela Siska
Cover Design Graham Geary
Photo Credit iStockphoto.com/fpm
Layout Design Vera Brauner
Production Kelly O'Callaghan, Graham Geary
Typesetting SatzPro, Krefeld (Germany)
Printed and bound in the United States of America

ISBN 978-1-59229-387-2

© 2012 by Galileo Press Inc., Boston (MA)
2nd edition 2012

Library of Congress Cataloging-in-Publication Data
Hilgefort, Ingo.
Reporting and analysis with SAP BusinessObjects / Ingo Hilgefort. -- 2nd ed.
    p. cm.
ISBN 978-1-59229-387-2 -- ISBN 1-59229-387-5
1. BusinessObjects. 2. SAP NetWeaver BW. 3. SAP ERP. 4. Management information systems. 5. Business intelligence--Data processing. I. Title.
HF5548.4.B875H55 2012
005.74--dc23
2011044767

All rights reserved. Neither this publication nor any part of it may be copied or reproduced in any form or by any means or translated into another language, without the prior consent of Galileo Press, Rheinwerkallee 4, 53227 Bonn, Germany.

Galileo Press makes no warranties or representations with respect to the content hereof and specifically disclaims any implied warranties of merchantability or fitness for any particular purpose. Galileo Press assumes no responsibility for any errors that may appear in this publication.

"Galileo Press" and the Galileo Press logo are registered trademarks of Galileo Press GmbH, Bonn, Germany. SAP PRESS is an imprint of Galileo Press.

All of the screenshots and graphics reproduced in this book are subject to copyright © SAP AG, Dietmar-Hopp-Allee 16, 69190 Walldorf, Germany.

SAP, the SAP logo, mySAP, mySAP.com, mySAP Business Suite, SAP NetWeaver, SAP R/3, SAP R/2, SAP B2B, SAPtronic, SAPscript, SAP BW, SAP CRM, SAP EarlyWatch, SAP ArchiveLink, SAP GUI, SAP Business Workflow, SAP Business Engineer, SAP Business Navigator, SAP Business Framework, SAP Business Information Warehouse, SAP interenterprise solutions, SAP APO, AcceleratedSAP, InterSAP, SAPoffice, SAPfind, SAPfile, SAPtime, SAPmail, SAP-access, SAP-EDI, R/3 Retail, Accelerated HR, Accelerated HiTech, Accelerated Consumer Products, ABAP, ABAP/4, ALE/WEB, Alloy, BAPI, Business Framework, BW Explorer, Duet, Enjoy-SAP, mySAP.com e-business platform, mySAP Enterprise Portals, RIVA, SAPPHIRE, TeamSAP, Webflow and SAP PRESS are registered or unregistered trademarks of SAP AG, Walldorf, Germany.

All other products mentioned in this book are registered or unregistered trademarks of their respective companies.

Contents at a Glance

1	Introduction to the SAP BusinessObjects Reporting and Analysis Tools	19
2	Customer Requirements and Usage Scenarios	31
3	The Role of the Semantic Layer	49
4	Enterprise Reporting with SAP Crystal Reports for Enterprise	57
5	Interactive Analysis with SAP BusinessObjects Web Intelligence	119
6	Dashboarding and Data Visualization with SAP BusinessObjects Dashboards	181
7	Using SAP BusinessObjects Analysis, Edition for Microsoft Office	251
8	Using SAP BusinessObjects Analysis, Edition for OLAP	297
9	Data Exploration and Searching with SAP BusinessObjects Explorer	339
10	Using SAP BusinessObjects Live Office	385
11	Using SAP BusinessObjects BI Workspaces	421
12	Navigating the BI Launch Pad	449
13	Best Practices and Tips and Tricks for SAP BusinessObjects BI Tools	469
14	Integration Outlook	491

Dear Reader,

If you are familiar with the SAP BusinessObjects BI platform, you know it has a lot to offer in terms of reporting and analysis capabilities. So the real question is: Which tool is right for your particular business need? Is it SAP Crystal Reports? SAP BusinessObjects Dashboards? SAP BusinessObjects Web Intelligence? All of them? Or...something else entirely? Well, worry not: Ingo Hilgefort has these answers, and more.

When I first became an editor on the SAP PRESS SAP BusinessObjects list, one of the biggest challenges was identifying the differences among all of the SAP BusinessObjects BI offerings. I can tell you now: If I had started reading this book first, I would have had a much easier time. Inside these pages, Ingo offers a concise explanation of what kinds of analysis different users require from reporting tools, and then assesses how each tool addresses—or doesn't address—them. It is, in short, exactly what someone new to the SAP BusinessObjects BI portfolio needs to get started.

I'm confident that you will find the information contained in this book as informative as I did, and we at SAP PRESS are always eager to hear reader feedback—your comments and suggestions are the most useful tools to help us make our books the best they can be. We encourage you to visit our website at *www.sap-press.com* and share your feedback about this work.

Thank you for purchasing a book from SAP PRESS!

Kelly Grace Harris
Editor, SAP PRESS

Galileo Press
Boston, MA

kelly.harris@galileo-press.com
www.sap-press.com

Contents

Introduction 13

1 Introduction to the SAP BusinessObjects Reporting and Analysis Tools 19

1.1 Overview of the SAP BusinessObjects Tools 19
    1.1.1 Reporting—SAP Crystal Reports 20
    1.1.2 Dashboards and Visualization—SAP BusinessObjects Dashboards 22
    1.1.3 Interactive Analysis—SAP BusinessObjects Web Intelligence 24
    1.1.4 Analysis—SAP BusinessObjects Analysis 26
    1.1.5 Data Exploration—SAP BusinessObjects Explorer 27
1.2 Other Capabilities of the SAP BusinessObjects Tools 28
    1.2.1 SAP BusinessObjects BI and Microsoft Office 28
    1.2.2 SAP BusinessObjects BI and Mobility 30
1.3 Summary 30

2 Customer Requirements and Usage Scenarios 31

2.1 General Guidelines for Establishing Business Requirements 31
2.2 Matching Business Requirements to BI Products 33
    2.2.1 Financial Reporting and Analysis Requirements 33
    2.2.2 Sales Reporting and Analysis Requirements 35
    2.2.3 Human Resources (HR) Reporting and Analysis Requirements 36
    2.2.4 C-Level Management and Leadership Reporting and Analysis Requirements 36
2.3 Mapping SAP BusinessObjects BI Tools to Capabilities 37
2.4 Mapping SAP BusinessObjects Tools to the Audience 42
2.5 Summary 48

3 The Role of the Semantic Layer 49

3.1 Semantic Layer Technology 49
3.2 Data Connectivity Options for SAP Systems 53

Contents

3.3		Recommendations for Semantic Layer Usage	55
3.4		Summary	56

4 Enterprise Reporting with SAP Crystal Reports for Enterprise ... 57

4.1		SAP Data Connectivity	57
4.2		Assessing the Business Requirements	62
	4.2.1	Financial Reporting and Analysis Requirements	63
	4.2.2	Sales Reporting and Analysis Requirements	63
	4.2.3	Human Resources (HR) Reporting and Analysis Requirements	64
	4.2.4	C-Level Management and Leadership Reporting and Analysis Requirements	65
4.3		Introduction to the Tool	65
	4.3.1	SAP Crystal Reports for Enterprise Designer Environment	66
	4.3.2	Data Explorer	69
	4.3.3	Establishing a Connection to SAP NetWeaver BW	70
	4.3.4	Groupings	78
	4.3.5	Section Expert	80
	4.3.6	Conditional Formatting	81
	4.3.7	Saving to SAP BusinessObjects	86
4.4		Building a Report for Financial Analysis	87
4.5		Building a Report for HR Analysis	101
4.6		Summary	118

5 Interactive Analysis with SAP BusinessObjects Web Intelligence ... 119

5.1		SAP Data Connectivity	119
5.2		Assessing the Business Requirements	124
	5.2.1	Financial Reporting and Analysis Requirements	124
	5.2.2	Sales Reporting and Analysis Requirements	126
	5.2.3	Human Resource (HR) Reporting and Analysis Requirements	126
	5.2.4	C-Level Management and Leadership Reporting and Analysis Requirements	127
5.3		Introduction to the Tool	128
	5.3.1	Creating Your First Report	128

Contents

	5.3.2	Using Filters	141
	5.3.3	Arranging Objects	147
	5.3.4	Using Breaks, Sections, and Summaries	151
5.4	Building a Report for Sales Analysis		154
5.5	Building a Report for Financial Analysis		170
5.6	Summary		179

6 Dashboarding and Data Visualization with SAP BusinessObjects Dashboards ... 181

6.1	SAP Data Connectivity		181
6.2	Assessment of Business Requirements		189
	6.2.1	Financial Reporting and Analysis Requirements	189
	6.2.2	Sales Reporting and Analysis Requirements	190
	6.2.3	Human Resources (HR) Reporting and Analysis Requirements	192
	6.2.4	C-Level Management and Leadership Reporting and Analysis Requirements	192
6.3	Introduction to the Tool		193
	6.3.1	SAP BusinessObjects Dashboards Designer Overview	193
	6.3.2	Setting Up Your Environment	195
	6.3.3	Role of Microsoft Excel	198
	6.3.4	Common Look and Feel	199
	6.3.5	Creating Your First Dashboard	200
6.4	Building a Dashboard for Sales Planning		224
6.5	Summary		250

7 Using SAP BusinessObjects Analysis, Edition for Microsoft Office ... 251

7.1	SAP Data Connectivity		251
7.2	Assessing the Business Requirements		256
	7.2.1	Financial Reporting and Analysis Requirements	256
	7.2.2	Sales Reporting and Analysis Requirements	257
	7.2.3	Human Resources (HR) Reporting and Analysis Requirements	258
	7.2.4	C-Level Management and Leadership Reporting and Analysis Requirements	258
7.3	Introduction to the Tool		259

9

7.4	Building a Workbook for Financial Analysis	272
7.5	Building a Workbook for Sales Analysis	284
7.6	Summary	295

8 Using SAP BusinessObjects Analysis, Edition for OLAP ... 297

8.1	SAP Data Connectivity		297
8.2	Assessing the Business Requirements		302
	8.2.1	Financial Reporting and Analysis Requirements	302
	8.2.2	Sales Reporting and Analysis Requirements	303
	8.2.3	Human Resources (HR) Reporting and Analysis Requirements	304
	8.2.4	C-Level Management and Leadership Reporting and Analysis Requirements	304
8.3	Introduction to the Tool		305
8.4	Building a Workbook for Financial Analysis		317
8.5	Building a Workbook for Sales Analysis		327
8.6	Summary		338

9 Data Exploration and Searching with SAP BusinessObjects Explorer ... 339

9.1	SAP Data Connectivity for SAP BusinessObjects Explorer		339
9.2	Assessing the Business Requirements		344
	9.2.1	Financial Reporting and Analysis Requirements	344
	9.2.2	Sales Reporting and Analysis Requirements	345
	9.2.3	Human Resource (HR) Reporting and Analysis Requirements	346
	9.2.4	C-Level Management and Leadership Reporting and Analysis Requirements	346
9.3	Introduction to the Tool		347
9.4	Creating an Information Space for Sales Analysis		368
9.5	Summary		383

10 Using SAP BusinessObjects Live Office ... 385

10.1	SAP BusinessObjects Live Office Configuration	385
10.2	SAP BusinessObjects BI Platform Content and Microsoft Office	387

10.3	Introduction to the Tool	388
	10.3.1 SAP BusinessObjects Live Office Environment	388
	10.3.2 Using SAP BusinessObjects Live Office and Microsoft Excel	391
	10.3.3 Using SAP BusinessObjects Live Office and Microsoft PowerPoint	404
	10.3.4 Using SAP BusinessObjects Live Office and Microsoft Outlook	404
	10.3.5 Using SAP BusinessObjects Live Office and SAP BusinessObjects Explorer	410
10.4	Summary	419

11 Using SAP BusinessObjects BI Workspaces 421

11.1	Overview	421
11.2	Creating Content for Your First SAP BusinessObjects BI Workspace	427
11.3	Creating Your First BI Workspace	440
11.4	Summary	447

12 Navigating the BI Launch Pad 449

12.1	User Authentication	449
12.2	User Interface (UI) Overview	452
12.3	Folders and Categories	455
12.4	Using Search in the BI Launch Pad	456
12.5	Configuring User Preferences	462
12.6	Summary	467

13 Best Practices and Tips and Tricks for SAP BusinessObjects BI Tools 469

13.1	Selection of the Right Tool	469
13.2	SAP NetWeaver BEx Query Design	470
	13.2.1 Relationship: BEx Query and Report	470
	13.2.2 Elements of an SAP NetWeaver BEx Query	471
	13.2.3 Using Variables in a BE Query	473
	13.2.4 Display Relevant Settings	473
13.3	Data Connectivity	475

13.4	User Security	478
13.5	Performance Considerations	479
13.6	Known Limitations	481
13.7	Report Design Topics	488
13.8	Tracing and Troubleshooting	488
13.9	Summary	489

14 Integration Outlook ... 491

14.1	SAP Crystal Reports for Enterprise	491
14.2	SAP BusinessObjects Dashboards	492
14.3	SAP BusinessObjects Web Intelligence	492
14.4	SAP BusinessObjects Analysis Suite	492
14.5	SAP BusinessObjects Explorer	492
14.6	Semantic Layer	493
14.7	Summary	493

The Author ... 495
Index ... 497

Introduction

Welcome to the updated edition of *Reporting and Analysis with SAP BusinessObjects*! The first edition was very well received by the SAP customer base, and as I am still frequently being asked questions like "Which tool should I use?" or "How do I create my balance sheet?", I decided to create an updated edition with a focus on the new SAP BusinessObjects 4.0 feature pack 3 (FP3) release. The goal of this book is to provide an overview of the SAP BusinessObjects toolset in the business intelligence (BI) area and to provide guidance as to the question "When do I use which tool?" This book tries to cover as much as possible in a single volume.

The first part offers a set of criteria that can be used to drive tool selection for your own implementation. The second part focuses on the actual creation of content and provides you with step-by-step guidance for certain types of reports in each of the tools based on Business Content in SAP NetWeaver Business Warehouse (BW), so you should be able to follow along in your own system.

I hope this book provides you with a sound overview of the capabilities of each tool, insight into the selection of the tools based on your business requirements, and a great reference for how you can use each tool to create content on top of your SAP data.

Target Group

The target audience for this book is twofold. On the one hand, I hope that BI team leads, BI project managers, and BI decision makers can use the book to understand the various tools and get a better understanding of which tool is best suited for which requirements.

On the other hand, the audience for this book is anyone who will implement and create content with the SAP BusinessObjects software. For this audience, I hope the book provides guidance as to tool selection and the information required to

Introduction

understand which metadata and data are available, and how they can be used in each tool.

The focus of the book is not on making you an expert in the installation and deployment of the SAP BusinessObjects software in an SAP landscape. If you are looking for material in this area, you might want to consider the updated edition of *Integrating SAP BusinessObjects BI Platform 4.x with SAP NetWeaver*.

As a reader, you should have some prior knowledge of SAP NetWeaver BW and SAP ERP. With SAP BusinessObjects, I tried to keep the need for prior knowledge to a minimum, so you should be able to follow this book even without any SAP BusinessObjects experience (although you should consider further training).

Technical Prerequisites

All steps and examples are based on SAP BusinessObjects 4.0 FP3 in combination with an SAP NetWeaver BW 7.01 SP08 and SAP ECC 6.0 system. However, you can also use higher releases from SAP NetWeaver BW as long as they are supported with the SAP BusinessObjects 4.0 FP3 release. All of the SAP BusinessObjects software can be downloaded from the SAP Service Marketplace, and you can receive temporary license keys from *http://service.sap.com/licensekeys*. As this book is very practical, I highly recommend that you download the following components so that you can follow all of the outlined steps:

- SAP BusinessObjects Enterprise 4.0
- SAP BusinessObjects BI client tools 4.0
- SAP Crystal Reports for Enterprise 4.0
- SAP BusinessObjects Dashboards 4.0
- SAP BusinessObjects Analysis, edition for Microsoft Office 1.1
- SAP BusinessObjects Live Office 4.0
- SAP BusinessObjects Explorer 4.0

This book is based on the 4.0 FP3 release of the SAP BusinessObjects BI suite. Please note that this is the first major update on top of the 4.0 release; therefore, you may have to download and install the 4.0 software first and apply the update for feature pack 3 accordingly. You should also make sure that you have access to an SAP NetWeaver BW and SAP ERP system so that you can follow the examples.

If you can't get access to an existing system, you can download a trial version of SAP NetWeaver via the DOWNLOAD section on the SAP Developer Network (SDN).

Structure of the Book

When I started this book and outlined all the topics I wanted to write about, it quickly became obvious that it would become a large book, which made its organization very important. I tried to keep it very practical with lots of examples and step-by-step guidance. Here is a short overview of the content of the chapters:

Chapter 1—SAP BusinessObjects Product Overview

This chapter introduces you to the SAP BusinessObjects platform and the SAP BusinessObjects BI client tools that you will use in the following chapters. We offer a short overview of the different BI tools.

Chapter 2—Customer Requirements and Usage Scenarios

In the second chapter we look at a list of typical requirements for your BI landscape and use this list to evaluate which tool is best used for which type of requirement.

Chapter 3—The Role of the Semantic Layer

In the third chapter we explain the different options for connecting to SAP systems, and we uncover the strengths and weaknesses of the different options available.

Chapters 4 through 10—SAP BusinessObjects BI Client Tools

In each of these chapters we look at several common business requirements, and how each of the areas in the SAP BusinessObjects portfolio is able to fulfill these requirements. You will also learn how to use the appropriate tool to create content for these areas. Each chapter will provide an overview on the usage of the tools, the connectivity, and concrete examples with step-by-step instructions.

Chapter 11—BI Workspaces

In this chapter, we show how you can leverage BI workspaces as part of your SAP BusinessObjects deployment and combine content from different sources and tools into compelling dashboards.

Chapter 12—BI Launch Pad

In this chapter we look at how you can use the BI launch pad to view, schedule, or edit content. You will learn how you can interface with your BI environment and leverage all BI related content.

Chapter 13—Best Practices

This chapter provides tips, recommendations, and best practices for the design of BEx queries and steps you can take to improve the overall performance and stability of your system.

Chapter 14—Outlook

Chapter 14 offers a short list of topics that might be of interest to you and your deployment. These topics are part of the integration roadmap given out by SAP and BusinessObjects, but were technically not final at the time of writing this book.

Acknowledgments

First, I would like to thank the team from SAP PRESS, especially Kelly Harris, for providing the opportunity to write this book and for providing such a smooth process.

In addition, special thanks go to the following people for reviewing early drafts of the book and providing their input and feedback:

- Tammy Powlas, Fairfax Water & ASUG BI Community
- Joyce Butler, Cameron International & ASUG BI Community
- Helle Knudsen, Vestas Wind Systems A/S
- Derek Loranca, Aetna Inc. & ASUG BI Community

Most of all, my thanks go out to Elvira Wallis and Juergen Lindner for supporting me on this journey, but most importantly for continuously being mentors for me and for bringing me back to earth from time to time.

In this chapter, you will learn about the SAP BusinessObjects reporting and analysis portfolio and how it relates to your SAP landscape.

1 Introduction to the SAP BusinessObjects Reporting and Analysis Tools

In this chapter, we look at the SAP BusinessObjects portfolio for business intelligence (BI) tools and offer a quick introduction to each tool. We also discuss the SAP BusinessObjects BI platform capabilities with respect to Microsoft Office and mobility.

A more detailed analysis of the portfolio, including which tool should be chosen for each type of usage, is provided in Chapter 2.

1.1 Overview of the SAP BusinessObjects Tools

Before we get into the overview of the SAP BusinessObjects BI portfolio, please note that even though not all of the products from the SAP BusinessObjects portfolio are mentioned in this book, their omission is not a statement about the importance of those products. The focus here is on the reporting and analysis capabilities of the SAP BusinessObjects products in the 4.0 FP3 release.

The SAP BusinessObjects BI portfolio consists of five main areas. These areas, and the question they each aim to answer, are listed below:

- **Reporting**
  How do I access and transform corporate data into highly formatted reports for greater insight?
- **Dashboards and visualization**
  How do I visualize data for better decision making?
- **Interactive analysis**
  How do I answer ad hoc questions and interact with information?

- **Analysis**
  How do I determine trends from complex historical data and possibly make better forecasts?
- **Data exploration**
  How do I find immediate answers to business questions?

In this book you will learn to identify which of these areas are best suited for your requirements and how you can use the products in each of these categories. These areas are the ones most often used by SAP, but remember that they are not the actual products. You will learn more about the products next.

1.1.1 Reporting—SAP Crystal Reports

SAP Crystal Reports is the de facto standard reporting tool in enterprise reporting. In this category, SAP Crystal Reports replaces the Business Explorer (BEx) Report Designer and provides the following reporting capabilities to the end user:

- Highly formatted and print-optimized reporting
- Layout-focused reporting
- Static reporting
- Parameterized reporting

Based on the above capabilities, you might think SAP Crystal Reports is capable only of creating well-formatted, pixel-perfect invoices (i.e., purchase orders, account balance statements, etc.) (see Figure 1.1). However, SAP Crystal Reports has evolved into a reporting tool capable of creating reports that include very sophisticated user interactivity, even an integration with SAP BusinessObjects Dashboards data visualizations as part of your report (see Figure 1.2).

SAP Crystal Reports is very easy to learn and use, as you will see yourself in the following chapters. It allows you to access any kind of data source and create a wide variety of reports and navigations inside them. Nevertheless, the primary purpose of SAP Crystal Reports as a reporting tool is to provide you with the functionality to create content while having complete control over the layout, font, positioning of objects, and rendering and printing on all different types of clients.

1.1 Overview of the SAP BusinessObjects Tools

G/L Accounts: Balances

Fiscal Year: 2008   Period: 1 - [OFIS]   Ledger: [OAC_I]   Page 1 of 3
Last Data Update: 7/7/2009   Printed by: on 7/7/2009

Selection Criteria
CompanyCode: [OCOMP_CODE].[1000]
Profit Center:
CurrencyType: 10

Company Code: 1000   SAP A.G.
Currency Type: 10   Currency: EUR

Account Number	G/L Account	Balance Carryforward	Balance Previous	Cum.Balance Previous	Debit Total	Credit Total	Cumulated Debit Balance	Cumulated Credit Balance	Cumulated Balance
INT/1000	Real estate and similar rights	-26,273.54	0.00	-26,273.54	225,216.24	939,007.93	0.00	-740,065.23	-740,065.23
INT/100000	Petty cash	-7,000.00	0.00	-7,000.00	0.00	0.00	0.00	-7,000.00	-7,000.00
INT/1010	Accumltd. Deprctn - Real Estate and Similar Rights	-644,077.00	0.00	-644,077.00	0.00	268,565.00	0.00	-912,642.00	-912,642.00
INT/11000	Machinery and equipment	2,000.00	0.00	2,000.00	2,000.00	0.00	4,000.00	0.00	4,000.00
INT/11010	Accumulated depreciation-plant and machinery	-493,188.00	0.00	-493,188.00	0.00	204,074.00	0.00	-697,262.00	-697,262.00
INT/113100	G/L Account	-3,322.00	0.00	-3,322.00	1,300.00	1,000.00	0.00	-3,022.00	-3,022.00
INT/113105	Bank 1 (other interim postings)	0.00	0.00	0.00	1,000.00	1,000.00	0.00	0.00	0.00
INT/140000	Customers - Domestic Receivables 1	0.00	0.00	0.00	2,100.00	1,100.00	1,000.00	0.00	1,000.00
INT/154000	Input tax	43.90	0.00	43.90	689.65	0.00	733.55	0.00	733.55
INT/160000	Accounts payable-domestic	-318.25	0.00	-318.25	0.00	7,300.00	0.00	-7,618.25	-7,618.25
INT/175000	Output tax	0.00	0.00	0.00	13.79	0.00	13.79	0.00	13.79
INT/191000	GR/IR clearing - own production	0.00	0.00	0.00	0.00	0.00	0.00	0.00	0.00

Figure 1.1 SAP Crystal Reports—Account Balances

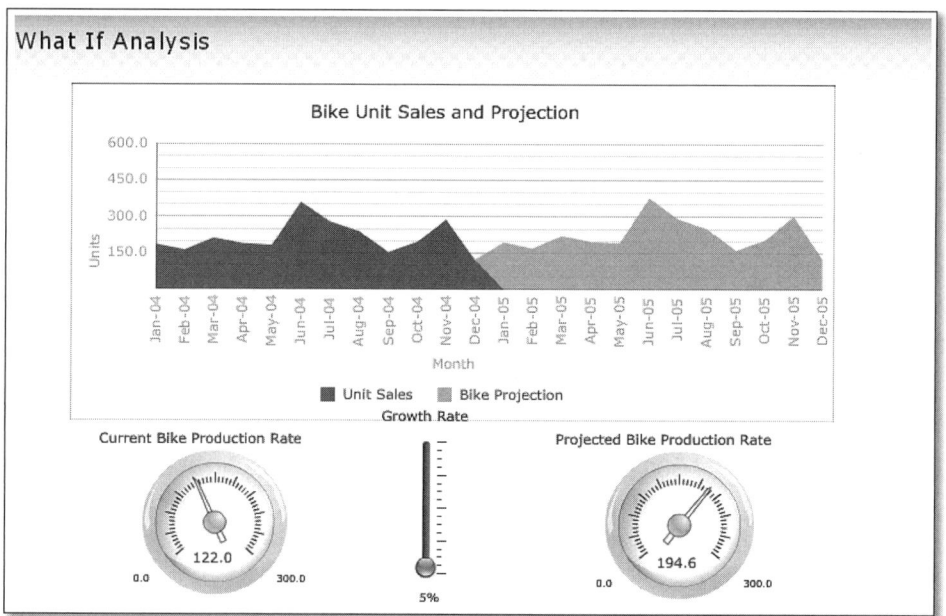

Figure 1.2 SAP Crystal Reports—Interactive Report

As part of the SAP BusinessObjects 4.0 release, you will notice that you receive two versions of SAP Crystal Reports:

- **SAP Crystal Reports for Enterprise**
    - Contains a major update and re-design of the SAP Crystal Reports Designer and associated processing servers.
    - Focuses on the needs of large enterprises and customers with SAP deployments.
    - Provides the foundation for all future releases of SAP Crystal Reports.
- **SAP Crystal Reports 2011**
    - Contains incremental updates to SAP Crystal Reports 2008 with a few new features.
    - Focuses on serving the needs of standalone customers (partners and volume customers).
    - Continues to deliver existing functionality with no regressions.

SAP Crystal Reports for Enterprise is a brand new and redesigned version of SAP Crystal Reports with the focus on large deployments and—most important for you as an SAP customer—with the focus on the integration with SAP landscapes. As part of this book, we will use SAP Crystal Reports for Enterprise for all our activities.

1.1.2 Dashboards and Visualization—SAP BusinessObjects Dashboards

SAP BusinessObjects Dashboards (formerly Xcelsius) provides the capabilities to create compelling dashboards and data visualizations. SAP BusinessObjects Dashboards is a very simple and intuitive tool that allows you to create a broad range of data visualizations, from a very simple chart (see Figure 1.3) to very complex interactive dashboards (see Figure 1.4).

As part of the 4.0 FP3 release, SAP BusinessObjects Dashboards is able to use the semantic layer directly, which tremendously reduces the need to use a spreadsheet as part of the design environment. You can easily use all of the components that are delivered as part of the SAP BusinessObjects Dashboards design environment. You can also extend the environment by using the software development kit (SDK) and create your own visualization components using Adobe Flex.

Overview of the SAP BusinessObjects Tools | 1.1

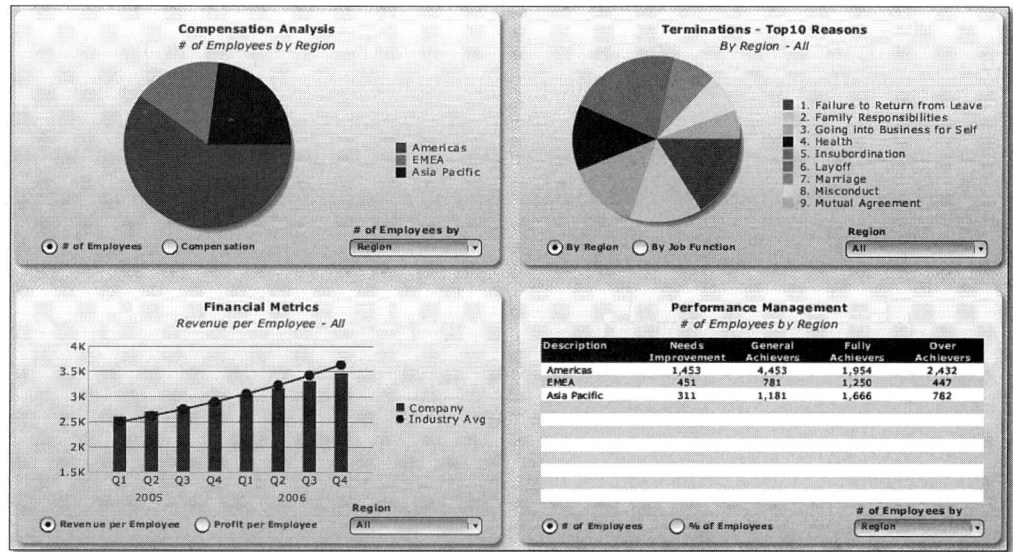

Figure 1.3 Simple Dashboard

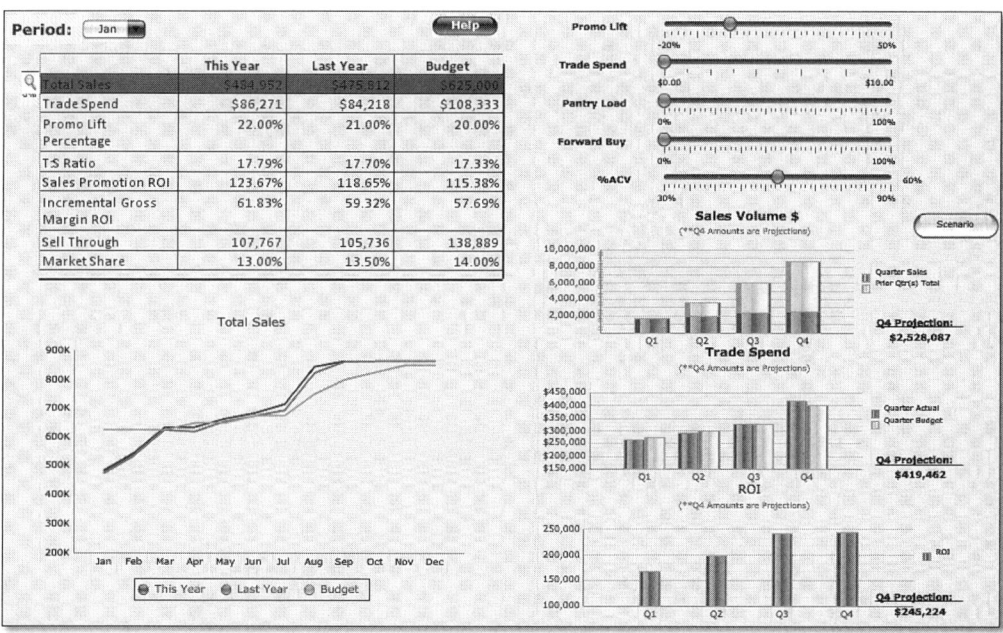

Figure 1.4 Complex Dashboard

23

SAP BusinessObjects Dashboards provides you with the capability to leverage several different data sources in a single dashboard. The most common options to leverage data from your available SAP data sources are either a direct link provided by the semantic layer to your SAP system—such as SAP ECC or SAP NetWeaver BW—or a combination of SAP BusinessObjects Live Office or BI Web Services and data provided by existing SAP Crystal Reports for Enterprise or SAP BusinessObjects Web Intelligence objects.

1.1.3 Interactive Analysis—SAP BusinessObjects Web Intelligence

In the category of interactive analysis—sometimes also referred to as ad-hoc query and reporting—SAP BusinessObjects Web Intelligence provides you with the functionality to establish a self-service environment for your end users to easily create, edit, and share reports based on any data source. This can be done from a web-based environment or a desktop-based version, and also includes the option to create offline reports.

You can use SAP BusinessObjects Web Intelligence to consume and analyze information in a self-service-oriented environment so that there is no need for you to rely on your information technology (IT) department to specify and create a new report for you. You can easily specify which data you would like to use in your report using the SAP BusinessObjects Web Intelligence query panel (see Figure 1.5).

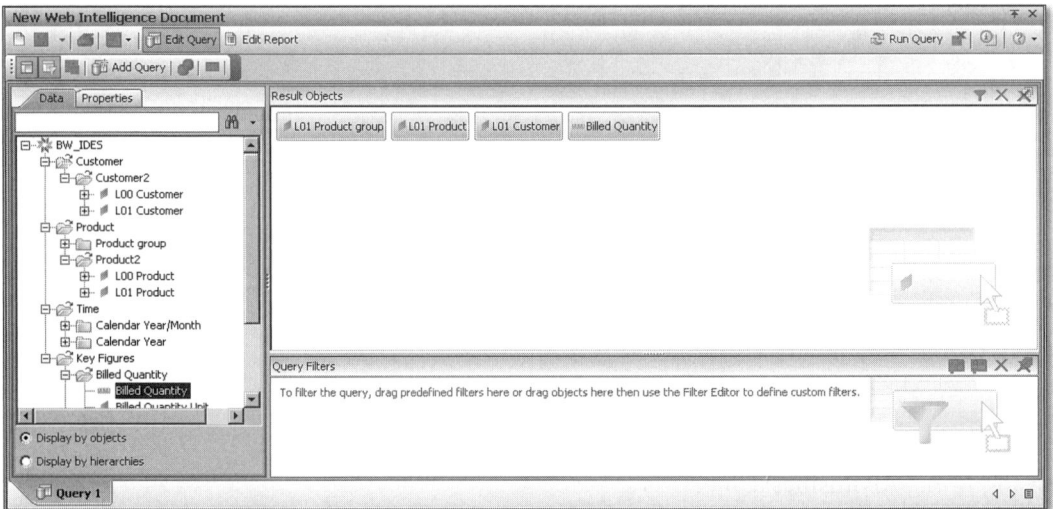

Figure 1.5 SAP BusinessObjects Web Intelligence—Query Panel

Overview of the SAP BusinessObjects Tools | **1.1**

You can also leverage SAP BusinessObjects Web Intelligence either to create a new report or to use an existing report, as shown in Figure 1.6, and to change the report based on your needs. With some very simple steps, covered in depth in the following chapters, you can change the report not only to provide a different layout, but to show different information, as shown in Figure 1.7.

L01 Product group	L01 Product	L01 Customer	Billed Quantity	Net Sales
Office	Lamy Pencil	9999 Hotel Ltd	502	2,535
Office	Lamy Pencil	Abbey Coffee & Tea Group Inc	1,760	8,873
Office	Lamy Pencil	Abbey Co Inc	1,446	7,288
Office	Lamy Pencil	Abbey Enterprises Group Inc	502	2,535
Office	Lamy Pencil	Abbey Fine Foods Inc	502	2,535
Office	Lamy Pencil	Abbey Foods Ltd	660	3,327
Office	Lamy Pencil	Abbey Group Inc	1,917	9,665
Office	Lamy Pencil	Abbey Ltd	4,651	23,449
Office	Lamy Pencil	Abbey Lumber Co Inc	1,288	6,496
Office	Lamy Pencil	Abbey Motor Group Inc	1,131	5,704
Office	Lamy Pencil	Abbey Services Co Inc	502	2,535
Office	Lamy Pencil	Abbey Solutions Group Inc	345	1,743

Figure 1.6 SAP BusinessObjects Web Intelligence—Simple Report

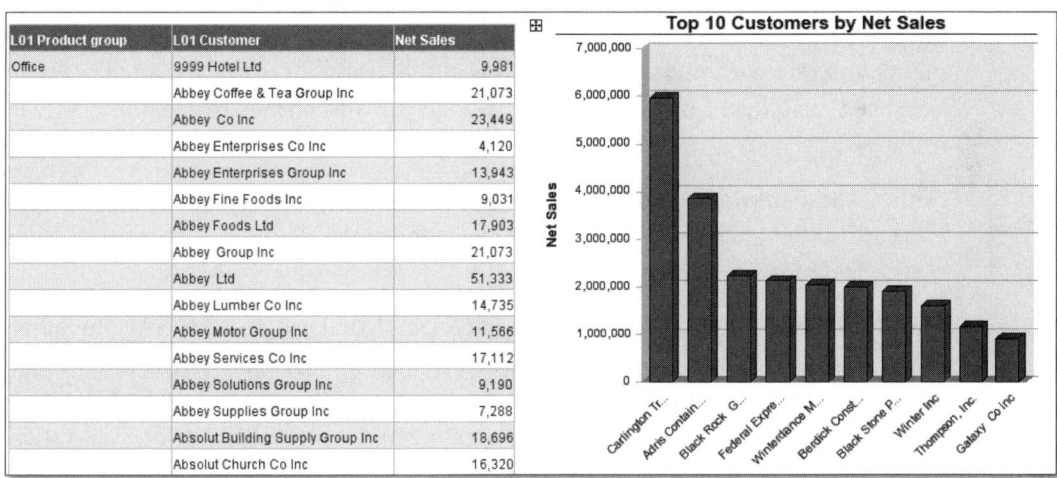

Figure 1.7 SAP BusinessObjects Web Intelligence—Modified Report

In addition, SAP BusinessObjects Web Intelligence offers you the choice of a fully web-based solution or a rich client solution for your ad-hoc reporting needs.

25

1.1.4 Analysis—SAP BusinessObjects Analysis

A key area in the BI tools portfolio is the functionality of an in-depth, online analytical processing (OLAP) analysis client that provides you with the capability to create predefined workbooks with guided navigation and the option to leverage the tool for an ad-hoc OLAP analysis. Most SAP users know this category very well based on their familiarity with BEx Analyzer and BEx Web Analyzer. SAP BusinessObjects Analysis is the premium successor to BEx Analyzer and BEx Web Analyzer and provides two versions of the product.

SAP BusinessObjects Analysis, edition for Microsoft Office is the version that fully integrates into the Microsoft Office environment; in this way, the product provides an alternative to your existing BEx Analyzer workbooks. It has a powerful application design that combines multiple data sources, allows for free formatting of text elements, and supports BW integrated planning. It also has the capability for live analyses embedded into Microsoft PowerPoint presentations, which allows you to embed the analysis as a live object, export current analysis from Microsoft Excel, and directly insert BEx query results.

The counterpart of the web deployment is SAP BusinessObjects Analysis, edition for OLAP, which is also a premium alternative to your existing BEx web reporting solution; it is the successor to SAP BusinessObjects Voyager. It allows you to uncover deep business insights with self-service analysis, leverage all your investments, interact with multiple dimensions and hierarchies, run deep analyses with advanced analytical functions, and break data silos to enrich analyses and visualizations.

Both of these products are designed to provide a real multidimensional workflow and capabilities such as analyzing data along multiple hierarchies or creating your own calculations on the fly.

The third member of the SAP BusinessObjects Analysis Suite is SAP BusinessObjects Analysis, edition for Application Design. This is an environment that allows you to create applications with the focus on BI and integrated planning. It has an Eclipse-based application design environment for planning and analytical applications, access to SAP NetWeaver BW via BI Consumer Services (BICS), and is integrated with SAP BusinessObjects. At the time of this writing (November 2011), SAP BusinessObjects Analysis, edition for Application Design is planned to become available in the first half of 2012, and will become the premium alternative to the the Web Application Designer.

1.1.5 Data Exploration—SAP BusinessObjects Explorer

SAP BusinessObjects Explorer provides the functionality to use a search interface on top of your data set. You can then use SAP BusinessObjects Explorer to navigate and explore the data further (see Figure 1.8).

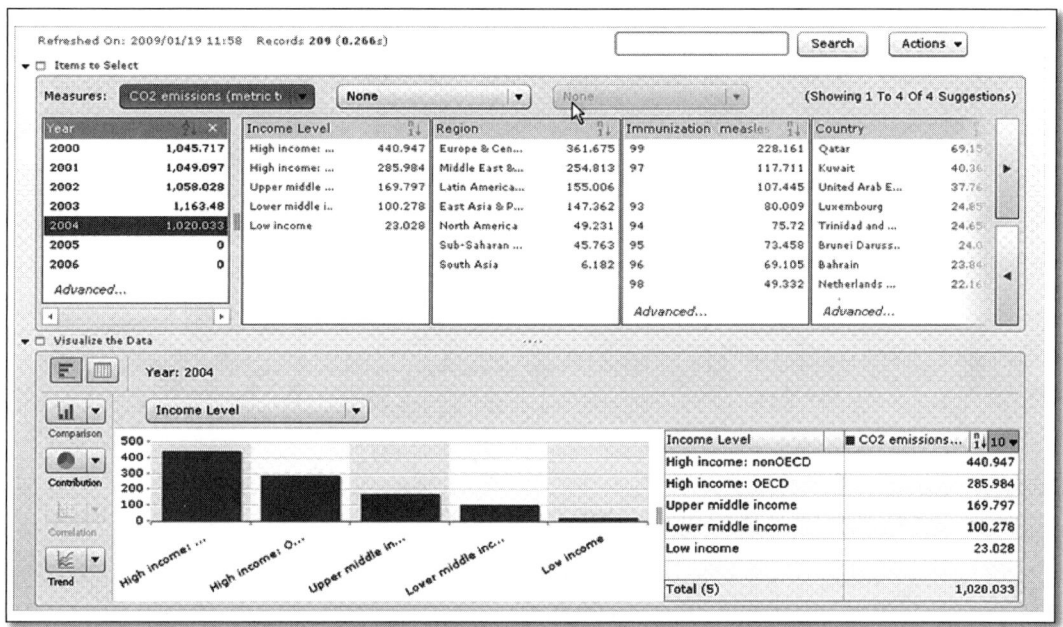

Figure 1.8 SAP BusinessObjects Explorer

SAP BusinessObjects Explorer is a product that affords access to a large volume of data, and, when used in conjunction with SAP NetWeaver BW Accelerator (BWA) or SAP HANA, offers access to tremendously large volumes of data with high performance. SAP BusinessObjects Explorer is also able to leverage the semantic layer from SAP BusinessObjects and to create indexes of the available data via the semantic layer in situations where you do not have access to SAP NetWeaver BWA or SAP HANA.

With the integration of SAP BusinessObjects Explorer and SAP BusinessObjects Web Intelligence, you can use SAP BusinessObjects Explorer to start analyzing data and then use SAP BusinessObjects Web Intelligence for further sharing and formatting purposes (see Figure 1.9).

1 | Introduction to the SAP BusinessObjects Reporting and Analysis Tools

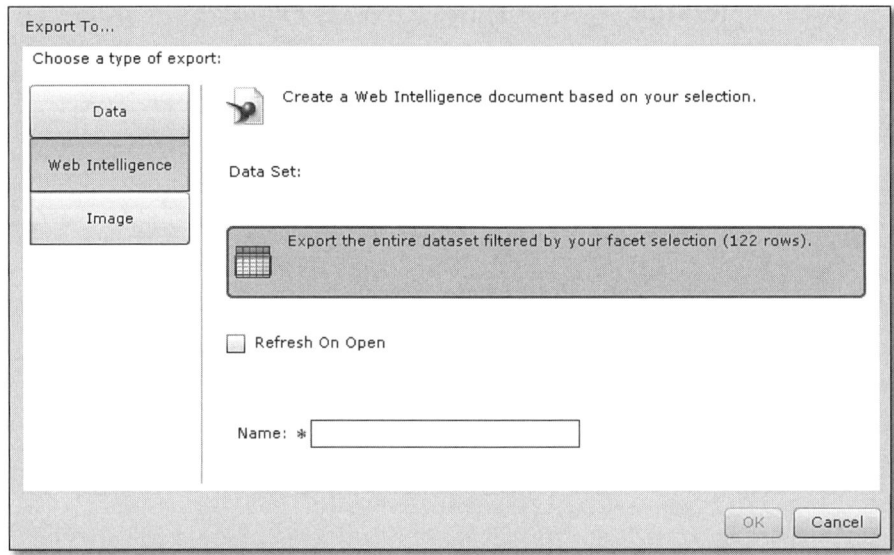

Figure 1.9 SAP BusinessObjects Explorer and SAP BusinessObjects Web Intelligence

1.2 Other Capabilities of the SAP BusinessObjects Tools

In addition to the capabilities discussed in the previous section (reporting, dashboards and visualization, interactive analysis, analysis, and data exploration), the SAP BusinessObjects BI platform also has the capabilities to integrate with Microsoft Office, and to offer mobile solutions. We discuss both of these next.

1.2.1 SAP BusinessObjects BI and Microsoft Office

In addition to all of the areas mentioned above, we should also highlight the integration of the SAP BusinessObjects BI portfolio into a Microsoft Office environment, which allows you to leverage your BI content as part of your day-to-day Microsoft Office environment, and at the same time keep the BI data and visualizations intact and refreshable (see Figure 1.10).

With SAP BusinessObjects Live Office you can provide accurate and trusted data via the SAP BusinessObjects BI toolset to Microsoft Excel, Microsoft Word, Microsoft PowerPoint, and Microsoft Outlook (see Figure 1.11).

1.2 Other Capabilities of the SAP BusinessObjects Tools

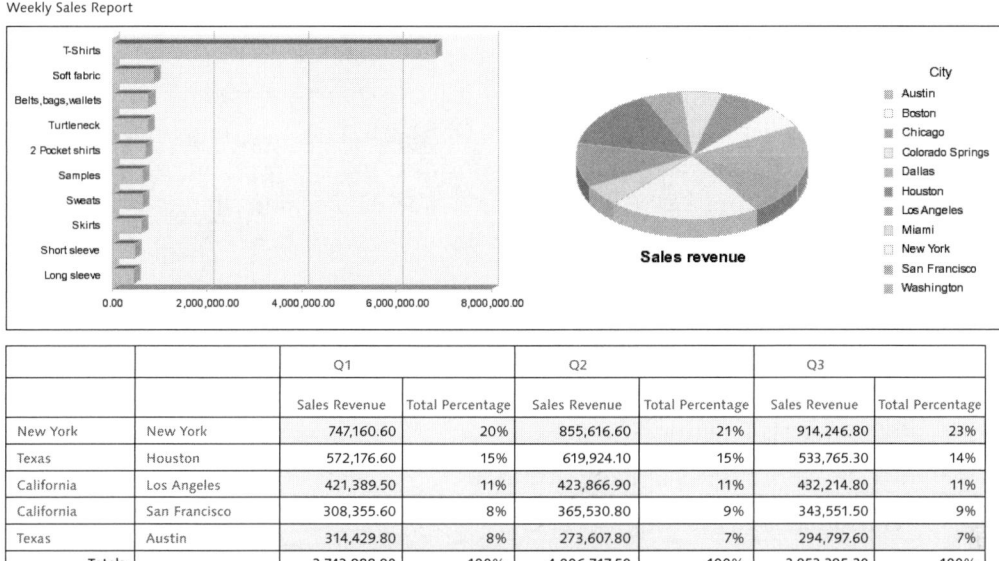

		Q1		Q2		Q3	
		Sales Revenue	Total Percentage	Sales Revenue	Total Percentage	Sales Revenue	Total Percentage
New York	New York	747,160.60	20%	855,616.60	21%	914,246.80	23%
Texas	Houston	572,176.60	15%	619,924.10	15%	533,765.30	14%
California	Los Angeles	421,389.50	11%	423,866.90	11%	432,214.80	11%
California	San Francisco	308,355.60	8%	365,530.80	9%	343,551.50	9%
Texas	Austin	314,429.80	8%	273,607.80	7%	294,797.60	7%
Totals		3,742,988.90	100%	4,006,717.50	100%	3,953,395.30	100%

Figure 1.10 SAP BusinessObjects Live Office and Microsoft PowerPoint

	2004		2005		2006	
	Salesrevenue	CategoryMargin %	Salesrevenue	CategoryMargin %	Salesrevenue	CategoryMargin %
Jewelry	1,138,562	37.94%	2,688,536	40.77%	47,856	1.27%
Hats,gloves,scarves	383,306	13.64%	877,699	14.33%	26,959	0.65%
Evening wear	295,862	10.86%	542,035	9.11%	284,506	19.85%
Long sleeve	235,123	8.23%	378,076	6.27%	336,208	22.02%
Day wear	242,601	8.93%	554,986	9.29%	5,889	0.10%
Cardigan	203,818	5.69%	483,776	6.67%	25,198	-1.39%
Lounge wear	72,270	2.53%	160,637	2.80%	199,705	11.66%
Casual dresses	48,734	1.35%	115,415	1.46%	137,287	9.03%
Hair accessories	62,740	1.50%	93,026	1.20%	105,999	4.22%
Jeans	53,301	1.87%	95,324	1.64%	73,346	4.80%
Boatwear	33,175	1.30%	15,879	0.23%	134,282	11.01%
Dry wear	50,596	1.98%	97,609	1.94%	29,588	0.62%
Full length	34,572	1.47%	72,886	1.47%	62,236	2.53%
Long lounge pants	32,778	1.08%	66,832	1.14%	37,688	1.92%

Figure 1.11 SAP BusinessObjects Live Office Used in Microsoft Outlook

1.2.2 SAP BusinessObjects BI and Mobility

In addition to the set of BI tools, the topic of mobility and the option to have information available on a mobile device are becoming more and more important. The 4.0 release of the SAP BusinessObjects BI platform delivers a mobile BI solution: SAP BusinessObjects Mobile Business Intelligence. This allows you to deliver content from SAP Crystal Reports and SAP BusinessObjects Web Intelligence to mobile devices, which enables you to:

- Make informed decisions with instance access to personalized information.
- Leverage existing BI investments and skills to quickly reach mobile users.
- Ensure secure access to information across a range of devices.
- Receive alerts on critical events.
- Investigate problems and opportunities.
- Take immediate action.

In addition to the SAP BusinessObjects Mobile BI solution, you can also use SAP BusinessObjects Explorer Mobile, which allows you to use the SAP BusinessObjects Explorer functionality on your mobile device. This functionality:

- Searches across all data sources.
- Offers contextual exploration.
- Enables automated relevancy and chart generation.
- Provides high performance and scalability.
- Allows you to share your results instantly.

1.3 Summary

In this chapter, we looked at the existing offerings in the BI portfolio from SAP. In the next chapter, we examine typical customer requirements from different areas, and show how those requirements can be mapped to the offerings in the BI portfolio.

By first understanding the typical customer requirements for a reporting and analysis solution, we can then map those requirements to the SAP BusinessObjects portfolio and to typical user profiles in the business intelligence (BI) area.

2 Customer Requirements and Usage Scenarios

In this chapter, we map the SAP BusinessObjects BI client tools to typical customer requirements and user profiles. Based on the scope of this book, coverage will be limited to the most common scenarios, but this should provide you with a good overview of the main criteria for the SAP BusinessObjects portfolio and how to select the right tool for the right job.

To start the chapter, we offer some general guidelines for identifying business requirements. Then we continue our discussion by actually establishing these business requirements for different areas of a fictional company. Finally, we evaluate each of the BI client tools against these requirements, and establish which requirements can and cannot be fulfilled by the tools.

2.1 General Guidelines for Establishing Business Requirements

At this point, SAP and SAP BusinessObjects have been a combined entity for over three years, and now offer a combined BI solutions portfolio. However, SAP users still struggle with one important question: "Which product is the right choice for my project?" Of course, users seek guidance about the overall BI portfolio—but they also have difficulty selecting the best BI tool for their project. Often, customers try to create a "simple fix" solution and try to focus on one or two BI client products without a complete evaluation of which product would be the best fit. In most cases, such projects fail in terms of user satisfaction. In such a situation, the business users often lose their trust and confidence in the products and systems. Not only is the selection of the right tool a critical factor for the project itself, but—given that selecting the right tool can greatly increase the adoption of the overall BI solution—a wrong selection can seriously impact not only a single project but the overall BI strategy in your company.

In this chapter, we establish a set of business requirements and then use those business requirements to evaluate which of the BI client products best fits these requirements. But before doing this, we would like to give a set of general guidelines for these topics:

- SAP BusinessObjects BI provides you with five different categories of reporting and their corresponding products. During your project, you should always evaluate which tool fits the best and keep one simple rule in mind: It is unlikely that your project requires all of the BI client tools, but it is also unrealistic that you will succeed with only one of them.

- When you start your BI project, you should make sure that you first collect the business requirements and that you involve the business users in the project right from the start. Remember that the business users will be using the products, so they have to become part of your decision process, and you will need their feedback on an ongoing basis.

- Please do not start with the data warehouse. Establishing a BI system and following a BI strategy does not start with building a data warehouse. Certainly, the data warehouse is a fundamental part of the final outcome, but first you need to understand the overall business needs. You can then establish the requirements for the BI layer, and for the data warehouse layer, based on what the business needs are.

- When you start collecting the business requirements, try to focus on smaller parts of the overall company. For example, collect the requirements by department, instead of collecting them for all departments at the same time. Each area of your business is different and has different needs. Also remember to consider the different types of users; for example, a business analyst in your finance department might have a very different set of requirements and skills from a business analyst in the sales department.

- During the project phase where you collect the business requirements, let the business user describe the problem in his own words, and keep asking questions. Find out how the user is using the information, in which form and format he is using the data, and how he is interacting with the data. For example:

- Is he exporting the information because the data are used as input to another system?
- Is he interacting with the data in form of drilldown, filtering, or slice and dice?
- Does he read the information in a browser on his desktop or on a mobile device?

All the guidelines listed above are just simple suggestions based on experience in helping several customers make the right choice. Always keep in mind that the most important aspect of your BI project is to understand the business requirements, and to fulfill those requirements in the best possible way. A business requirement does not start with the modeling in the data warehouse—it starts with the need for information so that your company can make informed decisions.

2.2 Matching Business Requirements to BI Products

In this section, we outline some common customer business requirements from different areas that we then match to the SAP BusinessObjects BI products. The requirements are broken into separate areas, which we then use in the following chapters to provide more detail about creating the actual reports and analytics. We focus on the following areas: financials, sales and distribution (SD), human resources (HR), and management/executive information systems. We do not explain each of these areas in full, but rather focus on typical requirements and scenarios; this will allow you to differentiate the tools and understand which scenarios lend themselves to which tools. Please keep in mind that the goal of this book is to explain the usage of the reporting and analysis tools from SAP BusinessObjects, not to describe all SAP NetWeaver BW-related or SAP ERP-related topics for each area.

2.2.1 Financial Reporting and Analysis Requirements

The following is a brief description of the typical requirements for financial reporting. These requirements represent a typical usage scenario and focus on reporting and analysis for customers in the financial area. Please note that references to "content" refer to the objects created with the SAP BusinessObjects BI tools.

- The content must be available in a web-based environment and in a Microsoft Office environment (especially Microsoft Excel).
- For specific content (such as an income statement or a balance sheet), the design needs to be layout focused with the actual print version of the report being a high priority.
- The reporting and analysis tools need to let the user create new calculations and formulas and share those with other consumers of the content.
- The reporting and analysis tools need to allow for the use of hierarchies and for easy navigation along those hierarchies.
- The reporting and analysis tools need to use custom structures that are defined as part of a BEx query.
- The content needs to resolve the time dependency defined for financial cost and profit center hierarchies.
- Consumers of the reports should have the option to receive real-time data but also be able to use pre-calculated data if needed.
- Users need to be able to navigate from aggregated data to more granular items; for example, to navigate from a cost center aggregated value to the actual line items per cost element.
- Some content requires navigation into the actual SAP transaction to retrieve further detail.
- Users need to be able to receive the data from multiple sources, such as multiple BEx queries, in a single report.
- Users need to be able to create planning scenarios and write information back into the source.

Commonly found example content in the financials area might include:

- Income statement
- Balance sheet
- Cost center—actual and plan comparison
- Profit center—actual/plan/variance comparison

As you can see, based on the preceding descriptions, there is a wide range of requirements in the financial area alone. Without going into detail, it should be clear that those requirements need more than one tool from the SAP BusinessObjects BI portfolio.

2.2.2 Sales Reporting and Analysis Requirements

The following is a brief description of the typical requirements for the sales area. We use these requirements in combination with the other reporting and analysis deliverables to determine which tools should be used to fulfill these requirements.

- Content must be available online, offline, and on mobile devices (for sales representatives on the road).
- Distribution of content via email may be required.
- Users need the capability to navigate within the data and change the view of the actual content. For example, they need to be able to change a weekly sales statistics broken down by country into a monthly sales statistics broken down by sales region and quarter.
- Content has to leverage real-time data in most reports. Historical data may be required for comparisons.
- Users need to be able to modify existing reports and, if needed, create new ad-hoc reports.
- Users should be able to drill down or navigate to more detail-oriented information.
- Users should be able to perform scenario-based analysis, where the user is able to see the data but can also influence certain factors and see the impact on the overall numbers; for example, a what-if analysis in a sales planning workflow.

Commonly found example content in the sales area might include:

- Opportunity pipeline analysis
- Sales opportunity planning
- Opportunity monitoring
- Incoming orders from customers
- Product profitability analysis

2.2.3 Human Resources (HR) Reporting and Analysis Requirements

Similar to the previous sections, the following is a list of requirements for reporting and analysis in the HR area.

- The content needs to leverage data from several different sources (SAP and non-SAP) and present it in a single report.
- The content needs to present highly textual information in a layout-focused format.
- Some of the content (such as employee appraisals or performance reviews) will likely be used as official documentation and therefore needs to follow strict layout rules.
- All of the tools need to leverage the security of the underlying system.
- The tools for the content need to offer specific features, such as date-organized aggregation to show the correct numbers for items (such as a headcount statistic or a salary at a given date for an employee). Resolving these time-dependent key figures is very important.

Commonly found example content in the HR area might include:

- Personal development—appraisals and qualifications
- Employee master sheet
- Employee termination statistics
- Termination trend analysis
- Employee recruitment planning
- Salary and bonus comparisons per year

2.2.4 C-Level Management and Leadership Reporting and Analysis Requirements

In this section, we highlight executive and management reporting requirements, which are applicable to all of the previously discussed areas—any business that needs a BI solution will also have a management team looking for specific numbers and information. The following are the typical requirements for the executive and management areas:

- The content needs to present highly aggregated information with alerts for important key performance indicators (KPIs).

- The data needs to be shown in a highly visualized manner and the main KPIs need to be presented in a single dashboard.
- The reports and analytics need to allow for further navigation to more detail-oriented reports and further analysis of the summarized data.
- The consumption of the reports and analytics needs to be simple and easy to use, and critical information needs to be easily identifiable.
- The information needs to be available on mobile devices.

> **Response Time as a Requirement**
> Performance and response time are important factors in the requirements for the management and leadership team. However, keep in mind that performance is not affected by the BI client tool itself; rather, it is related to the data warehouse and the BEx query design.

Some commonly found example content for the executive and management area might include:

- Sales management overview
- Sales pipeline overview and forecast
- Operational KPI dashboard
- Employee turnover

2.3 Mapping SAP BusinessObjects BI Tools to Capabilities

Before we go into the details of all our requirements, we look here at some of the main capabilities of the SAP BusinessObjects BI products and compare them to one another.

In Figure 2.1, you can see a ranking of the SAP BusinessObjects BI tools mapped to several key capabilities. Let's look at the details of these capabilities and provide more background and insight into the ranking.

- **Highly formatted layout**
  In this category, it's important that the tool provides full control over the layout, and that you are able to create a report that looks identical in all web clients or when exported to an external format (such as a PDF). The extreme

example of this is creating reports that are identical to legal forms; however, formatted layouts can be very important in other areas as well, such as a delivery notice, customer invoice, or a balance sheet.

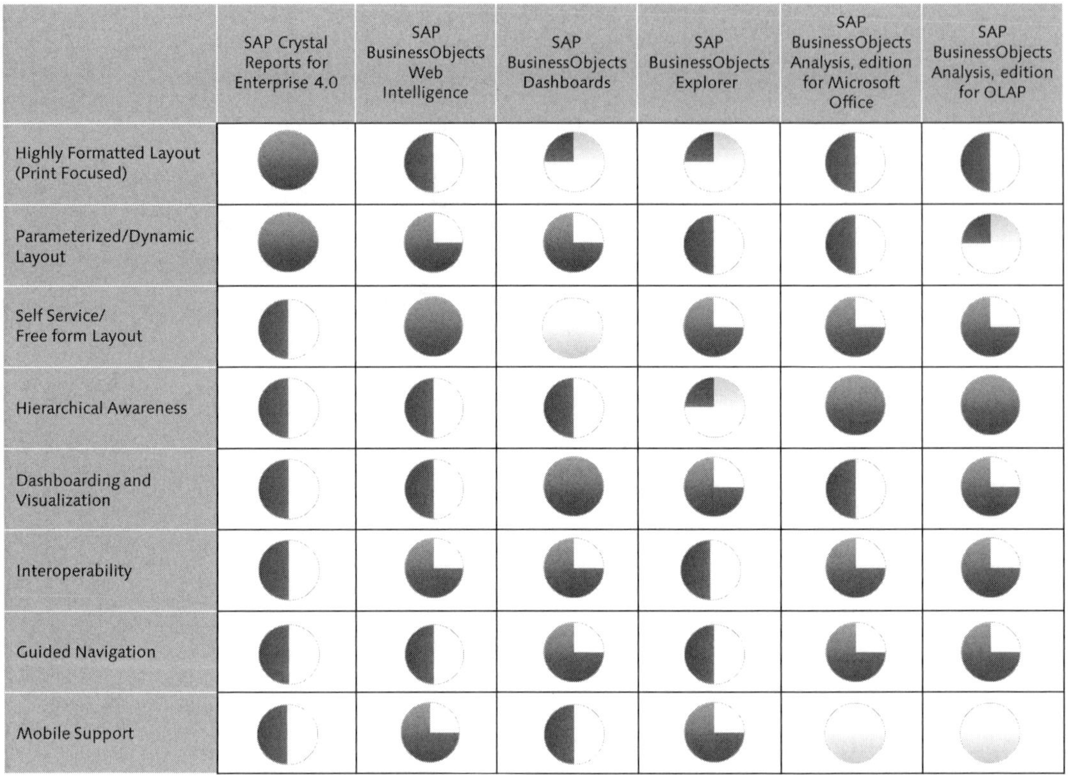

	SAP Crystal Reports for Enterprise 4.0	SAP BusinessObjects Web Intelligence	SAP BusinessObjects Dashboards	SAP BusinessObjects Explorer	SAP BusinessObjects Analysis, edition for Microsoft Office	SAP BusinessObjects Analysis, edition for OLAP
Highly Formatted Layout (Print Focused)	●	◐	◔	◔	◐	◐
Parameterized/Dynamic Layout	●	◐	●	◐	◐	◕
Self Service/Free form Layout	◐	●	○	◕	◕	◕
Hierarchical Awareness	◐	◐	◐	◔	●	●
Dashboarding and Visualization	◐	◐	●	◕	◐	◐
Interoperability	◐	◕	◕	◐	◕	◕
Guided Navigation	◐	◕	◕	◐	◕	◕
Mobile Support	◐	◕	◕	◕	○	○

Figure 2.1 SAP BusinessObjects BI Tools Mapped to Capabilities

- **Parameterized layout**
  A *parameterized layout* means that a report consumer can influence layout simply by changing some parameters. A good example is a report that allows you to see the data grouped as a simple list or as a chart. The user is able to influence the layout of the report by simply setting a value for a parameter that selects one of those options. Another example of a parameterized layout is one that has the capability of showing different types of data visualization based on user input; for example, showing a weekly, quarterly, or monthly comparison after the user has selected one of the three options. In addition, part of a parameterized layout is its ability to influence the layout based on defined

conditions and the data being retrieved. The simplest example of this functionality is the ability to highlight a key figure based on a value and thresholds. A more complete example is to completely suppress a Top 5 chart in cases where only three values exist and thus would all be shown.

- **Self-service/free form layout**
  Self-service reporting (sometimes referred to as *free form layout-driven reporting*) allows the user to create or change content without involving the information technology (IT) department in order to create a new report or make changes to an existing report. The concept of self-service reporting is more of an actual tool functionality than it is a type of report or analytics that can be created. Self-service reporting focuses on offering the consumer a tool that provides him with an easy-to-use environment that puts the user in the driver's seat of the report—enabling him to create or edit the report as needed.

- **Hierarchical awareness**
  In this category, the tools are compared based on the capability of leveraging an existing hierarchy from SAP NetWeaver BW and being able to present the hierarchy properly as part of the report. The tool should be able not only to actually identify the hierarchy but also to create a hierarchical organized report, to allow formatting of the report based on hierarchical information (such as the hierarchy level), and also to recognize things like a hierarchy variable and hierarchy node variable. In addition, this category also includes the actual hierarchy navigation that a consumer of the report can perform.

- **Dashboarding and visualization**
  This category focuses on the set of capabilities needed to visualize actual data and to provide dashboarding capabilities. It is important to recognize that this is not a comparison of all of the different charting options of the tools; charting is just one element of data visualization capabilities. Other elements include interactive navigation and the ease-of-use of the visualization.

- **Interoperability**
  Interoperability is the term used to describe the capability of the BusinessObjects BI client tools to work together. A typical workflow for this category could be that the sales manager starts in SAP BusinessObjects Explorer and searches for the revenue numbers for a specific product. After he finds the numbers and navigates in SAP BusinessObjects Explorer to see further details, he can then use the data and navigate to SAP BusinessObjects Web Intelligence so that he can conduct further analysis within that product.

As you can see in Figure 2.1, not all of the SAP BusinessObjects tools have the same ranking. These rankings are based on how easy or how difficult it is to set up the navigation from one tool to any other tool.

- **Guided navigation**

  The term *guided navigation* is used to describe the capability to provide ad-hoc analysis and to limit the scope of change for the user so that the user is able to change only specific parts of the analysis workflow. In addition, guided navigation refers to the functionality that allows the designer of the analysis workflow to create a pre-determined workflow for the actual consumer of the information. Think about a sales management analysis, where the user is able to see his top 10 customers and the top 10 opportunities in his pipeline upon the initial viewing of the analysis. In addition, he can see the top 10 opportunities with the highest risk factor of not getting closed in the current quarter. Instead of having to navigate through the data, the sales manager can click on a button and be "guided" to the second page of his analysis, where he sees more details regarding the 10 opportunities that are at risk. You can see that guided navigation helps create a predefined workflow for the consumer that is geared toward anticipating and providing answers to the most commonly asked questions.

- **Mobile support**

  Mobile support refers to the opportunity to access the content created by the BI tool on a mobile device. Explicitly, this category refers to supporting the mobile device as a native application, not to opening the BI content in a browser session on the mobile device. You will notice that there are different rankings among the tools, based on the fact that the support for different mobile devices—such as Android devices, iPads, or BlackBerry devices—varies among BI tools.

Now let's look at some technical capabilities, such as being able to connect to SAP NetWeaver BW and SAP ECC, and the hierarchical reporting capabilities.

As shown in Figure 2.2, you will notice that not all of the SAP BusinessObjects BI tools provide you with the same data connectivity options in regard to your SAP systems. A direct link to your SAP ECC system is possible for most of the products via the semantic layer. An alternative is the transient provider, which is part of enhancement package 5 for SAP ECC 6.0. When it comes to SAP NetWeaver BW, you will notice that some tools are able to leverage SAP NetWeaver BW data in a multidimensional way and, in addition, some products are also able to establish a relational view of the data in SAP NetWeaver BW via the semantic layer.

	SAP Crystal Reports 2011	SAP Crystal Reports for Enterprise 4.0	SAP BusinessObjects Web Intelligence	SAP BusinessObjects Dashboards	Analysis, edition for Microsoft Office	Analysis, editon for OLAP	SAP BusinessObjects Explorer
SAP ECC (Directly)	✓	✓	✓	✓	✗	✗	✓
SAP ECC (Via Transient Provider ECC 6—EhP05	✓	✓	✓	✓	✓	✓	✗
SAP NetWeaver BW (Multi-Dimensional)	✓	✓	✓	✓	✓	✓	✗
SAP NetWeaver BW (Relational)	✗	✓	✓	✓	✗	✗	✓
SAP NetWeaver BWA (Directly)	✗	✗	✗	✗	✗	✗	✓
SAP HANA	✗	✓	✓	✓	✓	✓	✓
Non-SAP Sources	✓	✓	✓	✓	✗	✓	✓

Figure 2.2 Selecting the Right SAP BusinessObject BI Client Product Using the Data Source as a Criterion

In Figure 2.3 you can see a comparison of the BI products in terms of hierarchical reporting capabilities. For SAP BusinessObjects Dashboards, you can identify the exclamation mark for the hierarchical parameters and the hierarchical report design. This exclamation mark indicates that SAP BusinessObjects Dashboards is able to create hierarchical parameters, but not able to create a relationship between a hierarchy and hierarchy node variable. On the item for the hierarchical report design, you will notice that the number of components that can visualize hierarchical information is very limited in the 4.0 FP3 release of SAP BusinessObjects Dashboards.

Based on the preceding reporting and analysis categories and the brief descriptions of the compared functionality in each of them, you should now have a much better understanding of the strengths and weaknesses of each tool—even though this chapter did not compare every detail of every tool. The material up to this point is meant to provide you with an overview. You will see how the tools are differentiated from one another in the following chapters, where you are going to use the products and create the reports, analytics, and dashboards yourself.

	SAP Crystal Reports 2011	SAP Crystal Reports for Enterprise 4.0 FP3	SAP Business-Objects Web Intelligence	SAP Business-Objects Dashboards	Analysis, edition for Microsoft Office	Analysis, edition for OLAP	SAP Business-Objects Explorer
Hierarchical Member Selection	✓	✓	✓	✓	✓	✓	✓
Hierarchical Parameters	✗	✓	✓	✓ (!)	✓	✓	✗
Hierarchical Charting	✗	✓	✓	✗	✓	✓	✗
Hierarchies in Crosstab	✗	✓	✓	✗	✓	✓	✗
Level Based Member Selection	✗	✓	✓	✓	✓	✓	✗
Selection Based on Nodes and Leafs	✗	✓	✓	✓	✓	✓	✓
Ad-Hoc Exchange of Hierarchies	✗	✗	✗	✗	✓	✓	✓
Hierarchical Report Design	✓	✓	✓	✗ (!)	✓	✓	✗

Figure 2.3 Selecting the Right SAP BusinessObject BI Client Product Using Hierarchical Reporting Capabilities as Criteria

2.4 Mapping SAP BusinessObjects Tools to the Audience

In this section, we look at the different user types of the BI solutions and how the tools align with those user types. We also look at the skills that define each user type. It's important to understand both the requirements and the audience when making a decision about actual product usage. For example, you might need a report that provides information about several characteristics, which can be created with SAP Crystal Reports for Enterprise, SAP BusinessObjects Web Intelligence, and SAP BusinessObjects Analysis. However, because your audience is a group of not-very-IT-oriented information consumers, you may decide to use prepared reports with a small set of parameters (category: parameterized layout) to offer such functionality. If this is the case, the best decision is probably to go with SAP Crystal Reports for Enterprise.

It's very important to understand the different user types for the SAP Business-Objects BI tools and how those user types map to the different products. Before we begin, it should be stated that not every product from the SAP Business-Objects BI portfolio has been created for each user type. Each tool delivers a specific reporting and analysis user experience to a defined group of user types;

however, it was impossible to consider each individual user type when creating each tool.

Before we start mapping the BI toolset to the user types, we need to clarify what those user types are, and, more importantly, the needs and skills associated with the user types. We must look at this issue from two sides: what the user wants and what he actually needs to do in his day-to-day job. Beyond these two points, you must also consider the skill level of the user. Sometimes the choice of tool can be based solely on product features and functionality, but other times you also have to consider the skills of the person using the tool.

To keep it relatively simple, we break down our user types into four categories:

- Information consumer/business user
- Business analyst/power user
- Middle management/line of business management
- C-level management and leadership

You may notice that these user types do not include roles such as report designers or IT administrators. The reason for this is that we want to focus on the *consumption* of information, and how a user can leverage the BI tools to make informed decisions based on the provided information. The person creating the reports and analytics may have a different skill set compared to the user. Although we focus on the actual creation of the content in this book, it is important to understand the types of people consuming the reporting and analytical content. By doing so, you'll be better equipped to provide them with the right information in the right tool.

In Table 2.1, Table 2.2, Table 2.3, and Table 2.4, we define the typical characteristics and skills of our user types. We characterize each user type based on the following questions:

- What are some typical goals of the user type when working in a BI environment?
- What are some typical tasks for the user type?
- What other software does the user type work with on a regular basis?

These tasks and goals are not meant to be specific to an area such as sales or finance, but rather should be seen as generic descriptions of a certain type of task or goal.

Goals	Tasks	Regularly-Used Software
▶ Review regular sales reports and monitor individual accounts and sales status. ▶ Review regular account statements to control customer invoices and vendor accounts. ▶ Review actual operational measures against goals. ▶ Fulfill management requests for information as simply as possible.	▶ Find a prepared report, view the information, and print or export the information. ▶ Receive and review alerts from prepared reports and analytics. ▶ Schedule prebuilt reports and review the resulting information. ▶ Use predefined navigation steps and alerts to receive needed information. ▶ If required, provide information to the IT department for additional reports and analytics based on the needed information.	▶ Microsoft Excel ▶ Microsoft PowerPoint ▶ Microsoft Word ▶ Microsoft Outlook ▶ Internet browser

Table 2.1 User Type: Information Consumer/Business User

Goals	Tasks	Regularly-Used Software
▶ Analyze KPIs to find areas for improvement. ▶ Create deeper analysis to find details about anomalies. ▶ Leverage actual data and historical data to create detailed planning scenarios to enable more realistic forecasting and planning of future company key goals. ▶ Leverage the data and tools to provide answers ad hoc to the management and leadership team so that decisions are based on solid information.	▶ Review prepared reports for KPIs and analyze the prepared data for anomalies. ▶ Edit existing reports and, if required, create new reports and analytics on the fly to answer related business questions. ▶ Share analysis and results with a larger audience and the management/leadership team. ▶ Act as the go-to person for the management/leadership team by providing required analysis for informed decisions.	▶ Microsoft Excel ▶ Microsoft PowerPoint ▶ Microsoft Word ▶ Microsoft Outlook ▶ Microsoft Access ▶ Internet browser

Table 2.2 User Type: Business Analyst/Power User

Goals	Tasks	Regularly-Used Software
▶ Review and analyze regional/departmental goals and KPIs and share findings with upper management. ▶ Analyze information to measure the progress toward set goals and KPIs. ▶ Fulfill executive level requests for information as simply as possible.	▶ Jointly set goals and targets on a department/line of business level and continuously monitor and review those goals and targets. ▶ Regularly analyze operational reports and prepare analytical summaries for upper management. ▶ Leverage prebuilt reports to further analyze the detailed information. ▶ If needed, leverage the tools to further analyze the information and to measure the current against the agreed-upon goals.	▶ Microsoft Excel ▶ Microsoft PowerPoint ▶ Microsoft Word ▶ Microsoft Outlook ▶ Internet browser

Table 2.3 User Type: Middle Management/Line of Business Management

Goals	Tasks	Regularly-Used Software
▶ Analyze overall companywide operational metrics and ensure that agreed-upon targets are met. ▶ Oversee cross department/line of business performance and evaluate different scenarios for planning and forecasting purposes. ▶ Leverage the information for analyzing, monitoring, and planning purposes to continuously improve company performance. ▶ Combine the analytics with company strategies and goals and integrate these strategies and goals into each employee's workflow and goals.	▶ Review companywide metrics (including past, actual, and forecasted values), make informed decisions, and take necessary actions. ▶ Set goals and targets for middle management and link them back to companywide goals and metrics. Continuously monitor and review those goals and targets. ▶ Regularly review operational KPIs and look for opportunities to improve operations and profit.	▶ Microsoft Excel ▶ Microsoft Outlook ▶ Internet browser

Table 2.4 User Type: C-Level Leadership and Management Team

Now that we've defined our user types, we need to map these user types (based on their needs and skills) to the SAP BusinessObjects BI tools.

Figure 2.4 shows the four user types and the tools to address their needs. This does not mean, for example, that you cannot use SAP BusinessObjects Explorer for a typical business analyst audience, but it is possible that business analysts will not be 100% satisfied with the tool, and may prefer a tool like SAP Business-Objects Analysis to perform their work.

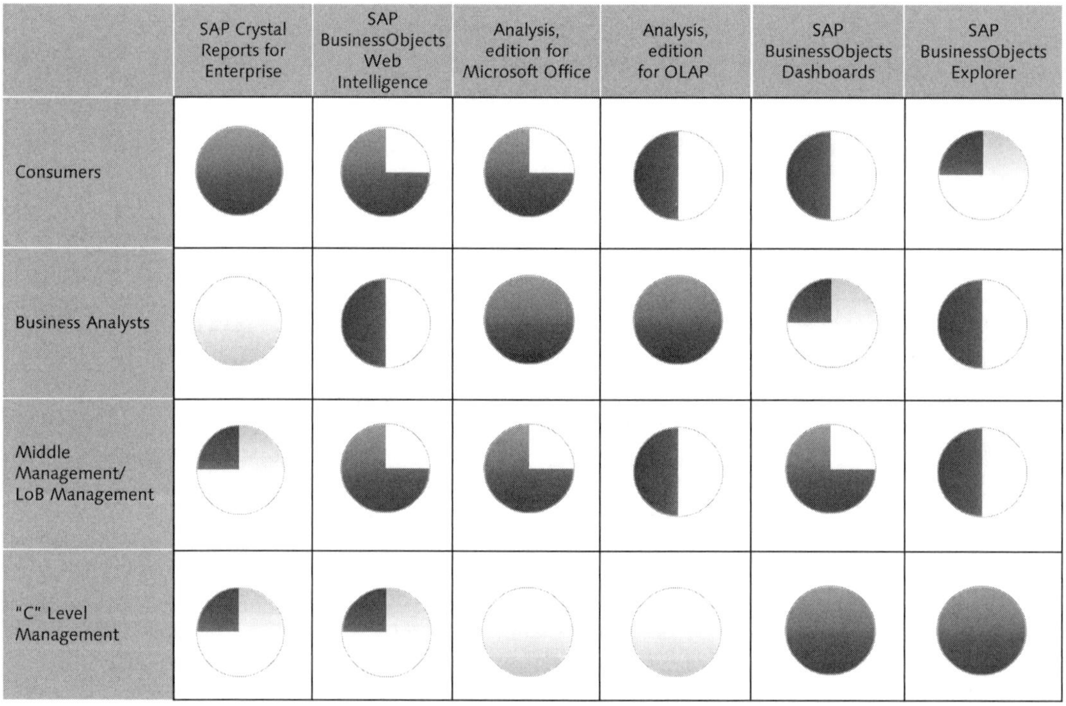

	SAP Crystal Reports for Enterprise	SAP BusinessObjects Web Intelligence	Analysis, edition for Microsoft Office	Analysis, edition for OLAP	SAP BusinessObjects Dashboards	SAP BusinessObjects Explorer
Consumers	●	◕	◕	◐	◐	◔
Business Analysts	○	◐	●	●	◑	●
Middle Management/ LoB Management	◔	◕	●	◐	◕	◐
"C" Level Management	◐	◕	○	○	●	●

Figure 2.4 Mapping SAP BusinessObjects BI Tools to User Types

Figure 2.4 is not an exclusive statement, meaning that the user types should use only the tools shown. It is a guide for tool selection. As you become more familiar with the tools in SAP BusinessObjects, you will be able to use your own judgment and add your own criteria to the decision-making process. In cases where a tool covers only part of a user type (for example, SAP BusinessObjects Web Intelligence for a business analyst), you can assume that you will be able to address some of the requirements and needs of that particular user type with the tool.

However, there will still be some areas that might be better addressed by a different tool. In addition, keep in mind that when selecting the tool, there is no single tool that provides all the functionality that you might need. However, each tool does have a main purpose (see Figure 2.1).

In addition to the capabilities, you also need to keep in mind the skills required by your consumers. In Figure 2.5 you can see the BI products along with the level of skills required by the user.

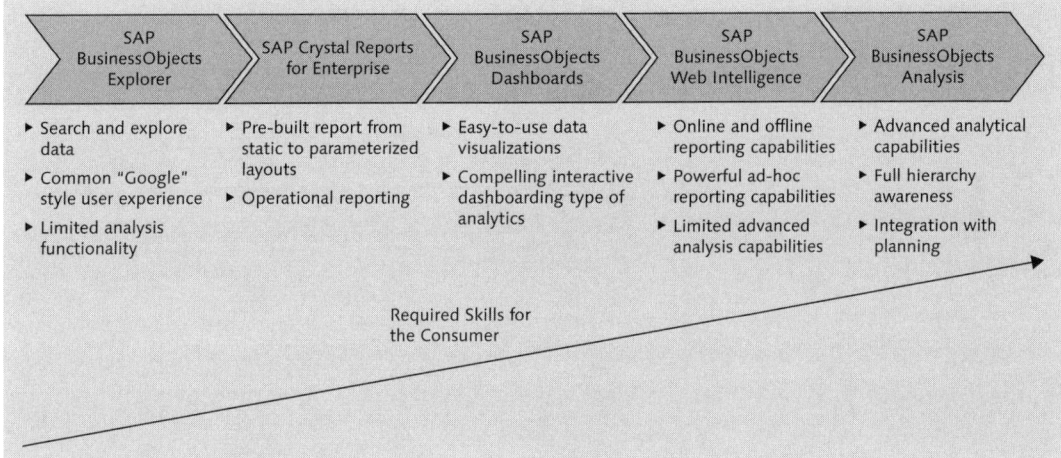

Figure 2.5 Required Skill Level

As you can see here, the required skill levels grow along with the self-service awareness that the tool offers. This is something to consider when selecting the right tool.

We are often asked whether there is a simple set of questions you can use that will lead to the right tool. In other words, people are always looking for some form of decision tree. In the previous edition of this book, we did include a decision tree to help people understand some of the major decision points along the way. In this updated edition, we decided not to include the decision tree, as we would rather see people really trying to understand the business requirements and using those requirements to select the right BI tool instead of simply following a small and limited set of questions.

2.5 Summary

In this chapter, you learned about the criteria that are important to consider when selecting a tool from the SAP BusinessObjects BI portfolio. In addition, you learned that not only are the functional criteria important, but the user type and skill set as well. In the next chapter, you will learn about the semantic layer as part of the overall SAP BusinessObjects BI suite, and which role the semantic layer plays for you as an SAP customer.

The semantic layer technology is a fundamental part of the SAP Business-Objects BI platform, and allows you to use existing metadata from your SAP landscape.

3   The Role of the Semantic Layer

In this chapter we explain more about the concept of the semantic layer as part of the overall SAP BusinessObjects BI landscape. In the second part of this chapter we review the role that the semantic layer plays in the overall SAP NetWeaver BW, SAP ECC, and SAP BusinessObjects BI platform systems.

3.1   Semantic Layer Technology

Before we discuss how you can leverage the semantic layer as part of your BI landscape accessing data from your SAP systems, you should be sure that you understand the basic concepts. This chapter is not about making you an expert in the semantic layer; it is about ensuring that you understand the basic concepts and terminology so that you know how to leverage the semantic layer as part of your overall SAP landscape.

As shown in Figure 3.1, the semantic layer provides your consumers a common experience when accessing information using the SAP BusinessObjects tools. The goal of the semantic layer is to allow your end users to leverage the information stored in different data sources by establishing a shared definition using business terms. This is achieved by hiding the complexity of the underlying data source and enabling the IT department to create a shared presentation layer.

You will notice in Figure 3.1 that you have a direct access and a universe access method. Figure 3.2 shows more details regarding what these different access methods include.

3   The Role of the Semantic Layer

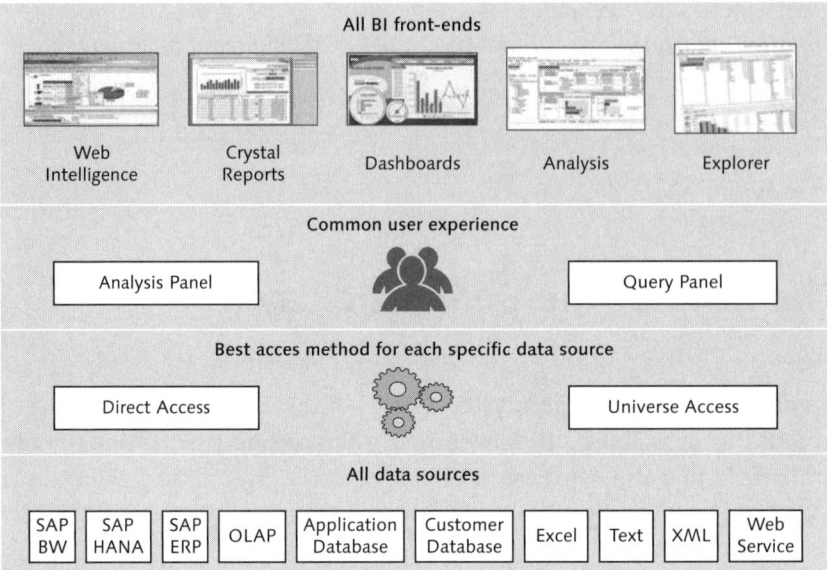

Figure 3.1 SAP BusinessObjects Semantic Layer

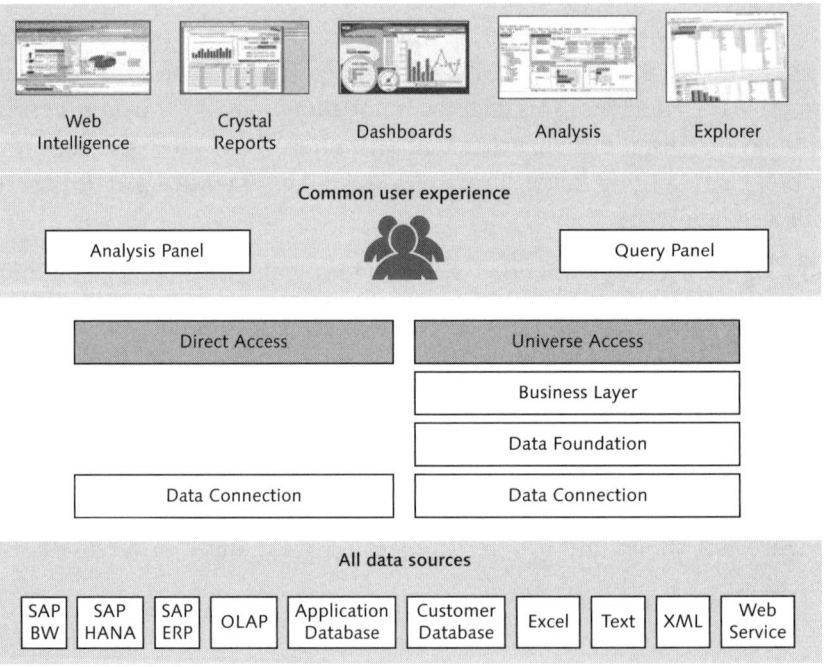

Figure 3.2 Access Methods

A direct access method is established under the assumption that the underlying data source provides enough information and metadata so that there is no need for an additional descriptive layer on top of the data source itself. A good example of such a data source is your BEx queries available in SAP NetWeaver BW. In SAP BusinessObjects 4.0 FP3, there is no need to create a universe, as your underlying BEx query provides enough information for your end user. In such a scenario, you simply establish a data connection to the underlying source and the semantic layer shows the retrieved information to the end user in the query panel.

The universe access method allows you to leverage all the capabilities of the semantic layer for those data sources that do not provide a rich set of metadata. In such a situation, you first set up a data connection (see Figure 3.2) to the underlying data source. In the second step, you create a data foundation, where you can define the joins between tables, setup parameters, list of values, and many other definitions that help you to enrich the metadata. The third step is to create a business layer, where you can leverage the definitions from the data foundation and provide a structure for your end users based on a business structure and using business terms. You can then export the established business layer to your SAP BusinessObjects BI system in the form of a universe, which is what the end user will see in the query panel.

Now that you have learned about the two different methods of connecting to the sources, let's clarify a few technical terms that you might come across:

- *The semantic layer* is a technology that is part of the SAP BusinessObjects stack; it allows you to expose a given data source to your end users using more user-friendly business terms.
- *Universes* are artifacts created using the Information Design Tool as part of the SAP BusinessObjects 4.0 FP3 release and using the Universe Designer as part of the SAP BusinessObjects XI 3.x release. Universes represent a model using a data connection and business terms. They can be used by the BI client tools to expose information to end users.
- *Dimensional universes* are one form of universes. They focus on multidimensional capabilities, such as hierarchies.
- *Relational universes* are another form of universes. They expose business terms in a flat view to end users.

- *Multisource universes* allow users to combine multiple data sources into a single universe and thus expose these multiple sources to end users in the form of a single logical view.
- *BI Consumer Services (BICS)* is a direct access option provided by the semantic layer. The BICS connectivity option allows the semantic layer to expose a BEx query directly to the BI client tool without the need to create a universe.
- The *Information Design Tool* is the client tool that allows you to connect to data sources and expose them in the form of business layers to your end users.
- *Universe Designer* is the previous version of the Information Design Tool for the SAP BusinessObjects XI 3.1 release.

You will notice that as part of the SAP BusinessObjects 4.0 FP3 release, all BI client products try to provide as much consistency as possible, including in the terms that are used. It is import to acknowledge that all the SAP BusinessObjects BI client products are moving away from using SAP NetWeaver BW-specific terms and toward using a common set of terms.

Table 3.1 shows previously-used SAP NetWeaver BW terms and the matching terms for the SAP BusinessObjects BI platform.

BEx Query Terms	SAP BusinessObjects 4.x Terms
Key figure	Measure
Characteristic	Dimension
Variable	Prompt
Characteristic values	Member
Condition	Filter by measure
Exception	Conditional formatting

Table 3.1 Terms Used in SAP BusinessObjects 4.0

In this section we reviewed the general concept of the semantic layer as part of the overall SAP BusinessObjects BI stack. In the next section we discuss the implications of the overall SAP landscape.

3.2 Data Connectivity Options for SAP Systems

In this section we review the overall options that you can use to connect from your SAP BusinessObjects BI client tools to the different SAP landscapes.

As shown in Figure 3.3, you can use the following options for a connection to SAP NetWeaver BW:

- SAP Crystal Reports for Enterprise; SAP BusinessObjects Web Intelligence; SAP BusinessObjects Dashboards; SAP BusinessObjects Analysis, edition for Microsoft Office; and SAP BusinessObjects Analysis, edition for OLAP are able to establish a direct connection to SAP NetWeaver BW using the BEx query.
- SAP Crystal Reports for Enterprise, SAP BusinessObjects Web Intelligence, SAP BusinessObjects Dashboards, and SAP BusinessObjects Explorer are able to connect to a universe using a relational data connectivity to SAP NetWeaver BW.
- SAP Crystal Reports 2011 is able to connect directly to SAP NetWeaver BW using the BEx queries without requiring a universe.

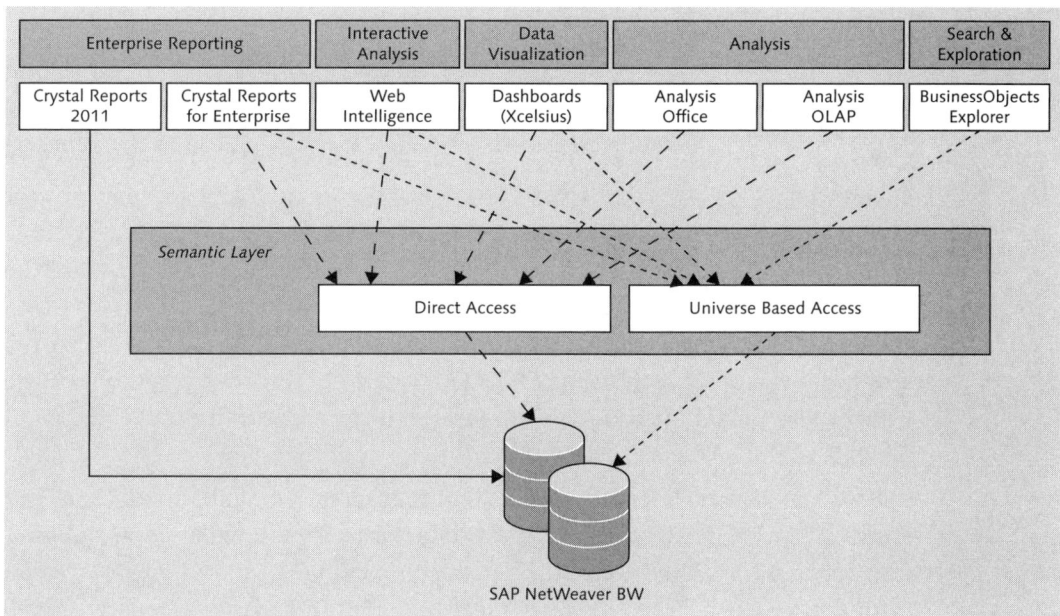

Figure 3.3 Data Connectivity Options for SAP NetWeaver BW

3 | The Role of the Semantic Layer

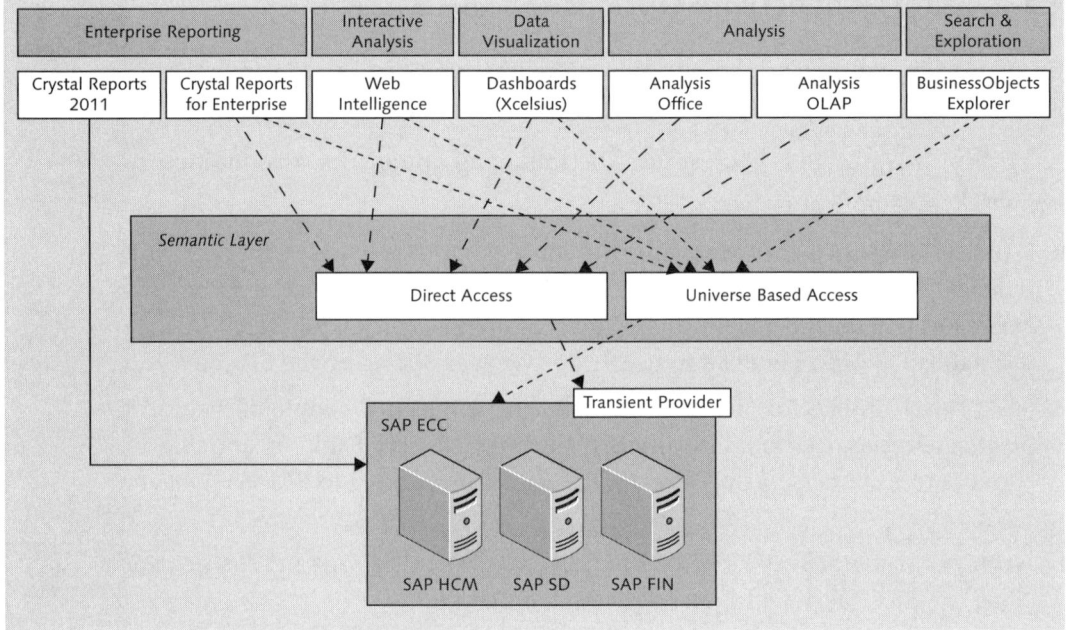

Figure 3.4 Data Connectivity Options for SAP ECC

As shown in Figure 3.4, you can use the following options for a connection toward SAP ECC:

- SAP Crystal Reports for Enterprise; SAP BusinessObjects Web Intelligence; SAP BusinessObjects Dashboards; SAP BusinessObjects Analysis, edition for Microsoft Office; and SAP BusinessObjects Analysis, edition for OLAP are able to establish a direct connection to SAP ECC using the transient provider. The transient provider is available with SAP ECC 6.0 enhancement package 05, and allows you to expose a classic InfoSet from the SAP ECC 6.0 system to the locally activated BI client of the SAP ECC system. In this way you can leverage a BEx query in combination with the transient provider and provide access to the data in the SAP ECC system.

- SAP Crystal Reports for Enterprise, SAP BusinessObjects Web Intelligence, SAP BusinessObjects Dashboards, and SAP BusinessObjects Explorer are able to connect to a universe establishing data connectivity to the SAP ECC system. With the release of SAP BusinessObjects 4.0 FP3, the semantic layer is able to establish a universe on top of InfoSet, ABAP functions, and SAP queries from the SAP ECC system.

- SAP Crystal Reports 2011 is able to connect directly to the SAP ECC system leveraging classic Infosets, ABAP functions, SAP queries, and the tables from the ABAP Dictionary.

In this section we reviewed the different options for using the information from your SAP system as part of the SAP BusinessObjects BI system. In the next section you will learn about some recommendations for these different options.

> **Details on SAP Connectivity Options**
>
> If you are interested in more details about the connectivity of SAP BusinessObjects 4.x BI tools to your SAP landscape, we recommend *Integrating SAP BusinessObjects BI Platform 4.x with SAP NetWeaver* (SAP PRESS, 2012), which explains installation, configuration, and data connectivity options in full detail.

3.3 Recommendations for Semantic Layer Usage

In the previous sections you received an overview of the different options available when establishing data connectivity from the SAP BusinessObjects BI system to your SAP system.

When connecting to your SAP NetWeaver BW system, we recommend the direct access method from the semantic layer, using the BEx query as your data source. This connectivity gives you the largest set of metadata and helps reduce the overall total cost of ownership (TCO) and administrative overhead, as it removes the need for a universe. If you are planning to leverage this data connectivity, please remember that your BEx query needs to contain all elements required for your reporting, as there is no additional layer involved that allows you to enrich the existing metadata.

The relational universe-based data access for SAP NetWeaver BW does have its place in the overall landscape. Customers looking to combine information from SAP NetWeaver BW with another data source are able to leverage the universe layer and use the multisource universe approach to combine multiple data sources into a single universe. Please note, though, that this connectivity is a relational-based data connectivity; as such, not all of the multidimensional concepts from SAP NetWeaver BW—such as a calculated key figure or an external hierarchy—are supported.

For data connectivity to your SAP ECC system, you can decide either to configure the transient provider as part of SAP ECC 6.0 enhancement package 05 and then to use direct connectivity, or to use the semantic layer on top of the SAP ECC system. In most cases your SAP ECC 6.0 environment might not have as rich metadata as your SAP NetWeaver BW system, so the semantic layer on top of the SAP ECC system can be an ideal option. If you are interested in a more analytical workflow and look to use SAP BusinessObjects Analysis, edition for Microsoft Office or SAP BusinessObjects Analysis, edition for OLAP, you will have to use the transient provider option; neither product yet supports the semantic layer from the SAP BusinessObjects BI platform.

3.4 Summary

In this chapter you received an overview of the semantic layer as part of the overall SAP BusinessObjects BI environment and you learned about the different data connectivity options available to you. In the next chapter we use SAP Crystal Reports for Enterprise to see which of our requirements can be fulfilled.

In this chapter we discuss enterprise reporting and how SAP Crystal Reports for Enterprise can be used to fulfill your requirements.

4   Enterprise Reporting with SAP Crystal Reports for Enterprise

In the first half of this chapter, we look at which business requirements established in Chapter 2 can be fulfilled by SAP Crystal Reports for Enterprise 4.0 FP3. In the second part, we use SAP Crystal Reports for Enterprise 4.0 FP3 to create reports based on those requirements.

> **Integrating SAP BusinessObjects 4.x with SAP NetWeaver**
>
> A complete discussion of the installation and deployment of the SAP BusinessObjects 4.x release in combination with your SAP landscape can be found in *Integrating SAP BusinessObjects BI Platform 4.x with SAP NetWeaver* (SAP PRESS, 2012).

4.1   SAP Data Connectivity

In this section, we provide a short overview of the options for data retrieval when using SAP Crystal Reports for Enterprise as part of your overall SAP landscape.

In Figure 4.1, you can see that SAP Crystal Reports for Enterprise is able to connect to the SAP ERP system and the SAP NetWeaver BW system. For the SAP ERP system, SAP Crystal Reports for Enterprise uses the semantic layer and in that way provides you with access to classic InfoSets, ABAP functions, and SAP queries.

On the SAP NetWeaver BW side, SAP Crystal Reports for Enterprise connects directly via BI Consumer Services (BICS) and is able to use BEx queries in that way. In addition, SAP Crystal Reports for Enterprise can use the semantic layer on top of SAP NetWeaver BW and provide you with a relational view on top of the InfoProvider.

4 | Enterprise Reporting with SAP Crystal Reports for Enterprise

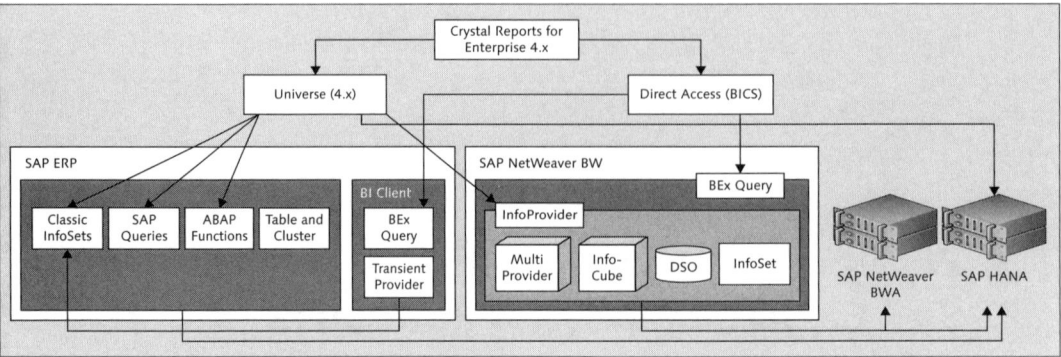

Figure 4.1 Data Connectivity Options

Table 4.1 shows the level of support for your existing metadata as part of your BEx queries.

	Direct Access using BICS	Relational Universe Access
Direct access to InfoCube and MultiProvider	No	Yes
Access to BEx queries	Yes	Limited
Characteristic Values		
Key	Yes	Yes
Short description	Yes	Yes
Medium and long description	Yes	Yes
BEx Query Features		
Support for hierarchies	Yes	No
Support for free characteristics	Yes	Yes
Support for calculated and restricted key figures	Yes	No
Support for currencies and units	Yes	Yes
Support for custom structures	Yes	No
Support for formulas and selections	Yes	No

Table 4.1 BEx Queries Metadata Support

	Direct Access using BICS	Relational Universe Access
Support for filters	Yes	Yes
Support for display and navigational attributes	Yes	Yes
Support for conditions in rows	No	No
Support for conditions in columns	No	No
Support for conditions for fixed characteristics	No	No
Support for exceptions	No	No
Compounded characteristics	Limited	No
Constant selection	Yes	No
Default values in BEx query	No	No
Number scaling factor	Yes	No
Number of decimals	No	No
Calculate rows as (local calculation)	No	No
Sorting	Yes	No
Hide/unhide	Yes	No
Display as hierarchy	No	No
Reverse sign	Yes	No
Support for reading master data	Yes	No
Data Types		
Support for CHAR (characteristics)	Yes	Yes
Support for NUMC (characteristics)	Yes as string value	Yes as string value
Support for DATS (characteristics)	Yes for value description. Key is supported as string value.	Yes for value description. Key is supported as string value.
Support for TIMS (characteristics)	Yes as string value	Yes as string value

Table 4.1 BEx Queries Metadata Support (Cont.)

	Direct Access using BICS	Relational Universe Access
Support for numeric key figures such as Amount and Quantity	Yes	Yes
Support for Date (key figures)	Yes	Yes
Support for Time (key figures)	Yes as string value	Yes as string value
SAP Variable—Processing Type		
User input	Yes	No
Authorization	Yes	No
Replacement path	Yes	No
SAP exit/custom exit	Yes	No
Precalculated value set	Yes	No
General Features for Variables		
Support for optional and mandatory variables	Yes	No
Support for key date dependencies	Yes	No
Support for default values	Yes	No
Support for personalized values	No	No
SAP Variables—Variable Type		
Single value	Yes	No
Multi-single value	Yes	No
Interval value	Yes	No
Selection option	Limited	No
Hierarchy variable	Yes	No
Hierarchy node variable	Yes	No
Hierarchy version variable	No	No
Text variable	Yes	No
EXIT variable	Yes	No

Table 4.1 BEx Queries Metadata Support (Cont.)

	Direct Access using BICS	Relational Universe Access
Single key date variable	Yes	No
Multiple key dates	Yes	No
Formula variable	Yes	No

Table 4.1 BEx Queries Metadata Support (Cont.)

> **Direct InfoCube Access**
>
> In addition to a different level of metadata support, when accessing the InfoCube directly, you should also consider that you do not have the functionality to create authorization variables to filter the data based on user authorizations.

With regard to the mapping of the SAP NetWeaver BEx query metadata, Table 4.2 lists further details.

BEx Query Element	SAP Crystal Reports for Enterprise
Characteristic	For each characteristic you'll receive a field representing the key value and a field for the description, including short, medium, and long description.
Hierarchy	Each available hierarchy is shown as an external hierarchy in SAP Crystal Reports for Enterprise.
Key figure	Each key figure can have up to four elements: numeric value, unit, scaling factor, and formatted value. The formatted value is based on the user preferences configured in the SAP system.
Calculated/restricted key figure	Each calculated and restricted key figure is treated like a key figure. The user does not have access to the underlying definition in the SAP Crystal Reports for Enterprise Designer.
Filter	Filters are applied to the underlying query but are not visible in the SAP Crystal Reports for Enterprise Designer.
Display attribute	Display attributes become standard fields in the query panel and are grouped as subordinates of the linked characteristic.

Table 4.2 SAP NetWeaver BW Metadata Mapping for SAP Crystal Reports for Enterprise

BEx Query Element	SAP Crystal Reports for Enterprise
Navigational attribute	Navigational attributes are treated the same way as characteristics.
Variables	Each variable with the READY FOR INPUT property activated results in a parameter field in SAP Crystal Reports for Enterprise.
Custom structures	A custom structure is available as an element in the query panel and each structure element can be selected or deselected for the report.

Table 4.2 SAP NetWeaver BW Metadata Mapping for SAP Crystal Reports for Enterprise (Cont.)

In addition to the BEx query connectivity we just discussed, you will notice in Figure 4.1 that you also have the option to leverage a BEx query on top of the newly available transient InfoProvider. The transient InfoProvider allows you to connect to an ERP data source—specifically an ERP InfoSet—without any data modeling required by SAP NetWeaver BW. The transient provider is available with enhancement package 05 for SAP ECC 6.0.

In the next section, we evaluate the requirements for enterprise reporting with respect to SAP Crystal Reports for Enterprise.

4.2 Assessing the Business Requirements

Now that you have learned about possible data connectivity options, we look at the enterprise reporting requirements and evaluate which of those requirements best fits SAP Crystal Reports for Enterprise.

We start with the financial area requirements mentioned in Chapter 2, Section 2.2.1. We filter the list to those requirements that cannot be fulfilled with SAP Crystal Reports for Enterprise or where we think SAP Crystal Reports for Enterprise is not a good match. It is important to realize that some requirements can be fulfilled with more than one tool, which does not mean that SAP Crystal Reports for Enterprise wouldn't be able to fulfill the requirements that we list here. However, we are trying to find the best combination of requirements for SAP Crystal Reports for Enterprise, and we need to understand that not all requirements will be satisfied using a single BI tool.

4.2.1 Financial Reporting and Analysis Requirements

Based on the list of requirements, there are only two requirements that we think SAP Crystal Reports for Enterprise will not be able to fulfill.

Unfulfilled Requirements
► The reporting and analysis tools need to let the user create new calculations and formulas and share those with other consumers of the content. ► Users need to be able to create planning scenarios and write information back into the source.

SAP Crystal Reports for Enterprise is not a tool that provides the end user or consumer of the report the capability to add new calculations and formulas; it provides highly formatted reports for the consumer to view information, but not to customize or change the actual content of the report. As such, this requirement is better suited for SAP BusinessObjects Web Intelligence or SAP BusinessObjects Analysis, edition for Microsoft Office or for OLAP, which all allow the user to add calculations and formulas on demand.

The second requirement that SAP Crystal Reports for Enterprise will not be able to fulfill is the need to create planning scenarios. SAP Crystal Reports for Enterprise is not designed to provide the consumer a very interactive user experience, and it also does not provide any write back or planning capabilities.

Especially the planning scenarios are much better suited for SAP BusinessObjects Analysis, edition for Microsoft Office.

4.2.2 Sales Reporting and Analysis Requirements

There are several requirements in the sales area that cannot be fulfilled with SAP Crystal Reports for Enterprise.

Unfulfilled Requirements
► Users need the capability to navigate within the data and change the view of the actual content. For example, they need to be able to change a weekly sales statistics broken down by country into a monthly sales statistics broken down by sales region and quarter.

> ► Users need to be able to modify existing reports and, if needed, create new ad-hoc reports.
>
> ► Users should be able to perform scenario-based analysis, where the user is able to see the data but can also influence certain factors and see the impact on the overall numbers; for example, a what-if analysis in a sales planning workflow.

Three out of the seven sales area requirements we identified cannot be fulfilled with SAP Crystal Reports for Enterprise. This may mean that most of the reports in the sales area will be delivered by another tool. Let's look at the three unfulfilled requirements and determine which tool is best suited to fulfill them:

- For users to modify existing reports or create new reports would mean that those users have access to the SAP Crystal Reports for Enterprise designer tool. Providing those users a tool like SAP BusinessObjects Web Intelligence or SAP BusinessObjects Analysis, edition for OLAP could offer such functionality in a web-based environment.

- For users to change the view of the report as previously described, SAP Crystal Reports for Enterprise can be used to a certain extent. However, if this is a very frequent requirement, another tool (such as SAP BusinessObjects Analysis or SAP BusinessObjects Web Intelligence) might be better.

- Scenario-based analysis is not possible with SAP Crystal Reports for Enterprise. You can integrate SAP BusinessObjects Dashboards (formerly Xcelsius) objects into SAP Crystal Reports for Enterprise content and provide such capabilities, but it is not something that SAP Crystal Reports for Enterprise can fulfill on its own. In addition, remember (from the financial area requirements) that if these what-if scenarios involve a write back, the best suited tool is SAP BusinessObjects Analysis, edition for Microsoft Office.

4.2.3 Human Resources (HR) Reporting and Analysis Requirements

Based on the list of requirements, there are no requirements that SAP Crystal Reports for Enterprise cannot fulfill, which is not surprising because SAP Crystal Reports for Enterprise is a tool that allows you to create content with highly textual information.

4.2.4 C-Level Management and Leadership Reporting and Analysis Requirements

There are a few requirements in the executive and management area that SAP Crystal Reports for Enterprise does not fulfill.

> **Unfulfilled Requirements**
>
> - The data needs to be shown in a highly visualized manner and the main KPIs need to be presented in a single dashboard.
>
> - The consumption of the reports and analytics needs to be simple and easy to use, and critical information needs to be easily identifiable.

SAP Crystal Reports for Enterprise lacks the functionality for data visualization and the ease of consumption such visualization offers. This does not mean that SAP Crystal Reports for Enterprise is not an easy-to-use tool. SAP Crystal Reports is, in fact, very easy to use, but the strength of the tool does not lie in its data visualization capabilities. Data visualization requirements are better fulfilled by other tools, such as SAP BusinessObjects Dashboards, SAP BusinessObjects Web Intelligence, and SAP BusinessObjects Analysis.

Based on the evaluation of SAP Crystal Reports for Enterprise against our requirements, we will use SAP Crystal Reports for Enterprise as the tool to fulfill most of our financial and HR area requirements. Requirements from the sales and executive/management area are better suited for another tool.

In the next section, you will learn the first basic steps for using SAP Crystal Reports for Enterprise as a design tool for reports.

4.3 Introduction to the Tool

Before we begin building reports, let's take a quick look at some of the basic functionality of SAP Crystal Reports for Enterprise. If you already have a basic familiarity with SAP Crystal Reports for Enterprise as a reporting tool, you can move on to the next section. However, if you are new to SAP Crystal Reports for Enterprise, you should spend time reading this section to become familiar with the new environment.

In the following sections, we look at some basic elements of SAP Crystal Reports for Enterprise and how to use them to build a compelling report. You won't become an expert after reading these sections, but they will provide you with an overview of the most important elements in SAP Crystal Reports for Enterprise. Throughout these sections, we explain the topics as simply as possible and offer examples so that you can see how each functionality works.

4.3.1 SAP Crystal Reports for Enterprise Designer Environment

When you start SAP Crystal Reports for Enterprise for the first time, you are presented with a start page. This page gives you the option of opening an existing report or using wizards to create a new report. In this exercise, we create an empty report without any data connectivity. This will allow us to concentrate on the tool itself.

1. Follow the FILE • NEW • FROM DATA SOURCE menu path.
2. In the next screen that comes up, click on CANCEL.
3. You should now have an empty report in front of you (see Figure 4.2).

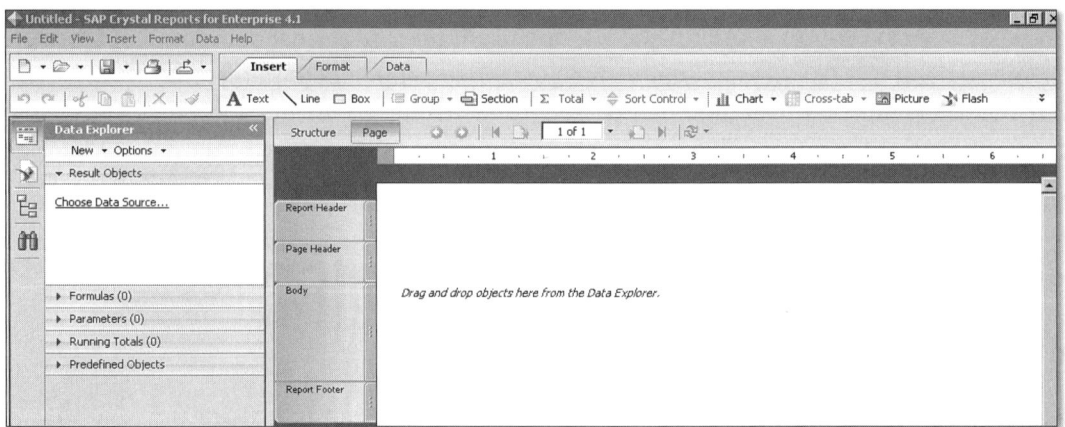

Figure 4.2 SAP Crystal Reports for Enterprise Designer with an Empty Report

Before we look at the menu items, let's look at the empty report. SAP Crystal Reports for Enterprise created a report with five areas called *sections*. These five sections are REPORT HEADER, PAGE HEADER, BODY, REPORT FOOTER, and PAGE FOOTER. These sections provide the basic structure of your report. The number and type of sections can change depending on the design of your report. For example, if you need your report to group the revenue by country, then your report will also receive a group header and a group footer section.

The report header and report footer sections are placed at the beginning and end of your report. These sections are often used to present summary information about the report or the data that is being shown.

The page header and page footer are shown on the top and bottom of each page and are mostly used to show information such as the page number or the date of the report.

The body section is the area that shows each record that has been received from the underlying data source. For example, a report with 500 records of data received from the SAP ERP system would have 500 detail sections—unless you suppress or hide them.

Based on the preceding descriptions, you should realize that SAP Crystal Reports for Enterprise is a well-designed tool that allows you to create structured, layout-driven reports. Let's look at the EDIT • PREFERENCES menu items to understand some of the available customization options (see Figure 4.3).

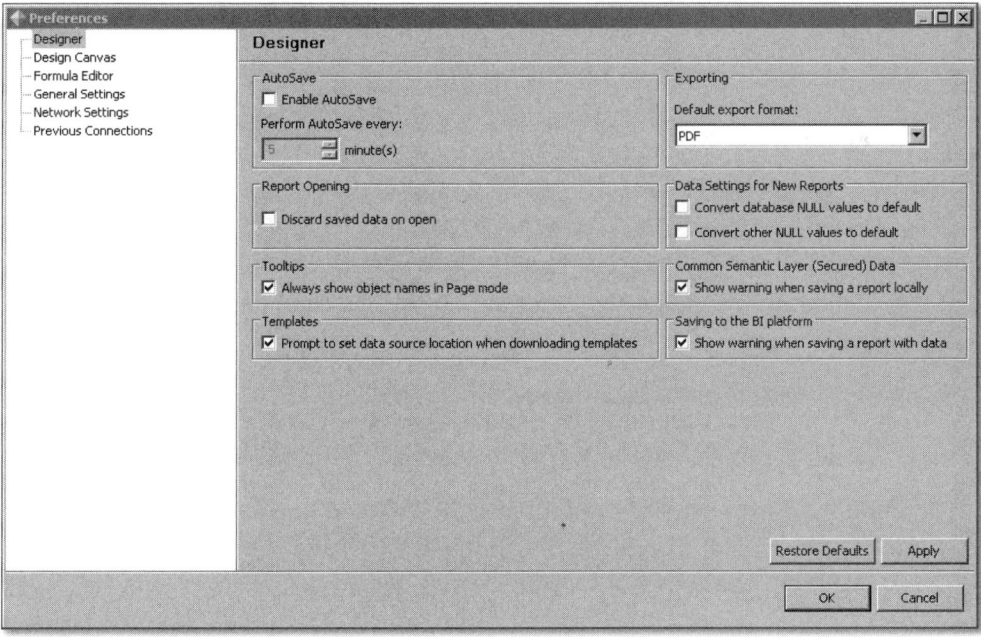

Figure 4.3 Preferences Menu in Crystal Reports for Enterprise

You can customize the look and feel of SAP Crystal Reports for Enterprise Designer on your system. Let's look at some of the customization settings that are available.

In the DESIGNER area you can specify how your designer should leverage different data connections, as well as establish settings for the export format and saving of reports.

In the DESIGN CANVAS area you can configure items such as the measurement units, rulers, and how the objects placed into the report are going to align with other elements and sections. Those familiar with SAP Crystal Reports 2008 will notice that Crystal Reports for Enterprise doesn't provide a DATABASE tab as SAP Crystal Reports 2008 did. This is simply because SAP Crystal Reports for Enterprise is much more closely integrated with the semantic layer, and those settings are handled as part of the semantic layer.

There are several menu items on the menu bar:

- The FILE menu is for creating, opening, and saving your reports.
- The EDIT menu has tasks similar to Microsoft Office (e.g., copy, paste, redo, undo, etc.) but also contains the PREFERENCES and SERVER CONNECTIONS menu items, where you configure the list of available SAP BusinessObjects systems.
- The VIEW menu allows you to select the elements and tools you want to see in your SAP Crystal Reports for Enterprise design environment. You can turn the Data Explorer or rules and guidelines on and off, for example.
- The INSERT menu is one of the most useful menus in SAP Crystal Reports for Enterprise. Here, you can find all of the available elements you can add to your report, such as creating a group, creating a chart, or adding a textbox.
- The FORMAT menu allows you not only to format the selected objects but also to configure conditional formatting and align and size several objects in a single step.
- The DATA menu concerns your data connectivity. For example, you can verify the database for changes or just simply log on to or log off of the database.

In addition to the standard menu items, SAP Crystal Reports for Enterprise also provides you with the typical tabbed approach, which you will recognize from other SAP BusinessObjects 4.x products (see Figure 4.4). During report design, these tabs directly provide the functionality offered via the INSERT, FORMAT, and DATA menus.

Figure 4.4 Tabbed Menus

Over time, you will start to use more and more of the toolbars with the respective icons for all of the menu items. When calling the menus, SAP Crystal Reports for Enterprise shows the icons that are shown on the toolbars in front of each of the menu items, which will help you remember them.

4.3.2 Data Explorer

The Data Explorer (see Figure 4.5) is an element of your SAP Crystal Reports for Enterprise design environment that you will use almost all the time. It provides you with all of the fields that you received from the underlying source, shown as result objects, or elements that you created yourself, such as FORMULAS, PARAMETERS, and RUNNING TOTALS. The list of PREDEFINED OBJECTS is a list of common elements, such as the actual date or time, page numbers, or the report title. In the VIEW • SIDE PANELS menu, you can switch the display of the Data Explorer on and off.

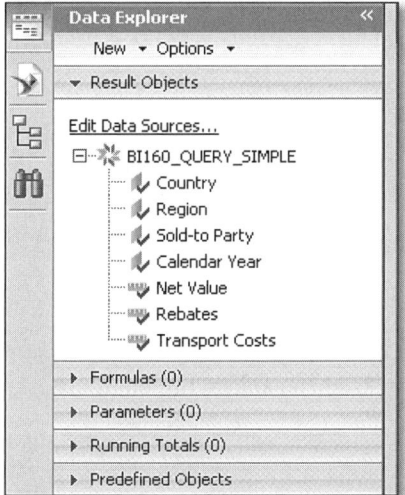

Figure 4.5 Data Explorer

4.3.3 Establishing a Connection to SAP NetWeaver BW

In the previous sections you learned about the design environment of SAP Crystal Reports for Enterprise. Now let's create a simple report on top of a simple BEx query. As you can see in Figure 4.6, we created a BEx query on top of the Info-Provider DalSegno Company Sales Data (technical name: 0D_DX_C01).

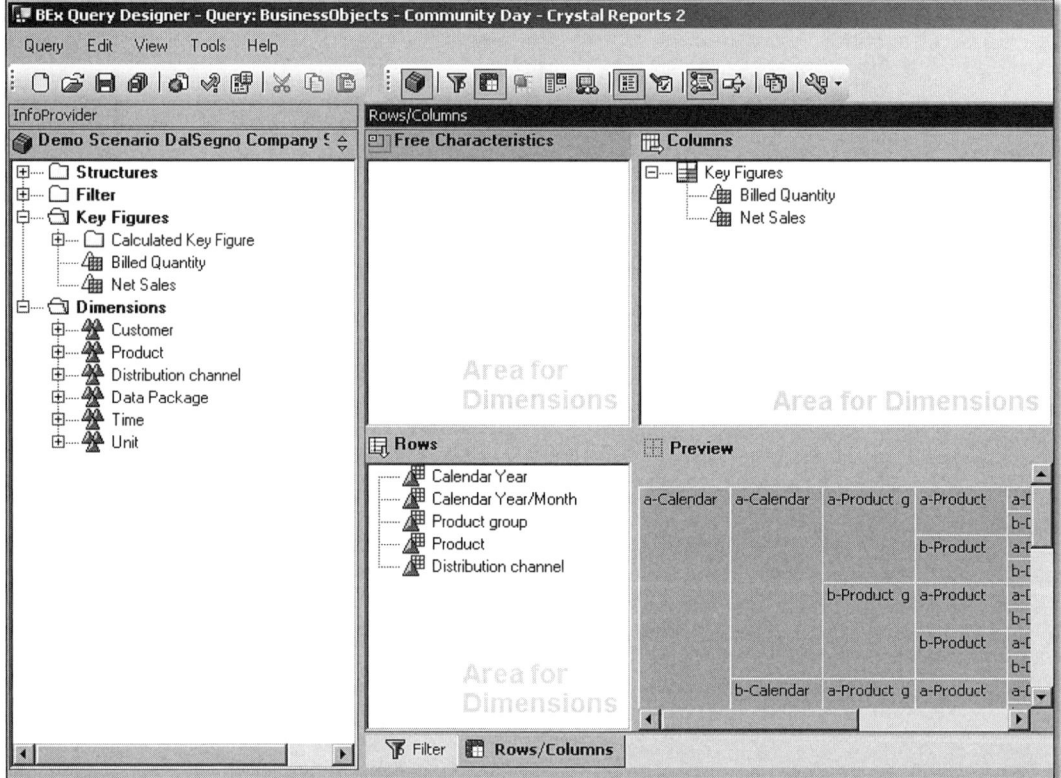

Figure 4.6 BEx Query

This is a standard demo content InfoCube, which means you can create the same query in your own system. In the BEx query we used the following elements:

- In the rows:
  - CALENDAR YEAR
  - CALENDAR YEAR/MONTH

- PRODUCT GROUP
- PRODUCT
- DISTRIBUTION CHANNEL
▶ In the columns:
  - BILLED QUANTITY
  - NET SALES

Before you can start using SAP Crystal Reports for Enterprise in combination with the BEx query, you need to establish data connectivity as part of the Central Management Console (CMC) of your SAP BusinessObjects system.

1. To start the configuration of data connection you need to log on to the CMC by opening the URL *http://localhost:8080/BOE/CMC* in your browser.
2. Log on with an administrative account.
3. Navigate to the area OLAP CONNECTIONS (see Figure 4.7)

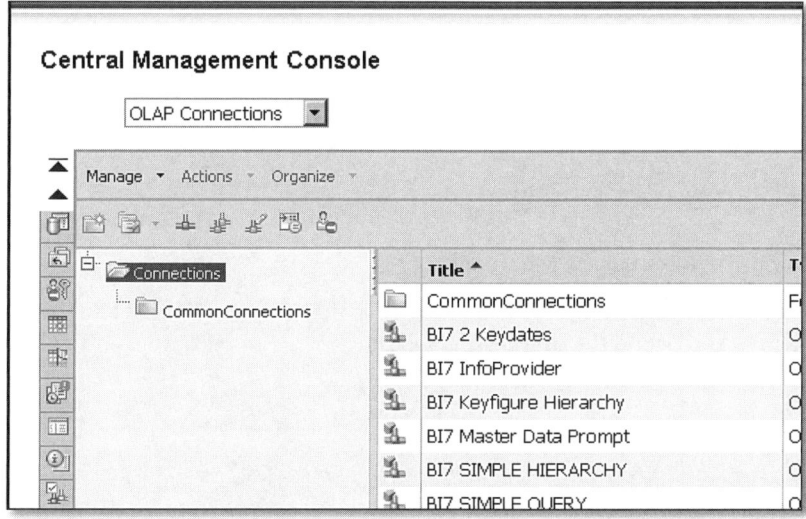

Figure 4.7 OLAP Connections

4. Use the CREATE icon ( ) to create a new OLAP connection.
5. Enter the details for your OLAP connection according to Table 4.3 with the values for your SAP system:

Field Name	Value Description
Name	The name of the connection the user sees in SAP Crystal Reports for Enterprise.
Description (optional)	Description of the connection. The value is optional.
Provider	The type of connection. For our example, select the SAP BUSINESS INFORMATION WAREHOUSE provider.
Server type	Here you can select between an application server (SERVER) or a message server with a logon group (GROUP).
System	The three-digit system ID of your SAP NetWeaver BW system. Example: IH1
Server	This is either the full qualified name of your application server or your message server, depending on the SERVER-TYPE you selected. Example: *ihilgefort.dyndns.org*
System number	The two-digit system number of your SAP NetWeaver BW system. Example: 00
Client	The client number you would like to connect to from your SAP NetWeaver BW system. Example: 800
Language	The two-digit letter code for the language. Example: EN for English
Save language	You can use this option to save the language, so that the setting in the user profile does not overwrite the setting in the connection.
Authentication	Here you can select one of three options: PROMPT, SSO, or USER SPECIFIED.

Table 4.3 OLAP Connection Parameters

6. Click on CONNECT (see Figure 4.8).
7. You are asked to enter your SAP credentials to log on to the SAP NetWeaver system. After doing so, you are presented with a list of InfoProviders and BEx queries (see Figure 4.9).

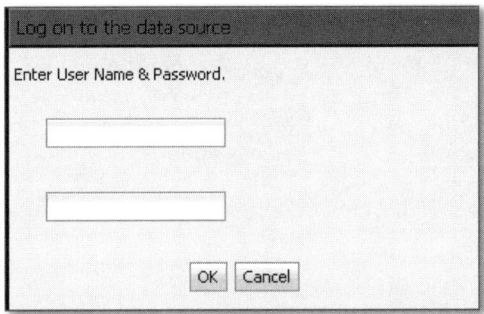

Figure 4.8 Log On to the Data Source

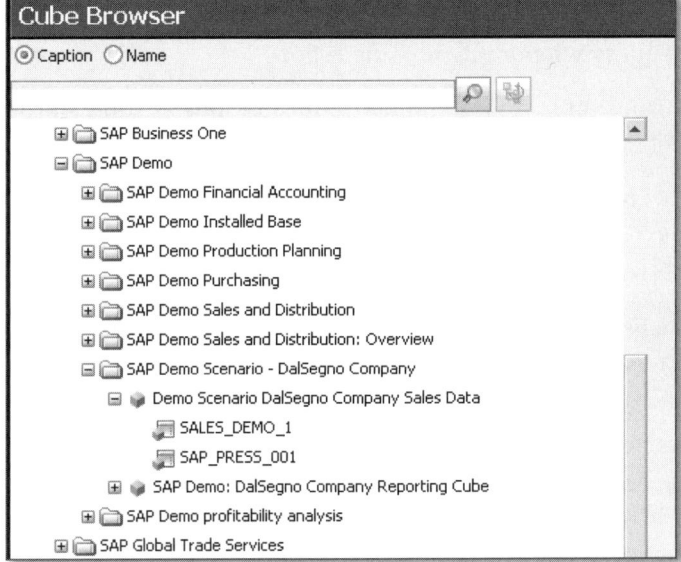

Figure 4.9 Cube Browser

8. Open the InfoArea SAP Demo.
9. Open the list of cubes from the InfoArea SAP Demo Scenario–DalSegno Company.
10. Open the list of BEx queries for the InfoProvider.
11. Select the BEx query you created previously and click on Select.
12. Set the Authentication to the value SSO.
13. Click on Save.

4 | Enterprise Reporting with SAP Crystal Reports for Enterprise

> **Setting Up the OLAP Connections**
>
> You can configure your OLAP connections to point to a BEx query, to an InfoProvider, or just to the SAP NetWeaver BW system. If you set up an OLAP connection that does not point to a BEx query, you will be asked, at the time of creating the report, which BEx query you would like to use.
>
> This is the case for all BI clients, except for SAP BusinessObjects Analysis, edition for Microsoft Office.

You have created an OLAP connection as part of your SAP BusinessObjects system. You can now build your first report using SAP Crystal Reports for Enterprise. In this case the OLAP connection points directly to the BEx query, but you can also establish an OLAP connection pointing to the InfoProvider and you will then be able to select the BEx query when designing the report.

Now we can start creating a simple report and take a further look at some of the common elements of SAP Crystal Reports for Enterprise.

1. Start SAP Crystal Reports for Enterprise by following the menu START • PROGRAMS • CRYSTAL REPORTS FOR ENTERPRISE 4 • CRYSTAL REPORTS FOR ENTERPRISE 4.

2. Select the menu FILE • NEW • FROM DATA SOURCE.

3. Select the menu option BROWSE REPOSITORY from the SAP BUSINESSOBJECTS BUSINESS INTELLIGENCE PLATFORM.

4. As this is the first time using SAP Crystal Reports for Enterprise, you do not have any SAP BusinessObjects server definitions (see Figure 4.10). SAP Crystal Reports for Enterprise relies on the semantic layer to provide the connection and therefore needs to connect first to the SAP BusinessObjects system to receive a list of connections.

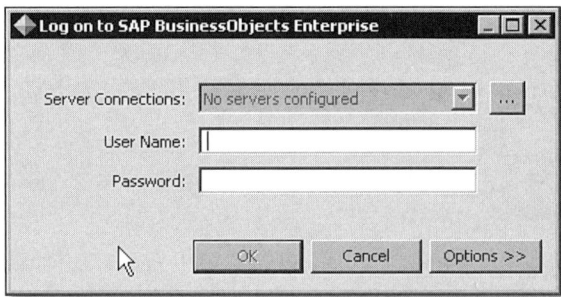

Figure 4.10 Log On to SAP BusinessObjects

5. Use the [...] button to open the SAP BusinessObjects server definition dialog (see Figure 4.11).

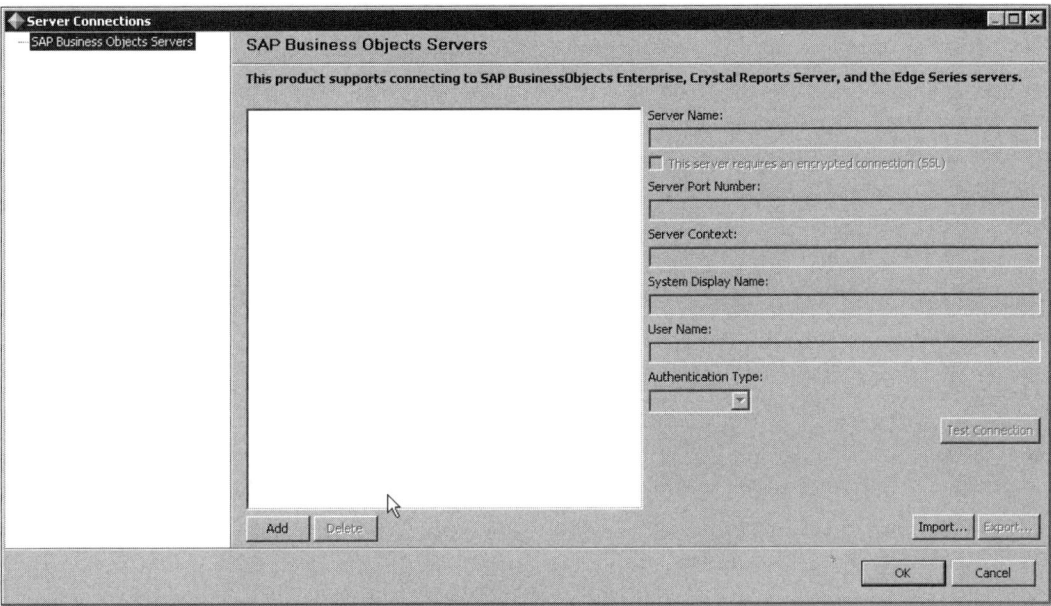

Figure 4.11 SAP BusinessObjects Server Definition

6. Click on ADD and enter the values according to Table 4.4.

Field Name	Value
Server name	This is the name of your Java Application server. Example: BOEXI4
Server port number	This is the port of your Java Application server. Example: 8080
Server context	This is the context for the deployment of the web services SDK. By default, this is /dswsbobje/services.
System display name	Here you can enter a display name for the server definition.

Table 4.4 SAP BusinessObjects Server Definition

Field Name	Value
User name	Here you can enter a user name that will be used as a default value.
Authentication type	Here you can select the default authentication type. Example: SAP

Table 4.4 SAP BusinessObjects Server Definition (Cont.)

In our example we configured the OLAP connection to leverage SSO to the SAP NetWeaver BW system; therefore, make sure you are using the SAP authentication when logging on to the SAP BusinessObjects system.

7. Click on OK.
8. Enter the necessary user and password. Remember to use your SAP credentials. The logon UI does not allow you to enter the system ID and client number; therefore, you need to enter your SAP credentials in the syntax: `<System ID>~<Client Number>/<User Name>`; for example `BW1~800/DEMO`.
9. Click on OK. You are presented with a list of available connections (see Figure 4.12).

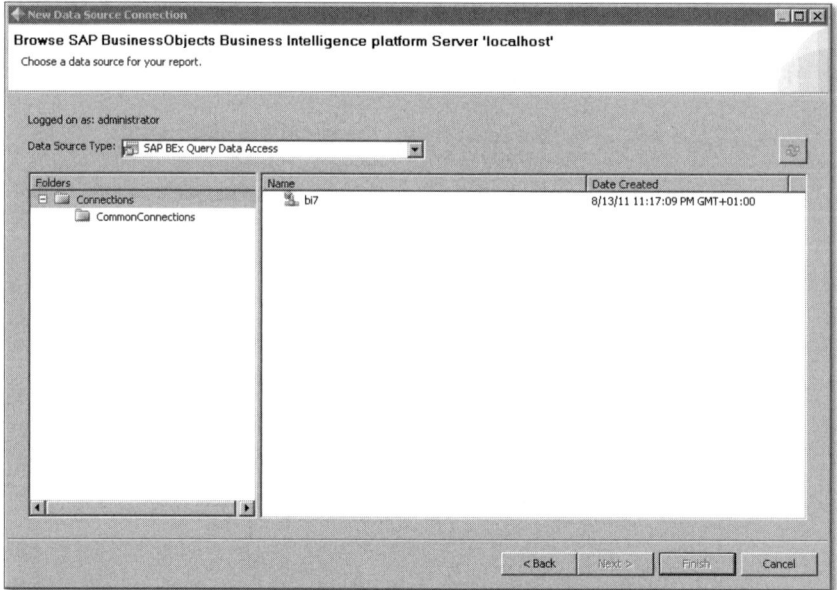

Figure 4.12 Available Connections

10. Select the previously established connection.
11. Click on NEXT. You are presented with the list of BEx queries.
12. Select the BEx query and click on OK.
13. You are presented with the query panel and you can select the objects and add them to RESULT OBJECTS (see Figure 4.13). Add the following items to the RESULT OBJECTS panel:
    - DISTRIBUTION CHANNEL KEY AND TEXT
    - PRODUCT GROUP KEY AND TEXT
    - CALENDAR YEAR
    - CALENDAR YEAR/MONTH
    - NET SALES VALUE
    - NET SALES CURRENCY

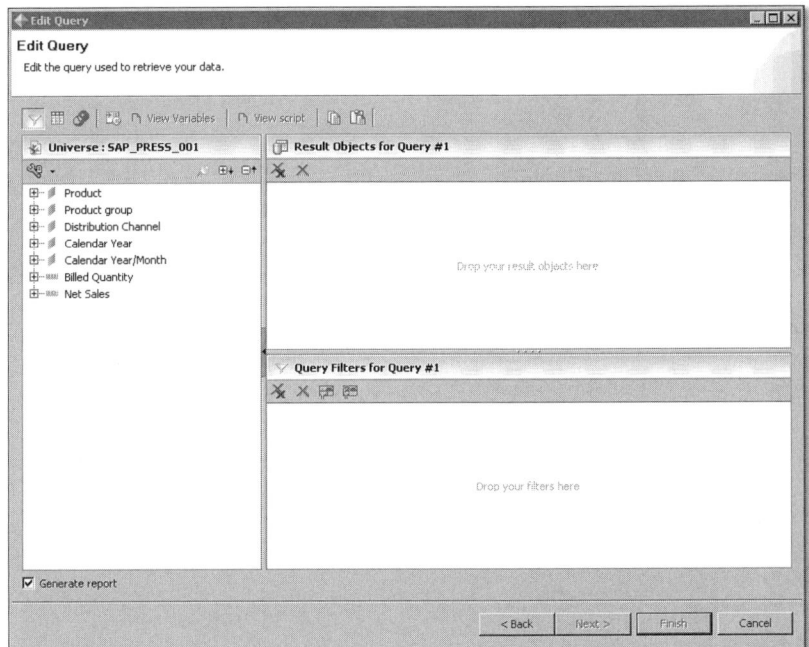

Figure 4.13 Query Panel

14. Uncheck the GENERATE REPORT option.
15. Click on FINISH.

16. Add the following elements shown in the Data Explorer to the body section of your report. You can simply drag and drop the fields from the Data Explorer onto the report.
    - DISTRIBUTION CHANNEL KEY AND TEXT
    - PRODUCT GROUP KEY AND TEXT
    - NET VALUE
    - NET VALUE CURRENCY
17. Reduce the height of the body section so that it fits the fields. You can reduce the height by simply reducing the height of the section (see Figure 4.14).

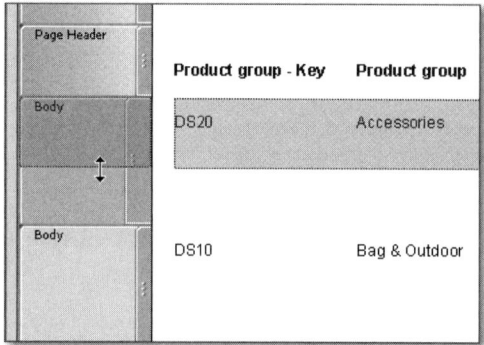

Figure 4.14 Body Height

4.3.4 Groupings

Let's now use the basic report we just created and create our first grouping in the report.

1. Follow the INSERT • GROUP menu path (see Figure 4.15).

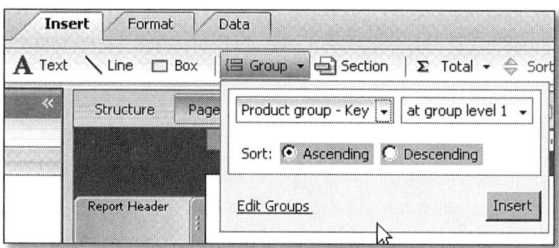

Figure 4.15 Insert Group

2. Using this example, select the CALENDAR YEAR field to group on. Configure the group to be ASCENDING.
3. Click on INSERT.
4. Select the STRUCTURE option to see your report structure (see Figure 4.16).

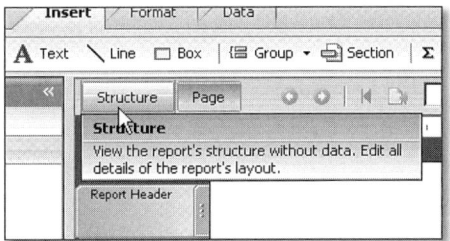

Figure 4.16 Menu Structure

5. Your report should look similar to Figure 4.17, and it should now contain a group header and group footer for the calendar year.

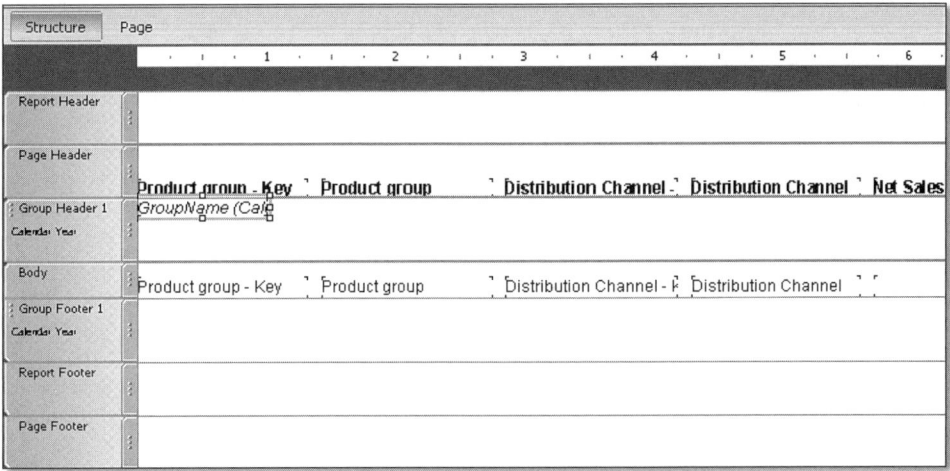

Figure 4.17 Report Structure

6. Click on the PAGE item to review your report with the data.
7. Select the NET VALUE object in the body section of your report.
8. Use a right-click and select the TOTAL NET VALUE option (see Figure 4.18).

Figure 4.18 Insert Summary

9. You can now select the summary type, for which group the summary is being created. You can also select where you want to place the subtotal.
10. In this example, select the DELEGATED option and the FOR EACH GROUPING OF CALENDAR YEAR option.
11. Select the ABOVE DATA option for the placement of the subtotal.
12. Click on INSERT.

Your report now has several fields in the body section, a group by calendar year, and a subtotal for the net sales key figure per calendar year.

> **Delegated Summaries**
>
> When connecting against a BEx query, all the key figures will be configured as delegated key figures, which means that SAP Crystal Reports for Enterprise will not aggregate the data but instead will request those from the underlying SAP NetWeaver BW system. You do have the option to select other types of aggregations in the SAP Crystal Reports for Enterprise designer, which means that SAP Crystal Reports for Enterprise has to calculate those numbers.

4.3.5 Section Expert

Now let's look at what kind of formatting options you have for the sections in your report.

1. Select the BODY section of your report.
2. Use a right-click and open the FORMAT BODY menu item (see Figure 4.19). You can now configure several settings for your body section, such as a drill-down or paging, or you can format your BODY section with multiple columns.
3. Navigate to the GENERAL area.
4. Select the SHOW ON DRILL ONLY option.
5. Click on CLOSE.

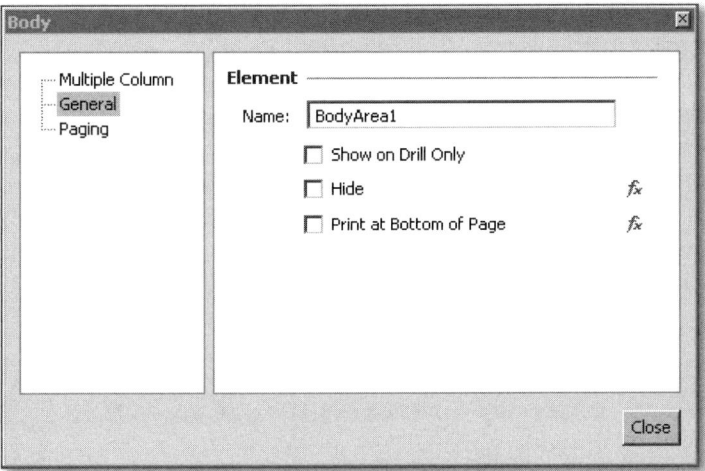

Figure 4.19 Body Section Formatting

6. Now your body section is hidden, but you can double-click on a calendar year and open a drill-down in the report. The drill-down will show as a separate page.
7. Because your group footer is now empty, you can suppress it. Right-click on the GROUP FOOTER 1 section and select the HIDE menu option.

> **SAP Crystal Reports for Enterprise: Designer vs. Viewing Experience**
>
> Keep in mind that all of the workflows that you are following right now are done with the SAP Crystal Reports for Enterprise Designer tool, but the user viewing your report can also perform most of these tasks, such as a drill-down.

4.3.6 Conditional Formatting

Now let's look at one of the most powerful tools in SAP Crystal Reports for Enterprise: the capability to influence formatting settings with formulas, called conditional formatting. Right now, your report shows net sales broken down by calendar year and, by drilling down, the user can see the distribution channel and each sold product with the net sales for each line item. You can add some highlighting to the report to identify the highest net sales products.

1. Open the STRUCTURE view of your report.
2. Select the NET SALES object in the BODY section of your report.

3. Use a right-click on the NET SALES field and select the CONDITIONAL FORMATTING menu item (see Figure 4.20).

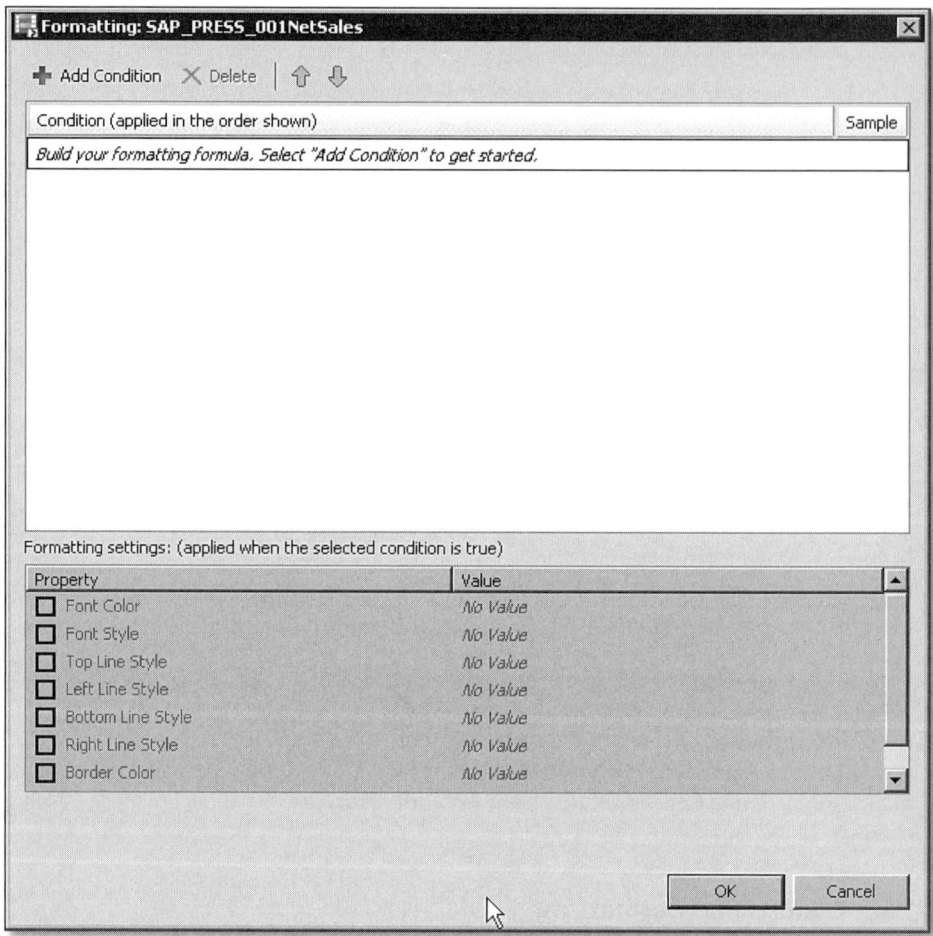

Figure 4.20 Conditional Formatting

4. Click on ADD CONDITION.
5. You can now set up a condition and configure the list of available properties for this condition.
6. User the GREATER THAN operator.
7. Enter the value "10000".

8. Select FONT COLOR and choose a yellow font.
9. Select BACKGROUND COLOR and choose a red color.
10. Click on OK.
11. Navigate back to the PAGE view of your report.
12. Drill down on one of the calendar years. Because you configured the CONDITIONAL FORMATTING on the value in the BODY section, you see the formatting only at a drill-down level.
13. Navigate back to the STRUCTURE view of your report.
14. Right-click on the BODY section and select FORMAT SECTION (see Figure 4.21).

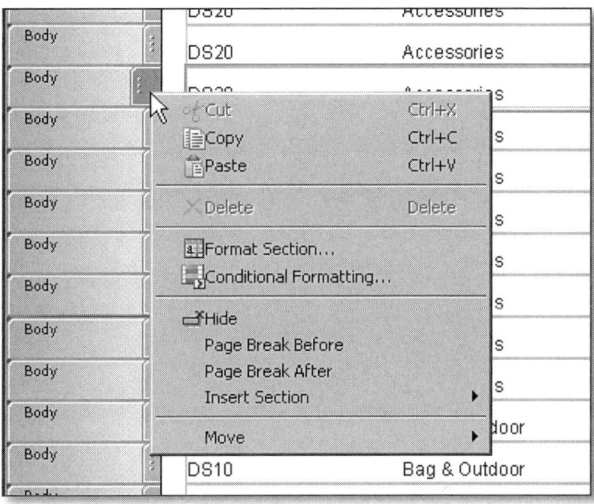

Figure 4.21 Format Section

> **Selecting Sections**
>
> You will notice that you can select the body section in its entirety or you can select the actual section. The complete body section can have multiple areas. Each configuration on the body section itself applies to all of the sections included in the body area.

15. Navigate to the GENERAL area (see Figure 4.22).
16. Click on the FORMULA icon (f_x) next to the COLOR (see Figure 4.23).

    You are now in the FORMULA WORKSHOP of SAP Crystal Reports for Enterprise. By default you are presented with the SIMPLE view.

4 | Enterprise Reporting with SAP Crystal Reports for Enterprise

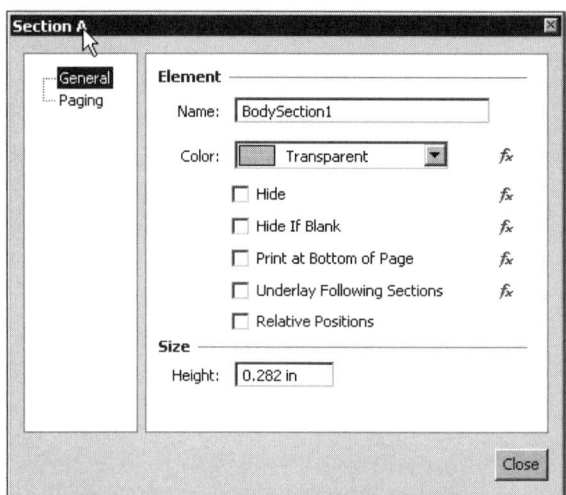

Figure 4.22 General Area

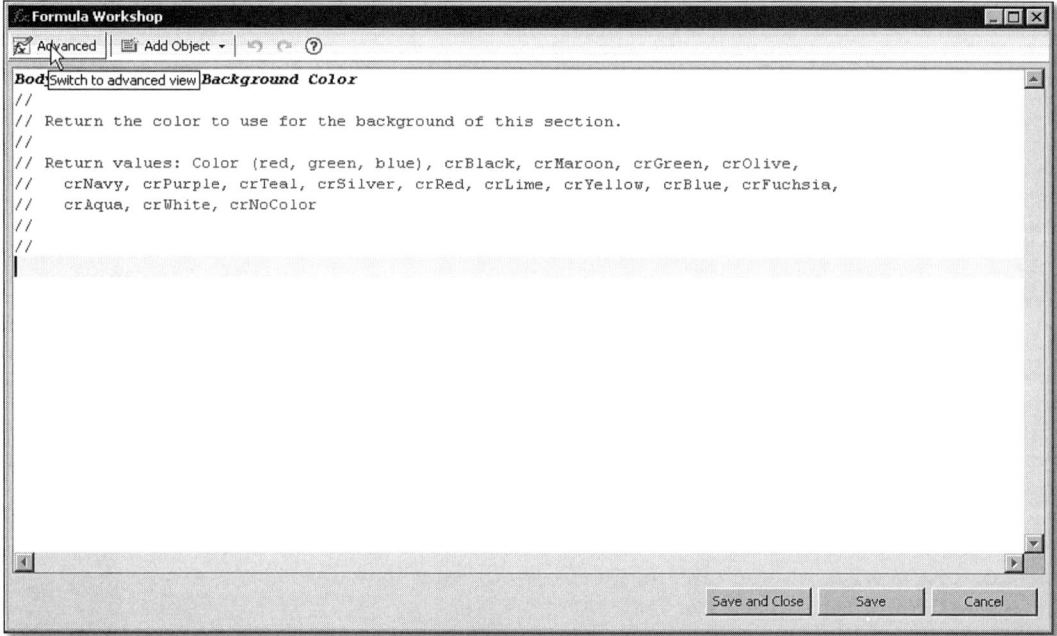

Figure 4.23 Formula Workshop

17. Click on ADVANCED (see Figure 4.24).

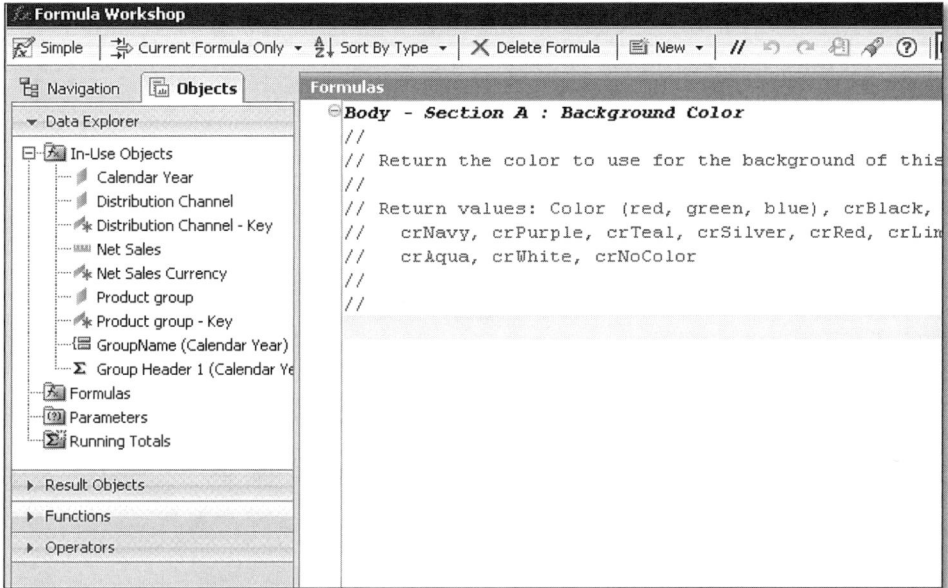

Figure 4.24 Advanced View

18. In the ADVANCED view you receive a complete list of FUNCTIONS, RESULT OBJECTS, and OPERATORS.

19. In this example, use a very simple formula:

```
if recordnumber mod 2 = 1 then crNoColor else crGreen
```

The formula divides the record number by 2. If there is a remainder, it sets the background color for the detail section to no color; if there is no remainder, it sets the background color to green. In simple terms, this means that the background for each second row becomes green.

You can type the formula manually but you can also use the functions. For example, you will find the color values in the FORMATTING FUNCTION • COLOR CONSTANTS area and you can add them to your formula with a simple double-click.

20. Click on SAVE AND CLOSE in the Formula Workshop. The symbol next to the color setting has changed to indicate that a formula has been created to influence the behavior.

21. Click on CLOSE.
22. Now when you drill down on one of the calendar years, you will see that every other row per calendar year has a green background. In addition, you will notice that the number highlighting has a higher priority than the background color (see Figure 4.25).

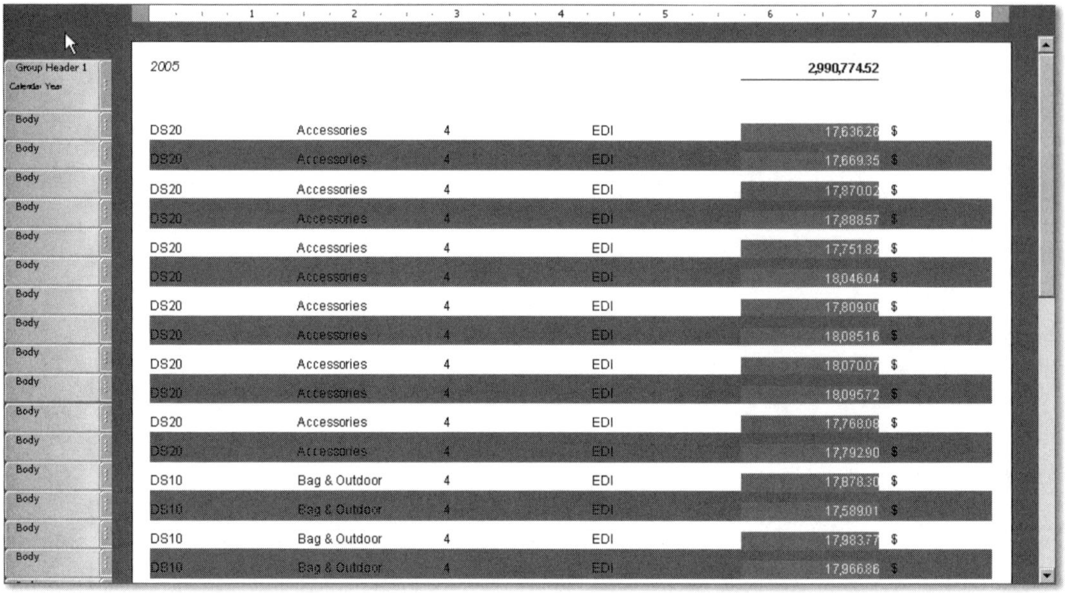

Figure 4.25 Formatted Report

4.3.7 Saving to SAP BusinessObjects

Now that you have finished the design of your report, you can save it to your SAP BusinessObjects system and share it with your consumers.

1. Follow the FILE • SAVE AS menu path.
2. Because you are already logged on to your SAP BusinessObjects system, you are presented with the list of available folders (see Figure 4.26).
3. You can now select a folder and enter a name for your report.
4. Click on SAVE.

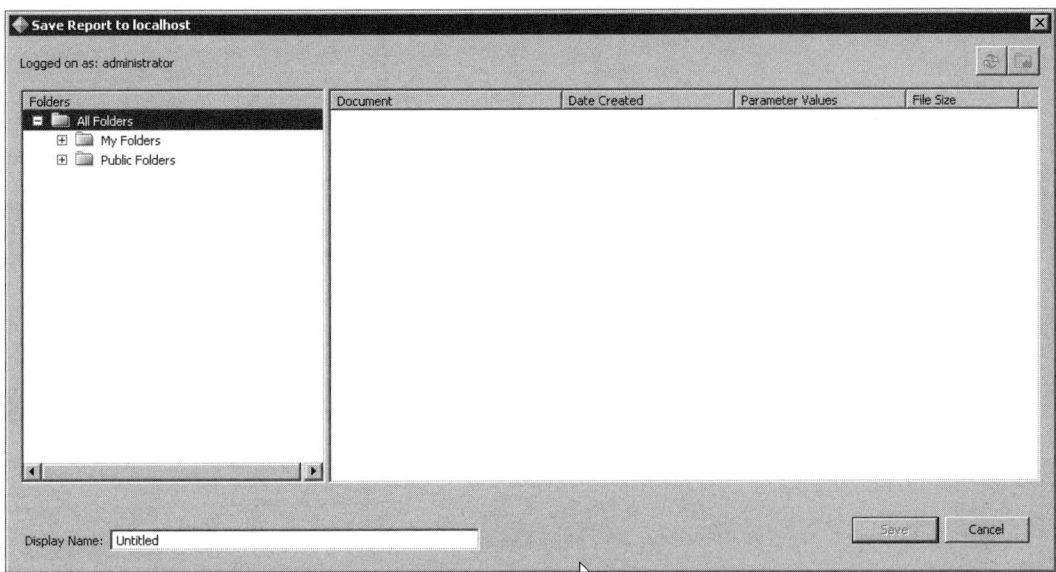

Figure 4.26 Save Report

Congratulations! You have created a new report on top of a BEx query and saved the report to your SAP BusinessObjects server so that other consumers can leverage the report in the BI launch pad.

4.4 Building a Report for Financial Analysis

Now that you have learned some basic functionality for SAP Crystal Reports for Enterprise, we will look at how you can realize the requirements from the previous section, and what steps you need to take to create a report with SAP Crystal Reports for Enterprise that matches these requirements. Based on the requirements and the tools that match these requirements, it is clear that SAP Crystal Reports for Enterprise is a great fit for the financial reporting part of the requirements. We start with reports from the financial area and take a look at how you can create a report for this area.

The first report that you are going to create is a profit and loss statement (see Figure 4.27) showing key figures such as balance, debit postings, and credit postings. The report should let the user select certain items when the report is being refreshed, such as the financial period, the currency, or the company code.

	Cumulative Balance	Total credit postgs	Total Debit Postings
Company Code 1000			
Selected Currency USD			
Fiscal Year 2011			
Profit and loss stat	-239,232,791.11	976,222,856.16	686,877,514.35
Depreciation	2,228,152.61	0.00	4,560,249.45
Depreciation on tang	2,228,152.61	0.00	4,560,249.45
scheduled	873,497.56	0.00	1,833,133.60
unplanned	1,354,655.05	0.00	2,727,115.85
Inventory changes	-357,414,570.52	745,198,585.29	400,746,363.08
Cost of goods sold	1,216,364.37	0.00	1,216,364.37
Cost of goods sold	3,921,221.71	2,479.97	4,849,613.15
Factory output of pr	-692,717,883.94	695,561,595.29	53,752.10
Inventory change - a	0.00	289,905.05	422,873.12
Inventory change - f	1,182.60	9,086.57	6,835.40
Inventory change - s	2,035,971.67	0.00	2,035,971.67
Inventory change - s	4,426,872.64	0.00	50,386,682.53
Inventory change CSA	-37,305,607.74	37,309,468.91	3,861.17
Inventory change -CGS	6,192,212.00	0.00	6,192,212.00
Scrapped material -	178,569.51	11,213,297.47	11,391,866.98
Semi-finished prod.	323,523,130.92	812,752.03	324,386,330.59
Other operating char	1,521,451.97	3,577,001.03	10,740,277.84
INT 3081000	288,802.05	4,852.16	3,417,495.24
Expense from allocat	288,802.05	4,852.16	3,417,495.24
INT 3083000	31,861.05	0.00	31,861.05
App operating costs	29,986.15	0.00	186.15

Figure 4.27 G/L Account Balances

To create this report, you will use a BEx query based on an InfoProvider from the Business Content. The BEx query is based on the General Ledger: Financial Statements cube, 0FIGL_VC1. The BEx query contains several variables that let you select the appropriate timeframe, financial periods, and currencies (see Figure 4.28). In addition, the BEx query organizes the information along the hierarchy for the accounts.

Before you continue creating the report, let's review the goal of the report. You want to create a detailed report showing all of the accounts with key figures and descriptions and the key figures for the balances. In addition, you want to show the information that was used as selection criteria for the report. In our example, we group the information per company code; if other groupings make more sense for your company, you should still be able to follow along. Based on these items, you might initially think that a cross tab is the perfect choice for such a report, but here are some points to consider:

Building a Report for Financial Analysis | **4.4**

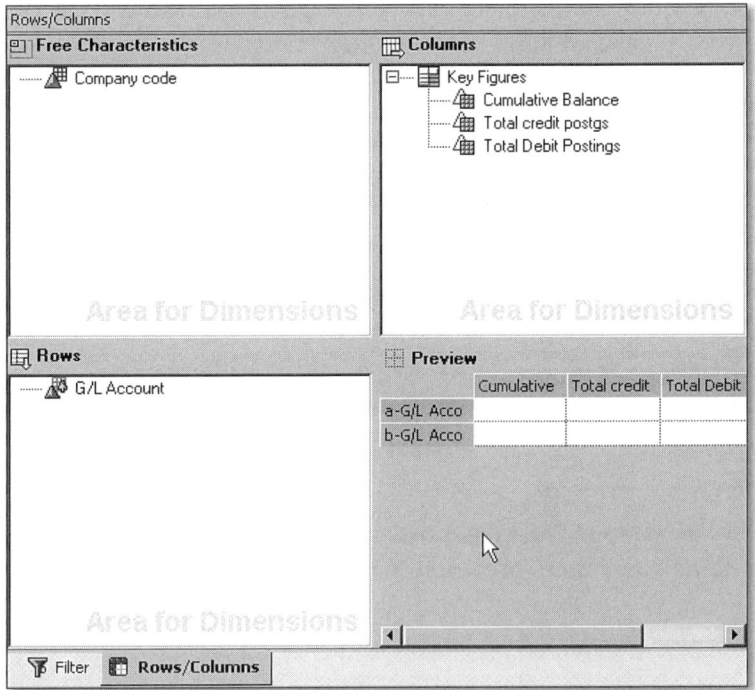

Figure 4.28 BEx Query

- When you use a cross tab, you can have only one field (similar to grouping) that distinguishes the groups. You can have several groups encapsulated, but each group is configured by one field. In our case, we want to show the key and description for the account, which means that we would have to combine the number and the description, but that would give us one field where the number would not be right-aligned with a left-aligned description—you can only align the combination of the text.

- The field that is used to distinguish the rows in the cross tab—in our example, the G/L account—loses the CAN GROW property for the field formatting. The CAN GROW option is relevant for our report because we might have G/L account descriptions that are relatively long and we want to ensure that the complete description is shown. In a cross tab, we would have to size all elements from the cross tab accordingly. Doing this would lead to a lot of wasted space in our report, because we would have to resize all of the rows—not just those where the description of the general ledger account field needs more than a single line.

89

Based on the preceding items, we will not use a cross tab; instead we will use the details sections of our report and build the structure.

Start with the report design:

1. To start the configuration of data connection, you need to log on to the CMC. To reach the CMC, open the URL *http://localhost:8080/BOE/CMC* in your browser.
2. Log on with an administrative account.
3. Navigate to the area OLAP CONNECTIONS.
4. Use the CREATE icon ( ) to create a new OLAP connection.
5. Enter the details for your OLAP connection to establish a connection to your SAP system.
6. Click on CONNECT.
7. You are asked to enter your SAP credentials to log on to the SAP NetWeaver system. After doing so, you are presented with the list of InfoProviders and BEx queries.
8. Select the BEx query you created previously and click on SELECT.
9. Set the AUTHENTICATION to the value SSO.
10. Click on SAVE.

Now we can start creating our report:

1. Start SAP Crystal Reports for Enterprise by following the menu START • PROGRAMS • CRYSTAL REPORTS FOR ENTERPRISE 4 • CRYSTAL REPORTS FOR ENTERPRISE 4.
2. Select the menu FILE • NEW • FROM DATA SOURCE.
3. Select the menu option BROWSE REPOSITORY from the SAP BUSINESSOBJECTS BUSINESS INTELLIGENCE PLATFORM.
4. Log on to your SAP BusinessObjects system. Remember to use your SAP credentials. The logon UI does not allow you to enter the system ID and client number; therefore, you need to enter your SAP credentials in the syntax: <System ID>~<Client Number>/<User Name>; for example BW1~800/DEMO.
5. Click on OK.
6. You are presented with a list of available connections.
7. Select the previously established connection.

8. Click on NEXT.
9. You are presented with the list of BEx queries.
10. Select the BEx query and click on OK.
11. You are presented with the query panel (see Figure 4.29).

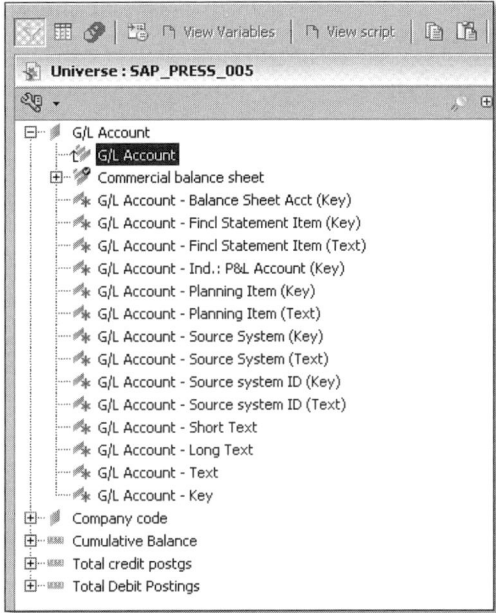

Figure 4.29 Query Panel

12. For our example, we will use the COMMERCIAL BALANCE SHEET hierarchy, which is the one we configured as part of the BEx query, and add it to RESULT OBJECTS.

> **Default Hierarchy in the Query Panel**
>
> In the query panel you will notice that if the InfoObjects contains hierarchies, you will retrieve a list of all hierarchies. You will also receive a so-called default hierarchy—shown in our example in Figure 4.29 as G/L ACCOUNT. The default hierarchy is the top entry of all hierarchies in the query panel, and is very useful in situations where you already defined a hierarchy in the BEx query or where you configured a hierarchy variable.
>
> The limitation of the default hierarchy is that you cannot leverage a level-based selection for the default hierarchy.

13. Add the G/L ACCOUNT KEY to RESULT OBJECTS.
14. Add all available key figures to RESULT OBJECTS. Also add COMPANY CODE to RESULT OBJECTS, because you want to group your report based on the company code.
15. Open the member selector for the hierarchy (see Figure 4.30). The member selector allows you to select the required nodes and leaves from the hierarchy.

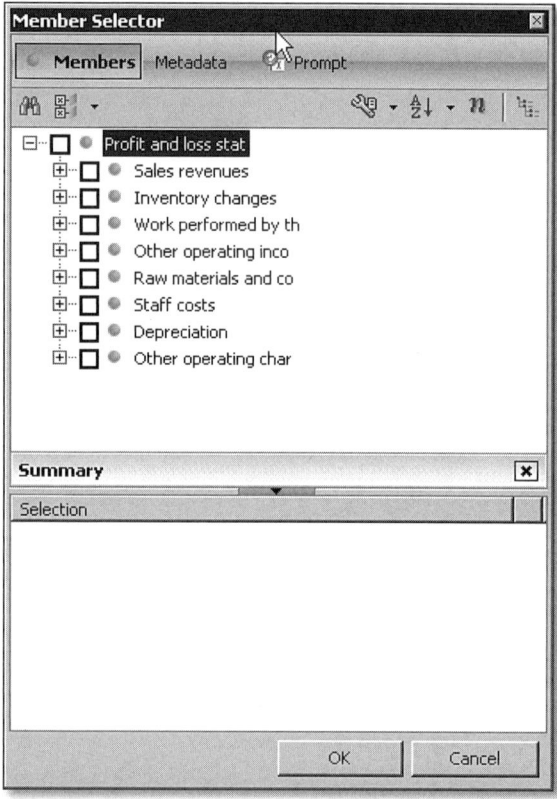

Figure 4.30 Members

16. For our example, we select all members of the hierarchy until LEVEL 04 (see Figure 4.31).
17. Click on OK.
18. Uncheck the GENERATE REPORT option.
19. Click on FINISH.

Building a Report for Financial Analysis | **4.4**

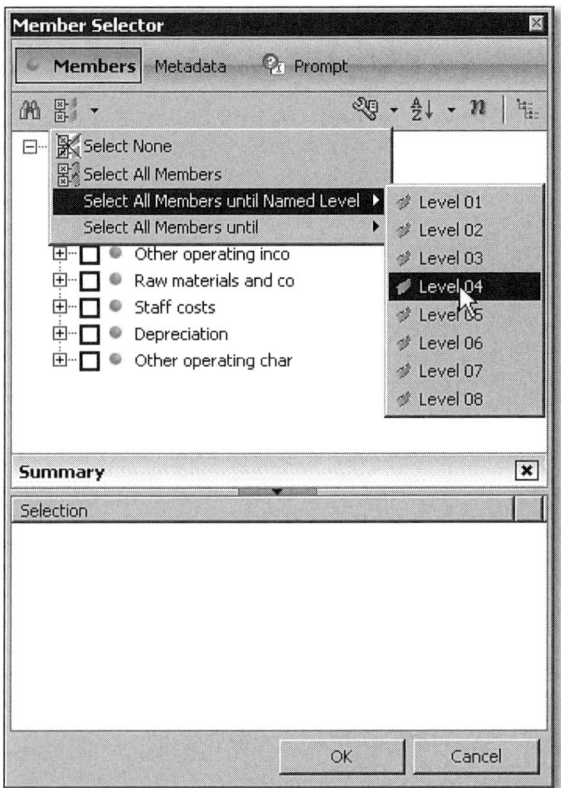

Figure 4.31 Member Selection

> **Level-Based Selection for Hierarchies**
>
> One of the major enhancements in the 4.0 FP3 release is the capability to select hierarchical members based on levels instead of selecting a fixed set of nodes and leaves. The metadata option in the member selector allows you to select those levels that you would like to include in the report. This functionality is available for SAP Crystal Reports for Enterprise, SAP BusinessObjects Web Intelligence, and SAP BusinessObjects Dashboards. SAP BusinessObjects Analysis is already offers such functionality as part of the 4.0 release.

As a first part of your report, you need to set up the hierarchical grouping.

1. Select the menu INSERT • GROUP (see Figure 4.32).
2. Select the COMMERCIAL BALANCE SHEET hierarchy as the field to group on.

93

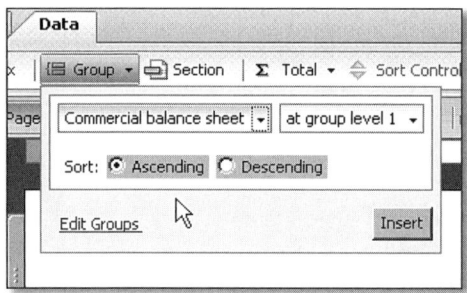

Figure 4.32 Insert Group

3. Set the SORT to ASCENDING.
4. Click on EDIT GROUPS.
5. Open the details for the group.
6. Set the value for the GROUP INDENT to 0.3.
7. Click on OK.
8. Right-click on GROUP FOOTER 1 and select the HIDE menu option.
9. Navigate to the STRUCTURE view of your report.
10. Place the three key figures CUMULATIVE BALANCE, TOTAL CREDIT POSTGS, and TOTAL DEBIT POSTINGS into the BODY section of your report.
11. Reduce the height of the BODY section.
12. Navigate back to the PAGE view of your report.
13. Right-click on the first key figure CUMULATIVE BALANCE and select the TOTAL CUMULATIVE BALANCE menu option (see Figure 4.33).

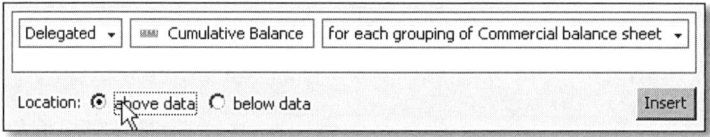

Figure 4.33 Insert Subtotal

14. Select the DELEGATED option and configure the subtotal to be FOR EACH GROUPING OF COMMERCIAL BALANCE SHEET.
15. Set the option ABOVE DATA for the location.
16. Click on INSERT.

17. Repeat the last four steps for the other two key figures.
18. Right-click on the BODY section and select the menu item HIDE.
19. Your report should look similar to Figure 4.34.

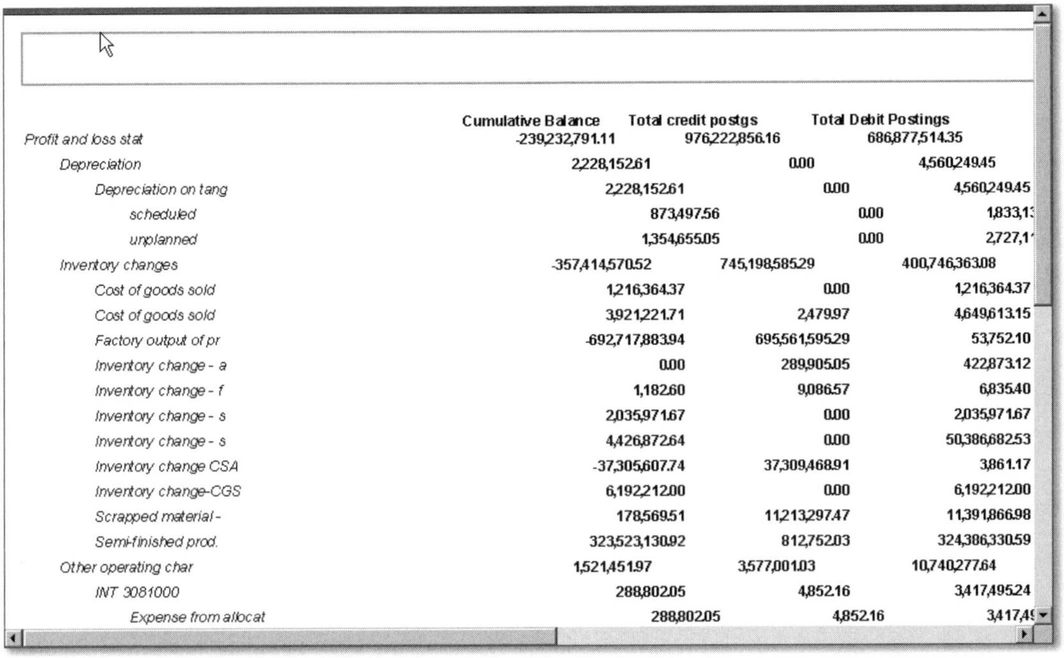

Figure 4.34 Report Preview

20. One of the major issues here is that not only the hierarchical group levels are indented but also the key figures.
21. To change this, right-click on GROUP HEADER 1 and select the EDIT GROUP menu item.
22. Set the value for the GROUP INDENT to 0.
23. Right-click on the GROUP NAME field for the hierarchy in your report and select the FORMAT GROUP NAME ELEMENT menu item (see Figure 4.35).
24. Click on FORMULA icon (*fx*) next to X in SIZE AND LOCATION.
25. Enter the following formula:
    ```
    hierarchylevel(GroupingLevel(< hierarchy >))
    *150
    ```

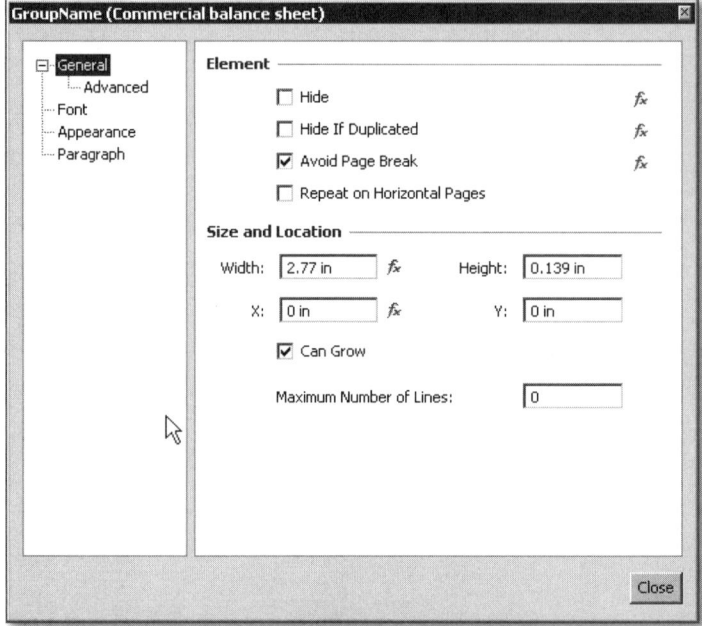

Figure 4.35 Formatting Group Name Element

26. As part of the formula, replace the placeholder <hierarchy> with the HIERARCHY from RESULT OBJECTS. The formula retrieves the hierarchical level of each element and multiplies the level number by 150. Because we enter the formula for the X property of the field, the outcome will be used to move the field to the value on the X axis.

27. Click on SAVE AND CLOSE.

28. Click on CLOSE.

29. The report look now similar to Figure 4.36.

30. You can add three more items to your report: grouping by company code, the values from the entered parameters, and some highlighting based on the hierarchy level.

31. Select the menu DATA • FORMULAS.

32. Select the menu NEW • NEW FORMULA.

33. Enter fn_Hierarchy_level as the formula name.

34. Click on OK.

Building a Report for Financial Analysis | 4.4

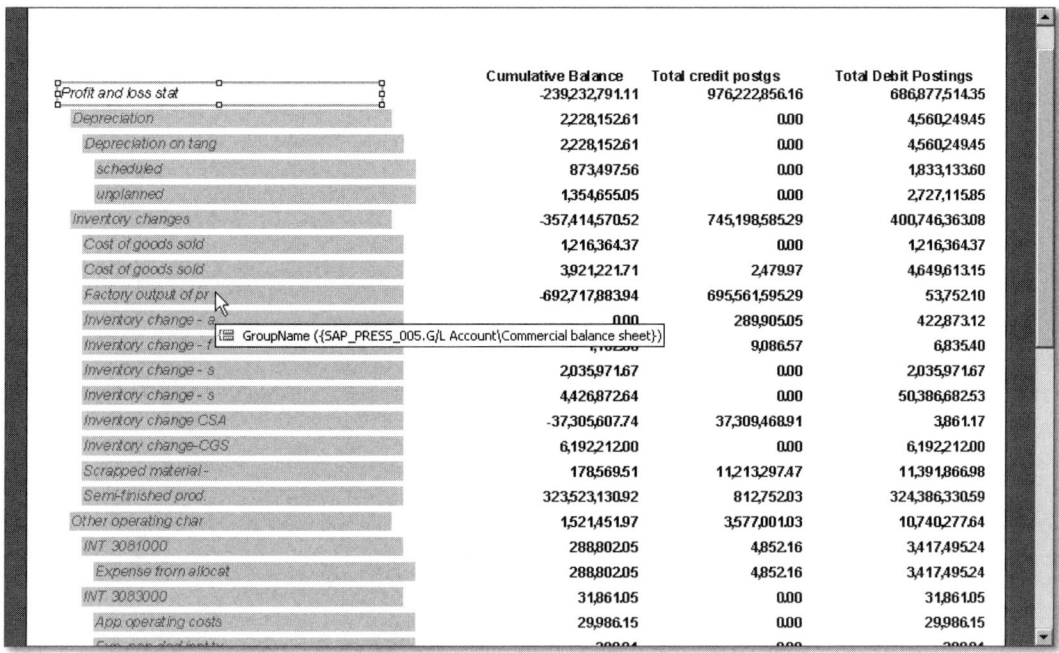

Figure 4.36 Report Preview

35. Enter the formula:

    ```
    hierarchylevel(GroupingLevel(< hierarchy >))
    ```

36. As part of the formula, replace the placeholder <hierarchy> with Hierarchy from RESULT OBJECTS.

37. Click on SAVE AND CLOSE. You have created a formula that returns the hierarchy level and you can use this formula now to color code levels of the hierarchy in your report to make the report easier to read.

38. Right click on the BODY section—not the BODY area (see Figure 4.37).

39. Select the CONDITIONAL FORMATTING option.

40. Click on ADD CONDITION.

41. Select the newly created formula as value.

42. User EQUAL TO as the operator.

43. Enter the value 1 and configure a background color. This background color will be used for all level 1 nodes of your hierarchy.

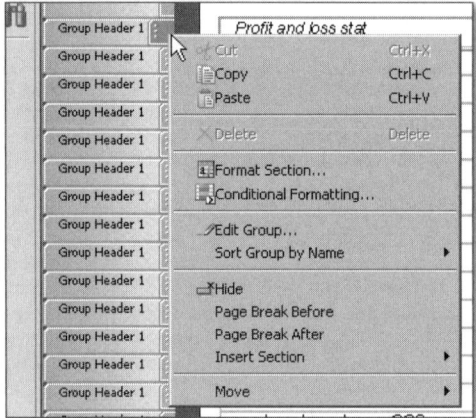

Figure 4.37 Body Section

44. Repeat the steps for level 2 of your hierarchy (see Figure 4.38).

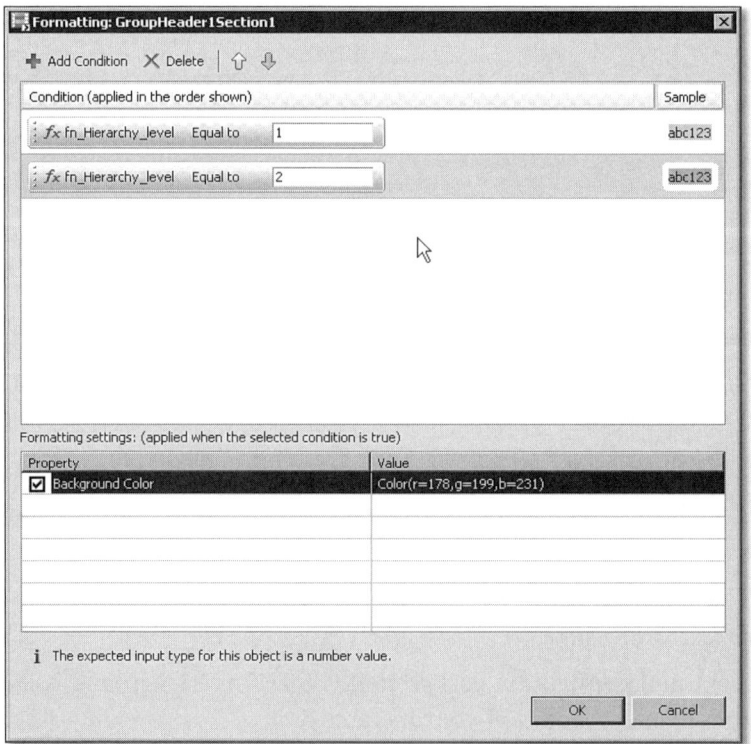

Figure 4.38 Conditional Formatting

45. Click on OK.
46. Navigate to the INSERT tab.
47. Select the menu option GROUP.
48. Select the COMPANY CODE as the field to group on.
49. Set it to be grouped on group level 1.
50. Click on INSERT (see Figure 4.39).

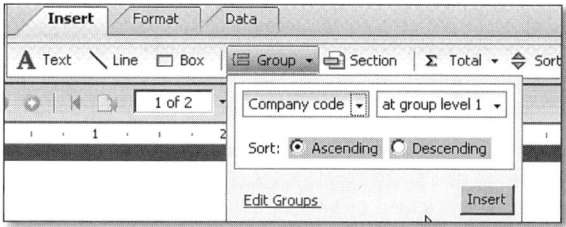

Figure 4.39 Insert Group

51. Right-click on GROUP HEADER 1 and select the menu INSERT SECTION • BELOW. You have just created an additional section in our GROUP HEADER 1. We will use this area to show the value selected for our parameters.

> **Display Parameter Values**
>
> One of the major limitations of SAP Crystal Reports for Enterprise is the capability to display selected values from a parameter on the report. You cannot show the value description from the selected values at all, and to display the key values, you may have to use a formula, as described in this section.

In cases where the parameter allows you to enter more than a single value, you need to create a formula to retrieve the selected values. The values are stored in an array from which you need to retrieve them.

A formula for retrieving the values of a parameter with multiple values would look like Listing 4.1.

```
stringVar variable_value := "";
  Local NumberVar i;
  FOR i := 1 To UBOUND(< Parameter >)
  DO
  if i=1 then
  variable_value:= (< Parameter > [i])
  else
```

```
variable_value:= variable_value + "; " + (< Parameter > [i])
;
  variable_value
```

Listing 4.1 Retrieving Values of a Parameter with Multiple Values

A formula for retrieving the values of a parameter with range values would look like Listing 1.2.

```
StringVar variable_value:="";
Local NumberVar i;
FOR i := 1 To UBOUND(<VARIABLE NAME>)
DO
if i=1 then
(
  IF MINIMUM(<VARIABLE NAME> [i]) = MAXIMUM<VARIABLE NAME> [i])
  THEN variable_value :=MINIMUM(<VARIABLE NAME> [i])
  ELSE variable_value :=MINIMUM(<VARIABLE NAME> [i]) + "-" +
    MAXIMUM(<VARIABLE NAME> [i]);
)
else
(
  IF MINIMUM(<VARIABLE NAME> [i]) = MAXIMUM(<VARIABLE NAME> [i])
  THEN variable_value:= variable_value + "; " + MINIMUM(<VARIABLE
    NAME> [i])
  ELSE variable_value:= variable_value + "; " + MINIMUM(<VARIABLE
    NAME> [i]) + "-" + MAXIMUM(<VARIABLE NAME> [i]);
);
variable_value
```

Listing 4.2 Retrieving Values of a Parameter with Range Values

52. Replace the placeholder <VARIABLE NAME> with the parameter from your Data Explorer. With such a formula per parameter, you should be able to display all selections made by the consumer.

You have created a report in SAP Crystal Reports for Enterprise, which shows the financial key figures along the hierarchy from your SAP BEx query. You highlighted certain levels from the hierarchy, aligned the key figures, and displayed the selected parameter values.

In the next section, we look at the requirements of HR and how we can use SAP Crystal Reports for Enterprise to fulfill them.

4.5 Building a Report for HR Analysis

Based on the previous sections, we identified SAP Crystal Reports for Enterprise as a good fit for the reporting requirements for the HR department. This does not mean that other tools would not be able to fulfill most of the requirements as well, but SAP Crystal Reports for Enterprise is the best fit for the requirements specified here.

The requirements for the HR department are:

- The content needs to leverage data from several different sources (SAP and non-SAP) and present it in a single report.
- The content needs to present highly textual information in a layout-focused format.
- Some of the content (such as employee appraisals or performance reviews) will likely be used as official documentation and therefore needs to follow strict layout rules.
- All of the tools need to leverage the security of the underlying system.
- The tools for the content need to offer specific features, such as date-organized aggregation to show the correct numbers for items (such as a headcount statistic or a salary at a given date for an employee). Resolving these time-dependent key figures is very important.

Next, we use SAP Crystal Reports for Enterprise to fulfill these requirements. We create a report showing the employee master data information, which is highly textual. In addition, we combine employee data with the qualifications for each employee in a single report (see Figure 4.40).

1. Start the Information Design Tool by following the menu START • PROGRAMS • SAP BUSINESSOBJECTS BI PLATFORM 4 • SAP BUSINESSOBJECTS BI PLATFORM CLIENT TOOLS • INFORMATION DESIGN TOOL.
2. Select the menu FILE • NEW • PROJECT to create a new project for your universe.
3. Enter a name for the new PROJECT and click on FINISH.
4. Select the menu FILE • NEW • RELATIONAL CONNECTION to start the process to set up the data connection toward your SAP ERP system.
5. Enter a name for the data connection and click on NEXT.

Employee details			
Personnel Number	00001000		
Employee name	MULLER ANJA		
Employee address	Gartenstr. 46		
	Karlsruhe		
Phone number	0721/12 12 12		

Company details			
Company Code	IDES AG	Cost Center	Human Resources
Personnel Area	Frankfurt	Personnel Subarea	Zentrale
Employee group	Active	Payroll area	HR-D: Sal. employees
Start date	1/1/1995		

Employment details	
Employed as	Director
Employment percentage	100.00
Weekly hours	37.50
Notice period	3 months/month's end

Qualifications		
Qualification	Scale	Proficiency
HR Management skills	Standard marks - 9	5.00
HR Management skills	5 Point Scale	5.00
HR Management skills	Standard	5.00
Perceptive faculty	Standard marks - 9	4.00
Ability to organize and act	Standard marks - 9	4.00
Verbal, written communicative skills	Standard marks - 9	4.00
Leadership skills	Standard marks - 9	4.00
Business Administration Degree	Yes/No	4.00
MBA	Yes/No	4.00
Knowledge of payroll	Standard marks - 9	3.00
HR Management skills	Standard marks - 9	5.00
Ability to organize and act	Standard marks - 9	4.00
Verbal, written communicative skills	Standard marks - 9	4.00
Leadership	Standard marks - 9	4.00
B.A. (Business Administration)	Yes/No	4.00
M.B.A.	Yes/No	4.00

Figure 4.40 Employee Master Report

6. Select SAP ERP from the list of available options (see Figure 4.41).

7. Click on NEXT.

8. Enter the necessary system details (see Figure 4.42).

9. Click on NEXT.

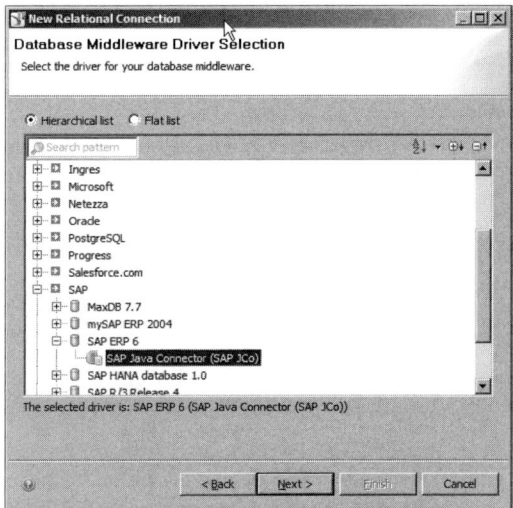

Figure 4.41 Database Selection

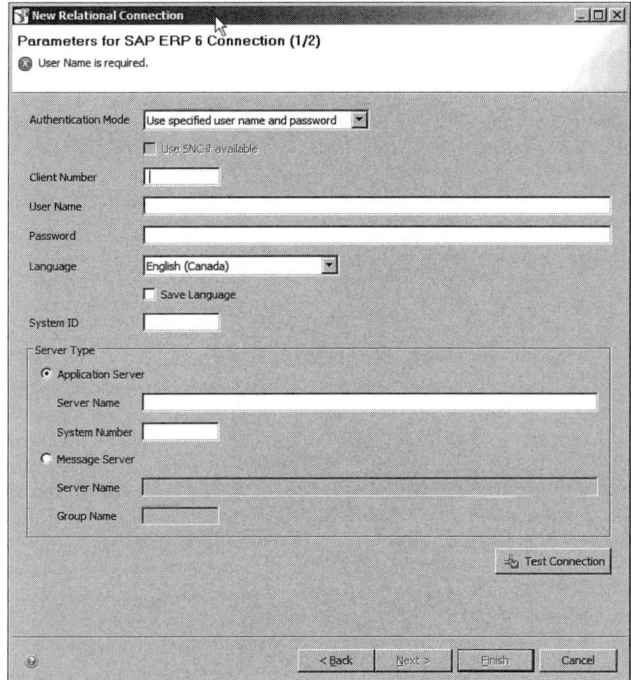

Figure 4.42 System Parameters

10. Activate the MAP TABLE PARAMETERS INTO INPUT COLUMNS option.
11. Activate the MAP SELECTION FIELDS INTO TABLE COLUMNS option.

These two options allow you to configure parameters and selections from the underlying SAP ERP source as input columns for your universe so that you will be able to configure parameters for them (see Figure 4.43).

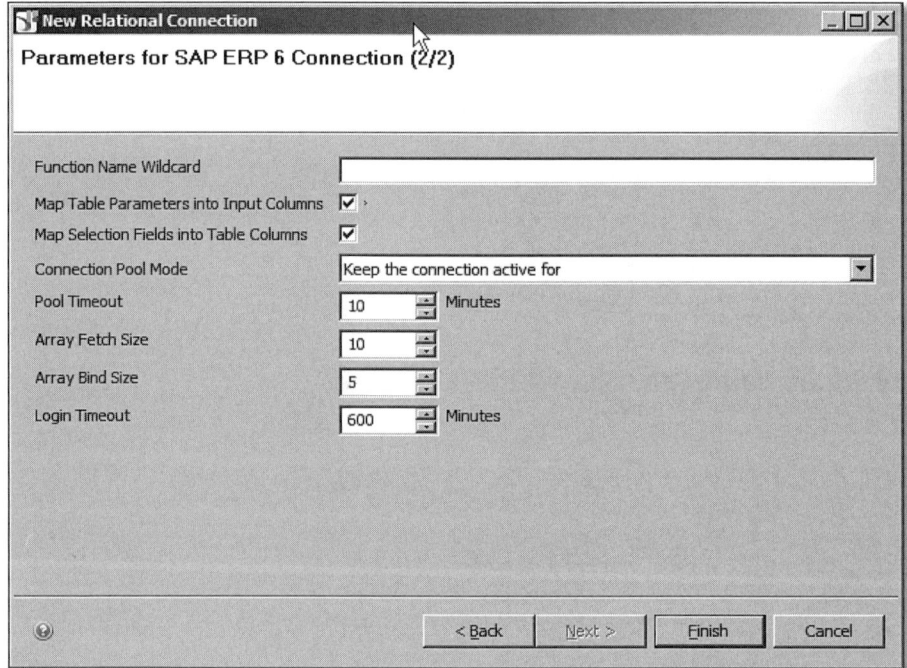

Figure 4.43 Connection Parameters

12. Click on FINISH.
13. Select the new connection in your project.
14. Right-click on the connection and select the PUBLISH CONNECTION TO REPOSITORY menu.
15. Log on to your SAP BusinessObjects BI platform.
16. Click on NEXT.
17. Select a folder for your connection and click on FINISH.
18. You are asked if you want to create a shortcut for the connection.
19. Click on YES.

20. Click on CLOSE.
21. Select the menu FILE • NEW • DATA FOUNDATION.
22. Enter a name for the data foundation and click on NEXT.
23. Select the MULTISOURCE-ENABLED option.
24. Click on NEXT.
25. Log on to your SAP BusinessObjects BI platform.
26. Click on NEXT.
27. Select the shortcut to your newly created connection.
28. Click on NEXT.
29. Click on FINISH (see Figure 4.44).

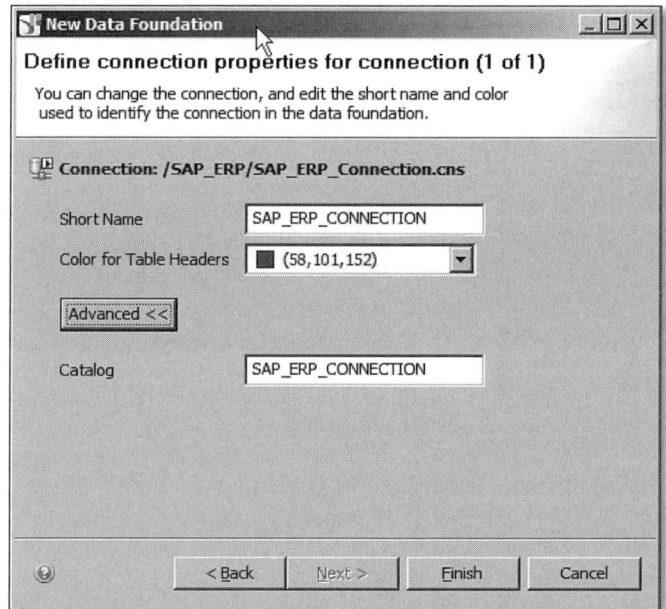

Figure 4.44 Data Foundation (Part 1)

30. Navigate to the DATA FOUNDATION.
31. From the Global.INFOSET area (see Figure 4.45) select the InfoSet /SAPQUERY/HR_ADM.
32. Add the InfoSet to the area for the selected tables.
33. Save your changes.

4 | Enterprise Reporting with SAP Crystal Reports for Enterprise

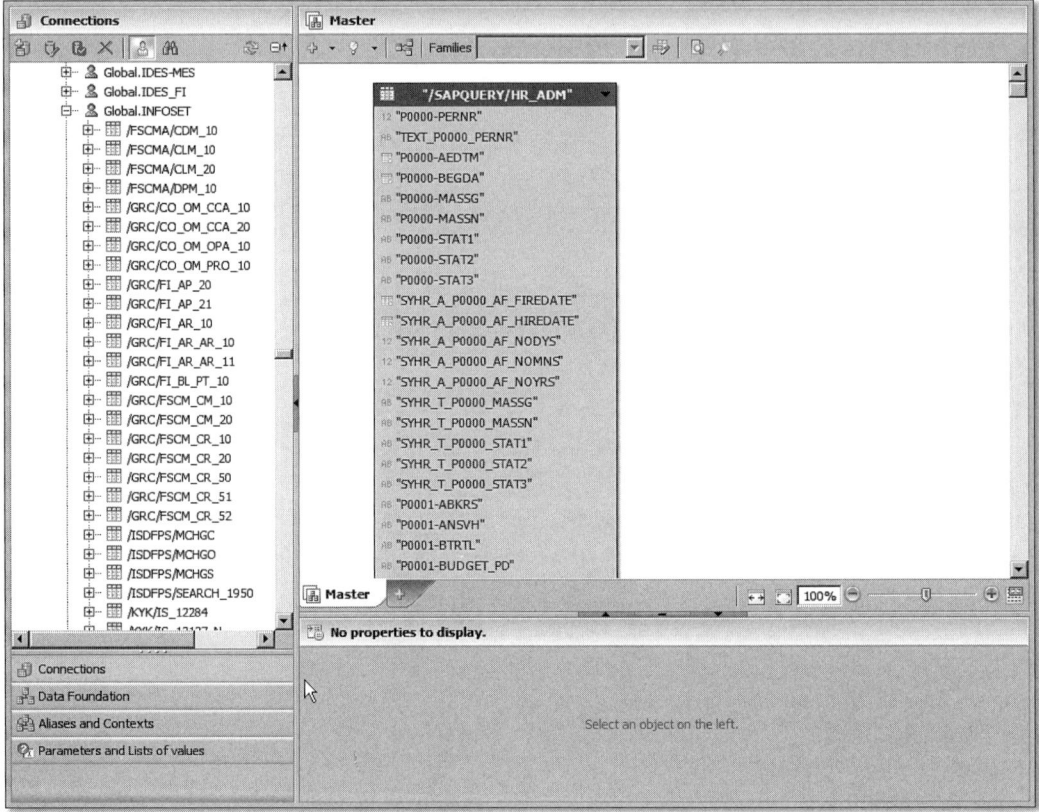

Figure 4.45 Data Foundation (Part 2)

34. Navigate to your local project.
35. Select the menu File • New • Business Layer.
36. Select the Relational Data Source option.
37. Enter a name for the business layer.
38. Click on Next.
39. Select the previously created data foundation.
40. Click on Next.
41. Activate the Automatically create classes and objects for all connections option.
42. Click on Finish.
43. Save your changes.

44. Navigate to the local project and select the business layer.
45. Right-click and open the context menu for the business layer.
46. Select the option PUBLISH • TO A REPOSITORY.
47. Click on NEXT.
48. Select a folder for the universe.
49. Click on FINISH.
50. Click on CLOSE.

Because there is a data type mismatch between the two InfoSets, we will set up two universes and then use the subreport option in SAP Crystal Reports for Enterprise. Follow the steps below:

1. Navigate to your local project.
2. Select the menu FILE • NEW • DATA FOUNDATION.
3. Enter a name for the data foundation and click on NEXT.
4. Select the option MULTISOURCE-ENABLED.
5. Click on NEXT.
6. Log on to your SAP BusinessObjects BI platform.
7. Click on NEXT.
8. Select the shortcut to your newly created connection.
9. Click on NEXT.
10. Click on FINISH.
11. Navigate to the data foundation.
12. From the Global.INFOSET area (see Figure 4.45) select the /SAPQUERY/HR_PD_Q InfoSet.
13. Add the InfoSet to the area for the selected tables.
14. Save your changes.
15. Navigate to your local project.
16. Select the menu FILE • NEW • BUSINESS LAYER.
17. Select the option RELATIONAL DATA SOURCE.
18. Enter a name for the business layer.
19. Click on NEXT.
20. Select the previously created data foundation.

21. Click on NEXT.
22. Activate the AUTOMATICALLY CREATE CLASSES AND OBJECTS FOR ALL CONNECTIONS option.
23. Click on FINISH.
24. Save your changes.
25. Navigate to the local project and select the business layer.
26. Use a right-click and open the context menu for the business layer.
27. Select the option PUBLISH • TO A REPOSITORY.
28. Click on NEXT.
29. Select a folder for the universe.
30. Click on FINISH.
31. Click on CLOSE.

Now you can start building the report using SAP Crystal Reports for Enterprise:

1. Start SAP Crystal Reports for Enterprise by following the menu START • PROGRAMS • CRYSTAL REPORTS FOR ENTERPRISE 4 • CRYSTAL REPORTS FOR ENTERPRISE 4.
2. Select the menu FILE • NEW • FROM DATA SOURCE.
3. Select the BROWSE REPOSITORY menu option from SAP BUSINESSOBJECTS BUSINESS INTELLIGENCE PLATFORM.
4. Log on to your SAP BusinessObjects BI platform.
5. Select the UNIVERSE data source option.
6. Select the first universe you created.
7. Click on NEXT.
8. You are presented with the query panel. Include the objects shown in Table 4.5 in RESULT OBJECTS.

Field Name	Description
P0000-PERNR	Personnel number
P0001-SNAME	Employee name
P0006-STRAS	House number and street
P0006-ADR03	Street 2

Table 4.5 Required Fields

Field Name	Description
P0006-ADR04	Street 3
P0006-ORT01	Location
P0006-TELNR	Telephone number
SYHR_T_P0001_BUKRS	Company code
SYHR_T_P0001_WERKS	Personnel areas
SYHR_T_P0001_BTRTL	Personnel subarea
SYHR_T_P0001_PERSG	Employee group
SYHR_T_P0001_ABKRS	Payroll area
SYHR_A_P0000_AF_HIREDATE	Start date
SYHR_T_P0001-KOSTL	Cost center
SYHR_T_P0001_STELL	Employed as
P0007-EMPCT	Employment percentage
P0007-WOSTD	Weekly hours
SYHR_T_P0016_KDGF2	Notice period

Table 4.5 Required Fields (Cont.)

9. Uncheck the option GENERATE REPORT.
10. Click on FINISH.
11. Navigate to the INSERT tab.
12. Click on GROUP (see Figure 4.46).

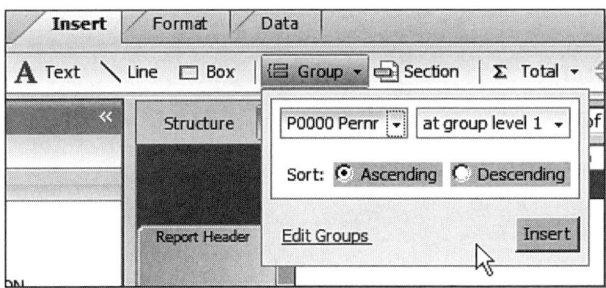

Figure 4.46 Insert Group

13. Insert a group based on P0000-PERNR.
14. Click on STRUCTURE in the toolbar to navigate to the more technical view of your report.
15. You need a total of four different areas in your report: Employee Details, Company Details, Employment Details, and Qualifications.
16. Right-click on the GROUP HEADER 1 section and use the menu option INSERT SECTION • BELOW (see Figure 4.47).

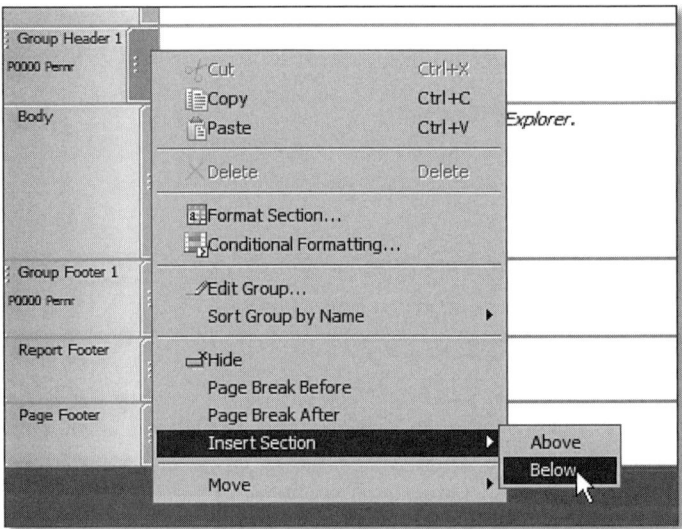

Figure 4.47 Insert Section

17. Insert a total of seven additional sections so that your report has eight sections in GROUP HEADER 1.
18. Navigate to the INSERT tab and use the TEXT button to insert the following headers into the sections (see Figure 4.48):
    - Section 1: EMPLOYEE DETAILS
    - Section 3: COMPANY DETAILS
    - Section 5: EMPLOYMENT DETAILS
    - Section 7: QUALIFICATIONS

Building a Report for HR Analysis | 4.5

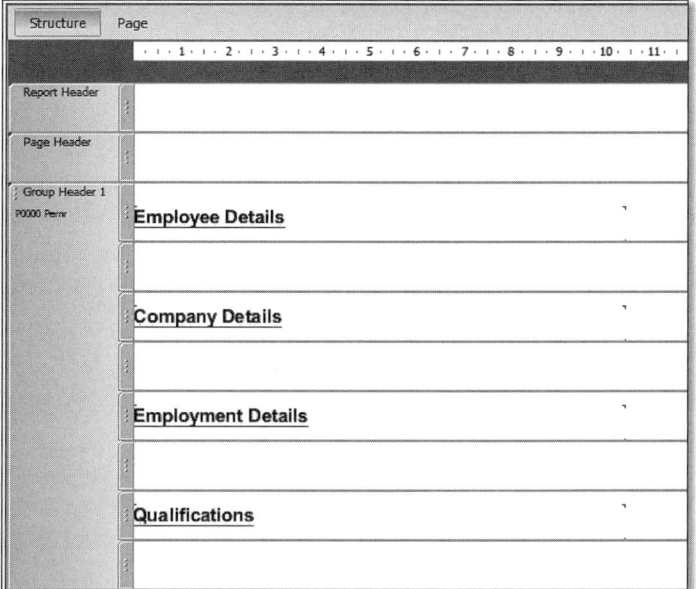

Figure 4.48 Report Structure

19. Now use the INSERT • TEXT option and add the following text objects to the first section below the EMPLOYEE DETAILS header (see Figure 4.49):

   ▸ PERSONNEL NUMBER
   ▸ EMPLOYEE NAME
   ▸ EMPLOYEE ADDRESS
   ▸ PHONE NUMBER

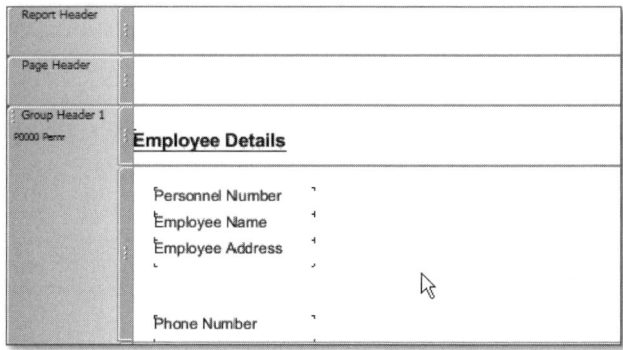

Figure 4.49 Employee Details

111

20. Place the fields shown in Table 4.6 into the section next to the corresponding text objects.

Field Name	Description
P0000-PERNR	Personnel number
P0001-SNAME	Employee name
P0006-STRAS	House number and street
P0006-ADR03	Street 2
P0006-ADR04	Street 3
P0006-ORT01	Location
P0006-TELNR	Telephone number

Table 4.6 Employee Details

21. Use the INSERT • TEXT option and add the following text objects to the first section below the COMPANY DETAILS header:
    - COMPANY CODE
    - PERSONNEL AREAS
    - PERSONNEL SUBAREA
    - EMPLOYEE GROUP
    - PAYROLL AREA
    - START DATE
    - COST CENTER

22. Place the fields shown in Table 4.7 into the section next to the corresponding text objects.

Field Name	Description
SYHR_T_P0001_BUKRS	Company code
SYHR_T_P0001_WERKS	Personnel areas
SYHR_T_P0001_BTRTL	Personnel subarea

Table 4.7 Company Details

Field Name	Description
SYHR_T_P0001_PERSG	Employee group
SYHR_T_P0001_ABKRS	Payroll area
SYHR_A_P0000_AF_HIREDATE	Start date
SYHR_T_P0001-KOSTL	Cost center

Table 4.7 Company Details (Cont.)

23. Use the INSERT • TEXT option and add the following text objects to the first section below the header EMPLOYMENT DETAILS:
    - EMPLOYED AS
    - EMPLOYMENT PERCENTAGE
    - WEEKLY HOURS
    - NOTICE PERIOD
24. Place the fields shown in Table 4.8 into the section next to the corresponding text objects.

Field Name	Description
SYHR_T_P0001_STELL	Employed as
P0007-EMPCT	Employment percentage
P0007-WOSTD	Weekly hours
SYHR_T_P0016_KDGF2	Notice period

Table 4.8 Employment Details

25. Your report should look similar to Figure 4.50.
26. Navigate to the FORMULAS area.
27. Use a right-click and select the NEW FORMULA menu.
28. Enter `fn_main_PersonnelNumber` as the name.
29. Click on OK.
30. Enter the following text as a formula:
    ```
    tonumber({SAP_ERP.SAP_ERP_CONNECTION\Sapquery Hr Adm\P0000 Pernr})
    ```

> **Formula Syntax**
>
> The formula shown in the previous step—`tonumber({SAP_ERP.SAP_ERP_CONNECTION\ Sapquery Hr Adm\P0000 Pernr})`—also shows the names of the underlying connection and data foundation.

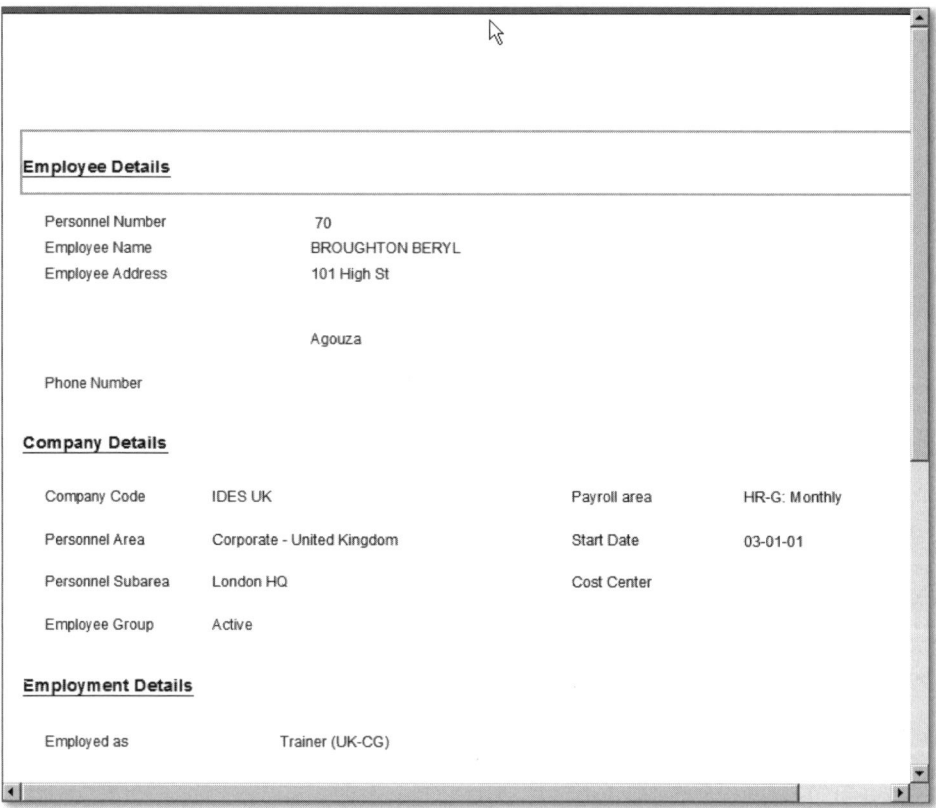

Figure 4.50 Report

31. Click on SAVE AND CLOSE.
32. Navigate to the QUALIFICATIONS area in your report.
33. Navigate to the INSERT tab.
34. Click on SUBREPORT.
35. Place the subreport into the empty section for the qualifications.
36. Select the option CONNECT TO A NEW DATA SOURCE (see Figure 4.51).

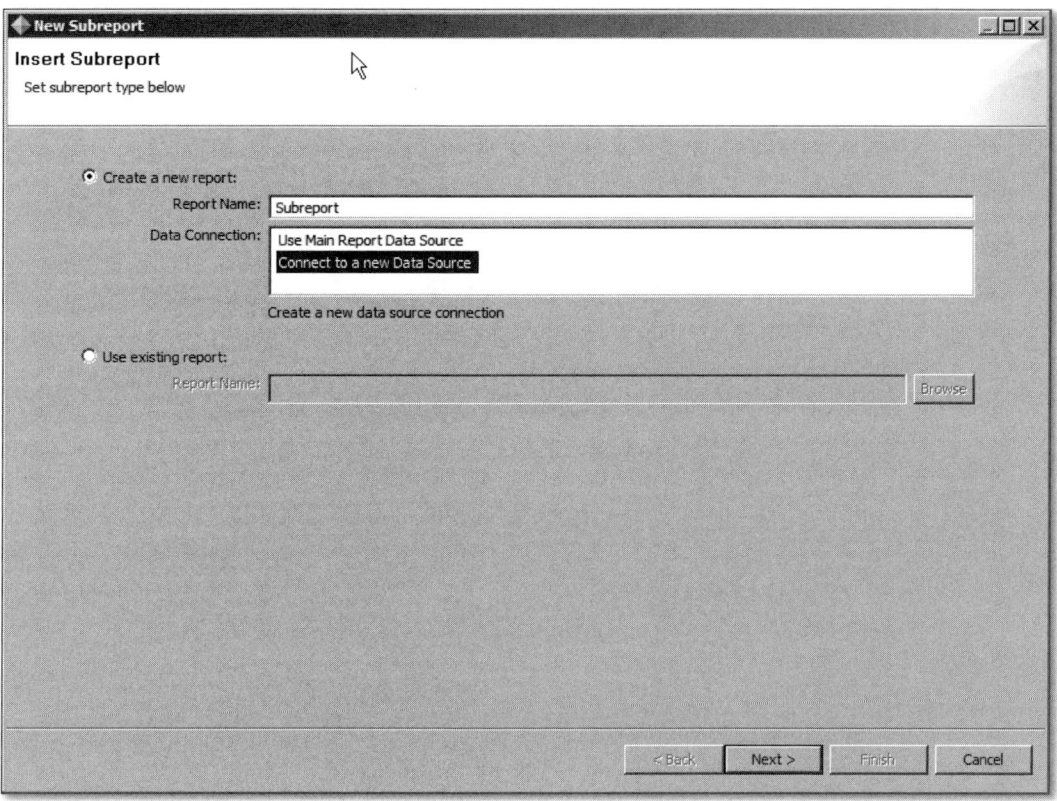

Figure 4.51 Subreport

37. Click on NEXT.
38. Click on BROWSE REPOSITORY.
39. Select the second universe you created.
40. Click on NEXT.
41. Insert the following objects into the RESULT OBJECTS area of the query panel:
    - P1000 OTYPE
    - P1000 STEXT
    - P1001 SCLAS
    - P1001 SOBID
    - P1002 TLINE
42. Drag and drop the P1000 OTYPE object to the query filters.

43. Set the operator to EQUAL TO.
44. Set the value to Q.
45. Click on NEXT.
46. Click on NEXT.
47. Select the option DETAIL ONLY.
48. Click on FINISH.
49. Double-click on the subreport. The subreport opens in a separate screen and you can now insert the needed fields.
50. Insert the P1000 STEXT object into the body area of the subreport.
51. Navigate to the FORMULAS area.
52. Right-click and select the NEW FORMULA menu (see Figure 4.52).

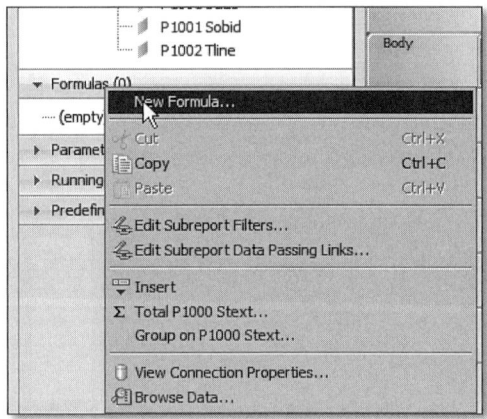

Figure 4.52 Formulas

53. Enter `fn_PersonnelNumber` as the name.
54. Click on OK.
55. Enter the following text as a formula:

    `tonumber({SAP_ERP_2.SAP_ERP_CONNECTION\Sapquery Hr Pd Q\P1001 Sobid})`

56. Click on SAVE AND CLOSE.

    You have created a subreport based on your second universe and a formula in the main and subreport so that you can link your main report to the subreport based on the personnel number.

57. In the subreport, navigate to the DATA tab (see Figure 4.53).

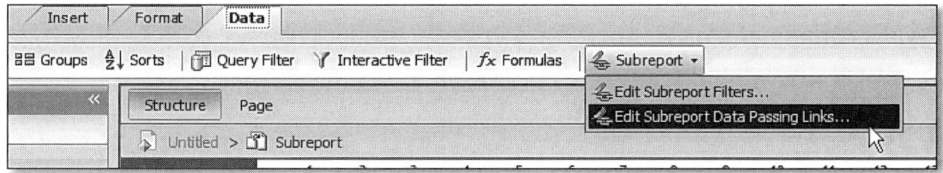

Figure 4.53 Data Tab

58. Select the menu SUBREPORT • EDIT SUBREPORT DATA PASSING LINKS.
59. Click on ADD.
60. Select the FN_MAIN_PERSONNELNUMBER object form the main report (see Figure 4.54)

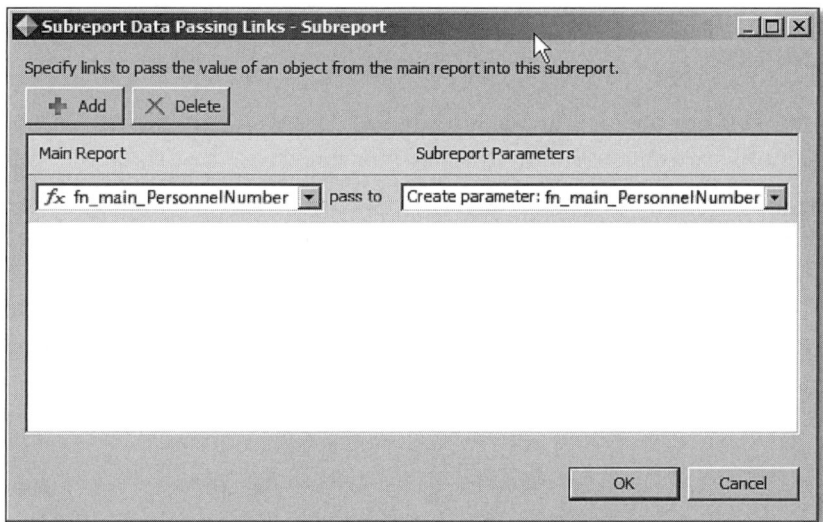

Figure 4.54 Subreport Data Passing

61. Click on OK.
62. Navigate to the DATA tab.
63. Click on FORMULAS.
64. Enter the following formula:

    {@fn_PersonnelNumber}={?MainReport.fn_main_PersonnelNumber}

65. Navigate back to the main report.
66. Right-click on the BODY section of the main report.
67. Select the menu item HIDE.
68. Right-click on the GROUP FOOTER section of the main report.
69. Select the menu item HIDE.
70. Refresh the main report.

Your report now shows several items of information retrieved from two data sources: employee details, company details, employment details, and qualifications for the employee.

In this section you used two universes to retrieve data from different ERP sources to fulfill the requirement for your HR area.

4.6 Summary

In this chapter, you not only learned about the basic functionality of SAP Crystal Reports for Enterprise as a design environment for enterprise reporting, but you reviewed the requirements and evaluated which requirements are a great fit for SAP Crystal Reports for Enterprise. You also used the requirements from the financial and HR area and created concrete reports to fulfill these requirements. In the next chapter, we continue our journey and try to fulfill our reporting requirements in the ad-hoc query and analysis areas using SAP BusinessObjects Web Intelligence.

In this chapter, we look at how you can use SAP BusinessObjects Web Intelligence for customer requirements in the area of interactive analysis reporting.

5 Interactive Analysis with SAP BusinessObjects Web Intelligence

After discussing the requirements for enterprise reporting, we now focus on interactive analysis-type reports—specifically with SAP BusinessObjects Web Intelligence. In this chapter, we look at the different connectivity options that you can use, and then evaluate how SAP BusinessObjects Web Intelligence can fulfill the business requirements established in Chapter 2.

5.1 SAP Data Connectivity

In this section, we consider the connectivity options for SAP BusinessObjects Web Intelligence as part of your SAP landscape. As shown in Figure 5.1, SAP BusinessObjects Web Intelligence can access the semantic layer as part of the 4.0 FP3 release; in this way, it establishes a direct connectivity to your SAP ERP system. As a result, SAP BusinessObjects Web Intelligence can connect to classic InfoSets, SAP queries, and ABAP functions. In addition, the tool is able to use a BEx query connected to the transient provider as part of the BI client of your SAP ERP system.

For SAP NetWeaver BW, SAP BusinessObjects Web Intelligence is able to access the semantic layer and establish a relational universe on top of the InfoProvider. It can use the direct BI Consumer Services (BICS) connectivity and read the metadata and data from the BEx queries as part of your SAP NetWeaver BW system.

For those customers using OLAP universes from the XI 3.1 release, you should take notice of the option to have the XI 3.1 OLAP universes simply deployed in a 4.x environment without having to migrate them. SAP BusinessObjects Web

Intelligence is capable of using these XI 3.1 universes, but you won't be able to use any new functionality, such as the new hierarchical features, in combination with the XI 3.1 OLAP universes. SAP BusinessObjects Web Intelligence is the only client tool that supports OLAP universes.

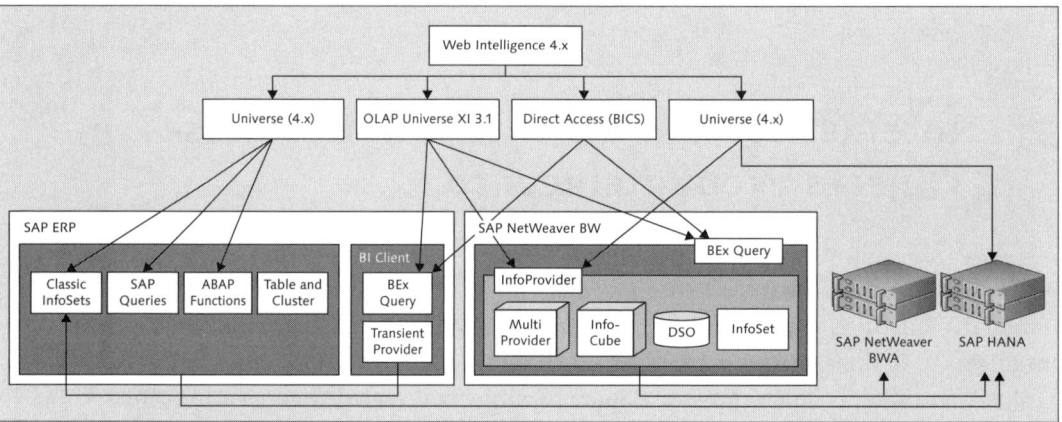

Figure 5.1 Data Connectivity

SAP ECC Transient Provider

The TRANSIENT PROVIDER lets you leverage a BEx query connecting directly to a classic InfoSet from your SAP ERP system without the requirement of modeling an InfoProvider. This functionality is available with enhancement package 5 for SAP ECC 6.0.

In Table 5.1, you can see the level of metadata support for SAP BusinessObjects Web Intelligence when connecting to SAP NetWeaver BW.

	Direct Access using BICS	Relational Universe Access
Direct access to InfoCube and MultiProvider	No	Yes
Access to BEx queries	Yes	Limited
Characteristic Values		
Key	Yes	Yes
Short description	Yes	Yes
Medium and long description	Yes	Yes

Table 5.1 Supported and Unsupported BEx Query Features for Web Intelligence

	Direct Access using BICS	Relational Universe Access
BEx Query Features		
Support for hierarchies	Yes	No
Support for free characteristics	Yes	Yes
Support for calculated and restricted key figures	Yes	No
Support for currencies and units	Yes	Yes
Support for custom structures	Yes	No
Support for formulas and selections	Yes	No
Support for filter	Yes	Yes
Support for display and navigational attributes	Yes	Yes
Support for conditions in rows	No	No
Support for conditions in columns	No	No
Support for conditions for fixed characteristics	No	No
Support for exceptions	No	No
Compounded characteristics	Limited	No
Constant selection	Yes	No
Default values in BEx query	No	No
Number scaling factor	Yes	No
Number of decimals	No	No
Calculate rows as (local calculation)	No	No
Sorting	Yes	No
Hide/unhide	Yes	No
Display as hierarchy	No	No
Reverse sign	Yes	No

Table 5.1 Supported and Unsupported BEx Query Features for Web Intelligence (Cont.)

	Direct Access using BICS	Relational Universe Access
Support for reading master data	Yes	No
Data Types		
Support for CHAR (characteristics)	Yes	Yes
Support for NUMC (characteristics)	Yes as string value	Yes as string value
Support for DATS (characteristics)	Yes for value description. Key is supported as string value.	Yes for value description. Key is supported as string value.
Support for TIMS (characteristics)	Yes as string value	Yes as string value
Support for numeric key figures such as Amount and Quantity	Yes	Yes
Support for Date (key figures)	Yes	Yes
Support for Time (key figures)	Yes as string value	Yes as string value
SAP Variable—Processing Type		
User Input	Yes	No
Authorization	Yes	No
Replacement path	Yes	No
SAP exit/custom exit	Yes	No
Precalculated value set	Yes	No
General Features for Variables		
Support for optional and mandatory variables	Yes	No
Support for key date dependencies	Yes	No
Support for default values	Yes	No
Support for personalized values	No	No
SAP Variables—Variable Type		
Single value	Yes	No

Table 5.1 Supported and Unsupported BEx Query Features for Web Intelligence (Cont.)

	Direct Access using BICS	Relational Universe Access
Multi-single value	Yes	No
Interval value	Yes	No
Selection option	Limited	No
Hierarchy variable	Yes	No
Hierarchy node variable	Yes	No
Hierarchy version variable	No	No
Text variable	Yes	No
EXIT variable	Yes	No
Single key date variable	Yes	No
Multiple key dates	No	No
Formula variable	Yes	No

Table 5.1 Supported and Unsupported BEx Query Features for Web Intelligence (Cont.)

Table 5.2 shows how SAP BusinessObjects Web Intelligence is able to leverage and support existing metadata from your existing BEx queries.

BEx Query Element	SAP BusinessObjects Web Intelligence
Characteristic	For each characteristic you'll receive a field representing the key value and a field for the description, including short, medium, and long description.
Hierarchy	Each available hierarchy is shown as an external hierarchy in SAP BusinessObjects Web Intelligence.
Key figure	Each key figure can have up to four elements: numeric value, unit, scaling factor, and formatted value. The formatted value is based on the user preferences configured in the SAP system.
Calculated/restricted key figure	Each calculated and restricted key figure is treated like a key figure. The user does not have access to the underlying definition in SAP BusinessObjects Web Intelligence.

Table 5.2 SAP NetWeaver Business Warehouse Metadata Mapping for Web Intelligence

BEx Query Element	SAP BusinessObjects Web Intelligence
Filter	Filters are applied to the underlying query but are not visible in SAP BusinessObjects Web Intelligence.
Display attribute	Display attributes become standard fields in the query panel and are grouped as subordinates of the linked characteristic.
Navigational attribute	Navigational attributes are treated the same way as characteristics.
Variables	Each variable with the READY FOR INPUT property activated results in a parameter field in SAP BusinessObjects Web Intelligence.
Custom structures	A custom structure is available as an element in the query panel and each structure element can be selected or deselected for the report.

Table 5.2 SAP NetWeaver Business Warehouse Metadata Mapping for Web Intelligence (Cont.)

In this section we reviewed the different options for connecting from SAP BusinessObjects Web Intelligence to your corporate information in SAP ERP and SAP NetWeaver BW.

5.2 Assessing the Business Requirements

In this section, we look into some common business requirements and see which ones we can fulfill with SAP BusinessObjects Web Intelligence, an interactive analysis reporting tool. Up to this point, you've learned the different options for data retrieval for SAP BusinessObjects Web Intelligence in an SAP landscape and how you can use the universe as a semantic layer to offer your end users a more business-oriented view of your data sources. Now we look at the requirements one by one and list those that we can't fulfill based on the overall list of requirements in Chapter 2.

5.2.1 Financial Reporting and Analysis Requirements

We start with requirements from the financial area. From the previous chapter, we know that SAP Crystal Reports for Enterprise is a very good fit for requirements from the financial area—but we also know that SAP Crystal Reports for

Enterprise can't fulfill all of these requirements. The following is a list of requirements that can't be fulfilled with SAP BusinessObjects Web Intelligence:

> **Unfulfilled Requirements**
>
> ▶ For specific content (such as an income statement or a balance sheet), the design needs to be layout focused with the actual print version of the report being a high priority.
>
> ▶ The reporting and analysis tools need to allow for the use of hierarchies and for easy navigation along those hierarchies.
>
> ▶ Users need to be able to create planning scenarios and write information back into the source.

As you can see, there are three main requirements that can't be fulfilled with SAP BusinessObjects Web Intelligence. The first requirement on the list, the focus on the layout of the report, is not a surprise because a detailed layout is not the strength and focus of SAP BusinessObjects Web Intelligence. The second requirement, the use of hierarchies, is listed because it is also not a major strength of SAP BusinessObjects Web Intelligence. In SAP BusinessObjects Web Intelligence 4.0 FP3, there have been several enhancements around hierarchical reporting; you can now leverage a hierarchy as part of your report and will be able to open and close the hierarchy in the report itself. However, hierarchy handling is a topic that needs to be carefully considered when selecting a reporting tool for your end users. In this case study, the audience is the financial department, which often means the usage of Microsoft Excel and the usage of several hierarchies in a single report. Based on those circumstances, SAP BusinessObjects Web Intelligence might not be the best choice for these requirements. We use a hierarchical report for the financial area in a later section so that you can learn about these new enhancements as part of SAP BusinessObjects Web Intelligence 4.0 FP3. The third requirement that cannot be fulfilled with SAP BusinessObjects Web Intelligence is the need for integration with your planning application. At this point (November 2011) SAP BusinessObjects Web Intelligence is not integrated with any of the planning applications or engines, and is not able to write back information into the underlying source.

Looking at these three requirements, the first requirement—layout-based reporting—is better accomplished in SAP Crystal Reports for Enterprise. The second requirement—navigation along hierarchies—is better accomplished in SAP BusinessObjects Analysis. And the third requirement—writing information back into the source—is better accomplished in SAP BusinessObjects Analysis, edition for Microsoft Office.

5.2.2 Sales Reporting and Analysis Requirements

Next, we look at all of the requirements from the sales area and see which ones can't be fulfilled. In this case, there is only one.

> **Unfulfilled Requirement**
>
> ▶ Users should be able to perform scenario-based analysis, where the user is able to see the data but can also influence certain factors and see the impact on the overall numbers; for example, a what-if analysis in a sales planning workflow.

As you can see, only one requirement from the sales area is listed as a requirement that can't be fulfilled. All the other requirements can be fulfilled with SAP BusinessObjects Web Intelligence. It should not be a surprise that the requirement to create a what-if analysis is listed; such a requirement is much better accomplished by a data visualization created with SAP BusinessObjects Dashboards, which you'll see in a later chapter.

5.2.3 Human Resource (HR) Reporting and Analysis Requirements

For the HR area, the following is a list of requirements that SAP BusinessObjects Web Intelligence can't fulfill:

> **Unfulfilled Requirements**
>
> ▶ The content needs to present highly textual information in a layout-focused format.
>
> ▶ Some of the content (such as employee appraisals or performance reviews) will likely be used as official documentation and therefore needs to follow strict layout rules.

It's clear that the requirements regarding the layout and textual information—similar to the requirements from the financial area—are better accomplished by SAP Crystal Reports for Enterprise. It is important, especially for the HR area, that these requirements are fully met and that the reports can be used as actual paper-based documents (for example, appraisal documents). SAP BusinessObjects Web Intelligence is capable of creating a report that will provide the necessary information, but SAP Crystal Reports for Enterprise is much better suited for such a requirement.

5.2.4 C-Level Management and Leadership Reporting and Analysis Requirements

For the leadership and management team, the following is a list of requirements that SAP BusinessObjects Web Intelligence can't fulfill.

> **Unfulfilled Requirements**
> - The data needs to be shown in a highly visualized manner and the main KPIs need to be presented in a single dashboard.
> - The consumption of the reports and analytics needs to be simple and easy to use, and critical information needs to be easily identifiable.

With regard to the first requirement, we would like to add a bit more context, as SAP BusinessObjects Web Intelligence offers a great user experience and is a tool that end users can learn very quickly. The reason that the requirement is listed here is not because SAP BusinessObjects Web Intelligence is a difficult tool to use or because it is not capable of offering highlighting or alerts as part of a report. The reason is the combination of highly visualized data and easily identifiable information with an executive and leadership management team audience. For executive and leadership management, though, the requirement is better fulfilled by using SAP BusinessObjects Dashboards to create an executive overview dashboard. SAP BusinessObjects Web Intelligence could provide virtually the same information, but the product might be too complex for an audience that needs critical information in a simple and easy-to-use manner.

Before we go into more detail and create a report to fulfill these requirements, let's look at some basic steps in SAP BusinessObjects Web Intelligence so that you can gain a basic understanding and overview of the tool.

5.3 Introduction to the Tool

Similar to the approach for enterprise reporting, we first provide you with an overview of the basic functionality of SAP BusinessObjects Web Intelligence before creating the reports and analytics to fulfill the requirements.

5.3.1 Creating Your First Report

Before you start a new report based on a BEx query, you need to look at some of the settings and preferences you can select as part of your user profile.

1. Launch the BI launch pad via the menu path START • PROGRAMS • SAP BUSINESS-OBJECTS BI PLATFORM 4 • SAP BUSINESSOBJECTS BI PLATFORM • SAP BUSINESS-OBJECTS BI PLATFORM JAVA BI LAUNCH PAD (see Figure 5.2).

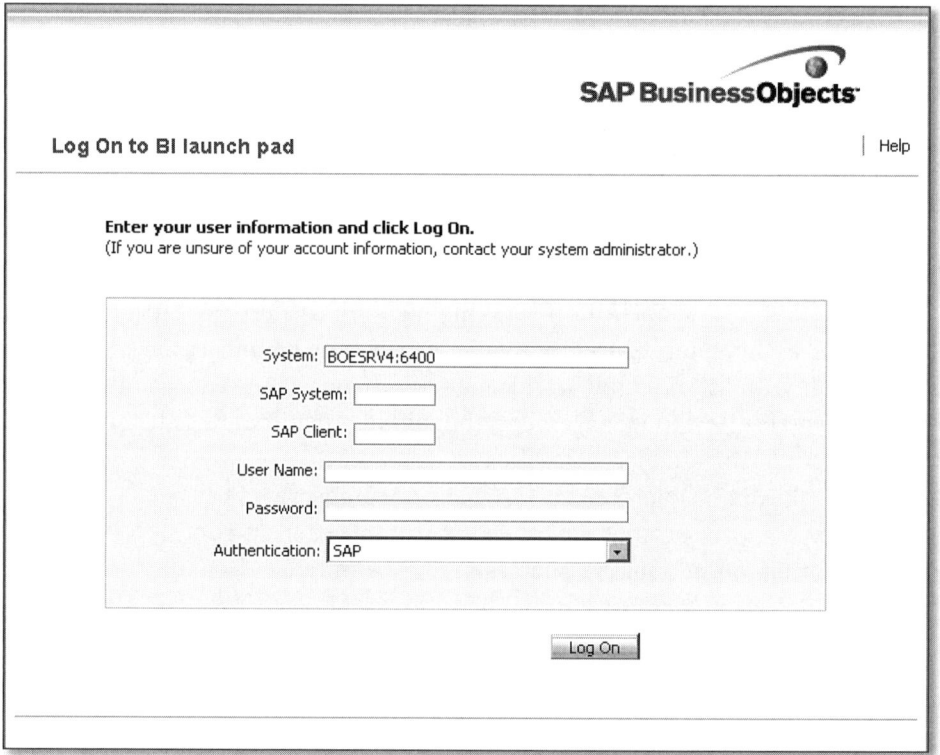

Figure 5.2 BI Launch Pad Logon Page

2. Use your SAP credentials to authenticate for the SAP system. Keep in mind that this requires the SAP authentication to be configured for your SAP BusinessObjects system. If the SAP authentication has not been configured, you can continue with the exercise using the enterprise authentication, but you will not be able to use single sign-on (SSO).

After authentication, you are presented with the standard entry page for BI launch pad (see Figure 5.3).

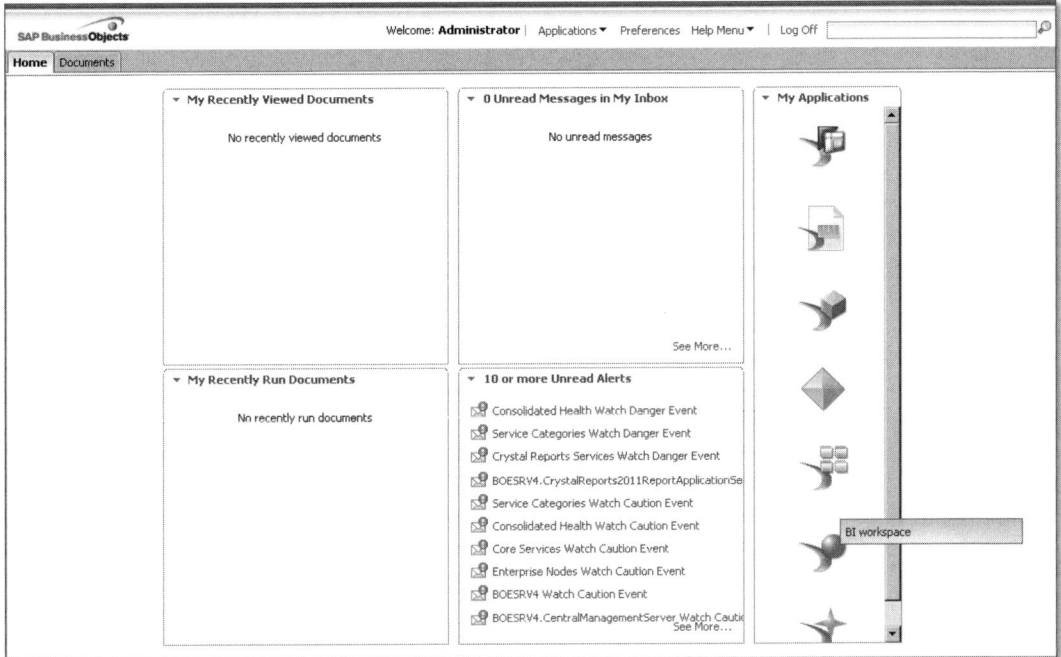

Figure 5.3 BI Launch Pad Start Page

3. Select the PREFERENCES option (see Figure 5.4).
4. Navigate to the WEB INTELLIGENCE section (see Figure 5.5).
5. As part of your user preferences, you can select a default VIEW format and a default CREATING/EDITING tool for SAP BusinessObjects Web Intelligence. Table 5.3 and Table 5.4 list more details of the different options.

5 | Interactive Analysis with SAP BusinessObjects Web Intelligence

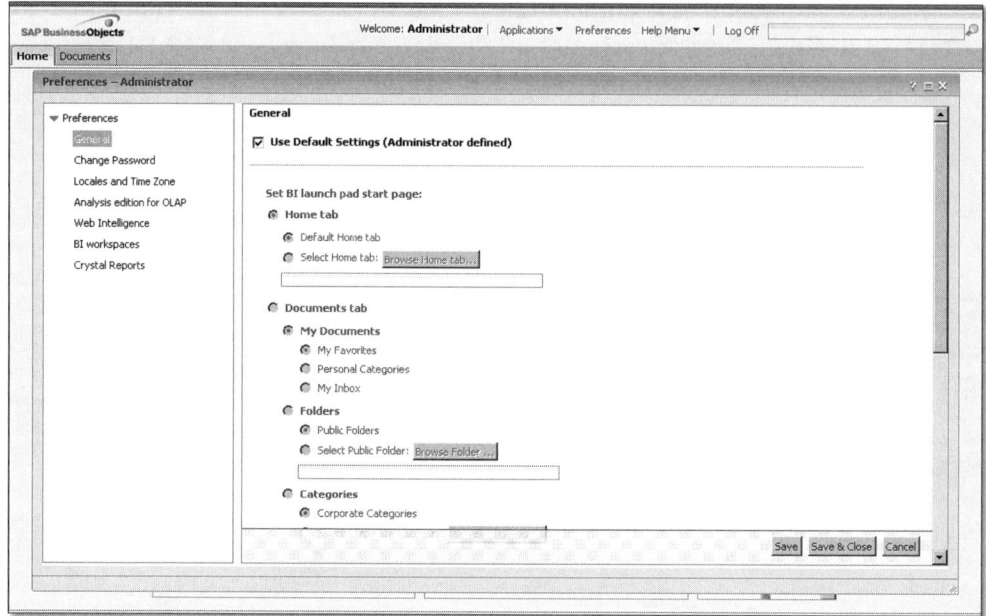

Figure 5.4 User Preferences

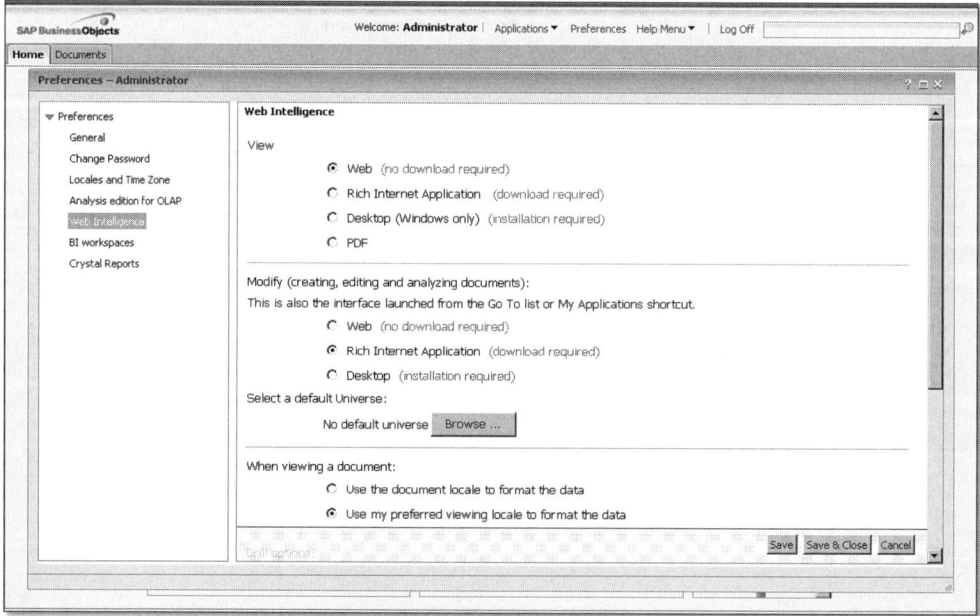

Figure 5.5 Web Intelligence Preferences

SAP BusinessObjects Web Intelligence View Format	Details
Web	You can view and print SAP BusinessObjects Web Intelligence documents. You can respond to prompts and perform drill operations. You view documents using the HTML interface.
Rich Internet application	You can view and print the SAP BusinessObjects Web Intelligence report. You leverage filters, sorting, and calculations, and format objects in the report. You view documents using the Java interface.
PDF	You can respond to prompts, view the document, and print the document.
Desktop	You can view documents using the Web Intelligence Desktop, a standalone interface that works outside of the BI launch pad.

Table 5.3 Web Intelligence View Formats

Web Intelligence Creation Tool	Details
Rich Internet application	You can use the Java interface to create and modify documents.
Desktop	You can create and modify documents using the Web Intelligence Desktop, a standalone interface that works outside of BI launch pad.
Web	You can create and edit documents using the HTML interface.

Table 5.4 Web Intelligence Creation and Editing Tools

6. For these activities, use RICH INTERNET APPLICATION as the VIEW and MODIFY option.
7. Configure the two options and click on SAVE.
8. Scroll down to the option WHEN VIEWING A DOCUMENT (see Figure 5.5). Here you can configure which language setting is used to format the documents. By default, the setting USE MY PREFERRED VIEWING LOCAL TO FORMAT DATA is activated.

9. Select the option LOCALES AND TIME ZONE in the left panel (see Figure 5.6).

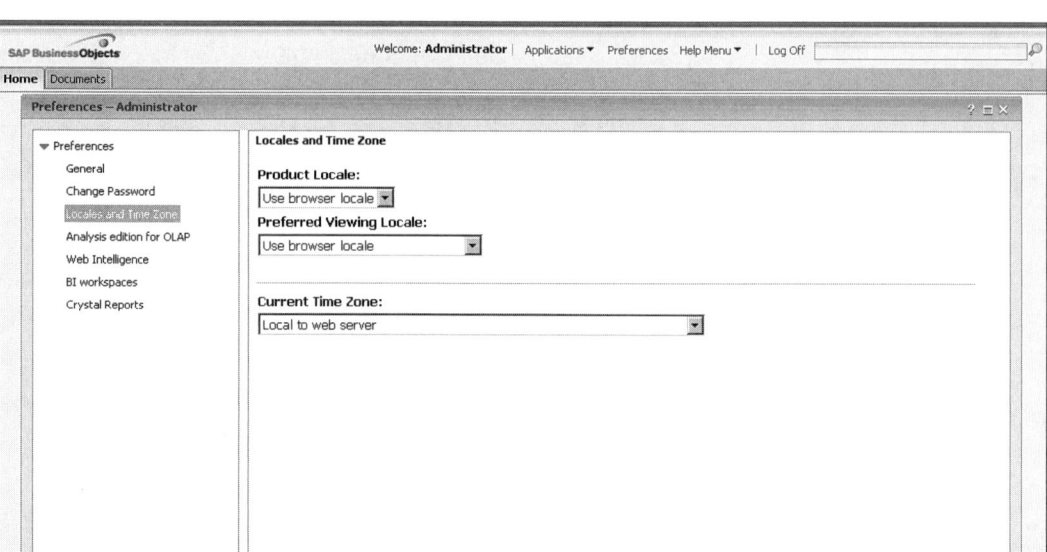

Figure 5.6 Locales and Time Zone

10. Here you can configure the PREFERRED VIEWING LOCALE. The PREFERRED VIEWING LOCALE is relevant for items such as translated text strings and number formatting. Configure the PREFERRED VIEWING LOCALE to your language. Here, English is used.

11. Click on SAVE & CLOSE.

12. You receive a notice that some changes will take effect only after a logoff and a new logon to the system. Confirm the message by clicking on OK. You can now use the APPLICATIONS menu to create a new Web Intelligence document.

13. Follow the menu path APPLICATIONS • WEB INTELLIGENCE APPLICATION. Depending on which option you selected for the viewing and creating of documents in the preferences, you may be asked to install the Java plug-in for Web Intelligence. Because SAP Crystal Reports for Enterprise and SAP BusinessObjectsWeb Intelligence share the connections toward SAP NetWeaver BW, there is no need to configure an additional new connection for your first steps

with SAP BusinessObjects Web Intelligence. Instead, you can re-use the previously created connection that you used with SAP Crystal Reports for Enterprise in Section 4.3.

After the installation of the plug-in finishes, you are presented with the Web Intelligence toolbar and an empty screen (see Figure 5.7). Now, let's create a new report.

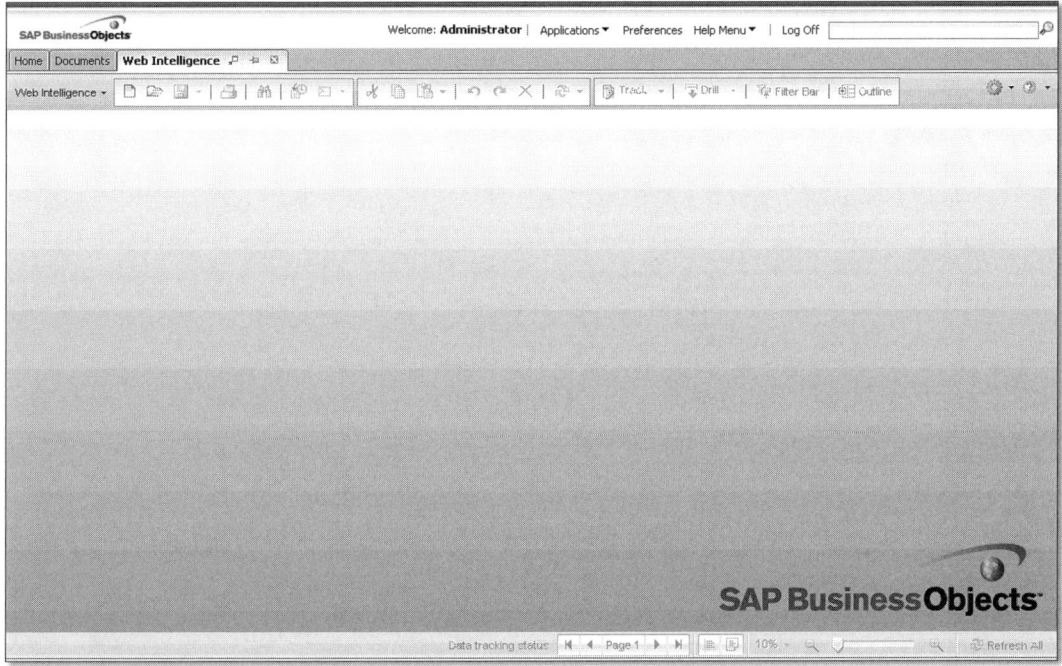

Figure 5.7 Web Intelligence Toolbar

1. Use the NEW (📄) button to start the process of creating a new report.
2. You are asked which type of data source you would like to use for your report (see Figure 5.8).
3. Select the BEx option.
4. Click on OK. You are presented with a list of available connections. As soon as you select one of the available connections, you are shown the available BEx queries on the right side of the dialog (see Figure 5.9).

5 | Interactive Analysis with SAP BusinessObjects Web Intelligence

Figure 5.8 Available Data Sources

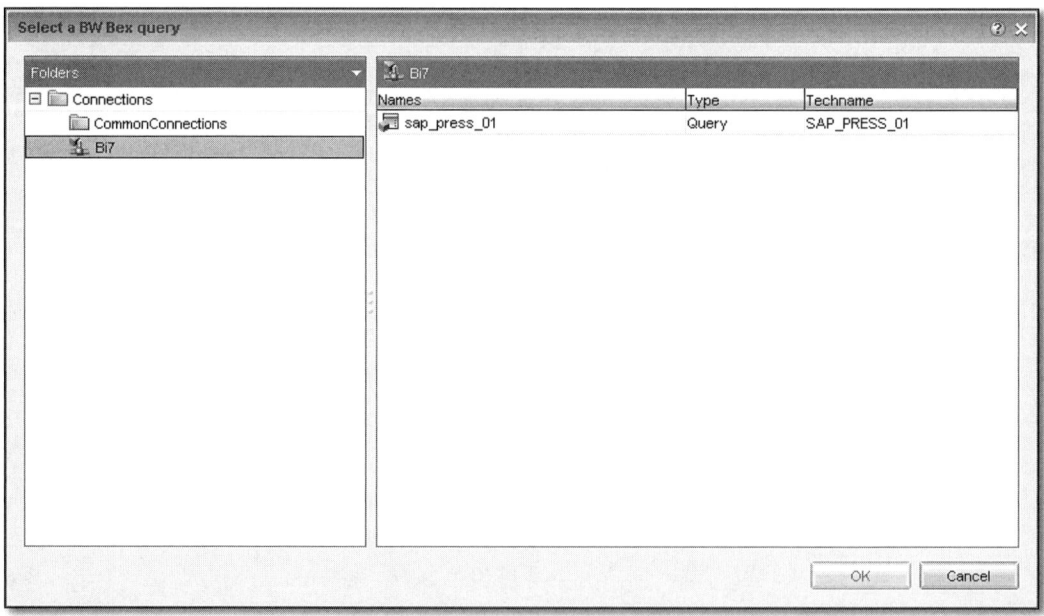

Figure 5.9 Available BEx Queries

5. Select the BEx query created previously and click on OK. You are presented with the SAP BusinessObjects Web Intelligence query panel containing all the available metadata for the selected BEx query (see Figure 5.10).

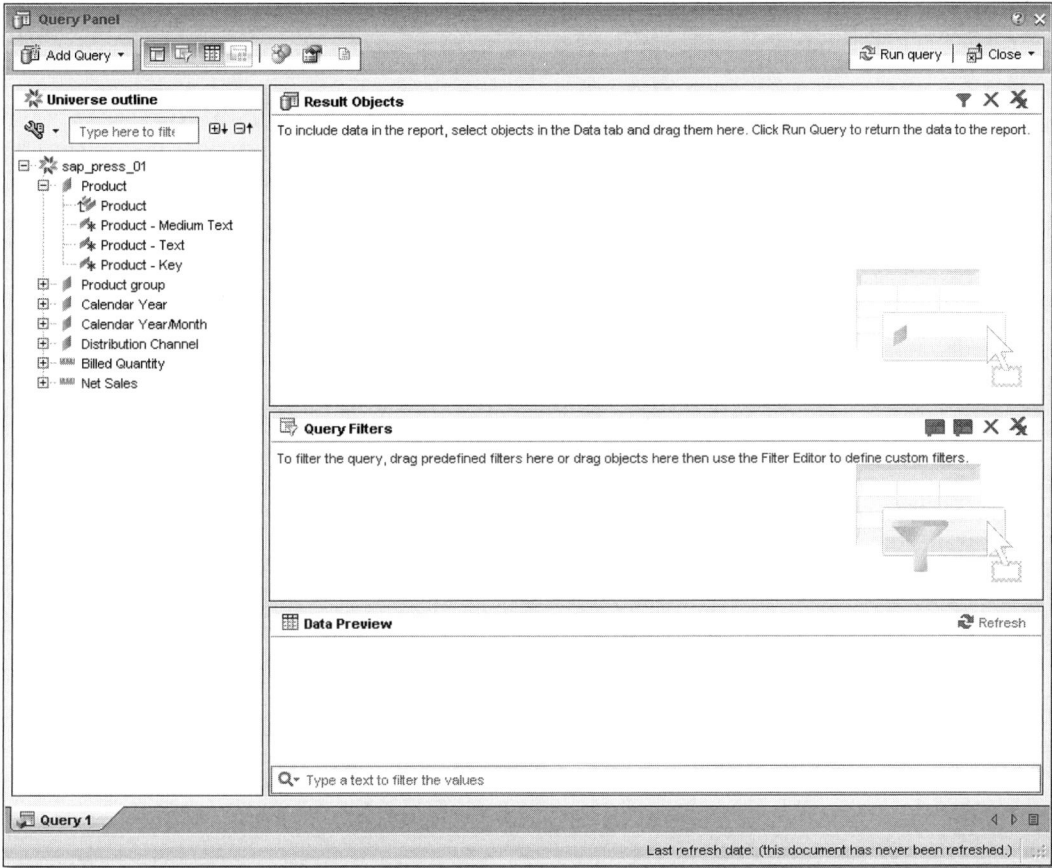

Figure 5.10 Web Intelligence Query Panel

The query panel consists of four major areas:

▸ The UNIVERSE OUTLINE panel, which provides you with the available objects from your selected data source.

▸ The RESULT OBJECTS panel, where you can include objects that you would like to offer to your end users and leverage in your report.

► The QUERY FILTERS panel, where you can—in addition to predefined prompts in the data source—create fixed filters and prompts for your report.

► The DATA PREVIEW PANEL, where you can receive a sample set of records from the underlying data source, before you start creating the actual report.

In addition to these panels, you also can use the PROPERTIES ( ) button in the toolbar to configure properties for the query, such as enabling query stripping or configuring the option to retrieve empty rows, which would mean that your report would be based on the master data in SAP NetWeaver BW (see Figure 5.11).

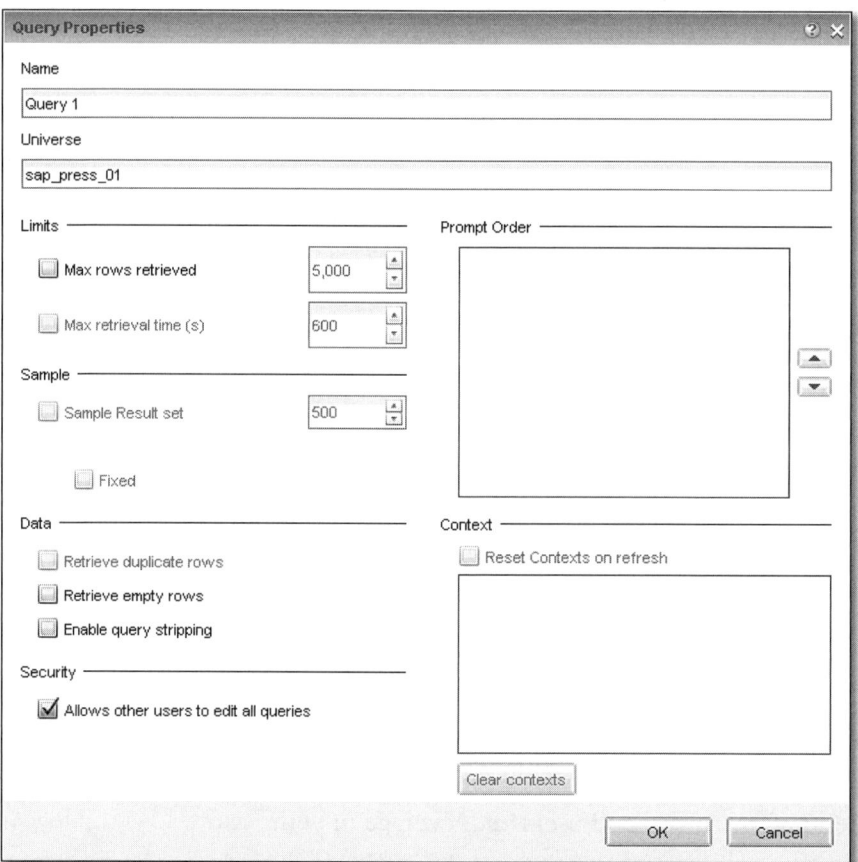

Figure 5.11 Web Intelligence Query Properties

Introduction to the Tool | **5.3**

> **Query Stripping**
>
> SAP BusinessObjects Web Intelligence does not use free characteristics by default, and therefore the functionality of query stripping was introduced. Without query stripping activated, SAP BusinessObjects Web Intelligence will create a data request based on all objects in the RESULT OBJECTS area of the query panel. With query stripping activated, SAP BusinessObjects Web Intelligence will create a data request based on the report design and not on the query panel.

Another important button in the toolbar is the SET VARIABLES option ([icon]), which allows you to set default values for predefined prompts. This capability is important for scenarios like the combination of a hierarchy and hierarchy node variable, or for the combination of a hierarchy node variable and a key date variable. In these scenarios you can use the SET VARIABLES option ([icon]) to ensure that you retrieve the correct list of values in the query panel.

> **Shared Query Panel**
>
> The query panel that provides you with the list of available objects based on the selected data source is shared among SAP BusinessObjects Web Intelligence, SAP Crystal Reports for Enterprise, and SAP BusinessObjects Dashboards. The described functionality—such as the SET VARIABLES option—is therefore available in all these BI client tools.

6. Add the following items to the RESULT OBJECTS panel (see Figure 5.12):
   - PRODUCT and PRODUCT KEY
   - PRODUCT GROUP and PRODUCT GROUP KEY
   - DISTRIBUTION CHANNEL and DISTRIBUTION CHANNEL KEY
   - CALENDAR YEAR
   - CALENDAR YEAR/MONTH and CALENDAR YEAR/MONTH KEY
   - BILLED QUANTITY
   - NET SALES

> **Detail Objects and Dimension Objects**
>
> In the universe outline panel, the dimension objects (blue square surrounded by a box) represent, by default, the description of the characteristic; the detail objects (blue square with a green star symbol, surrounded by a box) represent the key value and the display attributes from your underlying BEx query.

> It is especially important in cases where you would like to sort or group—such as the CALENDAR YEAR/MONTH in the example—to include the key value to make sure you are sorting properly.
>
> In addition, each characteristic will have one or multiple entries in the universe outline panel, representing the available hierarchies (set of stacked blue squares with upper arrow). The first hierarchy entry is known as the default hierarchy and should be used in scenarios where you would like to leverage a hierarchy variable at runtime.

Figure 5.12 Result Objects

7. Click on RUN QUERY in the toolbar.
8. Because you didn't define any specific report layout, SAP BusinessObjects Web Intelligence presents a standard table that includes all of the columns that you included in the result objects (see Figure 5.13).
9. On the left side of your report, you can see the AVAILABLE OBJECTS panel and several other panels that you can use to change your report (see Figure 5.14). The AVAILABLE OBJECTS panel provides access to the elements of our query; the REPORT MAP panel lets you navigate in the report; the INPUT CONTROLS panel lets you create items, such as a list box, for elements of your report. Make sure you can see the AVAILABLE OBJECTS panel selected.

Introduction to the Tool | 5.3

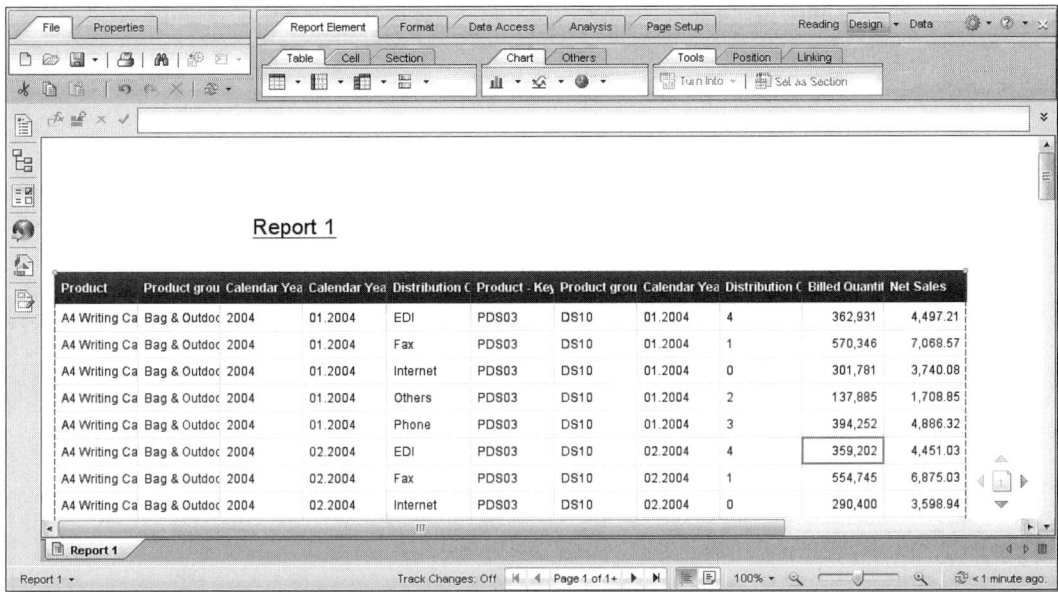

Figure 5.13 SAP BusinessObjects Web Intelligence Report

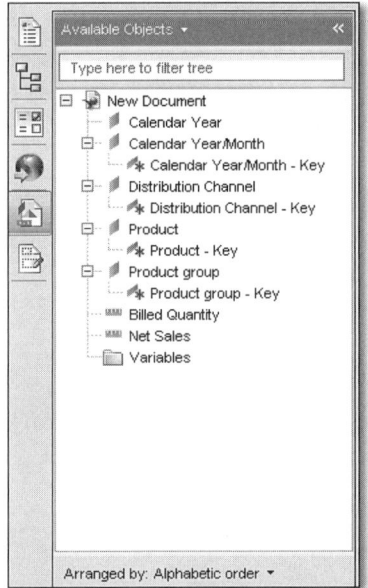

Figure 5.14 Available Objects

10. Drag and drop the following objects headers onto the AVAILABLE OBJECTS panel:

    ▶ PRODUCT GROUP KEY
    ▶ PRODUCT GROUP
    ▶ PRODUCT KEY
    ▶ PRODUCT
    ▶ CALENDAR YEAR/MONTH

    By dragging and dropping them onto the AVAILABLE OBJECTS panel, you are removing the objects from the report. Keep in mind that the data are still collected, because the objects are part of your result object in the query panel (see Figure 5.15).

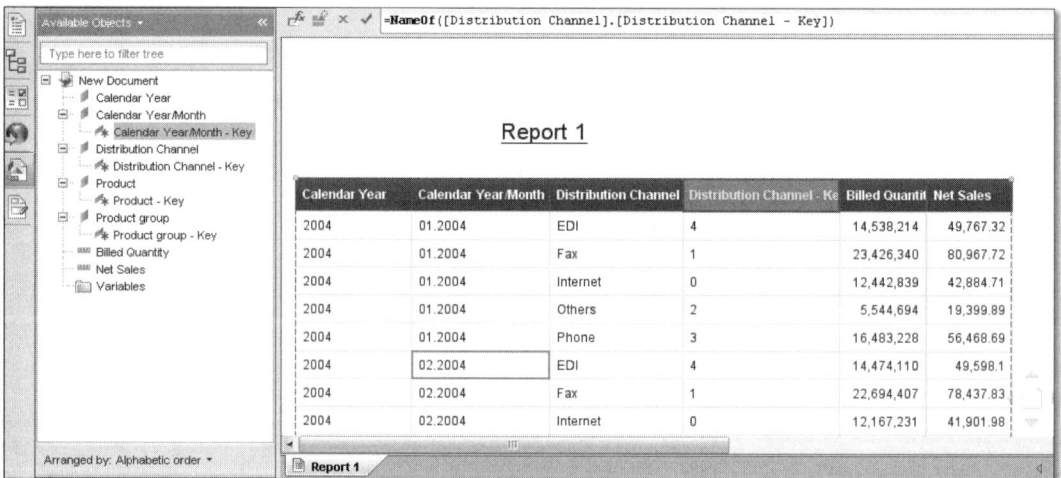

Figure 5.15 Web Intelligence Changed Report

11. Right-click on the BILLED QUANTITY column and select FORMAT NUMBER.
12. Select NUMBER as the FORMAT TYPE, scroll down the list of predefined options, and use the format type without decimals (see Figure 5.16).
13. Click on OK.

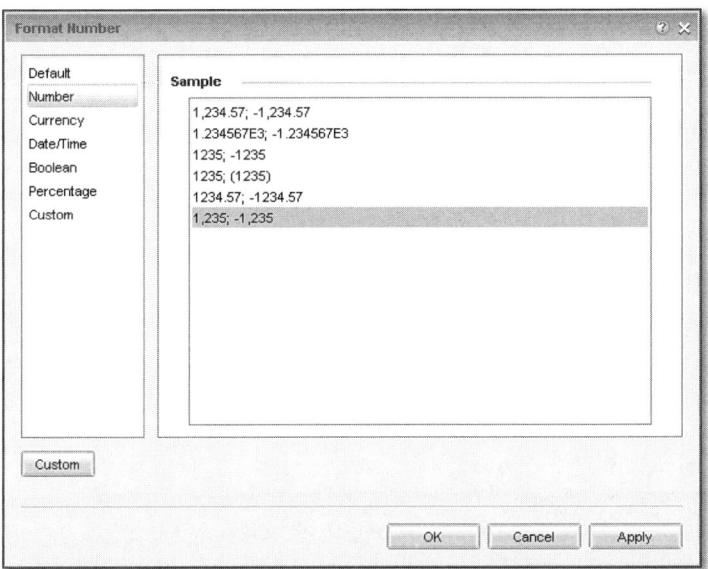

Figure 5.16 Format Number

> **Query Panel vs. Report Object**
>
> It is important to understand that SAP BusinessObjects Web Intelligence retrieves data based on the result objects defined in the query panel, unless you activate query stripping. Even though you might use only a small part of the selected objects from the result objects in your report, the query will ask for all of the elements and data based on the defined list of objects in the result objects panel. In case it's easier remember using the typical SAP Business Explorer (BEx) Analyzer terms, you can think of it this way: SAP BusinessObjects Web Intelligence without query stripping does not have free characteristics that are available for on demand usage. Query stripping needs to be activated in the properties of the query panel and in the properties of each report.

5.3.2 Using Filters

So far, you have created a very basic table output from your underlying BEx query. Let's build on this and leverage some filtering as part of your report.

1. Navigate to the DATA ACCESS tab.
2. Navigate to the DATA PROVIDERS tab.
3. Click on EDIT. You are back at the query panel.
4. Drag and drop the PRODUCT element to the QUERY FILTERS panel.

5. Use the IN LIST operator and select the PROMPT option (see Figure 5.17).

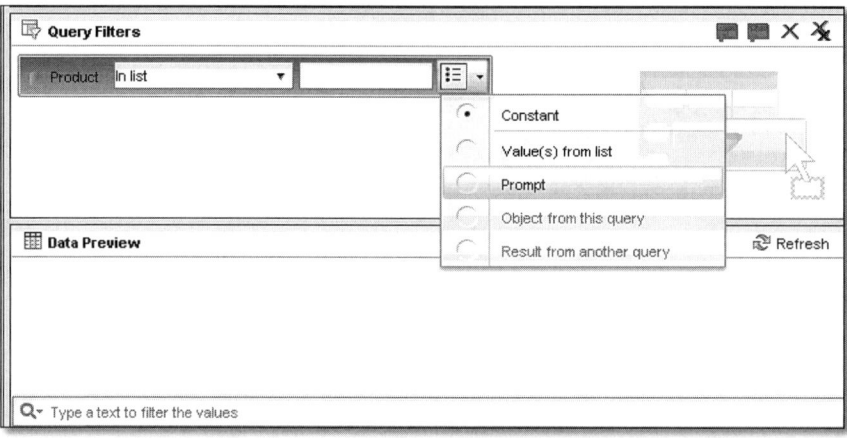

Figure 5.17 Query Filters

6. Click on the PARAMETER PROPERTIES button ( ) to define the details of your new prompt (see Figure 5.18).

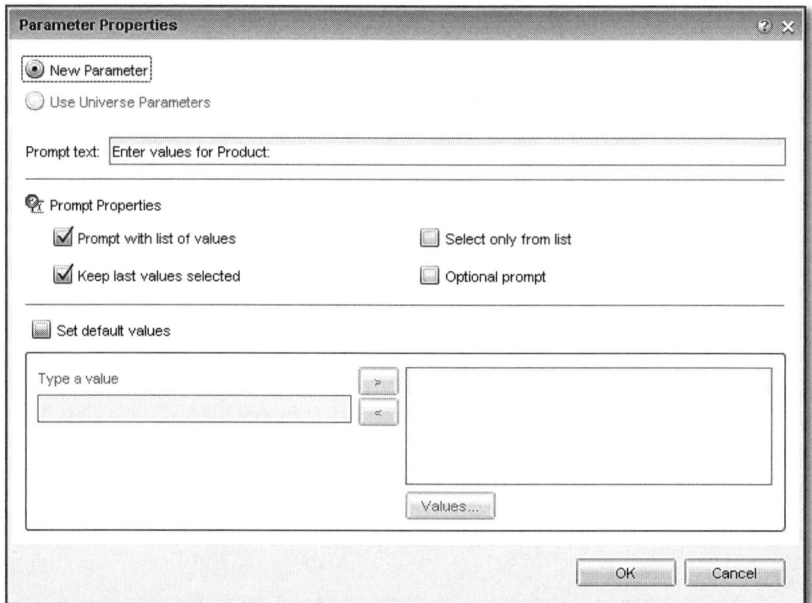

Figure 5.18 Parameter Properties

7. Activate the option OPTIONAL PROMPT.
8. Click on OK.
9. Click on RUN QUERY.
10. You are prompted for a value for the characteristic PRODUCT. Based on the IN LIST operator as part of your definition, you can enter multiple values (see Figure 5.19).

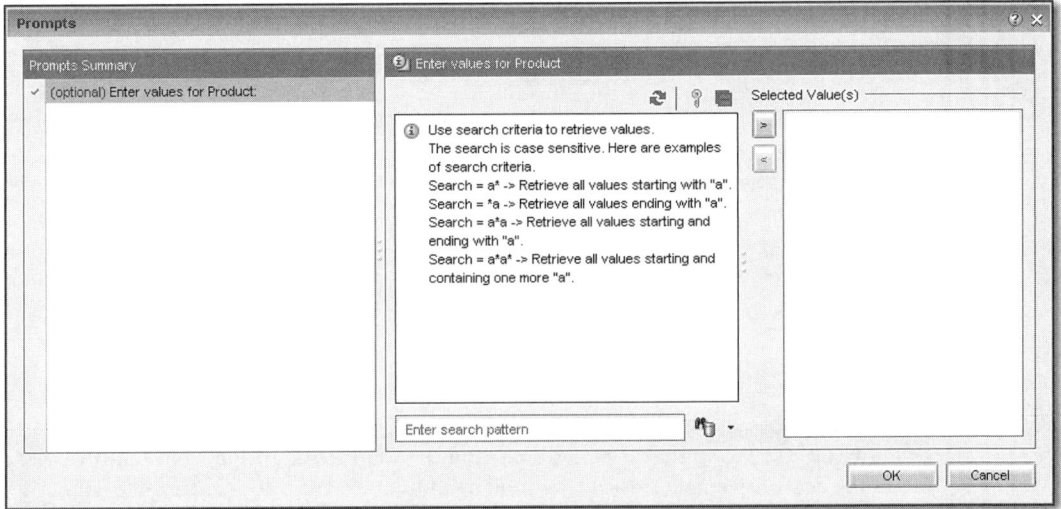

Figure 5.19 Prompt Dialog

11. Notice that the prompt does not provide a list of values; instead you are asked to enter search criteria. If you have only a short list of values, as in this example, you can enter "*" as search criteria and click on Enter.

> **Query Filter and Delegated Search**
>
> When updating this book (November 2011) the default behavior for prompts as part of the query filters area was to have the delegated search be enabled without an option for the user to configure the behavior. This behavior might change in the future.

12. You can then select a list of members for the prompt (see Figure 5.20) and use the arrow buttons (▶) to add the selected members to the list of SELECTED VALUE(S).

5 | Interactive Analysis with SAP BusinessObjects Web Intelligence

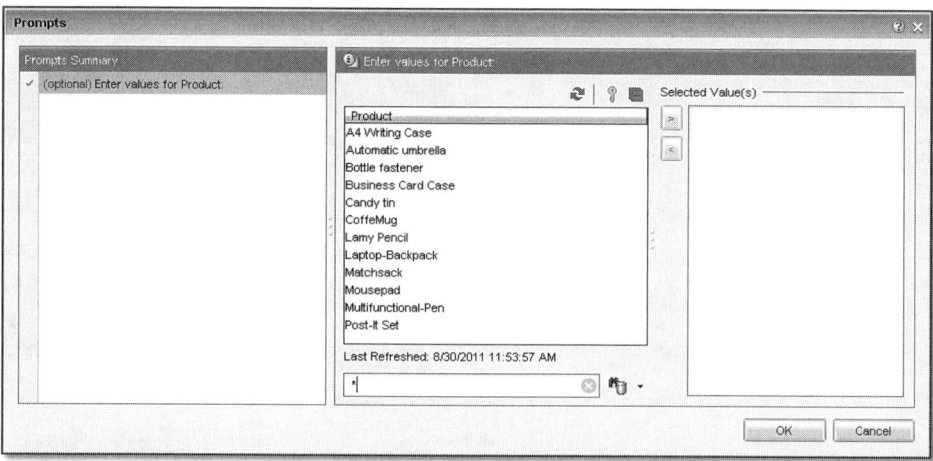

Figure 5.20 List of Values

13. Click on OK. You have now created a prompt as part of your report, which allows you to select the list of products each time you refresh the report.

Filtering in the SAP BusinessObjects Web Intelligence Report

When creating, editing, or viewing a report, you can also leverage the FILTER option from the FILTERS tab in the ANALYSIS area, and the FILTER BAR option from the INTERACT tab in the ANALYSIS area. (This can be done in addition to the options shown for filtering the data by creating a query filter.) Both options let you create filters based on the query. In addition, you can also leverage input controls in your report to offer a more interactive user experience for filtering.

14. Navigate to the ANALYSIS tab.
15. Navigate to the FILTERS tab (see Figure 5.21).

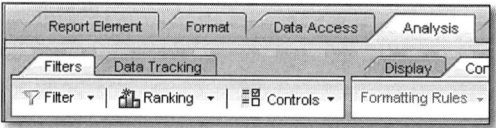

Figure 5.21 Filters and Controls

16. Click on CONTROLS (see Figure 5.22).
17. Select the CALENDAR YEAR.
18. Click on NEXT (see Figure 5.23).

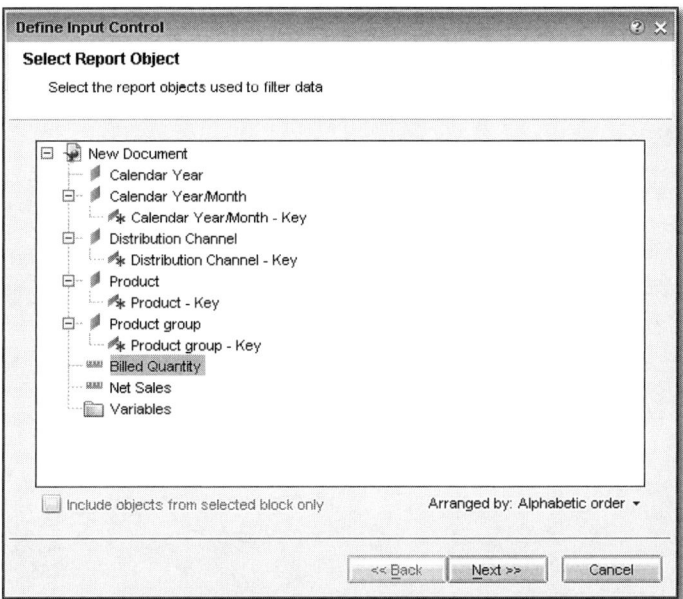

Figure 5.22 Define Input Control

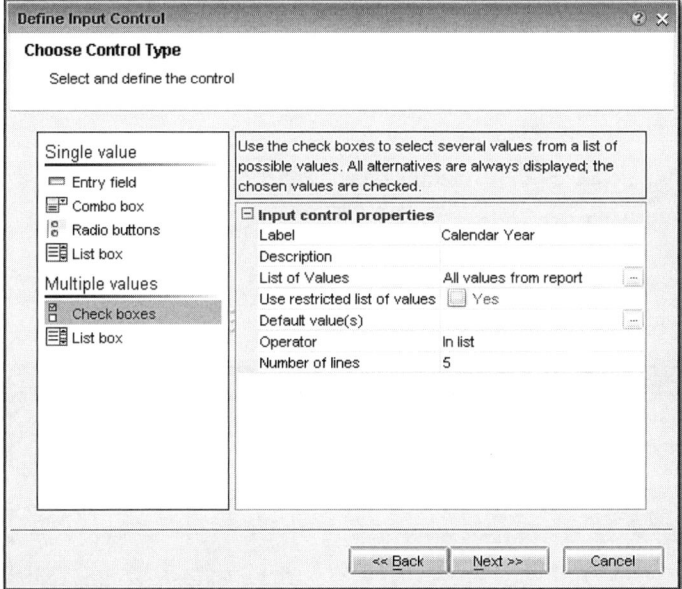

Figure 5.23 Control Type

19. Select the option CHECK BOXES for MULTIPLE VALUES.
20. Click on NEXT (see Figure 5.24).

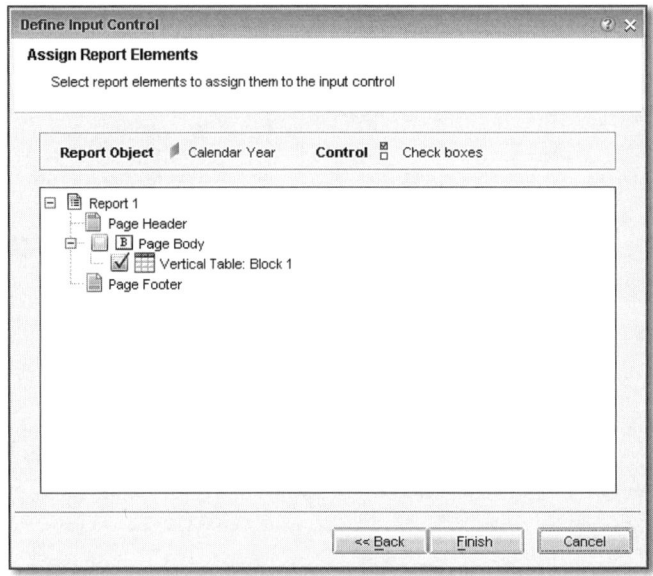

Figure 5.24 Assign Report Elements

21. Activate the option for the VERTICAL TABLE.
22. Click on FINISH (see Figure 5.25).

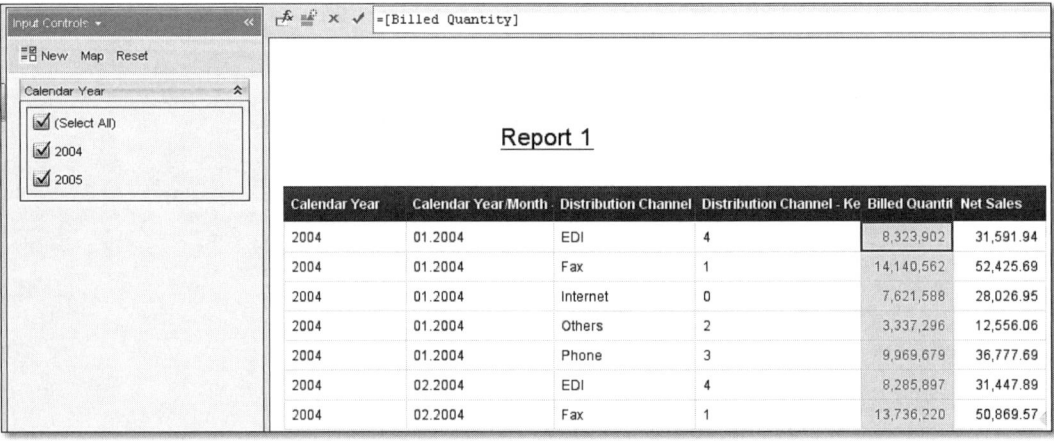

Figure 5.25 Report with Input Controls

You have now created an input control as part of your report, which allows the end user to select a set of years by using the checkboxes, and thus to filter the data shown in the report.

> **BEx Query Variables or SAP BusinessObjects Web Intelligence Prompts**
>
> In the XI 3.1 release of the SAP BusinessObjects suite, you were able to use OLAP universes to create your own filters, prompt as part of the OLAP universe, and share them across multiple reports. In the 4.0 FP3 release, you don't need the OLAP universe anymore, because you can connect directly to the BEx query. However, this also means that you need to create all the shared prompts as part of your BEx query in the form of BEx variables. You can still create your own filter and prompts—as shown in the activity here—but those are report-specific and cannot be shared across multiple reports.

5.3.3 Arranging Objects

At this point, you have created a report that consists of a single table. In the following steps, we look at how to use different objects in a single report, how to ensure that they are aligned, and how to influence the properties of the objects. We continue using the report from the previous sections.

1. Select the table in your report.
2. Right-click to open the context menu.
3. Select the menu item TURN INTO • CROSS TABLE (SEE Figure 5.26).

    Your table is automatically turned into a cross tab report.

4. Remove DISTRIBUTION CHANNEL KEY field from the cross tab by simply dragging the field outside of the report.
5. Navigate to the REPORT ELEMENT tab.
6. Navigate to the CHART tab.
7. Click on the LINE CHART option.
8. You now have a chart template attached to your mouse cursor and you can place the chart into your report. Place the chart above your cross tab but below the report title (see Figure 5.27).

    It is likely that your chart now overlaps with your table, but you will fix this in the next step.

9. Select the cross tab in your report.

5 | Interactive Analysis with SAP BusinessObjects Web Intelligence

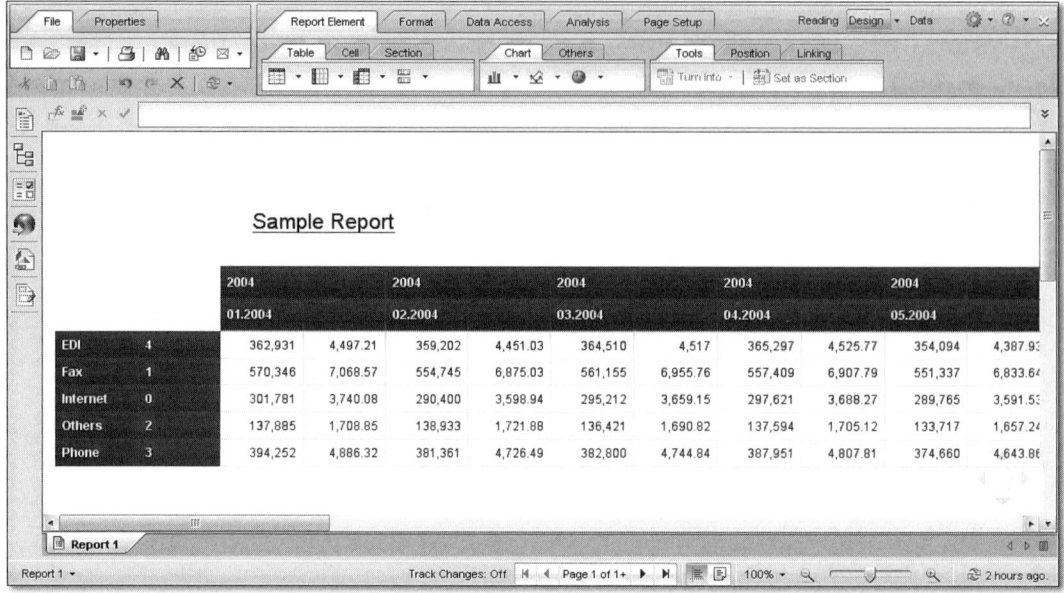

Figure 5.26 SAP BusinessObjects Web Intelligence Cross Tab

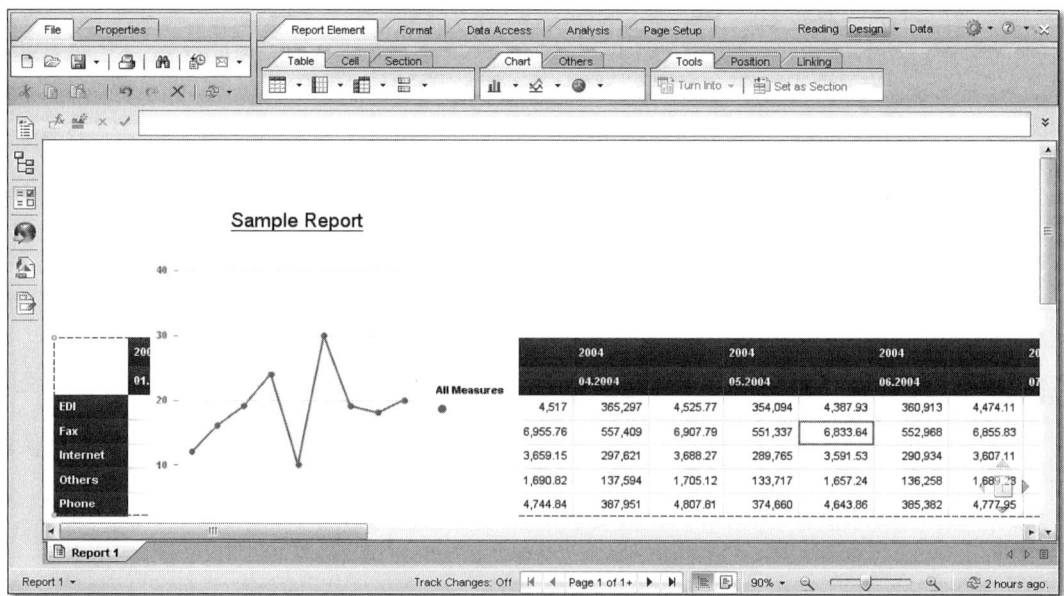

Figure 5.27 Report with Chart

10. Navigate to the REPORT ELEMENT tab.
11. Navigate to the POSITION tab.
12. Open the ALIGN menu and select the RELATIVE POSITION menu item (see Figure 5.28).

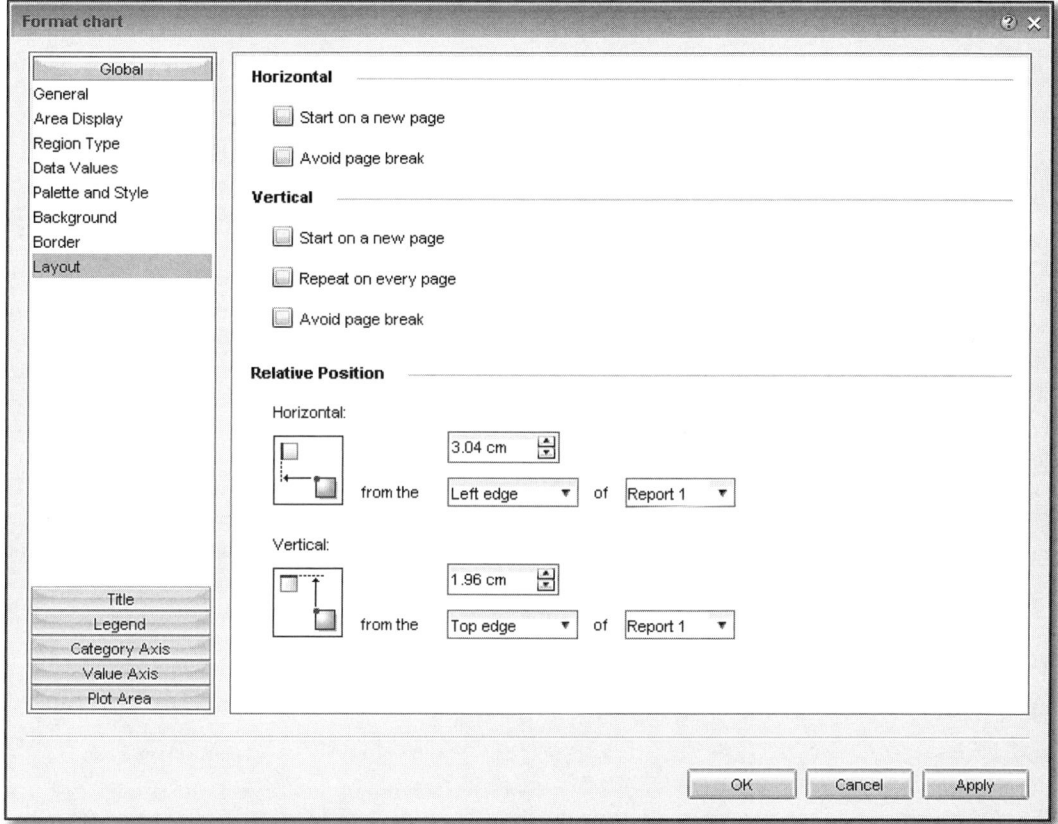

Figure 5.28 Relative Position

Here you can define the position of your cross tab in relation to other elements, such as the chart, in the report.

13. Set the cross tab to be 2 cm from the left edge of Report 1 for the horizontal position.
14. Set the cross tab to be 2 cm from the bottom edge of Block 2 for the vertical position. Block 2 is your chart.

15. Click on OK.
16. The cross tab automatically aligns when you resize the chart.
17. Right now the chart is still undefined and shows no data, so you need to configure which information you would like to surface in the chart.
18. Drag and drop the NET SALES key figure from the list of available objects onto the chart.
19. Drag and drop the CALENDAR YEAR/MONTH characteristic from the list of available objects onto the chart.
20. Resize the chart so that you can see all the information (see Figure 5.29).

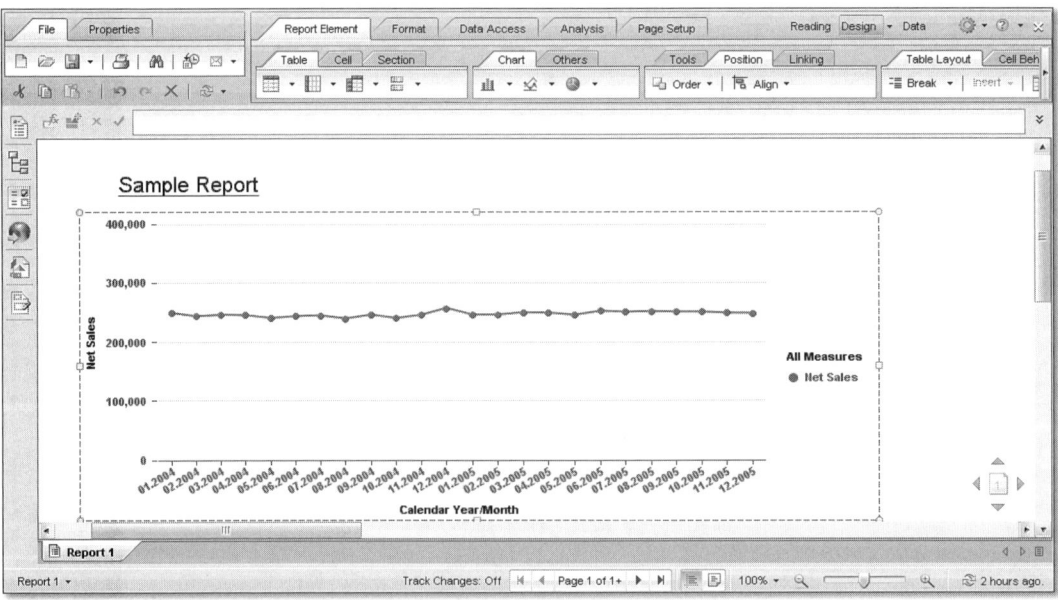

Figure 5.29 SAP BusinessObjects Web Intelligence Report with Chart

> **Identifying Report Elements**
>
> If you are not sure about the identification of the report part that you selected (for example, Block 2 for the chart in our report), you can use the document structure and filters panel to get a complete list of elements that are used in your report.

5.3.4 Using Breaks, Sections, and Summaries

So far, your report shows a table and a chart without any groupings or summaries. In the next couple of steps, we describe how you can continue using the report to create sections and summaries.

1. Your report shows the BILLED QUANTITY and NET SALES in a cross tab by CALENDAR YEAR/CALENDAR MONTH and DISTRIBUTION CHANNEL.
2. Select the CALENDAR YEAR in the cross tab.
3. Right-click to open the context menu.
4. Select the menu item SET AS SECTION (see Figure 5.30).

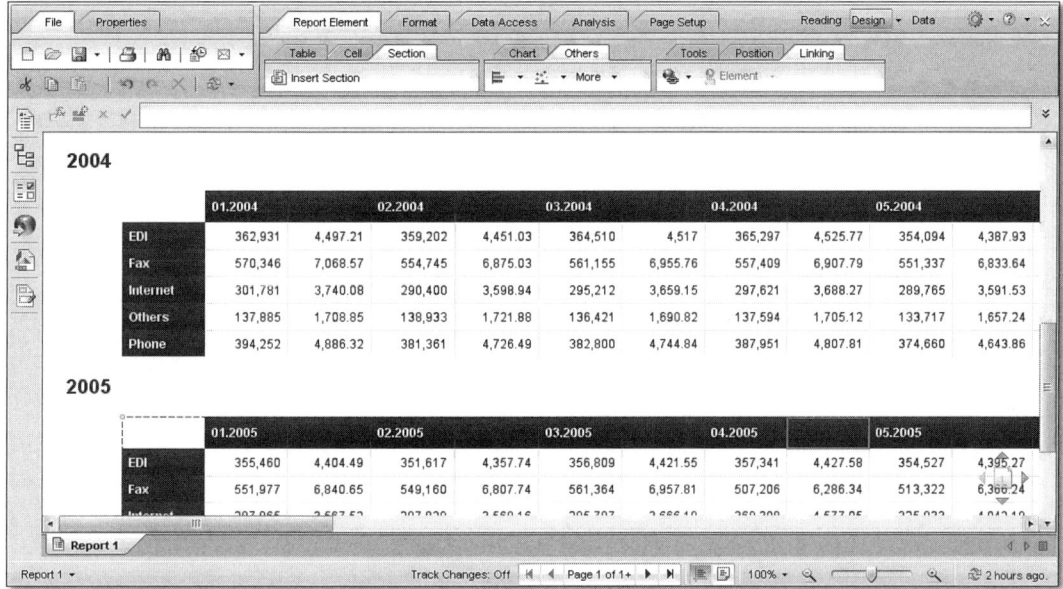

Figure 5.30 Report with Sections

Your report is now divided into sections based on the CALENDAR YEAR.

5. Open the REPORT MAP (see Figure 5.31).

   Your report now shows the sections of the report; you can use the report map to navigate to those sections.

6. Select the cross tab in your report.
7. Navigate to the REPORT ELEMENT tab.

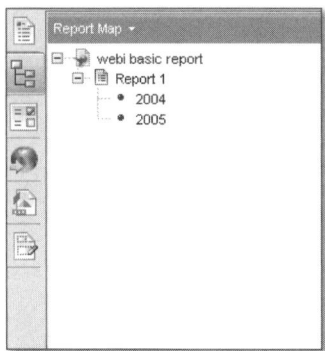

Figure 5.31 Report Map

8. Navigate to the TOOLS tab.
9. Select the menu path TURN INTO • VERTICAL TABLE.
10. Remove the DISTRIBUTION CHANNEL column from the table. Select the column, right-click to open the menu, and select the DELETE menu item.
11. Drag the PRODUCT and PRODUCT GROUP characteristics to your table from the list of available objects. Make sure your table shows the object in the following order: PRODUCT GROUP, PRODUCT, CALENDAR YEAR/MONTH (see Figure 5.32).

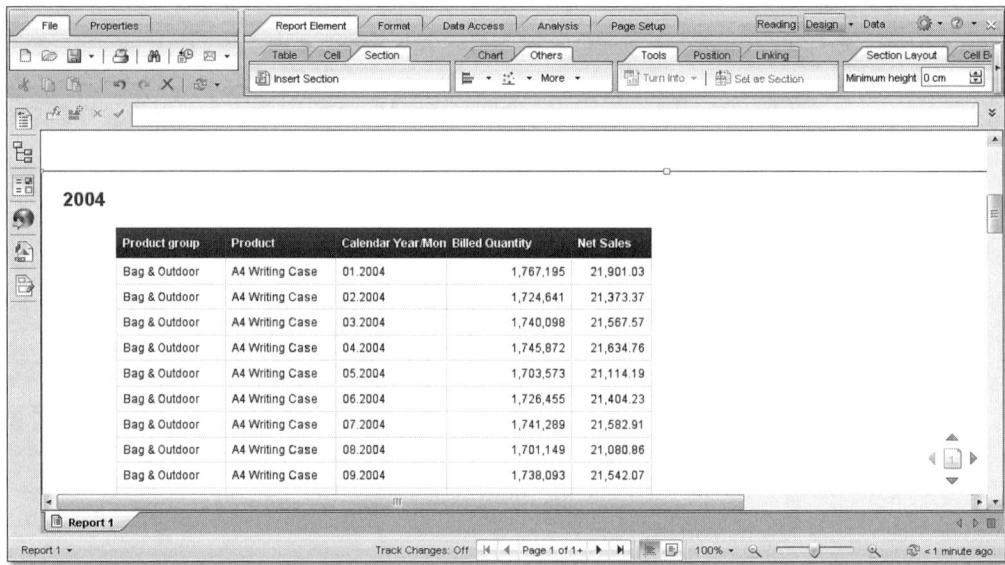

Figure 5.32 Updated Table

12. Select an entry from the column PRODUCT GROUP.
13. Navigate to the REPORT ELEMENT tab.
14. Navigate to the TABLE LAYOUT tab.
15. Select the menu path BREAK • ADD BREAK.
16. Repeat these steps for the PRODUCT column.
17. Select a member from the BILLED QUANTITY column.
18. Navigate to the ANALYSIS tab.
19. Navigate to the FUNCTION tab.
20. Use the SUM option to create subtotals for BILLED QUANTITY.
21. Repeat the steps for NET SALES.
22. Select the column PRODUCT GROUP.
23. Navigate to the ANALYSIS tab.
24. Navigate to the INTERACT tab.
25. Click on OUTLINE (see Figure 5.33).

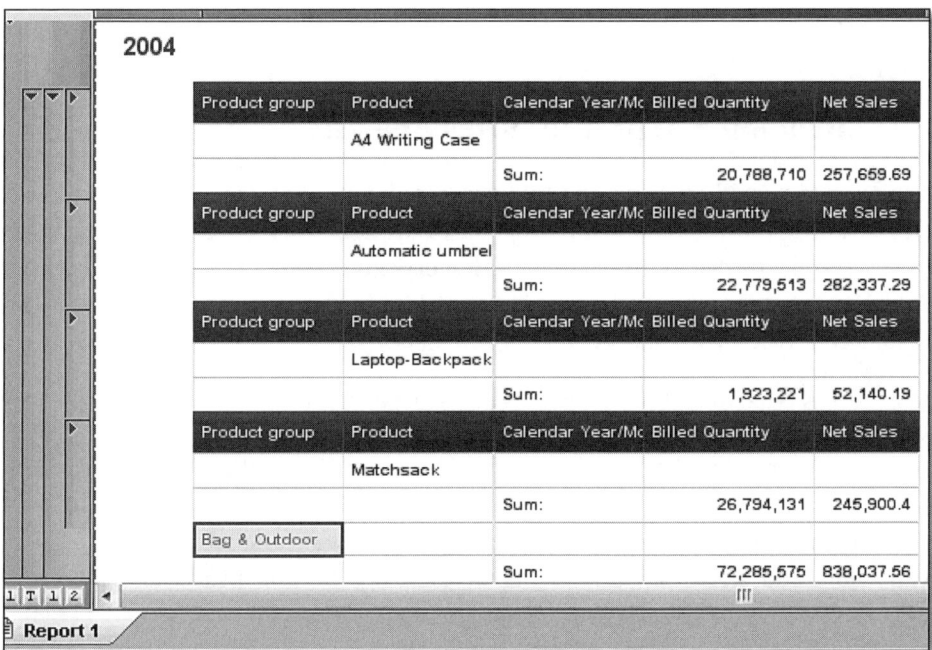

Figure 5.33 Report with Outline

You can now use the triangles on the left side or the numbers in the bottom left corner to open your previously configured breaks in the table independent of each other. In this way, you provide your end user a summarized view with the option to open for more detailed information.

26. Use the SAVE option ( ) from the menu FILE (see Figure 5.34) to save your report to the SAP BusinessObjects system.

Figure 5.34 Menu File

After saving your report, you can view the report with the different viewing options in the BI launch pad.

In this section, you learned the basics for how to use SAP BusinessObjects Web Intelligence for your reporting needs and how to create compelling analytics. We use this knowledge in the next section, by fulfilling the requirements from the sales area using SAP BusinessObjects Web Intelligence.

5.4 Building a Report for Sales Analysis

In this section we discuss using SAP BusinessObjects Web Intelligence to deliver sales area reports. We focus on how you can use SAP BusinessObjects Web Intelligence and the direct connectivity to SAP NetWeaver BW to provide the required reporting environment, and provide step-by-step instructions on how you can create a report for your sales team.

We're going to create a report that shows actual and planned sales in revenue and quantity based on different dimensions of the business, such as product group, product, region, and distribution channel. In addition, we'll provide the capability to drill down into more details, if required, and to filter the report based on dimensions. As part of the overall reporting, we will also deliver top and bottom performers and show some trending of the sales for the products (see Figure 5.35).

Building a Report for Sales Analysis | 5.4

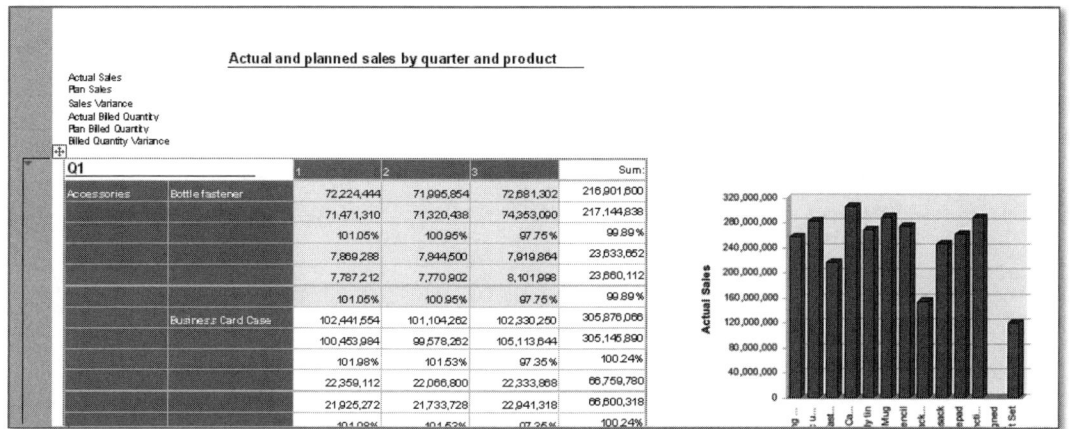

Figure 5.35 Web Intelligence Sales Report

In this example, we leverage a BEx query as the source for our reporting. This gives us the actual and planned sales revenue and quantity based on the SAP demo content cube 0D_DX_M01. The BW query that we are using contains the following characteristics (see Figure 5.36):

- CALENDAR MONTH
- DISTRIBUTION CHANNEL
- PRODUCT GROUP
- PRODUCT
- REGION CODE
- QUARTER
- CALENDAR YEAR
- CUSTOMER
- REASON — LOST DEALS

The BW query contains the following key figures:

- NET SALES
- SALES PLAN
- BILLED QUANTITY
- BILLED QUANTITY PLAN

155

- Lost Deals
- Number of Lost Deals

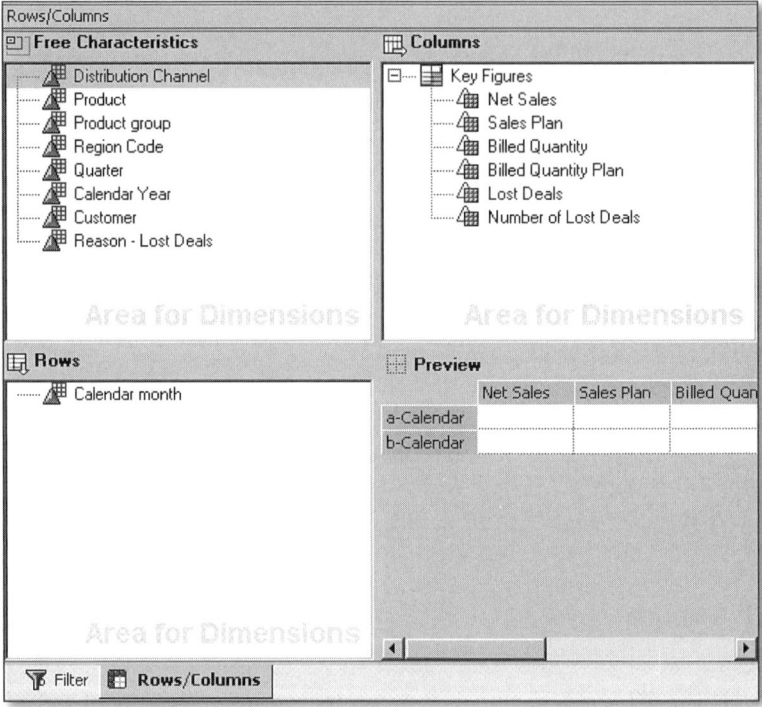

Figure 5.36 BEx Query for Sales Report

Before we can build our report using SAP BusinessObjects Web Intelligence, we need to set up the OLAP connection in the Central Management Console (CMC) of our SAP BusinessObjects system. You can find the detailed steps in Chapter 4, Section 4.3.3 as part of the overall SAP Crystal Reports for Enterprise chapter, but remember that SAP Crystal Reports for Enterprise and SAP BusinessObjects Web Intelligence are able to share the connections.

> **The "Non-Existence" of the Universe for BEx Query Connections**
>
> Because you do no longer have the actual universe between the BI client tool and the BEx query in the SAP BusinessObjects 4.0 FP3 release, you need to remind yourself of the following important items:

> ▶ You cannot create custom objects as part of the connection, so all elements needed should be part of the underlying BEx query. You can still create formulas, filters, and prompts as part of the SAP BusinessObjects Web Intelligence report, but those are report specific and cannot be shared with other reports.
>
> ▶ You cannot change the descriptions of elements. Any needed change needs to be done in the BEx query using the BEx Query Designer.

After you configure the OLAP connection as part of our SAP BusinessObjects system, you can start creating your sales report.

Before we continue, we should clarify what kind of report we want to create. The report should show the actual and planned number for the sales revenue and the quantity. The numbers should be broken down by month, product group, and product; in addition, the report user should be able to filter the report based on the available dimensions. Let's begin:

1. Launch the BI launch pad via the menu path START • PROGRAMS • SAP BUSINESSOBJECTS BI PLATFORM 4 • SAP BUSINESSOBJECTS BI PLATFORM • SAP BUSINESSOBJECTS BI PLATFORM JAVA BI LAUNCH PAD.

2. Use your SAP credentials to authenticate for the SAP system. Keep in mind that this requires the SAP authentication to be configured for your SAP BusinessObjects system. If the SAP authentication has not been configured, you can continue with the exercise using the Enterprise authentication, but you will not be able to use SSO.

3. Follow the menu path: APPLICATIONS • WEB INTELLIGENCE APPLICATION.

4. Use the NEW (🗋) button to start the process of creating a new report. You are asked which type of data source you would like to use for your report.

5. Select the BEx option.

6. Click on OK. You are presented with a list of available connections. As soon as you select one of the available connections, you are shown the available BEx queries on the right side of the dialog.

7. Select the connection and the BEx query you created for your sales report.

8. Click on OK. You are presented with the SAP BusinessObjects Web Intelligence query panel containing all the available metadata for the selected BEx query (see Figure 5.37).

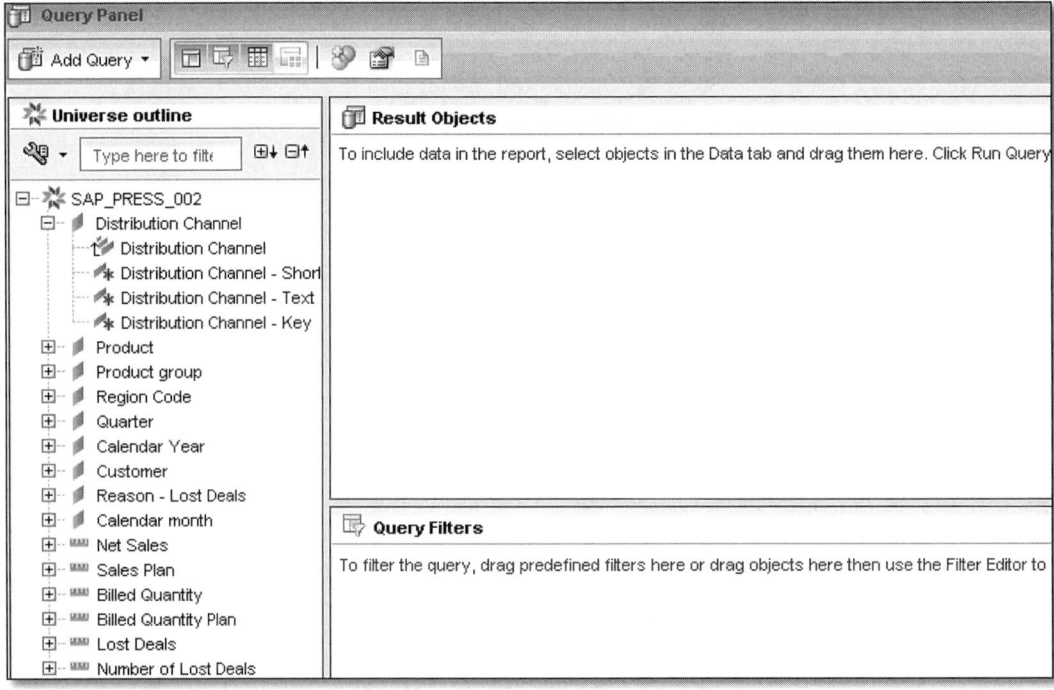

Figure 5.37 SAP BusinessObjects Web Intelligence Query Panel

9. Add the following objects to the RESULT OBJECTS panel:

   ▶ REGION CODE
   ▶ DISTRIBUTION CHANNEL
   ▶ PRODUCT GROUP
   ▶ PRODUCT
   ▶ CALENDAR MONTH KEY
   ▶ CALENDAR MONTH
   ▶ CALENDAR YEAR
   ▶ QUARTER
   ▶ REASON—LOST DEALS
   ▶ NET SALES
   ▶ SALES PLAN

- BILLED QUANTITY
- BILLED QUANTITY PLAN
- LOST DEALS
- NUMBER OF LOST DEALS

10. Use the QUERY PROPERTIES ( ) button from the toolbar to open the properties.
11. Activate the option ENABLE QUERY STRIPPING.
12. Click on OK.
13. Click on RUN QUERY to retrieve the data. The default table layout appears.

> **Note**
> Because you want to ensure proper sorting for the CALENDAR MONTH, you should first create a new formula/variable that represents the actual numeric value of the CALENDAR MONTH.

14. Click on the VARIABLE EDITOR ( ) symbol in the toolbar.
15. Enter "Calendar Month (numeric)" as the NAME.
16. Set the QUALIFICATION to DIMENSION.
17. Enter the following formula:

    `=ToNumber([Calendar month].[Calendar month – Key])`. Click on OK.

18. Replace the CALENDAR MONTH KEY column with the newly created CALENDAR MONTH (NUMERIC) object by dragging the objects from the data panel on top of the CALENDAR MONTH KEY column.
19. Remove the following objects from the table:
    - REGION CODE
    - DISTRIBUTION CHANNEL
    - CALENDAR MONTH
    - QUARTER
    - CALENDAR YEAR
    - REASON—LOST DEALS
    - LOST DEALS
    - NUMBER OF LOST DEALS

> **Note**
> You can remove the objects mentioned in the previous step by either dragging them outside the report or right-clicking and selecting the option DELETE in the context menu. You should remove these items from the table because you won't need them for your report. However, you will need them as filter objects and you want to offer them to the user as options in the report. Therefore, you should include them in your result objects panel.

20. Navigate to the PROPERTIES tab.
21. Click on DOCUMENT (see Figure 5.38).

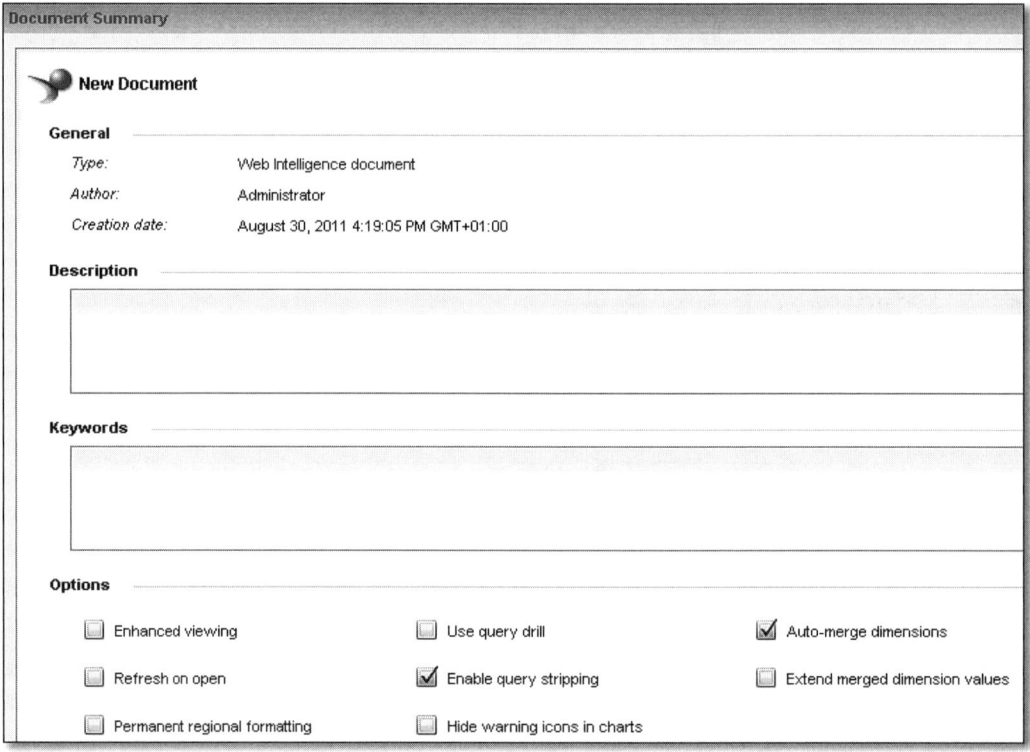

Figure 5.38 Document Properties

22. Activate the ENABLE QUERY STRIPPING option.
23. Click on OK.
24. Select the current VERTICAL TABLE in your report.

25. Navigate to the REPORT ELEMENT tab.
26. Navigate to the TOOLS tab.
27. Select the option TURN INTO • CROSS TABLE.
28. Arrange the objects in your cross tab so that the cross tab shows the PRODUCT GROUP and PRODUCT in the rows, and the CALENDAR MONTH (NUMERIC) in the columns. You can either simply drag and drop the elements or use the menu TURN INTO • MORE TRANSFORMATIONS for a more granular control.
29. Select the PRODUCT GROUP dimension in the rows.
30. Navigate to the REPORT ELEMENT tab.
31. Navigate to the TABLE LAYOUT tab.
32. Select the menu BREAK • MANAGE BREAKS.
33. Click on ADD.
34. Select PRODUCT GROUP.
35. Click on OK.
36. Select PRODUCT GROUP on the left side.
37. Uncheck the option BREAK HEADER (see Figure 5.39).

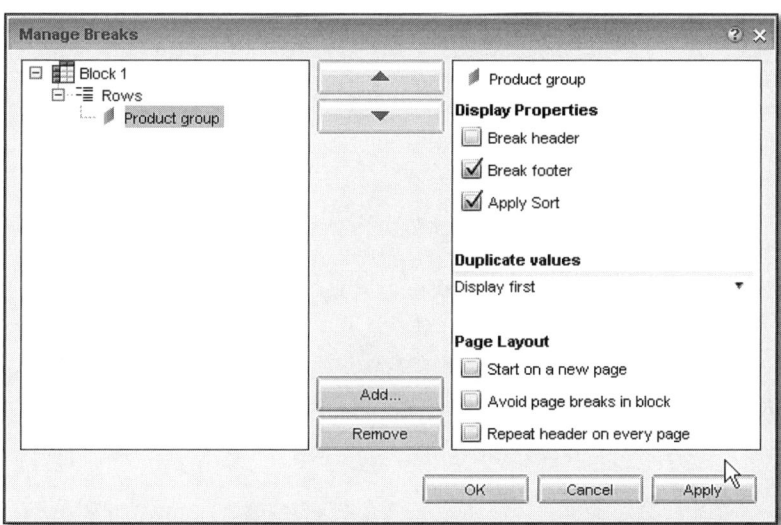

Figure 5.39 Manage Breaks

38. Click on OK.

39. Repeat the steps for the dimension PRODUCT.
40. Select the NET SALES key figure in the cross tab.
41. Navigate to the ANALYSIS tab.
42. Navigate to the FUNCTION tab.
43. Select the option SUM.
44. A dialog box will appear. Select AT THE END OF THE COLUMN.
45. Repeat these steps for all four key figures. You now have subtotals for the dimension PRODUCT GROUP and for the dimension PRODUCT. Notice that the labels for the subtotals simply state SUM: which is not very helpful knowing that we have four key figures.
46. Select the menu DESIGN • STRUCTURE ONLY. You are presented with the structural view of the report.
47. Select the cells with the labels for the subtotals one by one and change the formula in the cell to include the name of the key figure.
48. Select the cell of the subtotal for NET SALES.
49. Change the formula to the following syntax in the toolbar:

    ="Sum: " + Nameof([Net Sales])

50. Repeat this change for all four key figures on the product subtotal level and on the product group subtotal level.
51. Select the menu DESIGN • WITH DATA.
52. Navigate to the REPORT ELEMENT tab.
53. Navigate to the SECTION tab.
54. Click on INSERT SECTION.
55. Your mouse cursor now becomes a cross, asking you to position the mouse where you would like to insert the section. Place the cursor between the report title and your cross tab (see Figure 5.40).
56. You are asked to select the dimension for the section. Select the QUARTER dimension.
57. Click on OK.
58. Now all of the key figures are shown next to each other, which creates a very wide cross tab. Drag the key figures below each other in your cross tab (see Figure 5.41).

5.4 | Building a Report for Sales Analysis

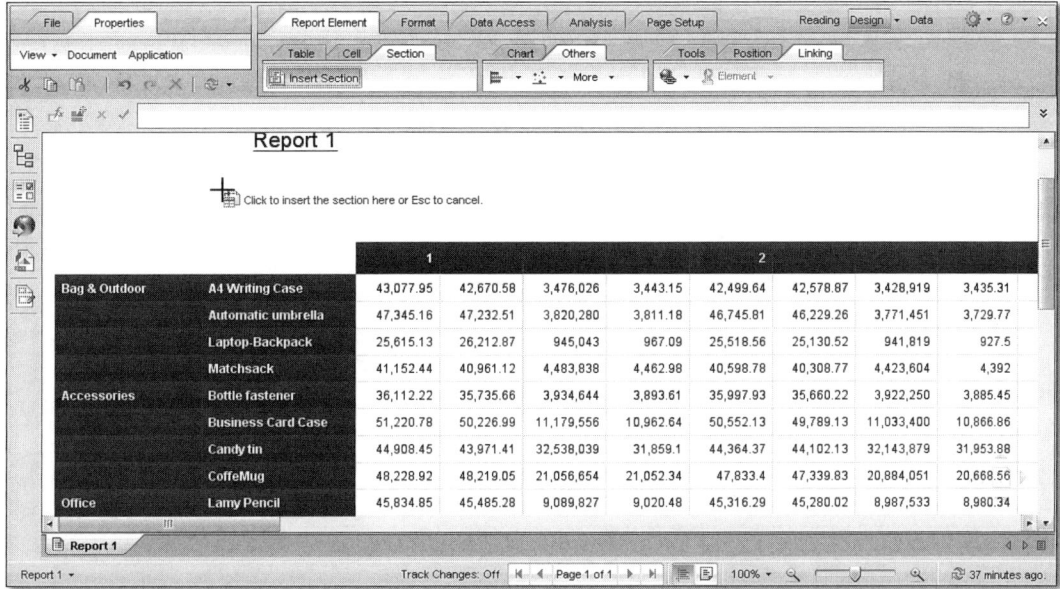

Figure 5.40 Insert Section

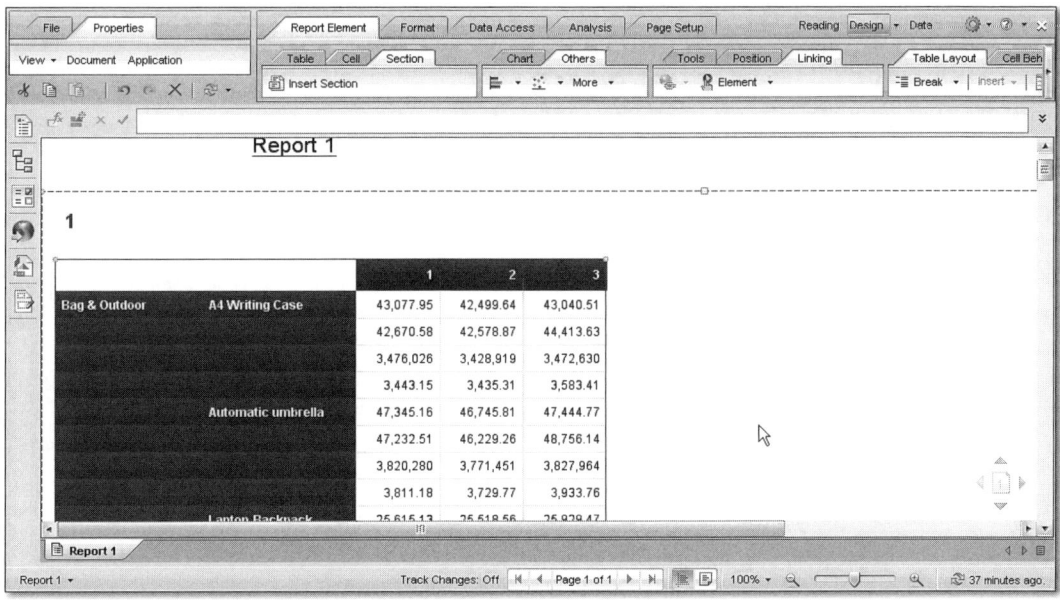

Figure 5.41 Changed Cross Tab Report

59. The cross tab does not show which numbers you're using, so you need to add the descriptions of the key figures. You have two options available to you: You can follow the steps and format the cross tab as outlined in the next steps or you can create a text block as outlined in the note below—choose the one you prefer.
60. Select the cross tab in your report.
61. Right-click to open the context menu and select the FORMAT TABLE menu item.
62. Select the GENERAL area.
63. Activate the SHOW OBJECT NAME option. Your cross tab will look like Figure 5.42.

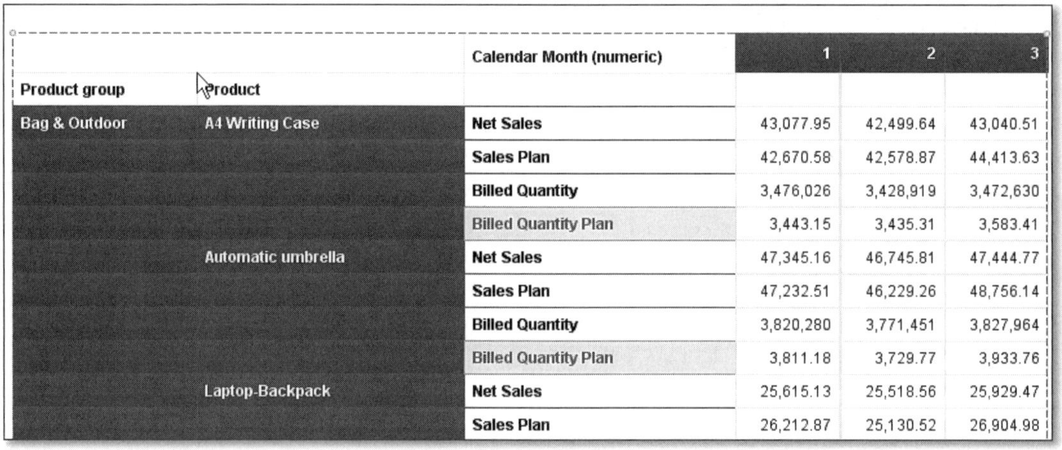

Product group	Product	Calendar Month (numeric)	1	2	3
Bag & Outdoor	A4 Writing Case	Net Sales	43,077.95	42,499.64	43,040.51
		Sales Plan	42,670.58	42,578.87	44,413.63
		Billed Quantity	3,476,026	3,428,919	3,472,630
		Billed Quantity Plan	3,443.15	3,435.31	3,583.41
	Automatic umbrella	Net Sales	47,345.16	46,745.81	47,444.77
		Sales Plan	47,232.51	46,229.26	48,756.14
		Billed Quantity	3,820,280	3,771,451	3,827,964
		Billed Quantity Plan	3,811.18	3,729.77	3,933.76
	Laptop-Backpack	Net Sales	25,615.13	25,518.56	25,929.47
		Sales Plan	26,212.87	25,130.52	26,904.98

Figure 5.42 SAP Business Objects Web Intelligence Cross Tab with Labels

> **Note**
> You can also create a text block that shows the same information but doesn't repeat it as part of the cross tab.

64. Make sure you have enough space between your report title and the section for the quarter. You can also use the menu DESIGN • STRUCTURE from the toolbar to view the report structure.
65. Navigate to the REPORT ELEMENT tab.
66. Navigate to the CELL tab.

67. Click on BLANK.
68. Place the blank cell between your report title and your cross tab.
69. Select the new object and click on the FORMULA EDITOR icon (f_x) in the toolbar. Use the NAME OF function to create description fields for your four key figures. For NET SALES the formula is =NameOf([Net Sales]).
70. Repeat the steps for the other three key figures and format the fields (see Figure 5.43).

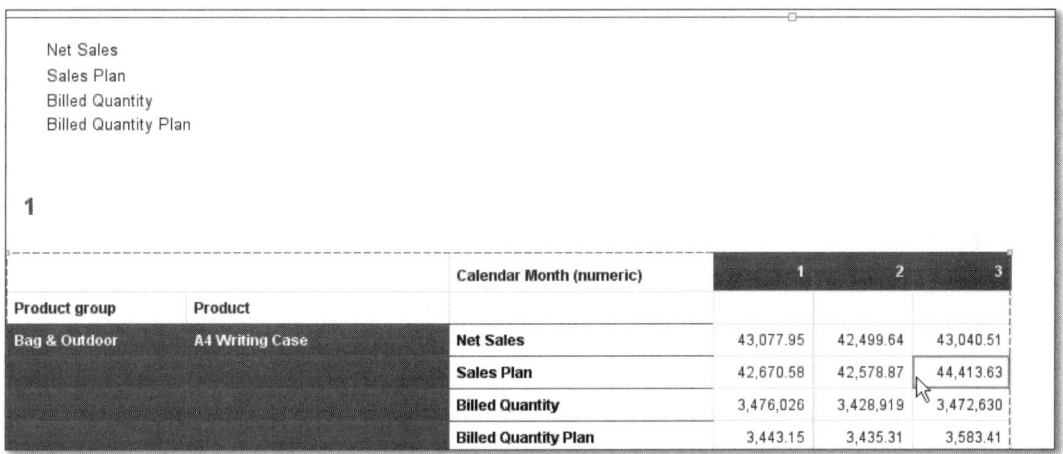

Figure 5.43 Formatted Labels

71. Navigate to the REPORT ELEMENT tab.
72. Navigate to the CHART tab.
73. Click on the bar chart and place the bar chart next to your cross tab.
74. Drag the NET SALES key figure from the list of AVAILABLE OBJECTS to the bar chart.
75. Drag the PRODUCT dimension from the list of AVAILABLE OBJECTS to the bar chart.
76. Right-click on the chart and follow the menu path ALIGN • RELATIVE POSITION.
77. Configure the chart to be 2 cm away from the right edge of BLOCK 1 for the HORIZONTAL configuration.
78. Configure the chart to be 2 cm away from the TOP EDGE of SECTION ON: QUARTER for the VERTICAL configuration.

79. Click on OK.
80. Select the PRODUCT GROUP in the cross tab.
81. Navigate to the ANALYSIS tab.
82. Navigate to the INTERACT tab.
83. Activate the OUTLINE option.
84. Now you can fold and unfold the following items:
    - The section, which in this example will then let you switch between the section header and the cross tab.
    - The product group in the cross tab, which lets you show either the totals per PRODUCT GROUP or per quarter.
    - The PRODUCT itself, which lets you switch between a summarized level on PRODUCT GROUP and PRODUCT level.
85. Enter a REPORT TITLE for your report.
86. For this part of your report, the only step left is to incorporate the functionality to filter the report in specific dimensions. To do this, there are two options:
    - You can use the FILTER BAR button from the INTERACT tab in the ANALYSIS area to show the FILTER BAR and drag and drop a dimension onto it.
    - You can use the INPUT CONTROLS to provide the filter capabilities.
87. In this example, use the INPUT CONTROLS to include the filter capabilities.
88. Navigate to the ANALYSIS tab.
89. Navigate to the FILTERS tab. Click on CONTROLS.
90. Select the DISTRIBUTION CHANNEL dimension.
91. Click on NEXT.
92. Select the RADIO BUTTONS option from the SINGLE VALUE area (see Figure 5.44).
93. Click on NEXT.
94. Select the section, bar chart, and cross tab as elements that will be assigned to the input control. By assigning an element to the input control, the element will be filtered based on the selection (see Figure 5.45).
95. Click on FINISH.
96. Select the value from the list and filter your report to a single DISTRIBUTION CHANNEL (see Figure 5.46).

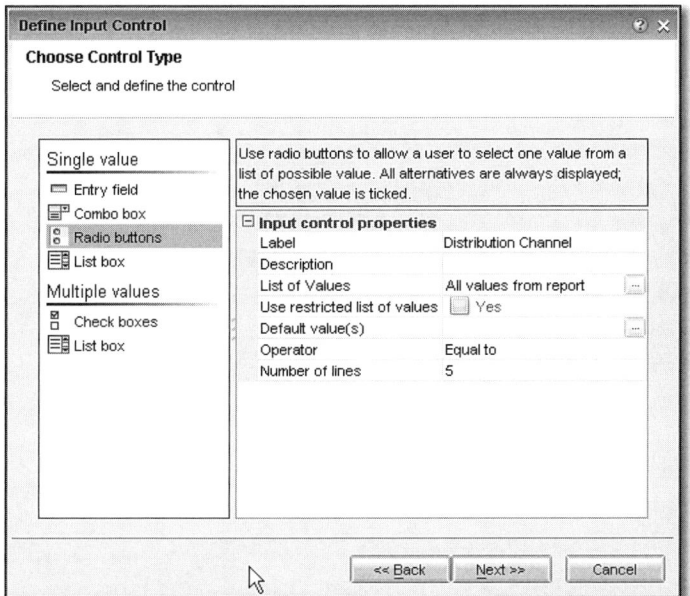

Figure 5.44 Input Controls

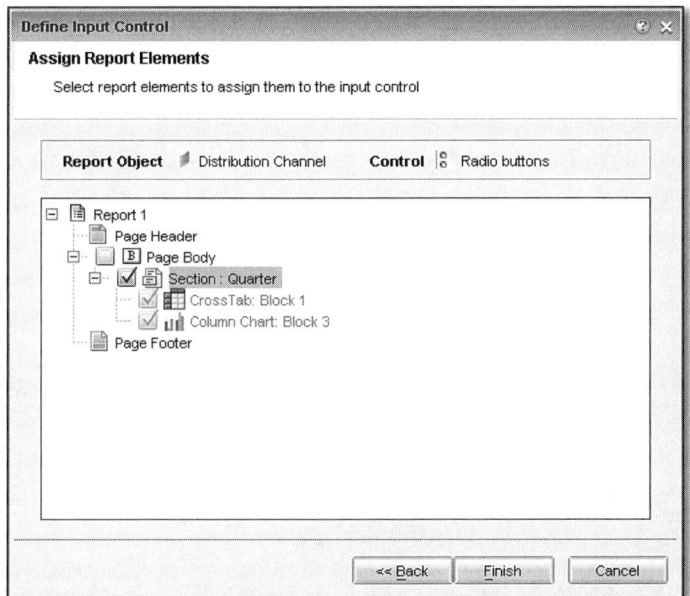

Figure 5.45 Assign Report Elements

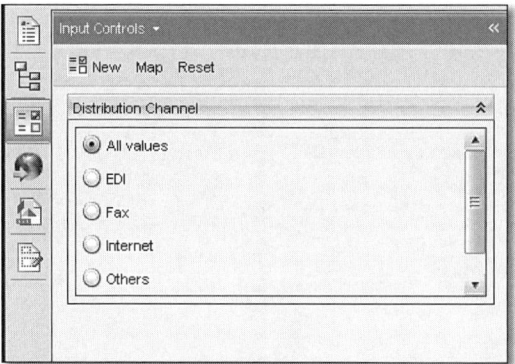

Figure 5.46 Input Controls

97. Navigate to the FILE tab.
98. Use the SAVE (![]) button to save your report to your SAP BusinessObjects system.

    In addition to the information we've discussed so far, your report should also now show LOST DEALS and the reasons behind them.

99. Create a second report tab. Right-click on the REPORT1 tab and select ADD REPORT.
100. Navigate to the REPORT ELEMENT tab.
101. Navigate to the TABLE tab.
102. Click on the INSERT CROSSTABLE option and insert a cross tab to the new report.
103. Navigate to the AVAILABLE OBJECTS panel.
104. Drag the REASON—LOST DEALS dimension into the rows from our cross tab and drag the CALENDAR MONTH (NUMERIC) into the columns. For a cell, use the LOST DEALS key figure.
105. Navigate to the REPORT ELEMENT tab.
106. Navigate to the CELL tab.
107. Click on BLANK to insert a new cell to the report.
108. Enter a report title into the new cell.
109. Navigate to the REPORT ELEMENT tab.
110. Navigate to the CHART tab.

111. Click on the PIE CHART option.
112. Place the pie chart below the cross tab.
113. Drag and drop the LOST DEALS key figure from the AVAILABLE OBJECTS panel to the pie chart.
114. Drag and drop the REASON—LOST DEALS dimension from the AVAILABLE OBJECTS panel to the pie chart.
115. Navigate to the REPORT ELEMENT tab.
116. Navigate to the CHART tab.
117. Click on the BAR CHART option.
118. Place the bar chart next to the pie chart.
119. Drag and drop the LOST DEALS key figure from the AVAILABLE OBJECTS panel to the bar chart.
120. Drag and drop the CALENDAR MONTH (NUMERIC) dimension from the AVAILABLE OBJECTS panel to the bar chart (see Figure 5.47).

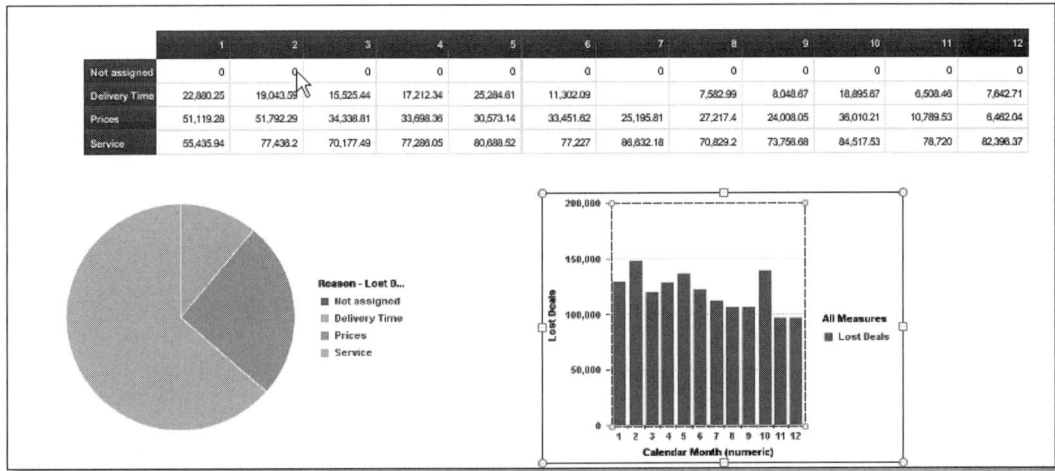

Figure 5.47 SAP BusinessObjects Web Intelligence Report

121. Right-click on the REPORT1 tab and select RENAME. Enter "Actual and Planned Sales" by quarter as the new report name.
122. Right-click on the REPORT2 tab and select RENAME. Enter "Lost Sales Revenue by Reason and Month" as the new report name.

Use the SAVE (🔳) button to save your report to your SAP BusinessObjects system. As you can see, we reused the data that we retrieved in two reports to show different views of the same information, which was the reasoning behind the last couple of steps. Just as we added an additional report, you can also add an additional query based on the same or a different connection to your SAP BusinessObjects Web Intelligence document, allowing you to store data from several sources in a single document.

Next, we continue to work with SAP BusinessObjects Web Intelligence and focus on the requirements for the financial department.

5.5 Building a Report for Financial Analysis

In this section, we look at how you can use SAP BusinessObjects Web Intelligence to fulfill the requirements for your financial area. We create a report on top of a BEx query showing a cost center hierarchy and the details broken down by cost elements. With regard to the key figures, we will leverage the actual and plan amounts and show the variance as an absolute value and as a percentage value. In addition, we enable alerting in the report and the tracking of changes with each refresh to make it easy for the cost center manager to keep track of the budget and identify changes in the numbers (see Figure 5.48).

In this example, we use a BEx query based on InfoProvider 0CCA_M20 from the cost center accounting area as the source for this SAP BusinessObjects Web Intelligence report. The BEx query contains the following elements (see Figure 5.49):

- In the rows:
  - COST CENTER
  - COST ELEMENT
- In the free characteristics:
  - FISCAL YEAR
  - FISCAL YEAR/PERIOD
- In the columns, the following key figures:
  - ACTUAL COSTS
  - PLANNED COSTS
  - VARIANCE
  - VARIANCE IN %

Building a Report for Financial Analysis | 5.5

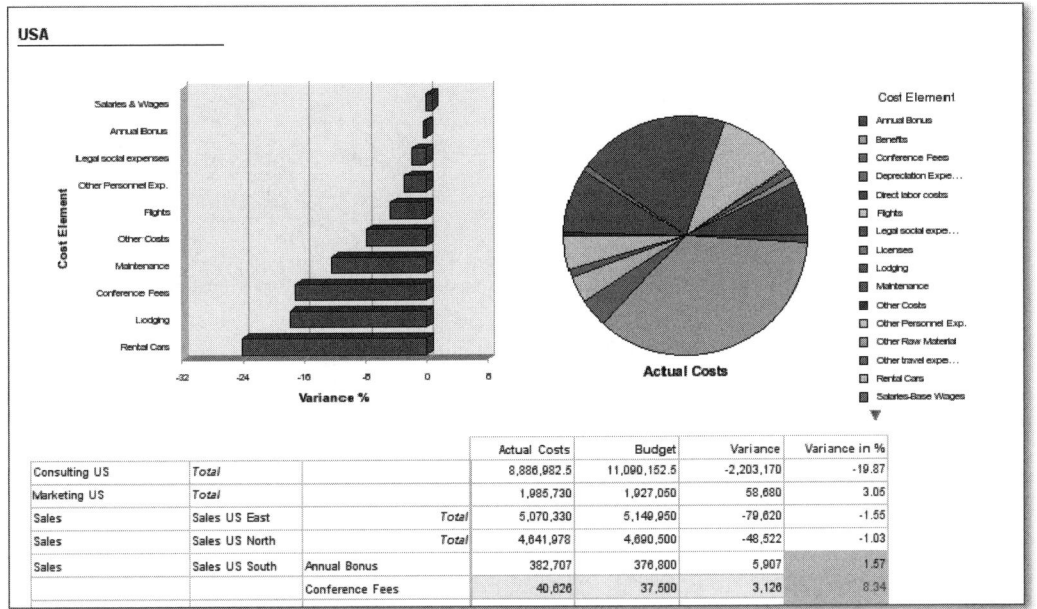

Figure 5.48 SAP BusinessObjects Web Intelligence Financial Report

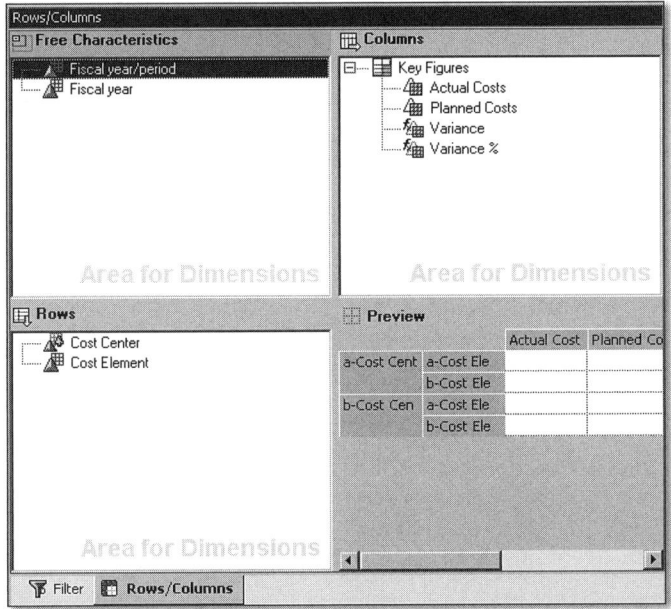

Figure 5.49 BEx Query for Financial Report

171

> **Currency Conversion and Selections**
>
> In currency-sensitive reports, like the report you're creating in this section, it is highly recommended that you either ensure that the query will return only a single currency per key figure or that you offer the user the option to use a variable from the BEx query to select the currency. The reporting tools do not offer an automatic functionality to split the totals per currency; therefore, you might mistakenly summarize numbers from different currencies.
>
> For the sake of simplicity, the following steps continue without a variable.

Before we can build our report using SAP BusinessObjects Web Intelligence, we need to set up the OLAP connection in the Central Management Console (CMC) of our SAP BusinessObjects system. You can find the detailed steps in Section 4.3.3, but remember that SAP Crystal Reports for Enterprise and SAP BusinessObjects Web Intelligence are able to share the connections.

After we configure the OLAP connection as part of our SAP BusinessObjects system, we can start creating our sales report. Follow the steps below:

1. Launch BI launch pad via the menu path START • PROGRAMS • SAP BUSINESSOBJECTS BI PLATFORM 4 • SAP BUSINESSOBJECTS BI PLATFORM • SAP BUSINESSOBJECTS BI PLATFORM JAVA BI LAUNCH PAD.

2. Use your SAP credentials to authenticate for the SAP system. Keep in mind that this requires the SAP authentication to be configured for your SAP BusinessObjects system. If the SAP authentication has not been configured, you can continue with the exercise using the Enterprise authentication, but you will not be able to use SSO.

3. Follow the menu path: APPLICATIONS • WEB INTELLIGENCE APPLICATION.

4. Click the NEW ( ) button to start the process of creating a new report.

5. You are asked which type of data source you would like to use for your report. Select the option BEx.

6. Click on OK.

7. Select the connection and BEx query you configured for the financial report.

8. Click on OK.

9. Add the following objects to the RESULT OBJECTS panel (see Figure 5.50):
   - DEFAULT HIERARCHY FROM COST CENTER
   - COST ELEMENT

► Actual Costs
► Budget Costs
► Variance
► Variance %

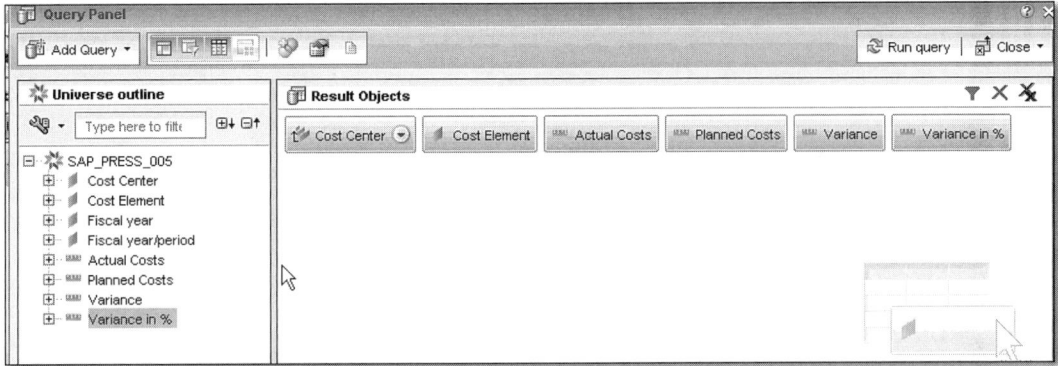

Figure 5.50 SAP BusinessObjects Web Intelligence Query Panel

> **Default Hierarchy**
>
> Each characteristic has a default hierarchy. In the SAP BusinessObjects Web Intelligence query panel, the default hierarchy is shown in addition to the list of available hierarchies. The default hierarchy is the first entry in the list of hierarchies and is shown with the name of the characteristic. The default hierarchy is useful when a hierarchy is already configured in the BEx query—as in our example—and in cases where you would like to leverage a hierarchy variable.

10. Use the small triangle shown at the Cost Center in the Result Objects to open the member list of Cost Center (see Figure 5.51).
11. Select specific members, nodes, or use the All Members ( ) button.
12. Click on OK.
13. Click on Run Query.
14. You are presented with the default layout of a table (see Figure 5.52).
15. Select the Actual Costs key figure in the table.
16. Right-click and select the Format Number menu.
17. Select the Number option and select the last entry from the list, formatting the number without decimals.

5 | Interactive Analysis with SAP BusinessObjects Web Intelligence

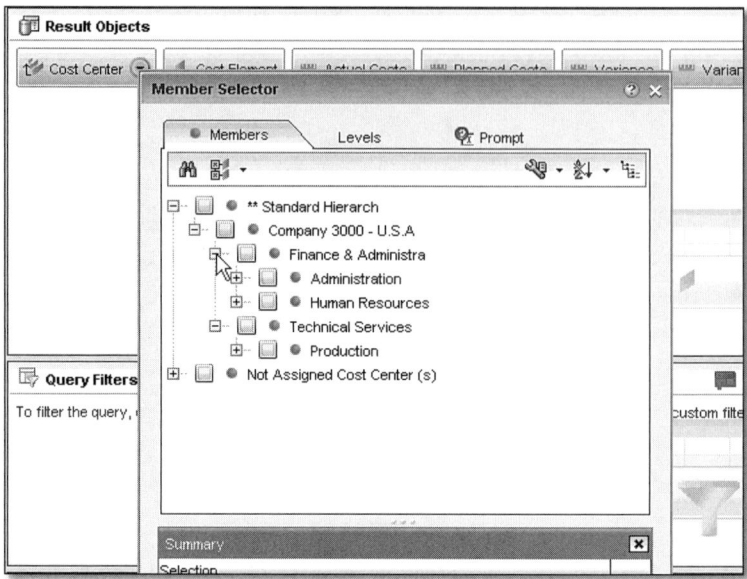

Figure 5.51 Member Selector

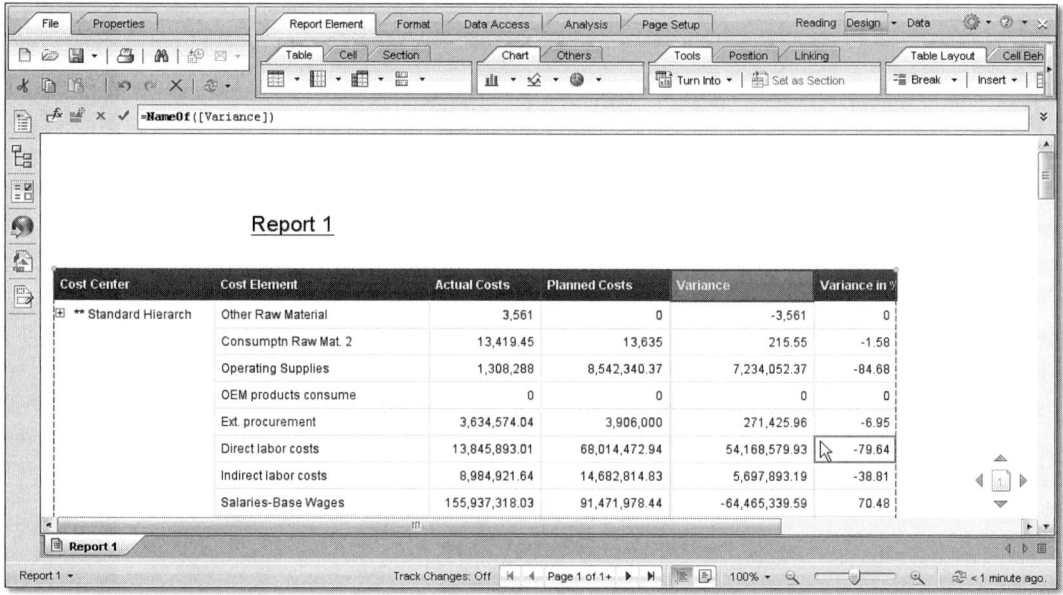

Figure 5.52 SAP BusinessObjects Web Intelligence Hierarchical Report

18. Repeat these steps for the other three key figures.
19. Select the hierarchy in the table.
20. Right-click and select the menu SET AS SECTION.

    The hierarchy is now being used to group the report. Each time you open another level, the corresponding sections are generated on the fly (see Figure 5.53).

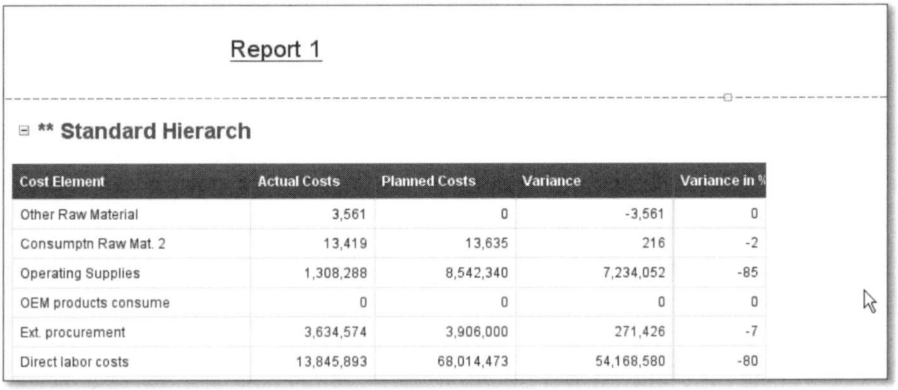

Report 1

**** Standard Hierarch**

Cost Element	Actual Costs	Planned Costs	Variance	Variance in %
Other Raw Material	3,561	0	-3,561	0
Consumptn Raw Mat. 2	13,419	13,635	216	-2
Operating Supplies	1,308,288	8,542,340	7,234,052	-85
OEM products consume	0	0	0	0
Ext. procurement	3,634,574	3,906,000	271,426	-7
Direct labor costs	13,845,893	68,014,473	54,168,580	-80

Figure 5.53 Hierarchical Sections

In addition to the information and navigation that is already part of the report, you may want to add alerts and highlighting to the report with some additional charts visualizing the most important information.

21. Move the cross table down so that you have enough space for two charts.
22. Navigate to the REPORT ELEMENT tab.
23. Navigate to the CHART tab.
24. Click on the bar chart and place the bar chart above the cross tab.
25. Drag and drop the COST ELEMENT dimension from the AVAILABLE OBJECTS panel to the bar chart.
26. Drag and drop the VARIANCE IN % key figure from the AVAILABLE OBJECTS panel to the bar chart.
27. Select the bar chart in the report.
28. Navigate to the ANALYSIS tab.
29. Navigate to the FILTERS tab.
30. Select the RANKING option (see Figure 5.54).

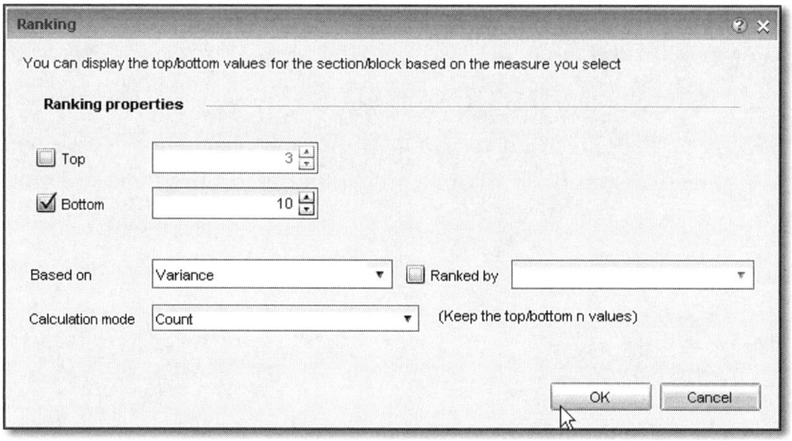

Figure 5.54 Ranking

31. Configure a BOTTOM 10 ranking based on the VARIANCE.
32. Click on OK.
33. Add another chart to your report, but this time a pie chart. Drag and drop the COST ELEMENT dimension from the AVAILABLE OBJECTS panel to the pie chart.
34. Drag and drop the ACTUAL COST key figure from the AVAILABLE OBJECTS panel to the pie chart.

After adding the two charts, you can add highlighting to your cross tab. If you would like to highlight cost centers or cost elements that are 5% or higher above budget, do the following:

1. Select the VARIANCE IN % key figure in the cross tab.
2. Navigate to the ANALYSIS tab.
3. Navigate to the CONDITIONAL tab.
4. Click on NEW RULE (see Figure 5.55).
5. Enter your description for the new rule.
6. Configure the rule to evaluate the VARIANCE % key figure above or equal to the value 5.
7. Click on FORMAT.
8. Configure the formatting with a yellow background and red font, as shown.
9. Click on OK.

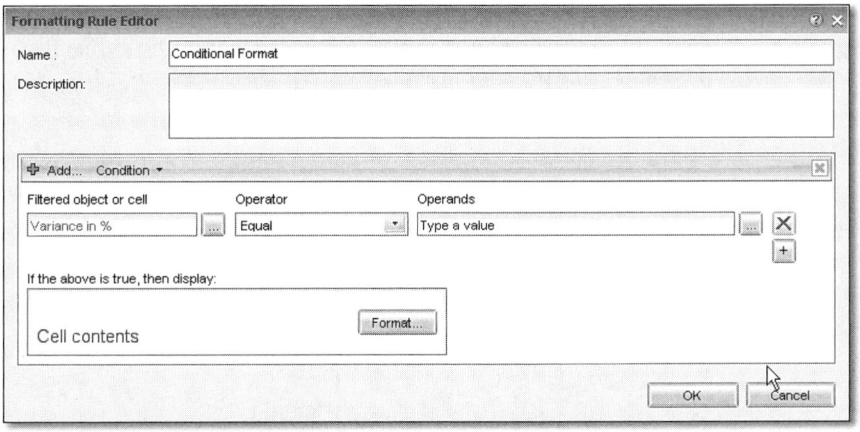

Figure 5.55 Formatting Rule

You just created a report that shows the actual and planned costs along a cost center hierarchy with the details per cost element. Users can see the top-ranked cost elements based on the variance in percentage and the distribution of the actual costs across the cost elements. In addition, the report is structured along the hierarchy, and all information is shown for each of the hierarchy nodes (see Figure 5.56).

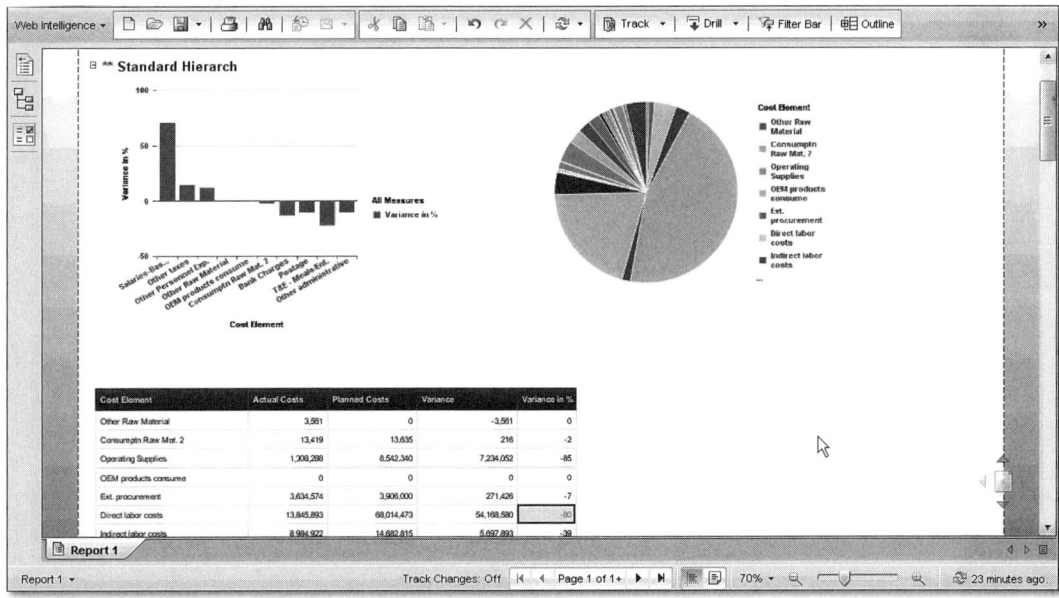

Figure 5.56 SAP BusinessObjects Web Intelligence Report

5 | Interactive Analysis with SAP BusinessObjects Web Intelligence

Next we highlight a very compelling functionality in SAP BusinessObjects Web Intelligence that is useful in the financial reporting area: the data tracking function. The DATA TRACKING tab is in the SAP BusinessObjects Web Intelligence toolbar in the ANALYSIS tab, and it lets you enable tracking of changes in your report. You can configure a baseline for the report, and each change in the report can then be highlighted, depending on the type of change in the DATA TRACKING OPTIONS (see Figure 5.57).

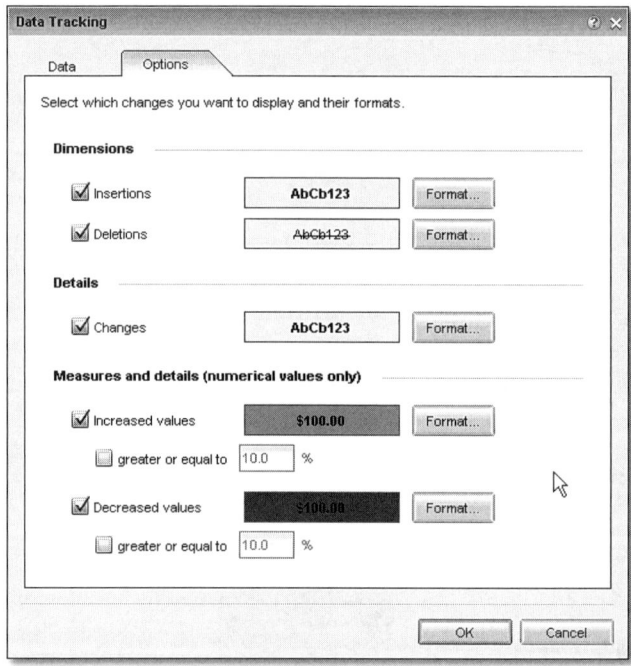

Figure 5.57 Data Tracking Options

1. Navigate to the ANALYSIS tab.
2. Navigate to the DATA TRACKING tab.
3. Click on TRACK (see Figure 5.58).
4. Specify which data you would like to compare with your next refresh. Select the COMPARE WITH LAST DATA REFRESH option.
5. Navigate to the OPTIONS. Specify how changes are going to be highlighted.
6. Click on OK.

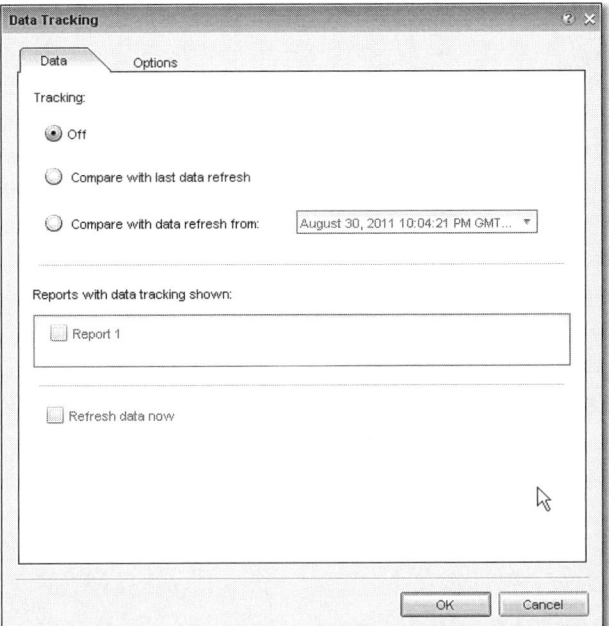

Figure 5.58 Data Tracking

Now any change in the data shown in the report will be highlighted. By using these options, your user can quickly visualize and analyze any changes in this report that happened since the last time the report was refreshed. This will save a lot of time and effort. This functionality is especially helpful in cases where you're also using a key date variable as part of the underlying SAP NetWeaver BW query to ask for the date to resolve a time-dependency, such as a time-dependent hierarchical structure. In such cases, the data tracking options visualize the changes based on a different key date in the report, allowing users to quickly identify the changes.

5.6 Summary

In this chapter, you learned about data connectivity options for universes and SAP BusinessObjects Web Intelligence on top of your SAP data source. Also, you learned how to evaluate SAP BusinessObjects Web Intelligence as an ad-hoc reporting tool against requirements from different areas and then created reports for the sales and finance areas to fulfill parts of their requirements.

In this chapter, we look at how to use SAP BusinessObjects Dashboards to create data visualization based on your SAP data.

6   Dashboarding and Data Visualization with SAP BusinessObjects Dashboards

This chapter introduces you to SAP BusinessObjects Dashboards, starting with a discussion of data connectivity, and then moving on to an explanation of how to fulfill business requirements from the different areas we established in Chapter 2.

6.1   SAP Data Connectivity

With regard to data connectivity for SAP BusinessObjects Dashboards, we separate the view into SAP ERP and SAP NetWeaver BW. If you want to leverage SAP ERP data in combination with SAP BusinessObjects Dashboards, your options are the following (see Figure 6.1):

- To leverage the semantic layer connectivity on top of SAP ERP as part of the 4.0 FP3 release.
- To leverage the transient provider as part of SAP ERP 6.0 enhancement package 05 in combination with a BEx query in the local BI client of your SAP ERP system.
- To use SAP BusinessObjects Live Office in combination with SAP Crystal Reports 2011 and in that way use the data connectivity toward SAP ERP from SAP Crystal Reports 2011.

6 | Dashboarding and Data Visualization with SAP BusinessObjects Dashboards

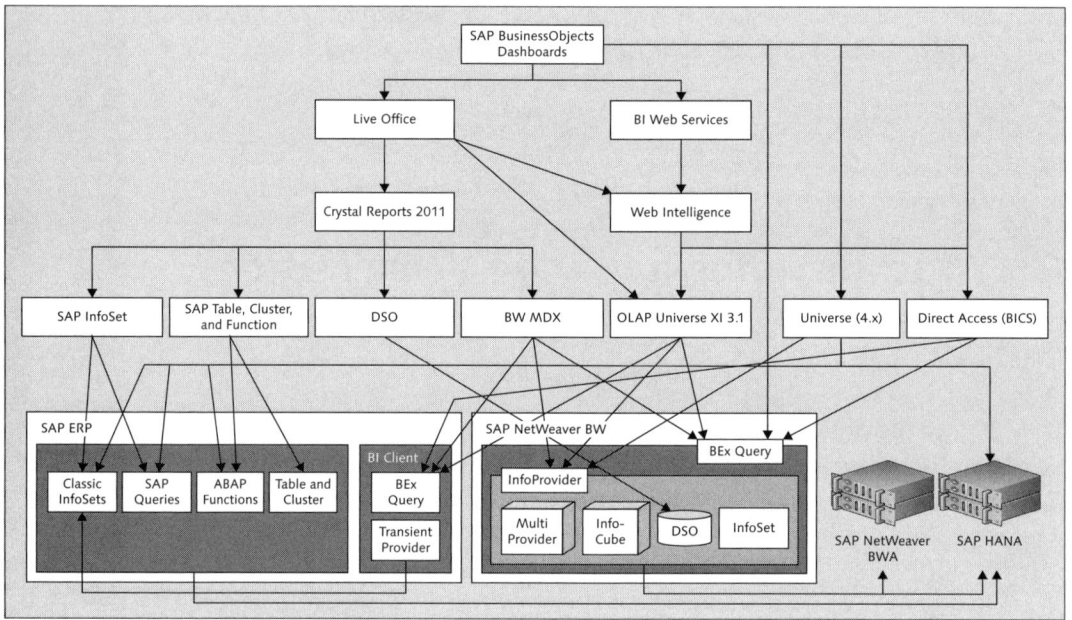

Figure 6.1 Data Connectivity

You have a much broader range of connectivity choices for SAP BusinessObjects Dashboards on top of SAP NetWeaver BW.

- As you can see in Figure 6.1, SAP BusinessObjects Dashboards has multiple options for connecting to the information stored in your SAP NetWeaver BW system. It can connect directly to SAP NetWeaver BEx queries without any additional middleware, and, as part of release 4.0 FP3, can also connect to BEx queries via the shared BI Consumer Services (BICS) connection from the SAP BusinessObjects BI platform.

- SAP BusinessObjects Dashboards can use the universe as part of the 4.0 FP3 platform and in that way use relational access to the SAP NetWeaver BW system.

- SAP BusinessObjects Dashboards can consume BI Web Services from the SAP BusinessObjects BI platfom and use SAP BusinessObjects Web Intelligence reports via BI Web Services as a data source for the dashboards.

- SAP BusinessObjects Dashboards, in combination with SAP BusinessObjects Live Office, can use SAP BusinessObjects Web Intelligence and SAP Crystal

Reports 2011 as a data source and use the connection to SAP NetWeaver BW from those tools.

> **SAP BusinessObjects BI Platform or SAP NetWeaver BW?**
>
> As outlined in the previous paragraph, SAP BusinessObjects Dashboards has two direct connectivity options for SAP NetWeaver BW:
>
> - A direct connectivity to BEx queries using BICS from SAP NetWeaver BW.
> - A direct connectivity to BEx queries using BICSfrom the SAP BusinessObjects BI platform.
>
> These options have two major distinctions:
>
> - Direct connectivity using BICS from SAP NetWeaver BW requires a BI Java part for your SAP NetWeaver BW system.
> - SAP BusinessObjects Dashboards data visualizations created using BICS direct connectivity from SAP NetWeaver BW cannot be hosted inside the SAP BusinessObjects BI platform; instead, they need to be hosted inside SAP NetWeaver BW.

Table 6.1 shows the level of support for your existing SAP NetWeaver BW metadata for the two data connectivity options that use the BICS layer.

	Direct Access using BICS as Part of SAP BusinessObjects BI Platform	Direct Access using BICS as Part of SAP NetWeaver BW
Direct access to InfoCube and MultiProvider	No	No
Access to BEx queries	Yes	Yes
Characteristic Values		
Key	Yes	Yes
Short description	Yes	Yes
Medium and long description	Yes	Yes
BEx Query Features		
Support for hierarchies	Yes	Limited
Support for free characteristics	Yes	Yes

Table 6.1 Supported and Unsupported BEx Query Features for SAP BusinessObjects Dashboards

	Direct Access using BICS as Part of SAP BusinessObjects BI Platform	Direct Access using BICS as Part of SAP NetWeaver BW
Support for calculated and restricted key figures	Yes	Yes
Support for currencies and units	Yes	Yes
Support for custom structures	Yes	Yes
Support for formulas and selections	Yes	Yes
Support for filters	Yes	Yes
Support for display and navigational attributes	Yes	Navigational attributes only
Support for conditions in rows	No	Yes
Support for conditions in columns	No	Yes
Support for conditions for fixed characteristics	No	Yes
Support for exceptions	No	No
Compounded characteristics	Limited	Yes
Constant selection	Yes	Yes
Default values in BEx query	No	Yes
Number scaling factor	Yes	Yes
Number of decimals	No	Yes
Calculate rows as (local calculation)	No	Yes
Sorting	Yes	Yes
Hide/unhide	Yes	Yes
Display as hierarchy	No	No
Reverse sign	Yes	Yes
Support for reading master data	Yes	Yes
Data Types		
Support for CHAR (characteristics)	Yes	Yes

Table 6.1 Supported and Unsupported BEx Query Features for SAP BusinessObjects Dashboards (Cont.)

	Direct Access using BICS as Part of SAP BusinessObjects BI Platform	Direct Access using BICS as Part of SAP NetWeaver BW
Support for NUMC (characteristics)	Yes as string value	Yes as string value
Support for DATS (characteristics)	Yes as string value	Yes as string value
Support for TIMS (characteristics)	Yes as string value	Yes as string value
Support for numeric key figures such as Amount and Quantity	Yes	Yes
Support for Date (key figures)	Yes as string value	Yes as string value
Support for Time (key figures)	Yes as string value	Yes as string value
SAP Variable—Processing Type		
User input	Yes	Yes
Authorization	Yes	Yes
Replacement path	Yes	Yes
SAP exit/custom exit	Yes	Yes
Precalculated value set	Yes	Yes
General Features for Variables		
Support for optional and mandatory variables	Yes	Yes
Support for key date dependencies	Yes	Yes
Support for default values	Limited	Limited
Support for personalized values	No	No
SAP Variables—Variable Type		
Single value	Yes	Yes
Multi-single value	Yes	Yes
Interval value	No	Yes
Selection option	No	Yes
Hierarchy variable	Limited	Yes
Hierarchy node variable	Limited	Yes

Table 6.1 Supported and Unsupported BEx Query Features for SAP BusinessObjects Dashboards (Cont.)

	Direct Access using BICS as Part of SAP BusinessObjects BI Platform	Direct Access using BICS as Part of SAP NetWeaver BW
Hierarchy version variable	Limited	Yes
Text variable	Yes	Yes
EXIT variable	Yes	Yes
Single key date variable	Yes	Yes
Multiple key dates	Yes	Yes
Formula variable	Yes	Yes

Table 6.1 Supported and Unsupported BEx Query Features for SAP BusinessObjects Dashboards (Cont.)

Table 6.2 shows the details of how SAP BusinessObjects Dashboards uses available BEx query elements when you use the direct access BICS method without using SAP BusinessObjects BI platform, which means that you are using the BICS as part of SAP NetWeaver BW.

BEx Query Element	SAP BusinessObjects Dashboards (BICS as Part of SAP NetWeaver BW)
Characteristic	Each characteristic is supported with the elements configured in the underlying BEx query. For example, if the characteristic is configured to be displayed with medium text only, SAP BusinessObjects Dashboards will show medium text only, even though the characteristic also has a key value.
Hierarchy	Hierarchies are transformed into levels, and SAP BusinessObjects Dashboards puts all levels into a single column; therefore, it is very difficult to create a hierarchical report.
Key figure	Each key figure is shown with the unit and scaling factor information. In addition, you have the option to switch between a raw and a formatted display of the key figures, where the formatted option incorporates the unit, thousand separator, and decimals into the display.
Calculated/restricted key figure	Each calculated and restricted key figure is treated like a key figure. The user does not have access to the underlying definition in SAP BusinessObjects Dashboards.

Table 6.2 SAP NetWeaver BW Metadata Mapping for SAP BusinessObjects Dashboards

6.1 SAP Data Connectivity

BEx Query Element	SAP BusinessObjects Dashboards (BICS as Part of SAP NetWeaver BW)
Filter	Filters are applied to the underlying query, and SAP BusinessObjects Dashboards provides the information about the predefined filters as part of the data connection.
Display attribute	Display attributes are not supported as part of this data connectivity.
Navigational attribute	Navigational attributes are treated the same way as characteristics.
Variables	Each variable with the READY FOR INPUT property activated results in an input variable as part of the data connection details. In addition, SAP BusinessObjects Dashboards is also able to leverage the run time from BEx Web Analyzer to prompt the users.
Custom structures	A custom structure is available as a single element in the data structure and users cannot select single structure elements.

Table 6.2 SAP NetWeaver BW Metadata Mapping for SAP BusinessObjects Dashboards (Cont.)

Table 6.3 shows the details of how SAP BusinessObjects Dashboards can leverage the shared connection from your SAP BusinessObjects BI platform system using the direct access method involving BICS.

BEx Query Element	SAP BusinessObjects Dashboards (BICS as Part of SAP BusinessObjects)
Characteristic	For each characteristic, you receive a field representing the key value and a field for the description, including short, medium, and long descriptions.
Hierarchy	Each available hierarchy is shown as an external hierarchy in SAP BusinessObjects Dashboards.
Key figure	Each key figure can have up to four elements: numeric value, unit, scaling factor, and formatted value. The formatted value is based on the user preferences configured in the SAP system.

Table 6.3 SAP NetWeaver BW Metadata Mapping for SAP BusinessObjects Dashboards with SAP BusinessObjects

BEx Query Element	SAP BusinessObjects Dashboards (BICS as Part of SAP BusinessObjects)
Calculated/restricted key figure	Each calculated and restricted key figure is treated like a key figure. The user does not have access to the underlying definition in SAP BusinessObjects Dashboards.
Filter	Filters are applied to the underlying query but are not visible in SAP BusinessObjects Dashboards.
Display attribute	Display attributes become standard fields in the query panel and are grouped as subordinates of the linked characteristic.
Navigational attribute	Navigational attributes are treated the same way as characteristics.
Variables	Each variable with the READY FOR INPUT property activated results in a prompt available in SAP BusinessObjects Dashboards.
Custom structures	A custom structure is available as an element in the query panel and each structure element can be selected or deselected for the report.

Table 6.3 SAP NetWeaver BW Metadata Mapping for SAP BusinessObjects Dashboards with SAP BusinessObjects (Cont.)

Deployment Considerations for SAP BusinessObjects Dashboards Connectivity
With release 4.0 FP3, SAP BusinessObjects Dashboards is able to use the shared connection from the SAP BusinessObjects BI platform and connect directly to BEx queries, while still hosting the dashboard in the SAP BusinessObjects BI platform.
The alternate option for connecting directly to the BEx queries inside the SAP NetWeaver BW system—using the BICS connection provided by SAP NetWeaver BW—allows you to cut out the middleware and does not require a SAP BusinessObjects BI platform system. On the other hand, it means that you now use two landscapes for your reporting needs (SAP NetWeaver BW for SAP BusinessObjects Dashboards and SAP BusinessObjects BI platform for SAP Crystal Reports for Enterprise, SAP BusinessObjects Web Intelligence, SAP BusinessObjects Analysis, and SAP BusinessObjects Explorer).
You should carefully consider which direct connectivity type best suits your overall landscape and deployment scenario.

In this section we reviewed the different data connectivity options for SAP ERP and SAP NetWeaver BW, as well as the level of support for SAP BusinessObjects

Dashboards in combination with your existing metadata in your SAP NetWeaver BW system. In the next section, we provide a detailed view of the direct connectivity to BEx queries provided by the SAP BusinessObjects BI platform.

> **SAP BusinessObjects Dashboards Connectivity Options**
>
> As shown in this section, SAP BusinessObjects Dashboards offers several ways to connect to your SAP NetWeaver BW data. In this book, we focus on the data connectivity available with the 4.0 FP3 release: the shared connections from the SAP BusinessObjects BI platform. If you're interested in more details on the other options for SAP NetWeaver BW, please read *Integrating SAP BusinessObjects BI Platform 4.x with SAP NetWeaver* (SAP PRESS, 2012).

6.2 Assessment of Business Requirements

Let's now take a look at the business requirements from our different established areas and evaluate the ones that can be best fulfilled by using SAP BusinessObjects Dashboards. As in previous chapters, we list those requirements that we don't think can be fulfilled with SAP BusinessObjects Dashboards or that are better suited for another tool.

6.2.1 Financial Reporting and Analysis Requirements

The following represents a list of requirements we don't think can be fulfilled with SAP BusinessObjects Dashboards, or scenarios where we would use a different tool to fulfill the requirement.

> **Unfulfilled Requirements**
>
> - For specific content (such as an income statement or a balance sheet), the design needs to be layout focused with the actual print version of the report being a high priority.
>
> - The reporting and analysis tools need to let the user create new calculations and formulas and share those with other consumers of the content.
>
> - The reporting and analysis tools need to allow for the use of hierarchies and for easy navigation along those hierarchies.
>
> - Users need to be able to create planning scenarios and write information back into the source.

As you can see, the requirements from the financial area that cannot be fulfilled have to do with layout-based reports, such as balance sheets or income statements, and the capability to create on-demand calculations and formulas in the report. The third requirement listed is the visualization of the data along hierarchies. In addition, there is the requirement to create an actual planning scenario, including the write-back of information to the source.

Looking at these requirements, it's clear that the first requirement is better met by SAP Crystal Reports for Enterprise—and we provided the proof in the previous chapter. The second requirement is better met by SAP BusinessObjects Web Intelligence, SAP BusinessObjects Analysis, edition for Microsoft Office, or SAP BusinessObjects Analysis, edition for OLAP, which allow the user to create calculations and formulas on demand. The consumption of hierarchies is limited in SAP BusinessObjects Dashboards, but it is now possible in release 4.0 FP3. However, it is important to recognize the differences in how the user wants to leverage the hierarchies.

In regard to the actual planning and rewriting of information, this capability, as of release 4.0 FP3, is solely possible with SAP BusinessObjects Analysis, edition for Microsoft Office.

> **SAP BusinessObjects Dashboards and SAP NetWeaver BW Hierarchies**
>
> With SAP BusinessObjects Dashboards 4.0 FP3, you can access hierarchies from your BEx queries. SAP BusinessObjects Dashboards provides a hierarchical prompt for a scenario in which you want to use a hierarchy node variable, and a hierarchical scorecard is available to you for visualization purposes.

6.2.2 Sales Reporting and Analysis Requirements

The following is a list of requirements from the sales area that are better suited for another tool or that cannot be fulfilled using SAP BusinessObjects Dashboards.

> **Unfulfilled Requirements**
>
> ▶ Content must be available online, offline, and on mobile devices (for sales representatives on the road).
>
> ▶ Distribution of content via email may be required.

- Users need the capability to navigate within the data and change the view of the actual content. For example, they need to be able to change a weekly sales statistics broken down by country into a monthly sales statistics broken down by sales region and quarter.
- Users need to be able to modify existing reports and, if needed, create new ad-hoc reports.

The preceding requirements are those that we think are better met by other tools or that cannot be fulfilled by SAP BusinessObjects Dashboards—especially the capability to make SAP BusinessObjects Dashboards available offline or to distribute an SAP BusinessObjects Dashboards via email. These are not standard functionalities offered as part of the SAP BusinessObjects BI platform.

The requirement to change the view of the data in the report can be fulfilled with SAP BusinessObjects Dashboards to a certain degree; namely, for those cases that are known when designing the dashboard. However, SAP BusinessObjects Dashboards cannot fulfill this requirement if it was not considered when creating the dashboard.

The requirement to modify reports or create new reports is not something the SAP BusinessObjects Dashboards tool can do. This is better suited for SAP BusinessObjects Web Intelligence, SAP BusinessObjects Analysis, edition for Microsoft Office, and SAP BusinessObjects Analysis, edition for OLAP.

You will also notice that we list the requirement to have content available on mobile devices as an unfulfilled requirement for SAP BusinessObjects Dashboards. Currently, content provided by SAP BusinessObjects Dashboards can be accessed only on mobile devices that support Flash, which excludes the iPhone and iPad.

SAP BusinessObjects Dashboards Offline Capabilities

SAP BusinessObjects Dashboards does not provide out-of-the-box the capability to create offline dashboards or to schedule a dashboard.

There are partner solutions available with such capabilities, and you can find them on the SAP EcoHub at *http://ecohub.sap.com/*.

6.2.3 Human Resources (HR) Reporting and Analysis Requirements

The following list represents the requirements that we think are better suited for another tool or that cannot be fulfilled by SAP BusinessObjects Dashboards.

Unfulfilled Requirements

- The content needs to present highly textual information in a layout-focused format.
- Some of the content (such as employee appraisals or performance reviews) will likely be used as official documentation and therefore needs to follow strict layout rules.

The requirements that can't be fulfilled with SAP BusinessObjects Dashboards should come as no surprise, because these are requirements that we already thought were better met by SAP Crystal Reports for Enterprise.

6.2.4 C-Level Management and Leadership Reporting and Analysis Requirements

The following list represents the requirements that we think are better suited for another tool or that cannot be fulfilled by SAP BusinessObjects Dashboards.

Unfulfilled Requirements

- The information needs to be available on mobile devices.

As we mentioned for the sales area requirements, SAP BusinessObjects Dashboards content can be consumed only on Flash-enabled mobile devices, which presently excludes the iPhone and iPad. All other requirements can be fulfilled by SAP BusinessObjects Dashboards. This should not be surprising, as SAP BusinessObjects Dashboards is a tool created for highly interactive and highly visualized dashboards, which is what the executive and leadership requirements demand.

We continue by offering an overview of the basic steps in SAP BusinessObjects Dashboards Designer.

6.3 Introduction to the Tool

In the following sections, we look at some basic steps in the SAP BusinessObjects Dashboards Designer and how you can leverage SAP BusinessObjects Dashboards to create data visualizations. The purpose of these sections is not to make you an SAP BusinessObjects Dashboards expert, but to give you a basic understanding of how you can use SAP BusinessObjects Dashboards with your SAP data.

6.3.1 SAP BusinessObjects Dashboards Designer Overview

When you start the SAP BusinessObjects Dashboards Designer for the first time, you will notice that your environment has six major areas, as shown in Figure 6.2.

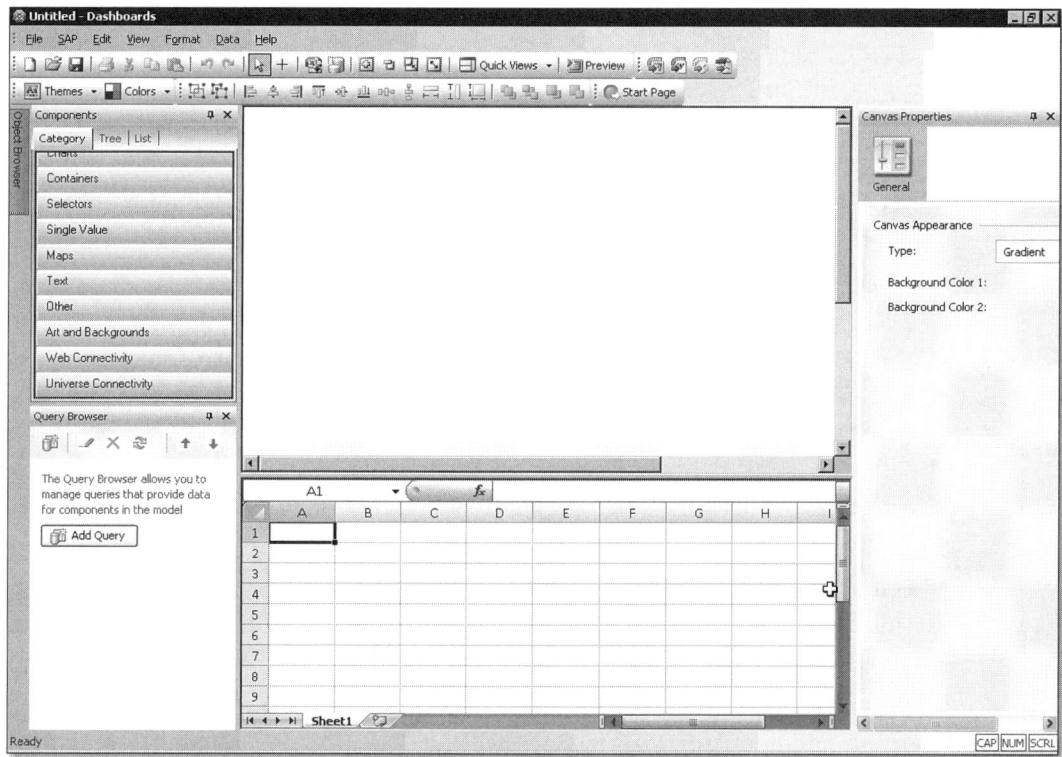

Figure 6.2 SAP BusinessObjects Dashboards Designer Environment

- COMPONENTS

  With the VIEW • COMPONENTS menu path, you can enable or disable a list of components that you can use in your SAP BusinessObjects Dashboards file. The COMPONENTS browser lets you view the list of components by CATEGORY, TREE control, or an alphabetical LIST.

- OBJECT BROWSER

  With the VIEW • OBJECT BROWSER menu path, you can enable or disable the OBJECT BROWSER as part of the SAP BusinessObjects Dashboards Designer environment. The OBJECT BROWSER shows you all of the components that you can include in your SAP BusinessObjects Dashboards visualization. You can select the objects, hide the objects, and lock the objects using the OBJECTS BROWSER; hiding components is especially helpful during the design of an SAP BusinessObjects Dashboards file.

- QUERY BROWSER

  The Query Browser is a new functionality as part of the SAP BusinessObjects Dashboards 4.x release. You can use the VIEW • QUERY BROWSER menu to enable or disable the display of the Query Browser. The Query Browser allows you to set up a data connection toward your universes or connections toward SAP NetWeaver BW, decide which elements of the source you would like to use, and then use the new direct binding capabilities in SAP BusinessObjects Dashboards for the components.

- CANVAS PROPERTIES

  The CANVAS PROPERTIES window is one of the most frequently used windows in the SAP BusinessObjects Dashboards Designer when creating an SAP BusinessObjects Dashboards dashboard. You can follow the VIEW • PROPERTIES menu path to activate the properties window, or you can right-click on the component and select PROPERTIES. The PROPERTIES window will show the properties and configuration options depending on the component.

- **Embedded spreadsheet**

  This embedded spreadsheet lets you define the area of data being used. You can use it to create further calculations.

- **Canvas**

  In the middle of the SAP BusinessObjects Dashboards Designer is an empty area. This is your canvas, which represents the area that you can use to create your SAP BusinessObjects Dashboards file.

6.3.2 Setting Up Your Environment

In this section, we look at some options for customizing your environment for your needs.

Preferences

Follow the FILE • PREFERENCES menu path to configure the global preferences that are accessed every time you create a new SAP BusinessObjects Dashboards file for your design environment (see Figure 6.3).

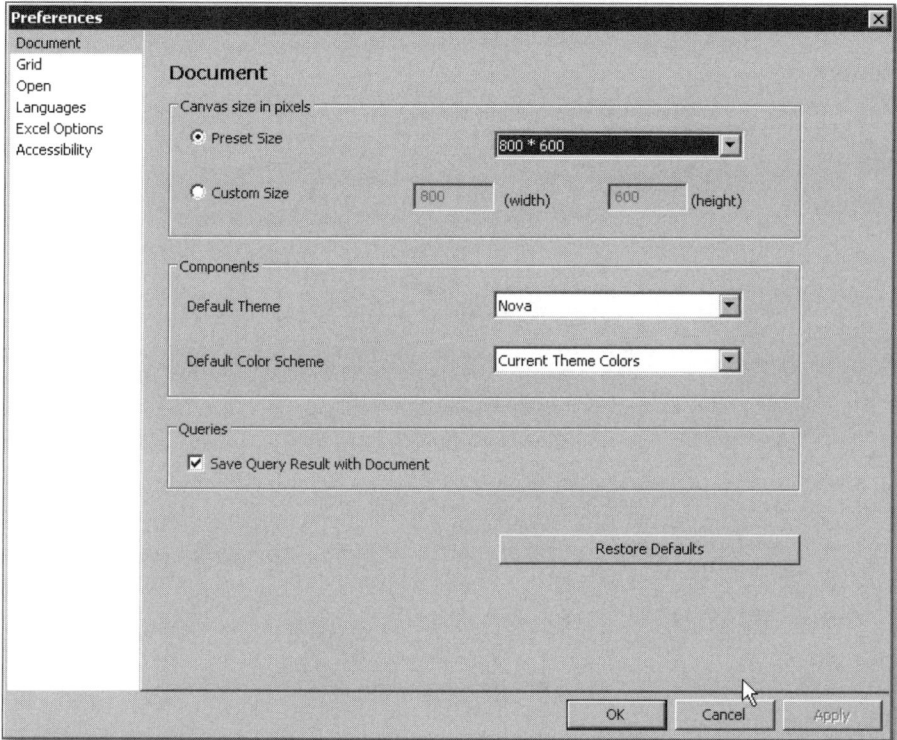

Figure 6.3 Preferences

- At DOCUMENT PREFERENCES, you can configure the size of your canvas based on either a list of preconfigured sizes or a custom size.
- In addition, you can preselect a DEFAULT THEME for your SAP BusinessObjects Dashboards canvas. At GRID PREFERENCES, you can activate a grid for your canvas

and configure whether or not components should snap to the grid. The WIDTH and HEIGHT are entered in pixels.

- EXCEL OPTIONS allows you to activate LIVE OFFICE COMPATIBILITY, which is important when planning to use SAP BusinessObjects Live Office functionality in the SAP BusinessObjects Dashboards Designer (see Figure 6.4).
- You can set the MAXIMUM NUMBER OF ROWS that can be leveraged for components. The default value is 512 rows.

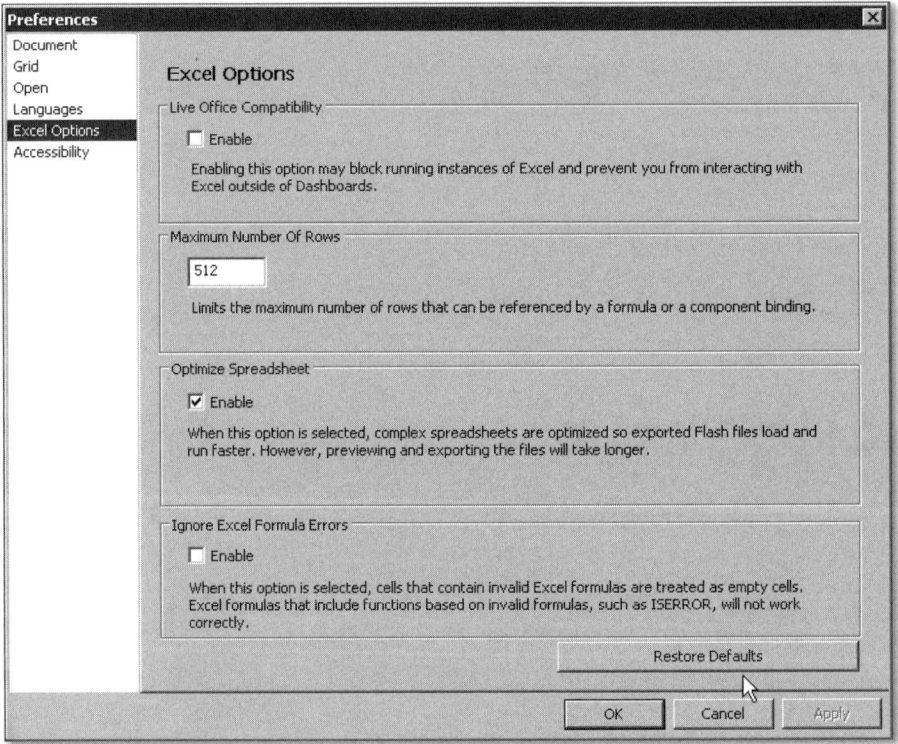

Figure 6.4 Excel Options

Document Properties

Follow the FILE • DOCUMENT PROPERTIES menu path to configure some of the global preferences specific to the SAP BusinessObjects Dashboards file you opened in the SAP BusinessObjects Dashboards Designer and, if required, to overwrite the global preferences (see Figure 6.5). As you can see, you can change the size of the canvas and you can configure a standard font for the SAP BusinessObjects Dashboards file.

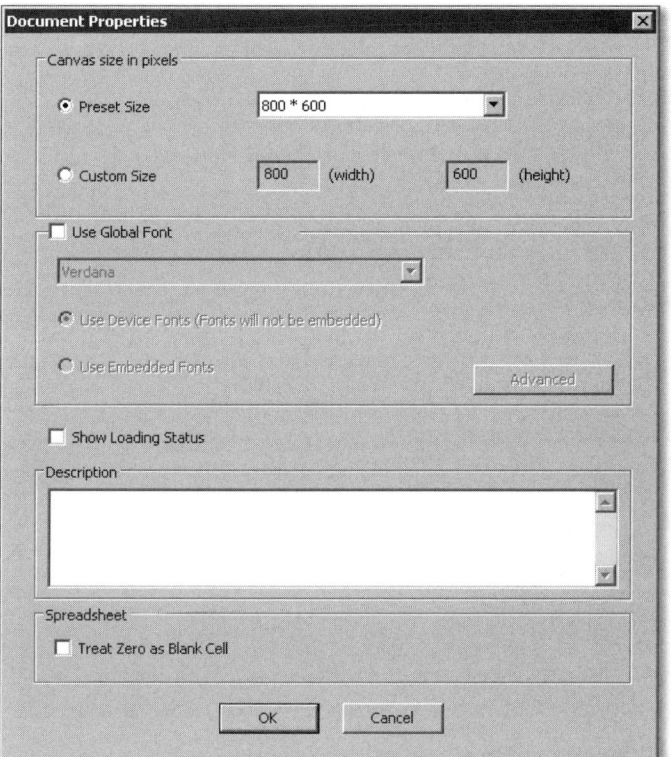

Figure 6.5 Document Properties

Saving vs. Exporting

In the SAP BusinessObjects Dashboards Designer, you can follow FILE • SAVE AS FILE • SAVE TO PLATFORM AS, and the FILE • EXPORT menu paths, which offers several export options. The SAP BusinessObjects Dashboards Designer distinguishes between saving the actual design of your SAP BusinessObjects Dashboards as an XLF file (which can be done using the FILE • SAVE AS or the FILE • SAVE TO PLATFORM AS menu path) and exporting your SAP BusinessObjects Dashboards file and generating a flash file (SWF) for end users to view your dashboard (which can be done with the menu FILE • EXPORT). Starting with the 4.x release of SAP BusinessObjects Dashboards, there is no need to export the flash file to your SAP

BusinessObjects BI platform because the flash file is generated at view time automatically.

6.3.3 Role of Microsoft Excel

Those who are new to SAP BusinessObjects Dashboards often ask why they need the embedded spreadsheet in the SAP BusinessObjects Dashboards Designer. The following list provides details on the role of the embedded spreadsheet:

- In the most simple case, the embedded spreadsheet provides an option for entering data directly into the spreadsheet and visualizing it with SAP BusinessObjects Dashboards. This can be helpful in cases where you don't have an underlying database or data warehouse.

- The embedded spreadsheet also lets you use formulas and calculations done in the spreadsheet so you can add calculations and possibly even aggregation to your data and use them in your SAP BusinessObjects Dashboards visualization. Nevertheless, you should avoid using calculations and data aggregation in the embedded spreadsheet where possible, because SAP BusinessObjects Dashboards is not a data calculation or aggregation engine—it is designed for visualization.

- The embedded spreasheet allows you to use *eventing*. Each time the value of a cell or a range changes, you can classify it as an event for your SAP BusinessObjects Dashboards dashboard and use it, for example, to hide or unhide components from the dashboard.

The first two roles of the embedded spreadsheet are irrelevant, especially in the SAP NetWeaver BW case, because you have an actual data source and data aggregation engine. In this case, the benefit you gain is the eventing model from the embedded spreadsheet that you can use to drive the interactive parts of your dashboard. In addition, as of the 4.x release of SAP BusinessObjects Dashboards and the capability to bind your components directly to the semantic layer or your shared connection from the SAP BusinessObjects BI platform, the role of the embedded spreadsheet becomes smaller and smaller.

Remember that with the new version of SAP BusinessObjects Dashboards, the use of the embedded spreadsheet becomes optional, because you can use the direct binding capabilities instead. We recommend that you avoid using the embedded spreadsheet every time you create a dashboard.

6.3.4 Common Look and Feel

After working with SAP BusinessObjects Dashboards for a while, you will notice that there is a need for a common look and feel for your dashboards. A common look and feel can mean anything from the placement of a component, such as a chart or gauge, to the color scheme. SAP BusinessObjects Dashboards offers several options to address this need, and below we look at the three most common ones.

Templates

From the FILE • TEMPLATES menu path, you can find a list of predefined templates and samples based on certain tasks.

SAP BusinessObjects Dashboards delivers a set of templates that represent more complex dashboards and that demonstrate the use of several components. These are worth spending some time with to see what you can do with SAP BusinessObjects Dashboards. In addition, you will find a category called LAYOUT, where you will find a set of templates for specific tasks.

More importantly, you can create your own templates, make them company-specific, and offer them to all your users.

To create a new template, you have to do the following:

1. Create the SAP BusinessObjects Dashboards design in the SAP BusinessObjects Dashboards Designer.
2. Follow the FILE • SAVE AS menu path and save the XLF file to the template folder. If you used a standard installation, you will find the templates at *Program Files\SAP Business Objects\Xcelsius 4.0\assets\template*.
3. Follow the FILE • EXPORT • FLASH (SWF) menu path and save the SWF file to the template folder.

After completing these steps, your SAP BusinessObjects Dashboards design will be available in the list of templates. If you would like to create your own category, you can create a subfolder in the template folder and store your SAP BusinessObjects Dashboards files there; the subfolder's name is used as the name of the category.

Themes

Themes are a collection of properties; think of them as a style sheet for a web page. Follow the FORMAT • THEME menu path to select a theme for your SAP BusinessObjects Dashboards design, and it will be applied to all of your components.

It's important to note that the themes have different components and that switching between themes can influence the look and feel of your components, because a component you used before may not be available in the new theme. In such cases, SAP BusinessObjects Dashboards will replace the component with one from the newly selected theme.

Color Schemes

Follow the FORMAT • COLOR SCHEME menu path to leverage a set of predefined color schemes and create your own custom color schemes. The main difference between the color scheme and the theme is that you can customize the colors in the color scheme, whereas in the themes you cannot. Because you can't create your own themes in the current version of the product, your best option is to create a custom color scheme, with some templates that you can share.

At this point, you have a good understanding of the SAP BusinessObjects Dashboards Designer environment. Let's move on to the next section and build the first SAP BusinessObjects Dashboards dashboard on top of a BEx query.

6.3.5 Creating Your First Dashboard

In this section, we focus on some simple steps in the SAP BusinessObjects Dashboards Designer to get you used to the data connectivity you will use to retrieve the information from SAP NetWeaver BW. This will also help you become familiar with designing a dashboard using the SAP BusinessObjects Dashboards Designer.

Defining the Dashboard Scope

Before you start building a dashboard with SAP BusinessObjects Dashboards, it's always good practice to have a clear understanding of the scope and goal of the dashboard you're going to create. In our case, for the first dashboard, we focus on some simple steps, but try to cover all of the major concepts in SAP BusinessObjects Dashboards.

Our dashboard should offer the sales revenue broken down either by product or month—this should be the user's choice. In addition, the dashboard should show details broken down by month when the user selects a single product from the chart, and it should show details broken down by product when the user selects a month from the chart.

Defining the Data Connectivity

In our dashboard, we want to show the numbers broken down by month and by product, and show some critical KPIs on an overall level. For our BEx query, this means we need to have the calendar month and product as part of the BEx query and we need to have all of the critical KPIs in the BEx query as well.

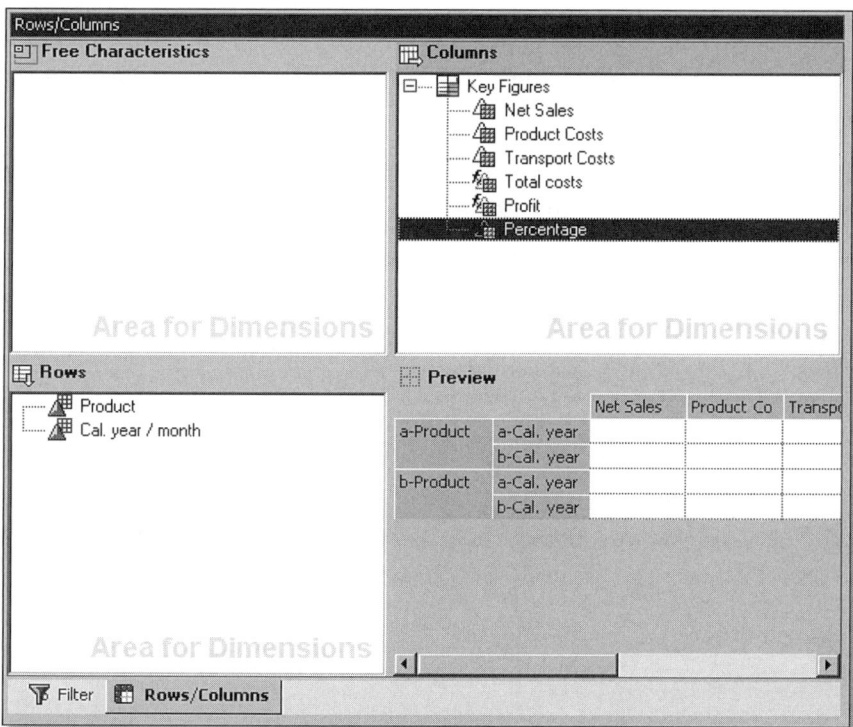

Figure 6.6 BEx Query

In the BEx query shown in Figure 6.6, we have the PRODUCT characteristic and the CAL. YEAR/MONTH characteristic in the rows and several key figures in the columns. The key figures represent the NET SALES, PRODUCT COSTS, TRANSPORT COSTS, TOTAL COSTS, PROFIT, and PERCENTAGE; the last three key figures are formulas created in the BEx query. The BEx query is based on the SAP NetWeaver Demo model InfoProvider 0D_NW_M01.

> **SAP NetWeaver Demo Model**
>
> If you are interested in using the SAP NetWeaver demo model for some simple exercises, you can find more information at *http://www.sdn.sap.com/irj/sdn/nw-demo-model*.

Because SAP BusinessObjects Dashboards, SAP Crystal Reports for Enterprise, and SAP BusinessObjects Web Intelligence share the connections toward SAP NetWeaver BW, the steps for setting up the OLAP connections are identical. You can find the detailed steps in Chapter 4, Section 4.3.3.

After we configure the OLAP connection in the Central Management Console (CMC), we can build our first dashboard:

1. Start the SAP BusinessObjects Dashboards Designer via the START • PROGRAMS • DASHBOARDS • DASHBOARDS menu path.
2. Select the menu FILE • NEW • NEW to create an empty model.
3. Use the menu VIEW • QUERY BROWSER to ensure that the Query Browser is shown as part of the design environment.
4. In the Query Browser, click ADD QUERY.
5. You are asked to authenticate your SAP BusinessObjects BI platform system. Log on to the system using your SAP credentials and the SAP authentication.

> **Logging On with SAP Credentials**
>
> You will notice that the SAP BusinessObjects Dashboards logon dialog for your SAP BusinessObjects BI platform does not provide separate fields for the SAP system ID, SAP client number, and language. You need to enter you SAP credentials using the following syntax:
>
> ```
> <SAP System ID>~<SAP Client number>/<SAP User>
> ```

> For example:
>
> `ABC~800/DEMO` for the SAP System ABC, client 800, and the user DEMO.

You are presented with the first step in adding a new query to your dashboard (see Figure 6.7).

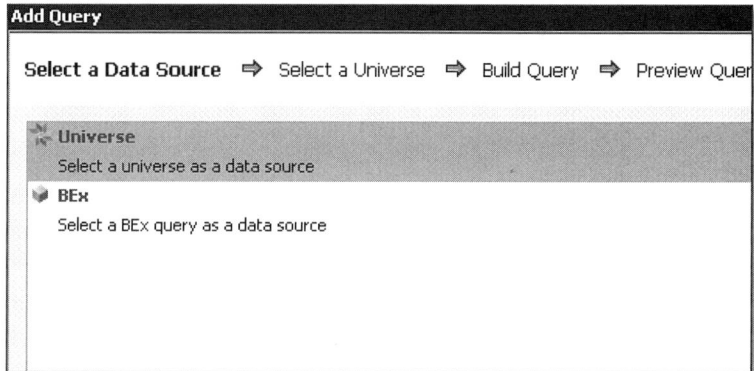

Figure 6.7 Add Query

6. Select the option BEx.
7. Click on NEXT.
8. You are presented with the list of available connections (see Figure 6.8). Select the connection you set up for the BEx query.

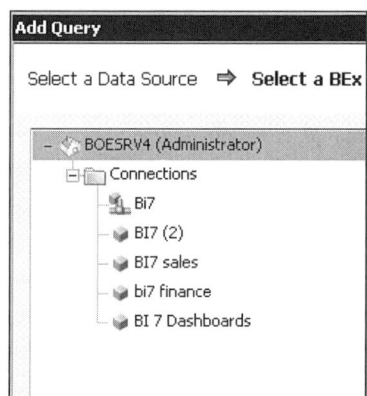

Figure 6.8 Available Connections

9. Click on NEXT.
10. You are presented with a list of BEx queries (see Figure 6.9) and you can select the BEx query you need for your dashboard. Select the BEx query and click on OK.

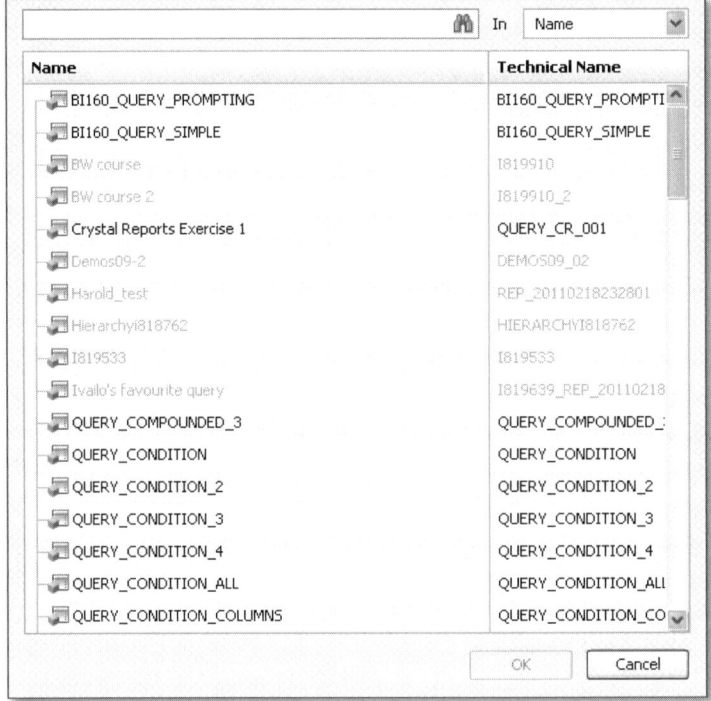

Figure 6.9 List of BEx Queries

11. You are presented with the query panel (see Figure 6.10), and you can now start creating your first query that you will use for your dashboard.
12. Add dimension PRODUCT to the RESULT OBJECTS.
13. Add measure NET SALES to the RESULT OBJECTS.
14. Click on NEXT.
15. You are shown a preview of the data (see Figure 6.11).
16. Click on NEXT.

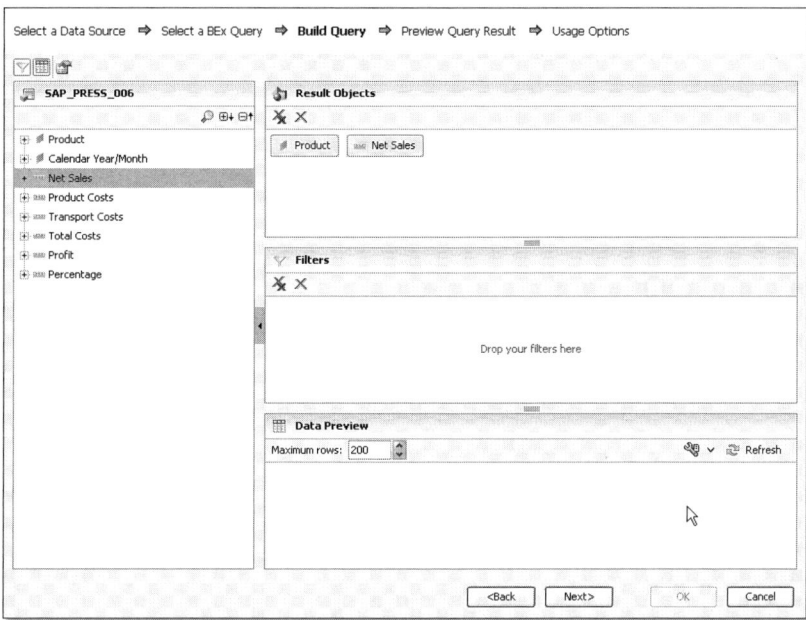

Figure 6.10 Query Panel

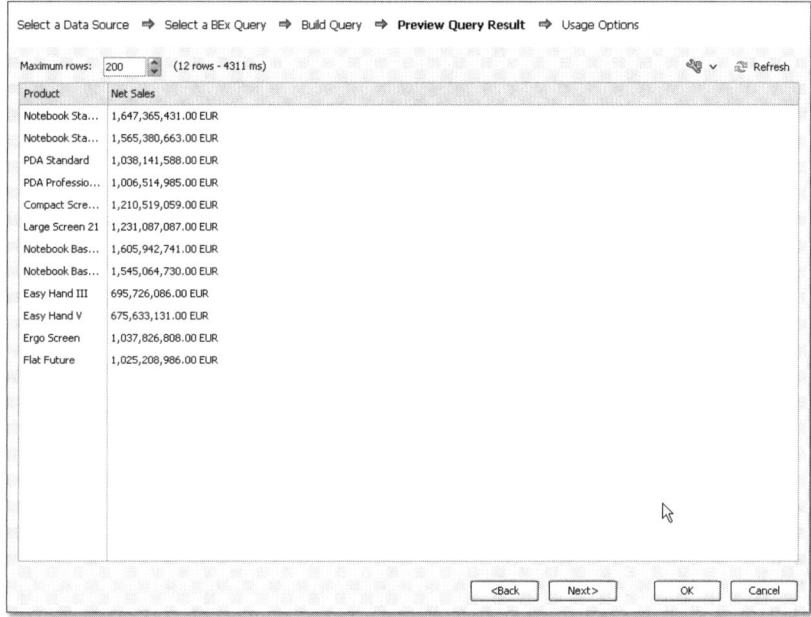

Figure 6.11 Data Preview

17. You can now configure several settings (see Figure 6.12) for the data connection. For now, we leave the default values and we will configure these settings later on.
18. Click on OK.

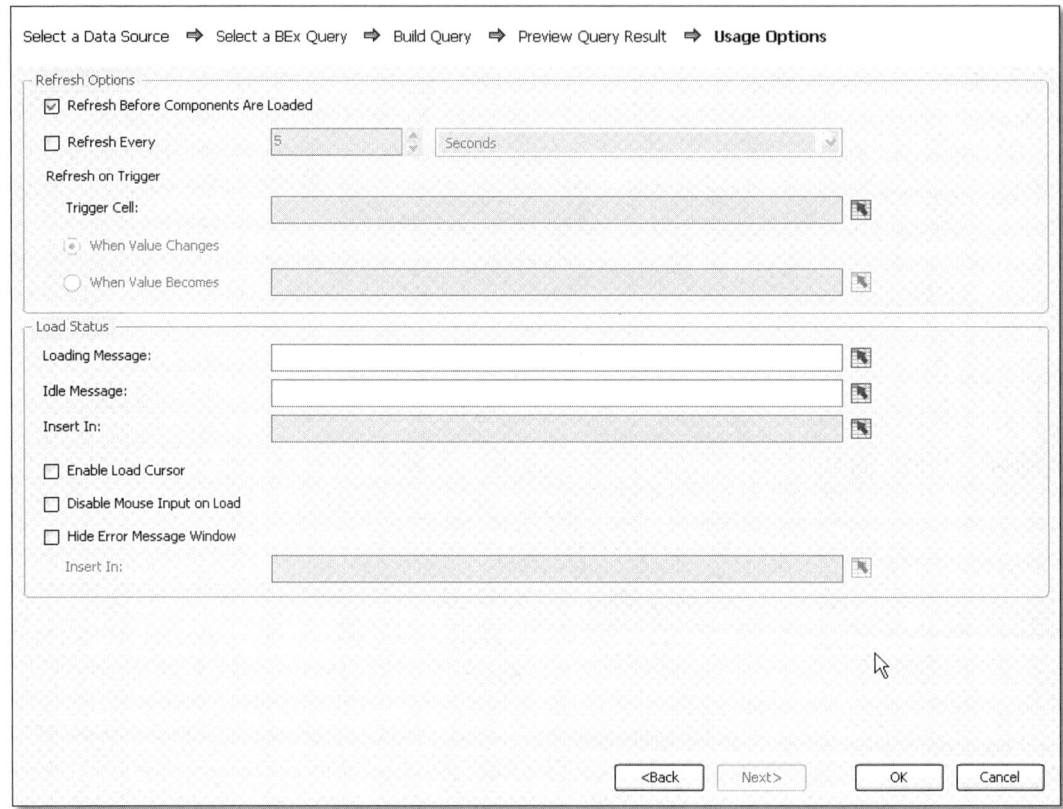

Figure 6.12 Connection Settings

19. Your new query is shown in the QUERY BROWSER and, if needed, you can use the toolbar to change the query or to configure the settings (see Figure 6.13).

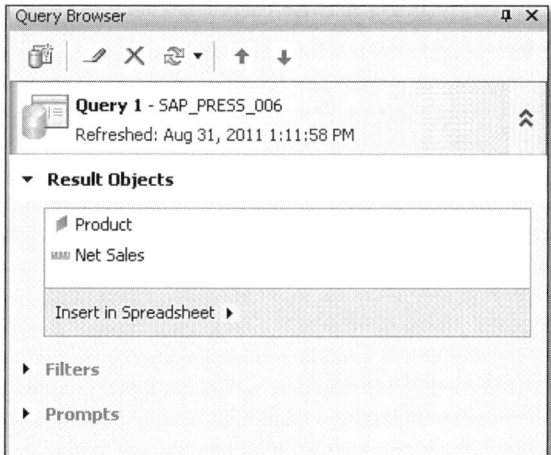

Figure 6.13 Query Browser

Remember that our final dashboard needs to provide the following options:

- The user can display the measure by product or by month depending on his choice.
- The user can drill down from the first chart to a second chart showing more details. Example: the first chart shows the revenue by product; the user can select one of the products in the chart and receive a second chart showing the revenue for the selected product broken down by month.

Overall, our dashboard will have four components, and we will also need four connections. For sure, there are other options for creating this dashboard with a single connection and receiving all the data up front, but such a design often leads to performance problems later on. Why do we need four connections?

- We have two main charts—one chart showing the measure by product and one chart showing the measure by month.
- These two charts allow the user to drill down into more details, such as another two charts showing the measure by month for a single product and showing the measure by product for a single month. These two charts are different because we want to filter the information and pass selected values to the connection; therefore, we can't re-use the connections from the two other charts.

In the following steps we set up the other three connections we will need.

1. Click on the EDIT option in the QUERY BROWSER for the existing query (see Figure 6.14).

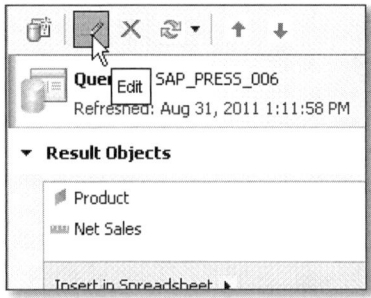

Figure 6.14 Editing Query

2. Use the PROPERTIES button (　) in the query panel to open the query properties.
3. Rename the query "Sales by Product".
4. Click on OK.
5. Go through the steps using the NEXT button until the end to save the changes.
6. Use the ADD QUERY button (　) in the QUERY BROWSER to create another query.
7. Select the BEx option.
8. Click on NEXT.
9. Select the connection you set up for the BEx query.
10. Click on NEXT.
11. Select the BEx query you need for your dashboard and click on OK.
12. You are presented with the query panel.
13. Add CALENDAR YEAR/MONTH to the RESULT OBJECTS.
14. Add NET SALES to the RESULT OBJECTS.
15. Use the PROPERTIES button (　) in the query panel to open the query properties.
16. Rename the query "SALES BY MONTH".
17. Click on OK.
18. Click on NEXT. You are shown a preview of the data.

19. Click on NEXT. You can now configure several settings for the data connection. For now, we leave the default values and we will configure these settings later on.
20. Click on OK.
21. Use the ADD QUERY button (📋) in the QUERY BROWSER to create another query.
22. Select the BEx option.
23. Click on NEXT.
24. Select the connection you set up for the BEx query.
25. Click on NEXT.
26. Select the BEx query you need for your dashboard and click on OK.
27. You are presented with the query panel.
28. Add PRODUCT to the RESULT OBJECTS.
29. Add NET SALES to the RESULT OBJECTS.
30. Add CALENDAR YEAR/MONTH to FILTERS.
31. Select the EQUAL TO operator.
32. Select the PROMPT option (see Figure 6.15).

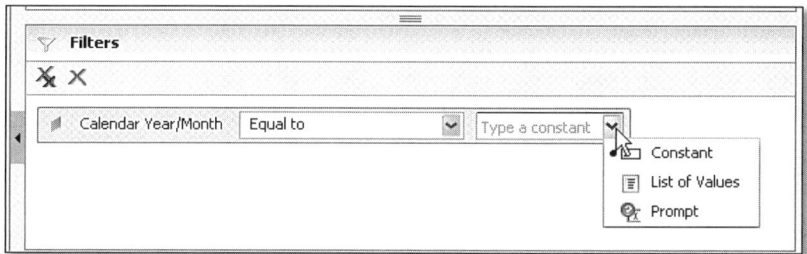

Figure 6.15 Filter Definition

33. A separate dialog comes up, providing you the option to configure details for the prompt. Configure the prompt to be an OPTIONAL PROMPT.
34. Uncheck the SELECT ONLY FROM LIST option.
35. Click on OK.
36. Use the PROPERTIES button (📋) in the query panel to open the query properties.
37. Rename the query "Sales by Product (Filtered)".

38. Click on OK.
39. Click on NEXT.
40. You are shown the prompt dialog. The prompt is optional, so we don't need to provide a value right now. Click on RUN.
41. You are shown a preview of the data.
42. Click on NEXT. You can now configure several settings for the data connection. For now, we leave the default values and we will configure these settings later on.
43. Click on OK.
44. Use the ADD QUERY button () in the QUERY BROWSER to create another query.
45. Select the BEx option.
46. Click on NEXT.
47. Select the connection you set up for the BEx query.
48. Click on NEXT.
49. Select the BEx query you need for your dashboard and click on OK.
50. You are presented with the query panel.
51. Add CALENDAR YEAR/MONTH to the RESULT OBJECTS.
52. Add NET SALES to the RESULT OBJECTS.
53. Add PRODUCT to the FILTERS.
54. Select the EQUAL TO operator.
55. Select the PROMPT option.
56. A separate dialog comes up, providing you the option to configure details for the prompt. Configure the prompt to be an OPTIONAL PROMPT.
57. Uncheck the SELECT ONLY FROM LIST option.
58. Click on OK.
59. Use the PROPERTIES button () in the query panel to open the query properties.
60. Rename the query to "Sales by Month (Filtered)".
61. Click on OK.
62. Click on NEXT.

63. You are shown the prompt dialog. The prompt is optional, so we don't need to provide a value right now. Click on RUN.
64. You are shown a preview of the data.
65. Click on NEXT. You can now configure several settings for the data connection. For now, we leave the default values and we will configure these settings later on.
66. Click on OK.

You should have now four connections listed in the query browser.

Including Charts and Selectors

We now start creating our dashboard and include the charts and the selection options in the canvas.

1. Follow the VIEW • COMPONENTS menu path.
2. Drag and drop the RADIO BUTTONS component from the SELECTORS category to the top left corner of your canvas.
3. Right-click on the new components and select PROPERTIES (see Figure 6.16).

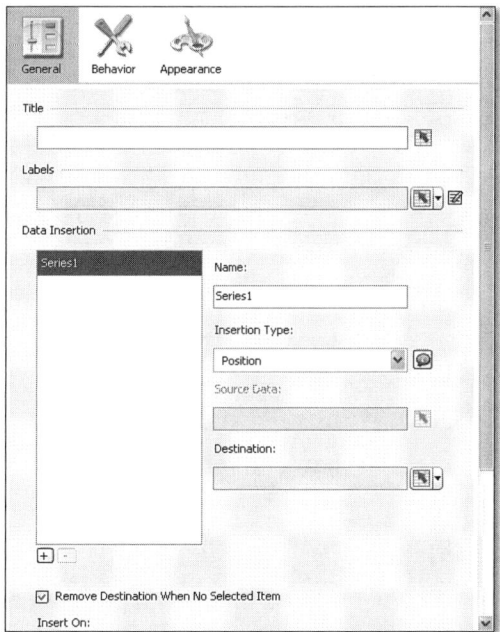

Figure 6.16 Radio Button Properties

4. Click on the SELECT A RANGE button (▣) next to LABELS and select cells B1 and B2 in the embedded spreadsheet.
5. Click on OK.
6. Set the INSERTION TYPE to VALUE.
7. Click on the SELECT A RANGE button (▣) next to SOURCE DATA and select cells A1 and A2 from the embedded spreadsheet.
8. Click on OK.
9. Click on the SELECT A RANGE button (▣) next to DESTINATION and select cell D1 from the embedded spreadsheet.

> **Why Do We Use the Embedded Spreadsheet?**
>
> You might ask yourself at this point why we use the embedded spreadsheet. The reason is that the radio buttons and the selected option by the user are not something our actual data source provides; therefore, we need a place to enter the labels and to store the selected value.

10. Enter the value 1 into cell A1.
11. Enter the value 2 into cell A2.
12. Enter the text "Summary by Product" into cell B1.
13. Enter the text "Summary by Month" into cell B2.

    You just created two radio buttons that will use text stored in the embedded spreadsheet for display purposes and the values as the selected value. The user selection will be stored in a cell so that we can use it later on to hide or unhide a chart depending on the choice the user made.

14. Drag and drop a COLUMN CHART from CHARTS to your canvas and resize it so that it uses about half of the height of your canvas and three-quarters of the width. This chart shows the NET SALES by PRODUCT.
15. Right-click on the COLUMN CHART in the canvas and select PROPERTIES.
16. Enter "Net Sales by Product" as the title for the chart and remove the subtitle.
17. Select the BY SERIES option for the DATA and use the "+" symbol to add a series.
18. Enter "Net Sales" as the NAME of the series.
19. Use the small arrow from the SELECT A RANGE button (▣) next to VALUES (Y) to open the list (see Figure 6.17) and select the QUERY DATA option.

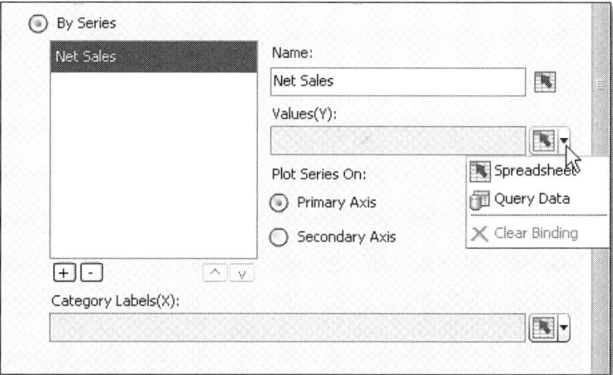

Figure 6.17 Direct Binding

20. Select the SALES BY PRODUCT (see Figure 6.18).

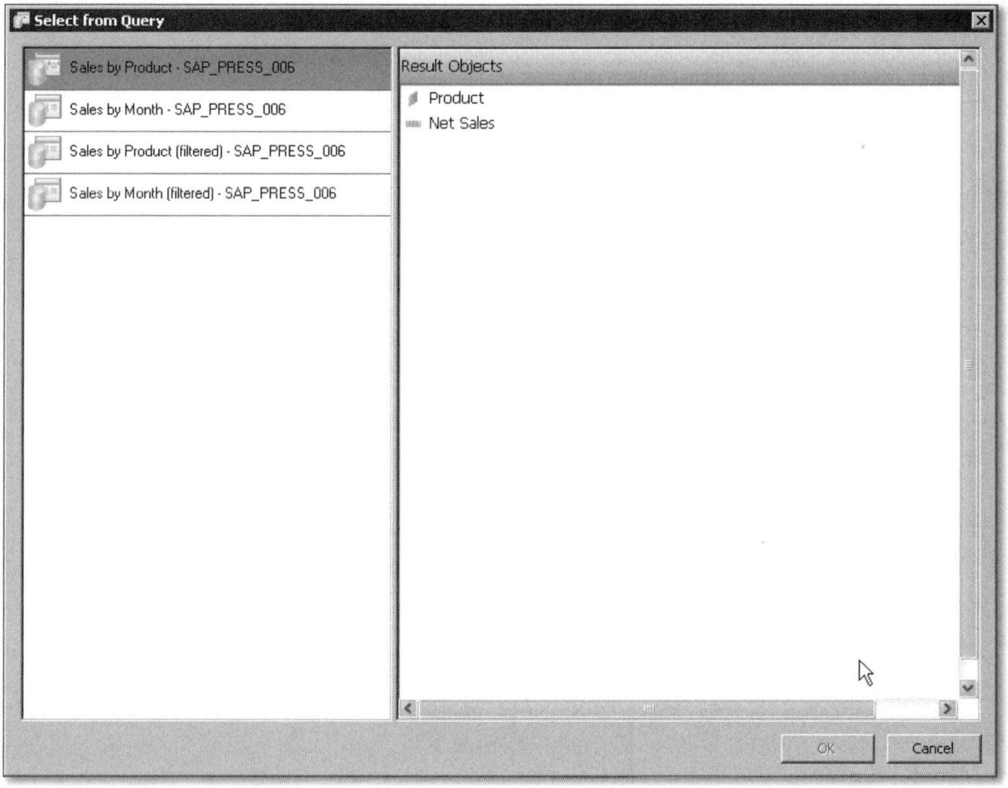

Figure 6.18 Binding Query Data

21. Select NET SALES.
22. Click on OK.
23. Use the small arrow from the SELECT A RANGE button (▣) next to CATEGORY LABELS (X) to open the list and select the QUERY DATA option.
24. Select the SALES BY PRODUCT.
25. Select PRODUCT.
26. Click on OK.
27. Navigate to the SCALE tab from BEHAVIOR.
28. Activate the FIXED LABEL SIZE option to shorten the numbers on the Y-axis.
29. Navigate to the COMMON tab from the BEHAVIOR area.
30. Click on the SELECT A RANGE button (▣) next to STATUS for DYNAMIC VISIBILITY. From your embedded spreadsheet, select cell D1, which is the cell where you store the user selection from the radio buttons.
31. Click on OK.
32. Set the KEY to the value 1, so that when the user selects the summary by product, the chart is shown; otherwise, it is hidden.

At this point you have a dashboard that allows you to select between a summary by PRODUCT or CALENDAR MONTH; if you select the PRODUCT, it shows the chart.

Now let's add the second chart to our canvas and use the OBJECT BROWSER to hide the current chart.

1. Follow the VIEW • OBJECT BROWSER menu path.
2. Right-click on the chart shown in the OBJECT BROWSER.
3. Select the RENAME menu item and enter the name "Sales by Product".
4. Click on ⏎ Enter.
5. Select the option to hide the chart from your canvas (see Figure 6.19).

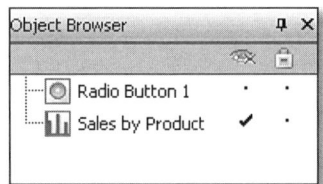

Figure 6.19 Object Browser

6. Drag and drop a COLUMN CHART from the CHARTS category to your canvas and resize it so that it uses about half of the height of your canvas and three-quarters of the width. It should overlap with the chart you created previously. Here, you can also select both charts in the OBJECT BROWSER (even when not visible on the canvas) and use the FORMAT • MAKE SAME SIZE and FORMAT • ALIGN menu paths to align the size and placement of both charts.
7. Right-click on COLUMN CHART in the canvas and select PROPERTIES.
8. Enter "Net Sales by Month" as the title for the chart and remove the subtitle.
9. Select the BY SERIES option for the DATA and use the "+" symbol to add a series.
10. Enter "Net Sales" as the NAME of the series.
11. Use the small arrow from the SELECT A RANGE button (▦) next to VALUES (Y) to open the list and select the QUERY DATA option.
12. Select SALES BY MONTH.
13. Select NET SALES.
14. Click on OK.
15. Use the small arrow from the SELECT A RANGE button (▦) next to CATEGORY LABELS (X) to open the list and select the QUERY DATA option.
16. Select SALES BY MONTH.
17. Select CALENDAR YEAR/MONTH.
18. Click on OK.
19. Navigate to the SCALE tab from BEHAVIOR.
20. Activate the option FIXED LABEL SIZE to shorten the numbers on the Y-axis.
21. Navigate to the COMMON tab from the BEHAVIOR area.
22. Click on the SELECT A RANGE button (▦) next to STATUS for DYNAMIC VISIBILITY and, from our embedded spreadsheet, select cell D1, which is the cell where we store the user selection from the radio buttons.
23. Click on OK.
24. Set the KEY to the value 2, so that the chart is shown when the user selects the summary by month; otherwise, it is hidden.
25. Follow the VIEW • OBJECT BROWSER menu path.
26. Right-click on the chart shown in the OBJECT BROWSER.

27. Select the RENAME menu item and enter the name "Sales by Month".

28. Click on [Enter].

In the next step, we will add two additional charts to show the details of the opposite chart. When you show the net sales by product and click on a single bar, you will see a chart showing the net sales by month for the selected product. If you show the net sales by month and select a single month in the chart, you will see a chart showing the net sales by product for a single month.

Setting Up Drill-Down

Up to this point, we have created an SAP BusinessObjects Dashboards dashboard showing two different charts based on our selection for either the month or the product. Now we will add a drill-down chart for both of these charts. In our example, we would like to show the numbers broken down by month in the lower level chart and broken down by product in the upper level chart.

1. Drag and drop a new COLUMN CHART to the canvas and place it below the existing two charts.

> **Naming of Elements**
>
> In the OBJECT BROWSER, you can right-click on a context menu for each element of your canvas and use RENAME to configure a name for each object. In that way, it is easy to differentiate each object from the others.

2. This chart should be displayed only when the upper chart shows the net sales by product, so we need to configure the DYNAMIC VISIBILITY property.
3. Right-click on the new chart and select PROPERTIES.
4. Navigate to the COMMON tab in the BEHAVIOR area.
5. Click on the SELECT A RANGE button (🔲) next to STATUS for DYNAMIC VISIBILITY and, from the embedded spreadsheet, select cell D1, which is the cell where we store the user selection from the radio buttons.
6. Click on OK.
7. Set the KEY to the value 1, so that when the user selects the summary by product, the chart is shown; otherwise, it is hidden.
8. Right-click on the chart and open PROPERTIES.

9. Navigate to the GENERAL area.
10. Enter "Monthly Sales" as the title and remove the subtitle.
11. Select the BY SERIES option for the DATA and use the "+" symbol to add a series.
12. Enter "Net Sales" as the NAME of the series.
13. Use the small arrow from the SELECT A RANGE button () next to VALUES (Y) to open the list and select the QUERY DATA option.
14. Select SALES BY MONTH (FILTERED).
15. Select NET SALES.
16. Click on OK.
17. Use the small arrow from the SELECT A RANGE button () next to CATEGORY LABELS (X) to open the list and select the QUERY DATA option.
18. Select SALES BY MONTH (FILTERED).
19. Select CALENDAR YEAR/MONTH.
20. Click on OK.
21. Navigate to the SCALE tab from BEHAVIOR.
22. Activate the FIXED LABEL SIZE option to shorten the numbers on the Y-axis.

Without doing anything further, the lower chart would show the data for the month. However, we want to show the net sales by month for a single product, which is selected in the upper level chart; therefore, we need to configure the drill-down.

1. Right-click on the upper level chart showing the net sales by product and select PROPERTIES, or you can also select the chart in the OBJECT BROWSER.
2. Navigate to the INSERTION area.
3. Activate the ENABLE DATA INSERTION option (see Figure 6.20).

   You will notice that the INSERTION TYPE field does not have the LABEL option, which means we can't just send the label from the selected product. The closest option is INSERTION TYPE ROW. For this option, you will notice that the source data do not provide the option to point to the query data, which means that you will have to point your query data to the spreadsheet to enable drill-down.
4. Select the menu VIEW • QUERY BROWSER to ensure the Query Browser is visible.
5. Select SALES BY PRODUCT.

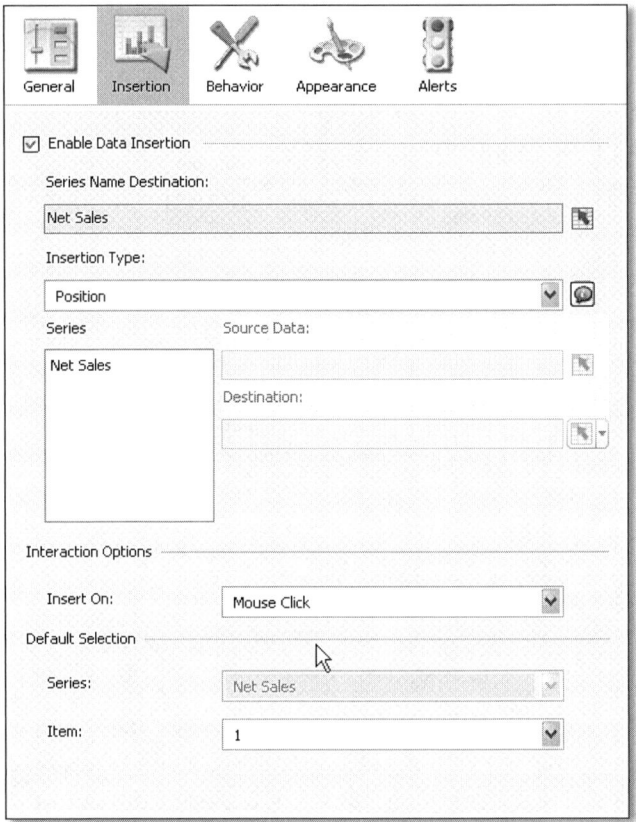

Figure 6.20 Data Insertion

6. Select PRODUCT in the query.
7. Click on INSERT IN SPREADSHEET.
8. Click on the SELECT A RANGE button (![icon]) next to INSERT IN SPREADSHEET and, from the embedded spreadsheet, select the range from cell G1 to cell G100.
9. Click on OK.
10. Now navigate back to the chart. Right-click on the upper level chart showing the net sales by product and select PROPERTIES. You can also select the chart in the OBJECT BROWSER.
11. Navigate to the INSERTION area.
12. Set the INSERTION TYPE to ROW.
13. Select the entry in the SERIES.

14. Click on the SELECT A RANGE button (▦) next to SOURCE DATA, and, from the embedded spreadsheet, select the range from cell G1 to cell G100.
15. Click on OK.
16. Use the SELECT A RANGE button (▦) next to DESTINATION to open the list and select cell D2 from the embedded spreadsheet.
17. Click on OK.

> **Excel Cell or Query Prompt?**
>
> In the previous step, you will notice that there is also an option to point the selected value directly to a query prompt. The reason we did not select the option is because we will need to refresh the data each time the value changes, which is configured using a trigger cell in SAP BusinessObjects Dashboards. Ideally, the trigger cell is able to react to changes for a defined prompt, but unfortunately, in release 4.0 FP3 this is not possible. Instead, the trigger cell can read a value only from the embedded spreadsheet. Therefore, we point our selected value to the embedded spreadsheet and our prompt will receive it from there.

18. Select the menu VIEW • QUERY BROWSER to ensure the QUERY BROWSER is visible.
19. Select SALES BY MONTH (FILTERED).
20. Select the prompt in the list.
21. Click on CONNECT TO SPREADSHEET (see Figure 6.21).
22. Click on the SELECT A RANGE button (▦) next to SELECTED VALUES and select cell D2 from the embedded spreadsheet.
23. Click on OK.
24. Select SALES BY MONTH (FILTERED) in the QUERY BROWSER.
25. Click on the EDIT option in the QUERY BROWSER.
26. Click on NEXT.
27. You can click on RUN at the prompt screen.
28. Click on NEXT at the data preview.
29. Click on the SELECT A RANGE (▦) button next to TRIGGER CELL and select cell D2 from the embedded spreadsheet (see Figure 6.22).
30. Click on OK.
31. Choose the WHEN VALUE CHANGES option.

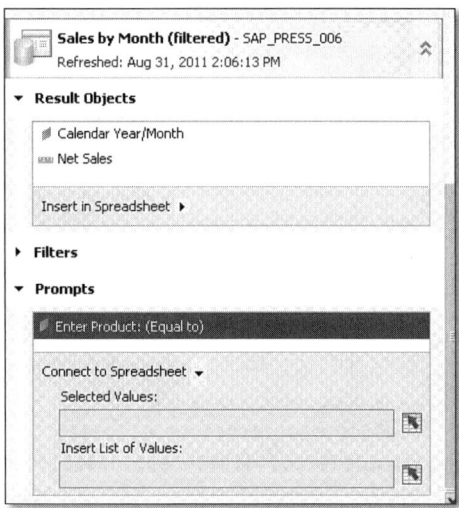

Figure 6.21 Prompts

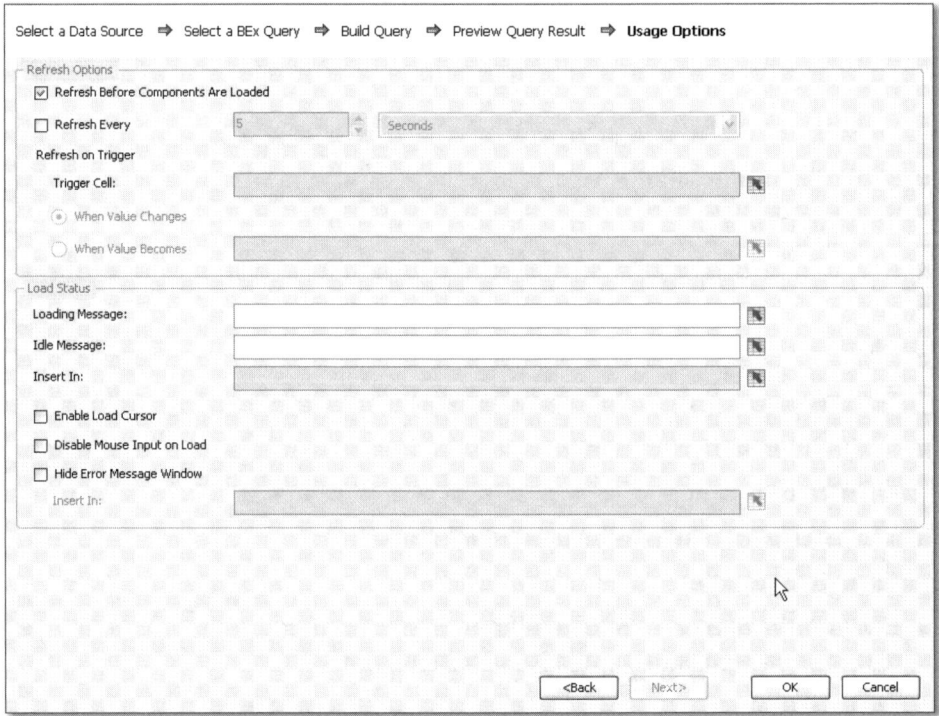

Figure 6.22 Trigger Cell Definition

32. Click on OK.
33. Select the menu VIEW • QUERY BROWSER to ensure the Query Browser is visible.
34. Select SALES BY MONTH.
35. Select CALENDAR YEAR/MONTH in the query.
36. Click on INSERT IN SPREADSHEET.
37. Click on the SELECT A RANGE button (🔲) next to INSERT IN SPREADSHEET, and, from the embedded spreadsheet, select the range from cell H1 to cell H100.
38. Click on OK.
39. Right-click on the upper level chart showing the net sales by month and select PROPERTIES. You can also select the chart in the Object Browser.
40. Navigate to the INSERTION area.
41. Activate the ENABLE DATA INSERTION option.
42. Set the INSERTION TYPE to ROW.
43. Select the entry in the SERIES.
44. Click on the SELECT A RANGE (🔲) button next to SOURCE DATA, and, from the embedded spreadsheet, select the range from cell H1 to cell H100.
45. Click on OK.
46. Use the SELECT A RANGE button (🔲) next to DESTINATION to open the list and select cell D3 from our embedded spreadsheet.
47. Click on OK.
48. Select the menu VIEW • QUERY BROWSER to ensure that the QUERY BROWSER is visible.
49. Select the query SALES BY PRODUCT (FILTERED).
50. Select the prompt in the list.
51. Click on CONNECT TO SPREADSHEET.
52. Click on the SELECT A RANGE button (🔲) next to SELECTED VALUES and select cell D3 from the embedded spreadsheet.
53. Click OK.
54. Select SALES BY PRODUCT (FILTERED) in the QUERY BROWSER.
55. Click on the EDIT option in the QUERY BROWSER.

56. Click on Next.
57. You can click on Run at the prompt screen.
58. Click on Next at the data preview.
59. Click on the Select a Range button (▨) next to Trigger Cell and select cell D3 from the embedded spreadsheet.
60. Click on OK.
61. Choose the When Value Changes option.
62. Click on OK.
63. Drag and drop a new Column Chart to the canvas and place it below the existing two charts on top of the other chart in the lower level.

This chart should be displayed only when the upper chart shows the net sales by month, so now we need to configure the Dynamic Visibility property.

1. Right-click on the new chart and select Properties.
2. Navigate to the Common tab in the Behavior area.
3. Click on the Select a Range button (▨) next to Status for Dynamic Visibility and, from the embedded spreadsheet, select cell D1, which is the cell where we store the user selection from the radio buttons.
4. Click on OK
5. Set the Key to the value 2, so that when the user selects the summary by product, the chart is shown; otherwise, it is hidden.
6. Right-click on the chart and open Properties.
7. Navigate to the General area.
8. Enter "Product Sales" as the title and remove the subtitle.
9. Select the by Series option for the Data and use the "+" symbol to add a series.
10. Enter "Net Sales" as the Name of the series.
11. Use the small arrow from the Select a Range button (▨) next to Values (Y) to open the list and select the Query Data option.
12. Select Sales by Product (Filtered).
13. Select Net Sales.
14. Click on OK.
15. Use the small arrow from the Select a Range button (▨) next to Category Labels (X) to open the list and select the Query Data option.

16. Select SALES BY PRODUCT (FILTERED).
17. Select PRODUCT.
18. Click on OK.
19. Navigate to the SCALE tab from BEHAVIOR.
20. Activate the FIXED LABEL SIZE option to shorten the numbers on the Y-axis.
21. Right-click on the lower level chart showing net sales by month and select PROPERTIES.
22. Navigate to the GENERAL area.
23. Click on the SELECT A RANGE button (▣) next to SUBTITLE and select cell D2 from the embedded spreadsheet so that the selected product name becomes the subtitle.
24. Click on OK.
25. Right-click on the lower level chart showing net sales by product and select PROPERTIES.
26. Navigate to the GENERAL area.
27. Click on the SELECT A RANGE (▣) button next to SUBTITLE and select cell D3 from our embedded spreadsheet so that the selected month becomes the subtitle.
28. Click on OK.

You have created a dashboard that not only lets you select a different chart on the highest level but also allows you to drill down into more details depending on the chart type you selected in the beginning. Now it's time to save the dashboard.

1. Follow the menu FILE • SAVE TO PLATFORM.
2. Select a folder in you SAP BusinessObjects platform.
3. Enter a name for your SAP BusinessObjects Dashboard object.
4. Click on SAVE.
5. Follow the menu FILE • PREVIEW to view your dashboard.

You have created a dashboard that allows several types of interaction and data display, and learned how to ensure a common look and feel for your dashboards. All of this is based directly on SAP NetWeaver BW data.

In the next section, we put this newly gained knowledge to work and use SAP BusinessObjects Dashboards to fulfill parts of the requirements from the sales department.

6.4 Building a Dashboard for Sales Planning

In our first example, we look at how you can use SAP BusinessObjects Dashboards not only to show the numbers from your sales organization, but also to offer a planning scenario where people can influence the planned numbers by using sliders in the dashboard. In the next couple of steps, we create an SAP BusinessObjects Dashboards dashboard that provides information about our sales revenue by product and regions, and also provides a planning scenario in which we can see the impact of reducing or increasing our product costs or our sales forecast.

Both queries that we use are based on InfoProvider 0D_NW_M01 from the SAP NetWeaver demo model. The first query shows the key figures PRODUCT COSTS, TRANSPORTS COSTS, NUMBER OF DEALS, and NET SALES along with the characteristics REGION, PRODUCT CATEGORY, and CAL. YEAR/MONTH (see Figure 6.23).

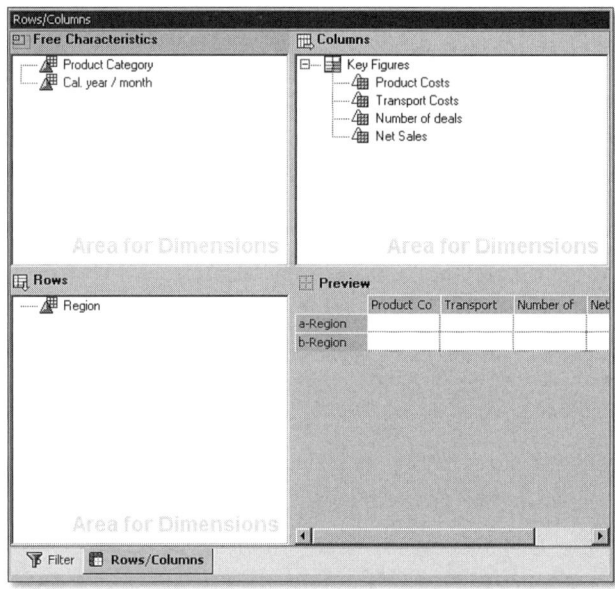

Figure 6.23 BEx Query

The second query we use for the planning scenario shows the identical key figures broken down by a structure that aggregates the key figures into quarters (see Figure 6.24).

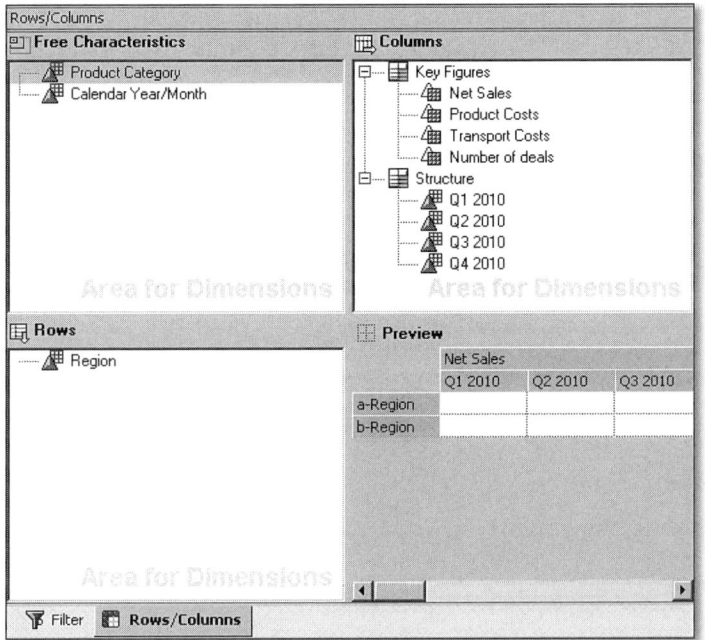

Figure 6.24 Second BEx Query

Overall, our dashboard should show key information, such as the transport costs, product costs, and the revenue of the last 12 months either by region or product category. In addition, we would like to enable the user to see the three measures broken down by region or product group, combined with the capability to simulate a what-if scenario, such as "How would the overall revenue be impacted if the product costs increased by 2%?"

Before we build our dashboard, we need to set up the OLAP connection in the CMC of our SAP BusinessObjects system. You can find the detailed steps in Section 4.3.3 as part of the overall SAP Crystal Reports for Enterprise chapter, but remember that SAP Crystal Reports for Enterprise and SAP BusinessObjects Web Intelligence and SAP BusinessObjects Dashboards are able to share the connections.

6 | Dashboarding and Data Visualization with SAP BusinessObjects Dashboards

We created the necessary BEx queries and OLAP connections, so we can now create our dashboard:

1. Start the SAP BusinessObjects Dashboards Designer by following the menu START • PROGRAMS • DASHBOARDS • DASHBOARDS.
2. Select the menu FILE • NEW • NEW to create an empty model.
3. Use the menu VIEW • QUERY BROWSER to ensure the Query Browser is shown as part of the design environment.
4. In the Query Browser, click on ADD QUERY.
5. You are asked to authenticate your SAP BusinessObjects BI platform system. Log on to the system using your SAP credentials and the SAP authentication.
6. Select the BEx data source option.
7. Click on NEXT.
8. Select the OLAP connection, which you created for the BEx query.
9. Click on NEXT.
10. Select the first BEx query from the list and click on OK.
11. You are presented with the query panel and you can now define the RESULT OBJECTS.
12. Add the REGION dimension and all measures to the RESULT OBJECTS.
13. Use the PROPERTIES button ( ) to open the properties for the query.
14. Enter "Measures by Region" as the NAME for the query.
15. Click on OK.
16. Click on NEXT.
17. In the data preview, click on NEXT.
18. In the connection properties, click on OK.
19. Use the ADD QUERY button ( ) in the QUERY BROWSER to create another query.
20. Select the BEx option.
21. Click on NEXT.
22. Select the OLAP connection, which you created for the BEx query.
23. Click on NEXT.
24. Select the first BEx query from the list and click on OK.

25. You are presented with the query panel and you can now define the Result Objects.
26. Add Product Category and all measures to Result Objects.
27. Use the Properties (📄) button to open the properties for the query.
28. Enter "Measures by Product Category" as the Name for the query
29. Click on OK.
30. Click on Next.
31. In the data preview, click on Next.
32. In the connection properties, click on OK.
33. Use the Add Query button (📄) in the Query Browser to create another query.
34. Select the BEx option.
35. Click on Next.
36. Select the OLAP connection, which you created for the BEx query.
37. Click on Next.
38. Select the first BEx query from the list and click on OK.
39. You are presented with the query panel and you can now define the Result Objects.
40. Add the dimension Calendar Year/Month and all measures to the Result Objects.
41. Use the Properties button (📄) to open the properties for the query.
42. Enter "Measures by Calendar Month Filtered by Region" as the Name for the query.
43. Click on OK.
44. Drag and drop the Region dimension to the Filters area.
45. Set the operator to Equal to.
46. Select the Prompt option.
47. Configure the prompt to be an optional prompt.
48. Click on OK.
49. Click on Next. The prompt is optional, so we don't need to provide a value at this point in time.

50. Click on RUN.
51. In the data preview, click on NEXT.
52. In the connection properties, click on OK.
53. Use the ADD QUERY button ( ) in the QUERY BROWSER to create another query.
54. Select the option BEx.
55. Click on NEXT.
56. Select the OLAP connection, which you created for the BEx query.
57. Click on NEXT.
58. Select the first BEx query from the list and click on OK.
59. You are presented with the query panel and you can now define the RESULT OBJECTS.
60. Add CALENDAR YEAR/MONTH and all measures to RESULT OBJECTS.
61. Use the PROPERTIES button ( ) to open the properties for the query.
62. Enter "Measures by Calendar Month Filtered by Product Category" as the NAME for the query.
63. Click on OK.
64. Drag and drop PRODUCT CATEGORY to the FILTERS area.
65. Set the operator to EQUAL TO.
66. Select the PROMPT option.
67. Configure the prompt to be an optional prompt.
68. Click on OK.
69. Click on NEXT. The prompt is optional, so we don't need to provide a value at this point in time.
70. Click on RUN.
71. In the data preview, click on NEXT.
72. In the connection properties, click on OK.
73. Drag and drop a TAB SET component from the CONTAINERS category to your canvas and resize it so that it uses all of the canvas space.
74. Select the first tab. To select the tab, do not click on the actual tab but instead click on the empty area below the selected tab.

75. Use a right-click and open PROPERTIES.
76. Enter "Sales Revenue" into the LABEL property.
77. Select the TAB SET component and use the "+" symbol to add a second tab.
78. Enter "Sales Planning" as the LABEL for the tab.
79. Drag and drop a RADIO BUTTON component from the SELECTORS category to the top left of the first tab.
80. Right-click on the new RADIO BUTTON component and select PROPERTIES.
81. Click on the SELECT A RANGE button ([icon]) next to LABELS and select cells B1 to B2 in the embedded spreadsheet.
82. Click on OK.
83. Set the INSERTION TYPE to VALUE option.
84. Click on the SELECT A RANGE button ([icon]) next to SOURCE DATA and select cell A1 to A2 in the embedded spreadsheet.
85. Click on the SELECT A RANGE ([icon]) button next to DESTINATION and select cell D1 the embedded spreadsheet.
86. Set the option ORIENTATION to HORIZONTAL.
87. Enter the value 1 into cell A1.
88. Enter the value 2 into cell A2.
89. Enter the text "by Product Category" into cell B1.
90. Enter the text "by Region" into cell B2.
91. Drag and drop a line chart to the first tab and size it so that it uses the complete width but about half of the height from the tab set.
92. Right-click on the line chart and select PROPERTIES.
93. Enter "Sales Revenue" as the title for the chart and remove the subtitle.
94. Right-click on the line chart and open PROPERTIES.
95. Select the GENERAL area.
96. Select the BY SERIES option for the DATA.
97. Use the "+" symbol to add a new series.
98. Enter the text "Sales Revenue" as the NAME for the series.
99. Use the small arrow from the SELECT A RANGE button ([icon]) next to VALUES (Y) to open the list and select the QUERY DATA option.

100. Select Measures by Calendar Month filtered by Region.
101. Select Net Sales (see Figure 6.25).

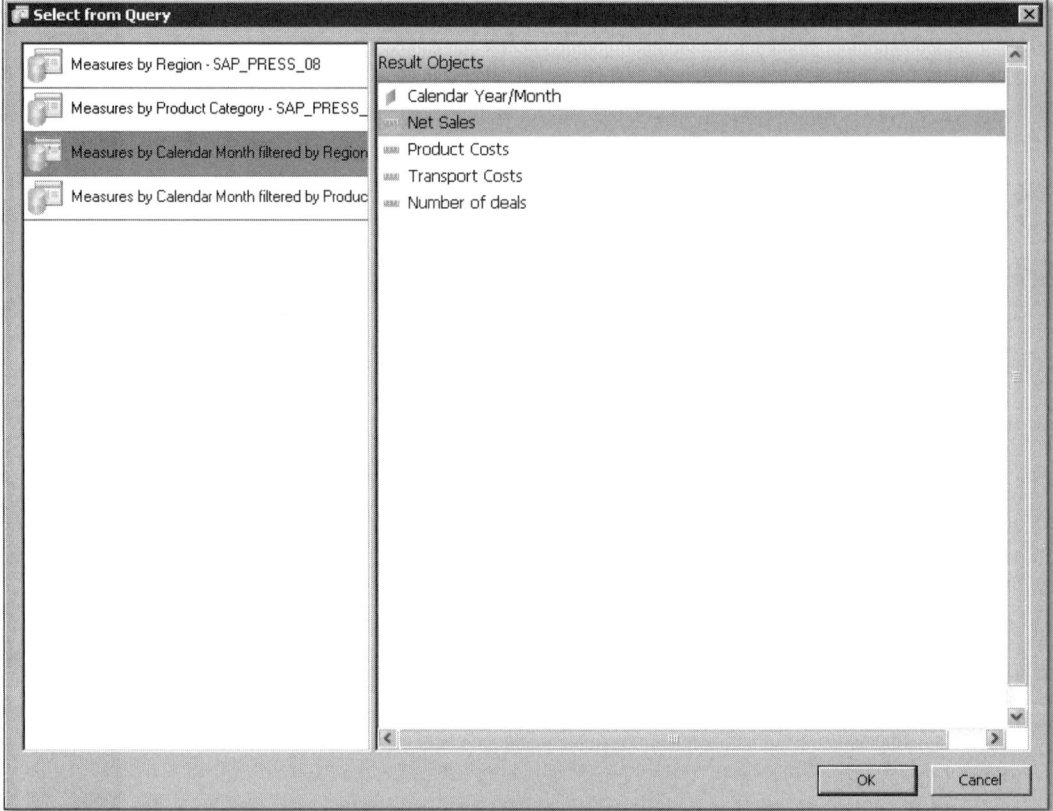

Figure 6.25 Select from Query

102. Click on OK.
103. Use the small arrow from the Select a Range button (▣) next to Category Labels (X) to open the list and select the Query Data option.
104. Select Measures by Calendar Month filtered by Region.
105. Select Calendar Year/Month.
106. Click on OK.
107. Navigate to the Common tab in the Behavior area.

108. Click on the SELECT A RANGE button (📋) next to STATUS FOR DYNAMIC VISIBILITY and select cell D1.
109. Click on OK.
110. Enter the value 2 for the key. The chart just created is shown only when the user selects the option BY REGION.
111. Drag and drop a COMBO BOX from the SELECTORS to the first tab next to the RADIO BUTTONS.
112. Use the small arrow from the SELECT A RANGE button (📋) next to LABELS and select the QUERY DATA option.
113. Select MEASURES BY REGION.
114. Select REGION.
115. Click on OK.
116. Set the INSERTION TYPE to LABEL.
117. Click on the SELECT A RANGE button (📋) next to DESTINATION and select cell E1 from the embedded spreadsheet.
118. Click on OK.
119. Navigate to the COMMON area in BEHAVIOR.
120. Click on the SELECT A RANGE button (📋) next to STATUS FOR DYNAMIC VISIBILITY and select cell D1.
121. Click on OK.
122. Enter the value 2 for the key. The combo box just created is shown only when the user selects the BY REGION option.
123. Select MEASURES BY CALENDAR MONTH FILTERED BY REGION in the Query Browser.
124. Click on the EDIT button (✏️) to change the query (see Figure 6.26).
125. Click on NEXT.
126. You are prompted for a value. Click on RUN. The prompt is optional, so we don't need to enter a value right now.
127. Click on NEXT.
128. Click on the SELECT A RANGE (📋) button next to TRIGGER CELL.
129. Select cell E1.
130. Click on OK.

6 | Dashboarding and Data Visualization with SAP BusinessObjects Dashboards

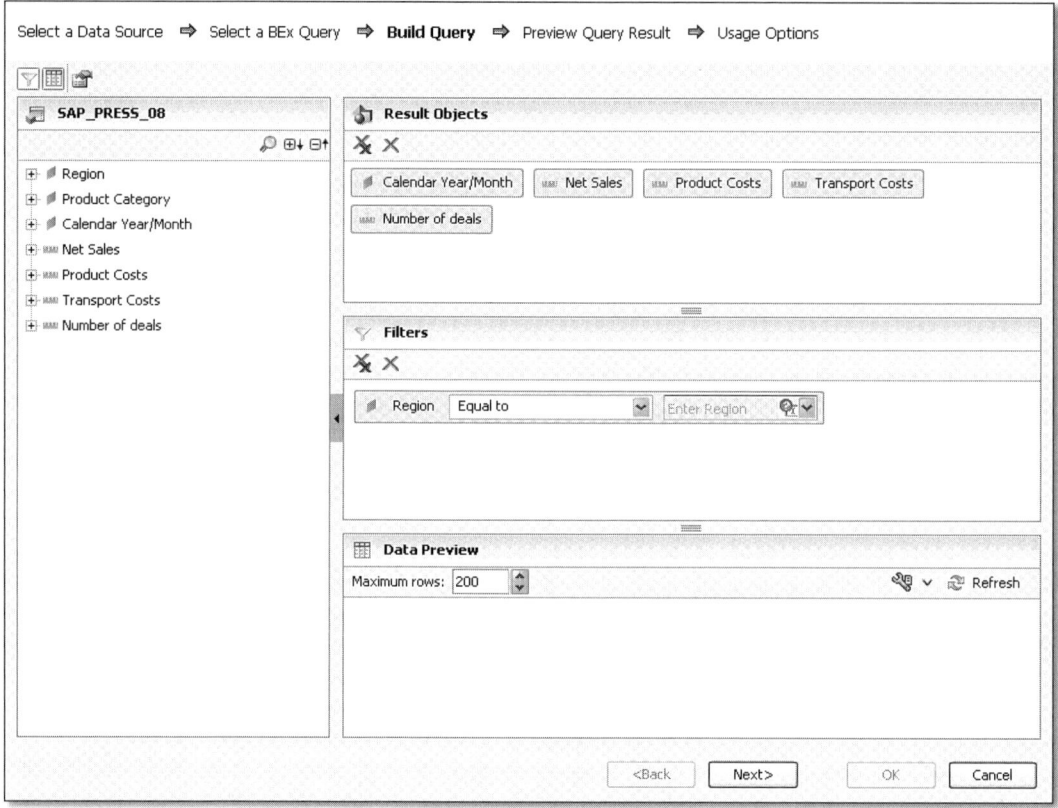

Figure 6.26 Edit Query

131. Ensure the option WHEN VALUE CHANGES is activated.
132. Click on OK.
133. Select the query MEASURES BY CALENDAR MONTH FILTERED BY REGION in the Query Browser.
134. Select the prompt in the list.
135. Click on CONNECT TO SPREADSHEET.
136. Click on the SELECT A RANGE button () next to SELECTED VALUES and select cell E1 from the embedded spreadsheet.
137. Click on OK.
138. Drag and drop a COMBO BOX from the SELECTORS to the first tab next to the RADIO BUTTONS so that it overlaps with the first combo box.

139. Use the small arrow from the SELECT A RANGE ( ) button next to LABELS and select the QUERY DATA option.
140. Select MEASURES BY PRODUCT CATEGORY.
141. Select PRODUCT CATEGORY.
142. Click on OK.
143. Set the INSERTION TYPE to LABEL.
144. Click on the SELECT A RANGE button ( ) next to DESTINATION and select cell F1 from the embedded spreadsheet.
145. Click on OK.
146. Navigate to the COMMON area in BEHAVIOR.
147. Click on the SELECT A RANGE ( ) button next to STATUS FOR DYNAMIC VISBILIY and select cell D1.
148. Click on OK.
149. Enter the value 1 for the key. The combo box just created is shown only when the user selects the option BY PRODUCT CATEGORY.
150. Select MEASURES BY CALENDAR MONTH FILTERED BY PRODUCT CATEGORY in the Query Browser.
151. Click on the EDIT ( ) button to change the query.
152. Click on NEXT.
153. You are prompted for a value. Click on RUN. The prompt is optional, so we don't need to enter a value right now.
154. Click on NEXT.
155. Click on the SELECT A RANGE ( ) button next to TRIGGER CELL.
156. Select cell F1 from the embedded spreadsheet.
157. Click on OK.
158. Ensure that the option WHEN VALUE CHANGES is activated.
159. Click on OK.
160. Select MEASURES BY CALENDAR MONTH FILTERED BY PRODUCT CATEGORY in the Query Browser.
161. Select the prompt in the list.
162. Click on CONNECT TO SPREADSHEET.

163. Click on the SELECT A RANGE (▣) button next to SELECTED VALUES and select cell F1 from the embedded spreadsheet.
164. Click on OK.
165. Drag and drop a second line chart into the first tab and size it so that it overlaps with the first line chart.
166. Right-click on the line chart and select PROPERTIES.
167. Enter SALES REVENUE as the title and remove the subtitle.
168. Select the GENERAL area.
169. Select the BY SERIES option for the DATA.
170. Use the "+" symbol to add a new series.
171. Enter the text "Sales Revenue" as the NAME for the series.
172. Use the small arrow from the SELECT A RANGE button (▣) next to VALUES (Y) to open the list and select the QUERY DATA option.
173. Select MEASURES BY CALENDAR MONTH FILTERED BY PRODUCT CATEGORY.
174. Select NET SALES.
175. Click on OK.
176. Use the small arrow from the SELECT A RANGE button (▣) next to CATEGORY LABELS (X) to open the list and select the QUERY DATA option.
177. Select MEASURES BY CALENDAR MONTH FILTERED BY PRODUCT CATEGORY.
178. Select CALENDAR YEAR/MONTH.
179. Click on OK.
180. Navigate to the COMMON tab in the BEHAVIOR area.
181. Click on the SELECT A RANGE button (▣) next to STATUS FOR DYNAMIC VISIBILITY and select cell D1.
182. Click on OK.
183. Enter the value 1 for the key. The chart just created is shown only when the user selects the BY PRODUCT CATEGORY option.
184. Drag and drop a PIE CHART in the first tab and size it so that it covers the lower left area below the line chart and half of the width.
185. Right-click on the PIE CHART and select PROPERTIES.
186. Enter "Revenue Mix by Region" as the title and remove the subtitle.

187. Select the Data in Columns option.
188. Use the small arrow from the Select a Range button (■) next to Values to open the list and select the Query Data option.
189. Select Measures by Region.
190. Select Net Sales.
191. Click on OK.
192. Use the small arrow from the Select a Range button (■) next to Labels to open the list and select the Query Data option.
193. Select Measures by Region.
194. Select Region.
195. Click on OK.
196. Navigate to the Common tab in the Behavior area.
197. Click on the Select a Range button (■) next to Status for Dynamic Visibility and select cell D1.
198. Click on OK.
199. Enter the value 2 for the key. The chart just created is shown only when the user selects the by Region option.
200. Drag and drop a Pie Chart into the first tab so that it overlaps with the first pie chart.
201. Right-click on the Pie Chart and select Properties.
202. Enter "Revenue Mix by Product Category" as the title and remove the subtitle.
203. Select the Data in Columns option.
204. Use the small arrow from the Select a Range (■) button next to Values to open the list and select the Query Data option.
205. Select Measures by Product Category.
206. Select Net Sales.
207. Click on OK.
208. Use the small arrow from the Select a Range button (■) next to Labels to open the list and select the Query Data option.
209. Select Measures by Product Category.
210. Select Product Category.

211. Click on OK.
212. Navigate to the COMMON tab in the BEHAVIOR area.
213. Click on the SELECT A RANGE ( ) button next to STATUS FOR DYNAMIC VISIBILITY and select cell D1.
214. Click on OK.
215. Enter the value 1 for the key. The chart just created is shown only when the user selects the option BY PRODUCT CATEGORY.

You should now have a dashboard that lets you switch from a view of the data by product category to a view by region. In addition, it lets you filter the top chart for a single region or product category. Next, we'll add a pie chart for cost distribution and then build the planning section.

1. Drag and drop a pie chart into the first tab and size it so that it covers the lower right area below the line chart and half of the width.
2. Right-click on the pie chart and select PROPERTIES.
3. Enter "Transport Cost Mix by Region" as the title and remove the subtitle.
4. Select the DATA IN COLUMNS option.
5. Use the small arrow from the SELECT A RANGE button ( ) next to VALUES to open the list and select the QUERY DATA option.
6. Select MEASURES BY REGION.
7. Select TRANSPORT COSTS.
8. Click on OK.
9. Use the small arrow from the SELECT A RANGE button ( ) next to LABELS to open the list and select the QUERY DATA option.
10. Select MEASURES BY REGION.
11. Select REGION.
12. Click on OK.
13. Navigate to the COMMON tab in the BEHAVIOR area.
14. Click on the SELECT A RANGE button ( ) next to STATUS FOR DYNAMIC VISIBILITY and select cell D1.
15. Click on OK.

16. Enter the value 2 for the key. The chart just created is shown only when the user selects the REGION option.
17. Drag and drop a pie chart into the first tab so that it overlaps with the previous pie chart.
18. Right-click on the pie chart and select PROPERTIES.
19. Enter "Transport Cost Mix by Product Category" as the title and remove the subtitle.
20. Select the DATA IN COLUMNS option.
21. Use the small arrow from the SELECT A RANGE button (▥) next to VALUES to open the list and select the QUERY DATA option.
22. Select MEASURES BY PRODUCT CATEGORY.
23. Select TRANSPORT COSTS.
24. Click on OK.
25. Use the small arrow from the SELECT A RANGE button (▥) next to LABELS to open the list and select the QUERY DATA option.
26. Select MEASURES BY PRODUCT CATEGORY.
27. Select PRODUCT CATEGORY.
28. Click on OK.
29. Navigate to the COMMON tab in the BEHAVIOR area.
30. Click the SELECT A RANGE (▥) button next to STATUS FOR DYNAMIC VISIBILITY and select cell D1.
31. Click on OK.
32. Enter the value 1 for the key. The chart just created is shown only when the user selects the option by PRODUCT CATEGORY.
33. Select the menu FILE • SAVE TO PLATFORM.
34. Log on to your SAP BusinessObjects BI platform.
35. Select a folder and enter a name for your dashboard.
36. Click on SAVE.
37. Select the menu FILE • PREVIEW.

Your dashboard should now look like Figure 6.27. Now we add the what-if analysis to our second tab.

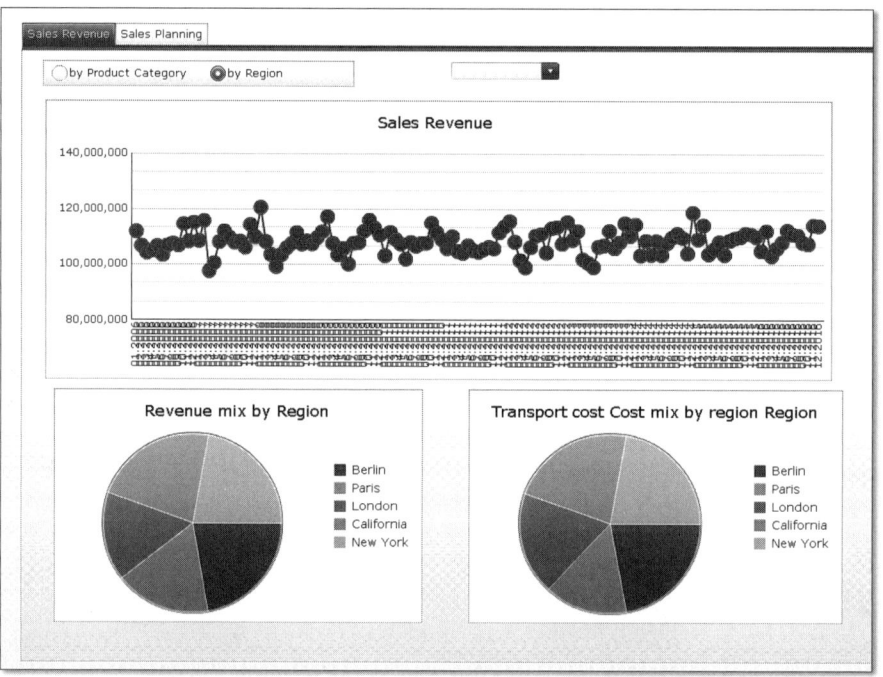

Figure 6.27 Dashboard Preview

Given that we cannot add new objects to the query panel (for example, in our case the need to calculate forecasted measures) and given that we cannot arrange the objects from the query in form of a cross tab, we have to use an alternate method to provide SAP BusinessObjects Dashboards with the necessary data. In this case, we could use SAP BusinessObjects Live Office or BI Web Services, as both would be able to provide us the data and both would allow us to arrange the necessary information in the form of a cross tab. For our example, we will use SAP BusinessObjects Live Office, but you can achieve the same results using BI Web Services.

You might think that we could have simply put the necessary objects into the underlying BEx query. However, if we did this, we could not arrange the data in the form of a cross tab, which would have made it impossible to show the information as we need it.

1. Start the BI launch pad by following the menu START • PROGRAMS • SAP BUSINESSOBJECTS BI PLATFORM 4 • SAP BUSINESSOBJECTS BI PLATFORM • SAP BUSINESSOBJECTS BI PLATFORM JAVA BI LAUNCH PAD.

2. Log on to the BI launch pad with your SAP credentials using SAP authentication.
3. Select the menu APPLICATIONS • WEB INTELLIGENCE APPLICATION.
4. Use the NEW REPORT button (□) to start creating a new report.
5. Select the BEx option.
6. Click on OK.
7. Select the connection you configured for the BEx query.
8. Select the second BEx query for our report from the list.
9. Click on OK.
10. Add REGION to RESULT OBJECTS.
11. Add the structure for the quarters to RESULT OBJECTS.
12. Add NET SALES, PRODUCT COSTS, and TRANSPORT COSTS to RESULT OBJECTS.
13. Click on RUN QUERY.
14. Select the table in the report.
15. Navigate to the REPORT ELEMENT tab.
16. Navigate to the TOOLS tab.
17. Select the menu TURN INTO • MORE TRANSFORMATIONS (SEE Figure 6.28).

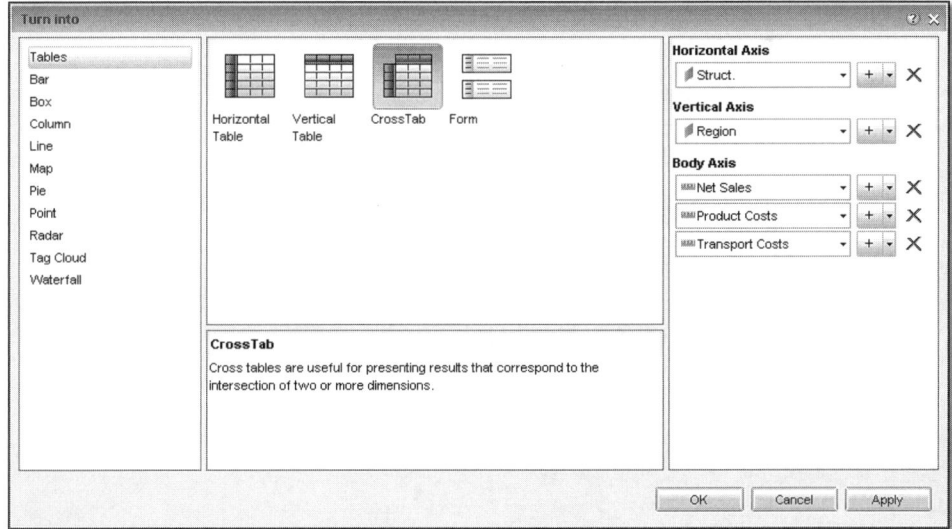

Figure 6.28 Transformations

18. Select the CROSS TAB option.
19. Select the STRUCTURE for the HORIZONTAL AXIS.
20. Set the REGION for the VERTICAL AXIS.
21. Set the measures to the BODY AXIS.
22. Click on OK.
23. Save the SAP BusinessObjects Web Intelligence report to your SAP BusinessObjects BI platform.
24. Close SAP BusinessObjects Web Intelligence.
25. Make sure that the SAP BusinessObjects Live Office compatibility mode is enabled for the SAP BusinessObjects Dashboards Designer. You can configure the option in the menu FILE • PREFERENCES.
26. After you activate the SAP BusinessObjects Live Office compatibility mode, go back to your existing SAP BusinessObjects Dashboard model.
27. In the embedded spreadsheet, add another sheet.
28. Navigate to the new sheet.
29. Select the APPLICATION OPTIONS menu item in the Live Office ribbon.
30. Navigate to the ENTERPRISE tab (see Figure 6.29).

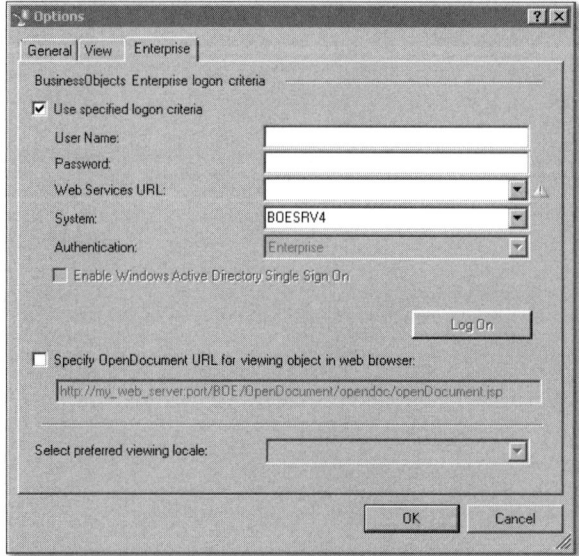

Figure 6.29 SAP BusinessObjects Live Office Application Options

31. Enter the Web Service URL for your SAP BusinessObjects system following the syntax:

    http://<application server>:<port>/dswsbobje/services/session

    Replace the *<application server>* placeholder with the name of your application server for the SAP BusinessObjects system and replace the placeholder *<port>* with the port number.

32. Set the AUTHENTICATION to the value SAP.
33. Enter your SAP credentials.
34. Enter the password.
35. Click on OK.
36. Navigate to the INSERT WEB INTELLIGENCE menu option in the Live Office ribbon (see Figure 6.30).

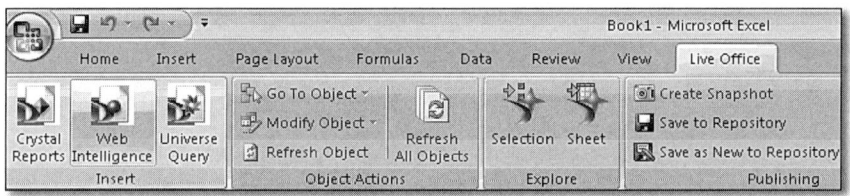

Figure 6.30 Live Office Ribbon

37. Select the previously saved SAP BusinessObjects Web Intelligence report.
38. Click on NEXT (SEE Figure 6.31).
39. Select the cross tab in the SAP BusinessObjects Web Intelligence report.
40. Click on NEXT.
41. Click on FINISH.
42. Select the menu DATA • CONNECTIONS.
43. Click on ADD.
44. Select LIVE OFFICE CONNECTIONS (see Figure 6.32).
45. Replace the placeholder *<webserver>* in the session URL with the name of your application server.
46. Click on CLOSE.

6 | Dashboarding and Data Visualization with SAP BusinessObjects Dashboards

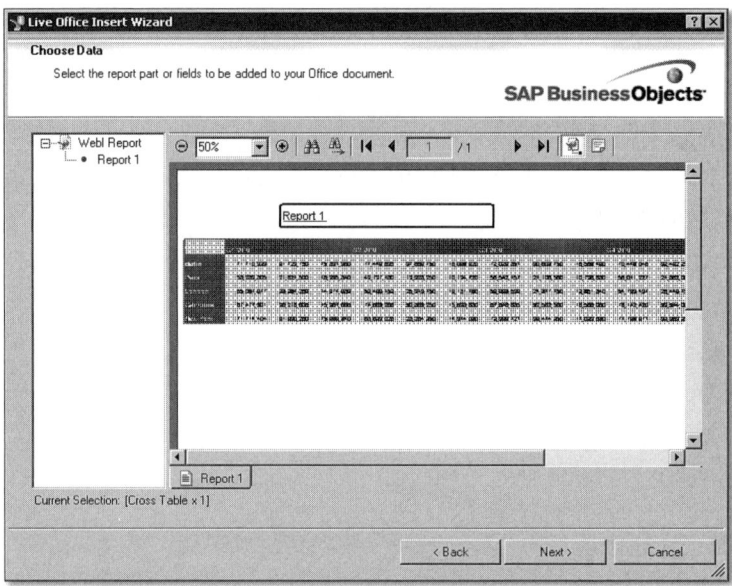

Figure 6.31 SAP BusinessObjects Live Office Wizard

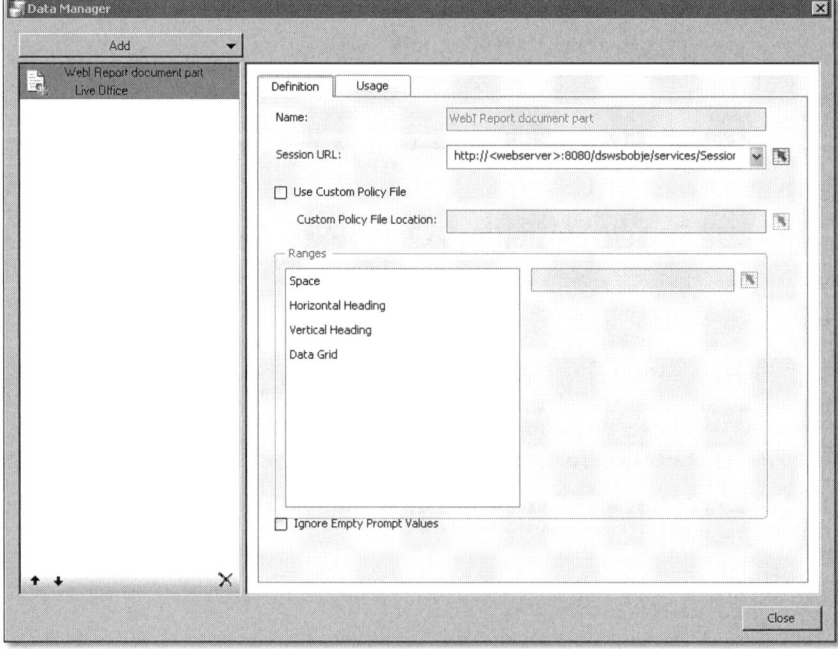

Figure 6.32 SAP BusinessObjects Live Office Connection

6.4 Building a Dashboard for Sales Planning

In our planning scenario we want to provide our users the capability to retrieve the current values and the option to leverage interactive slides to influence the current numbers as part of the overall dashboard. Therefore, we will create an additional sheet where we will use Microsoft Excel formulas to calculate those numbers.

1. Navigate to the new sheet showing the data from the SAP BusinessObjects Live Office document.
2. Select cell O2 in the spreadsheet. Enter the following formula:

    =B2*(1+Sheet1!$B$6)

    You will notice that the formula also points to cell B6 in the first sheet of the embedded spreadsheet, which we will use to configure later on the increase in percentages.
3. Copy and paste the formula to fill the column.
4. Select cell P2 in the spreadsheet. Enter the following formula:

    =E2*(1+Sheet1!$B$6).
5. Copy and paste the formula to fill the column.
6. Select cell Q2 in the spreadsheet. Enter the following formula:

    =H2*(1+Sheet1!$B$6).
7. Copy and paste the formula to fill the column.
8. Select cell R2 in the spreadsheet. Enter the following formula:

    =K2*(1+Sheet1!$B$6)
9. Copy and paste the formula to fill the column.

Based on the structure of our cross tab, columns B, E, H, and F show the net sales measure. We have created four columns showing the net sales number increased by the percentage value, which the user will be able to configure. We will now do the same for the product costs and transport costs.

1. Select cell T2 in the spreadsheet. Enter the following formula:

    =C2*(1+Sheet1!$B$7).
2. Copy and paste the formula to fill the column.
3. Select cell U2 in the spreadsheet. Enter the following formula:

    =F2*(1+Sheet1!$B$7)

4. Copy and paste the formula to fill the column.
5. Select cell V2 in the spreadsheet. Enter the following formula:
   =I2*(1+Sheet1!$B$7).
6. Copy and paste the formula to fill the column.
7. Select cell W2 in the spreadsheet. Enter the following formula:
   =L2*(1+Sheet1!$B$7).
8. Copy and paste the formula to fill the column.
9. Select cell Y2 in the spreadsheet. Enter the following formula:
   =D2*(1+Sheet1!$B$8)
10. Copy and paste the formula to fill the column.
11. Select cell Z2 in the spreadsheet. Enter the following formula:
    =G2*(1+Sheet1!$B$8).
12. Copy and paste the formula to fill the column.
13. Select cell AA2 in the spreadsheet. Enter the following formula:
    =J2*(1+Sheet1!$B$8).
14. Copy and paste the formula to fill the column.
15. Select cell AB2 in the spreadsheet. Enter the following formula:
    =M2*(1+Sheet1!$B$8)
16. Copy and paste the formula to fill the column.
17. Enter the following into SHEET1 of the embedded spreadsheet:
    - Cell A6: Net Sales Forecast
    - Cell B6: 0.01
    - Cell A7: Product Cost Increase
    - Cell B7: 0.01
    - Cell A8: Transport Cost Increase
    - Cell B8: 0.01

We use Microsoft Excel functions in our embedded spreadsheet so we can use percentage values and increase or decrease the numbers in our SAP BusinessObjects Dashboards dashboard. Now we can add the necessary components to our canvas.

1. Drag and drop a BAR CHART to the SALES PLANNING tab and place it in the top-left corner.
2. Right-click on the new chart and open PROPERTIES.
3. Enter "Net Sales by Quarter" as the title and remove the subtitle.
4. Select the GENERAL area.
5. Select the BY SERIES option for the DATA.
6. Use the "+" symbol to add a new series.
7. Enter Q1 as the NAME of the series.
8. Click on the SELECT A RANGE button ( ) next to VALUES (X).
9. Select the range O2 to O50 in the second sheet of the embedded spreadsheet.
10. Click on OK.
11. Click on the SELECT A RANGE button ( ) next to CATEGORY LABELS (Y).
12. Select the range A2 to A50 in the second sheet of the embedded spreadsheet.
13. Click on OK.
14. Use the "+" symbol to add a new series.
15. Enter Q2 as the NAME of the series.
16. Click on the SELECT A RANGE button ( ) next to VALUES (X).
17. Select the range P2 to P50 in the second sheet of the embedded spreadsheet.
18. Click on OK.
19. Use the "+" symbol to add a new series.
20. Enter Q3 as the NAME of the series.
21. Click on the SELECT A RANGE button ( ) next to VALUES (X).
22. Select the range Q2 to Q50 in the second sheet of the embedded spreadsheet.
23. Click on OK.
24. Use the "+" symbol to add a new series.
25. Enter Q4 as the NAME of the series.
26. Click on the SELECT A RANGE button ( ) next to VALUES (X).
27. Select the range R2 to R50 in the second sheet of the embedded spreadsheet.
28. Click on OK.
29. Navigate to the BEHAVIOR tab and activate the IN SERIES and IN VALUES options.

30. Select the Common tab and activate the Fixed Label Size option.
31. Drag and drop a Bar Chart into the Sales Planning tab and place it in the top-right corner.
32. Right-click on the new chart and open Properties.
33. Enter "Transport Costs by Quarter" as the title and remove the subtitle.
34. Select the General area.
35. Select the by Series option for the Data.
36. Use the "+" symbol to add a new series.
37. Enter Q1 as the name of the series.
38. Click on the Select a Range button ([icon]) next to Values (X).
39. Select the range Y2 to Y50 in the second sheet of the embedded spreadsheet.
40. Click on OK.
41. Click on the Select a Range button ([icon]) next to Category Labels (Y).
42. Select the range A2 to A50 in the second sheet of the embedded spreadsheet.
43. Click on OK.
44. Use the "+" symbol to add a new series.
45. Enter Q2 as the name of the series.
46. Click on the Select a Range button ([icon]) next to Values (X).
47. Select the range Z2 to Z50 in the second sheet of the embedded spreadsheet.
48. Click on OK.
49. Use the "+" symbol to add a new series.
50. Enter Q3 as the name of the series.
51. Click on the Select a Range button ([icon]) next to Values (X).
52. Select the range AA2 to AA50 in the second sheet of the embedded spreadsheet.
53. Click on OK.
54. Use the "+" symbol to add a new series.
55. Enter Q4 as the name of the series.
56. Click on the Select a Range button ([icon]) next to Values (X).
57. Select the range AB2 to AB50 in the second sheet of the embedded spreadsheet.

58. Click on OK.
59. Navigate to the BEHAVIOR tab and activate the IN SERIES and IN VALUES options.
60. Select the COMMON tab and activate the FIXED LABEL SIZE option.
61. Drag and drop a BAR CHART into the SALES PLANNING tab and place it in the bottom-right corner.
62. Right-click on the new chart and open PROPERTIES.
63. Enter "Product Costs by Quarter" as the title and remove the subtitle.
64. Select the GENERAL area.
65. Select the BY SERIES option for the DATA.
66. Use the "+" symbol to add a new series.
67. Enter Q1 as the NAME of the series.
68. Click on the SELECT A RANGE () button next to VALUES (X).
69. Select the range T2 to T50 in the second sheet of the embedded spreadsheet.
70. Click on OK.
71. Click on the SELECT A RANGE button () next to CATEGORY LABELS (Y).
72. Select the range A2 to A50 in the second sheet of the embedded spreadsheet.
73. Click on OK.
74. Use the "+" symbol to add a new series.
75. Enter Q2 as the NAME of the series.
76. Click on the SELECT A RANGE button () next to VALUES (X).
77. Select the range U2 to U50 in the second sheet of the embedded spreadsheet.
78. Click on OK.
79. Use the "+" symbol to add a new series.
80. Enter Q3 as the NAME of the series.
81. Click on the SELECT A RANGE button () next to VALUES (X).
82. Select the range V2 to V50 in the second sheet of the embedded spreadsheet.
83. Click on OK.
84. Use the "+" symbol to add a new series.
85. Enter Q4 as the NAME of the series.
86. Click on the SELECT A RANGE button () next to VALUES (X).

87. Select the range W2 to W50 in the second sheet of the embedded spreadsheet.
88. Click on OK.
89. Navigate to the BEHAVIOR tab and activate the IN SERIES and IN VALUES options.
90. Select the COMMON tab and activate the FIXED LABEL SIZE option.
91. Follow the VIEW • COMPONENTS menu path.
92. Drag and drop a HORIZONTAL SLIDER from the SINGLE VALUE area to the bottom-left area of the SALES PLANNING tab.
93. Right-click on the new slider and open PROPERTIES.
94. Enter "Sales Forecast Increase" as the title.
95. Click on the SELECT A RANGE button (▣) next to DATA and select cell B6 in the first sheet of the embedded spreadsheet.
96. Set the MAXIMUM LIMIT to 0.5.
97. Select the BEHAVIOR area and set the value for the INCREMENT to 0.025.
98. Select the APPEARANCE area and select the TEXT tab. Select VALUE in the list.
99. Set the NUMBER FORMAT to the value PERCENT and set the number of DECIMAL PLACES to 0.
100. Drag and drop an additional HORIZONTAL SLIDER from the SINGLE VALUE area to the bottom-left area of the SALES PLANNING tab.
101. Right-click on the new slider and open PROPERTIES.
102. Enter "Product Cost Increase" as the title.
103. Click on the SELECT A RANGE (▣) button next to DATA and select cell B7 in the first sheet of the embedded spreadsheet.
104. Set the MAXIMUM LIMIT to 0.5.
105. Select the BEHAVIOR area and set the value for the INCREMENT to 0.025.
106. Select the APPEARANCE area and select the TEXT tab. Select the entry VALUE in the list.
107. Set the NUMBER FORMAT to PERCENT and set the number of DECIMAL PLACES to 0.
108. Drag and drop an additional HORIZONTAL SLIDER from the SINGLE VALUE area to the bottom-left area of the SALES PLANNING tab.
109. Right-click on the new slider and open PROPERTIES.

110. Enter "Transport Cost Increase" as the title.
111. Click on the SELECT A RANGE ( ) button next to DATA and select cell B8 in the first sheet of the embedded spreadsheet.
112. Set the MAXIMUM LIMIT to 0.5.
113. Select the BEHAVIOR area and set the value for the INCREMENT to 0.025.
114. Select the APPEARANCE area and select the TEXT tab. Select VALUE in the list.
115. Set the NUMBER FORMAT to PERCENT and set the number of DECIMAL PLACES to 0.
116. Select the menu FILE • SAVE TO PLATFORM.
117. Select a folder and enter a name.
118. Click on SAVE.
119. Select the menu FILE • PREVIEW.

You have just created a dashboard (see Figure 6.33) that allows you to increase or decrease specific numbers and to see the impact on your business right away. Remember: this dashboard only displays the information; it does not write any information back to SAP NetWeaver BW.

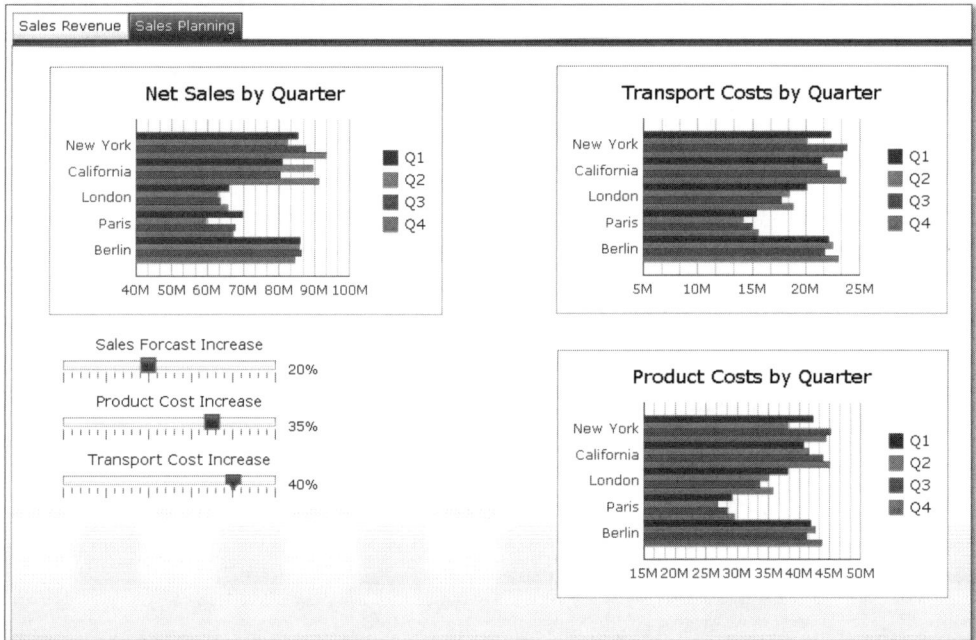

Figure 6.33 SAP BusinessObjects Dashboard

6.5 Summary

In this chapter, you learned how to use SAP BusinessObjects Dashboards for your data visualizations needs. You also received an overview of the data connectivity options of SAP BusinessObjects Dashboards as part of your overall SAP landscape. You then reviewed the requirements against the capabilities of SAP BusinessObjects Dashboards as a data visualization and dashboarding tool, and used SAP BusinessObjects Dashboards to fulfill those requirements and to create compelling dashboards.

SAP BusinessObjects Analysis, edition for Microsoft Office is the premium successor to BEx Analyzer.

7   Using SAP BusinessObjects Analysis, Edition for Microsoft Office

In this chapter, you will learn how SAP BusinessObjects Analysis, edition for Microsoft Office can help you fulfill the need for a user experience offering a rich Online Analytical Processing (OLAP) type of reporting client. We will discuss the data connectivity options, as well as how the product can be used to fulfill user requirements.

7.1   SAP Data Connectivity

In this section we address the options for connecting SAP BusinessObjects Analysis, edition for Microsoft Office to your SAP data source. SAP BusinessObjects Analysis, edition for Microsoft Office can be used in combination with your SAP BusinessObjects BI platform. In regard to data connectivity, as shown in Figure 7.1, SAP BusinessObjects Analysis, edition for Microsoft Office is able:

- To use a direct access method via BI Consumer Services (BICS) to connect to BEx queries and InfoProviders in your SAP NetWeaver BW system.

- To use a direct access method via BICS to connect to BEx queries based on transient providers in the SAP ERP system. The transient provider requires SAP ECC 6.0 enhancement package 5.

- To use the shared connections from SAP BusinessObjects and the direct access method via BICS to connect to the BEx queries and InfoProvider in SAP NetWeaver BW, as well as to the BEx queries combined with the transient provider.

- To establish a direct link to SAP HANA.

7 Using SAP BusinessObjects Analysis, Edition for Microsoft Office

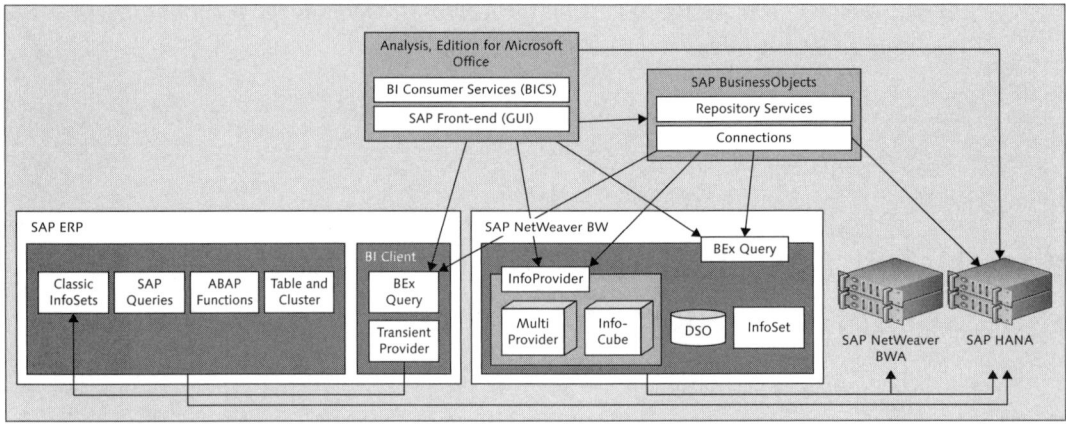

Figure 7.1 Data Connectivity

As you will notice, SAP BusinessObjects Analysis, edition for Microsoft Office does not have an integration with the semantic layer, nor does it have direct connectivity to your SAP ERP system. So far, the available version of SAP BusinessObjects Analysis, edition for Microsoft Office focuses on the integration with SAP NetWeaver BW and SAP HANA.

Table 7.1 shows which objects are supported when using SAP BusinessObjects Analysis, edition for Microsoft Office as a BI client tool.

	Direct Access using BICS
Direct access to InfoCube and MultiProvider	Yes
Access to BEx queries	Yes
Characteristic Values	
Key	Yes
Short description	Yes
Medium and long description	Yes
BEx Query Features	
Support for hierarchies	Yes
Support for free characteristics	Yes

Table 7.1 Supported and Unsupported BEx Query Features for SAP BusinessObjects Analysis, Edition for Microsoft Office

	Direct Access using BICS
Support for calculated and restricted key figures	Yes
Support for currencies and units	Yes
Support for custom structures	Yes
Support for formulas and selections	Yes
Support for filter	Yes
Support for display and navigational attributes	Yes
Support for conditions in rows	Yes
Support for conditions in columns	Yes
Support for conditions for fixed characteristics	Yes
Support for exceptions	Yes
Compounded characteristics	Yes
Constant selection	Yes
Default values in BEx query	Yes
Number scaling factor	Yes
Number of decimals	Yes
Calculate rows as (local calculation)	Yes
Sorting	Yes
Hide/unhide	Yes
Display as hierarchy	Yes
Reverse sign	Yes
Support for reading master data	Yes
Data Types	
Support for CHAR (characteristics)	Yes
Support for NUMC (characteristics)	Yes
Support for DATS (characteristics)	Yes

Table 7.1 Supported and Unsupported BEx Query Features for SAP BusinessObjects Analysis, Edition for Microsoft Office (Cont.)

	Direct Access using BICS
Support for TIMS (characteristics)	Yes
Support for numeric key figures such as Amount and Quantity	Yes
Support for type Date (key figures)	Yes
Support for type Time (key figures)	Yes
SAP Variables—Processing Type	
User input	Yes
Authorization	Yes
Replacement path	Yes
SAP exit/custom exit	Yes
Precalculated value set	Yes
General Features for Variables	
Support for optional and mandatory variables	Yes
Support for key date dependencies	Yes
Support for default values	Yes
Support for personalized values	No
SAP Variables—Variable Type	
Single value	Yes
Multi-single value	Yes
Interval value	Yes
Selection option	Yes
Hierarchy variable	Yes
Hierarchy node variable	Yes
Hierarchy version variable	Yes
Text variable	Yes

Table 7.1 Supported and Unsupported BEx Query Features for SAP BusinessObjects Analysis, Edition for Microsoft Office (Cont.)

	Direct Access using BICS
EXIT variable	Yes
Single key date variable	Yes
Multiple key dates	Yes
Formula variable	Yes

Table 7.1 Supported and Unsupported BEx Query Features for SAP BusinessObjects Analysis, Edition for Microsoft Office (Cont.)

Table 7.2 shows how the direct access method using the BICS option uses the elements from the BEx query and how the objects are mapped to the navigation panel for SAP BusinessObjects Analysis, edition for Microsoft Office.

BEx Query Element	SAP BusinessObjects Analysis, Edition for Microsoft Office
Characteristic	For each characteristic you receive a field and with the menu members you can decide which part of the characteristic is shown as part of the overall result.
Hierarchy	Each available hierarchy is shown as an external hierarchy and can be used as part of the cross tab. In addition, you can use hierarchy levels as part of your cross tab; for example, you can show all members of Level 2 of the hierarchy.
Key figure	Each key figure is shown with the unit and scaling factor information.
Calculated/restricted key figure	Each calculated and restricted key figure is treated like a key figure. The user does not have access to the underlying definition in SAP BusinessObjects Analysis, edition for Microsoft Office.
Filters	Filters are applied to the underlying query and are visible in the navigation panel as part of the FILTER area in the INFORMATION tab.
Display attribute	Display attributes become standard fields in the navigation panel and are grouped as subordinates of the linked characteristic.
Navigational attribute	Navigational attributes are treated the same way as characteristics.

Table 7.2 SAP NetWeaver Business Warehouse Metadata Mapping for SAP BusinessObjects Analysis, Edition for Microsoft Office

BEx Query Element	SAP BusinessObjects Analysis, Edition for Microsoft Office
Variables	Each variable with the READY FOR INPUT property results in a prompt. You can use the prompts menu to provide the necessary input values.
Custom structures	A custom structure is available as an element in the navigation panel, and each structure element can be selected or de-selected for the report.

Table 7.2 SAP NetWeaver Business Warehouse Metadata Mapping for SAP BusinessObjects Analysis, Edition for Microsoft Office (Cont.)

> **Deployment Considerations**
>
> As shown in Figure 7.1, SAP BusinessObjects Analysis, edition for Microsoft Office can be used without SAP BusinessObjects BI platform—a so-called lean deployment—or in combination with the SAP BusinessObjects BI platform. If you are interested in further details on the installation and deployment of SAP BusinessObjects Analysis, edition for Microsoft Office we recommend the books *Integrating SAP BusinessObjects BI Platform 4.x with SAP NetWeaver* (SAP PRESS, 2012) and *Inside SAP BusinessObjects Advanced Analysis* (SAP PRESS, 2011).

In this section we reviewed the various data connectivity options available with SAP BusinessObjects Analysis, edition for Microsoft Office.

7.2 Assessing the Business Requirements

In this section we look at our overall requirements and see which ones we can fulfill with SAP BusinessObjects Analysis, edition for Microsoft Office. We start with requirements from the financial area.

7.2.1 Financial Reporting and Analysis Requirements

There is only one requirement that we think can't be fulfilled with SAP BusinessObjects Analysis, edition for Microsoft Office. However, this does not necessarily mean that SAP BusinessObjects Analysis, edition for Microsoft Office is the best choice for all of the requirements: you also need to consider who and what type of user the audience is. SAP BusinessObjects Analysis, edition for Microsoft Office is capable of delivering the requirements, but, in some situations, a different tool may be a better choice because it is better suited to the consumer.

> **Unfulfilled Requirements**
>
> - For specific content (such as an income statement or a balance sheet), the design needs to be layout focused with the actual print version of the report being a high priority.

With regard to the content being available in Microsoft Office and a web-based environment, we would use a combination of SAP BusinessObjects Analysis, edition for Microsoft Office and SAP BusinessObjects Analysis, edition for OLAP.

With regard to the navigation between different sets of data or even different sets of BI client tools, SAP BusinessObjects Analysis, edition for Microsoft Office provides the capability to create an analysis view, which then can be consumed by SAP Crystal Reports for Enterprise or SAP BusinessObjects Web Intelligence.

7.2.2 Sales Reporting and Analysis Requirements

When looking at the requirements from the sales area, only a few requirements are unable to be fulfilled by SAP BusinessObjects Analysis, edition for Microsoft Office. While the product does provide users with analytical capabilities, an actual what-if analysis model is better suited to a tool like SAP BusinessObjects Dashboards. On the other hand, SAP BusinessObjects Analysis, edition for Microsoft Office is integrated with SAP NetWeaver BW Integrated Planning (BW-IP) and you are able to write back to your SAP NetWeaver BW system, which you cannot do with SAP BusinessObjects Dashboards at this time.

> **Unfulfilled Requirements**
>
> - Content must be available online, offline, and on mobile devices (for sales representatives on the road).
> - Distribution of content via email may be required.
> - Users should be able to perform scenario-based analysis, where the user is able to see the data but can also influence certain factors and see the impact on the overall numbers; for example, a what-if analysis in a sales planning workflow.

As you will notice, the first requirement that we cannot fulfill with SAP BusinessObjects Analysis, edition for Microsoft Office concerns the capability to provide online, offline, and mobile access. For the online and offline options, you can use SAP BusinessObjects Analysis, edition for Microsoft Office, but there is no mobile device support yet.

The second unfulfilled requirement is the need to have content distributed via email, which, as of the 4.0 FP3 release, is not yet possible. There are plans for a future release to integrate SAP BusinessObjects Analysis, edition for Microsoft Office with the scheduling and publication mechanism of your SAP BusinessObjects BI platform.

7.2.3 Human Resources (HR) Reporting and Analysis Requirements

There are two unfulfilled requirements for the HR area.

Unfulfilled Requirements

- The content needs to present highly textual information in a layout-focused format.
- Some of the content (such as employee appraisals or performance reviews) will likely be used as official documentation and therefore needs to follow strict layout rules.

SAP BusinessObjects Analysis, edition for Microsoft Office is a multidimensional analysis client; therefore, it should not be a surprise that it is unable to fulfill the highly textual-based requirements for the HR area.

7.2.4 C-Level Management and Leadership Reporting and Analysis Requirements

There are three unfulfilled requirements for the executive and leadership area.

Unfulfilled Requirements

- The content needs to present highly aggregated information with alerts for important key performance indicators (KPIs).
- The information needs to be available on mobile devices.
- The consumption of the reports and analytics needs to be simple and easy to use, and critical information needs to be easily identifiable.

The first unfulfilled requirement concerns highly aggregated information and alerting on key measures. SAP BusinessObjects Analysis, edition for Microsoft Office clearly is capable of providing access to highly aggregated information, but in release 4.0 FP3 there is no proactive alerting capability. As for mobile device support, SAP BusinessObjects Analysis, edition for Microsoft Office does not yet support mobile devices.

Some may argue about the last requirement we list here as unfulfilled: that the information needs to be easily identifiable and easy to consume. If we received this requirement from, for example, our financial area or our sales area, then clearly this requirement could be fulfilled using SAP BusinessObjects Analysis, edition for Microsoft Office. But we received this requirement from our C-level management, and given the type of audience, tools such as SAP BusinessObjects Explorer or SAP BusinessObjects Dashboards will be a better choice.

In this section we reviewed our requirements and learned which of them we can fulfill using SAP BusinessObjects Analysis, edition for Microsoft Office.

7.3 Introduction to the Tool

In this section we look at some simple steps for using SAP BusinessObjects Analysis, edition for Microsoft Office and explain more about the tool and its functionality. In the following steps, we use a BEx query based on the SAP NetWeaver demo model InfoProvider 0D_NW_N01 (see Figure 7.2).

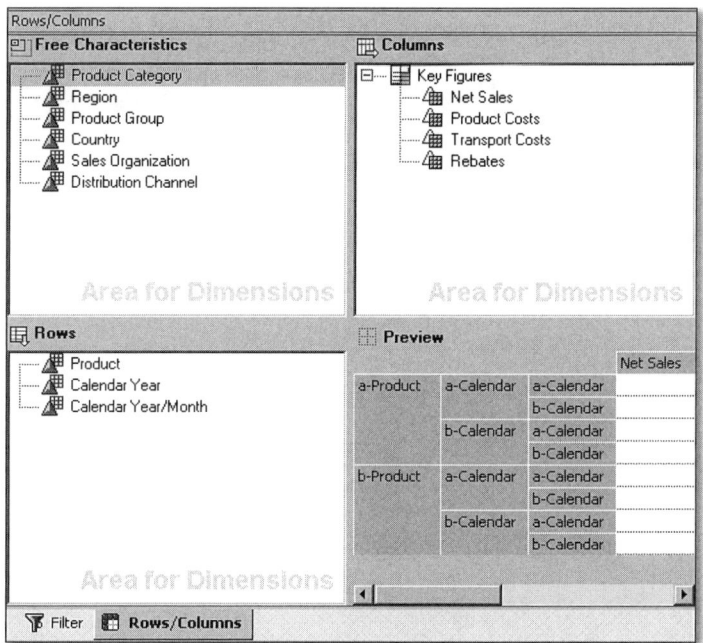

Figure 7.2 BEx Query

Because BI client products are able to share connections toward SAP NetWeaver BW, the steps for how to set up the OLAP connections are identical. You can find detailed steps in Section 4.3.3.

> **OLAP Connections for SAP BusinessObjects Analysis, Edition for Microsoft Office**
>
> As you should know from previous chapters, if your OLAP connection is configured to point to the InfoProvider and not to the BEx query, the BI client product will still ask which BEx query you want to use for the report design.
>
> SAP BusinessObjects Analysis, edition for Microsoft Office in the current version (release 1.1 from September 2011) can leverage the OLAP connections from the SAP BusinessObjects BI platform, but will use the connection as is. There is no separate step to ask which BEx query to use. This means that the OLAP connection configured on the SAP BusinessObjects BI platform for SAP BusinessObjects Analysis, edition for Microsoft Office should already point to the BEx query.

After we configure the OLAP connection in the Central Management Console (CMC), we can build our first workbook using SAP BusinessObjects Analysis, edition for Microsoft Office.

> **Microsoft Office 2007 vs. Microsoft Office 2003**
>
> As part of the activities in this book, we use SAP BusinessObjects Analysis, edition for Microsoft Office in combination with Microsoft Office 2007. If you use Microsoft Office 2003, you will not have the ribbon we mention throughout; instead, the items are part of an SAP BusinessObjects Analysis menu structure.

1. Start SAP BusinessObjects Analysis, edition for Microsoft Office with Microsoft Excel via the menu path: START • PROGRAMS • SAP BUSINESSOBJECTS • ANALYSIS FOR MICROSOFT EXCEL.
2. Select the INSERT • SELECT DATA SOURCE option from the Analysis ribbon (see Figure 7.3).

Figure 7.3 Analysis Ribbon

3. In the next screen you have the option either to use a connection from your SAP BusinessObjects BI platform or to use a local connection configured via the SAP GUI. If you want to use the local connection, click on the SKIP button. In our example, we want to use the shared connection and therefore we replace the placeholder <boe server hostname> with the name of our SAP BusinessObjects application server and the placeholder <port> with the corresponding port (see Figure 7.4).

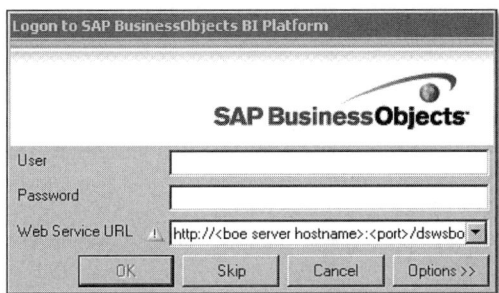

Figure 7.4 Logon Dialog

4. Click on OPTIONS.
5. Set the AUTHENTICATION to SAP.
6. Enter your SAP credentials and the password. Because the dialog does not provide you the option to enter the SAP system ID and the SAP client number, you need to enter your SAP credentials in the following syntax:

   <SAP System ID>~<SAP Client Number>/<User Name>;

   for example:

   IH1~800/DEMO for system ID IH1, client 800, and user DEMO.

7. Click on OK.
8. Select the configured connection.
9. Click on OK.
10. Depending on your configuration, you may be asked to log on to your SAP NetWeaver BW system again.
11. The result set is shown as configured in the BEx query (see Figure 7.5).

7 | Using SAP BusinessObjects Analysis, Edition for Microsoft Office

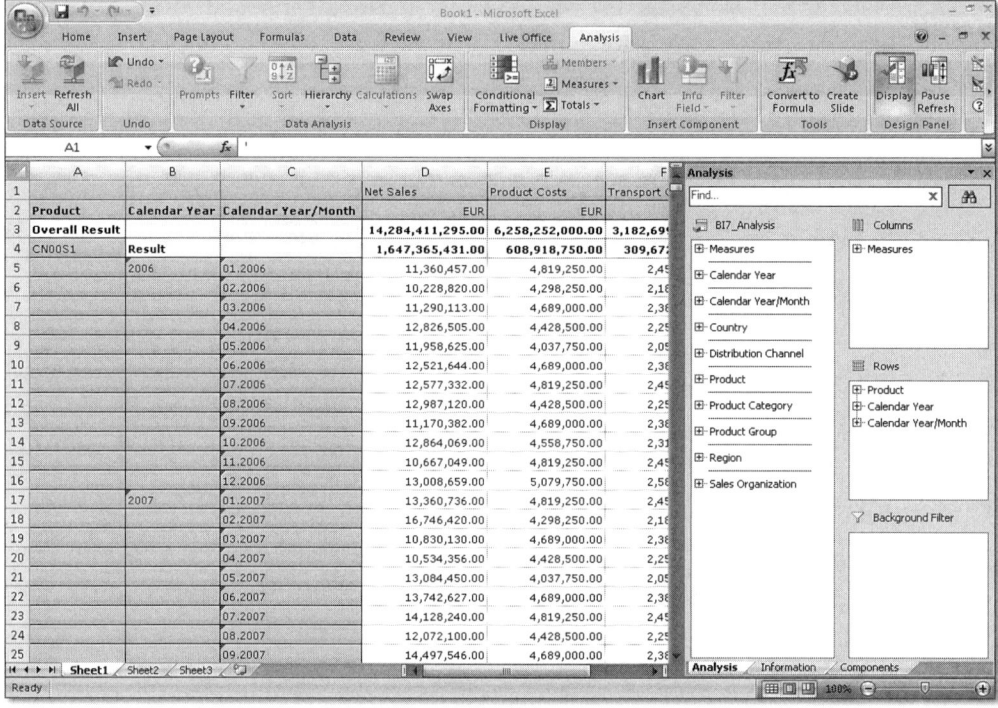

Figure 7.5 Resultset

On the right-hand side of the screen, you can see the navigation panel, which you can enable or disable using the DISPLAY button in the Analysis ribbon. You can use the panel for filtering and for navigating data.

12. Select the PRODUCT entry in the cross tab.
13. Select the menu MEMBERS in the Analysis ribbon (see Figure 7.6).

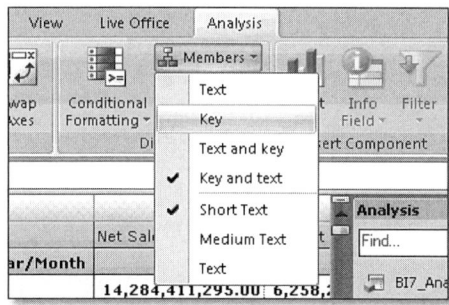

Figure 7.6 Members Options

262

14. Select the option to display KEY and TEXT for the PRODUCT dimension.
15. Select the column header for the NET SALES measure.
16. Select the menu MEASURES in the Analysis ribbon.
17. Select the NUMBER FORMAT menu item (see Figure 7.7).

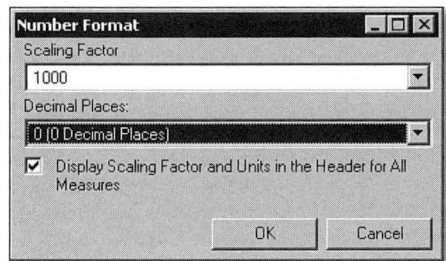

Figure 7.7 Number Format

18. Configure net sales with a 1000 scaling factor and 0 decimal places.
19. Click on OK.
20. In the navigation panel right-click on MEASURES (see Figure 7.8).

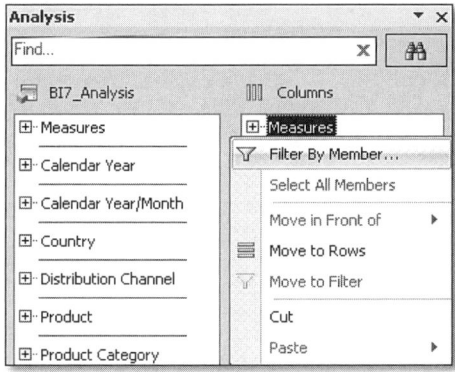

Figure 7.8 Measures

21. Select the FILTER BY MEMBER option (see Figure 7.9).
22. Select all measures except REBATES.
23. Click on OK.
24. Drag and drop CALENDAR YEAR from the Rows to the BACKGROUND FILTER.

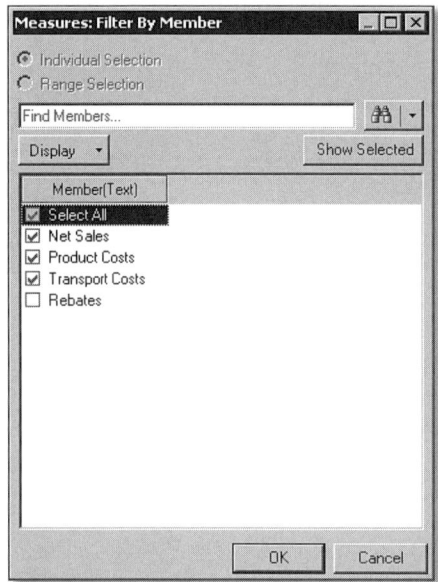

Figure 7.9 Filter By Member

25. Open the list of members for CALENDAR YEAR in the navigation panel (see Figure 7.10).

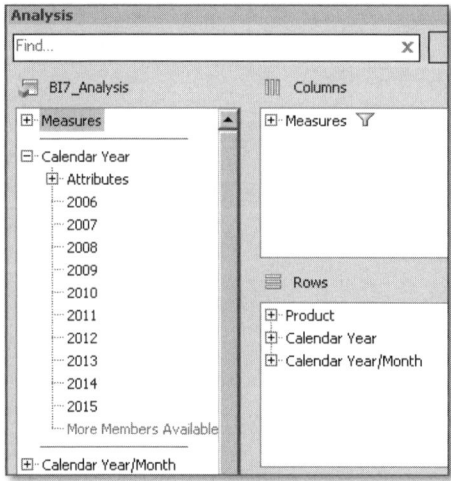

Figure 7.10 List of Members

26. Select the values for the years 2009, 2010, and 2011.

27. Drag and drop the values to the BACKGROUND FILTER (see Figure 7.11).

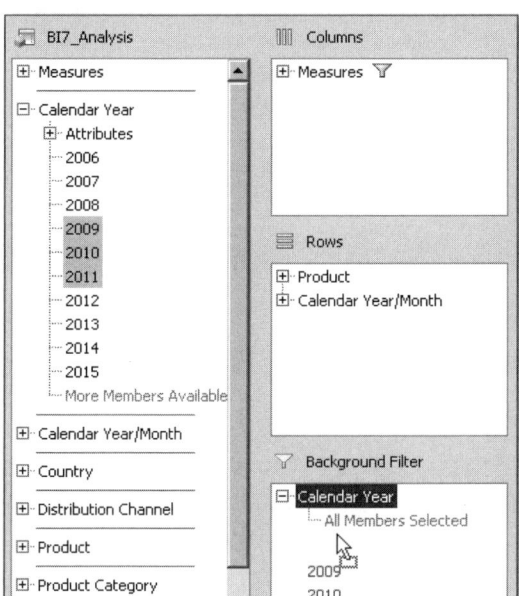

Figure 7.11 Background Filter

28. Click on PAUSE REFRESH in the Analysis ribbon (see Figure 7.12).

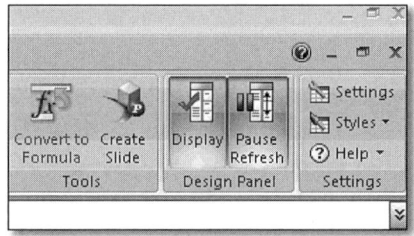

Figure 7.12 Pause Refresh

29. Remove all dimensions from ROWS by dragging them into an empty area in the navigation panel.
30. Drag and drop COUNTRY to ROWS.
31. Drag and drop REGION to ROWS.
32. Click on PAUSE REFRESH again, and your cross tab is updated.

> **Pause Refresh**
>
> The PAUSE REFRESH option allows you to stop the interactivity with the underlying SAP NetWeaver BW server. You can still navigate in the data, but the cross tab in the spreadsheet does not reflect the actual changes until you disable PAUSE REFRESH. In this way you can minimize interaction with the SAP NetWeaver BW system.

33. Open the list of members for COUNTRY (see Figure 7.13).

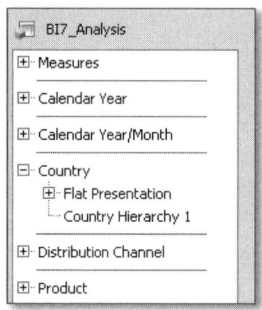

Figure 7.13 List of Members

If the dimension also contains hierarchies, all available hierarchies are shown, as in our example in Figure 7.13, with COUNTRY HIERARCHY 1. The list of available members is shown as a separate entry called FLAT PRESENTATION.

34. Drag and drop COUNTRY HIERARCHY 1 to ROWS so that it replaces COUNTRY (see Figure 7.14).

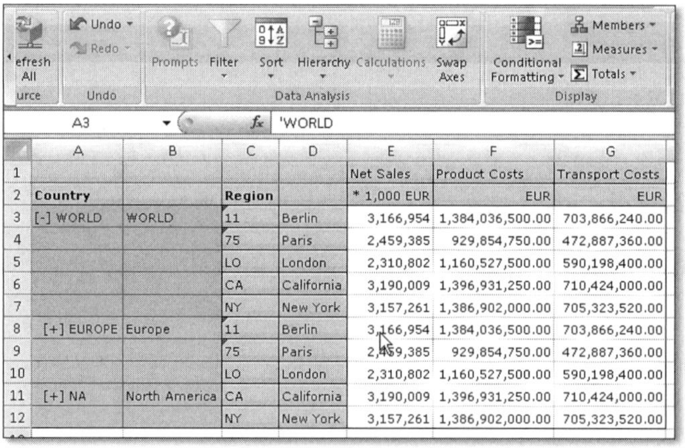

Figure 7.14 Hierarchical Report

35. Select WORLD in the cross tab.
36. Select the menu HIERARCHY • EXPAND NODE TO LEVEL • LEVEL 03 (see Figure 7.15).

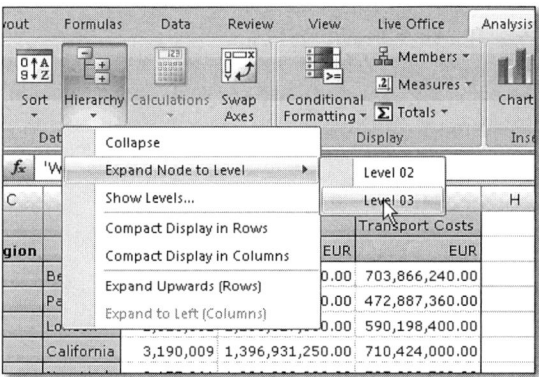

Figure 7.15 Menu Hierarchy

37. Select the menu HIERARCHY • SHOW LEVELS.
38. Select LEVEL 02.
39. Click on OK.
40. Select the column header for TRANSPORT COSTS.
41. Hold down the [Ctrl] button and select the column header for PRODUCT COSTS.
42. Select the menu CALCULATIONS • ADD CALCULATION • ADD. The calculation is added as a new measure to the list of measures, and you can edit and rename it (see Figure 7.16).

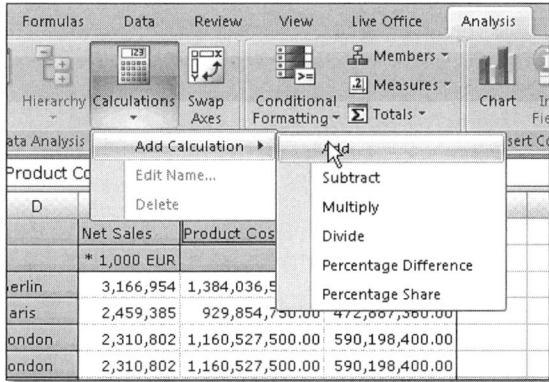

Figure 7.16 Insert Calculations

Calculations

As shown in the previous steps, the calculations in SAP BusinessObjects Analysis, edition for Microsoft Office depend on the order of selected elements. The first selected element is used as the first operant and the second selected element is used as the second operant.

43. Remove COUNTRY from the ROWS.
44. Remove REGION from the ROWS.
45. Add PRODUCT TO THE ROWS.
46. Select the column header for NET SALES.
47. Select the menu FILTER • FILTER BY MEASURE • MOST DETAILED DIMENSION IN ROWS • EDIT (see Figure 7.17).

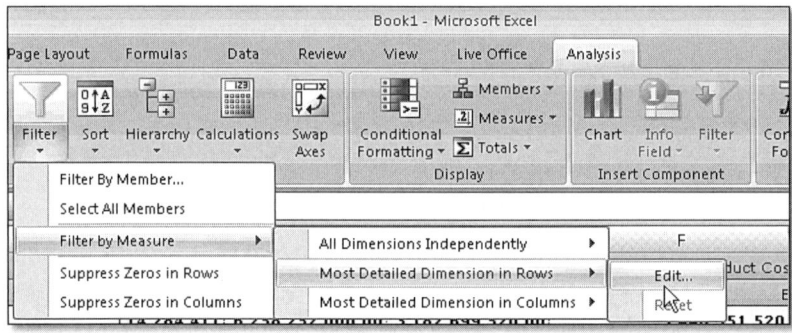

Figure 7.17 Menu Filter

48. Select the operator TOP N.
49. Set the value to 3 (see Figure 7.18).
50. Click on ADD.
51. Click on OK.
52. You are shown the top 3 products based on net value (see Figure 7.19).
53. Drag and drop PRODUCT GROUP to the ROWS so that it replaces PRODUCT. You can do so in the navigation panel or you can drag the dimension to the cross tab.
54. You are now shown the top 3 product groups, because the filter is dynamic in the rows.

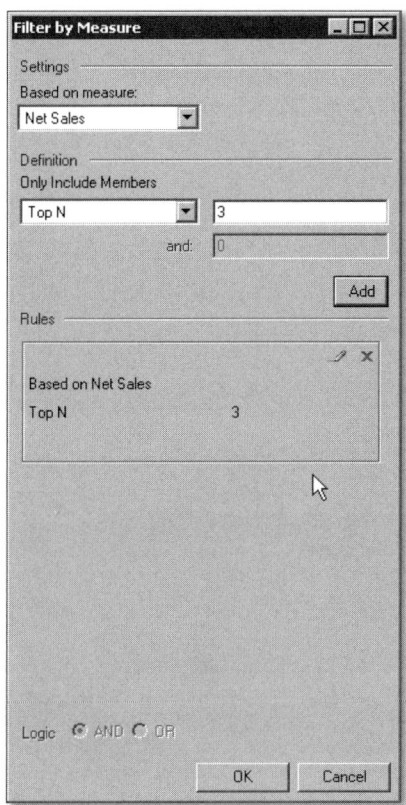

Figure 7.18 Filter by Measure

	A	B	C	D
1			Net Sales	Product Costs
2	**Product**		* 1,000 EUR	EUR
3	**Overall Result**		14,284,411	6,258,252,000.00
4	CN00S1	Notebook Standard 15	1,647,365	608,918,750.00
5	CN00S2	Notebook Standard 17	1,565,381	598,889,500.00
6	HT1000	Notebook Basic 15	1,605,943	990,030,250.00
7				

Figure 7.19 Top 3 Products

55. Select a cell in your cross tab.
56. Select the CREATE SLIDE menu item in the Analysis ribbon (see Figure 7.20).
57. SAP BusinessObjects Analysis for Microsoft PowerPoint starts. As a first step, you need to log on to your SAP NetWeaver BW system.

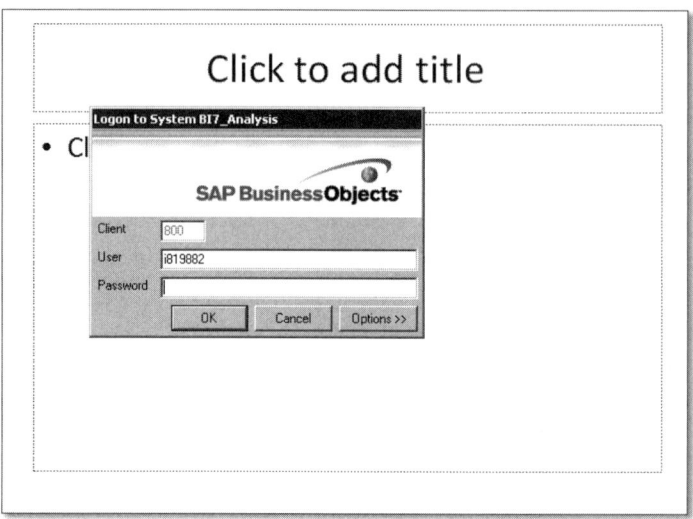

Figure 7.20 SAP BusinessObjects Analysis for Microsoft PowerPoint

58. Enter your SAP credentials and password.
59. Click on OK.
60. You are presented with a default layout for the table as part of your slides (see Figure 7.21).

	Net Sales	Product Costs	Transport Costs	Transport Costs + Product Costs
Product Group	* 1,000 EUR	EUR	EUR	EUR
Overall Result	14,284,411	6,258,252,000.00	3,182,699,520.00	9,440,951,520.00
MON2	2,256,296	945,615,000.00	480,902,400.00	1,426,517,400.00
NB1	3,253,308	1,598,949,000.00	813,162,240.00	2,412,111,240.00
NB2	3,110,445	1,545,937,250.00	786,202,560.00	2,332,139,810.00

Figure 7.21 Table as Part of Slides

61. Select a cell in the table.
62. Select the menu items FIT TABLE in the Analysis ribbon.

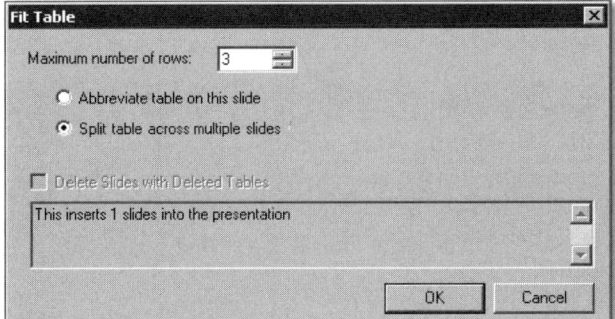

Figure 7.22 Fit Table

63. You can now decide how many rows of the table are being shown on each slide. Set the value to 3 and use the option SPLIT TABLE ACROSS MULTIPLE SLIDES.
64. Click on OK.
65. The table is split across multiple slides.
66. You can now use the MICROSOFT OFFICE button to save your work. Click on the MICROSOFT OFFICE button.
67. Select the menu item SAVE PRESENTATION (see Figure 7.23).

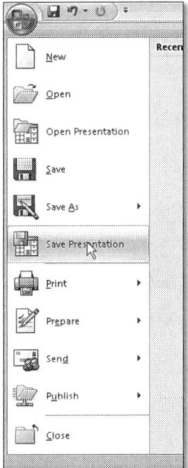

Figure 7.23 Save Presentation

68. Log on to your SAP BusinessObjects BI platform.
69. Select a folder for your presentation.
70. Enter a name for your presentation.
71. Click on SAVE.

> **Integration with Microsoft Office**
>
> SAP BusinessObjects Analysis, edition for Microsoft Office is tightly integrated with the Microsoft Office environment. For example, charts in the Microsoft Excel environment use the Microsoft Excel charting engine and can be formatted and configured using the standard Microsoft Excel charting functionality. Another example is tables in Microsoft PowerPoint, which can be formatted and configured using the standard layout and design options available with Microsoft PowerPoint.

In this section you learned some basic steps in SAP BusinessObjects Analysis, edition for Microsoft Office. In the next section we use our business requirements and see which of those we can fulfill using SAP BusinessObjects Analysis, edition for Microsoft Office.

7.4 Building a Workbook for Financial Analysis

In our first example we seek to fulfill the requirements from the finance department by delivering a cost center analysis using SAP BusinessObjects Analysis, edition for Microsoft Office. We will use the BEx query, which we already used in combination with SAP BusinessObjects Web Intelligence in Section 5.5. In this example our main interest is to see which of the assigned cost centers have used more than allocated and which of the cost centers have still a budget left. In addition, we are interested in the most used cost elements.

As you learned in the previous section, SAP BusinessObjects Analysis, edition for Microsoft Office is able to share connections from the SAP BusinessObjects BI platform with the other BI client products, but SAP BusinessObjects Analysis, edition for Microsoft Office uses the connection "as is," which means that if the connection points to the InfoProvider, you do not have the option to select a BEx query as you do with the other BI client products. Based on this situation, you will have to create an OLAP connection pointing to the BEx query for SAP BusinessObjects Analysis, edition for Microsoft Office. You can find more detailed steps in Section 4.3.3.

After we configure the OLAP connection in the CMC we can build our cost center analysis workbook using SAP BusinessObjects Analysis, edition for Microsoft Office:

1. Start SAP BusinessObjects Analysis, edition for Microsoft Office with Microsoft Excel via the menu path: START • PROGRAMS • SAP BUSINESSOBJECTS • ANALYSIS FOR MICROSOFT EXCEL.
2. Select the INSERT • SELECT DATA SOURCE option from the Analysis ribbon.
3. Enter your SAP credentials and password.
4. Click on OK.
5. Select the connection you established for the BEx query.
6. Click on OK.
7. You may be asked to log on to the SAP NetWeaver BW system again.
8. The BEx query is presented based on the default layout as defined in the BEx Query Designer (see Figure 7.24).

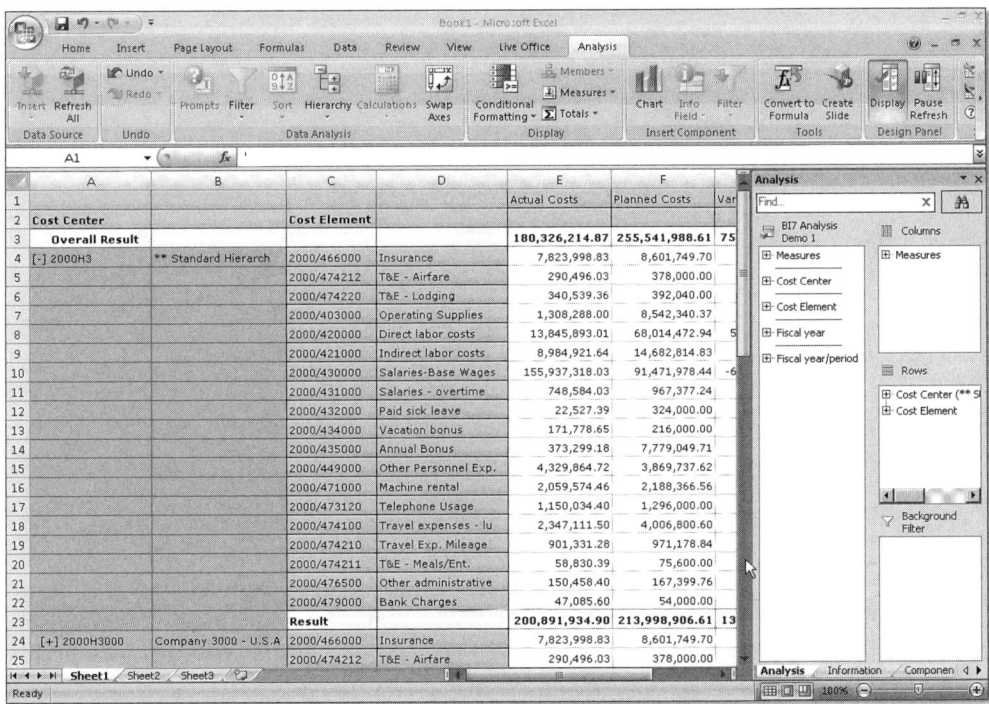

Figure 7.24 Cross Tab (Part 1)

9. Remove COST ELEMENT from ROWS.
10. Click on a member of the hierarchy in the cross tab.
11. Select the menu HIERARCHY • EXPAND TO NODE LEVEL • LEVEL 05.
12. Click on a member of the hierarchy in the cross tab.
13. Select the MEMBERS menu in the Analysis ribbon.
14. Configure the hierarchy to display only the text (see Figure 7.25).

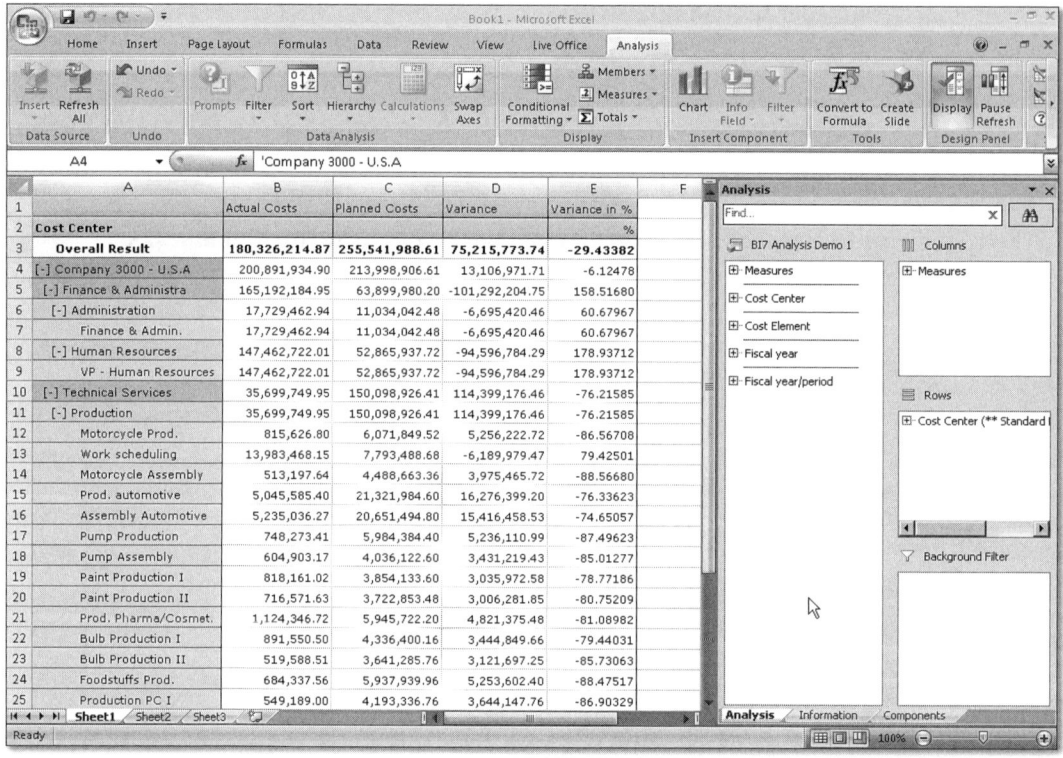

Figure 7.25 Cross Tab (Part 2)

15. Select the column header of VARIANCE IN %.
16. Select the menu CONDITIONAL FORMATTING • NEW.
17. Configure two sets of conditional formatting so that values above 50% are highlighted in red and values above 0% are highlighed in orange (see Figure 7.26).

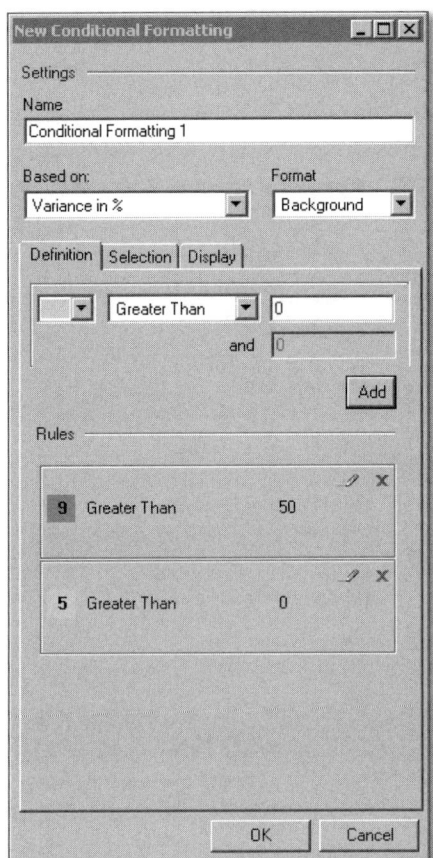

Figure 7.26 Conditional Formatting

18. In the cross tab the corresponding numbers are highlighed (see Figure 7.27).

    You may ask yourself why we did not use the FILTER BY MEASURE option to filter the cross tab to the bottom 10 cost centers based on the VARIANCE IN %. You will notice, when trying to do so, that a ranking is not possible with an active hierarchy in the display.

    Based on the highlighted values, we can now quickly identify which areas of our hierarchy we need to concentrate on.

19. Select those cost centers that are highlighted now in the cross tab. You can use the `Ctrl` key on the keyboard to select multiple entries.

7 | Using SAP BusinessObjects Analysis, Edition for Microsoft Office

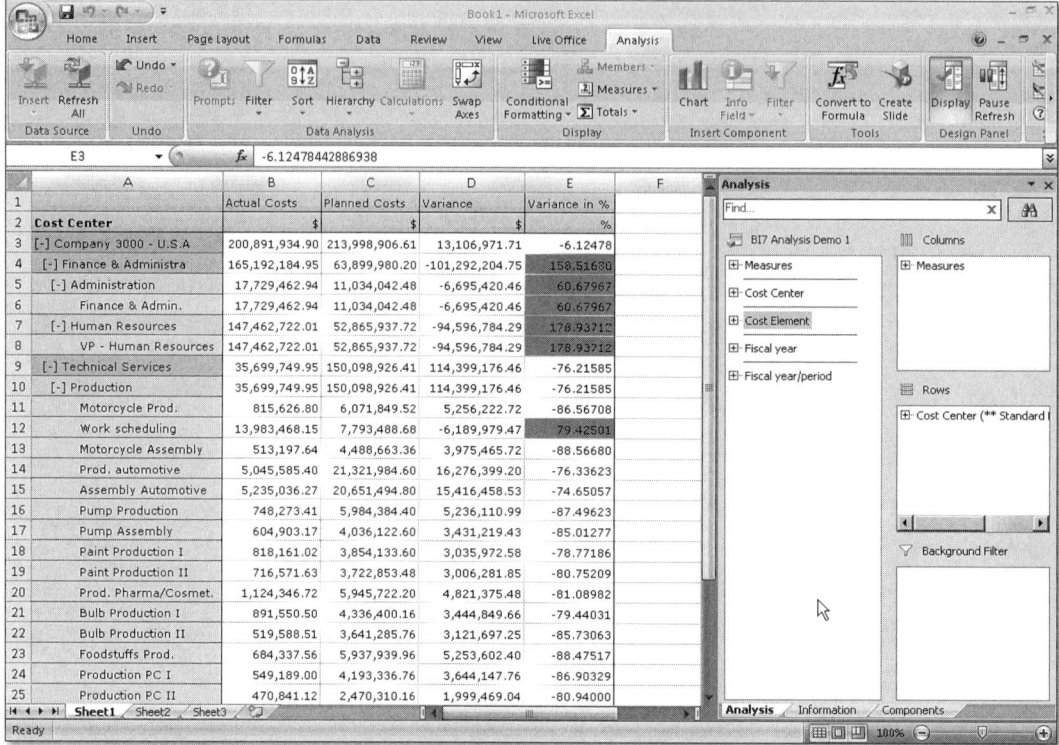

Figure 7.27 Highlighted Resultset

20. After you select the entries, right-click and select the menu entry FILTER MEMBERS (see Figure 7.28).

	A	B	C	D	E	F
1		Actual Costs	Planned Costs	Variance	Variance in %	
2	**Cost Center**	$	$	$	%	
3	[-] Finance & Administra	165,192,184.95	63,899,980.20	-101,292,204.75	158.51680	
4	[-] Administration	17,729,462.94	11,034,042.48	-6,695,420.46	60.67967	
5	Finance & Admin.	17,729,462.94	11,034,042.48	-6,695,420.46	60.67967	
6	[-] Human Resources	147,462,722.01	52,865,937.72	-94,596,784.29	178.93712	
7	VP - Human Resources	147,462,722.01	52,865,937.72	-94,596,784.29	178.93712	
8	Work scheduling	13,983,468.15	7,793,488.68	-6,189,979.47	79.42501	
9						

Figure 7.28 Filtered Members

By using simple highlighting and filtering, we were able to quickly identify those cost centers where the actual cost is larger than the planned costs.

21. Select a member of the hierarchy.
22. Click on the menu item CREATE SLIDE in the Analysis ribbon.
23. Microsoft PowerPoint starts and you are asked to log on to SAP NetWeaver BW.
24. Enter your SAP credentials and password.
25. Click on OK. You can then decide if you would like to split the table or abbreviate it.
26. Set the maximum number of rows to the highest number possible.
27. Select the option ABBREVIATE TABLE ON THIS SLIDE.
28. Click on OK (see Figure 7.29), and Figure 7.30 appears.

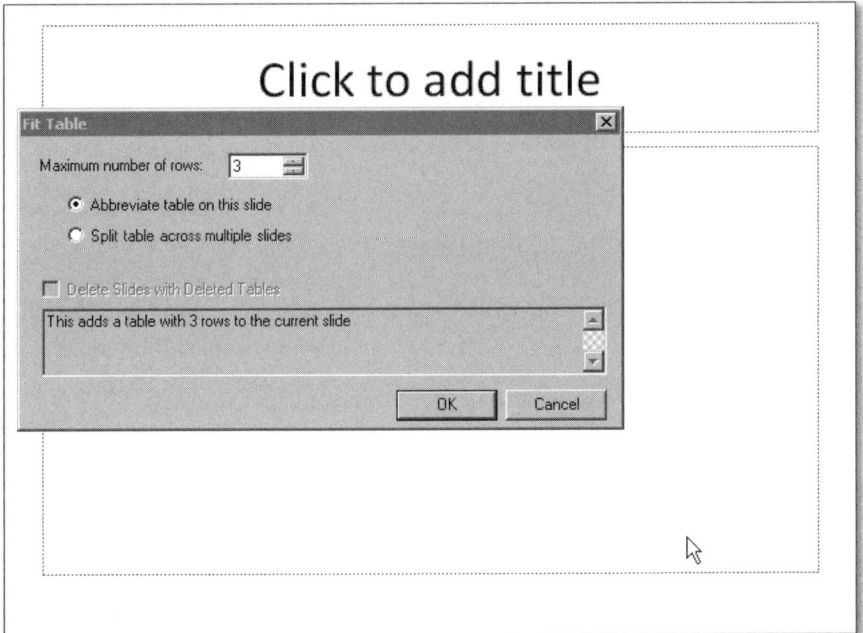

Figure 7.29 Analysis for Microsoft PowerPoint

29. You can now use the standard Microsoft PowerPoint formatting features and table layout and design options to format your table.

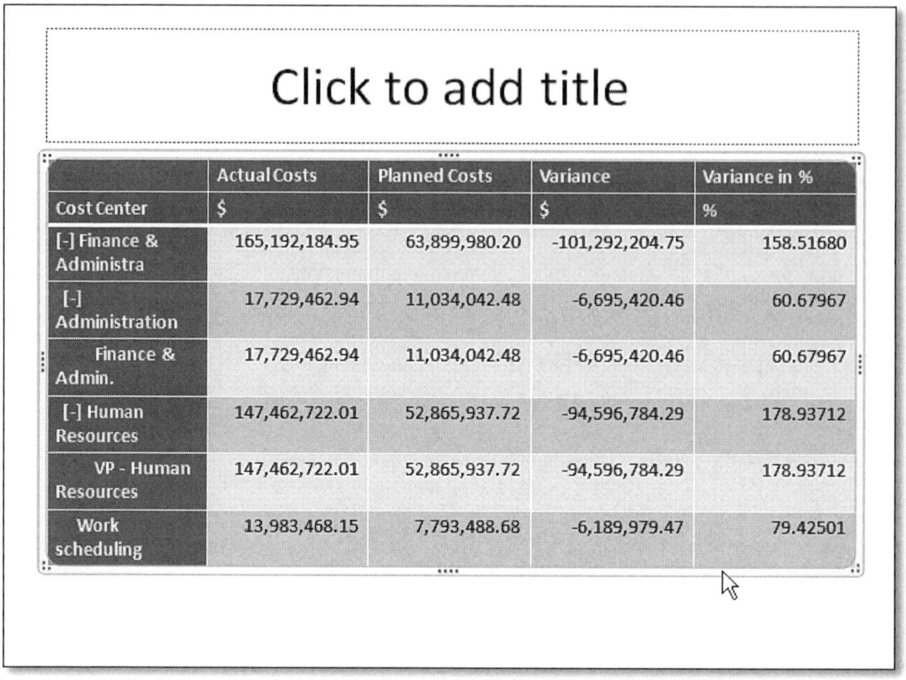

	Actual Costs	Planned Costs	Variance	Variance in %
Cost Center	$	$	$	%
[-] Finance & Administra	165,192,184.95	63,899,980.20	-101,292,204.75	158.51680
[-] Administration	17,729,462.94	11,034,042.48	-6,695,420.46	60.67967
Finance & Admin.	17,729,462.94	11,034,042.48	-6,695,420.46	60.67967
[-] Human Resources	147,462,722.01	52,865,937.72	-94,596,784.29	178.93712
VP - Human Resources	147,462,722.01	52,865,937.72	-94,596,784.29	178.93712
Work scheduling	13,983,468.15	7,793,488.68	-6,189,979.47	79.42501

Figure 7.30 Analysis Workbook in Microsoft PowerPoint

You now have the first part of your summary report that you want to create for your management level. The next step is to add a slide for the cost elements:

1. In Analysis for Microsoft PowerPoint, select a cell in the cross tab.
2. Select the CHART menu in the Analysis ribbon. A chart is created on top of the cross tab, and you can use the standard Microsoft PowerPoint capabilities to format the chart.
3. Select the chart.
4. Select the MOVE TO menu item in the Analysis ribbon.
5. Create an empty slide, and then move the chart to a new slide.
6. Click on OK.
7. Navigate back to your Analysis for Microsoft Excel spreadsheet.
8. Move the hierarchy from the ROWS area to the BACKGROUND FILTER area.
9. Move COST ELEMENT to ROWS.

10. Select the column header for VARIANCE IN %.
11. Select the menu FILTER • FILTER BY MEASURE • MOST DETAILED DIMENSION IN ROWS • EDIT.
12. Select the operator TOP N.
13. Enter the value 10 (see Figure 7.31).

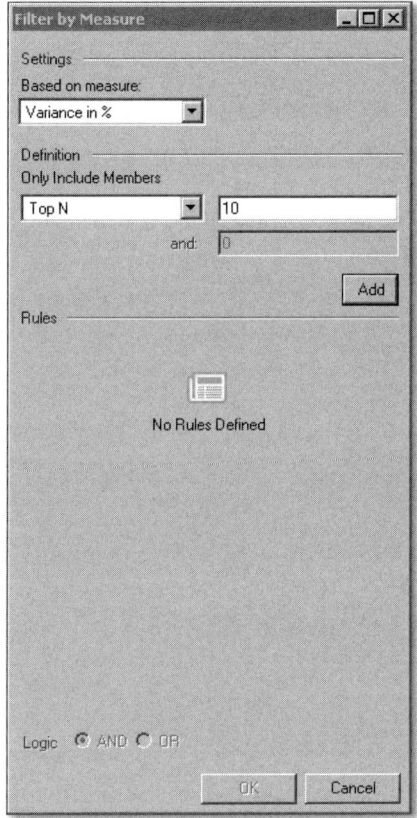

Figure 7.31 Filter By Measure

14. Click on ADD.
15. Click OK.
16. Select a member of the cross tab.
17. Select the menu CREATE SLIDE in the Analysis ribbon.
18. Use the highest number of rows possible.

19. Select the option SPLIT TABLE ACROSS MULTIPLE SLIDES.
20. Click on OK.
21. The top 10 cost elements are populated onto a slide using SAP BusienssObjects Analysis for Microsoft PowerPoint (see Figure 7.32).

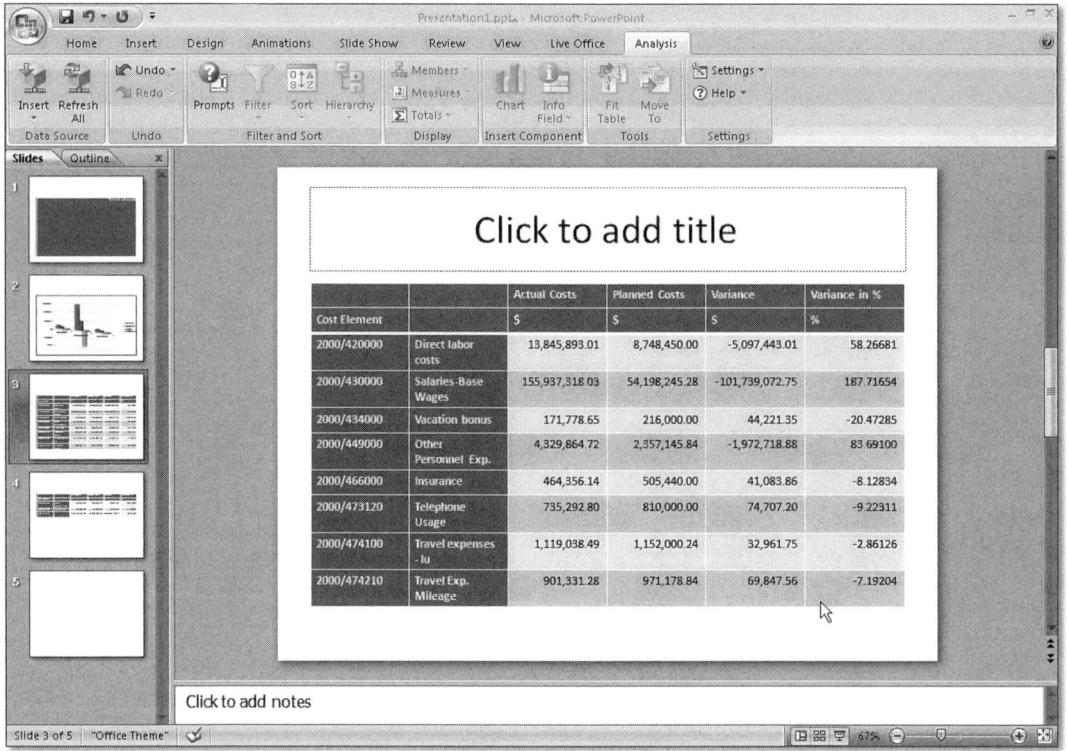

Figure 7.32 Extended PowerPoint Slides

At this point we have an Analysis for Microsoft Excel workbook showing the top 10 cost elements, which have a higher actual cost compared to the planned cost. In addition, we have created a slide deck outlining these numbers so that we can use the slides for our management meeting.

So far, we have been able to find those cost center and cost elements that have the highest actual costs compared to the planned costs. We will now analyze the information from SAP NetWeaver BW to analyze those cost centers with the smallest amount spent compared to the planned costs, and include this information in our presentation.

1. Navigate back to your Analysis for Microsoft Excel spreadsheet.
2. Select a cell in an empty area below the existing cross tab of your spreadsheet.
3. Navigate to the COMPONENTS tab of the navigation panel (see Figure 7.33).

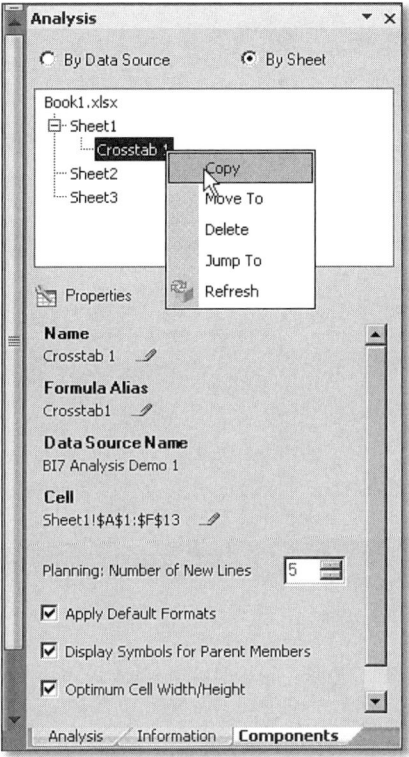

Figure 7.33 Components

4. Select the CROSSTAB 1 entry in SHEET 1.
5. Right-click and select the COPY menu.
6. A dialog with a cell selection comes up. The cell should be the one that you selected previously.
7. Click on OK (see Figure 7.34).

    You now have two cross tabs that you can navigate independent of each other, but both of the cross tabs share the same underlying BEx query.

8. Select the column header of the VARIANCE IN % of the second cross tab.

7 | Using SAP BusinessObjects Analysis, Edition for Microsoft Office

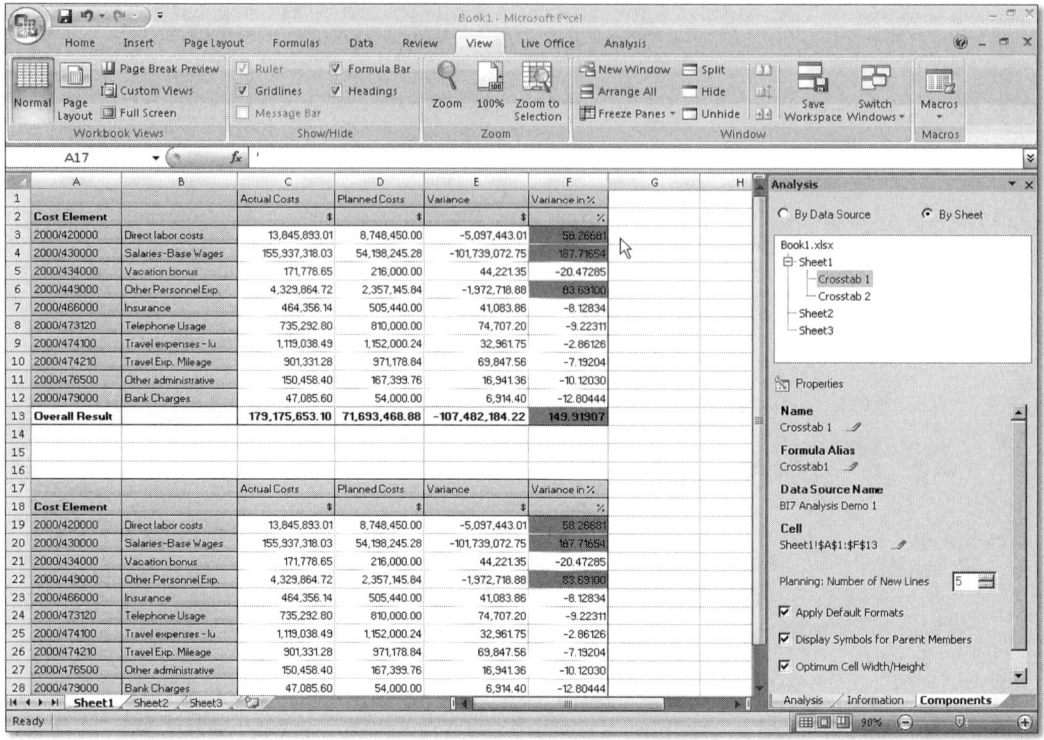

Figure 7.34 Updated Spreadsheet

9. Select the menu FILTER • FILTER BY MEASURE • MOST DETAILED DIMENSION IN ROWS • EDIT.

10. You can use the EDIT button ( ) to change the existing filter (see Figure 7.35).

11. Set the operator to BOTTOM N.

12. Click on OK.

13. Select a member of the second cross tab.

14. Select the CREATE SLIDE menu in the Analysis ribbon.

15. Use the highest number of rows possible.

16. Select the option SPLIT TABLE ACROSS MULTIPLE SLIDES.

17. Click on OK.

18. The bottom 10 cost elements are populated onto a slide using Analysis for Microsoft PowerPoint. You can now use the MICROSOFT OFFICE button to save your work. Click on the MICROSOFT OFFICE button.

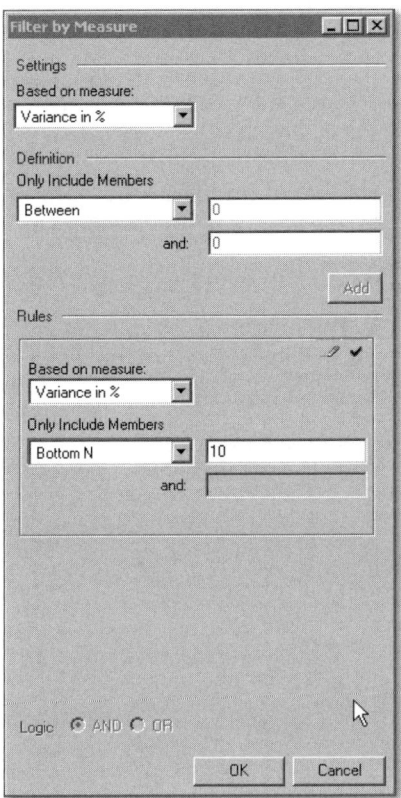

Figure 7.35 Edit Filter by Measure

19. Select the SAVE PRESENTATION menu item.
20. Log on to your SAP BusinessObjects BI platform.
21. Select a folder for your presentation.
22. Enter a name for your presentation.
23. Click on SAVE.

In this example we used a BEx query from the financial area and were quickly able to analyze the cost centers and cost elements using conditional formatting. We were also able to use filter by measure functionality to highlight those cost centers and cost elements that use the most and the least of their assigned budgets. In addition, we were able to create a slide deck visualizing the information so that we can use those slides as part of our regular update to the management level.

7.5 Building a Workbook for Sales Analysis

In our second example we seek to fulfill requirements from the sales department by delivering a profitability analysis for our products. We use a BEx query based on the demo cube 0D_COPA (see Figure 7.36). In this example, our main interest is to see which of the products we should focus on (based on the profit margin), as well as which of our market segments contribute the most to our revenue and profit. We also compare the sales groups against each other.

As in the previous example, we will need an OLAP connection pointing to the BEx query (see Figure 7.36). You can find detailed steps in Chapter 4, Section 4.3.3.

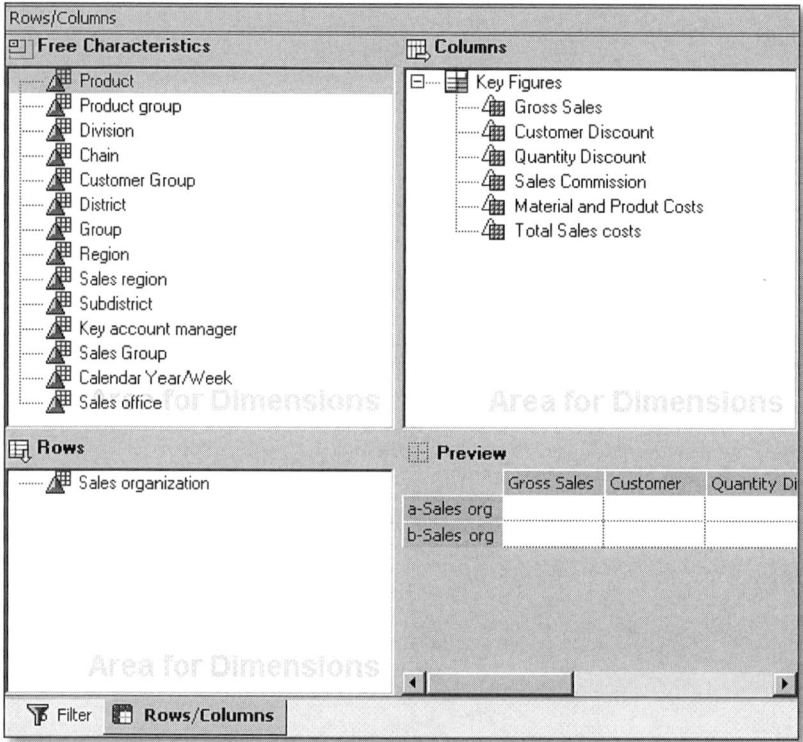

Figure 7.36 BEx Query

After we configure the OLAP connection in the CMC, we can build our cost center analysis workbook using SAP BusinessObjects Analysis, edition for Microsoft Office:

1. Start SAP BusinessObjects Analysis, edition for Microsoft Office with Microsoft Excel via the menu path: START • PROGRAMS • SAP BUSINESSOBJECTS • ANALYSIS FOR MICROSOFT EXCEL.
2. Select the INSERT • SELECT DATA SOURCE option from the Analysis ribbon.
3. Log on to your SAP BusinessObjects BI platform using your SAP credentials.
4. Click on OK.
5. Select the connection you established for the BEx query.
6. Click on OK.
7. You may be asked to log on to the SAP NetWeaver BW system again.
8. The BEx query is presented based on the default layout as defined in the BEx Query Designer (see Figure 7.37).

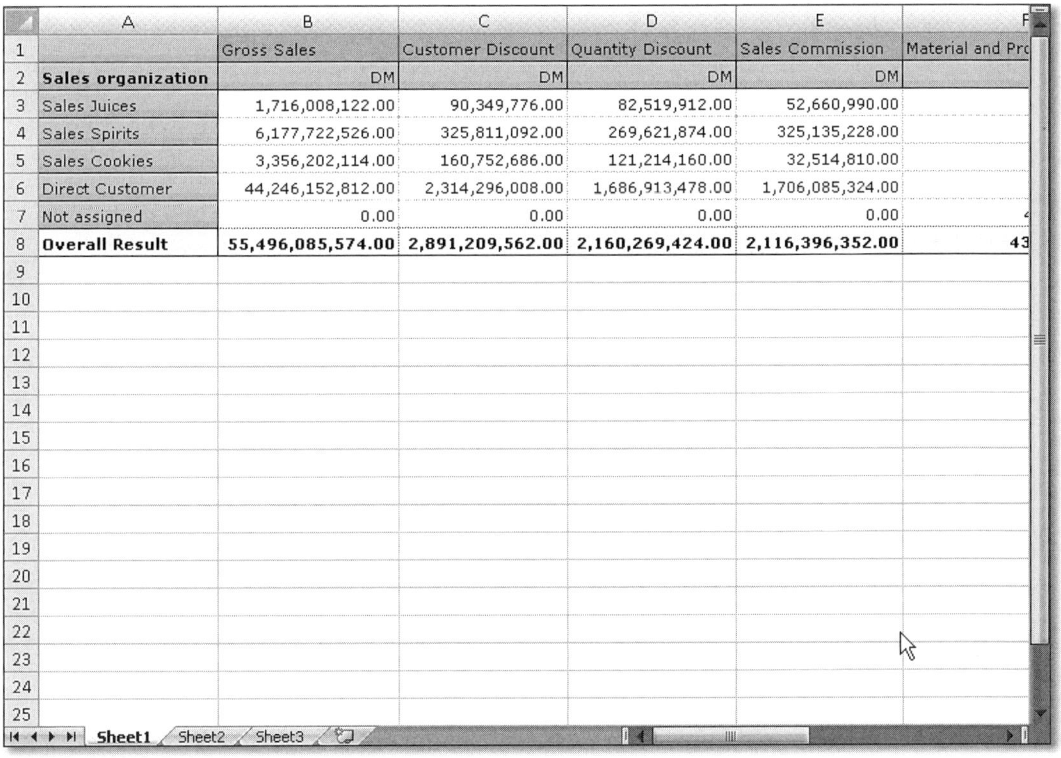

	A	B	C	D	E	F
1		Gross Sales	Customer Discount	Quantity Discount	Sales Commission	Material and Pro
2	**Sales organization**	DM	DM	DM	DM	
3	Sales Juices	1,716,008,122.00	90,349,776.00	82,519,912.00	52,660,990.00	
4	Sales Spirits	6,177,722,526.00	325,811,092.00	269,621,874.00	325,135,228.00	
5	Sales Cookies	3,356,202,114.00	160,752,686.00	121,214,160.00	32,514,810.00	
6	Direct Customer	44,246,152,812.00	2,314,296,008.00	1,686,913,478.00	1,706,085,324.00	
7	Not assigned	0.00	0.00	0.00	0.00	
8	**Overall Result**	**55,496,085,574.00**	**2,891,209,562.00**	**2,160,269,424.00**	**2,116,396,352.00**	43

Figure 7.37 Cross Tab

9. As the first step, look at the profitability of the products and remove the SALES ORGANIZATION dimension from Rows.
10. Click on PAUSE REFRESH in the Analysis ribbon.
11. Add PRODUCT GROUP to ROWS.
12. Add PRODUCT to ROWS.
13. Click on PAUSE REFRESH in the Analysis ribbon.

    You will notice that some key measures are missing from the BEx query. As such, you will need to create some calculations, which you can use later when you analyze the data by sales region.

14. Select the column header of CUSTOMER DISCOUNT.
15. Press the [Ctrl] button on the keyboard and select the column header of QUANTITY DISCOUNT.
16. Select the menu CALCULATIONS • ADD CALCULATION • ADD from the Analysis ribbon.
17. Navigate to the far right of the cross tab and select the column header of the newly created measure (see Figure 7.38).

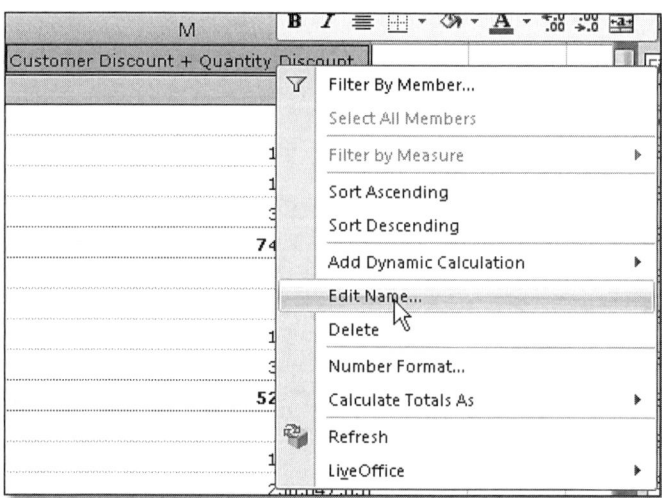

Figure 7.38 Edit Name

18. Right-click and select the menu EDIT NAME. Enter "Total Discount" as the name and click on OK.

19. Navigate to the MEASURE AREA in the navigation panel.
20. Select the newly created measure and move it up so that it is displayed after the calculated members.
21. Select the column header of GROSS SALES.
22. Press the [Ctrl] button on the keyboard and select the newly created measure, TOTAL DISCOUNT.
23. Select the menu CALCULATIONS • ADD CALCULATION • SUBTRACT from the Analysis ribbon.
24. Navigate to the far right of the cross tab and select the column header of the newly created measure.
25. Use a right click and select the menu EDIT NAME. Enter "Net Sales" as the name and click on OK.
26. Navigate to the MEASURE area in the navigation panel.
27. Select the newly created measure and move it up so that it is displayed after the calculated members.
28. Select the column header of NET SALES.
29. Press the [Ctrl] button on the keyboard and select SALES COMMISSION.
30. Press the [Ctrl] button on the keyboard and select MATERIAL AND PRODUCT COSTS.
31. Press the [Ctrl] button on the keyboard and select TOTAL SALES COSTS.
32. Select the menu CALCULATIONS • ADD CALCULATION • SUBTRACT from the Analysis ribbon.
33. Navigate to the far right of the cross tab and select the column header of the newly created measure.
34. Right-click and select the menu EDIT NAME. Enter "Operating Profit" as the name and click on OK.
35. Navigate to the MEASURES area in the navigation panel.
36. Right-click on MEASURES and select the FILTER BY MEMBER menu.
37. Select GROSS SALES, TOTAL DISCOUNT, NET SALES, and OPERATING PROFIT.
38. Select a member from PRODUCT GROUP.
39. Select the menu HIERARCHY • COMPACT DISPLAY IN ROWS (see Figure 7.39).

	A	B	C	D	E
1		Gross Sales	Total Discount	Net Sales	Operating Profit
2	**Product group**	$	$	$	$
3	**Overall Result**	**318,665,887.22**	**27,793,790.68**	**290,872,096.54**	**177,514,728.16**
4	[+] Apple 10%	7,599,617.61	745,327.46	6,854,290.15	5,145,105.02
5	[+] Apple cond	5,552,235.22	523,908.24	5,028,326.98	3,824,008.05
6	[+] Apple nat.	6,874,457.82	622,397.25	6,252,060.57	4,676,704.91
7	[+] Applejuice	3,731,475.56	356,321.37	3,375,154.19	2,522,793.00
8	[+] Brandy 20%	52,535,535.31	4,381,580.56	48,153,954.75	35,270,868.18
9	[+] Brandy 30%	38,890,395.74	3,191,766.18	35,698,629.56	26,010,202.49
10	[+] Brandy 40%	60,307,310.95	5,327,866.43	54,979,444.52	40,339,220.90
11	[+] Brandy lite	48,782,864.67	4,282,678.33	44,500,186.34	32,030,652.64
12	[+] Chocookies	16,877,943.43	1,425,809.68	15,452,133.75	11,896,837.75
13	[+] Crisps	12,214,218.96	1,079,236.94	11,134,982.02	8,510,279.00
14	[+] Orange 10%	4,997,784.73	492,679.18	4,505,105.55	3,302,088.85
15	[+] Orange 40%	7,509,512.12	733,155.92	6,776,356.20	5,002,859.19
16	[+] Orange cond	6,734,452.68	588,903.79	6,145,548.89	4,595,299.85
17	[+] Orangejuice	6,796,980.48	590,071.97	6,206,908.51	4,715,535.18
18	[+] Pumpkincook	20,262,411.97	1,695,181.70	18,567,230.27	14,335,274.37
19	[+] Softcookies	18,998,689.97	1,756,905.68	17,241,784.29	13,247,764.94
20	[+] #	0.00	0.00	0.00	-37,910,766.16
21					

Figure 7.39 Compact Display

40. You can now use PRODUCT GROUP and PRODUCT like a hierarchical display.
41. Select the column header of OPERATING PROFIT.
42. Use the [Ctrl] key on the keyboard and select the column header of NET SALES.
43. Select the menu CALCULATION • ADD CALCULATION • PERCENTAGE SHARE.
44. Select the column header for the newly calculated measure.
45. Select the menu CONDITIONAL FORMATTING • NEW.
46. Set the FORMAT to STATUS SYMBOL.
47. Define a condition using green for values greater than 75.
48. Click on ADD.
49. Define a condition using orange for values between 50 and 75.
50. Click on ADD (see Figure 7.40).

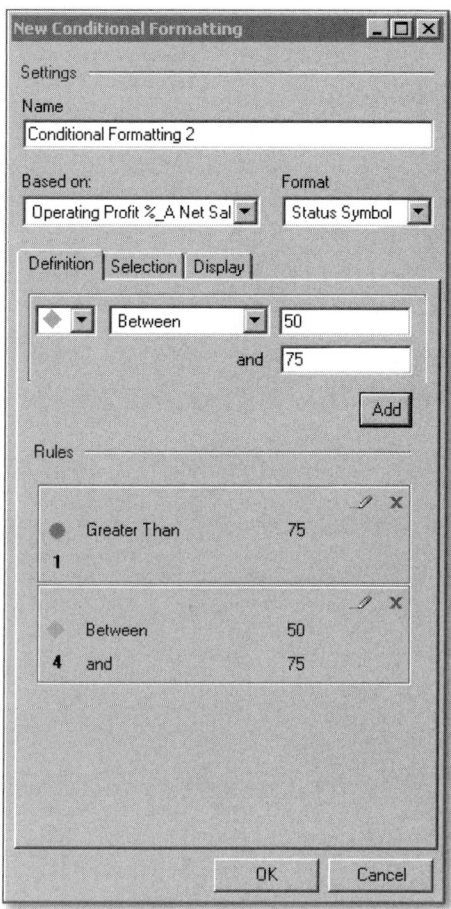

Figure 7.40 Conditional Formatting

51. Navigate to the DISPLAY tab.
52. Select the ROW HEADERS option and uncheck all other options.
53. Click on OK.

Based on the hierarchical display, the conditional formatting displays the color for the product group; for example, showing a green circle for orange juice in line 17. The product is also included in the conditional formatting and the highlighting can be different there, as shown in Figure 7.41 in lines 18 to 21.

7 | Using SAP BusinessObjects Analysis, Edition for Microsoft Office

	A	B	C	D	E	F
1		Gross Sales	Total Discount	Net Sales	Operating Profit	Operating Profit %_A Net Sales
2	Product group	$	$	$	$	%
3	Overall Result	318,665,887.22	27,793,790.68	290,872,096.54	177,514,728.16	61.02845
4	[+] Apple 10%	7,599,617.61	745,327.46	6,854,290.15	5,145,105.02	75.06401
5	[+] Apple cond	5,552,235.22	523,908.24	5,028,326.98	3,824,008.05	76.04931
6	[+] Apple nat.	6,874,457.82	622,397.25	6,252,060.57	4,676,704.91	74.80262
7	[+] Applejuice	3,731,475.56	356,321.37	3,375,154.19	2,522,793.00	74.74601
8	[+] Brandy 20%	52,535,535.31	4,381,580.56	48,153,954.75	35,270,868.18	73.24605
9	[+] Brandy 30%	38,890,395.74	3,191,766.18	35,698,629.56	26,010,202.49	72.86051
10	[+] Brandy 40%	60,307,310.95	5,327,866.43	54,979,444.52	40,339,220.90	73.37146
11	[+] Brandy lite	48,782,864.67	4,282,678.33	44,500,186.34	32,030,652.64	71.97869
12	[+] Chocookies	16,877,943.43	1,425,809.68	15,452,133.75	11,896,837.75	76.99155
13	[+] Crisps	12,214,218.96	1,079,236.94	11,134,982.02	8,510,279.00	76.42831
14	[+] Orange 10%	4,997,784.73	492,679.18	4,505,105.55	3,302,088.85	73.29659
15	[+] Orange 40%	7,509,512.12	733,155.92	6,776,356.20	5,002,859.19	73.82816
16	[+] Orange cond	6,734,452.68	588,903.79	6,145,548.89	4,595,299.85	74.77444
17	[-] Orangejuice	6,796,980.48	590,071.97	6,206,908.51	4,715,535.18	75.97236
18	Orangejuice 0,2	684,123.00	64,630.48	619,492.52	463,752.32	74.86004
19	Orangejuice 0,7	1,345,516.77	122,311.36	1,223,205.41	900,285.16	73.60049
20	Orangejuice 1,0	3,178,065.78	288,715.79	2,889,349.99	2,204,936.02	76.3125
21	Orangejuice 2,0	1,589,274.93	114,414.34	1,474,860.59	1,146,561.68	77.74034
22	[+] Pumpkincook	20,262,411.97	1,695,181.70	18,567,230.27	14,335,274.37	77.20739
23	[+] Softcookies	18,998,689.97	1,756,905.68	17,241,784.29	13,247,764.94	76.83523
24	[+] #	0.00	0.00	0.00	-37,910,766.16	

Figure 7.41 Cross Tab with Highlighting

At this point we have found the most profitable products and product groups. In the next steps we are interested in comparing the different sales regions and chain groups with each other.

1. Navigate to a new empty sheet inside Microsoft Excel.
2. Select cell A1 in the empty sheet.
3. Navigate to the COMPONENTS tab of the navigation panel.
4. Select CROSSTAB 1 in the list of elements.
5. Right-click and select the COPY menu (see Figure 7.42).
6. Confirm the cell selection and click on OK. You have created a copy of your existing cross tab on a new sheet in the spreadsheet.
7. Navigate to the ANALYSIS tab of the navigation panel.
8. Remove PRODUCT AND PRODUCT GROUP from ROWS.
9. Add SALES REGION to the ROWS.
10. Add GROUP to the ROWS.

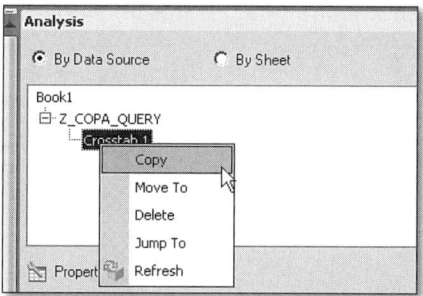

Figure 7.42 Components

11. Navigate to the menu CONDITIONAL FORMATTING • CONDITIONAL FORMATTING 1 • ACTIVE. By unchecking the ACTIVE option you can disable the conditional formatting.

12. Select the HIERARCHY menu and uncheck the COMPACT DISPLAY IN ROWS option (see Figure 7.43).

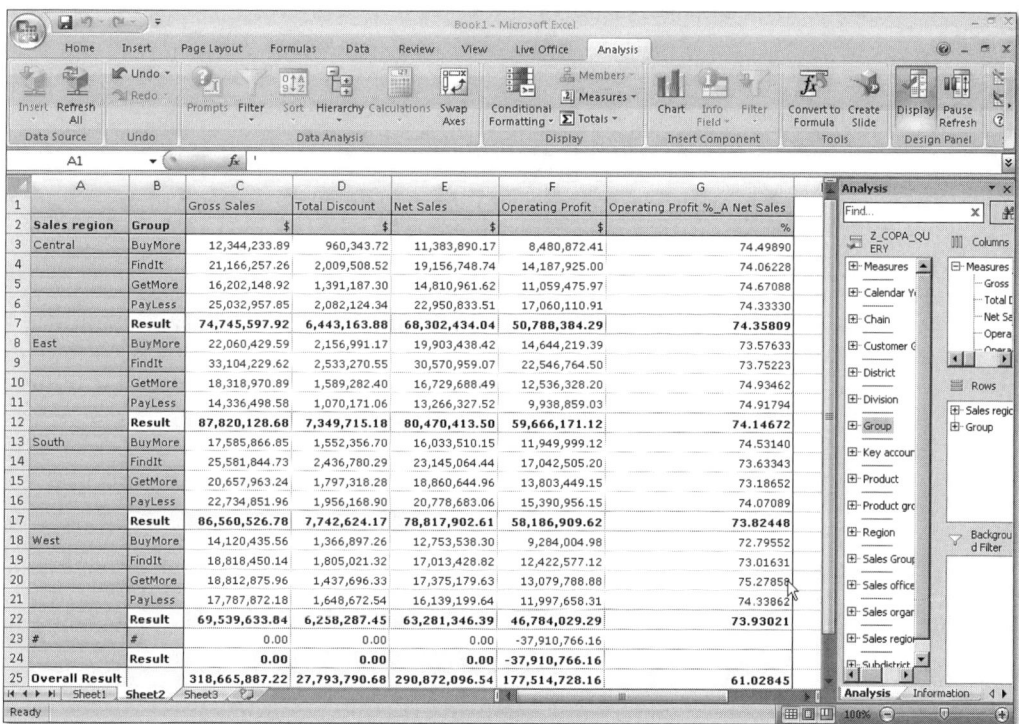

Figure 7.43 Cross Tab

You can see from Figure 7.43 that across the sales region your groups are between 73% and 75% operating profit. Let's drill down further.

1. Remove SALES GROUP from ROWS.
2. Add CHAIN as the inner row so that the display shows GROUP first and then CHAIN.
3. Add PRODUCT to ROWS.
4. Select the column header for GROSS SALES.
5. Select the menu FILTER • FILTER BY MEASURE • MOST DETAILED DIMENSION IN ROWS • EDIT.
6. Select the BOTTOM N option.
7. Enter the value 5.
8. Click on ADD.

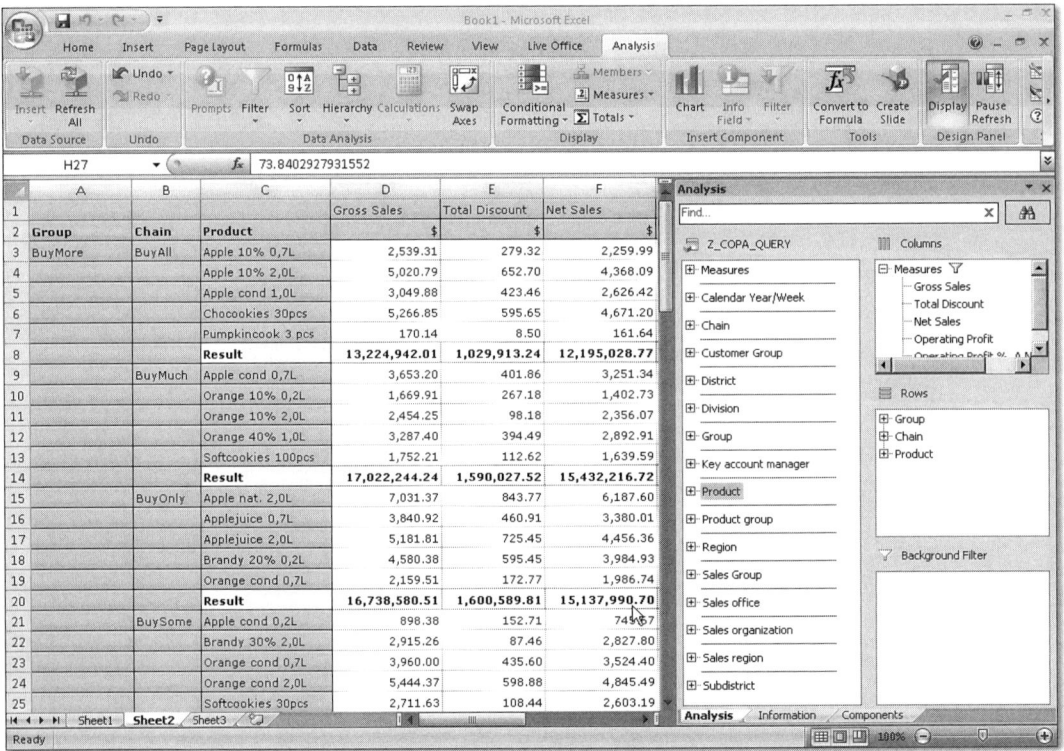

Figure 7.44 Changed Cross Tab

We are shown the bottom 5 products for each group and chain combination (see Figure 7.44). We can quickly identify a pattern and a set of products that repeat themselves in the bottom 5 across multiple chains. In the next steps we focus on this pattern to get more details.

1. Remove CHAIN from ROWS (see Figure 7.45).

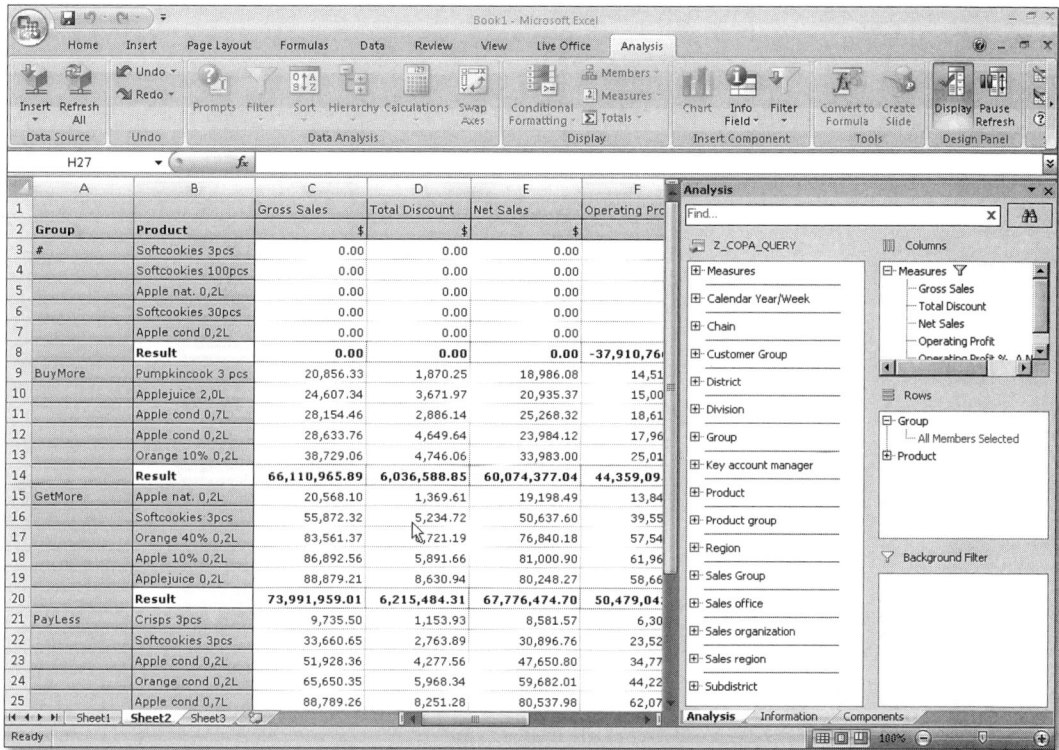

Figure 7.45 Cross Tab

Now the pattern becomes even more obvious. You can recognize that a small set of apple juice products across all groups has the lowest sales revenue.

2. Remove GROUP from ROWS.
3. Select a cell in the cross tab.
4. Select the menu item CHART in the Analysis ribbon.

A chart is created, which you can design and format using the common Microsoft Excel functionality.

7 | Using SAP BusinessObjects Analysis, Edition for Microsoft Office

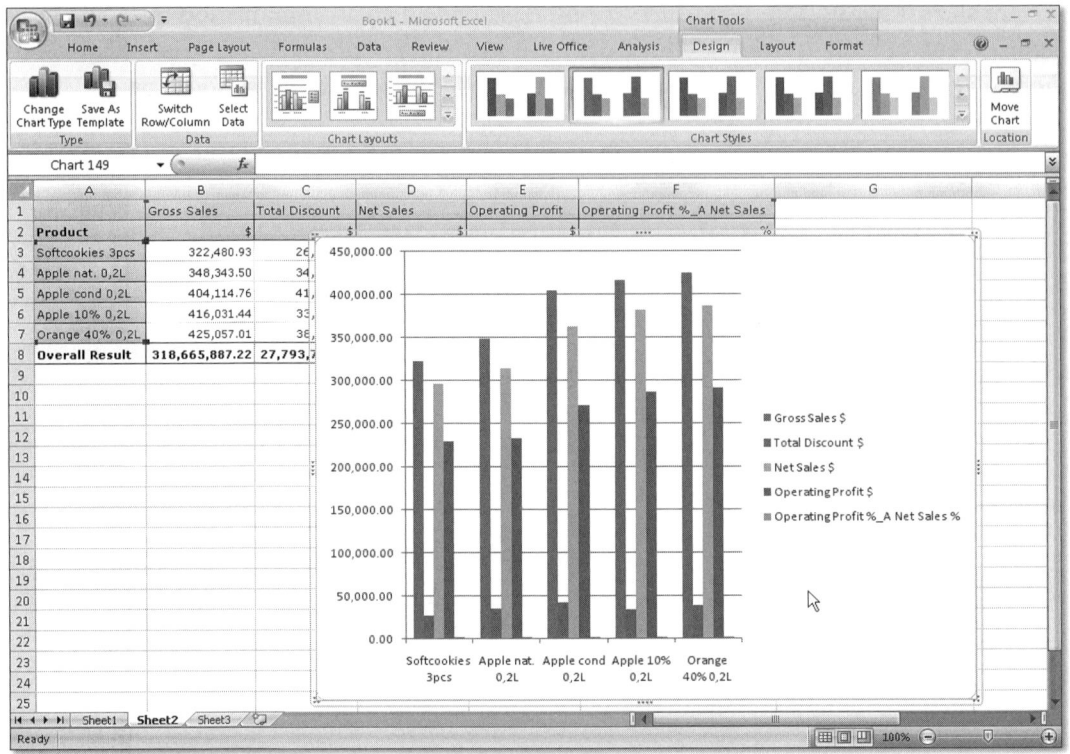

Figure 7.46 Chart

5. Use the MICROSOFT OFFICE button to save your work. Click on the MICROSOFT OFFICE button.
6. Select the SAVE WORKBOOK menu item.
7. Log on to your SAP BusinessObjects BI platform.
8. Select a folder for your workbook.
9. Enter a name for your workbook.
10. Click on SAVE.

In this example we used SAP BusinessObjects Analysis, edition for Microsoft Office to analyze profitability, and were quickly able to identify the most profitable products. In the second part of our example, we used SAP BusinessObjects Analysis, edition for Microsoft Office to compare the profitability of our sales groups and chains. We were then able to identify the set of products that—across all our sales areas—were the products with the lowest profits.

7.6 Summary

In this chapter, you used SAP BusinessObjects Analysis, edition for Microsoft Office and learned about possible deployment and data connectivity. In addition, you learned some of the basics of using SAP BusinessObjects Analysis, edition for Microsoft Office, and then created a cost center report for your financial area and a profitability report for sales management. In the next chapter we use SAP BusinessObjects Analysis, edition for OLAP to fulfill our established business requirements.

SAP BusinessObjects Analysis, edition for OLAP is your analytical BI client deployment option for the web. In this chapter, you will learn how SAP BusinessObjects Analysis, edition for OLAP is able to fulfill some of your business requirements and provide your users with a rich multi-dimensional user experience.

8   Using SAP BusinessObjects Analysis, Edition for OLAP

In this chapter we focus on SAP BusinessObjects Analysis, edition for OLAP. We begin by explaining data connectivity options, and then we describe the first steps for using the product to fulfill business requirements.

8.1   SAP Data Connectivity

In this section, you will learn about the different options you can use in combination with SAP BusinessObjects Analysis, edition for OLAP to connect to your SAP data sources. SAP BusinessObjects Analysis, edition for OLAP is part of your SAP BusinessObjects BI platform and uses the shared connections from the platform (see Figure 8.1).

SAP BusinessObjects Analysis, edition for OLAP is able:

- To directly access shared connections from the SAP BusinessObjects BI platform via BI Consumer Services (BICS).
- To connect to BEx queries and InfoProviders in SAP NetWeaver BW, as well as BEx queries combined with the transient provider.
- To establish a direct link to SAP HANA.

8 | Using SAP BusinessObjects Analysis, Edition for OLAP

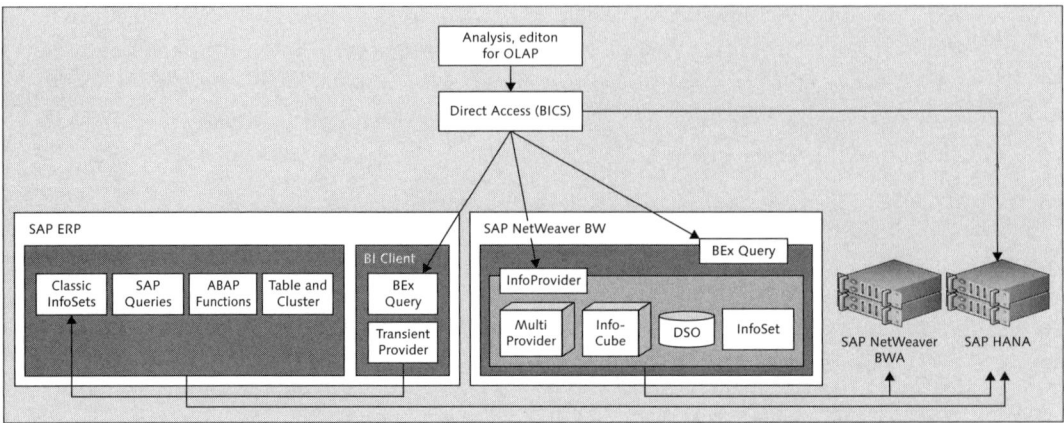

Figure 8.1 Data Connectivity

As you will notice, SAP BusinessObjects Analysis, edition for OLAP—like SAP BusinessObjects Analysis, edition for Microsoft Office—does not yet integrate with the semantic layer from SAP BusinessObjects. Therefore, the only option for using SAP BusinessObjects Analysis, edition for OLAP in combination with your SAP ERP data is either to use the transient provider as part of the local BI client, or to use SAP HANA. With the latter option, you can replicate the data from your SAP ERP system to SAP HANA and then establish a connection from SAP BusinessObjects Analysis, edition for OLAP to SAP HANA.

Table 8.1 shows the elements supported when using SAP BusinessObjects Analysis, edition for OLAP in combination with a BEx query.

	Direct Access using BICS
Direct access to InfoCube and MultiProvider	Yes
Access to BEx queries	Yes
Characteristic Values	
Key	Yes
Short description	Yes
Medium and long description	Yes

Table 8.1 Supported and Unsupported BEx Query Features for SAP BusinessObjects Analysis, Edition for OLAP

298

	Direct Access using BICS
BEx Query Features	
Support for hierarchies	Yes
Support for free characteristics	Yes
Support for calculated and restricted key figures	Yes
Support for currencies and units	Yes
Support for custom structures	Yes
Support for formulas and selections	Yes
Support for filter	Yes
Support for display and navigational attributes	Yes
Support for conditions in rows	Yes
Support for conditions in columns	Yes
Support for conditions for fixed characteristics	Yes
Support for exceptions	Yes
Compounded characteristics	Yes
Constant selection	Yes
Default values in BEx query	Yes
Number scaling factor	Yes
Number of decimals	Yes
Calculate rows as (local calculation)	Yes
Sorting	Yes
Hide/unhide	Yes
Display as hierarchy	Yes
Reverse sign	Yes
Support for reading master data	Yes

Table 8.1 Supported and Unsupported BEx Query Features for SAP BusinessObjects Analysis, Edition for OLAP (Cont.)

	Direct Access using BICS
Data Types	
Support for CHAR (characteristics)	Yes
Support for NUMC (characteristics)	Yes
Support for DATS (characteristics)	Yes
Support for TIMS (characteristics)	Yes
Support for numeric key figures such as Amount and Quantity	Yes
Support for Date (key figure)	Yes
Support for Time (key figure)	Yes
SAP Variables—Processing Type	
User input	Yes
Authorization	Yes
Replacement path	Yes
SAP exit/custom exit	Yes
Precalculated value set	Yes
General Features for Variables	
Support for optional and mandatory variables	Yes
Support for key date dependencies	Yes
Support for default values	Yes
Support for personalized values	No
SAP Variables—Variable Type	
Single value	Yes
Multi-single value	Yes
Interval value	Yes
Selection option	Yes

Table 8.1 Supported and Unsupported BEx Query Features for SAP BusinessObjects Analysis, Edition for OLAP (Cont.)

	Direct Access using BICS
Hierarchy variable	Yes
Hierarchy node variable	Yes
Hierarchy version variable	Yes
Text variable	Yes
EXIT variable	Yes
Single key date variable	Yes
Multiple key dates	Yes
Formula variable	Yes

Table 8.1 Supported and Unsupported BEx Query Features for SAP BusinessObjects Analysis, Edition for OLAP (Cont.)

Table 8.2 shows how the direct access BICS option uses the elements from the BEx query, and how the objects are used in SAP BusinessObjects Analysis, edition for OLAP.

BEx Query Element	SAP BusinessObjects Analysis, Edition for OLAP
Characteristic	For each characteristic you receive a field and with the context menu you can decide which part of the characteristic you would like to show.
Hierarchy	Each available hierarchy is shown as an external hierarchy and can be used as part of the cross tab. In addition, you can use hierarchy levels as part of your cross tab; for example, you can show all members of Level 2 of the hierarchy.
Key figure	Each key figure is shown with the unit and scaling factor information.
Calculated/restricted key figure	Each calculated and restricted key figure is treated like a key figure. The user does not have access to the underlying definition in SAP BusinessObjects Analysis, edition for OLAP.
Filters	Filters are applied to the underlying query but are not visible in the navigation panel as part of the background filter area.

Table 8.2 SAP NetWeaver BW Metadata Mapping for SAP BusinessObjects Analysis, Edition for OLAP

8   Using SAP BusinessObjects Analysis, Edition for OLAP

BEx Query Element	SAP BusinessObjects Analysis, Edition for OLAP
Display attribute	Display attributes are available in the layout panel and can be shown as part of your result set.
Navigational attribute	Navigational attributes are treated the same way as characteristics.
Variables	Each variable with the READY FOR INPUT property activated results in a prompt. You can use the prompts menu to provide the necessary input values.
Custom structures	A custom structure is available as an element in the navigation panel and each structure element can be selected or de-selected for the report using the members dialog.

Table 8.2 SAP NetWeaver BW Metadata Mapping for SAP BusinessObjects Analysis, Edition for OLAP (Cont.)

So far we have reviewed the different data connectivity options available with SAP BusinessObjects Analysis, edition for OLAP. As the next step, we map the product capabilities against our business requirements, so that we can evaluate which of our requirements can be fulfilled.

8.2   Assessing the Business Requirements

In this section, we use our list of requirements and compare them with product capabilities. Knowing that SAP BusinessObjects Analysis, edition for Microsoft Office and SAP BusinessObjects Analysis, edition for OLAP are very similar in terms of functional capabilities, it should not come as a surprise that SAP BusinessObjects Analysis, edition for OLAP fulfills similar requirements as SAP BusinessObjects Analysis, edition for Microsoft Office.

8.2.1   Financial Reporting and Analysis Requirements

The only financial requirement that we can not fulfill using SAP BusinessObjects Analysis, edition for OLAP is the requirement to create very layout-focused and print-oriented reports.

> **Unfulfilled Requirements**
>
> ▶ For specific content (such as an income statement or a balance sheet), the design needs to be layout focused with the actual print version of the report being a high priority.
>
> ▶ Users need to be able to create planning scenarios and write information back into the source.

Just because the product capabilities allow us to fulfill all other requirements from the financial area, it does not mean that SAP BusinessObjects Analysis, edition for OLAP will always be the best option. SAP BusinessObjects Analysis, edition for OLAP is a BI environment that mainly targets business analysts and power users; as such, other BI products might be a better option for certain situations.

Unlike SAP BusinessObjects Analysis, edition for Microsoft Office, the current release of SAP BusinessObjects Analysis, edition for OLAP does not integrate with the planning capabilities of SAP NetWeaver BW and is not able to write back into the underlying source. Therefore, this requirement can't be fulfilled.

For the requirement to offer analytical content in a web-based environment and in a Microsoft Office-based environment, the solution is based on the combination of SAP BusinessObjects Analysis, edition for Microsoft Office and SAP BusinessObjects Analysis, edition for OLAP.

8.2.2 Sales Reporting and Analysis Requirements

Just as SAP BusinessObjects Analysis, edition for Microsoft Office is able to fulfill most of the requirements in the sales area, SAP BusinessObjects Analysis, edition for OLAP is able to provide similar functionalities (and limitations).

> **Unfulfilled Requirements**
>
> ▶ Content must be available online, offline, and on mobile devices (for sales representatives on the road).
>
> ▶ Distribution of content via email may be required.
>
> ▶ Users should be able to perform scenario-based analysis, where the user is able to see the data but can also influence certain factors and see the impact on the overall numbers; for example, a what-if analysis in a sales planning workflow.

As discussed in Chapter 7, the limitations concern the ability to provide access to the information on a mobile device and the ability to provide offline access to corporate information. Both requests are not possible with SAP BusinessObjects Analysis, edition for OLAP.

At the time of this writing (November 2011) the ability to schedule a SAP BusinessObjects Analysis, edition for Microsoft Office or SAP BusinessObjects Analysis, edition of OLAP document is already part of the product roadmap, but it is not available in the 4.0 FP3 current release.

8.2.3 Human Resources (HR) Reporting and Analysis Requirements

The unfulfilled requirements from the HR area shouldn't come as a surprise, as SAP BusinessObjects Analysis, edition for OLAP focuses not on layout-driven reporting but instead on providing strong analytical functionality to your end user.

Unfulfilled Requirements

- The content needs to present highly textual information in a layout-focused format.
- Some of the content (such as employee appraisals or performance reviews) will likely be used as official documentation and therefore needs to follow strict layout rules.

These requirements are much better suited for a BI client product like SAP Crystal Reports for Enterprise.

8.2.4 C-Level Management and Leadership Reporting and Analysis Requirements

Looking at the requirements from our management and leadership team, we notice that several of the requirements can be fulfilled using SAP BusinessObjects Analysis, edition for OLAP. However, we do have a set of unfulfilled requirements.

Unfulfilled Requirements

- The content needs to present highly aggregated information with alerts for important key performance indicators (KPIs).
- The information needs to be available on mobile devices.

> ► The consumption of the reports and analytics needs to be simple and easy to use, and critical information needs to be easily identifiable.

Again, in the same way that we are able to provide highly aggregated data using SAP BusinessObjects Analysis, edition for Microsoft Office, we are able to do so using SAP BusinessObjects Analysis, edition for OLAP. However, we lack the capability to create alerts and provide these alerts in a proactive way to our end users. In addition, we are also unable to provide a solution for SAP BusinessObjects Analysis, edition for OLAP on mobile devices.

Based on the audience—our management and leadership team—the requirement to provide critical information in an easy way is not something for which we would use SAP BusinessObjects Analysis, edition for OLAP. In terms of features and functions, the product is more than capable of providing access to critical information, but SAP BusinessObjects Analysis, edition for OLAP is not well suited for this type of audience and the information is better delivered using a different BI client product.

We reviewed all the requirements and decided which of the requirements we can fulfill using SAP BusinessObjects Analysis, edition for OLAP and which are better suited for a different product. In the next section, we describe some basic steps for using the product.

8.3 Introduction to the Tool

Before we use SAP BusinessObjects Analysis, edition for OLAP to fulfill some of our requirements, we will learn the first steps in navigating and analyzing the data from SAP NetWeaver BW. We will leverage the BEx query that we configured for our first steps using SAP BusinessObjects Analysis, edition for Microsoft Office (see Figure 7.2).

As we mentioned in all other previous chapters, BI clients are able to share connections, so there is no need to specifically set up the connection for SAP BusinessObjects Analysis, edition for OLAP. You can find the detailed steps on how to set up the OLAP connections in Chapter 4, Section 4.3.3.

After we configure the OLAP connection in the Central Management Console (CMC) we can build our first workbook using SAP BusinessObjects Analysis, edition for OLAP.

1. Start the BI launch pad by following the menu START • PROGRAMS • SAP BUSINESS-OBJECTS BI PLATFORM 4 • SAP BUSINESSOBJECTS BI PLATFORM • SAP BUSINESS-OBJECTS BI PLATFORM • JAVA BI LAUNCH PAD.
2. Log on using your SAP credentials.
3. Select the menu APPLICATION • ANALYSIS, EDITION FOR OLAP.
4. You are presented with a list of available connections. Select the connection you created previously.
5. Click on NEXT. You are presented with the list of available BEx queries (see Figure 8.2).

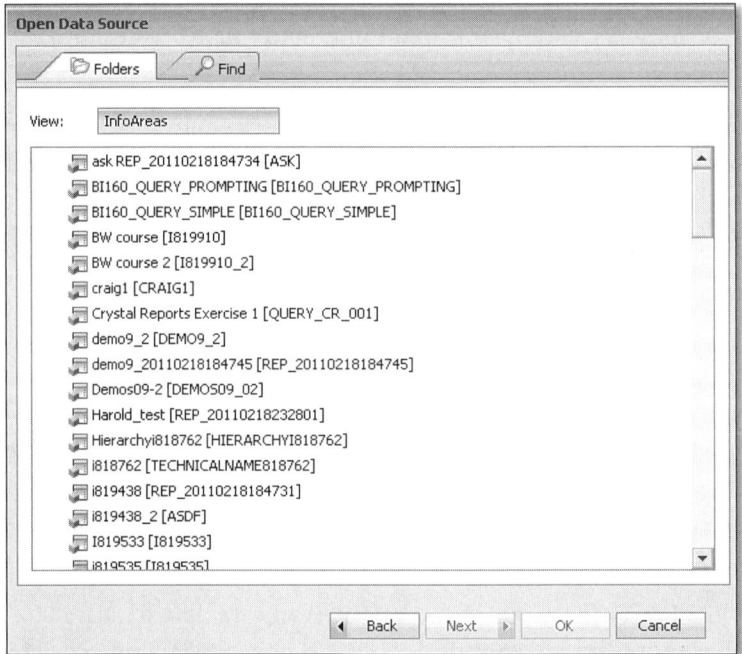

Figure 8.2 BEx Queries

6. Select the BEx query and click on OK.

7. The result set is shown based on the layout configured in the BEx query (see Figure 8.3).

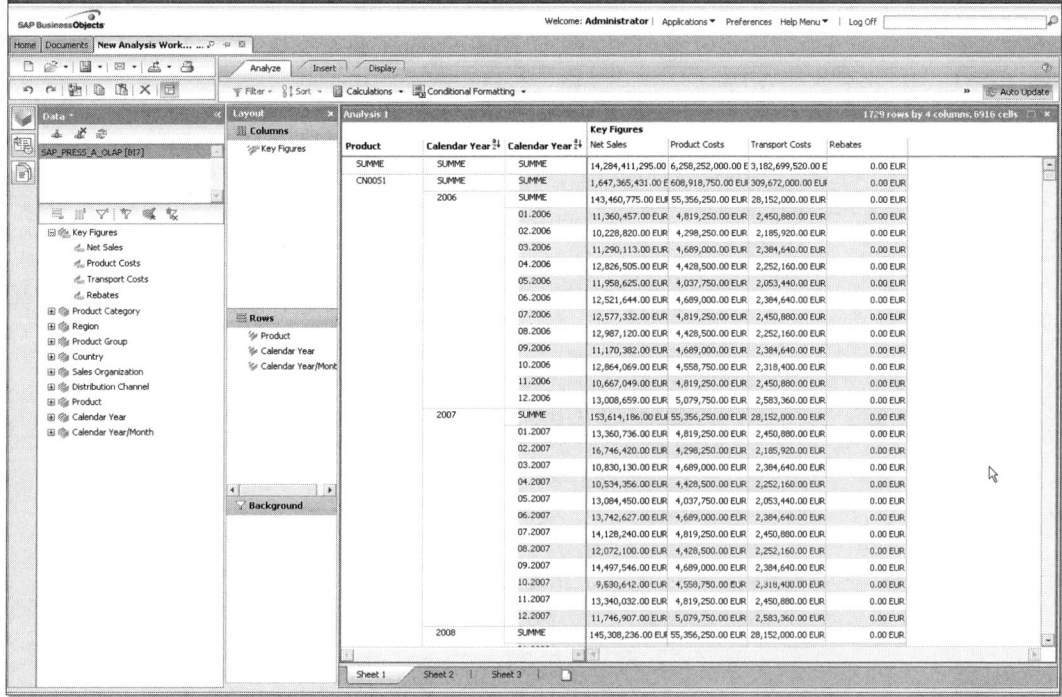

Figure 8.3 Default Resultset

SAP BusinessObjects Analysis, edition for OLAP has three main panels. On the far left, you can see the list of connections and the available metadata, which you can use to analyze the information.

Next to that, you can see the layout panel, which provides you with the option to navigate the data. It also provides you access to the ROWS, COLUMNS, and BACKGROUND FILTER areas.

The area on the far right displays the actual data from your report. Each sheet can have up to four components, where a component could be a cross tab or a chart.

1. Select the entry for PRODUCT in the LAYOUT tab.
2. Right-click and select DISPLAY AS (see Figure 8.4).
3. Select the option KEY : TEXT for the product.

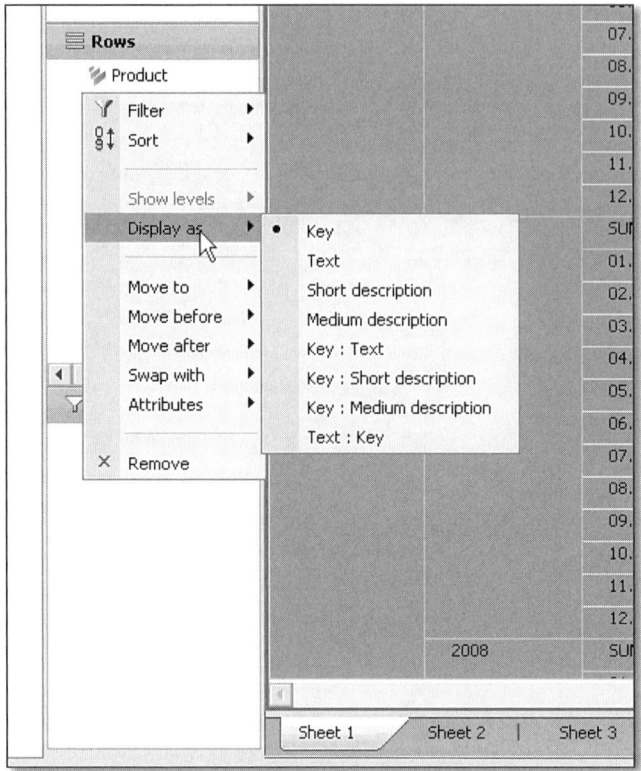

Figure 8.4 Display As

4. Select the column header for NET SALES.
5. Navigate to the DISPLAY tab.
6. Click on MEASURE FORMAT (see Figure 8.5).
7. Ensure the SERVER option is selected for all measures.
8. Click on OK.
9. Right-click on CALENDAR YEAR in ROWS.
10. Select the REMOVE menu entry.
11. Right-click on CALENDAR YEAR/MONTH in ROWS.
12. Select the REMOVE menu entry.
13. Right-click on PRODUCT in ROWS.
14. Select the option FILTER • BY MEASURE (see Figure 8.6).

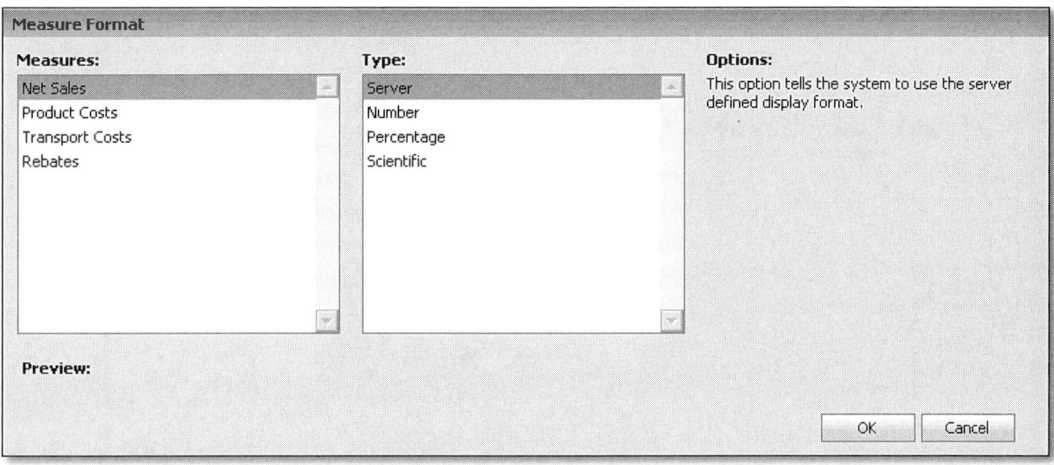

Figure 8.5 Measure Format

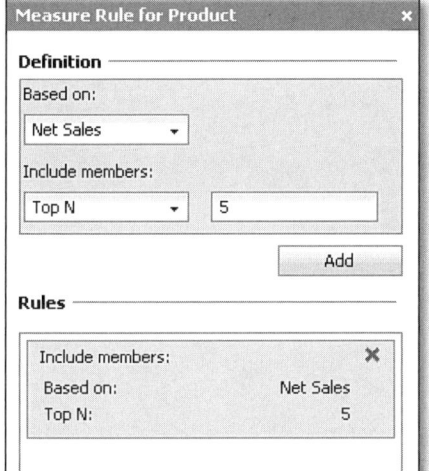

Figure 8.6 Filter by Measure

15. Select the option TOP N and enter the value 5.
16. Click on ADD.
17. Click on OK.
18. Open the entry for CALENDAR YEAR in the list of available dimensions.
19. Drag and drop CALENDAR YEAR to the BACKGROUND area (see Figure 8.7).

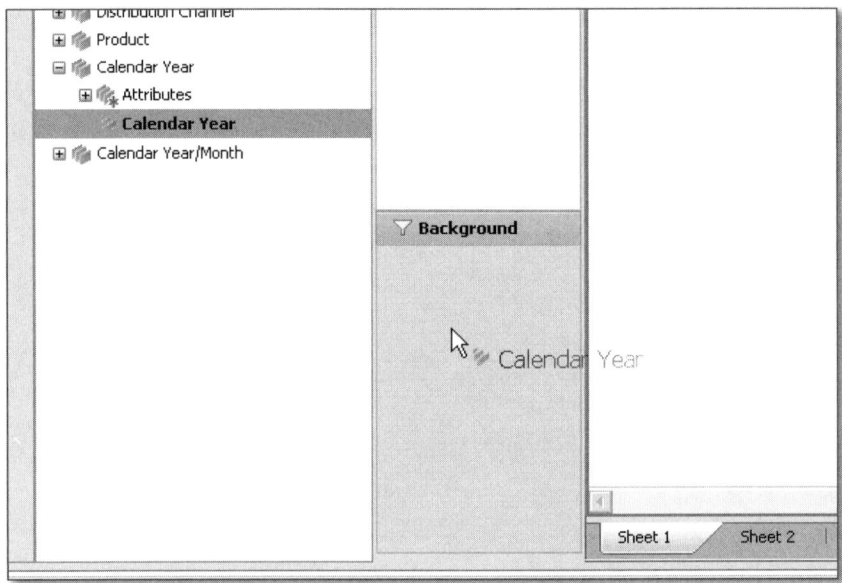

Figure 8.7 Background Filter

20. Because you moved CALENDAR YEAR to the BACKGROUND area, you are asked to select the actual filter vales (see Figure 8.8).

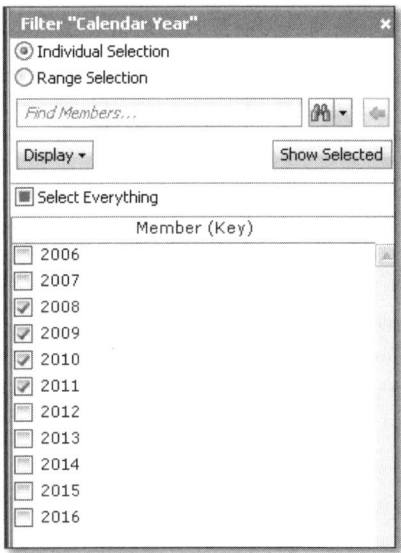

Figure 8.8 Filter by Member

21. Select the years 2008, 2009, 2010, and 2011.
22. Click on OK.
23. Click on AUTO UPDATE (top right corner).
24. Remove PRODUCT from ROWS by dragging the object to an empty area (see Figure 8.9).

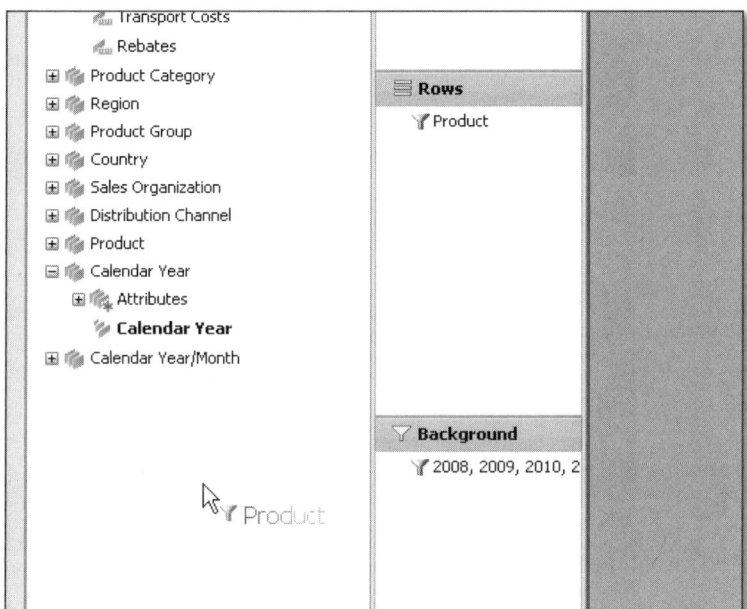

Figure 8.9 Remove Product

25. Click on AUTO UPDATE again and your cross tab is updated.

> **Auto Update**
> The AUTO UPDATE option allows you to stop the interactivity with the underlying SAP NetWeaver BW server. You can still navigate in the data but the changes are not reflected in the actual result set until you enable the AUTO UPDATE. In that way, you can minimize the interaction with the SAP NetWeaver BW system.

26. Open the list of available objects for COUNTRY (see Figure 8.10).
27. Drag and drop COUNTRY HIERARCHY 1 to ROWS (Figure 8.11).
28. Right-click on COUNTRY HIERARCHY 1 in the layout panel.

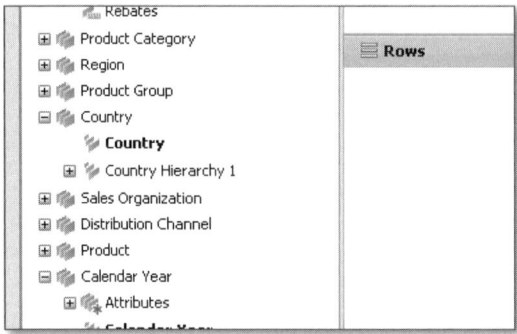

Figure 8.10 List of Available Objects

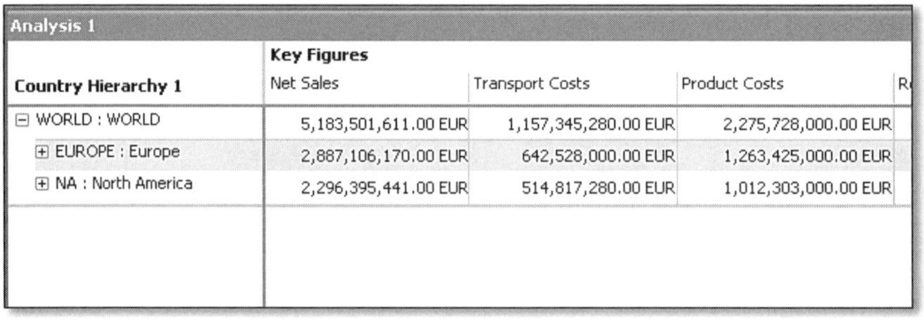

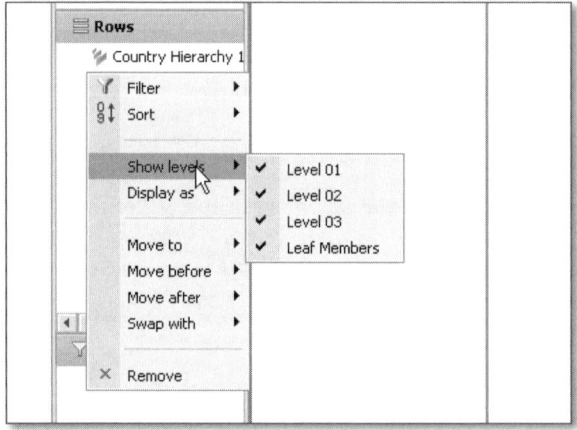

Figure 8.11 Hierarchical Data

29. Select the SHOW LEVELS menu (see Figure 8.12).

Figure 8.12 Show Levels

30. Select LEAF MEMBERS.
31. Right-click on COUNTRY HIERARCHY 1 in the layout panel and select SHOW LEVELS.
32. Activate the display of the leaf members.
33. You can also use the available levels and leaf member entries below COUNTRY HIERARCHY 1 in the list of available objects (see Figure 8.13). These entries are used for visual filters, meaning that only the display is filtered, not the actual data.

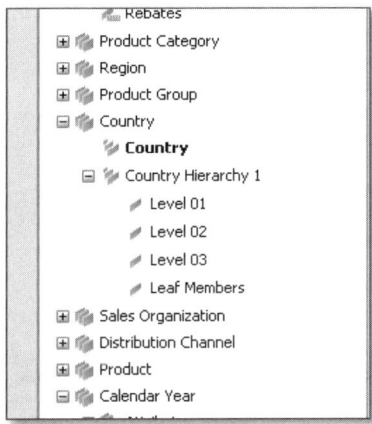

Figure 8.13 Visual Filtering

34. Click on the column header for TRANSPORT COSTS.
35. Hold the Ctrl button on the keyboard and click on the column header for PRODUCT COSTS.
36. Navigate to the ANALYZE tab.
37. Click on CALCULATIONS.
38. Select the ADD option (see Figure 8.14).

> **Calculations**
> As shown in the previous steps, the calculations in SAP BusinessObjects Analysis, edition for OLAP rely on the order of selecting the elements. The first selected element is used as the first operant and the second selected element is used as the second operant.

39. Click on the column header for NET SALES.

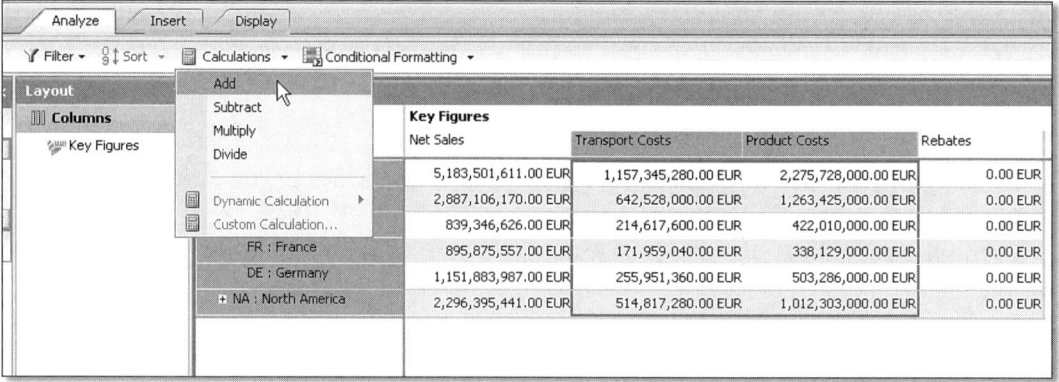

Figure 8.14 Calculations

40. Navigate to the ANALYZE tab.
41. Click on CALCULATIONS.
42. Select the option DYNAMIC CALCULATION • RANK NUMBER (see Figure 8.15).

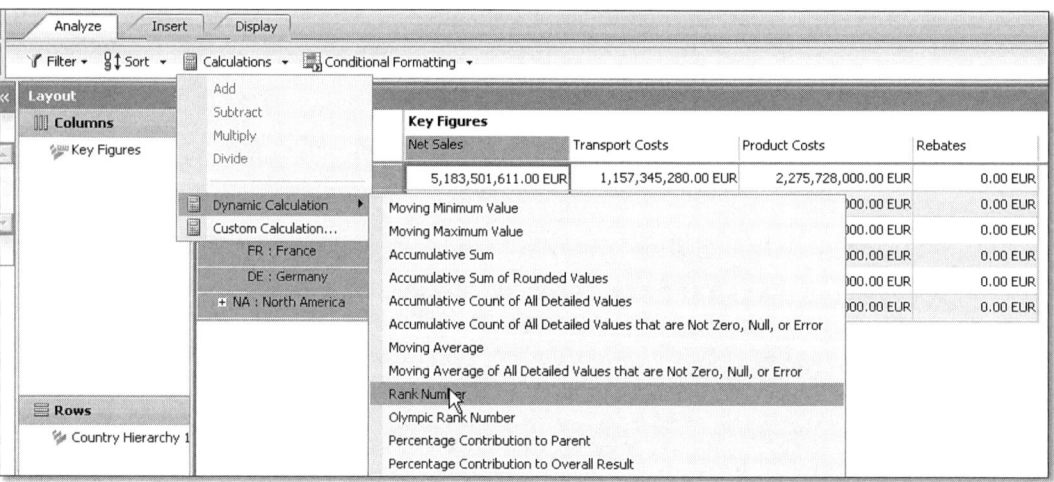

Figure 8.15 Ranking

43. NET SALES is now ranked along the hierarchy.
44. Navigate to the INSERT tab.
45. Click on the column chart symbol and select the CLUSTERED COLUMN option (see Figure 8.16).

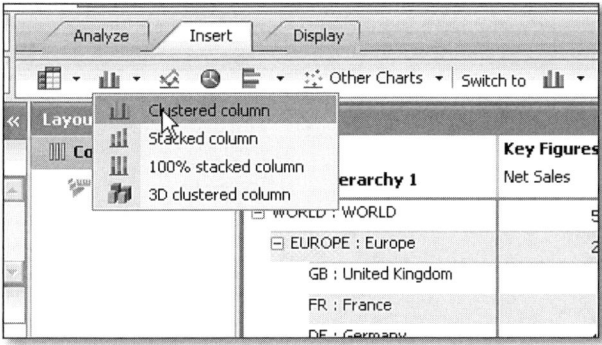

Figure 8.16 Clustered Column

46. A column chart is added to the sheet (see Figure 8.17).

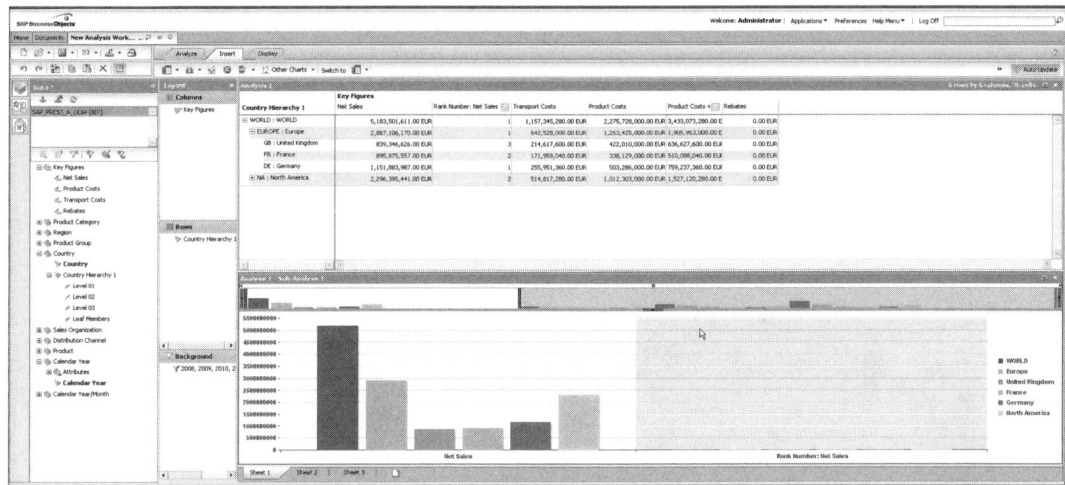

Figure 8.17 Example Workbook

47. Select the chart.
48. Select PROPERTIES in the far left panel (see Figure 8.18).
49. Activate the option SHOW HIERARCHICAL LABELING.
50. Click on APPLY.
51. Navigate to the DISPLAY tab.
52. Click on SWAP AXES.

8 | Using SAP BusinessObjects Analysis, Edition for OLAP

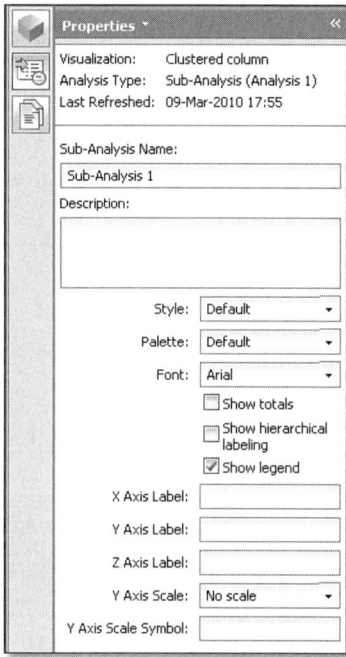

Figure 8.18 Properties

53. Put the chart in full screen mode (see Figure 8.19).

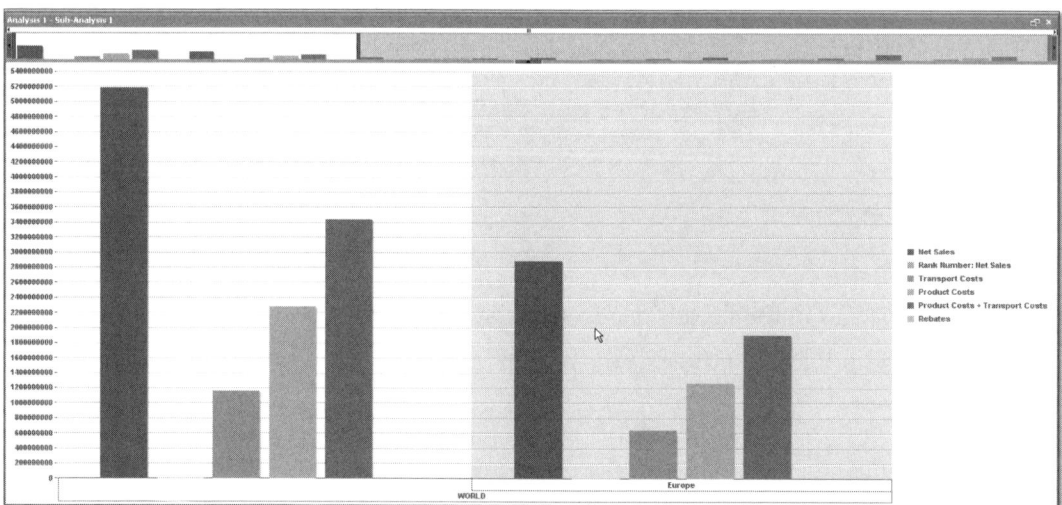

Figure 8.19 Chart in Full Screen Mode

54. Use the small area above the chart to focus on a specific area of your chart in cases where you visualize larger amounts of data.
55. Minimize the chart again so that you can see the table and the chart.
56. Use the SAVE AS menu to store your workbook (see Figure 8.20).

Figure 8.20 Save As Menu

57. Select a folder for your workbook.
58. Enter a name for your workbook.
59. Click on SAVE.

You can now view your workbook via the BI launch pad.

In this section you learned some basic steps in SAP BusinessObjects Analysis, edition for OLAP. In the next section we discuss which business requirements we can fulfill using SAP BusinessObjects Analysis, edition for OLAP.

8.4 Building a Workbook for Financial Analysis

Just as we created a financial report using SAP BusinessObjects Analysis, edition for Microsoft Office, we will use those same queries to create an analytical report using SAP BusinessObjects Analysis, edition for OLAP.

We will use the BEx query, which we already used in combination with SAP BusinessObjectsWeb Intelligence in Section 5.5. As with all other BI client products in the SAP BusinessObjects 4.x suite, SAP BusinessObjects Analysis, edition for OLAP is able to share connections with the other BI client products, so at this stage there is no need to create an additional connection.

1. Start the BI launch pad by following the menu START • PROGRAMS • SAP BUSINESSOBJECTS BI PLATFORM 4 • SAP BUSINESSOBJECTS BI PLATFORM • SAP BUSINESSOBJECTS BI PLATFORM • JAVA BI LAUNCH PAD.

8 | Using SAP BusinessObjects Analysis, Edition for OLAP

2. Log on using your SAP credentials.
3. Select the menu APPLICATION • ANALYSIS, EDITION FOR OLAP.
4. You are first presented with a list of available connections. Select the connection created previously for the needed BEx query.
5. Click on NEXT.
6. Select the BEx query.
7. Click on OK.
8. Right-click on COST ELEMENT in ROWS.
9. Select REMOVE.
10. Right-click on the hierarchy for COST CENTER in ROWS.
11. Select the menu DISPLAY AS • TEXT.
12. Use the + symbol in the cross tab to open the levels of your hierarchy (see Figure 8.21).

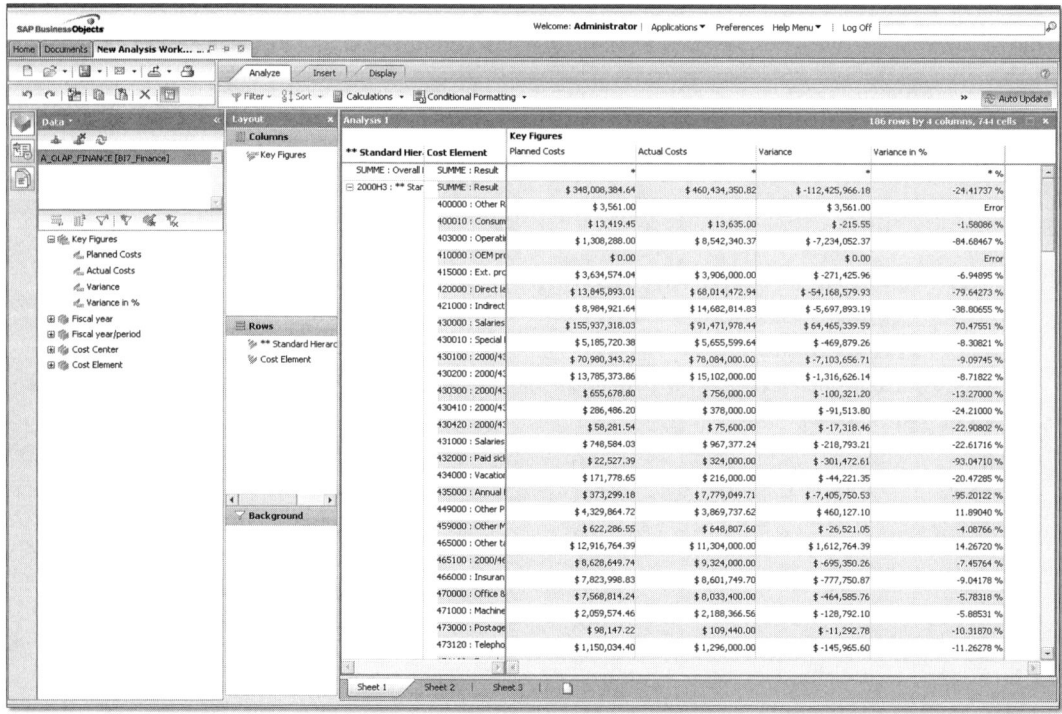

Figure 8.21 Hierarchy Levels in Cross Tab

318

13. Select the column header of the measure VARIANCE IN %.
14. Right-click and select CONDITIONAL FORMATTING • NEW.
15. Configure two sets of conditional formatting so that values smaller than -50% are highlighted in red and values between 0% and -50% are highlighted in orange (see Figure 8.22).

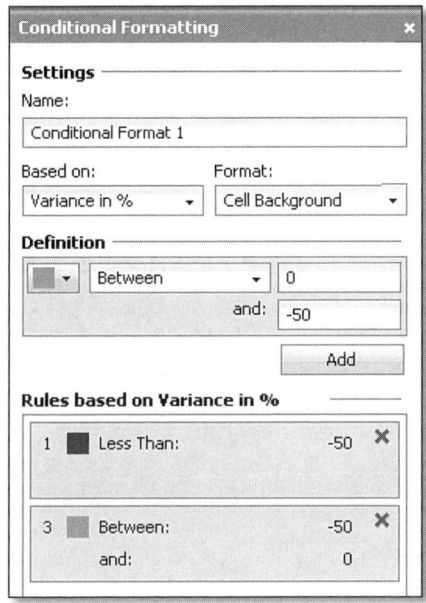

Figure 8.22 Conditional Formatting (Part 1)

16. Activate the PREVIEW option. The PREVIEW option allows you to recognize the impact of the conditional formatting on your cross tab before confirming it.
17. Click on OK (see Figure 8.23).
18. Select the column header for measure VARIANCE IN %.
19. Right-click on the top header of the hierarchy and use the menu FILTER • BY MEASURE (see Figure 8.24).
20. Select the option VARIANCE IN % for BASED ON.
21. Select the LESS THAN option.
22. Enter the value 0.

8 | Using SAP BusinessObjects Analysis, Edition for OLAP

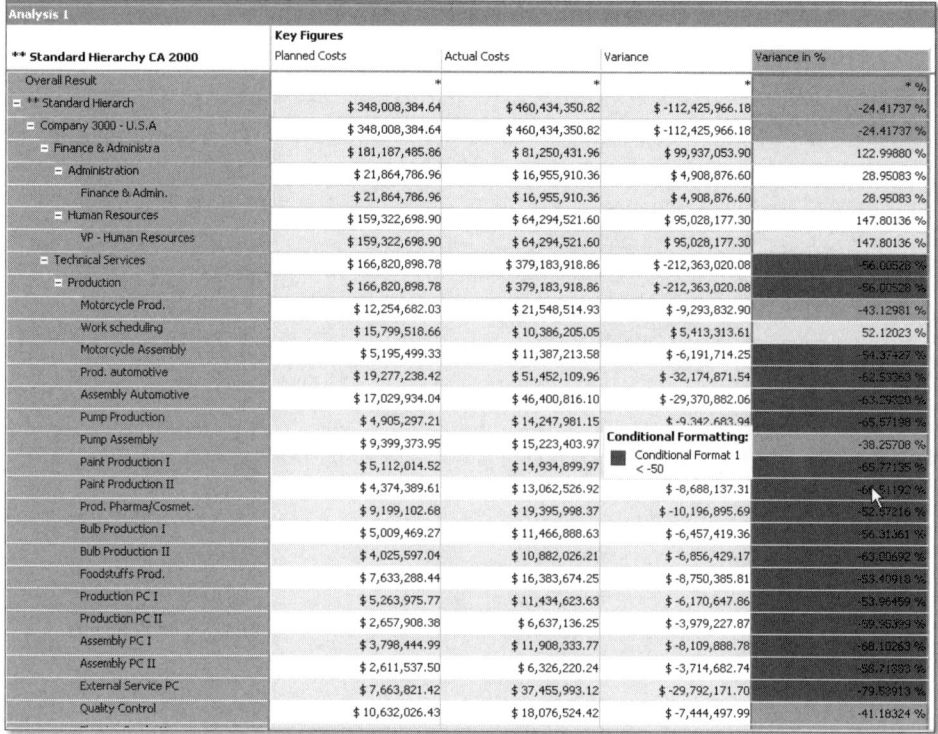

Figure 8.23 Conditional Formatting (Part 2)

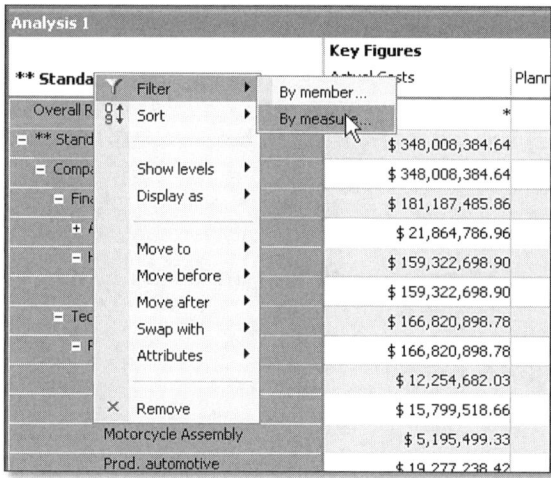

Figure 8.24 Context Menu

23. Click on ADD (see Figure 8.25).

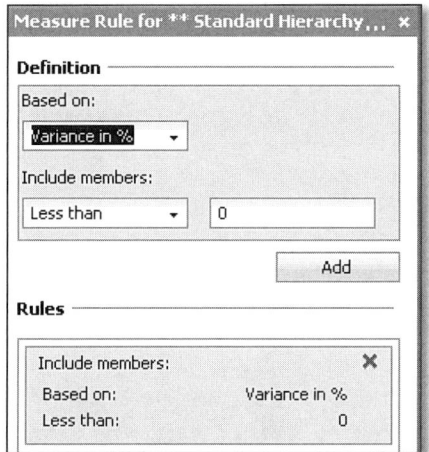

Figure 8.25 Filter by Measure

24. Click on OK. Your cross tab—including the hierarchical nodes and leaves—are now filtered based on a measure. Based on highlighting and filtering by measure, we are able to quickly identify those areas of our business that have used more of the allocated budget than planned.
25. Move the hierarchy from the ROWS area to the BACKGROUND FILTER area.
26. Add COST ELEMENT to ROWS.
27. Select the column header for VARIANCE IN %.
28. Right-click on dimension COST ELEMENT in the ROWS area (see Figure 8.26).
29. Select the menu FILTER • BY MEASURE.
30. Select VARIANCE IN % for BASED ON.
31. Select BOTTOM N.
32. Enter the value 10.
33. Click on ADD.
34. Click on OK (see Figure 8.27).
35. Navigate to the INSERT tab.
36. Click on the column chart symbol.

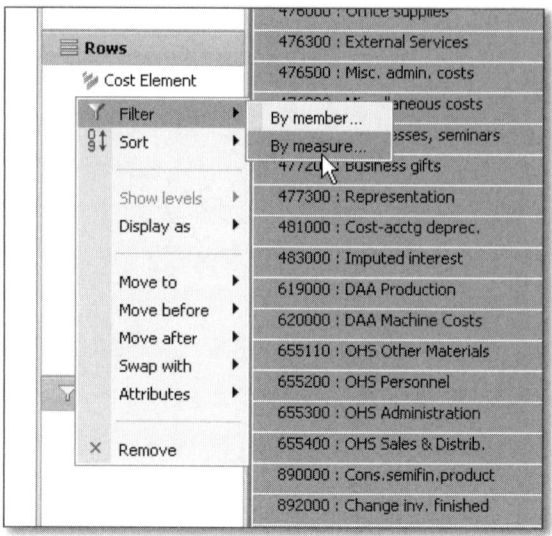

Figure 8.26 Filter Menu

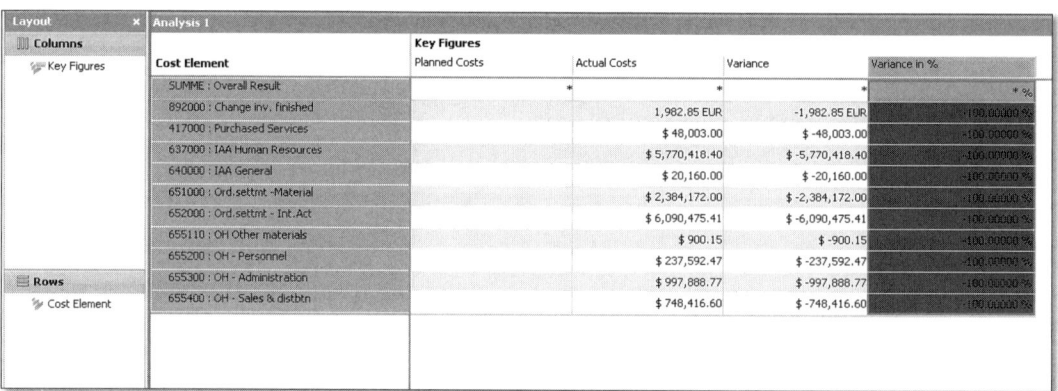

Figure 8.27 Bottom N Ranking

37. Select the option CLUSTERED COLUMN.
38. Right-click on the entry KEY FIGURES in the COLUMNS.
39. Use the menu FILTER • BY MEMBER.
40. Filter your data to show only the VARIANCE and VARIANCE IN % key figures.
41. Click on OK. Your chart will be automatically updated to the change.

So far we have been able to show the bottom 10 cost elements based on those cost centers that have a higher actual cost than the allocated budget. We will now add a second sheet to our analytical report and look for those cost centers that spend the least amount of money.

1. Click on SHEET 2 to navigate to an empty area.
2. Double-click on the INSERT NEW ANALYSIS hyperlink (see Figure 8.28).

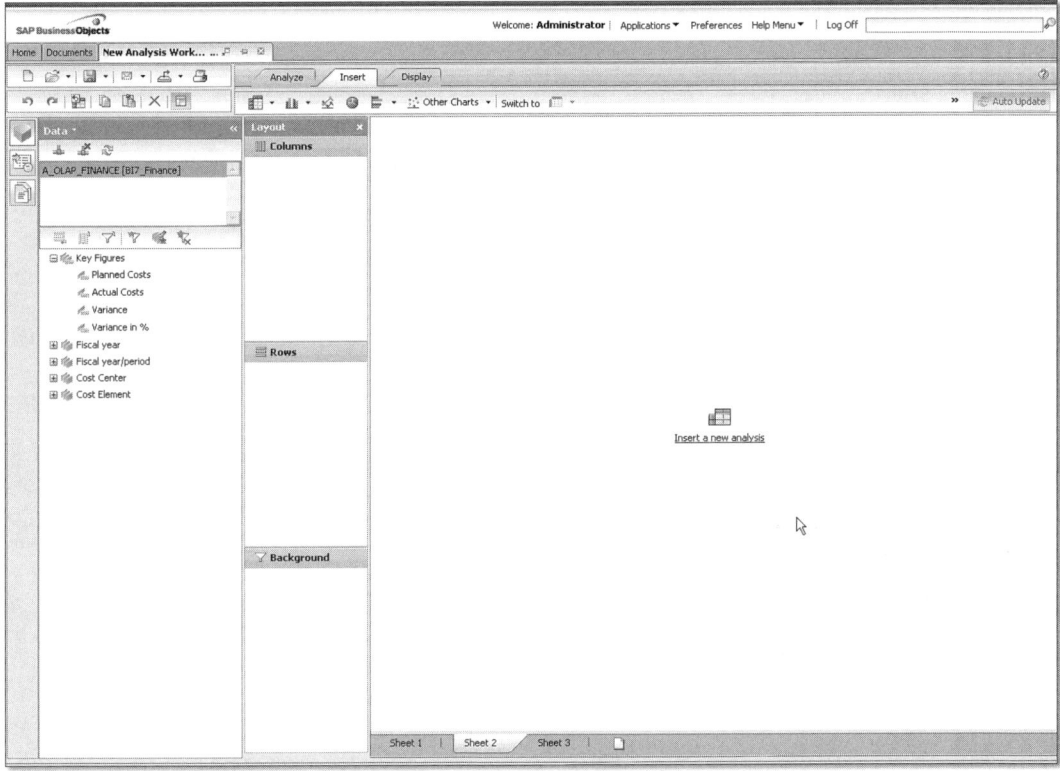

Figure 8.28 New Analysis

3. Remove COST ELEMENT from ROWS.
4. Navigate to the INSERT tab.
5. Select the menu INSERT A SUB-ANALYSIS (see Figure 8.29).
6. Navigate to the DISPLAY tab.
7. Select the first cross tab you inserted.

8 | Using SAP BusinessObjects Analysis, Edition for OLAP

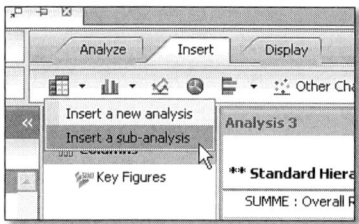

Figure 8.29 Sub-Analysis

> **Sub-Analysis Linking**
>
> SAP BusinessObjects Analysis, edition for OLAP allows you to insert sub-analysis components, which by default are linked and share the definition of the layout. By clicking on the UNLINK SUB-ANALYSIS button, you can separate these components and each of them can have its own layout.

8. Click on FOCUSED ANALYSIS.
9. Select the second cross tab you inserted.
10. Navigate to the INSERT tab.
11. Select the menu SWITCH TO • COLUMN • CLUSTERED COLUMN (see Figure 8.30).

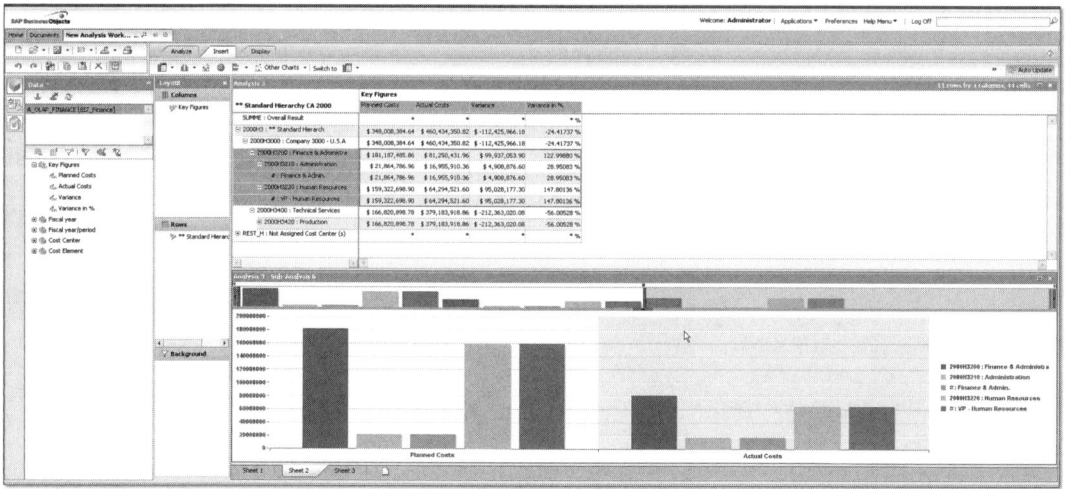

Figure 8.30 Focused Navigation

Based on the focused navigation, we can now select parts of our cross tab on the top and the measures are shown in the chart for the selected area.

1. Select the column header for VARIANCE.
2. Navigate to the ANALYZE tab.
3. Select the menu CALCULATIONS • DYNAMIC CALCULATION • RANK NUMBER. The variance is now shown as a rank in the cross tab across the shown hierarchy (see Figure 8.31).

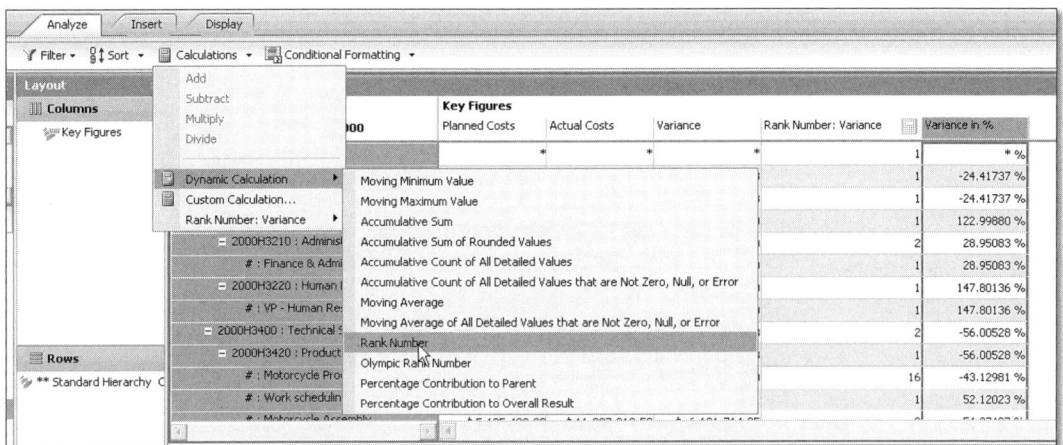

Figure 8.31 Dynamic Calculation

4. Open the list of available levels for the shown hierarchy in the data panel (see Figure 8.32).

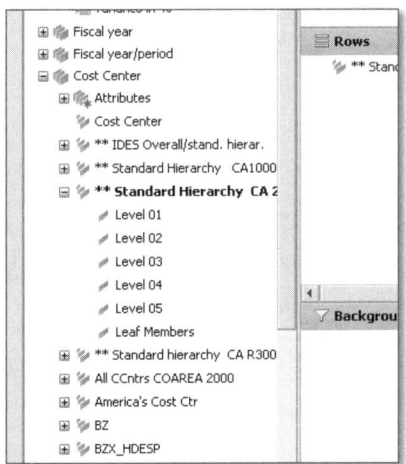

Figure 8.32 List of Available Levels

5. Select the entry LEAF MEMBERS. By using the LEAF MEMBER entry, you can filter the hierarchy by simply dragging and dropping the element onto the cross tab.

6. Drag and drop the entry LEAF MEMBERS to the hierarchy for COUNTRY (see Figure 8.33).

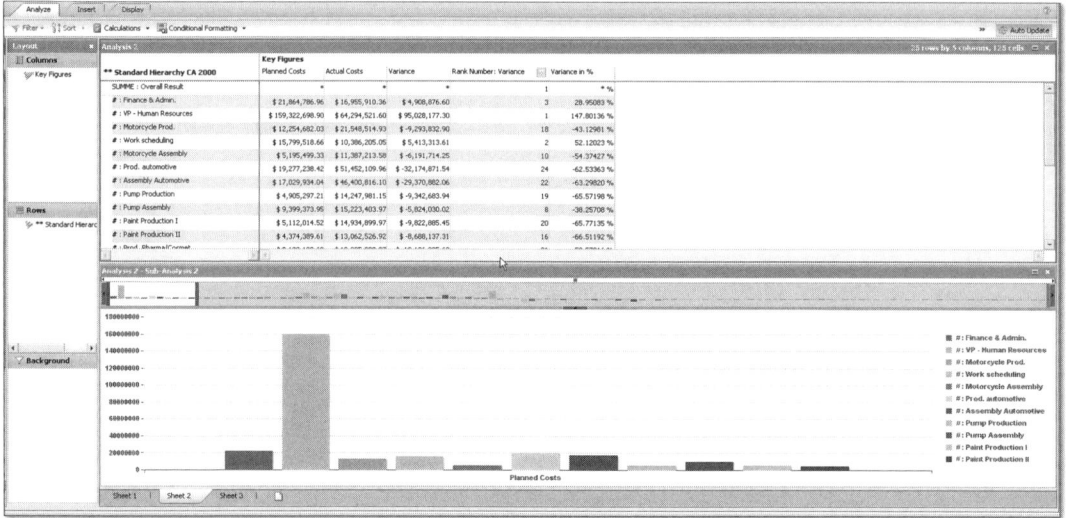

Figure 8.33 Example Workbook

7. Select the column header for RANK NUMBER.
8. Navigate to the ANALYZE tab.
9. Select the menu SORT.
10. Select the ASCENDING option.

Based on the focused navigation being activated, you can select an element in the upper portion, and the lower chart shows only those elements in the chart that have been selected in the upper portion.

We created a sheet that shows those cost elements that have the largest consumption of the actual budget compared to their planned budget. We added a second sheet where, based on a focused navigation and ranking, we are able to quickly select those areas in the hierarchy that so far have used the least amount of the allocated budget. To finish your work, save your workbook as we've explained previously.

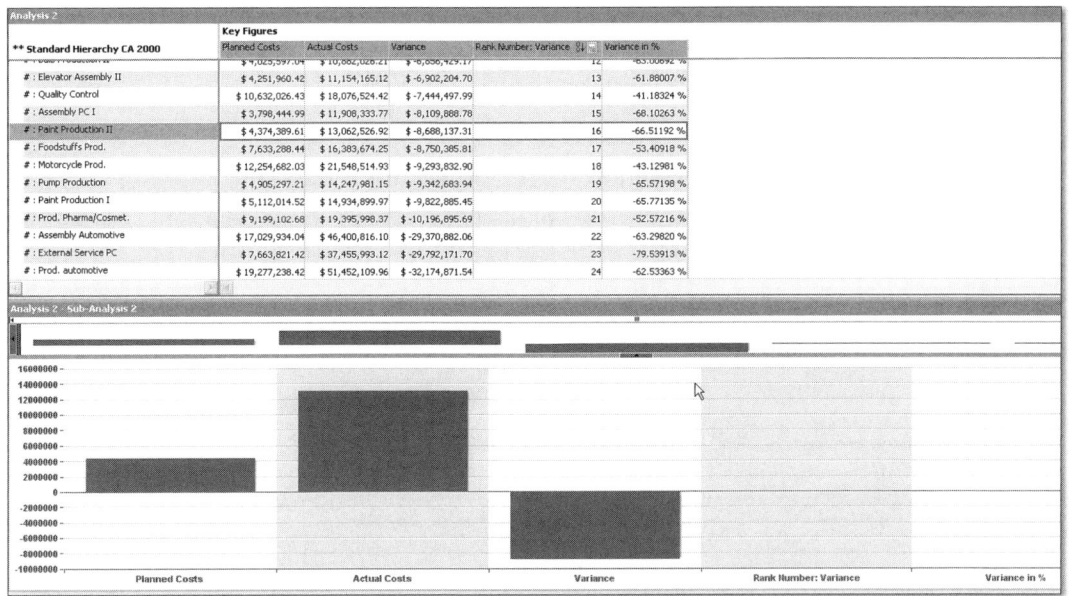

Figure 8.34 Focused Navigation

In this example we used a BEx query from the financial area and were quickly able to analyze the cost centers and cost elements using conditional formatting and filter by measure functionality. We were able to highlight specific cost centers and cost elements based on our needs, and we were able to use a focused navigation to quickly visualize a subset of the data.

8.5 Building a Workbook for Sales Analysis

In our second usage scenario for SAP BusinessObjects Analysis, edition for OLAP we are going to create a cost and profitability analysis using the BEx query from Section 7.5. If you followed the steps from the previous chapter, your SAP BusinessObjects BI platform already provides the OLAP connection pointing to the BEx query; otherwise, you can follow the steps outlined in Section 4.3.3 to set up an OLAP connection for this activity.

Assuming you configured the OLAP connection in the CMC, you can now start building your analytical workbook.

8 | Using SAP BusinessObjects Analysis, Edition for OLAP

1. Start the BI launch pad by following the menu START • PROGRAMS • SAP BUSINESS-OBJECTS BI PLATFORM 4 • SAP BUSINESSOBJECTS BI PLATFORM • SAP BUSINESS-OBJECTS BI PLATFORM • JAVA BI LAUNCH PAD.
2. Log on using your SAP credentials and SAP authentication.
3. Select the menu APPLICATION • ANALYSIS, EDITION FOR OLAP.
4. You are presented with a list of available connections. Select the connection you created previously for the needed BEx query.
5. Click on NEXT.
6. Select the BEx query for this scenario.
7. Click on OK.
8. You are presented with the view as defined in the BEx query (see Figure 8.35).

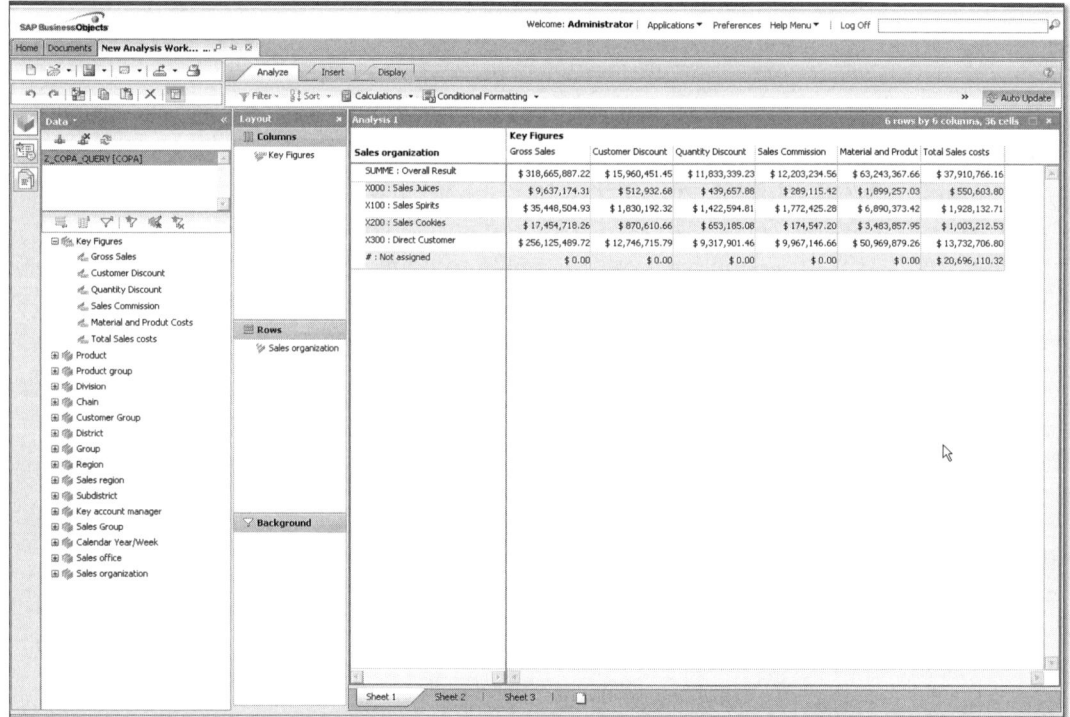

Figure 8.35 View as Defined in the BEx Query

9. Select PRODUCT GROUP from the data panel and drag it on top of SALES ORGANIZATION in the layout panel so that it replaces the hierarchy (see Figure 8.36).

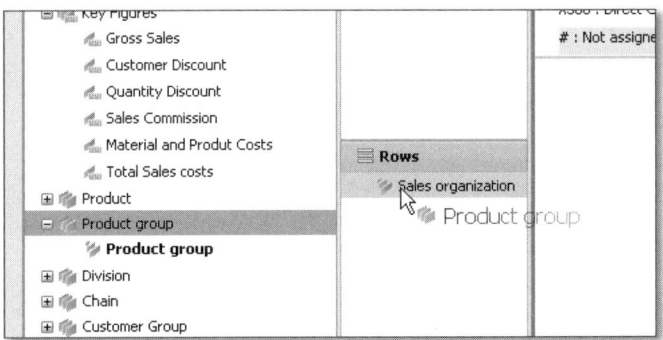

Figure 8.36 Exchanging Dimensions

10. Add PRODUCT to ROWS.
11. Navigate to the DISPLAY tab.
12. Select the menu TOTALS & PARENTS and disable the option DISPLAY SUB-TOTALS.
13. Select the column header for CUSTOMER DISCOUNT.
14. Press the `Ctrl` button on the keyboard and select the column header for QUANTITY DISCOUNT.
15. Navigate to the ANALYZE tab.
16. Select the menu CALCULATIONS • ADD.
17. Right-click on the column header for the newly created measure.
18. Select the menu CUSTOM CALCULATION • EDIT (Figure 8.37).

Figure 8.37 Editing Calculation

19. Enter "Total Discount Amount" in the NAME field.
20. Click on OK.
21. Select the column header for TOTAL DISCOUNT AMOUNT.
22. Drag and drop the column for the measure next to GROSS SALES.
23. Navigate to the ANALYZE tab.
24. Select the menu CALCULATION • CUSTOM CALCULATION.
25. Click on ADD MEMBER.
26. Select GROSS SALES.
27. Click on OK.
28. Enter a `-` after the measure GROSS SALES.
29. Click on ADD MEMBER.
30. Select TOTAL COSTS AMOUNT.
31. Enter "Net Sales" in the NAME field.
32. Click on OK.
33. Select the column header for NET SALES.
34. Drag and drop the column for the measure next to TOTAL DISCOUNT AMOUNT.
35. Select the menu CALCULATION • CUSTOM CALCULATION.
36. Click on ADD MEMBER.
37. Select NET SALES.
38. Click on OK.
39. Enter a `-` AFTER NET SALES.
40. Click on ADD MEMBER.
41. Select SALES COMMISSION.
42. Click on OK.
43. Enter a `-` after SALES COMMISSION.
44. Click on ADD MEMBER.
45. Select MATERIAL AND PRODUCT COSTS.
46. Click on OK.
47. Enter a `-` after MATERIAL AND PRODUCT COSTS.
48. Click on ADD MEMBER.

49. Select TOTAL SALES COSTS.
50. Click on OK.
51. Enter "Operating Profit" in the NAME field.
52. Click on OK.
53. Right-click on KEY FIGURES in COLUMNS.
54. Select the menu FILTER • BY MEMBER.
55. Select GROSS SALES, TOTAL DISCOUNT AMOUNT, NET SALES, and OPERATING PROFIT (see Figure 8.38).

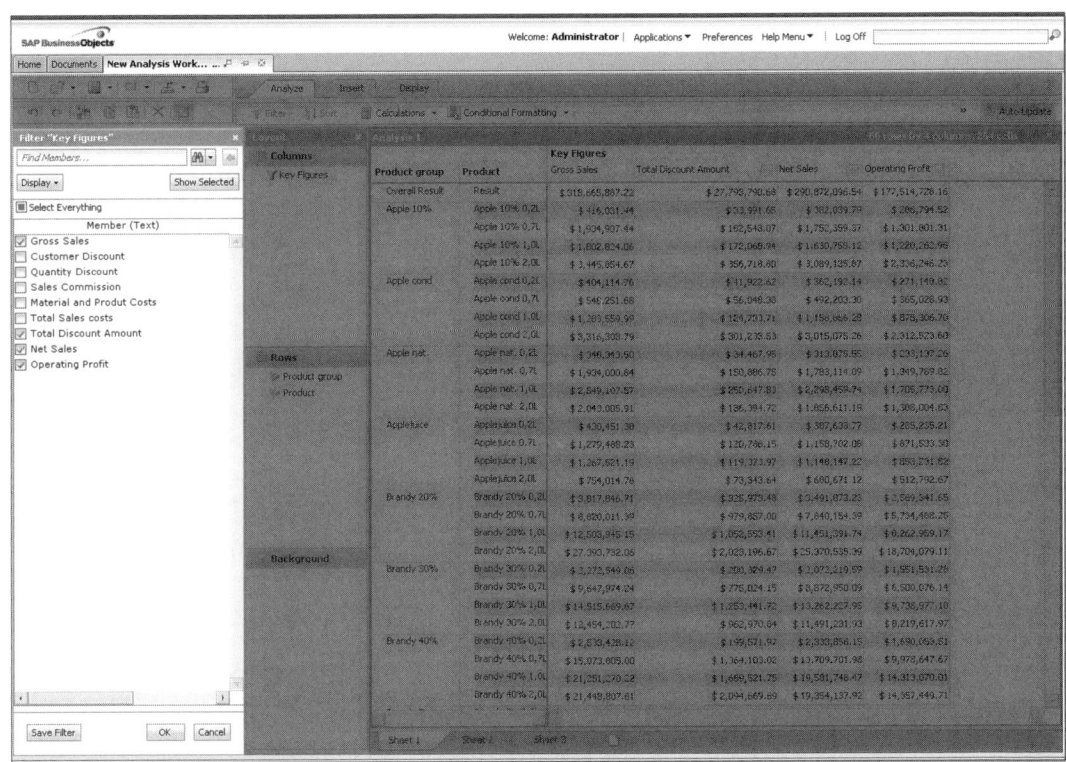

Figure 8.38 Selecting Key Figures

56. Select PRODUCT GROUP in the cross tab.
57. Navigate to the DISPLAY tab.
58. Select the menu HIERARCHY • COMPACT DISPLAY IN ROWS (see Figure 8.39).

8 | Using SAP BusinessObjects Analysis, Edition for OLAP

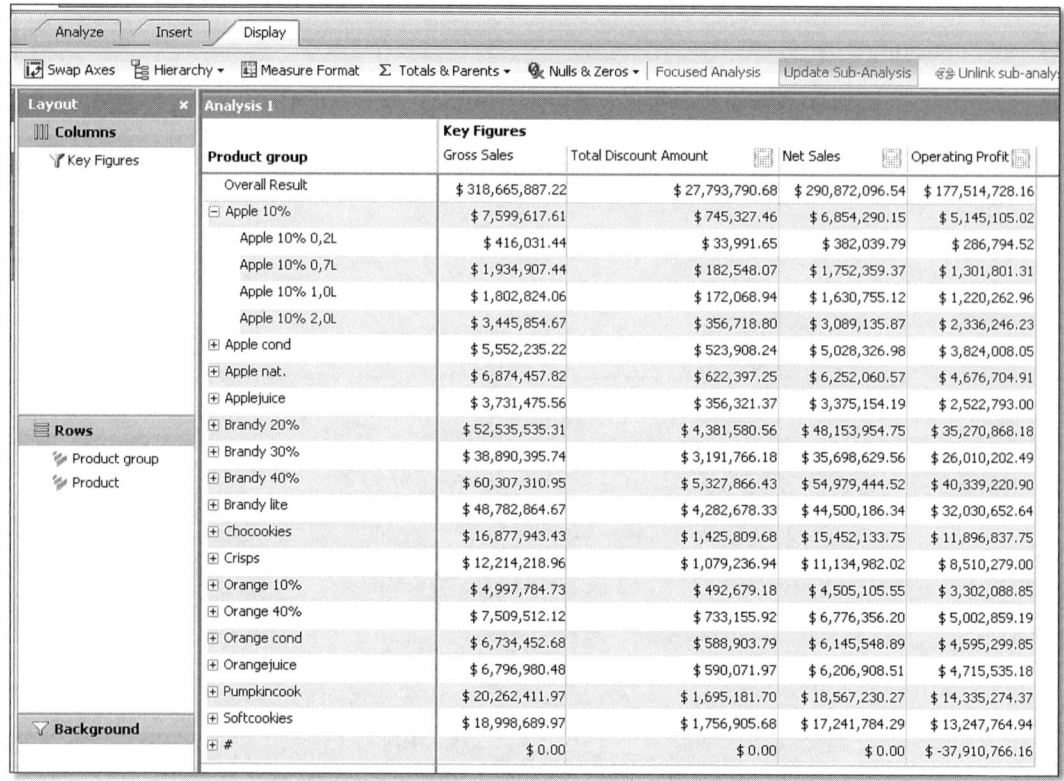

Figure 8.39 Compact Display

59. Select the menu TOTALS & PARENTS and enable the option DISPLAY SUB-TOTALS. PRODUCT GROUP and PRODUCT now behave like a hierarchy.

60. Select the menu CALCULATION • CUSTOM CALCULATION.

61. Click on ADD MEMBER.

62. Select OPERATING PROFIT.

63. Click on OK.

64. Enter "%_A" after OPERATING PROFIT.

65. Click on ADD MEMBER.

66. Select NET SALES.

67. Click on OK.

68. Enter "Profit in %" in the NAME field.

69. Click on OK.
70. Select the newly created measure PROFIT IN %.
71. Navigate to the ANALYZE tab.
72. Select the menu CONDITIONAL FORMATTING • NEW.
73. Set the FORMAT to SYMBOL.
74. Define a condition using green for values greater than 75.
75. Click on ADD.
76. Define a condition using orange for values between 50 and 75.
77. Click on ADD (see Figure 8.40).

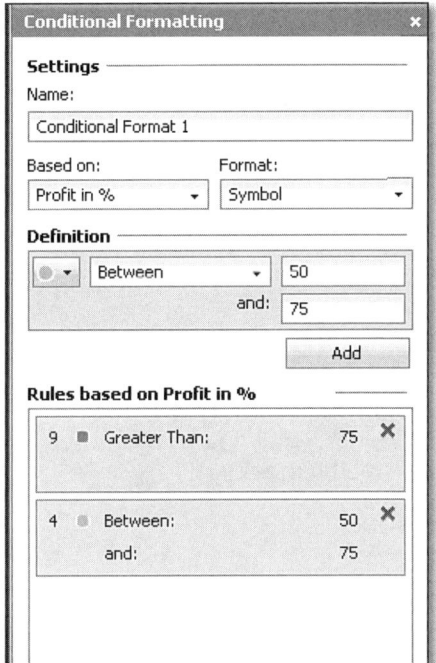

Figure 8.40 Conditional Formatting

78. Activate the PREVIEW option.
79. Click on OK (see Figure 8.41).

8   Using SAP BusinessObjects Analysis, Edition for OLAP

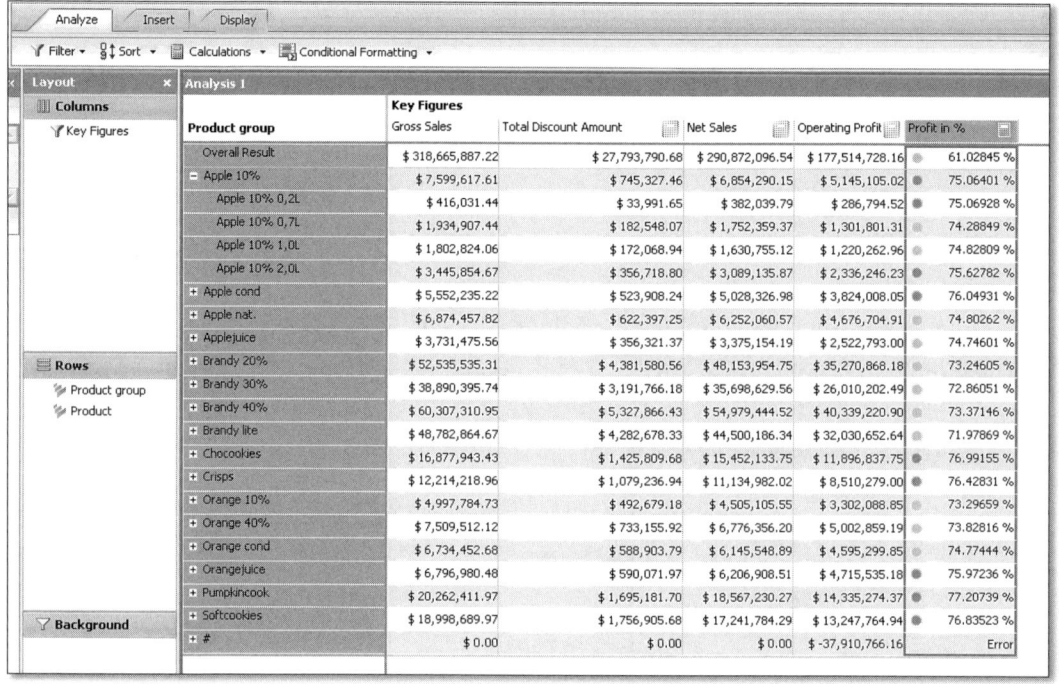

Figure 8.41 Preview Cross Tab

By using conditional formatting and a set of calculations, we are able to identify our most profitable product groups and products. In the next steps, we look into our sales regions in more details.

1. Navigate to the OUTLINE of your workbook (see Figure 8.42).
2. Select the cross tab from Sheet 1 in the outline.
3. Click on the COPY ( ) button.
4. Click on Sheet 2 to navigate to an empty area.
5. Click on the PASTE ( ) button to create a copy of your existing cross tab on Sheet 2.
6. Click on AUTO UPDATE.
7. Remove all dimensions from ROWS.
8. Add SALES REGION to ROWS.
9. Add GROUP to ROWS.
10. Click on AUTO UPDATE to refresh your workbook.

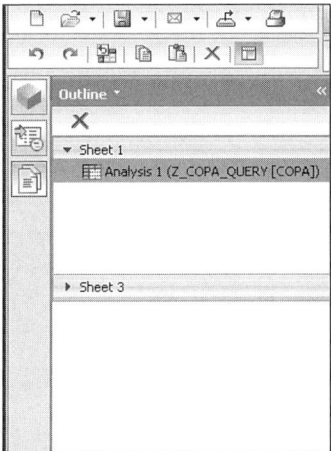

Figure 8.42 Outline

Based on the still active conditional highlighting, we can see that the sales regions are all around 75% profit (see Figure 8.43). At this point we decide to look into the products by retail chain.

Copy of Analysis 1					
	Key Figures				
Sales region	Gross Sales	Total Discount Amount	Net Sales	Operating Profit	Profit in %
Overall Result	$ 318,665,887.22	$ 27,793,790.68	$ 290,872,096.54	$ 177,514,728.16	61.02845 %
⊟ Central	$ 74,745,597.92	$ 6,443,163.88	$ 68,302,434.04	$ 50,788,384.29	74.35809 %
BuyMore	$ 12,344,233.89	$ 960,343.72	$ 11,383,890.17	$ 8,480,872.41	74.49890 %
FindIt	$ 21,166,257.26	$ 2,009,508.52	$ 19,156,748.74	$ 14,187,925.00	74.06228 %
GetMore	$ 16,202,148.92	$ 1,391,187.30	$ 14,810,961.62	$ 11,059,475.97	74.67088 %
PayLess	$ 25,032,957.85	$ 2,082,124.34	$ 22,950,833.51	$ 17,060,110.91	74.33330 %
⊟ East	$ 87,820,128.68	$ 7,349,715.18	$ 80,470,413.50	$ 59,666,171.12	74.14672 %
BuyMore	$ 22,060,429.59	$ 2,156,991.17	$ 19,903,438.42	$ 14,644,219.39	73.57633 %
FindIt	$ 33,104,229.62	$ 2,533,270.55	$ 30,570,959.07	$ 22,546,764.50	73.75223 %
GetMore	$ 18,318,970.89	$ 1,589,282.40	$ 16,729,688.49	$ 12,536,328.20	74.93462 %
PayLess	$ 14,336,498.58	$ 1,070,171.06	$ 13,266,327.52	$ 9,938,859.03	74.91794 %
⊟ South	$ 86,560,526.78	$ 7,742,624.17	$ 78,817,902.61	$ 58,186,909.62	73.82448 %
BuyMore	$ 17,585,866.85	$ 1,552,356.70	$ 16,033,510.15	$ 11,949,999.12	74.53140 %
FindIt	$ 25,581,844.73	$ 2,436,780.29	$ 23,145,064.44	$ 17,042,505.20	73.63343 %
GetMore	$ 20,657,963.24	$ 1,797,318.28	$ 18,860,644.96	$ 13,803,449.15	73.18652 %
PayLess	$ 22,734,851.96	$ 1,956,168.90	$ 20,778,683.06	$ 15,390,956.15	74.07089 %
⊟ West	$ 69,539,633.84	$ 6,258,287.45	$ 63,281,346.39	$ 46,784,029.29	73.93021 %
BuyMore	$ 14,120,435.56	$ 1,366,897.26	$ 12,753,538.30	$ 9,284,004.98	72.79552 %
FindIt	$ 18,818,450.14	$ 1,805,021.32	$ 17,013,428.82	$ 12,422,577.12	73.01631 %
GetMore	$ 18,812,875.96	$ 1,437,696.33	$ 17,375,179.63	$ 13,079,788.88	75.27858 %
PayLess	$ 17,787,872.18	$ 1,648,672.54	$ 16,139,199.64	$ 11,997,658.31	74.33862 %
⊞ #	$ 0.00	$ 0.00	$ 0.00	$ -37,910,766.16	Error

Figure 8.43 Cross Tab Showing Regional Sales

11. Drag and drop CHAIN to ROWS so that it replaces SALES REGION.
12. Drag and drop PRODUCT to ROWS so that it replaces GROUP.
13. Right-click on CHAIN in the ROWS of the layout panel.
14. Select the menu FILTER • BY MEASURE (see Figure 8.44).

Figure 8.44 Filter by Measure

15. Select GROSS SALES FOR BASED ON.
16. Select the option TOP N for INCLUDE MEMBERS.
17. Enter the value 10.
18. Click on ADD.
19. Click on OK.
20. Right-click on PRODUCT in the ROWS of the layout panel.
21. Select the menu FILTER • BY MEASURE (see Figure 8.45).
22. Select GROSS SALES for BASED ON.
23. Select TOP N for INCLUDE MEMBERS.
24. Enter the value 5.
25. Click on ADD.
26. Click on OK.

You are shown the top 5 products for the top 10 retail chains. You can quickly see that—based on profit in %—there is a small group of products that is more profitable than others.

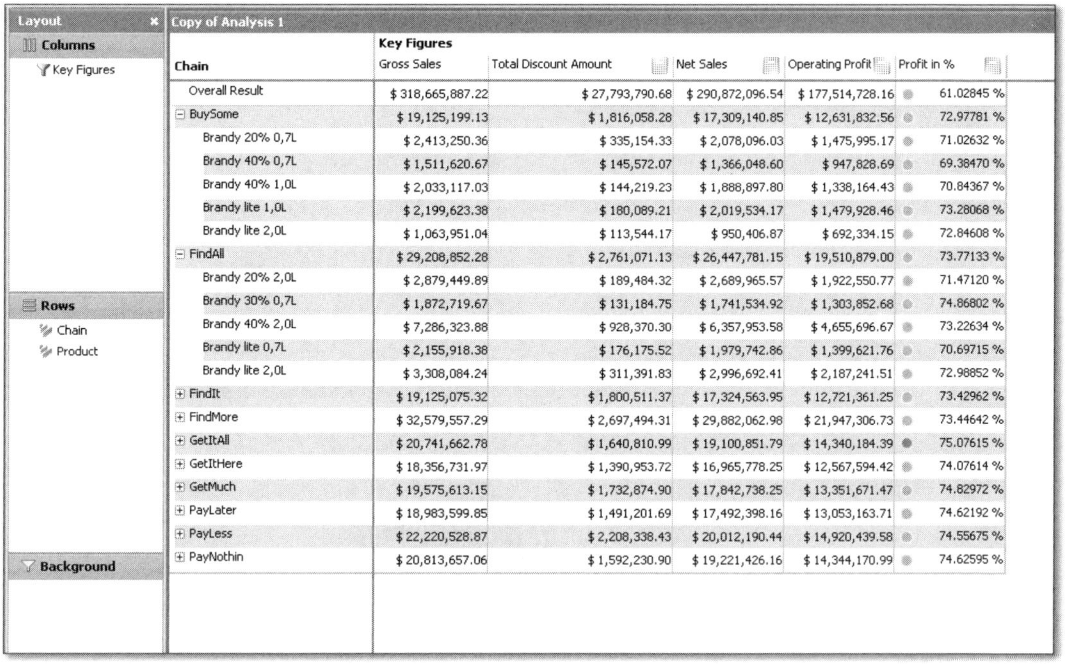

Building a Workbook for Sales Analysis | 8.5

Layout	Copy of Analysis 1					
Columns		**Key Figures**				
Key Figures	Chain	Gross Sales	Total Discount Amount	Net Sales	Operating Profit!	Profit in %
	Overall Result	$ 318,665,887.22	$ 27,793,790.68	$ 290,872,096.54	$ 177,514,728.16	61.02845 %
	⊟ BuySome	$ 19,125,199.13	$ 1,816,058.28	$ 17,309,140.85	$ 12,631,832.56	72.97781 %
	Brandy 20% 0,7L	$ 2,413,250.36	$ 335,154.33	$ 2,078,096.03	$ 1,475,995.17	71.02632 %
	Brandy 40% 0,7L	$ 1,511,620.67	$ 145,572.07	$ 1,366,048.60	$ 947,828.69	69.38470 %
	Brandy 40% 1,0L	$ 2,033,117.03	$ 144,219.23	$ 1,888,897.80	$ 1,338,164.43	70.84367 %
	Brandy lite 1,0L	$ 2,199,623.38	$ 180,089.21	$ 2,019,534.17	$ 1,479,928.46	73.28068 %
	Brandy lite 2,0L	$ 1,063,951.04	$ 113,544.17	$ 950,406.87	$ 692,334.15	72.84608 %
Rows	⊟ FindAll	$ 29,208,852.28	$ 2,761,071.13	$ 26,447,781.15	$ 19,510,879.00	73.77133 %
Chain	Brandy 20% 2,0L	$ 2,879,449.89	$ 189,484.32	$ 2,689,965.57	$ 1,922,550.77	71.47120 %
Product	Brandy 30% 0,7L	$ 1,872,719.67	$ 131,184.75	$ 1,741,534.92	$ 1,303,852.68	74.86802 %
	Brandy 40% 2,0L	$ 7,286,323.88	$ 928,370.30	$ 6,357,953.58	$ 4,655,696.67	73.22634 %
	Brandy lite 0,7L	$ 2,155,918.38	$ 176,175.52	$ 1,979,742.86	$ 1,399,621.76	70.69715 %
	Brandy lite 2,0L	$ 3,308,084.24	$ 311,391.83	$ 2,996,692.41	$ 2,187,241.51	72.98852 %
	⊞ FindIt	$ 19,125,075.32	$ 1,800,511.37	$ 17,324,563.95	$ 12,721,361.25	73.42962 %
	⊞ FindMore	$ 32,579,557.29	$ 2,697,494.31	$ 29,882,062.98	$ 21,947,306.73	73.44642 %
	⊞ GetItAll	$ 20,741,662.78	$ 1,640,810.99	$ 19,100,851.79	$ 14,340,184.39	75.07615 %
	⊞ GetItHere	$ 18,356,731.97	$ 1,390,953.72	$ 16,965,778.25	$ 12,567,594.42	74.07614 %
	⊞ GetMuch	$ 19,575,613.15	$ 1,732,874.90	$ 17,842,738.25	$ 13,351,671.47	74.82972 %
	⊞ PayLater	$ 18,983,599.85	$ 1,491,201.69	$ 17,492,398.16	$ 13,053,163.71	74.62192 %
	⊞ PayLess	$ 22,220,528.87	$ 2,208,338.43	$ 20,012,190.44	$ 14,920,439.58	74.55675 %
Background	⊞ PayNothin	$ 20,813,657.06	$ 1,592,230.90	$ 19,221,426.16	$ 14,344,170.99	74.62595 %

Figure 8.45 Cross Tab with Filter by Measure

> **Filter by Measure**
>
> As you might have noticed, the definition of the filter by measure functionality is different between SAP BusinessObjects Analysis, edition for Microsoft Office and SAP BusinessObjects Analysis, edition for OLAP. In the edition for Microsoft Office, you can set up a filter by measure for the most inner rows or columns, and the filter will be dynamic based on the navigation. In the edition for OLAP, the filter by measure functionality is defined based on the selected dimension and is not dynamic based on the overall navigation.

27. Remove CHAIN from ROWS.
28. Navigate to the INSERT tab.
29. Click on the PIE CHART icon ( ).
30. Navigate to the DISPLAY tab.
31. Click on FOCUSED NAVIGATION (see Figure 8.46).

You can now use the option to select a measure in the cross tab in the upper part, and the pie chart will show only the selected measure.

337

8 | Using SAP BusinessObjects Analysis, Edition for OLAP

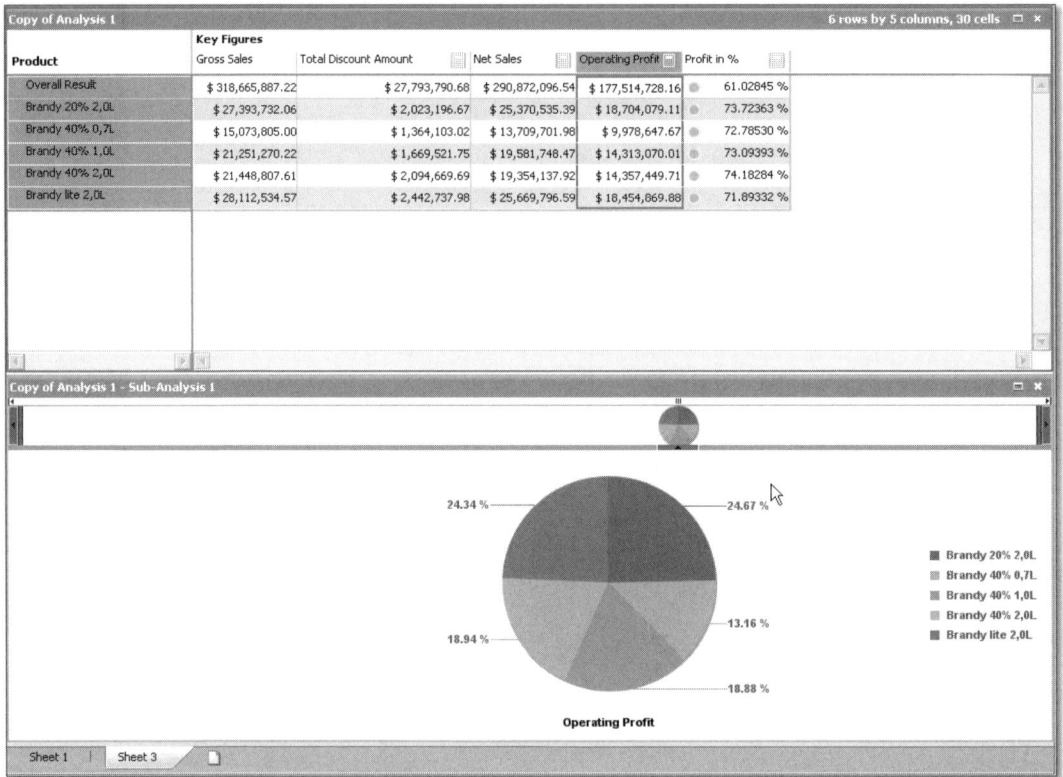

Figure 8.46 Focused Navigation

In this example we used SAP BusinessObjects Analysis, edition for OLAP to analyze the profitability of our products. We identified those products with the best profitability and we were also able to extend our analysis to the sales regions and retail chains. By using conditional formatting and filtering by measure settings, we are able to quickly find the information that we need.

8.6 Summary

In this chapter you learned where SAP BusinessObjects Analysis, edition for OLAP can help to fulfill business requirements, as well as the first steps in using the product. You then were able to create two scenarios for your end users. In the next chapter you will learn how to use SAP BusinessObjects Explorer to fulfill some of your requirements.

SAP BusinessObjects Explorer offers a unique user experience by providing search and exploration functionality.

9   Data Exploration and Searching with SAP BusinessObjects Explorer

In this chapter, you will learn how to consume your SAP data by using SAP BusinessObjects Explorer. In addition to providing a compelling user experience, SAP BusinessObjects Explorer offers a search and explore interface on top of the data warehouse. We explain the different options for connecting to the information and we discuss which of our establish business requirements can be fulfilled using SAP BusinessObjects Explorer.

9.1   SAP Data Connectivity for SAP BusinessObjects Explorer

SAP BusinessObjects Explorer can use a universe or an existing index from SAP NetWeaver BW Accelerator (BWA), or SAP HANA as a data source. SAP BusinessObjects Explorer is not able to leverage direct BI Consumer Services (BICS) connectivity in the current release.

Figure 9.1 shows the different options for data connectivity available for SAP BusinessObjects Explorer as part of the 4.0 FP3 release. SAP BusinessObjects Explorer can:

- Use a relational universe connecting to the InfoProvider in the SAP NetWeaver BW system.
- Use a relational universe on top of SAP ECC, connecting to ABAP functions, InfoSets, and SAP queries.
- Connect directly to SAP NetWeaver BW BWA and re-use existing indexes.

9 | Data Exploration and Searching with SAP BusinessObjects Explorer

- Connect directly to SAP HANA and re-use analytical views and calculation views.
- Use universe connectivity to SAP HANA, which allows it to receive the information being returned and create a disk-based index. Here it is important to recognize that when using the universe-based approach for SAP BusinessObjects Explorer on top of SAP HANA, SAP BusinessObjects Explorer does not use the pre-built indexes from SAP HANA.
- Create a disk-based index on Microsoft Excel spreadsheets.

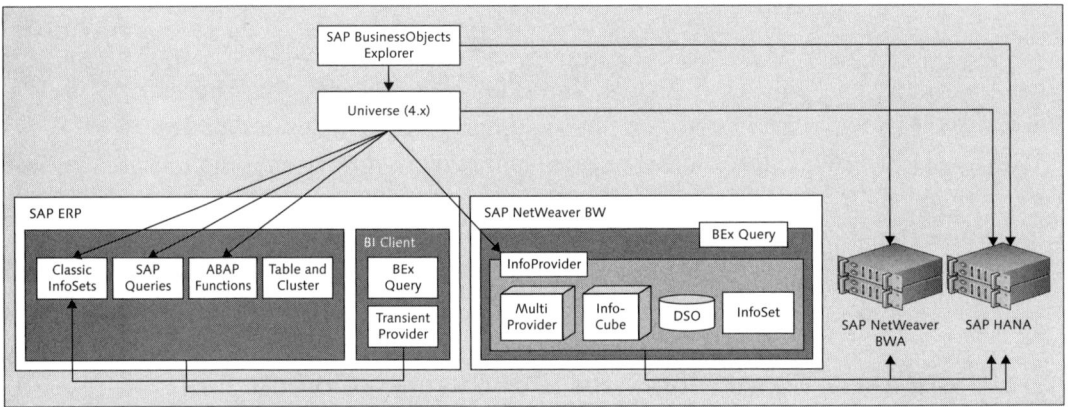

Figure 9.1 SAP BusinessObjects Explorer—Data Connectivity

For any connectivity based on a universe, SAP BusinessObjects Explorer has to generate its own disk-based index, which has a data volume limit. Usually, 2.5 to 3 million rows is considered the maximum for a disk-based index.

As shown in Table 9.1, a large set of existing metadata from SAP NetWeaver BW is not available when using the relational universe access method. Table 9.2 offers a list of possible workarounds as part of establishing a relational universe on top of SAP NetWeaver BW.

	Relational Universe Access
Direct access to InfoCube and MultiProvider	Yes
Access to BEx queries	Limited

Table 9.1 Supported and Unsupported BEx Query Features for SAP BusinessObjects Explorer

340

	Relational Universe Access
Characteristic Values	
Key	Yes
Short description	Yes
Medium and long description	Yes
BEx Query Features	
Support for hierarchies	No
Support for free characteristics	Yes
Support for calculated and restricted key figures	No
Support for currencies and units	Yes
Support for custom structures	No
Support for formulas and selections	No
Support for filter	Yes
Support for display and navigational attributes	Yes
Support for conditions in rows	No
Support for conditions in columns	No
Support for conditions for fixed characteristics	No
Support for exceptions	No
Compounded characteristics	No
Constant selection	No
Default values	No
Number scaling factor	No
Number of decimals	No
Calculate rows as (local calculation)	No
Sorting	No
Hide/unhide	No

Table 9.1 Supported and Unsupported BEx Query Features for SAP BusinessObjects Explorer (Cont.)

	Relational Universe Access
Display as hierarchy	No
Reverse sign	No
Support for reading master data	No
Data Types	
Support for CHAR (characteristics)	Yes
Support for NUMC (characteristics)	Yes as string value
Support for DATS (characteristics)	Yes as string value
Support for TIMS (characteristics)	Yes as string value
Support for Date (key figures)	Yes
Support for Time (key figures)	Yes as string value
SAP Variable—Processing Type	
User input	No
Authorization	No
Replacement path	No
SAP exit/custom exit	No
Precalculated value set	No
General Features for Variables	
Support for optional and mandatory variables	No
Support for key date dependencies	No
Support for default values	No
Support for personalized values	No
SAP Variables—Variable Type	
Single value	No
Multi-single value	No
Interval value	No

Table 9.1 Supported and Unsupported BEx Query Features for SAP BusinessObjects Explorer (Cont.)

	Relational Universe Access
Selection option	No
Hierarchy variable	No
Hierarchy node variable	No
Hierarchy version variable	No
Text variable	No
EXIT variable	No
Single key date variable	No
Multiple key dates	No
Formula variable	No

Table 9.1 Supported and Unsupported BEx Query Features for SAP BusinessObjects Explorer (Cont.)

BEx Query Elements	Relational Universe
Calculated/restricted key figures	Define calculated measures as part of the universe.
Variables	Define prompts as part of the universes. Not possible for EXIT variables or variables filled through authorizations
Currency and unit conversion	Possible with manual modeling of tables with conversion rates in the SAP BusinessObjects Universe Designer and joins in Data Federator.
Display attributes	Possible with joins from InfoProvider to the master data tables in the universe.
External BW hierarchies	No workaround.
Conditions	Use filters on measures.

Table 9.2 Possible Workarounds

Based on the level of support for your existing metadata in SAP NetWeaver BW and the missing option to leverage the BICS layer to leverage more of the pre-existing metadata, such as hierarchies and calculated key figures, we recommend that you evaluate the option to add SAP NetWeaver BWA or SAP HANA to your overall SAP landscape to leverage larger volumes of data and achieve a higher degree of metadata support. For integration with SAP ERP, you can either leverage the connectivity from the semantic layer and establish a universe or use SAP HANA as part of your overall SAP landscape (in that case, SAP BusinessObjects Explorer simply consumes the information from SAP HANA).

In this section we have reviewed the available data connectivity for SAP BusinessObjects Explorer as part of your SAP landscape. In the next section we evaluate which requirements can be met by SAP BusinessObjects Explorer.

9.2 Assessing the Business Requirements

In this section, we use the requirements from the previous section and see which ones are a good fit for using SAP BusinessObjects Explorer as a BI tool. Before looking at the requirements, we must note a major difference between SAP BusinessObjects Explorer and other BI tools, such as SAP BusinessObjects Web Intelligence, SAP Crystal Reports for Enterprise, SAP BusinessObjects Analysis, and SAP BusinessObjects Dashboards. SAP BusinessObjects Explorer focuses on the search and exploration aspect of the user experience, while the other tools focus on providing well-structured answers to consumer questions (see Chapter 2). Based on the focus of SAP BusinessObjects Explorer, most of the requirements are not seen as a best fit for SAP BusinessObjects Explorer. This does not mean that SAP BusinessObjects Explorer can't fulfill some of the requirements; it can be a great starting point for a consumer in situations where a report or analytics does not exist for a user's question. In this case, the information provided by SAP BusinessObjects Explorer can then be used in SAP BusinessObjects Web Intelligence for further analysis. Based on these assumptions, let's look at the requirements.

9.2.1 Financial Reporting and Analysis Requirements

The following list represents the requirements for which SAP BusinessObjects Explorer is not the best fit.

> **Unfulfilled Requirements**
>
> - For specific content (such as an income statement or a balance sheet), the design needs to be layout focused with the actual print version of the report being a high priority.
>
> - The reporting and analysis tools need to let the user create new calculations and formulas and share those with other consumers of the content.
>
> - The reporting and analysis tools need to allow for the use of hierarchies and for easy navigation along those hierarchies.
>
> - The reporting and analysis tools need to use custom structures that are defined as part of a BEx query.
>
> - The content needs to resolve the time dependency defined for financial cost and profit center hierarchies.
>
> - The content must be available in a web-based environment and in a Microsoft Office environment (especially Microsoft Excel).
>
> - Users need to be able to create planning scenarios and write information back into the source.

As you can see, based on the preceding list of requirements, the functionality to create custom calculations or structures is not the best fit for SAP BusinessObjects Explorer. The requirement to use hierarchies as part of the search and exploration workflow has been acknowledged, and you can use hierarchies for filtering but not for visualization. When it comes to integration with the Microsoft Office environment, it is important to mention that it is possible to export data from SAP BusinessObjects Explorer to Microsoft Excel—but it is an export and not live data, as with SAP BusinessObjects Live Office. In regard to the planning scenarios and writing back into the data source, it should be clear that SAP BusinessObjects Explorer does not have any capability to write back to the source system.

9.2.2 Sales Reporting and Analysis Requirements

In the sales area, only a few requirements cannot be fulfilled with SAP BusinessObjects Explorer.

> **Unfulfilled Requirements**
> - Content must be available online, offline, and on mobile devices (for sales representatives on the road).
> - Users should be able to perform scenario-based analysis, where the user is able to see the data but can also influence certain factors and see the impact on the overall numbers; for example, a what-if analysis in a sales planning workflow.

The requirement to provide what-if scenarios is better suited for SAP BusinessObjects Dashboards, as we have already acknowledged in previous chapters. In regard to the first requirement listed above, SAP BusinessObjects Explorer is able to provide an online and mobile user experience, but there is no offline capability; such a requirement is better suited for SAP Crystal Reports for Enterprise or SAP Business Objects Web Intelligence.

9.2.3 Human Resource (HR) Reporting and Analysis Requirements

Based on the nature of the requirements for the HR area, there are some key deliverables that we can't fulfill using SAP BusinessObjects Explorer.

> **Unfulfilled Requirements**
> - The content needs to present highly textual information in a layout-focused format.
> - Some of the content (such as employee appraisals or performance reviews) will likely be used as official documentation and therefore needs to follow strict layout rules.

SAP BusinessObjects Explorer can't create highly textual reports or deliver official documents. These requirements are much better suited for SAP Crystal Reports for Enterprise.

9.2.4 C-Level Management and Leadership Reporting and Analysis Requirements

There is only one requirement on the list for the executive leadership and management area that can't be fulfilled with SAP BusinessObjects Explorer.

> **Unfulfilled Executive Leadership and Management Reporting Requirements**
>
> ▶ The content needs to present highly aggregated information with alerts for important key performance indicators (KPIs).

SAP BusinessObjects Explorer can show and visualize highly aggregated information, but it can't provide alerts on specific KPIs in a proactive manner.

Overall, we strongly recommend that you become familiar with the SAP BusinessObjects Explorer BI tool and experience the different focus in the user experience yourself. You should use all of the guidance and decision criteria that we discussed in Chapter 2 to ensure that you choose the right tool for the job. SAP BusinessObjects Explorer is a unique user experience, which can be a great help in terms of your overall solution, but it can also be overwhelming for some users. It is meant to provide an easy-to-use BI experience—which it does—but it is not meant for those looking to receive a structured answer to a repeatable question. SAP BusinessObjects Explorer can present a large volume of data to the consumer, who can then use common techniques, search, and simple navigation steps to explore the data.

Now that we've reviewed how SAP BusinessObjects Explorer can help us fulfill some of our requirements, we can go into more detail about the tool itself.

9.3 Introduction to the Tool

In this section, you will learn how to use SAP BusinessObjects Explorer on an indexed data set created using SAP BusinessObjects Explorer without SAP NetWeaver BWA; we focus on the UI instead. For these steps we use the option to create a relational universe based on an InfoProvider and then set up an index based on the universe.

> **User Rights for Activities**
>
> For the following steps, we need a user that has the necessary rights to create, edit, and view information spaces from SAP BusinessObjects Explorer. The easiest way to ensure you have enough authorizations to follow along is to make your user part of the user group administrator in the Central Management Console (CMC).

1. Start the Information Design Tool by following the menu: START • PROGRAMS • SAP BUSINESSOBJECTS BI PLATFORM 4 • SAP BUSINESSOBJECTS BI PLATFORM CLIENT TOOLS • INFORMATION DESIGN TOOL.
2. Select the menu FILE • NEW • PROJECT to create a new project for your universe.
3. Enter a name for the new project and click on FINISH.
4. Select the WINDOW menu and make sure the REPOSITORY RESOURCES window is shown.
5. In the REPOSITORY RESOURCES window, select the INSERT SESSION menu to establish a session to your SAP BusinessObjects BI platform (see Figure 9.2).

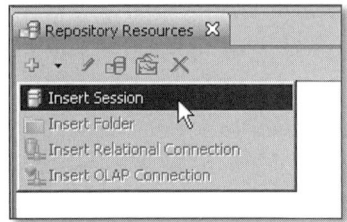

Figure 9.2 Repository Resources

6. Log on with your SAP credentials using the SAP authentication.
7. Click on OK.
8. Open the context menu of your established server connection in the CONNECTIONS area (see Figure 9.3).

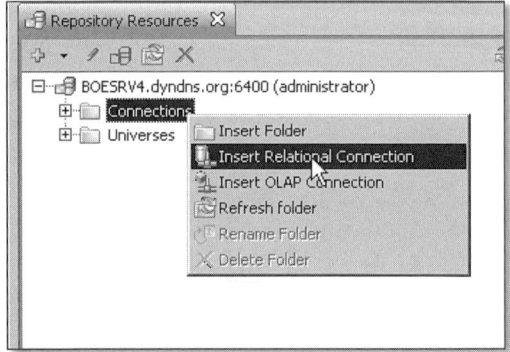

Figure 9.3 Relational Connection

9. Select the INSERT RELATIONAL CONNECTION menu item.

SAP NetWeaver BW Connection via Information Design Tool

To establish a relational connection to SAP NetWeaver BW, you first need to establish a session with the SAP BusinessObjects BI platform, and then create a connection starting with the repository of your SAP BusinessObjects BI platform, which is slightly different than the usual workflow.

10. Enter a name for the connection.
11. Click on NEXT (see Figure 9.4).

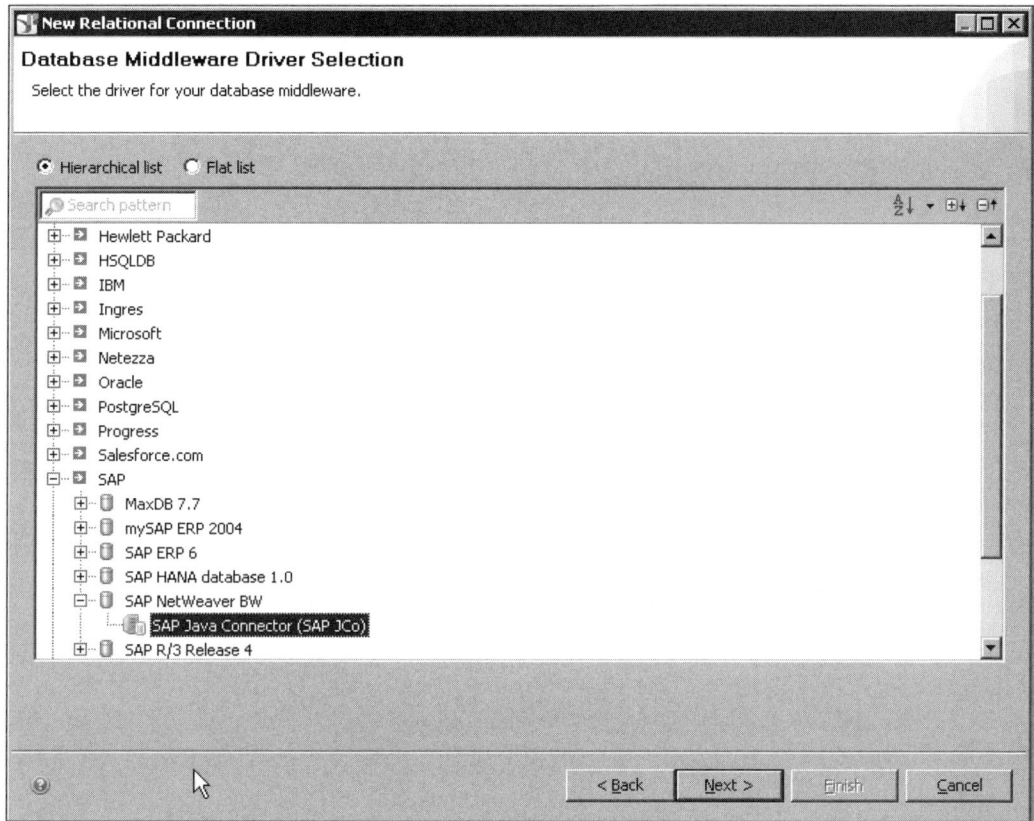

Figure 9.4 Driver Selection

12. Select the entry for SAP NETWEAVER BW.
13. Click on NEXT (see Figure 9.5).
14. Fill in the necessary details as shown in Figure 9.5.

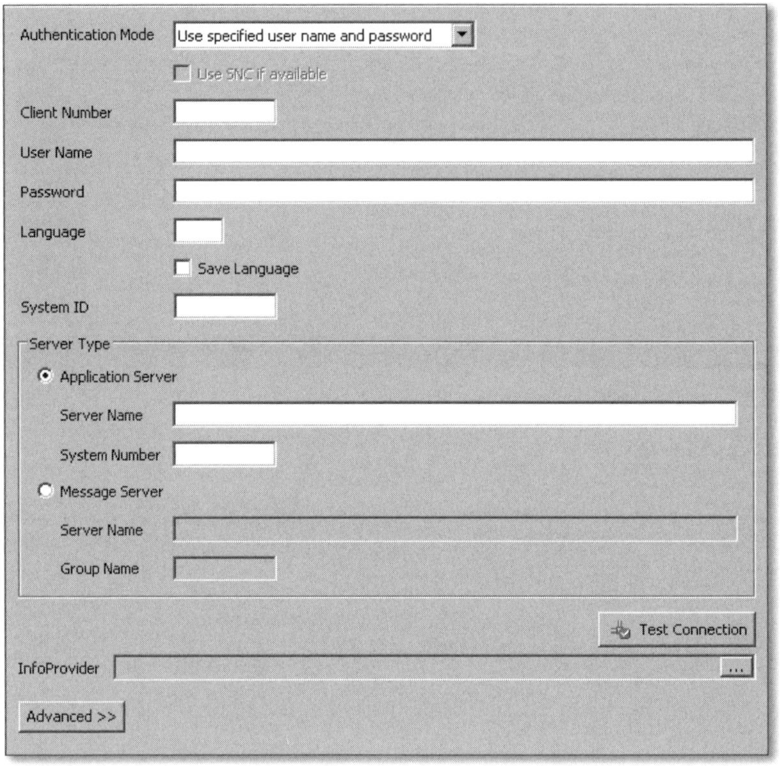

9 | Data Exploration and Searching with SAP BusinessObjects Explorer

Figure 9.5 Connection Details

> **Authentication Mode**
>
> You can set the authentication mode to USE SINGLE SIGN-ON, but doing this requires your SAP BusinessObjects system to be configured with SAP authentication.

15. Use the SAVE LANGUAGE option to save your settings as configured in the relational connection. If you leave the checkbox open, the user can change the language by setting the user preferences in the BI launch pad.

16. Use the [...] button next to INFOPROVIDER to obtain a list of possible INFO-PROVIDERS (see Figure 9.6).

17. Use the filter as part of the screen to limit the list of InfoProviders based on the type of InfoProvider:

    ▶ IOBJ = InfoObject
    ▶ CUBE = InfoCube

350

- ODSO = Operational Data Store
- MRPO = MultiProvider
- VIRT = Virtual InfoProvider

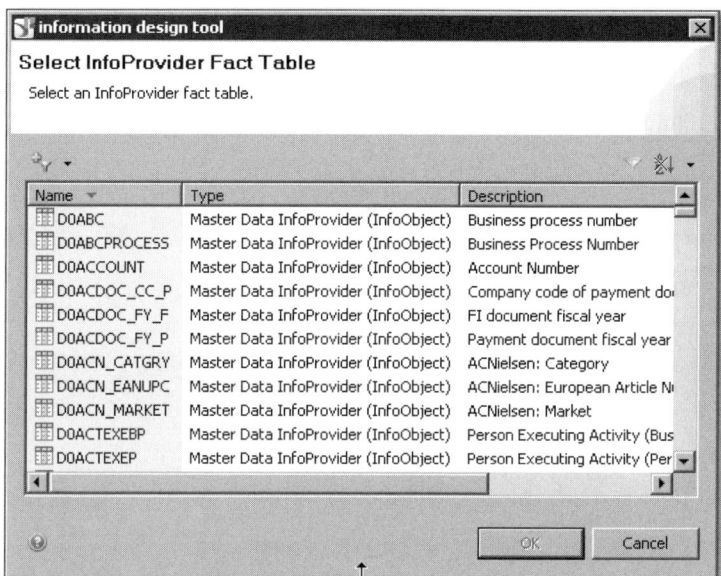

Figure 9.6 List of InfoProviders

18. In our example we use the MultiProvider 0D_NW_M01 from the NetWeaver demo model.
19. Click on OK.
20. Click on FINISH.
21. You are asked whether you want to create a shortcut for your connection. Click on YES.
22. Click on CLOSE.
23. Select your local project.
24. Select the menu FILE • NEW • DATA FOUNDATION.
25. Enter a name for the data foundation.
26. Click on NEXT.
27. Select the MULTI-SOURCE ENABLED option. The connection toward SAP NetWeaver BW is not available when using the single source option.

28. Click on Next.
29. You are asked to log on to your SAP BusinessObjects system.
30. Enter your credentials.
31. Click on Next.
32. Select the shortcut that was created for the connection you established previously.
33. Click on Next (see Figure 9.7).

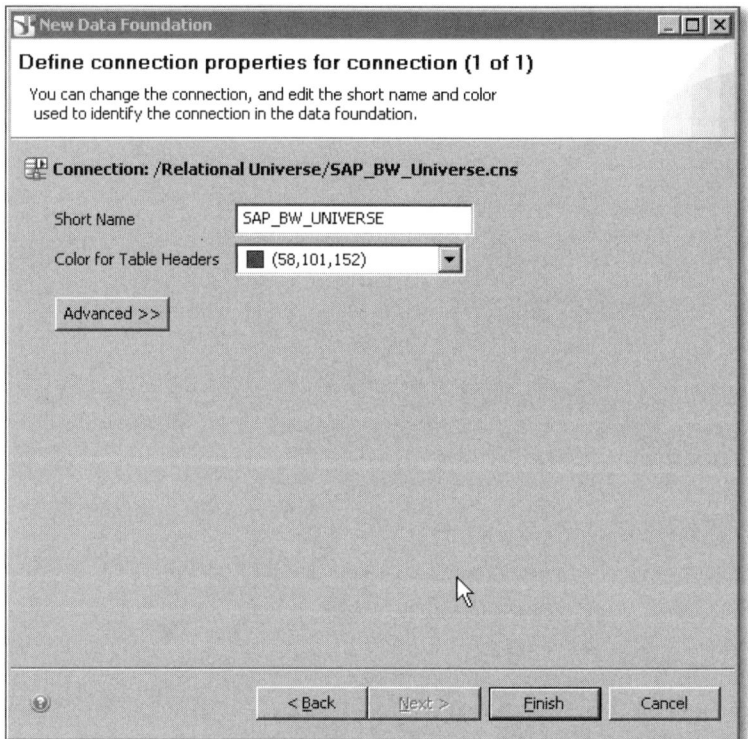

Figure 9.7 Define Connection Properties

34. Click on Advanced.
35. Ensure that the Automatically Creates Tables and Joins option is activated.
36. Click on Finish. You are presented with a default generated star schema for the selected InfoProvider.
37. Select your local project.

38. Select the menu File • New • Business Layer.
39. Select the Relational Data Source entry.
40. Click on Next.
41. Enter a name for the Business Layer.
42. Click on Next.
43. Use the [...] button and select the newly created data foundation (see Figure 9.8).

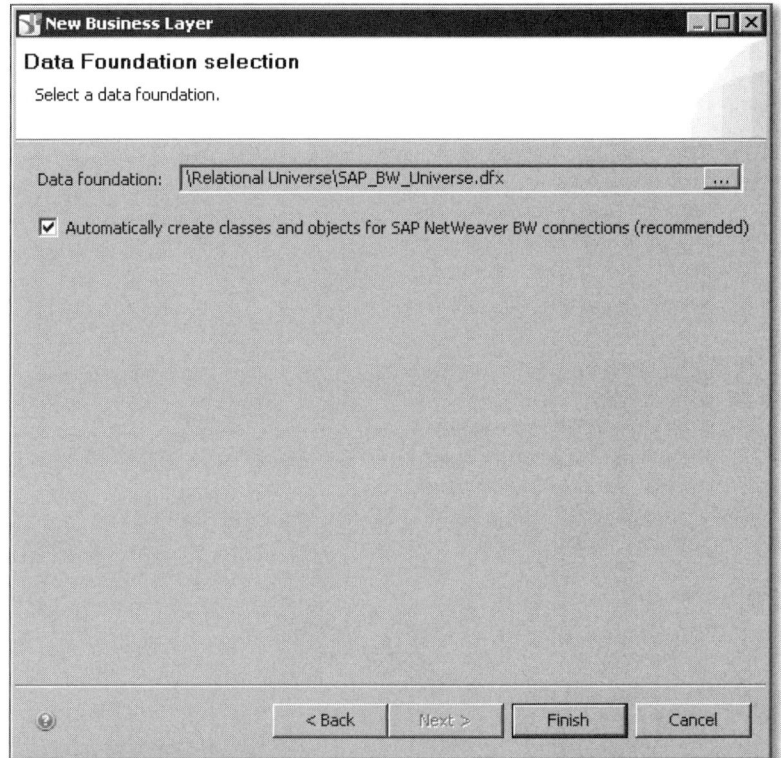

Figure 9.8 Data Foundation

44. Ensure that Automatically create classes and objects for SAP NetWeaver BW connections (recommended) is activated.
45. Click on Finish. You are presented (see Figure 9.9) with a list of classes, dimensions, and measures that have been generated based on the information retrieved from SAP NetWeaver BW.

9 Data Exploration and Searching with SAP BusinessObjects Explorer

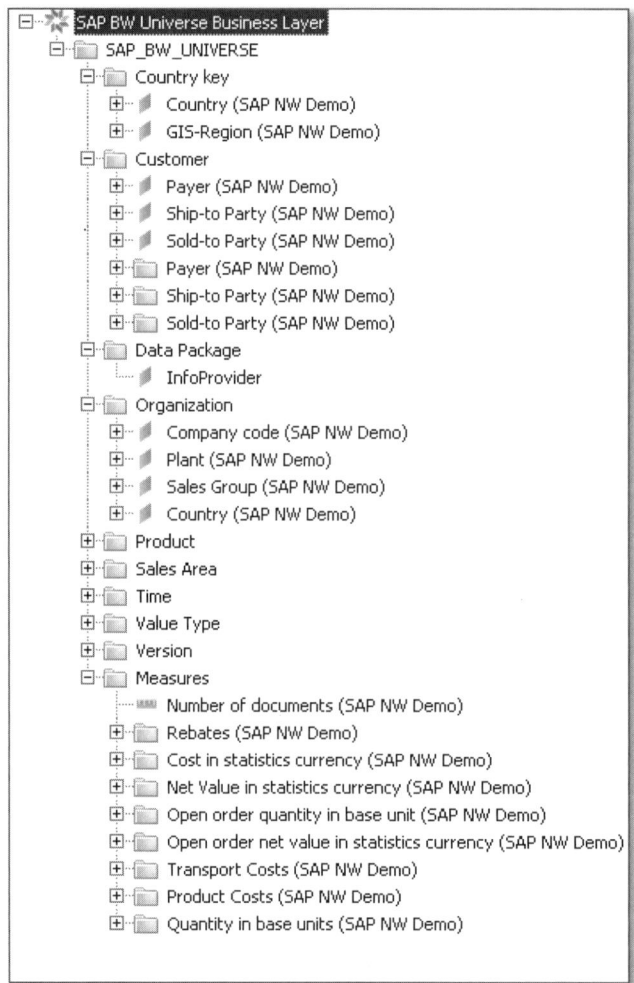

Figure 9.9 Business Layer

Default Layout for SAP NetWeaver BW Universe
When you generate a relational universe on top of the SAP NetWeaver BW InfoProvider, the Information Design Tool creates a default layout in the business layer for you. You will notice that all the dimensions in the business layer point to the key values of the InfoObjects in SAP NetWeaver BW and not to the descriptions. This is because all the descriptions are generated as detail objects. If you plan to use the universe for SAP BusinessObjects Explorer, you may want to change the definitions to point to the description and add a detail object manually pointing to the key value.

46. Right-click on the newly generated BUSINESS LAYER entry as part of your local project.
47. Select the menu PUBLISH • TO A REPOSITORY.
48. Select the integrity checks you would like to perform.
49. Click on NEXT.
50. Select a folder for the universe.
51. Click on FINISH.
52. Click on CLOSE.

You have created a relational universe on top of SAP NetWeaver BW, which you can use in the next steps to create a new information space.

1. Log on to the BI launch pad via the menu START • PROGRAMS • SAP BUSINESS-OBJECTS BI PLATFORM 4.0 • SAP BusinessObjects BI PLATFORM • SAP BUSINESS-OBJECTS BI PLATFORM JAVA BI LAUNCHPAD.
2. Select SAP as the authentication mode.
3. User your SAP credentials to log on.
4. Navigate to the menu APPLICATIONS.
5. Select EXPLORER (see Figure 9.10).

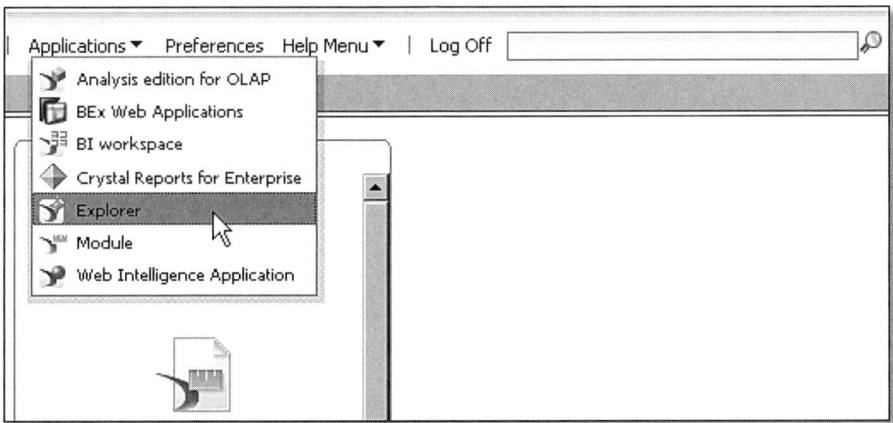

Figure 9.10 Applications Menu

6. Select the MANAGE SPACES menu (see Figure 9.11).
7. Select the previously generated universe.

9 | Data Exploration and Searching with SAP BusinessObjects Explorer

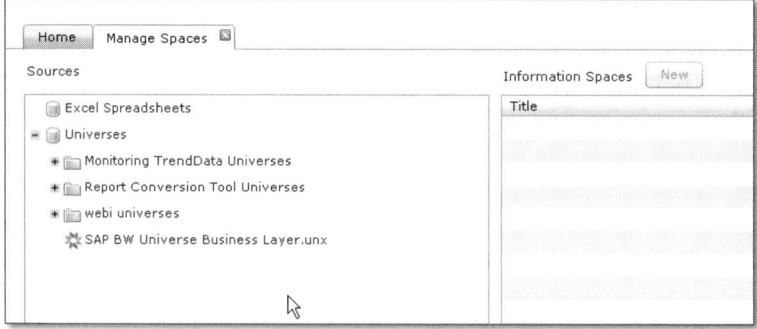

Figure 9.11 Manage Spaces

8. Click on NEW (see Figure 9.12).

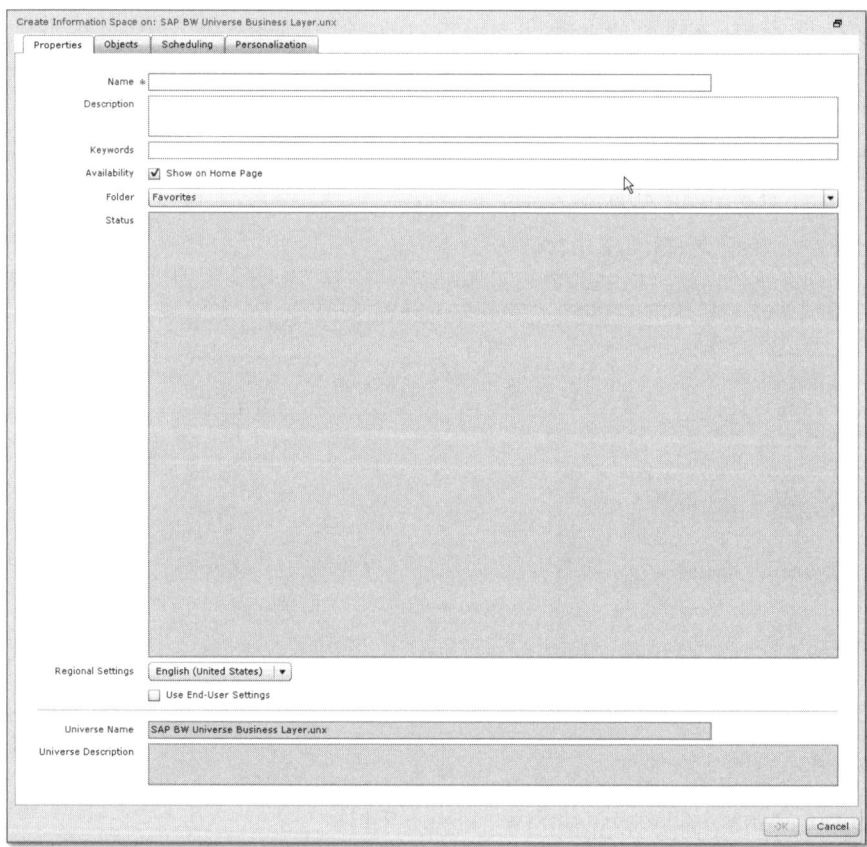

Figure 9.12 New Information Space

9. Enter a name for the new information space.
10. Navigate to the OBJECTS tab (see Figure 9.13).

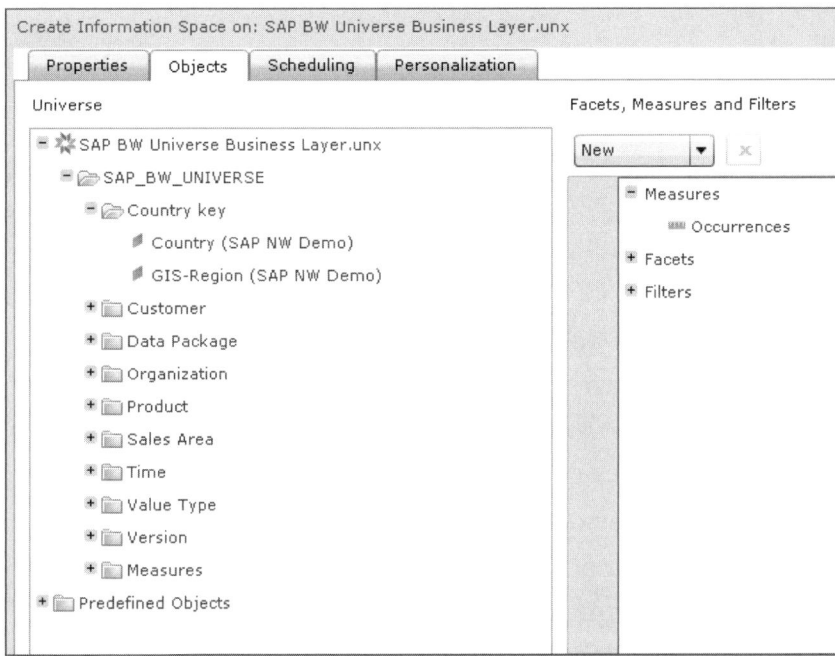

Figure 9.13 Objects

11. Add the following objects from the list of available objects to the facets. The list shows the class from the universe so that it is easier to locate the objects:

    ▶ COUNTRY KEY
        – COUNTRY (SAP NW DEMO)
        – GIS-REGION (SAP NW DEMO)
    ▶ CUSTOMER
        – SOLD-TO-PARTY (SAP NW DEMO)
    ▶ PRODUCT
        – PRODUCT CATEGORY (SAP NW DEMO)
        – PRODUCT GROUP (SAP NW DEMO)
        – PRODUCT (SAP NW DEMO)

- Sales area
  - Distribution Channel (SAP NW Demo)
  - Sales Organization (SAP NW Demo)
- Time
  - Calendar Year/Month
  - Calendar Year

12. Add the following objects from the list of available objects in the Measures class to the Measures area on the right-hand side. The list shows the class from the universe so that it is easier to locate the objects:

- Rebates (SAP NW Demo)
  - Rebates (SAP NW Demo)
- Cost in Statistics Currency (SAP NW Demo)
  - Cost in Statistics Currency (SAP NW Demo)
- Net Value in Statistics Currency (SAP NW Demo)
  - Net Value in Statistics Currency (SAP NW Demo)
- Open Order Quantity in Base Unit (SAP NW Demo)
  - Open Order Quantity in Base Unit (SAP NW Demo)
- Transport Costs (SAP NW Demo)
  - Transport Costs (SAP NW Demo)
- Product Costs (SAP NW Demo)
  - Product Costs (SAP NW Demo)

13. Select Country (SAP NW Demo) in the list of facets.

14. In the Details area, set the Dimension Kind to Toponym (see Figure 9.14).

15. Click on the [...] button next to Toponym (see Figure 9.15).

16. Click on Load (see Figure 9.16).

17. You can now see the values from SAP NetWeaver BW and the proposed values for the countries. If the match is not correct, you are able to change the configuration.

18. Click on OK. The information space is now listed as an available information space, which means that you can start the indexing process.

19. Use the Index Now ([icon]) button to start the indexing process.

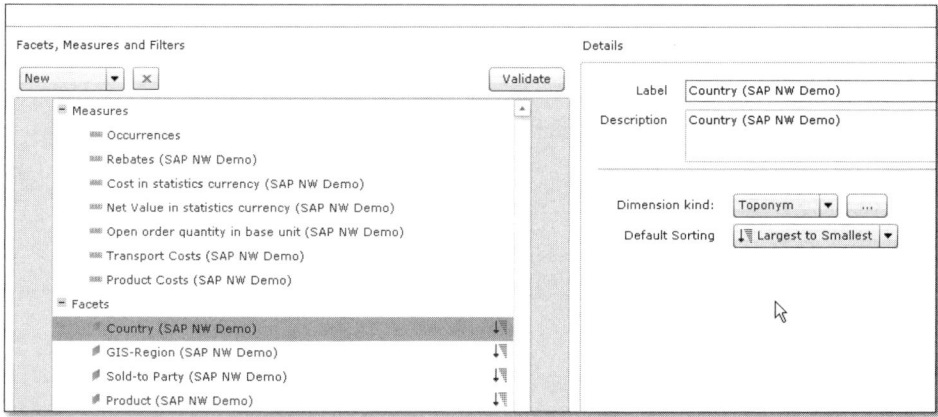

Figure 9.14 Details

Figure 9.15 Configure Matches

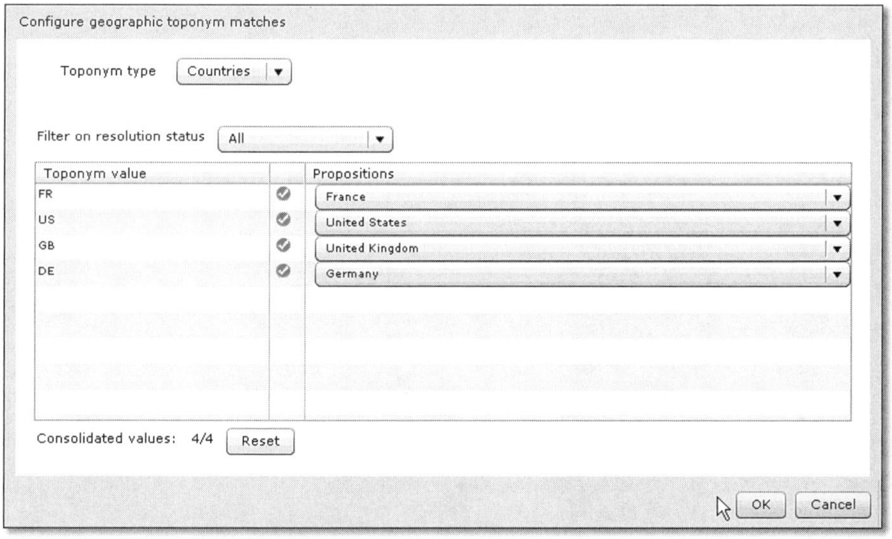

Figure 9.16 Loaded Values and Matches

9 | Data Exploration and Searching with SAP BusinessObjects Explorer

> **Geographic Information**
>
> Part of SAP BusinessObjects Explorer 4.0 FP3 is the ability to define dimensions as dimensions with geographic information and then to use those dimensions as part of the visualization in the form of maps in SAP BusinessObjects Explorer.

20. After the indexing is finished, navigate to the HOME tab.
21. Your new information space is listed on the HOME tab. Click on the link to open the data (see Figure 9.17).

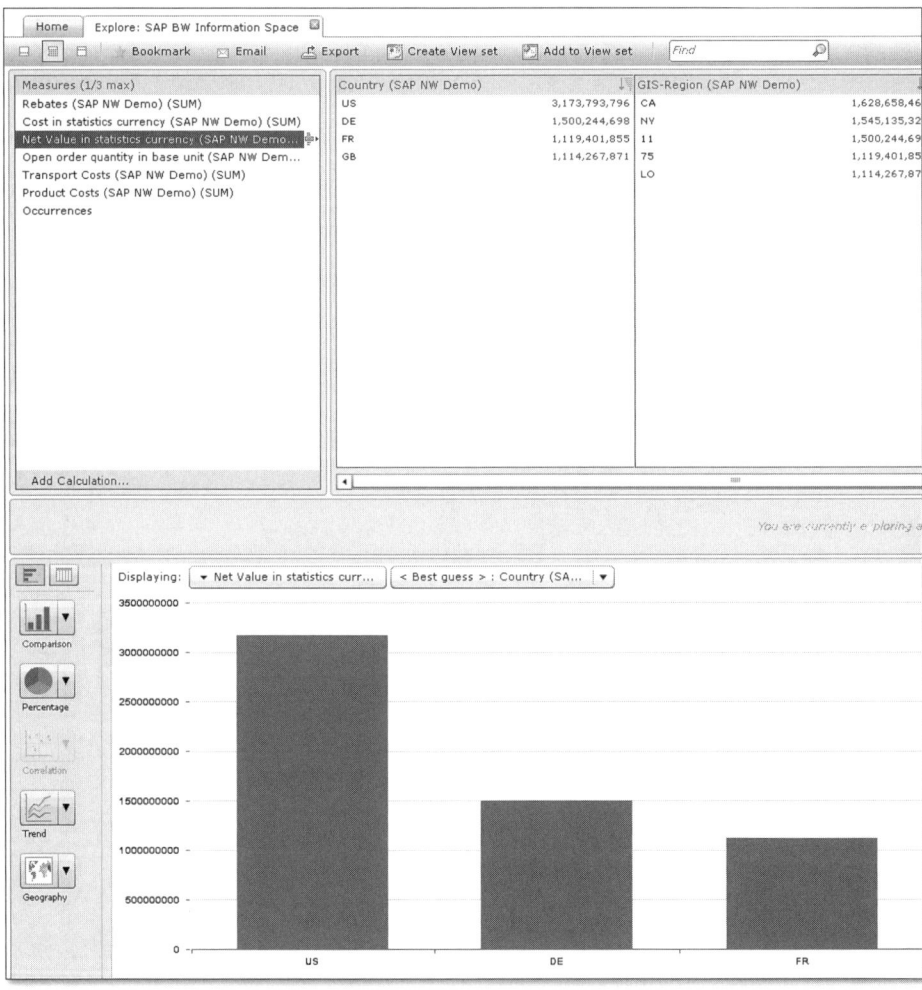

Figure 9.17 Information Space

You can now navigate in the complete set of index data, change the visualization type, search for information using the FIND dialog, and rank values using the TOP N functionality. In the next steps, we uncover some basic steps using SAP BusinessObjects Explorer.

1. In MEASURES, select NET VALUE.
2. In CALENDAR YEAR, click on the entry for 2011. The value is shown as a filter in the Information Space. You can change or remove the value at any time (see Figure 9.18).

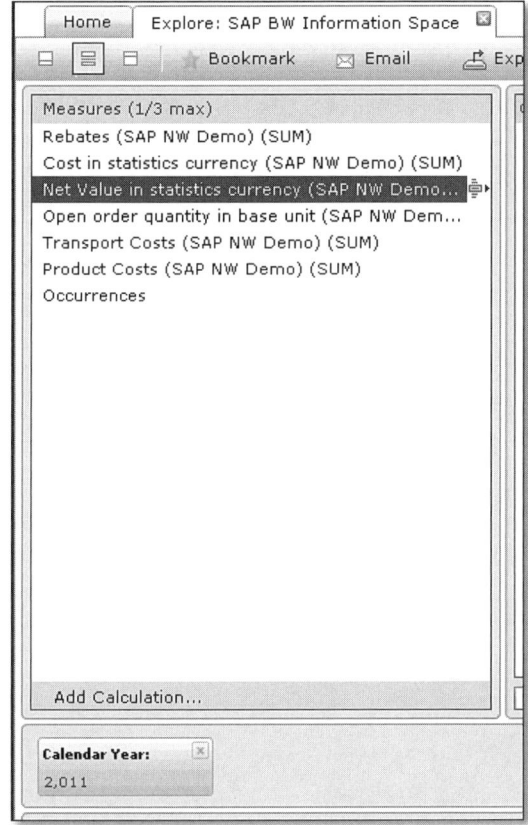

Figure 9.18 Filtered Values

3. Select PRODUCT COST as the second measure for the visualization (see Figure 9.19).

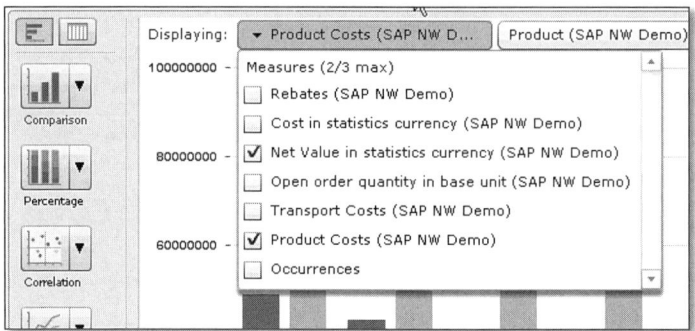

Figure 9.19 Selecting Measures

4. Select PRODUCT as the dimension for the visualization (see Figure 9.20).

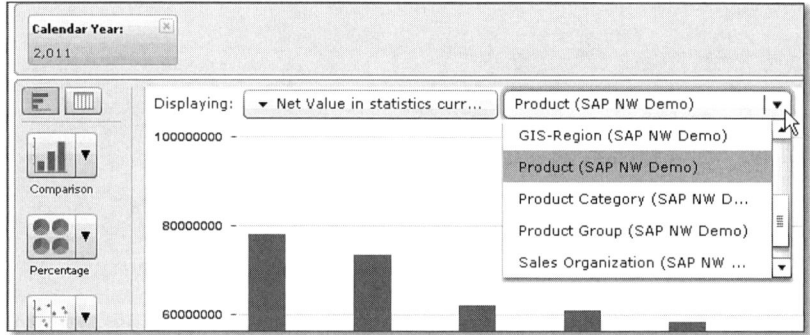

Figure 9.20 Selecting Dimension

5. Select the COMPARISON chart type with two axes (see Figure 9.21).

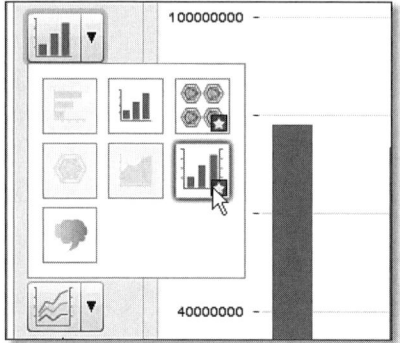

Figure 9.21 Comparison Charts

6. Navigate to the table in the bottom right corner and click on the column header for NET VALUE (see Figure 9.22).

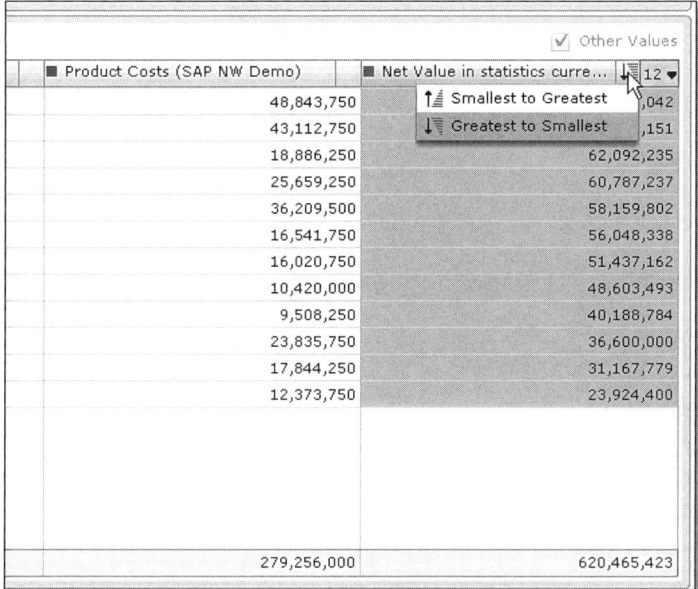

Figure 9.22 Ranking Values

7. Select the option GREATEST TO SMALLEST.
8. Click on the option to specify the number of values that are shown (see Figure 9.23) and specify the value 5.

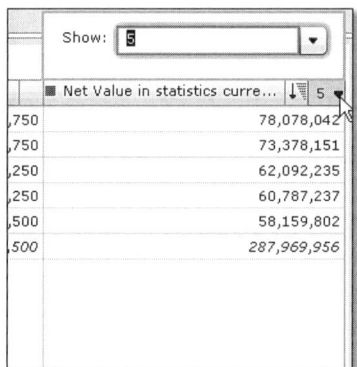

Figure 9.23 Select Top 5

You have filtered the values shown in the visualization to the top 5 values based on NET VALUE. This applies only to the visualization and not to the data facets shown in the upper part.

9. Uncheck the OTHER VALUES option.
10. Select the values shown in the chart either by drawing a box around them with the mouse or using the Ctrl key on the keyboard and selecting them one by one.

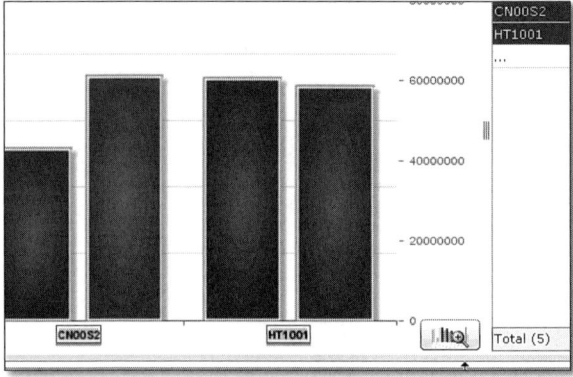

Figure 9.24 Filtering

11. After you select the values, you have the option to use the FILTER ( ) icon to use the selected values as a filter.
12. Click on the selected filter value 2011 for the CALENDAR YEAR (see Figure 9.25).

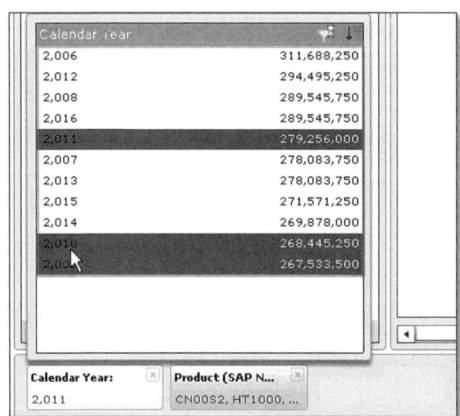

Figure 9.25 Changing Filter Value

13. In addition to the year 2011, also select the values 2009 and 2010 now.
14. Select CALENDAR YEAR as the dimension for the visualization.
15. Select TREND as the visualization type (see Figure 9.26).

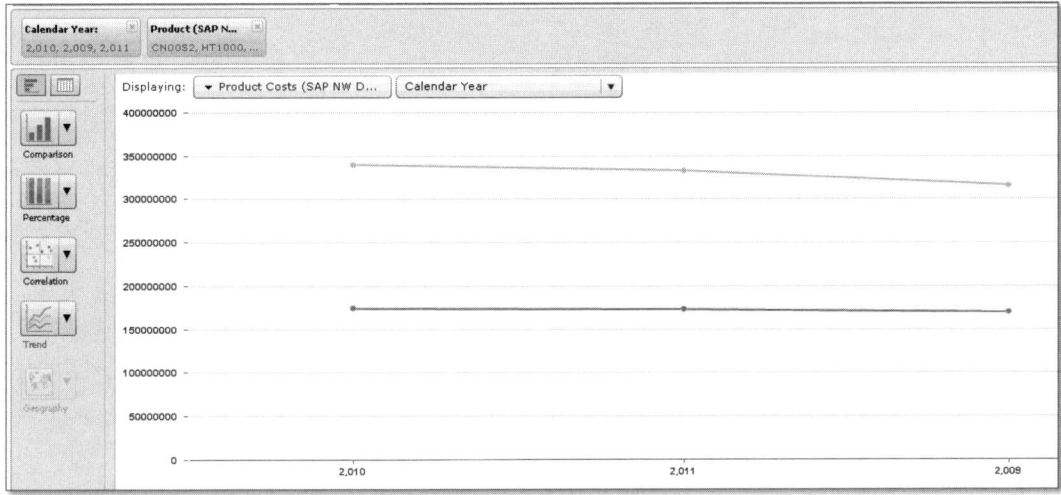

Figure 9.26 Trend Visualization

16. In addition to the NET VALUE and PRODUCT COSTS, also select the TRANSPORT COSTS for the visualization.
17. Click on the ADD CALCULATION button in MEASURES to create a new custom calculation (see Figure 9.27).

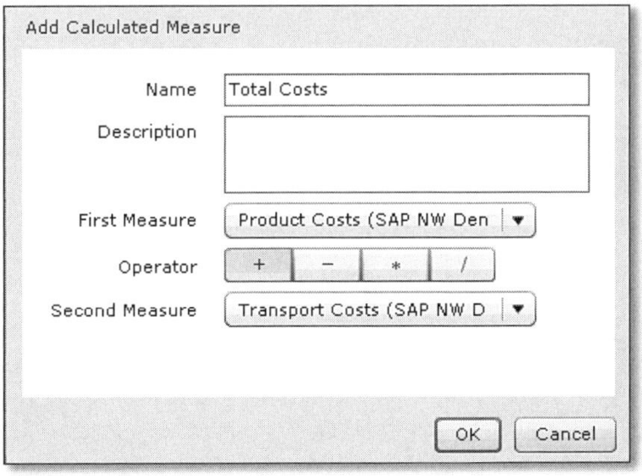

Figure 9.27 Add Calculated Measure

18. Enter TOTAL COSTS as NAME.
19. Select PRODUCT COSTS as FIRST MEASURE.
20. Select the + OPERATOR.
21. Select TRANSPORT COSTS as SECOND MEASURE.
22. Click on OK.

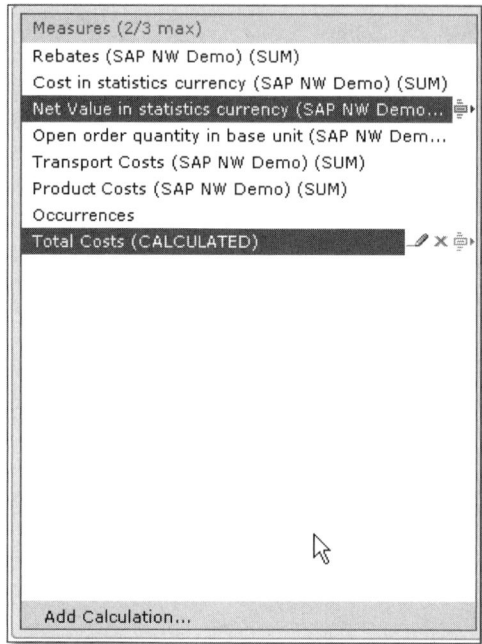

Figure 9.28 Facet Measures

The custom calculation is listed in MEASURES with the hint (CALCULATED) to show that this is a calculated measure, but you can use the calculated measure like any other measure in the product.

23. Select the measure NET VALUE and TOTAL COSTS for the visualization.
24. Click on the EXPORT button.
25. Select the option WEB INTELLIGENCE (see Figure 9.29).
26. Click on OK.

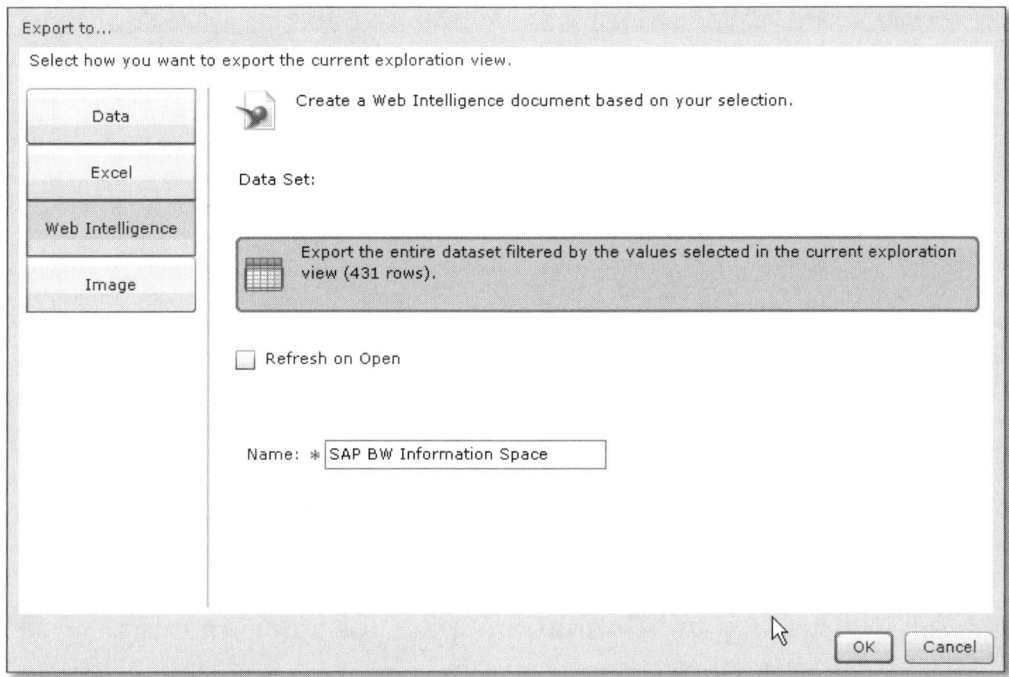

Figure 9.29 Export Options

27. You receive a message with a link to the SAP BusinessObjects Web Intelligence report (see Figure 9.30).

Figure 9.30 Link to SAP BusinessObjects Web Intelligence Report

28. Click on the link to the report (see Figure 9.31).
29. You can now use SAP BusinessObjects Web Intelligence to analyze the information further.

Country (SAF	GtS-Region (t	Sold-to Party	Product (SAF	Product Cate	Product Grou	Sales Organi	Distribution C	Calendar Ye:	Calendar Ye:	Rebates (SAI	Cost in statis	Net Value in :	Open order q	Transport Co	Product Cost	Occurrences	Total Costs
DE	11		CN00S2	NB	NB2	1514		200,901	2,009	0	0	4,600,000	0	1,523,520	2,995,750	1	4,519,270
DE	11		CN00S2	NB	NB2	1514		200,902	2,009	0	0	2,600,000	0	861,120	1,693,250	1	2,554,370
DE	11		CN00S2	NB	NB2	1514		200,903	2,009	0	0	3,400,000	0	1,126,080	2,214,250	1	3,340,330
DE	11		CN00S2	NB	NB2	1514		200,904	2,009	0	0	4,000,000	0	1,324,800	2,605,000	1	3,929,800
DE	11		CN00S2	NB	NB2	1514		200,905	2,009	0	0	3,600,000	0	1,192,320	2,344,500	1	3,536,820
DE	11		CN00S2	NB	NB2	1514		200,906	2,009	0	0	4,000,000	0	1,324,800	2,605,000	1	3,929,800
DE	11		CN00S2	NB	NB2	1514		200,907	2,009	0	0	4,200,000	0	1,391,040	2,735,250	1	4,126,290
DE	11		CN00S2	NB	NB2	1514		200,908	2,009	0	0	4,000,000	0	1,324,800	2,605,000	1	3,929,800
DE	11		CN00S2	NB	NB2	1514		200,909	2,009	0	0	3,400,000	0	1,126,080	2,214,250	1	3,340,330
DE	11		CN00S2	NB	NB2	1514		200,910	2,009	0	0	3,600,000	0	1,192,320	2,344,500	1	3,536,820
DE	11		CN00S2	NB	NB2	1514		200,911	2,009	0	0	4,200,000	0	1,391,040	2,735,250	1	4,126,290
DE	11		CN00S2	NB	NB2	1514		200,912	2,009	0	0	4,400,000	0	1,457,280	2,865,500	1	4,322,780
DE	11		CN00S2	NB	NB2	1514		201,001	2,010	0	0	4,600,000	0	1,523,520	2,995,750	1	4,519,270
DE	11		CN00S2	NB	NB2	1514		201,002	2,010	0	0	2,600,000	0	861,120	1,693,250	1	2,554,370
DE	11		CN00S2	NB	NB2	1514		201,003	2,010	0	0	3,400,000	0	1,126,080	2,214,250	1	3,340,330

Figure 9.31 SAP BusinessObjects Web Intelligence Report

In this section you learned some basic steps for using SAP BusinessObjects Explorer and how to create your own information space based on data from your SAP NetWeaver BW system. In the next section we use SAP BusinessObjects Explorer to fulfill the requirements from the sales area.

9.4 Creating an Information Space for Sales Analysis

Now that we have covered the basic steps for using SAP BusinessObjects Explorer, we can set up SAP BusinessObjects Explorer to fulfill the requirements from our sales department. We use the MultiProvider 0D_DX_M01—SAP Demo Scenario Reporting Cube. We first set up a relational universe based on the InfoProvider, customize the universe, and then create a new information space for the sales area.

1. Start the Information Design Tool by following the menu START • PROGRAMS • SAP BUSINESSOBJECTS BI PLATFORM 4 • SAP BUSINESSOBJECTS BI PLATFORM CLIENT TOOLS • INFORMATION DESIGN TOOL.
2. Select the menu FILE • NEW • PROJECT to create a new project for your universe.
3. Enter a name for the new project and click on FINISH.
4. Select the WINDOW menu and make sure that the REPOSITORY RESOURCES window is shown.
5. In the REPOSITORY RESOURCES window, select the INSERT SESSION menu to establish a session to your SAP BusinessObjects BI platform.
6. Log on with your SAP credentials using the SAP authentication.

7. Click on OK.
8. Open the context menu of your established server connection in the CONNECTIONS area.
9. Select the menu item INSERT RELATIONAL CONNECTION.
10. Enter a name for the connection.
11. Click on NEXT.
12. Select the entry for SAP NETWEAVER BW.
13. Click on NEXT.
14. Fill in the needed details to establish the connection to your SAP NetWeaver BW system.
15. Use the SAVE LANGUAGE option to save your settings as configured in the relational connection. If you leave the checkbox open, the user can change the language by setting the user preferences in the BI launch pad.
16. Use the [...] button next to INFOPROVIDER to receive a list of possible InfoProviders.
17. You can use the filter as part of the screen to limit the list of InfoProviders based on the type of InfoProvider:
    - IOBJ = InfoObject
    - CUBE = InfoCube
    - ODSO = Operational Data Store
    - MRPO = MultiProvider
    - VIRT = Virtual InfoProvider
18. In our example we use the MultiProvider 0D_DX_M01.
19. Click on OK.
20. Click on FINISH.
21. You are asked whether you want to create a shortcut for your connection. Click on YES.
22. Click on CLOSE.
23. Select your local project.
24. Select the menu FILE • NEW • DATA FOUNDATION.
25. Enter a name for the data foundation.

26. Click on NEXT.
27. Select the MULTI-SOURCE ENABLED option. The connection toward SAP NetWeaver BW is not available when using the single source option.
28. Click on NEXT.
29. You are asked to log on to your SAP BusinessObjects system.
30. Enter your credentials.
31. Click on NEXT.
32. Select the shortcut that was created for the connection you established previously.
33. Click on NEXT.
34. Click on ADVANCED.
35. Ensure that AUTOMATICALLY CREATES TABLES AND JOINS is activated.
36. Click on FINISH.
37. Select your local project.
38. Select the menu FILE • NEW • BUSINESS LAYER.
39. Select the RELATIONAL DATA SOURCE entry.
40. Click on NEXT.
41. Enter a name for the BUSINESS LAYER.
42. Click on NEXT.
43. Use the ... button and select the newly created DATA FOUNDATION.
44. Ensure that AUTOMATICALLY CREATE CLASSES AND OBJECTS FOR SAP NETWEAVER BW CONNECTIONS (RECOMMENDED) is activated.
45. Click on FINISH.
46. Right-click on the newly generated BUSINESS LAYER entry as part of your local project.
47. Select the menu PUBLISH • TO A REPOSITORY.
48. Select the integrity checks you would like to perform.
49. Click on NEXT
50. Select a folder for the universe.
51. Click on FINISH.
52. Click on CLOSE.

You are presented with a list of classes, dimensions, and measures that have been generated based on the information retrieved from SAP NetWeaver BW. The universe uses standard settings; in the next series of steps, we will customize these settings.

1. In BUSINESS LAYER, select CALENDAR YEAR/MONTH (see Figure 9.32).

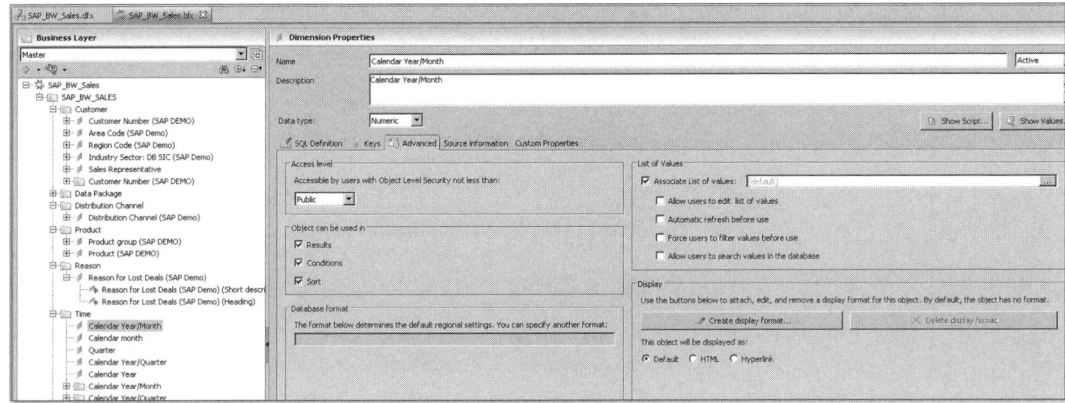

Figure 9.32 Business Layer

2. Click on CREATE DISPLAY FORMAT.
3. Select NUMERIC in FORMAT CATEGORIES.
4. Click on CUSTOM FORMAT.
5. Enter the custom format in the syntax `0000.00` as shown in Figure 9.33.
6. Click on OK.
7. Click on OK.
8. In BUSINESS LAYER, select CALENDAR MONTH.
9. Click on CREATE DISPLAY FORMAT.
10. Select the entry NUMERIC in the FORMAT CATEGORIES.
11. Click on CUSTOM FORMAT.
12. Enter the custom format in the syntax `00`.
13. Click on OK.
14. Click on OK.
15. In the BUSINESS LAYER select CALENDAR YEAR/QUARTER.

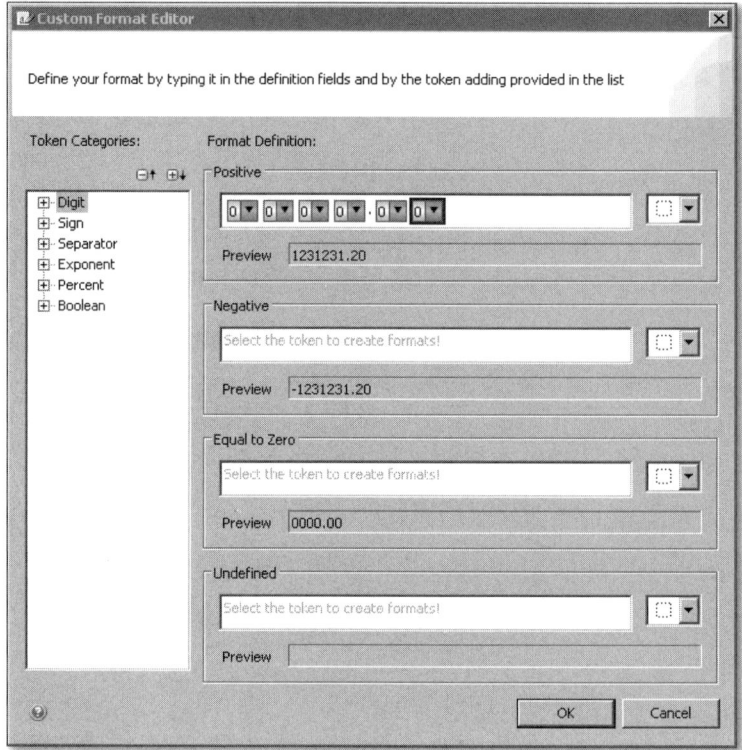

Figure 9.33 Custom Format Editor

16. Click on CREATE DISPLAY FORMAT.
17. Select NUMERIC in FORMAT CATEGORIES.
18. Click CUSTOM FORMAT.
19. Enter the custom format in the syntax `0000.00`.
20. Click on OK.
21. Click on OK.
22. In the BUSINESS LAYER select CUSTOMER NUMBER.
23. Right-click and select NEW • ATTRIBUTE from the menu (see Figure 9.34).
24. Enter "Customer Number" in the NAME field.
25. Select the dimension object CUSTOMER NUMBER.
26. Select the SELECT clause from the properties:

    `@catalog('SAP_BW_SALES')."PUBLIC"."IOD_DX_M01"."0D_CUSTOMER"`

Creating an Information Space for Sales Analysis | **9.4**

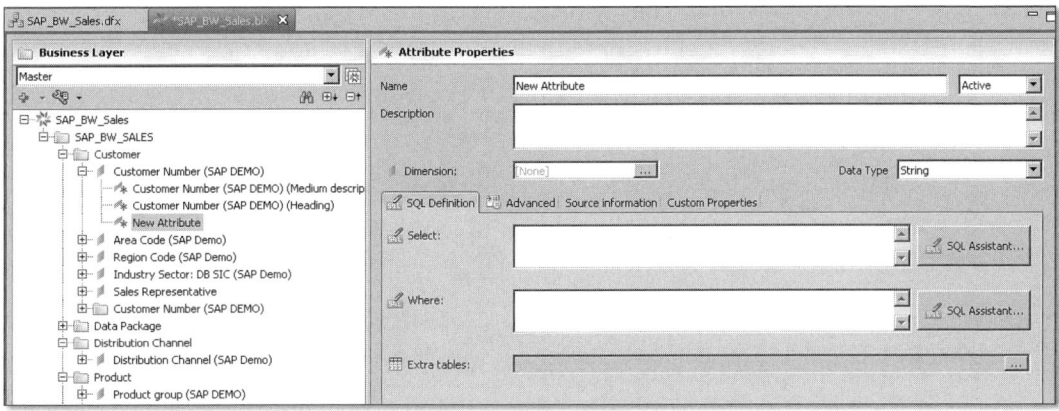

Figure 9.34 New Attribute

27. Copy the SELECT clause from CUSTOMER NUMBER.
28. Navigate to the new CUSTOMER NUMBER attribute.
29. Paste the content into the SELECT property.
30. Now navigate to the CUSTOMER NUMBER (SAP DEMO) (MEDIUM DESCRIPTION) attribute.
31. Copy the content from the SELECT property.
32. Paste the content of the SELECT property of the CUSTOMER NUMBER (SAP DEMO) (MEDIUM DESCRIPTION) attribute into the SELECT property of the CUSTOMER NUMBER dimension object (see Figure 9.35).

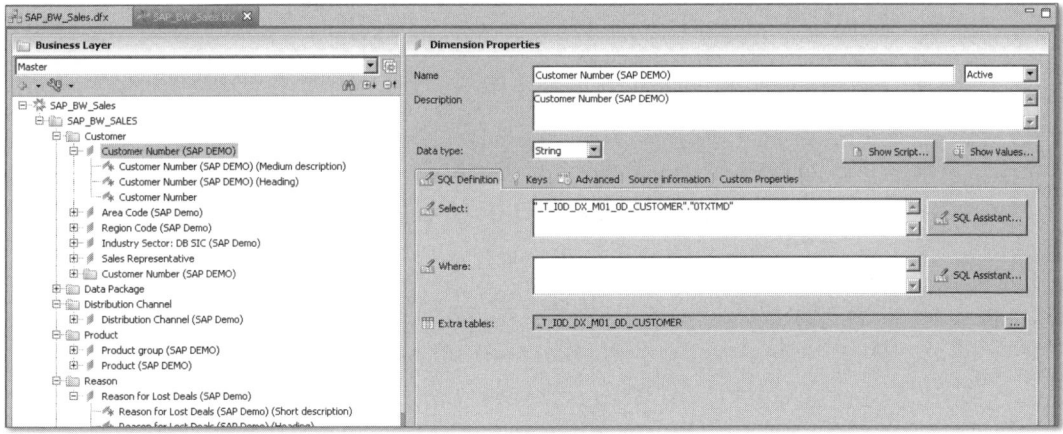

Figure 9.35 Customer Number

373

33. Click on SHOW VALUES. The values of the CUSTOMER NUMBER dimension should show actual customer names instead of customer numbers.
34. In BUSINESS LAYER, select the REGION CODE dimension.
35. Right-click and select the menu NEW • ATTRIBUTE from the menu.
36. Enter "Region Code (numeric)" in the NAME field.
37. Select the REGION CODE dimension object.
38. Select the SELECT clause from the properties:
    @catalog('SAP_BW_SALES')."PUBLIC"."IOD_DX_M01"."0D_DBREGCOD"
39. Copy the SELECT clause from the REGION CODE dimension.
40. Navigate to the new REGION CODE (NUMERIC) attribute.
41. Paste the content into the SELECT property.
42. Navigate to the REGION CODE (SAP DEMO) (LONG DESCRIPTION) attribute.
43. Copy the content from the property SELECT.
44. Paste the content of the property SELECT of the REGION CODE (SAP DEMO) (LONG DESCRIPTION) attribute into the SELECT property of the REGION CODE dimension object.
45. The values of the REGION CODE dimension should now show actual region descriptions instead of numeric values.
46. In BUSINESS LAYER, select the SALES REPRESENTATIVE dimension.
47. Right-click and select NEW • ATTRIBUTE from the menu.
48. Enter "Sales Representative (numeric)" in the NAME field.
49. Select the SALES REPRESENTATIVE dimension object.
50. Select the SELECT clause from the properties:
    @catalog('SAP_BW_SALES')."PUB-
    LIC"."IOD_DX_M01"."0D_CUSTOMER__PM_SREP"
51. Copy the SELECT clause from the SALES REPRESENTATIVE dimension.
52. Navigate to the new SALES REPRESENTATIVE (NUMERIC) attribute.
53. Paste the content into the SELECT property.
54. Navigate to the SALES REPRESENTATIVE (MEDIUM DESCRIPTION) attribute.
55. Copy the content from the SELECT property.

56. Paste the content of the SELECT property of the SALES REPRESENTATIVE (MEDIUM DESCRIPTION) attribute into the SELECT property of the SALES REPRESENTATIVE dimension object.
57. The values of the SALES REPRESENTATIVE dimension should now show actual names of the sales representatives instead of numeric values.
58. Repeat the steps outlined above for the following dimensions:
    - DISTRIBUTION CHANNEL
    - PRODUCT GROUP
    - PRODUCT
    - REASON FOR LOST DEALS

> **Default Layout for SAP NetWeaver BW Universe**
>
> When you generate a relational universe on top of the SAP NetWeaver BW InfoProvider, the Information Design Tool creates a default layout in the business layer for you. You will notice that all the dimensions in the business layer point to the key values of the InfoObjects in SAP NetWeaver BW and not to the descriptions. This is because all the descriptions are generated as detail objects. If you plan to use the universe for SAP BusinessObjects Explorer, you may want to change the definitions to point to the description and add a detail object manually pointing to the key value.

59. Select the menu FILE • SAVE to save the changes.
60. Right-click on the changed BUSINESS LAYER entry as part of your local project.
61. Select the menu PUBLISH • TO A REPOSITORY.
62. Select the integrity checks you want to perform.
63. Click on NEXT.
64. Select a folder for the universe.
65. Click on FINISH.
66. Click on CLOSE.

You have created a relational universe on top of SAP NetWeaver BW, which you can use in the next steps to create a new information space.

1. Log on to the BI launch pad via the menu START • PROGRAMS • SAP BUSINESSOBJECTS BI PLATFORM 4.0 • SAP BUSINESSOBJECTS BI PLATFORM • SAP BUSINESSOBJECTS BI PLATFORM JAVA BI LAUNCHPAD.

2. Select SAP as the authentication mode.
3. Use your SAP credentials to log on.
4. Navigate to the APPLICATIONS menu.
5. Select EXPLORER.
6. Select the menu MANAGE SPACES.
7. Select the previously generated universe.
8. Click on NEW.
9. Enter a name for the new information space.
10. Navigate to the OBJECTS tab.
11. Add the following objects from the list of available objects to the facets. The list shows the class from the universe so that it is easier to locate the objects:
    - CUSTOMER
        - CUSTOMER NUMBER (SAP DEMO)
        - REGION CODE (SAP DEMO)
        - SALES REPRESENTATIVE
    - DISTRIBUTION CHANNEL
        - DISTRIBUTION CHANNEL (SAP DEMO)
    - PRODUCT
        - PRODUCT GROUP (SAP DEMO)
        - PRODUCT (SAP DEMO)
    - REASON
        - REASON FOR LOST DEALS (SAP DEMO)
    - TIME
        - CALENDAR YEAR
        - CALENDAR MONTH
        - QUARTER
12. Select CALENDAR YEAR in the list of defined facets (see Figure 9.36).
13. Set the DEFAULT SORTING in the DETAILS to A to Z.
14. Repeat these steps for the CALENDAR MONTH and the QUARTER.

Creating an Information Space for Sales Analysis | **9.4**

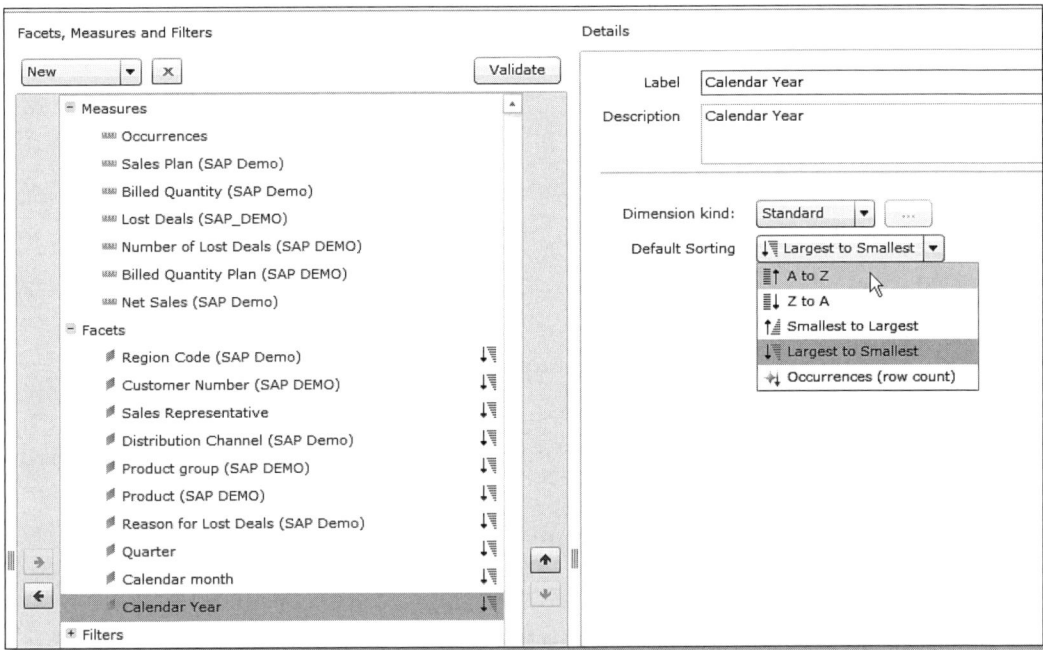

Figure 9.36 Defining Details

Default Sorting

By default, sorting is configured to be based on the selected measure and will be a largest-to-smallest sorting, which means it will sort the top values first. For time-based dimensions such as CALENDAR MONTH, it might be better to configure the sorting based on the dimension itself. By doing this, charts especially will show the time dimension properly.

15. Add the following objects from the list of available objects in the measures class to the MEASURES area on the right hand side. The list shows the class from the universe so that it is easier to locate the objects:

- SALES PLAN (SAP DEMO)
  - SALES PLAN (SAP DEMO)
- BILLED QUANTITY (SAP DEMO)
  - BILLED QUANTITY (SAP DEMO)
- LOST DEALS (SAP DEMO)
  - LOST DEALS (SAP DEMO)

377

- Number of Lost Deals (SAP Demo)
  - Number of Lost Deals (SAP Demo)
- Net Sales (SAP Demo)
  - Net Sales (SAP Demo)
- Billed Quantity Plan (SAP Demo)
  - Billed Quantity Plan (SAP Demo)

16. Click on OK. The information space is now listed as available, and you can start the indexing process.
17. Use the Index Now ( ) button to start the indexing process.
18. After the indexing is finished, navigate to the Home tab.
19. Your new information space is listed on the Home tab. Click on the link to open the data.
20. Select Net Sales as the measure (see Figure 9.37).

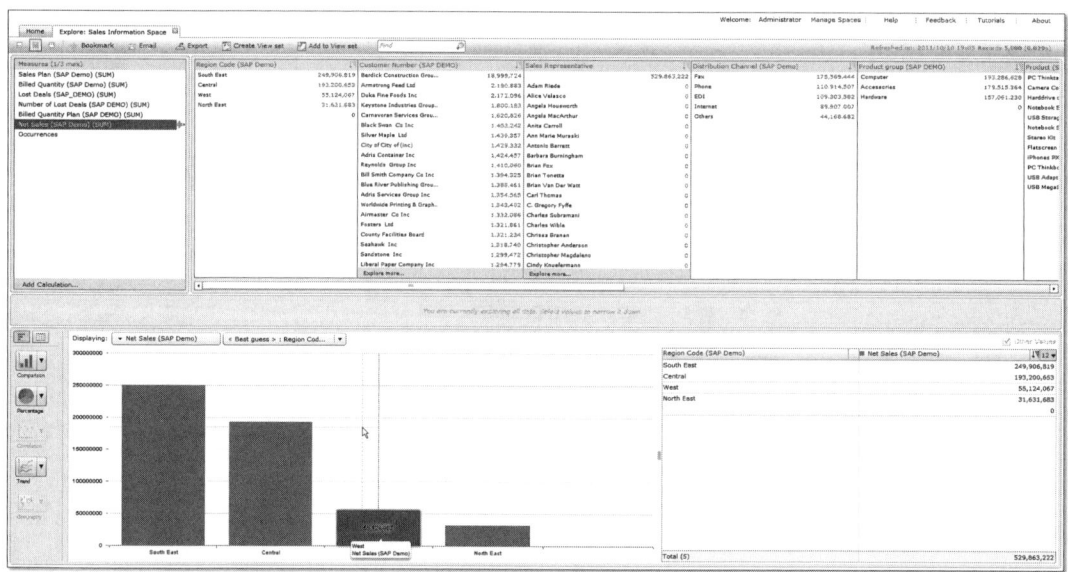

Figure 9.37 SAP BusinessObjects Explorer

21. Add Sales Plan as a second measure.
22. Select the current year in the Calendar Year (Key) facet so that the data will be filtered for the current year.

23. Set the dimension of the lower part of the visualization to CALENDAR MONTH (see Figure 9.38).

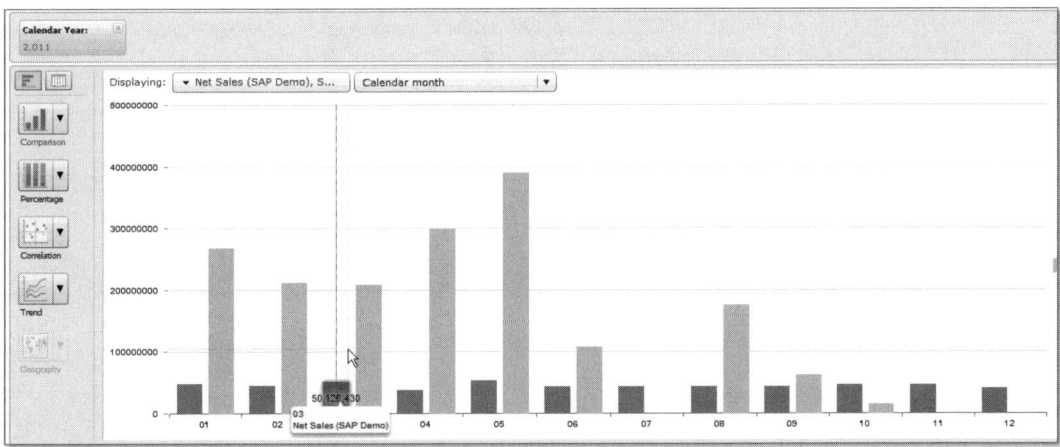

Figure 9.38 Visualization by Calendar Month

24. Set the visualization type to TREND (see Figure 9.39).

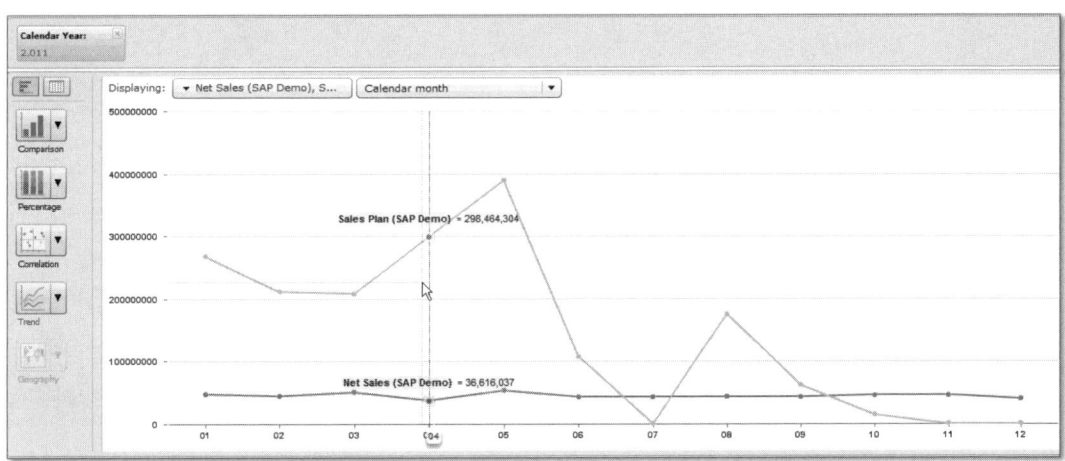

Figure 9.39 Trend Visualization

As you can see, NET SALES is always far below SALES PLAN. Now let's look at the third measure, LOST DEALS.

1. Add the third measure, LOST DEALS, to the visualization (see Figure 9.40)

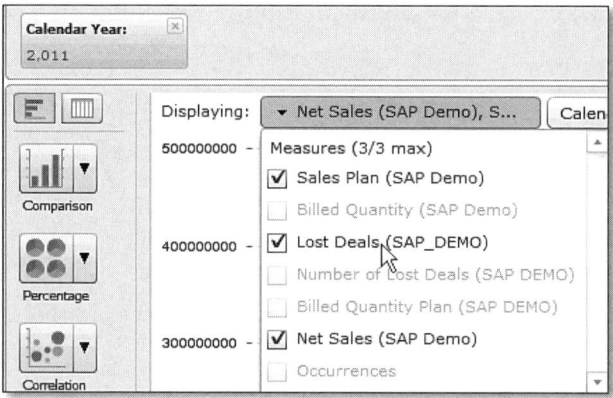

Figure 9.40 Configuring Measures for Visualization

2. Click on LOST DEALS in MEASURES so that all facets show the values for LOST DEALS.

3. Select REASON FOR LOST deals for the visualization.

4. Select the PERCENTAGE option for the visualization (see Figure 9.41).

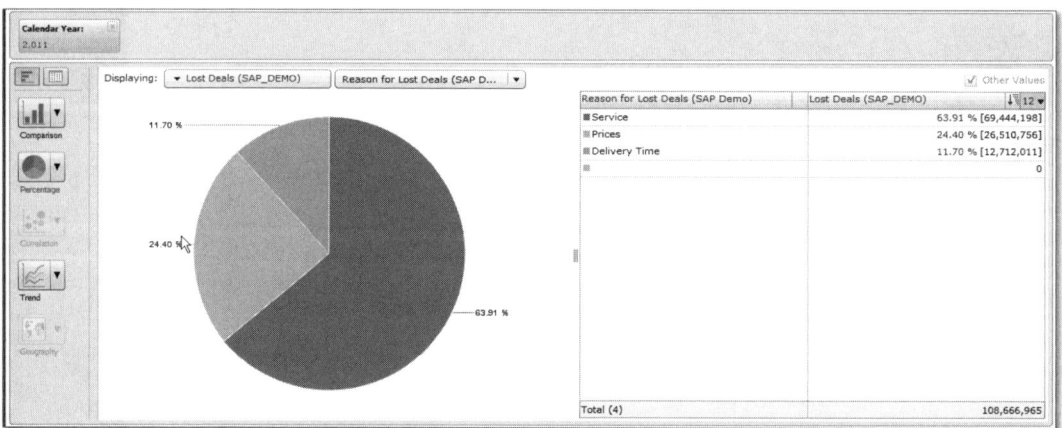

Figure 9.41 Percentage Contribution

5. You can see that over 60% of the lost deals occurred based on issues with SERVICE.

6. Select the SERVICE value in the chart.

7. Use the [ ] button to use the selected value as a filter.

8. Set the dimension for the visualization to REGION.
9. Add NUMBER OF LOST DEALS as a second measure to the visualization (see Figure 9.42).

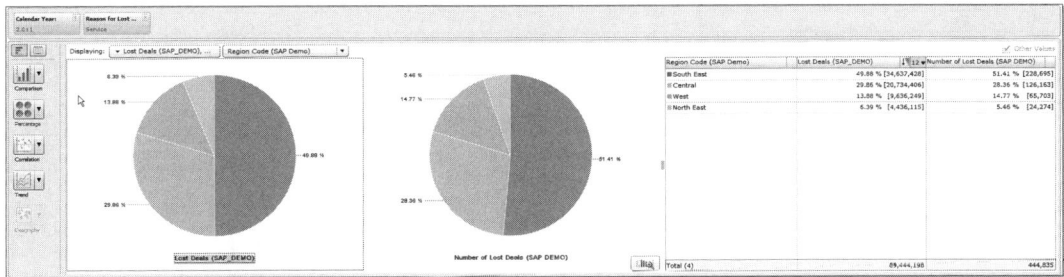

Figure 9.42 Contribution Summary

10. You can see that over 50% of the lost deals happened in the south east region. To find out more, select SOUTH EAST as a filter value in the chart.
11. Select CUSTOMER for the visualization.
12. Select the COMPARISON visualization type.
13. Uncheck the OTHER VALUES option so that you can focus on the top values (see Figure 9.43).

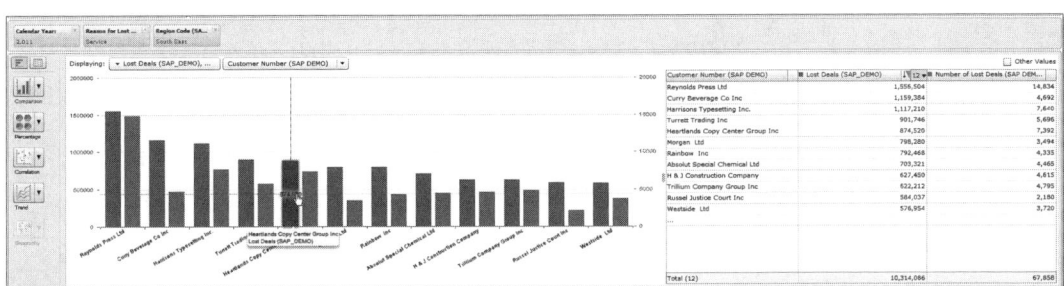

Figure 9.43 Comparison

14. You can see a significant difference in the amount and value of the lost deals between the top 3 customers and other customers.
15. Select the top 3 customers in the chart and select them as a filter value.
16. Select the SALES REPRESENTATIVE dimension for the visualization (see Figure 9.44).

9 | Data Exploration and Searching with SAP BusinessObjects Explorer

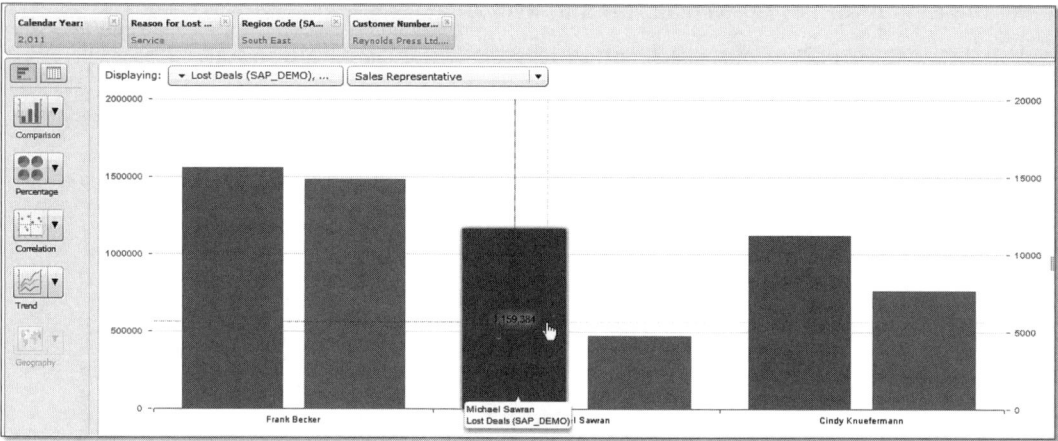

Figure 9.44 Visualization by Sales Representative

You can see the top 3 sales representatives in regard to the measures LOST DEALS and NUMBER OF LOST DEALS. By using SAP BusinessObjects Explorer you are quickly able to identify not only the sales region with the most lost deals, but also the customers and the assigned sales representatives. You can use this information and share it with colleagues in the sales management department to find the root cause of this phenomenon.

To conclude your work, send the report via email:

17. Click on the EMAIL button in the toolbar. Your email system generates a new message with a link to the information space, including your navigations (see Figure 9.45).

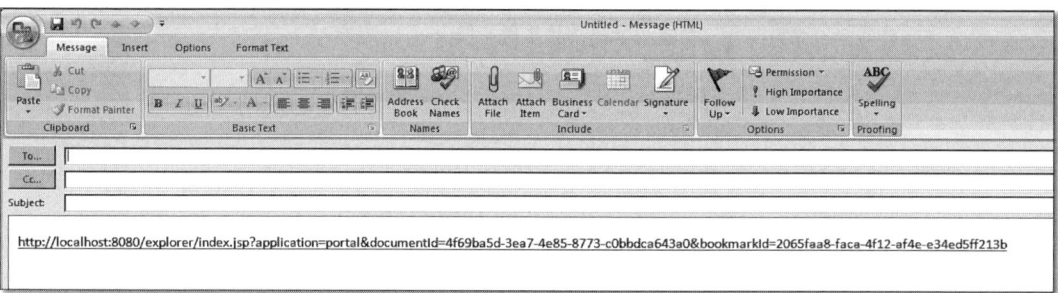

Figure 9.45 Email Message

You can now send colleagues in the sales management department the link to the information space from SAP BusinessObjects Explorer. By following the link, they will see exactly the same information that you just did. They are also able to navigate to further details if required.

9.5 Summary

In this chapter, you learned how to use SAP BusinessObjects Explorer to provide users with a unique and easy-to-use BI tool that lets them explore data and use common search workflows to find answers. You discovered the different data connectivity options for SAP BusinessObjects Explorer, started taking basic steps, and fulfilled the requirements for the sales department.

In this chapter we look at how you can use SAP BusinessObjects Live Office in combination with your BI content inside the Microsoft Office environment.

10   Using SAP BusinessObjects Live Office

In this chapter we use SAP BusinessObjects Live Office to provide content from the SAP BusinessObjects BI platform inside the Microsoft Office environment. You will learn how you can use data that is still live and that can be refreshed inside the different tools available with Microsoft Office. This chapter is not intended to cover the combination of SAP BusinessObjects Live Office and SAP BusinessObjects Dashboards, but instead to explore SAP BusinessObjects Live Office as your vehicle to share your BI content inside the Microsoft Office environment. In this chapter we focus less on the fulfillment of business requirements and more on the integration of your BI environment into the Microsoft Office products such as Microsoft Excel, Microsoft PowerPoint, and Microsoft Outlook.

10.1   SAP BusinessObjects Live Office Configuration

Before we can use SAP BusinessObjects Live Office in combination with our SAP BusinessObjects environment, we need to perform some very simple configuration steps. These steps need to be done on each client and in each product from the Microsoft Office environment that we would like to use in combination with SAP BusinessObjects Live Office.

In the next couple of steps, we use Microsoft Excel as the example, but the steps are identical for the other Microsoft Office products.

1. Start Microsoft Excel.
2. Navigate to the Live Office ribbon (see Figure 10.1).
3. Navigate to the menu LIVE OFFICE • APPLICATION OPTIONS (SEE Figure 10.2).

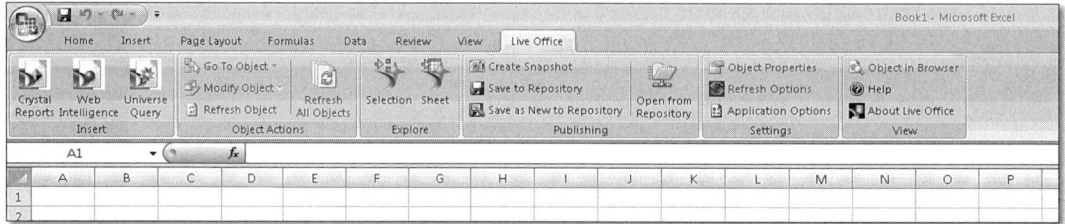

Figure 10.1 Live Office Ribbon

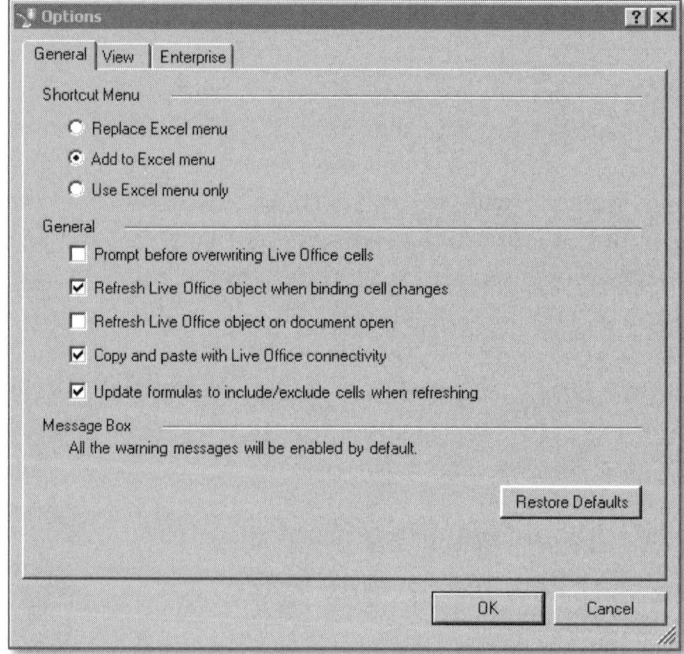

Figure 10.2 SAP BusinessObjects Live Office Options

4. Navigate to the ENTERPRISE tab.
5. Activate the option USE SPECIFIC LOGON CRITERIA.
6. Enter the URL to the web services deployment of your SAP BusinessObjects BI platform system. In a default installation the URL is:

   http://<Application Server>:<port>/dswsbobje/services/session

   Replace the placeholder *<Application Server>* and the placeholder *<port>* with values from your SAP BusinessObjects BI platform system.

7. As soon as the URL has been validated, you can set the AUTHENTICATION to SAP.

8. Leave the USER NAME and PASSWORD empty; you will then get asked each time when using SAP BusinessObjects Live Office to authenticate against the SAP BusinessObjects BI platform.

9. Uncheck the option USE SPECIFIC LOGON CRITERIA; otherwise, SAP BusienssObjects Live Office will use the empty entries and will try to log on to the system.

10. Click on OK and you are now ready to use SAP BusinessObjects Live Office.

As mentioned at the beginning of this section, these configuration steps need to be repeated in each of the Microsoft Office products that you would like to use with SAP BusinessObjects Live Office.

10.2 SAP BusinessObjects BI Platform Content and Microsoft Office

With SAP BusinessObjects Live Office, you are able to use content from different sources inside the Microsoft Office environment. As shown in Figure 10.3, SAP BusinessObjects Live Office is capable of retrieving content from SAP Crystal Reports 2011, SAP BusinessObjects Web Intelligence, and universes from the XI 3.1 release. It is important to mention here that SAP BusinessObjects Live Office is able to leverage all the investments you made in your reporting and analysis content; for example, you can use a well laid out chart from a SAP Business Objects Web Intelligence directly in Microsoft PowerPoint without having to reformat anything.

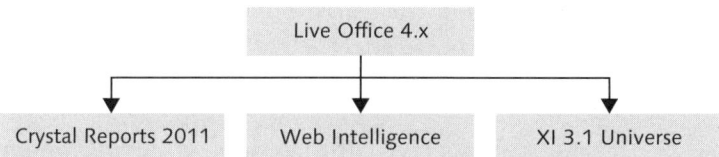

Figure 10.3 SAP BusinessObjects Live Office Content Options

Not only can you use the actual reporting content from these report types, but you can also use the underlying data source. In regard to your SAP landscape this means that you can use data from your SAP NetWeaver BW system and from your SAP ERP system inside the Microsoft Office environment.

> **Support for SAP BusinessObjects 4.x Universes**
>
> At the point of writing this book (November 2011) SAP BusinessObjects Live Office was not able to support universes created with the new Information Design Tool; instead, SAP BusinessObjects Live Office was only able to leverage universes from the XI 3.1 release. Future versions will address this limitation.

In general, SAP BusinessObjects Live Office has two main use cases:

- You would like to provide the information from your reporting and analysis environment to your end users and you would like to use the Microsoft Office environment as the client tool for viewing and refreshing the content.

- You would like to use SAP BusinessObjects Live Office as the "data engine" for pushing data into your SAP BusinessObjects Dashboards objects. SAP BusinessObjects Dashboards is capable of retrieving data from an SAP BusinessObjects Live Office document inside of Microsoft Excel and to use the SAP BusinessObjects Live Office functionality directly inside the SAP BusinessObjects Dashboards Designer. The benefit of using SAP BusinessObjects Live Office to provide data to SAP BusinessObjects Dashboards is the capability to leverage not only live data but also pre-scheduled data from an instance or a publication that you created on the SAP BusinessObjects BI platform. (A publication is the BusinessObjects counterpart to Information Broadcasting on the SAP NetWeaver BW side.)

10.3 Introduction to the Tool

In this section we look at some simple steps for how to use the information from our SAP BusinessObjects BI platform inside the Microsoft Office environment.

10.3.1 SAP BusinessObjects Live Office Environment

Before we start using SAP BusinessObjects Live Office with the different content types, let's configure our environment and look at some of the common menus in SAP BusinessObjects Live Office.

1. Start Microsoft Excel.
2. Navigate to the LIVE OFFICE ribbon.
3. Navigate to the menu LIVE OFFICE • APPLICATION OPTIONS (see Figure 10.4).

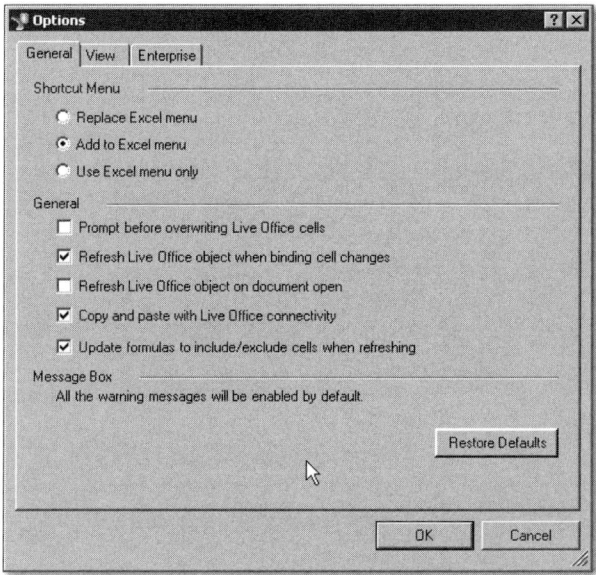

Figure 10.4 SAP BusinessObjects Live Office Options in Microsoft Excel

4. On the GENERAL tab in the SHORTCUT MENU area, you can configure how the SAP BusinessObjects Live Office menu is presented to you upon right-clicking. The SAP BusinessObjects Live Office menu will be shown only on SAP BusinessObjects Live Office relevant content.

5. In the GENERAL area on the GENERAL tab, you can configure several options:

    ▸ You can activate the option PROMPT BEFORE OVERWRITING LIVE OFFICE CELLS to prevent a situation in which you overwrite the content of a cell that is connected via Live Office to live data.

    ▸ You can use the option REFRESH LIVE OFFICE OBJECT WHEN BINDING CELL CHANGES to force a complete refresh of your SAP BusinessObjects Live Office-related data in cases where the binding of a cell to SAP BusinessObjects Live Office data is changing.

    ▸ You can use the option REFRESH LIVE OFFICE OBJECT ON DOCUMENT OPEN to enforce a refresh each time you open up a document with SAP BusinessObjects Live Office content.

    ▸ You can use the option COPY AND PASTE WITH LIVE OFFICE CONNECTIVITY to keep the connectivity intact for cases in which you use the standard copy and paste functionality in Microsoft Office.

You will see that some of these options differ, depending on which Microsoft Office product you are using.

6. Navigate to the VIEW tab (see Figure 10.5):

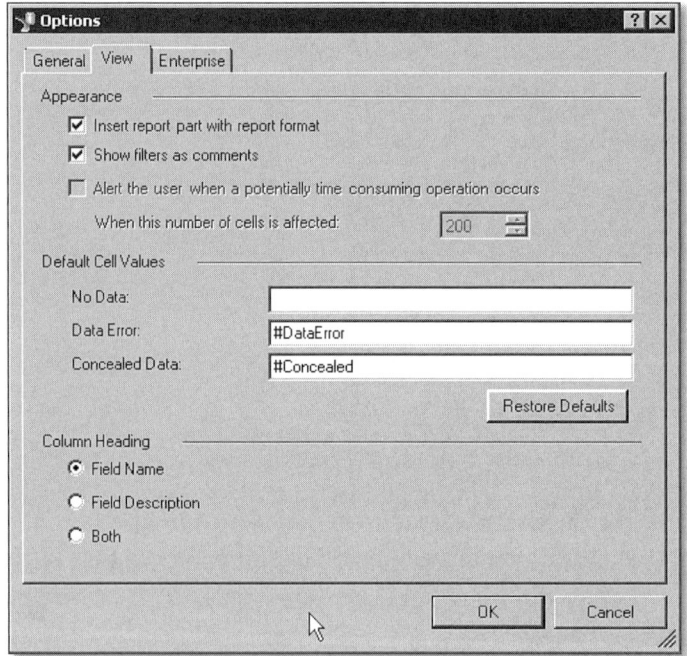

Figure 10.5 View

- In the APPEARANCE area, please take note of the option INSERT REPORT PART WITH REPORT FORMAT. This option allows you to insert (for example) a fully formatted SAP BusinessObjects Web Intelligence table into a Microsoft Office document and keep all the formatting intact.
- The option DEFAULT CELL VALUES allows you to specify values for certain default cases, like a field that contains no data.
- The option COLUMN HEADING allows you to specify how the fields in the menus and dialogs are shown to you as well as which option is used for the column header.

7. Activate the option FIELD DESCRIPTION in the COLUMN HEADING area.

In the following sections we look at how you can use the content from your SAP BusinessObjects BI platform in the different Microsoft Office products.

10.3.2 Using SAP BusinessObjects Live Office and Microsoft Excel

In this section we use Microsoft Excel and look at how you can use SAP Crystal Reports 2011, SAP BusinessObjects Web Intelligence, and XI 3.1 universes inside Microsoft Excel.

1. Start Microsoft Excel.
2. Navigate to the Live Office ribbon (see Figure 10.6).

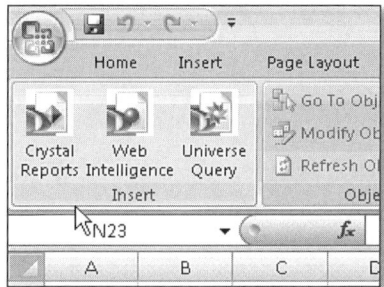

Figure 10.6 Live Office Ribbon

3. Select the CRYSTAL REPORTS menu item from the ribbon.
4. You are asked to provide your credentials. You configured Live Office to use SAP authentication; however, the SAP BusinessObjects Live Office screen does not provide the typical SAP logon dialog. Therefore, you need to use the following syntax:

   `<SAP System ID>~<SAP Client Number>/<SAP User name>`

   For example:

   `ABC~800/DEMO`

5. Enter your SAP credentials and your password. If you haven't configured your SAP BusinessObjects BI platform with SAP authentication, you can continue with an Enterprise account, but you will not be able to use SSO.
6. Click on OK.
7. You are presented with the repository (see Figure 10.7) from your SAP BusinessObjects BI platform, and you can navigate to the folder where you have stored the objects so far.
8. In our case, we will use SAP Crystal Report 2011 from the set of sample reports.

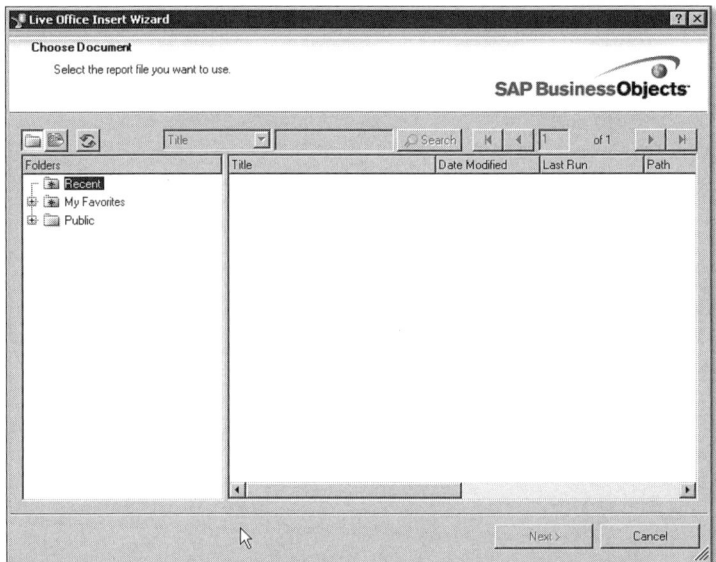

Figure 10.7 Live Office Insert Wizard (Part 1)

9. Select the report and click on NEXT.

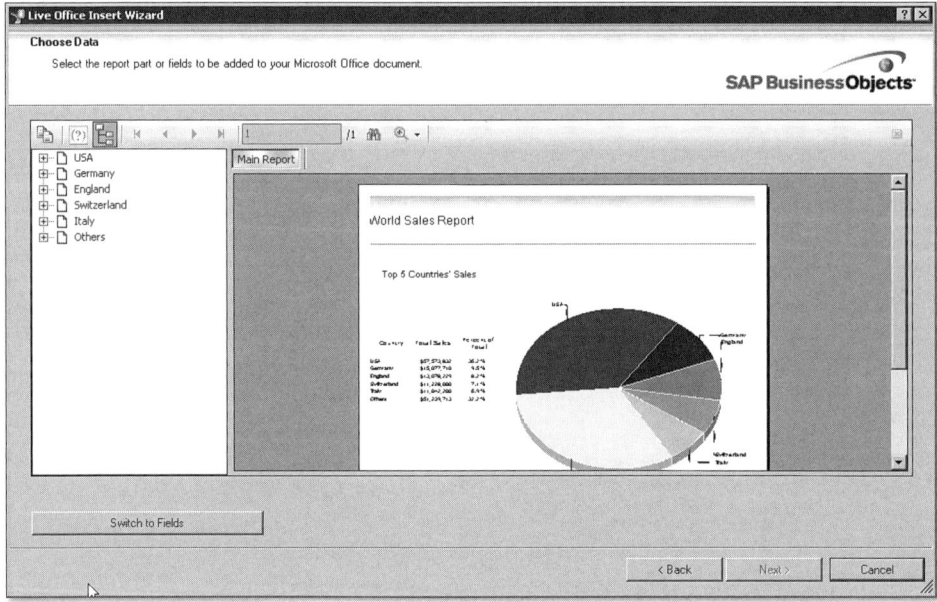

Figure 10.8 Live Office Insert Wizard (Part 2)

10. The SAP Crystal Reports 2011 content (see Figure 10.8) is shown to you in the SAP Crystal Reports 2011 viewer. You are now able to select content from the report. If you select content now, you are able to select parts of your report and use the formatting you have done in the report.

11. Use the SWITCH TO FIELDS option to see the complete list of fields available (see Figure 10.9).

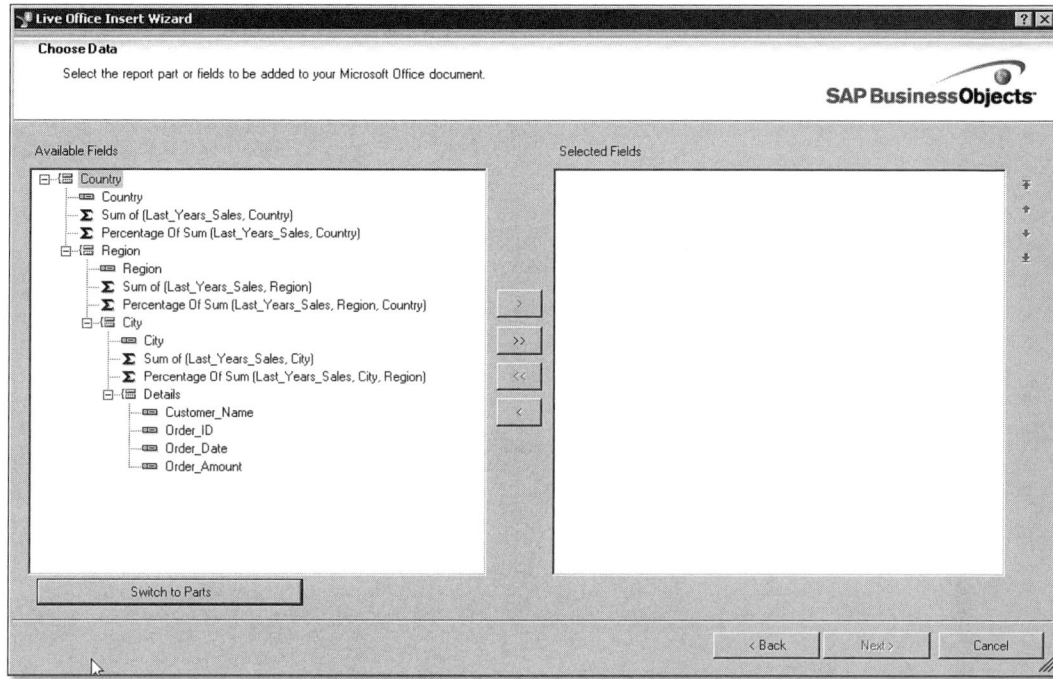

Figure 10.9 Live Office Insert Wizard (Part 3)

12. Select all fields from the DETAILS area and move them to the SELECTED FIELDS list by clicking on the > button.
13. Click on NEXT.
14. In the next screen you can add a filter to your SAP BusinessObjects Live Office document, but, for now, skip this step (see Figure 10.10).
15. Click on NEXT.
16. In the next screen you can enter the name for your LIVE OFFICE OBJECT (see Figure 10.11).

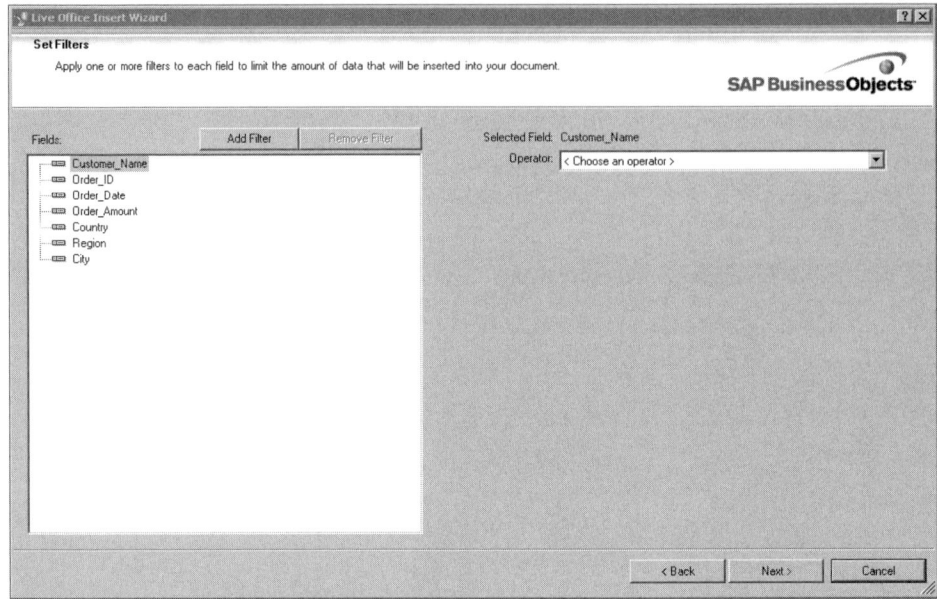

Figure 10.10 Live Office Insert Wizard (Part 4)

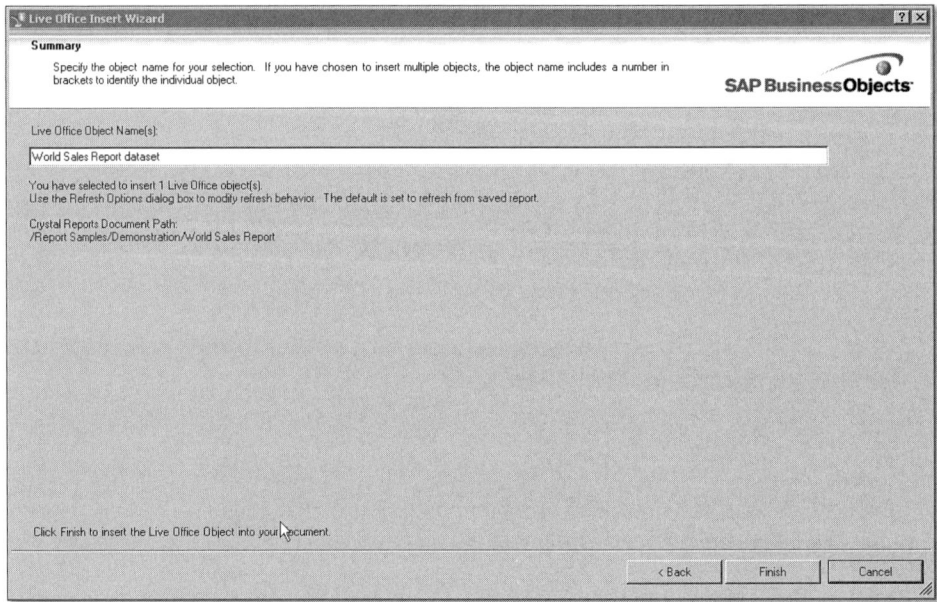

Figure 10.11 Live Office Insert Wizard (Part 5)

17. Click on FINISH.
18. Click on NEXT.
19. The content from the SAP Crystal Reports 2011 object is inserted into your Microsoft Excel sheet (see Figure 10.12).

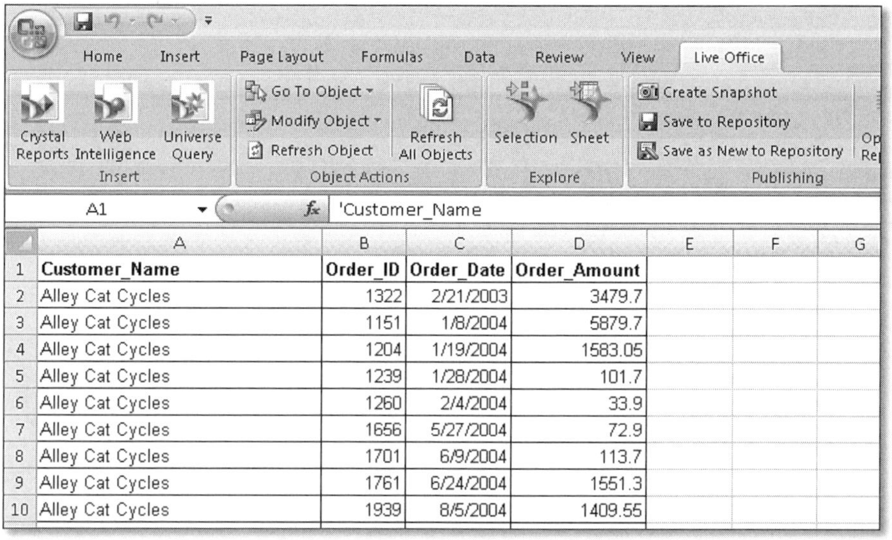

Figure 10.12 SAP BusinessObjects Live Office Document

In our first example, we used Microsoft Excel. As soon as you insert the content, you can use the data inside the spreadsheet and still use all the functionality and capabilities from Microsoft Excel in combination with the data. The important factor is that you can refresh the data from the SAP BusinessObjects Live Office document at any time. In the next steps we explore the options from the SAP BusinessObjects Live Office menu:

1. Navigate to the menu LIVE OFFICE • MODIFY OBJECTS (SEE Figure 10.13).
2. The ADD/REMOVE FIELDS option will bring you back to the wizard and allows you to add or remove fields from your spreadsheet.
3. The FILTER SETTINGS option allows you to create additional filters for your data.
4. Navigate to the PROPERTIES option (see Figure 10.14).
5. With the CHOOSE option, you can change to a different report or a different folder location if the actual source document has been renamed or has been moved.

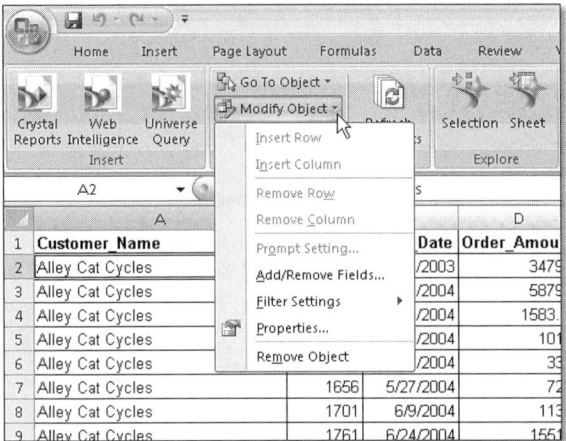

Figure 10.13 SAP BusinessObjects Live Office Menu

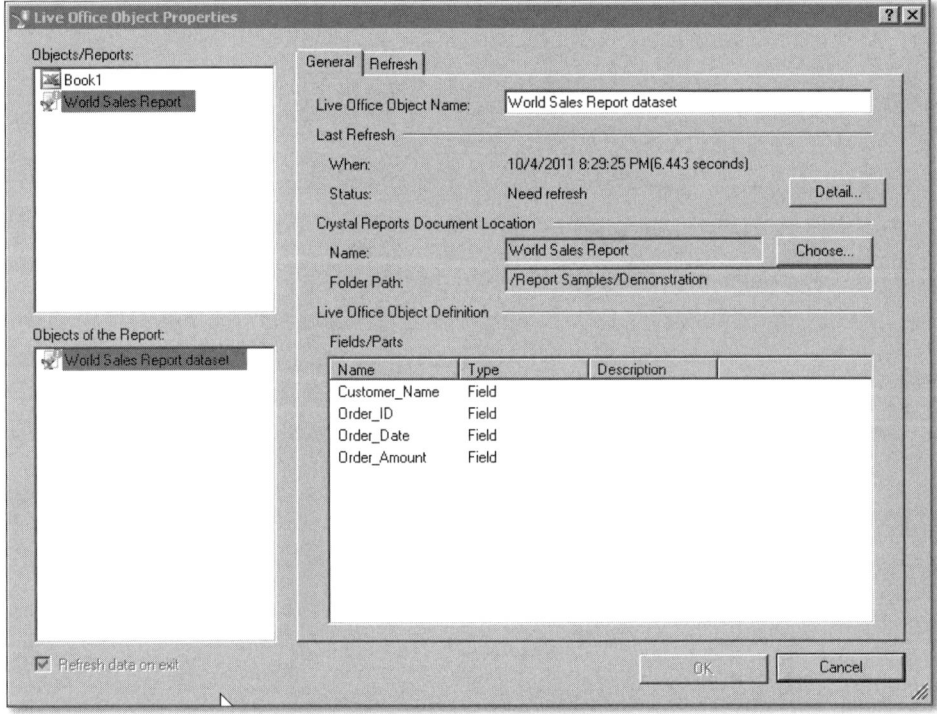

Figure 10.14 SAP BusinessObjects Live Office Document Properties

6. Navigate to the REFRESH tab (see Figure 10.15).

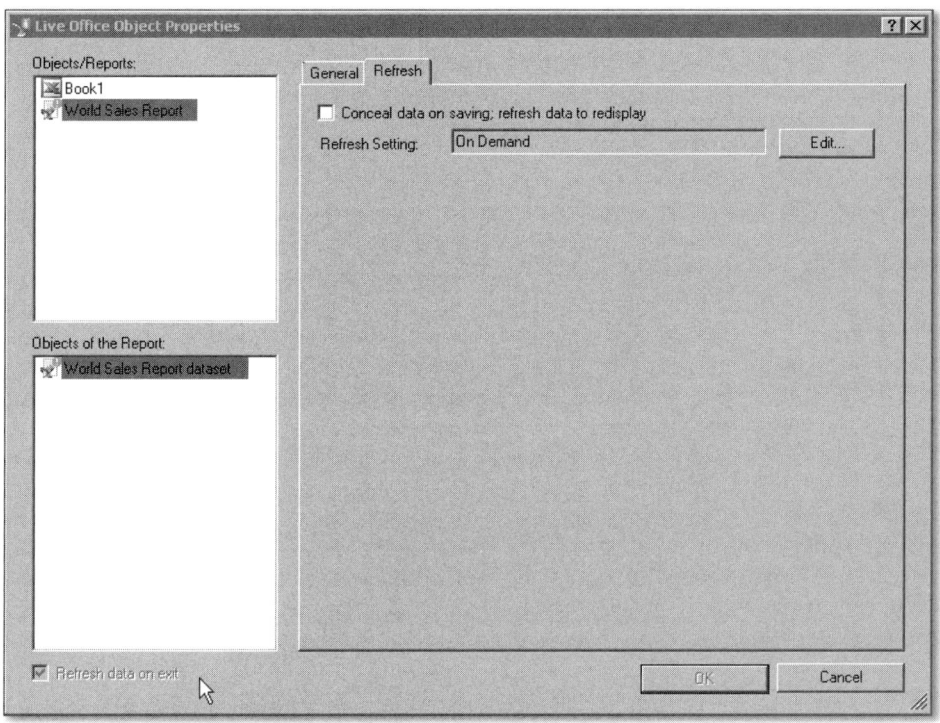

Figure 10.15 Refresh Options (Part 1)

7. Click on EDIT (see Figure 10.16).

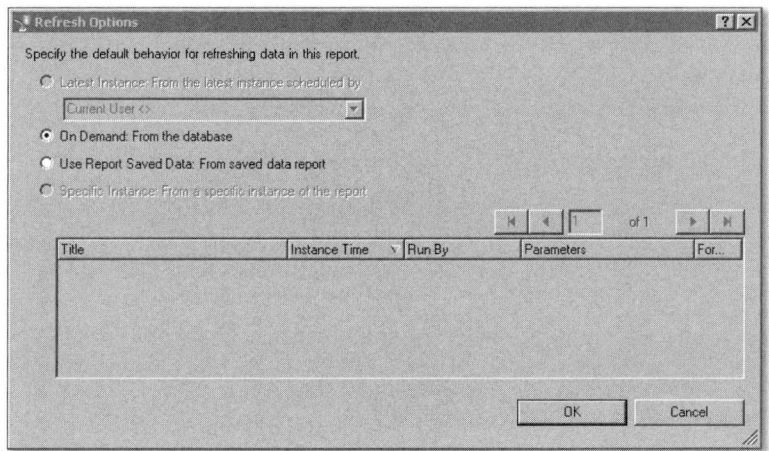

Figure 10.16 Refresh Options (Part 2)

8. Here you have the option to decide whether your report should show live data or data from a pre-scheduled report.
9. Close the dialogs and navigate back to the LIVE OFFICE menu.
10. Select the SAVE AS NEW TO REPOSITORY menu item (see Figure 10.17).

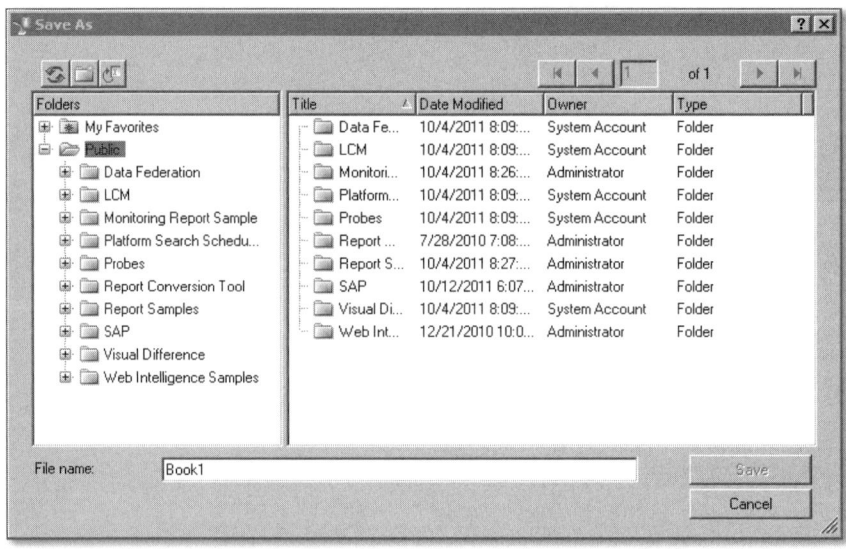

Figure 10.17 Save to BI Platform

With the option to store your SAP BusinessObjects Live Office document to your SAP BusinessObjects BI platform, you also have the option to secure your SAP BusinessObjects Live Office document. For example, you can store a weekly sales slide deck created with Microsoft PowerPoint and containing data from SAP BusinessObjects Live Office in your SAP BusinessObjects BI platform.

1. Create a new empty sheet in your Microsoft Excel file.
2. Select the menu LIVE OFFICE • WEB INTELLIGENCE from the ribbon.
3. You are presented with the repository from your SAP BusinessObjects BI platform.
4. Navigate to the folder where you stored the SAP BusinessObjects Web Intelligence reports that you created so far.
5. Select an SAP BusinessObjects Web Intelligence report and click on NEXT (see Figure 10.18).

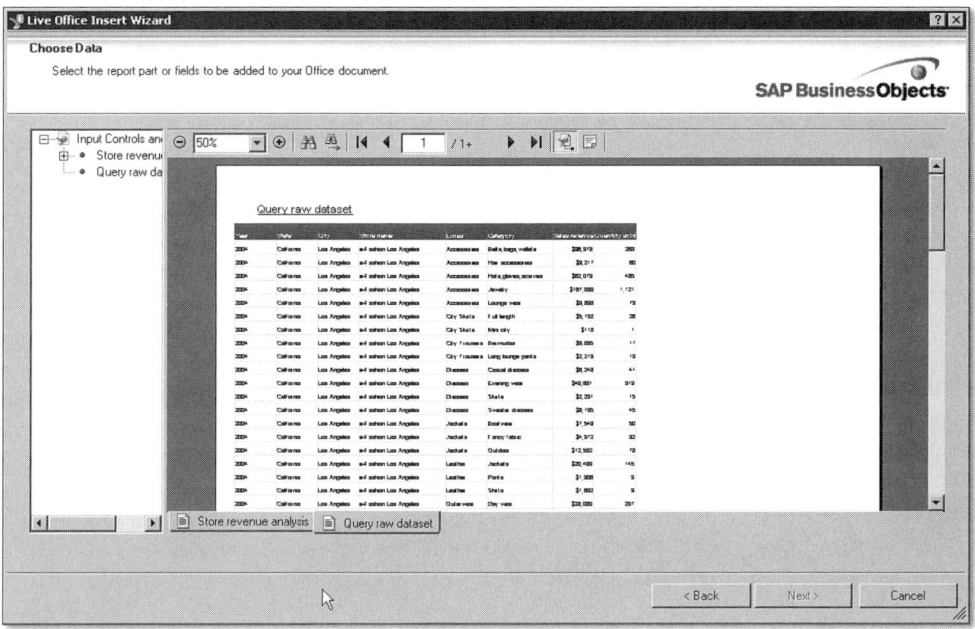

Figure 10.18 Live Office Insert Wizard

6. You will see that SAP BusinessObjects Live Office in this case does not offer any option to switch to the list of fields, which makes sense because SAP BusinessObjects Live Office offers the option to insert content based on a universe as a separate menu item.

7. Select the table object from the report.

8. Click on NEXT.

9. Click on FINISH.

10. In our case, the report had several parameters based on variables; therefore, we will refresh the report and change these values.

11. Select the menu LIVE OFFICE • REFRESH OBJECT. The prompt screen appears and you can select the values (see Figure 10.19).

12. Select the necessary values and click on OK.

13. After the refresh, select the menu LIVE OFFICE • OBJECT PROPERTIES.

14. Select the SAP BusinessObjects Web Intelligence report in the list of available reports.

15. Navigate to the PROMPTS tab (see Figure 10.20).

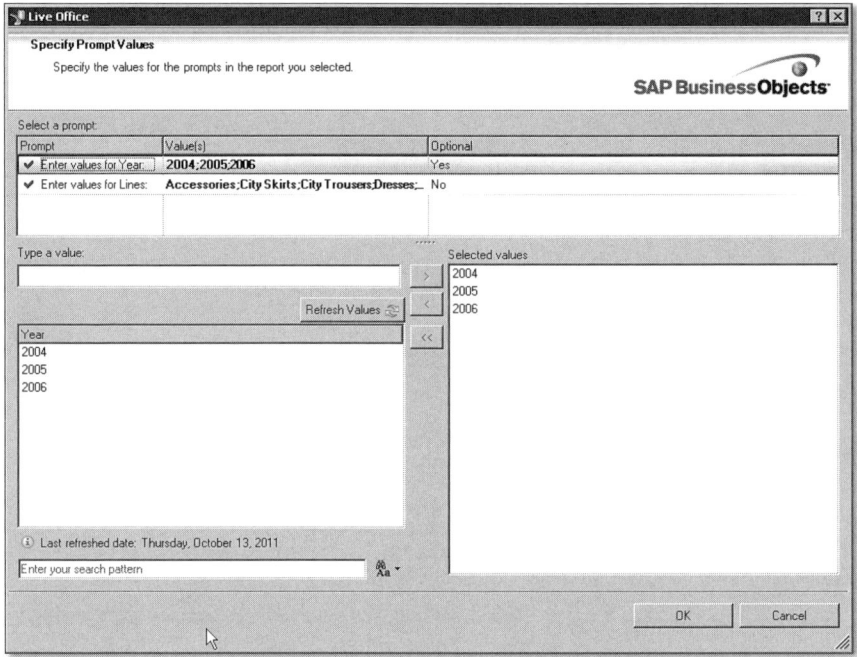

Figure 10.19 SAP BusinessObjects Live Office Prompting Screen

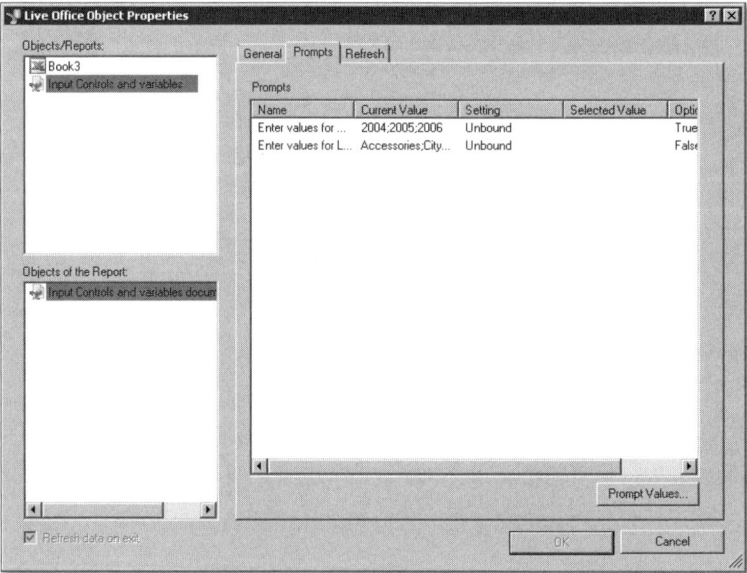

Figure 10.20 SAP BusinessObjects Live Office Object Properties

16. Click on PROMPT VALUES (see Figure 10.21).

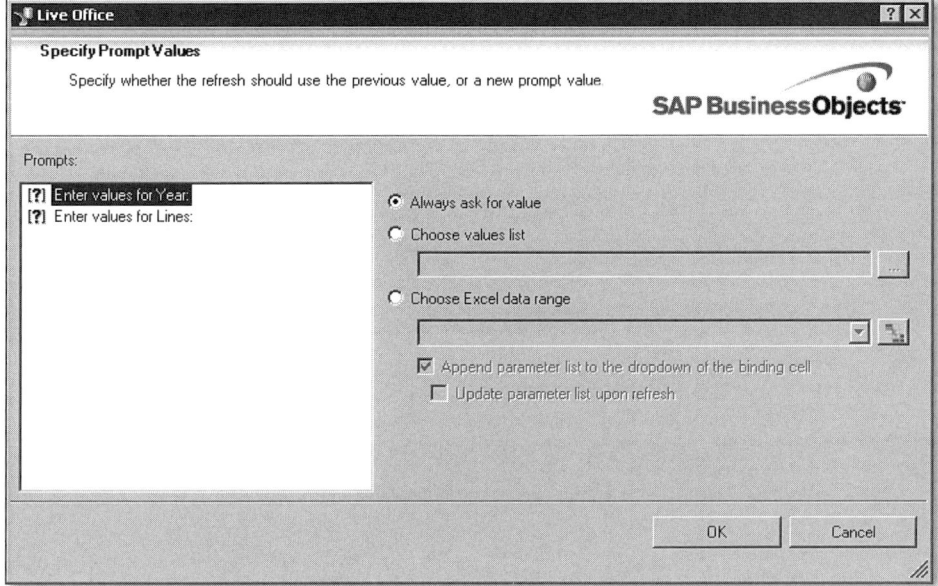

Figure 10.21 Live Office Prompt Values (Part 1)

17. You now have three options:
    - You can always be prompted for a value by using the ALWAYS ASK FOR VALUE option.
    - You can use the CHOOSE VALUES LIST option and select the values.
    - You can bind the parameter to an Excel range by using the CHOOSE EXCEL DATA RANGE option.
18. The most flexible option is the CHOOSE EXCEL DATA RANGE. Activate this option and click on the [icon] button to specify a range on your spreadsheet (see Figure 10.22).
19. Select the range in the spreadsheet and click on OK.
20. Activate APPEND PARAMETER LIST TO THE DROPDOWN OF THE BINDING CELL.
21. Repeat the steps for all parameters and bind each of them to a cell range in the spreadsheet.

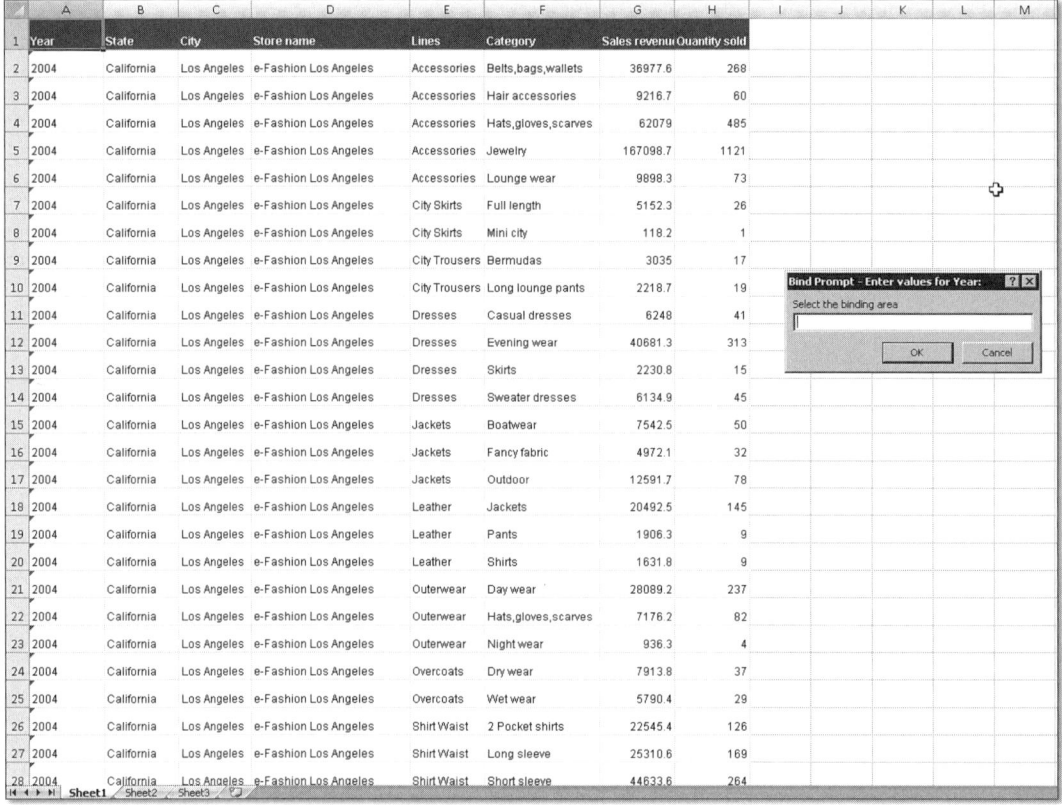

Figure 10.22 Live Office Prompt Values (Part 2)

22. Click on OK to close all the dialogs. You now have the option to use the cells that you defined as bounded cells for each of the parameters to enter the values and refresh your SAP BusinessObjects Live Office document.

23. Navigate to the menu LIVE OFFICE • OBJECT PROPERTIES.

24. Select the SAP BusinessObjects Web Intelligence report.

25. Navigate to the REFRESH tab.

26. Note the option CONCEAL DATA ON SAVING; REFRESH DATA TO DISPLAY. This option allows you to remove data from the SAP BusinessObjects Live Office document when the document is being saved locally or to your SAP BusinessObjects BI platform. In that way you can secure the data to a certain degree by removing the option to access the data offline.

In the next steps we look at how you can leverage a universe in Microsoft Excel.

1. Close the dialogs and create a new empty sheet in your Microsoft Excel file.
2. Select the menu LIVE OFFICE • UNIVERSE QUERY.
3. You receive a list of universes from your system. In our example, we use the eFashion Sample Universe.
4. Select the first universe you created and click on NEXT.
5. You are presented with a query panel similar to the SAP BusinessObjects Web Intelligence query panel. You can define which objects you would like to use (see Figure 10.23). In our example, we use:
   - YEAR
   - STATE
   - LINES
   - SALES REVENUE

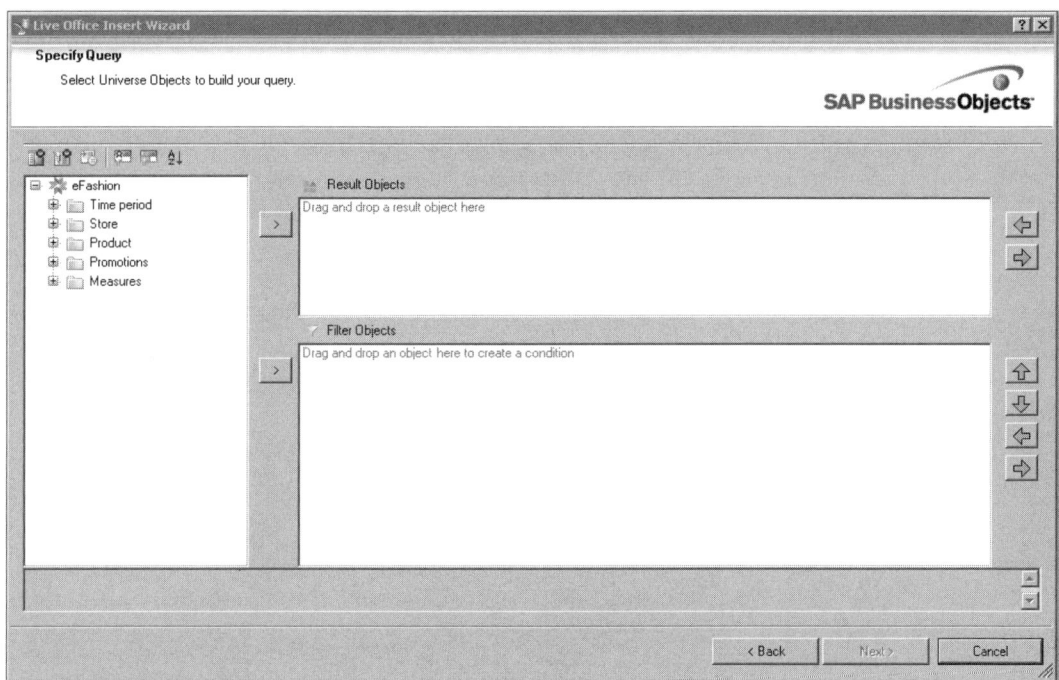

Figure 10.23 Query Panel

6. Click on NEXT.

7. In the next screen, click on FINISH to present the data in the spreadsheet. You can now use the live data as part of Microsoft Office. In addition, you can use the menu LIVE OFFICE • MODIFY OBJECT to change the dimension and key figures used or to configure filter values.

When you use data from a universe directly via this approach, you can use all the functionalities from Live Office in the same way as you are able to use them with SAP Crystal Reports and SAP BusinessObjects Web Intelligence-based content. There is only one capability of SAP BusinessObjects Live Office that you cannot leverage when using universe-based content: the functionality to retrieve data from instances or from a publication. A universe cannot be pre-scheduled and therefore the data retrieved by a universe-based query are always on-demand.

10.3.3 Using SAP BusinessObjects Live Office and Microsoft PowerPoint

When using SAP BusinessObjects Live Office inside of Microsoft PowerPoint, all of the above mentioned items shown in combination with Microsoft Excel are possible as well, with one exception: You can't bind parameters from underlying sources (such as SAP Crystal Reports, SAP BusinessObjects Web Intelligence, or a universe) to an area in your Microsoft PowerPoint slide deck to change the parameters. If you want to change the parameters, you either have to configure the document to prompt you for the values or use the menu LIVE OFFICE • OBJECT PROPERTIES to specify the values that will be used.

10.3.4 Using SAP BusinessObjects Live Office and Microsoft Outlook

In addition to being able to leverage content from your SAP BusinessObjects BI platform in Microsoft Excel and Microsoft PowerPoint, you can also integrate SAP BusinessObjects Live Office with Microsoft Outlook. After you configured the details of your SAP BusinessObjects BI platform in the menu LIVE OFFICE • OPTIONS as we did before for Microsoft Excel, you can use SAP BusinessObjects Live Office with Microsoft Outlook.

In Microsoft Outlook you can then see the Live Office panel (see Figure 10.24).

Figure 10.24 Live Office Panel

In the following steps we use the panel to share content from our SAP Business-Objects BI platform and learn more about ASSOCIATIONS and SUGGESTIONS.

1. Start Microsoft Outlook.
2. Create a new email message.
3. Navigate to the Live Office panel.
4. Enter a search term in the Live Office panel. In our example, we use the term "sales" (see Figure 10.25). SAP BusinessObjects Live Office returns a list of reports that match the search criteria.
5. In this step, you can decide how you want to include the report as part of your email (see Figure 10.26). You can decide to view the report in your browser, you can insert the report as a Live Office object or as a link, and you can associate the report with this email thread. Including the content as a link will result in a link to the actual report as part of your SAP BusinessObjects BI platform that is used as part of your email.

10 Using SAP BusinessObjects Live Office

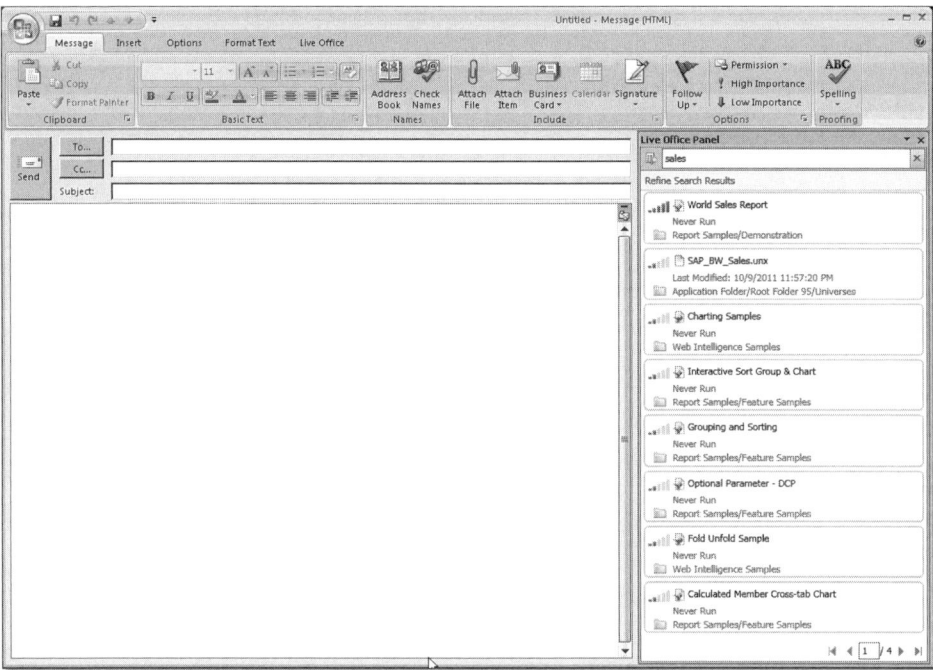

Figure 10.25 New Message with Live Office Panel

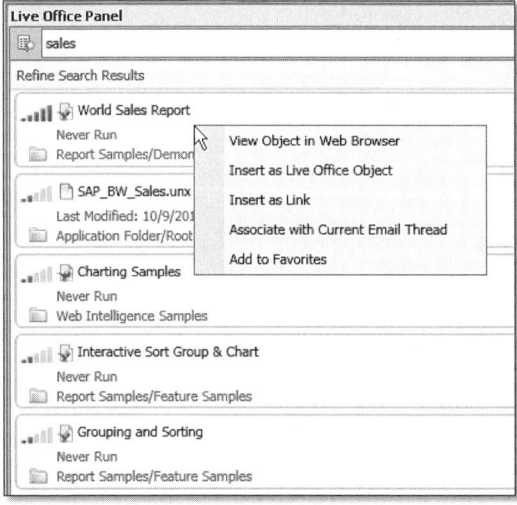

Figure 10.26 Search Result

6. Select the option INSERT AS LIVE OFFICE OBJECT (see Figure 10.27).

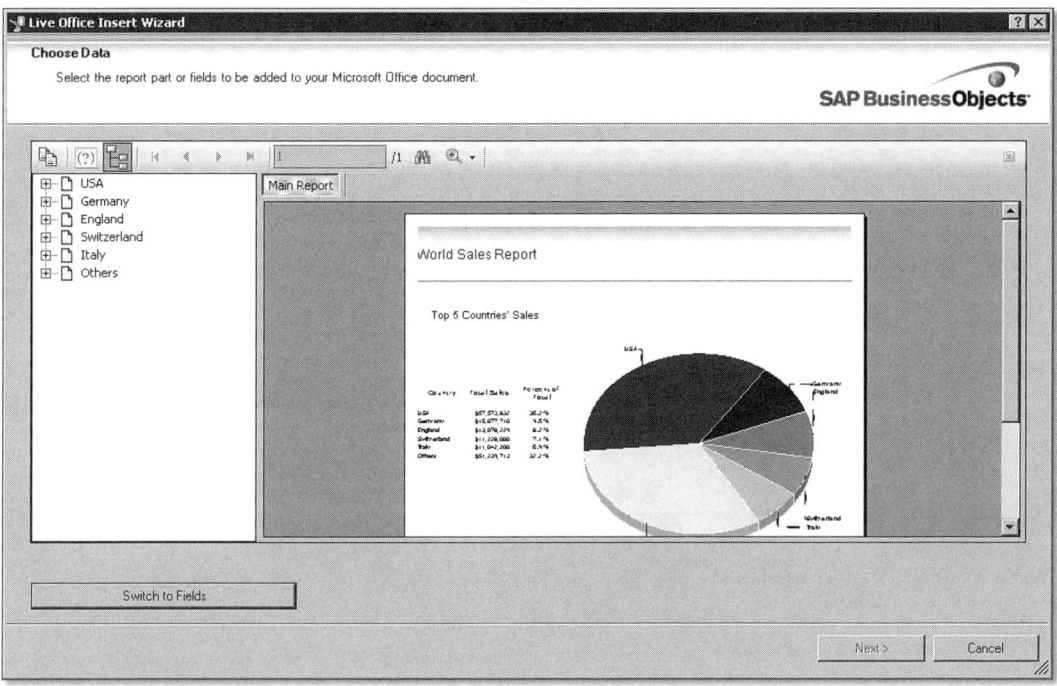

Figure 10.27 Live Office Wizard

7. You are presented with the report in the same way as if you tried to insert the report into Microsoft Excel. You can decide to select parts of a report—for example, a chart—or the data from the report into the email. Select a part of the report.
8. Click on NEXT.
9. Click on FINISH (see Figure 10.28).
10. The data of the report or the element of the report is inserted as a refreshable object.
11. Select the report in the Live Office panel.
12. Right-click to open the context menu (see Figure 10.29).
13. Select the menu option ASSOCIATE WITH CURRENT EMAIL THREAD. In our example, the subject line for the email is "Sales Report" and the recipient is *Ingo.Hilgefort@sap.com*. The association is based on the subject line.
14. Send the email.

10 | Using SAP BusinessObjects Live Office

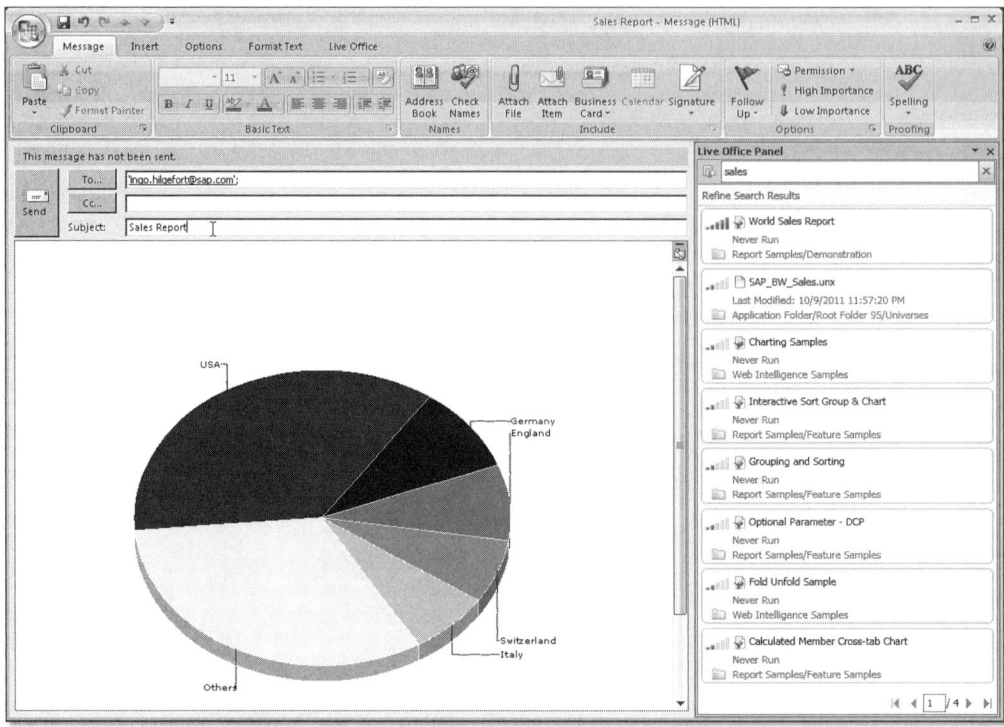

Figure 10.28 Message with SAP BusinessObjects Live Office Objects

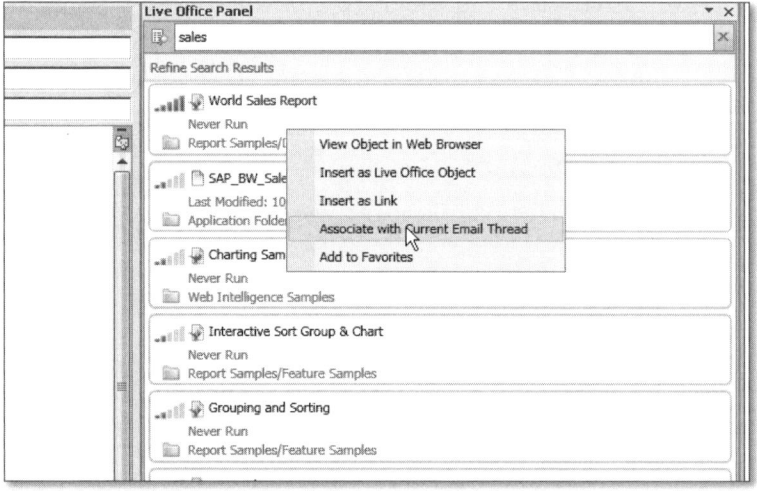

Figure 10.29 Association

You may have noticed the ASSOCIATIONS and SUGGESTIONS in the Live Office panel. ASSOCIATIONS are based on the subject line of email messages and SUGGESTIONS are based on the recipients. For example, the message we created previously included the report we selected with the subject line "Sales Report." If the recipient responds to our message, the report will be listed as one entry in ASSOCIATIONS (see Figure 10.30).

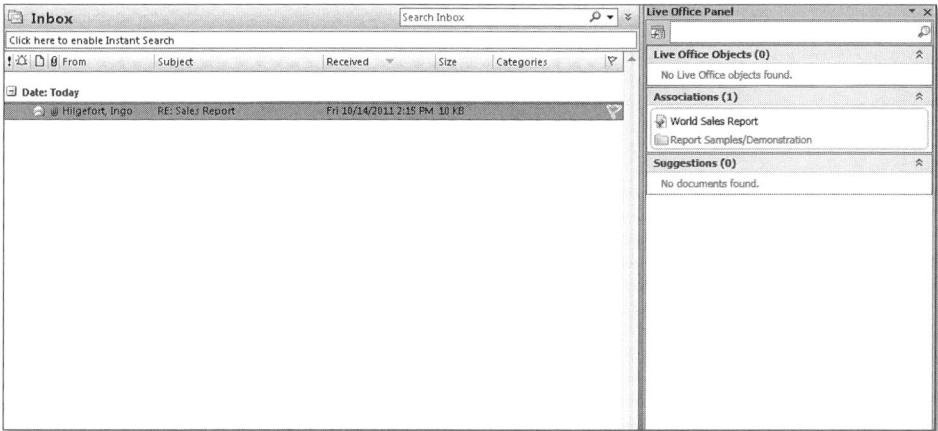

Figure 10.30 Associations Based on Subject

The second option is a new email message to a recipient that was used previously. In such a scenario, the Live Office panel lists all reports that have been used previously in email conversations with the recipient in the SUGGESTIONS area (see Figure 10.31).

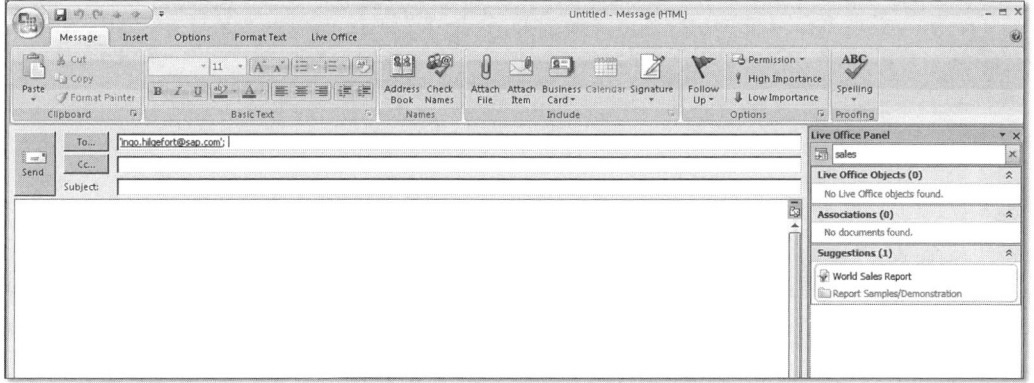

Figure 10.31 New Message

If you closed the Live Office panel but are selecting a email message that is associated with a report from your SAP BusinessObjects BI platform, you still will receive a notification (see Figure 10.31).

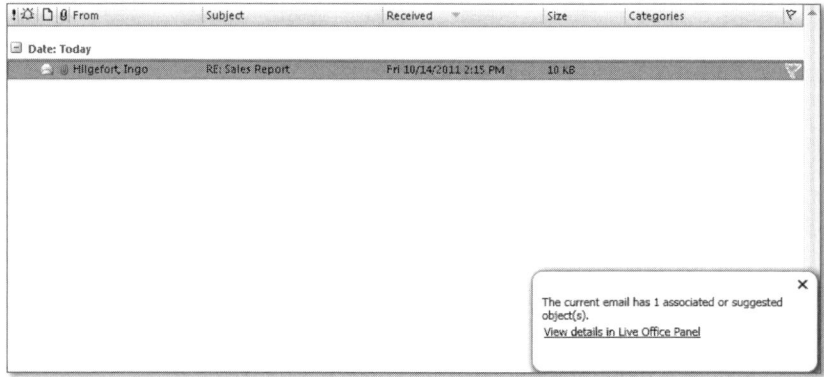

Figure 10.32 Notification

In this section we reviewed how you can use SAP BusinessObjects Live Office in combination with Microsoft Outlook. In the next section we use SAP BusinessObjects Live Office to share data with SAP BusinessObjects Explorer.

10.3.5 Using SAP BusinessObjects Live Office and SAP BusinessObjects Explorer

Part of SAP BusinessObjects Live Office is the capability to send the data that you are using as part of Microsoft Excel to SAP BusinessObjects Explorer for further analysis. In the next steps we use an SAP Crystal Reports object as a source, display the data from this report in Microsoft Excel, and then send the data to SAP BusinessObjects Explorer.

1. Start Microsoft Excel.
2. Navigate to the LIVE OFFICE ribbon.
3. Select the CRYSTAL REPORTS menu item from the ribbon.
4. You are asked to provide your credentials. Remember that you configured SAP BusinessObjects Live Office to leverage SAP authentication, but the SAP BusinessObjects Live Office screen does not provide the typical SAP logon dialog; therefore, you need to use the following syntax:

    <SAP System ID>~<SAP Client Number>/<SAP User name>

For example:

ABC~800/DEMO

5. Enter your SAP credentials and your password. If you haven't configured your SAP BusinessObjects BI platform with SAP authentication, you can continue with an enterprise account, but you will not be able to use SSO.

6. Click on OK (see Figure 10.33).

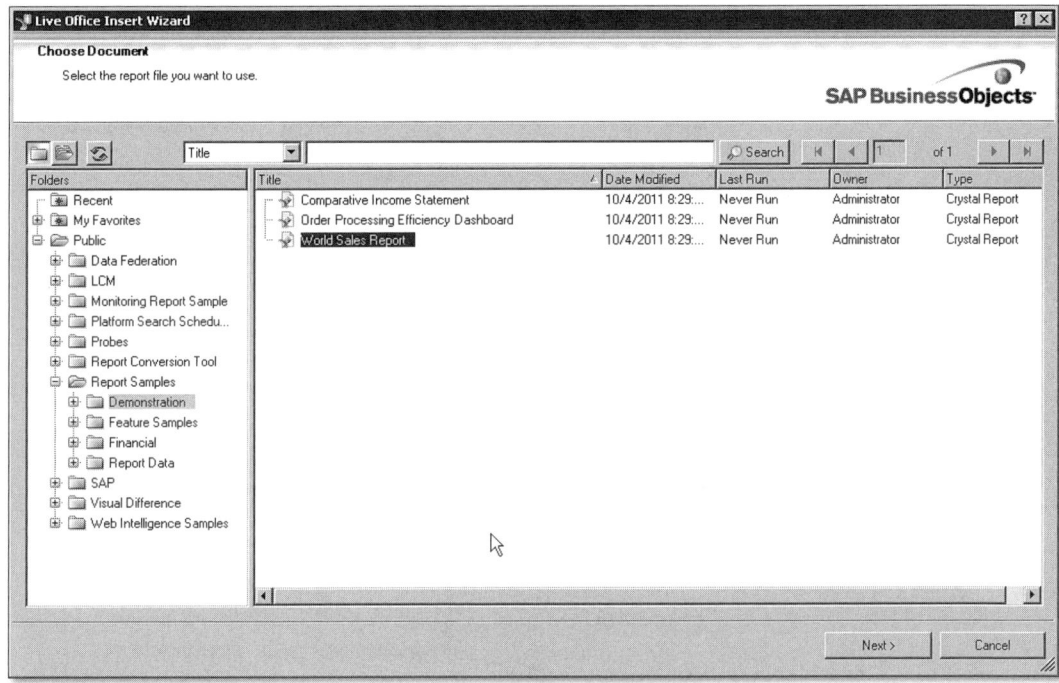

Figure 10.33 Live Office Wizard

7. You are presented with the repository from your SAP BusinessObjects BI platform, and you can navigate to the folder where you have stored the objects so far. In this example, we use the WORLD SALES REPORT from REPORT SAMPLES.

8. Select the report and click on NEXT.

9. The SAP Crystal Reports 2011 content is shown (see Figure 10.34) to you in the SAP Crystal Reports 2011 viewer. You are able to select content from the report. If you select content now, you are able to select parts of your report and leverage the formatting you have done in the report.

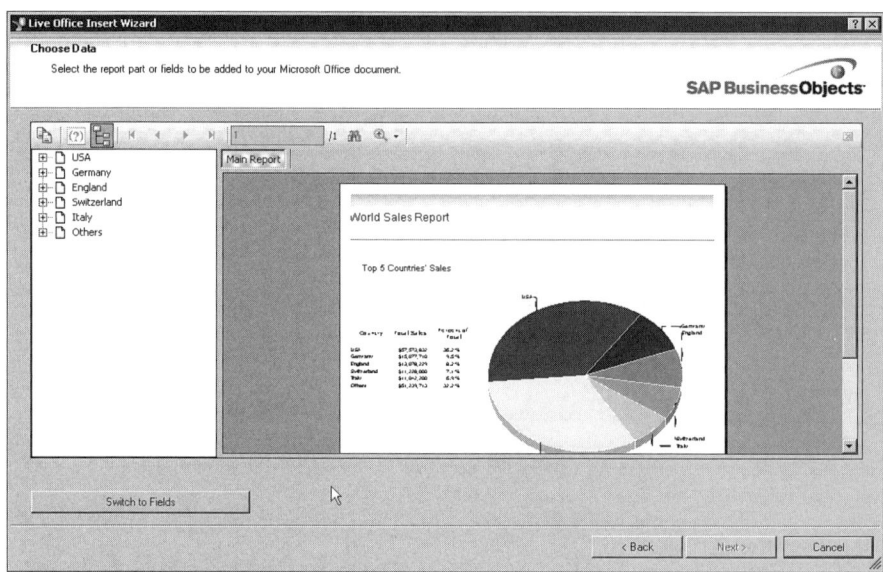

Figure 10.34 Sample Report

10. Use the option SWITCH TO FIELDS to see the complete list of fields available (see Figure 10.35).

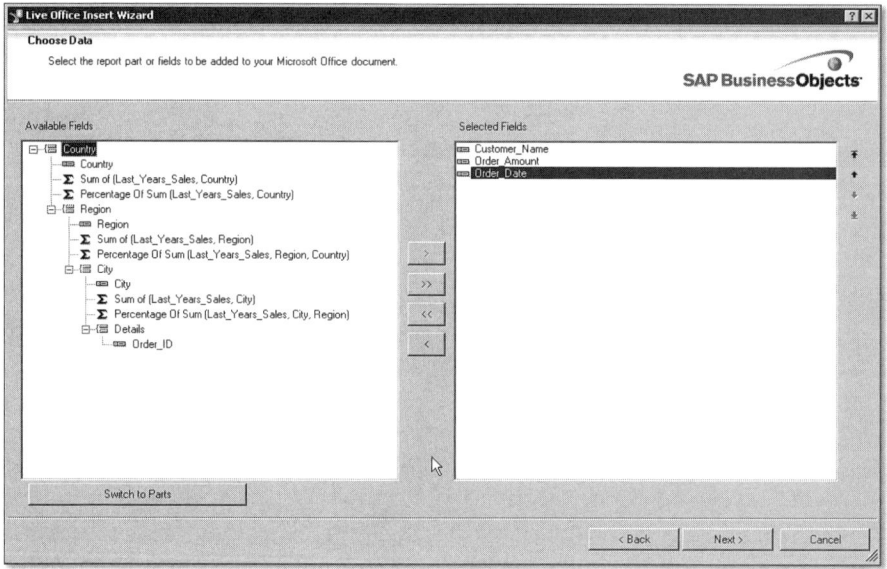

Figure 10.35 Available Fields

11. Select the fields CUSTOMER NAME, ORDER AMOUNT, and ORDER DATE from the DETAILS area and move them to the SELECTED FIELDS list by clicking on the > button.
12. Click on NEXT.
13. In the next screen you can add a filter to your SAP BusinessObjects Live Office document, but, for now, skip this step (see Figure 10.36).

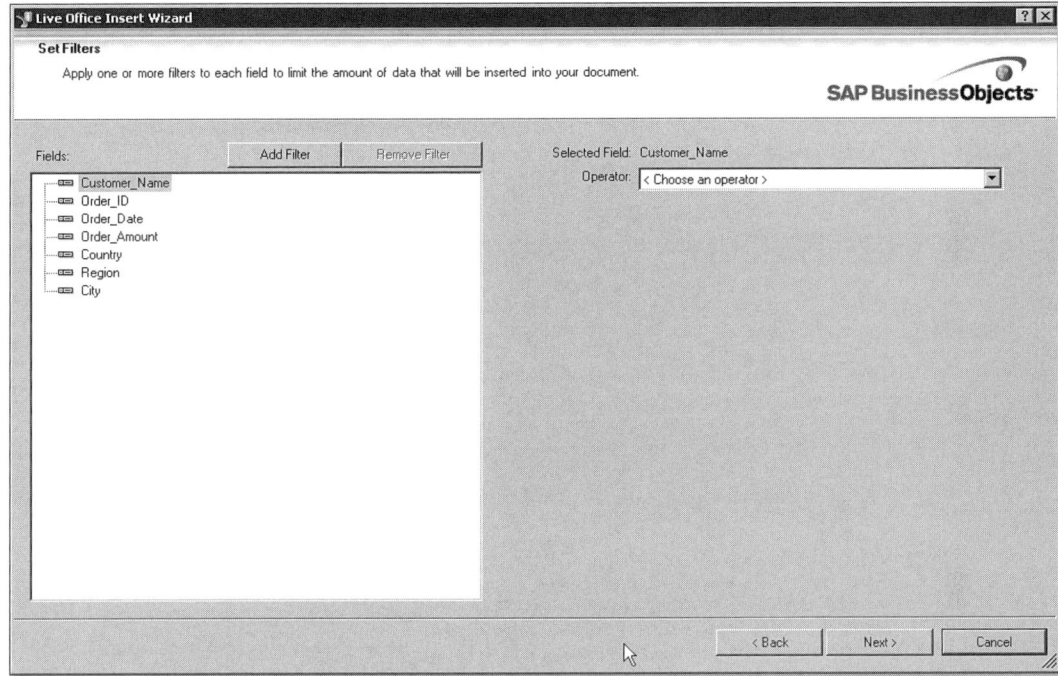

Figure 10.36 Configuring Filter Values

14. Click on NEXT.
15. In the next screen you can enter the name for your LIVE OFFICE OBJECT (see Figure 10.37).
16. Click on FINISH.
17. You now have the data from your SAP Crystal Reports object displayed in Microsoft Excel (see Figure 10.38).

10 | Using SAP BusinessObjects Live Office

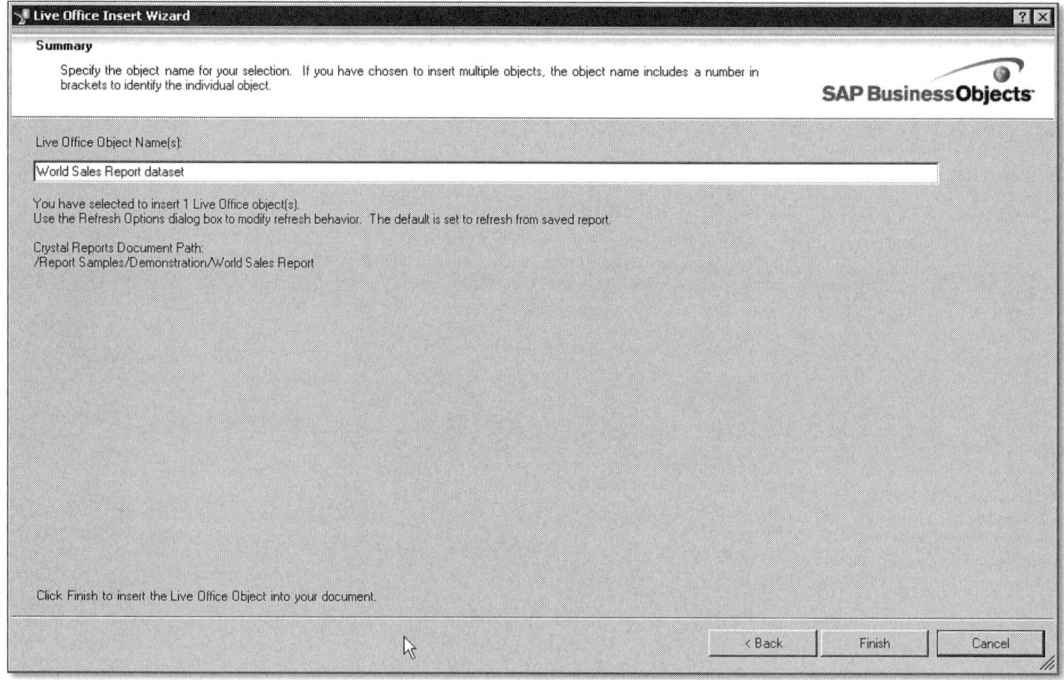

Figure 10.37 Naming SAP BusinessObjects Live Office Object

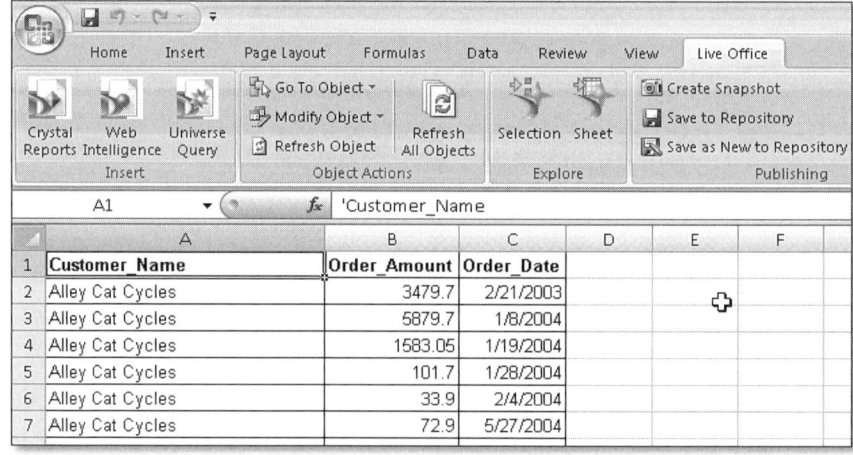

Figure 10.38 SAP Crystal Reports Data

18. Click on SHEET from the LIVE OFFICE • EXPLORE area in the ribbon (see Figure 10.39).

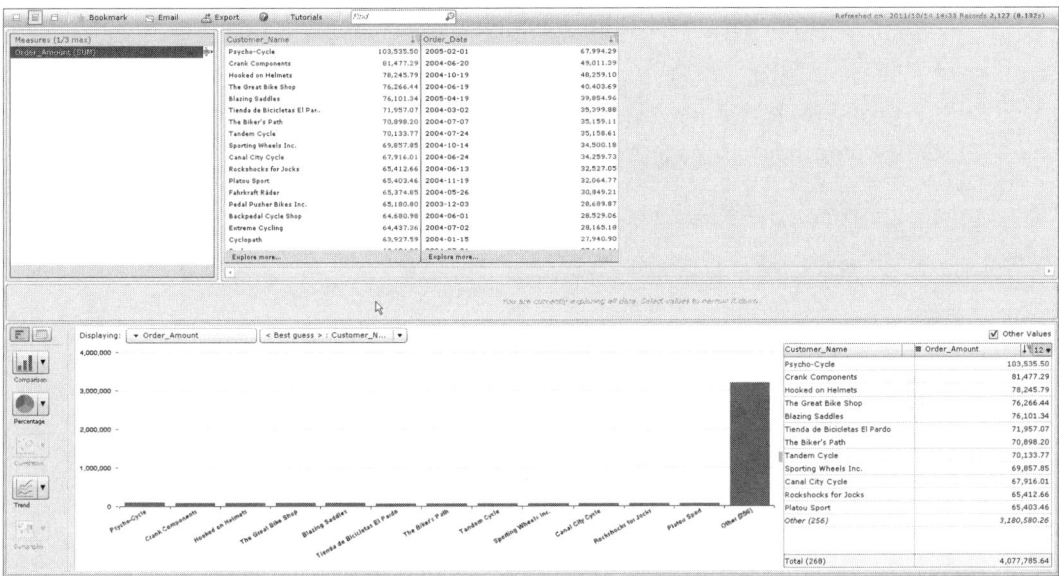

Figure 10.39 SAP BusinessObjects Explorer

The data from the spreadsheet are sent to SAP BusinessObjects Explorer and you are now able to explore the data for further analysis.

You also have the option to select an area in the Microsoft Excel spreadsheet and then to use the menu item LIVE OFFICE • EXPLORE • SELECTION, which then will transfer only the selected range to SAP BusinessObjects Explorer.

> **Saving the Information Space**
>
> You might have noticed that the navigation to SAP BusinessObjects Explorer from SAP BusinessObjects Live Office does not provide the option to save the created information space to your SAP BusinessObjects BI platform. You have two options to create a permanent link to the SAP BusinessObjects Explorer information space. The first option is to leverage the BOOKMARK menu in SAP BusinessObjects Explorer, which will provide you a URL to the information space. This URL is still valid even after closing the SAP BusinessObjects Live Office document. The second option is to save the SAP BusinessObjects Live Office document as a Microsoft Excel spreadsheet to your SAP BusinessObjects BI platform and to create an information space based on the Microsoft Excel spreadsheet using MANAGE SPACES in SAP BusinessObjects Explorer.

In addition to being able to send data from an SAP BusinessObjects Live Office spreadsheet, you can use the same functionality with any spreadsheet in Microsoft Excel. Another interesting option is to use SAP BusinessObjects Live Office to send data from SAP BusinessObjects Analysis, edition for Microsoft Office to SAP BusinessObjects Explorer.

In our example, we have an SAP BusinessObjects Analysis, edition for Microsoft Office workbook (see Figure 10.40).

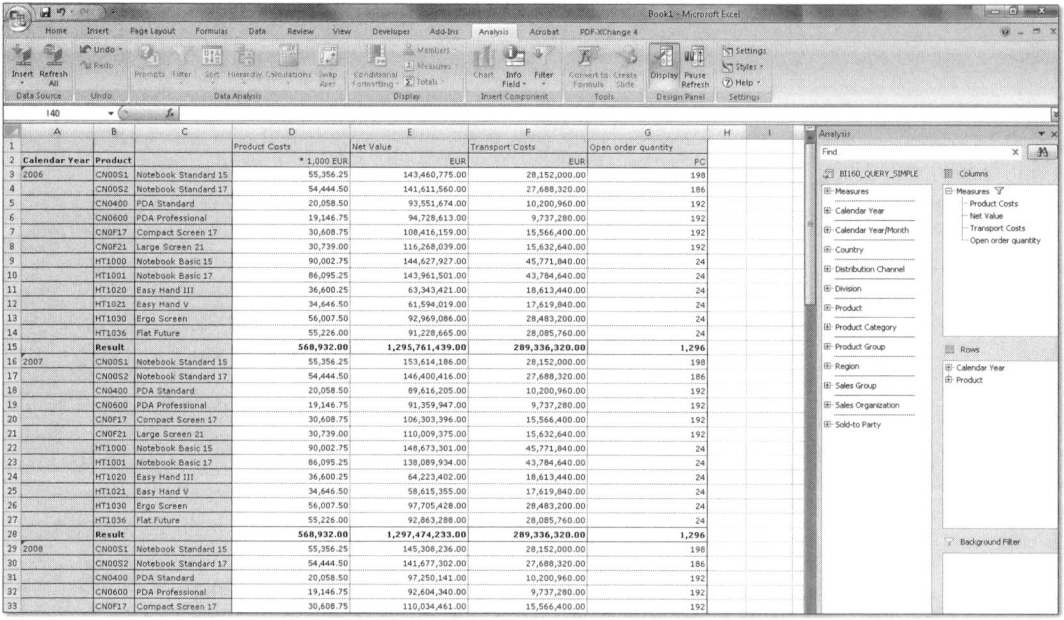

Figure 10.40 SAP BusinessObjects Analysis Workbook

You will notice in Figure 10.40 that the values for the calendar year are not repeated for each row; this would result in problems when we send the data as is to SAP BusinessObjects Explorer, because SAP BusinessObjects Explorer would be unable to index the information. Navigate to the COMPONENTS tab of the NAVIGATION panel in your workbook (see Figure 10.41) and activate the REPEAT MEMBERS option.

You will also see that, by default, SAP BusinessObjects Analysis, edition for Microsoft Office displays scaling factors for the measures, which you have to disable before pushing the data to SAP BusinessObjects Explorer (see Figure 10.42).

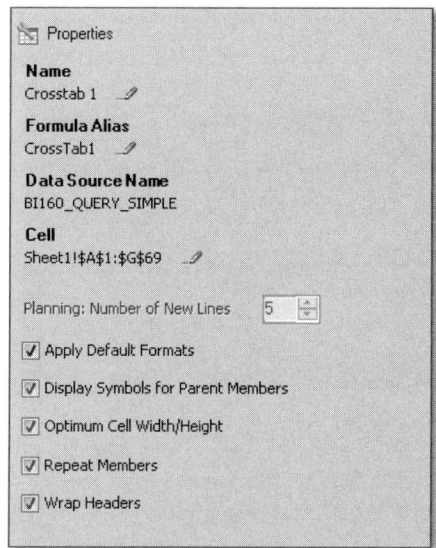

Figure 10.41 Workbook Components

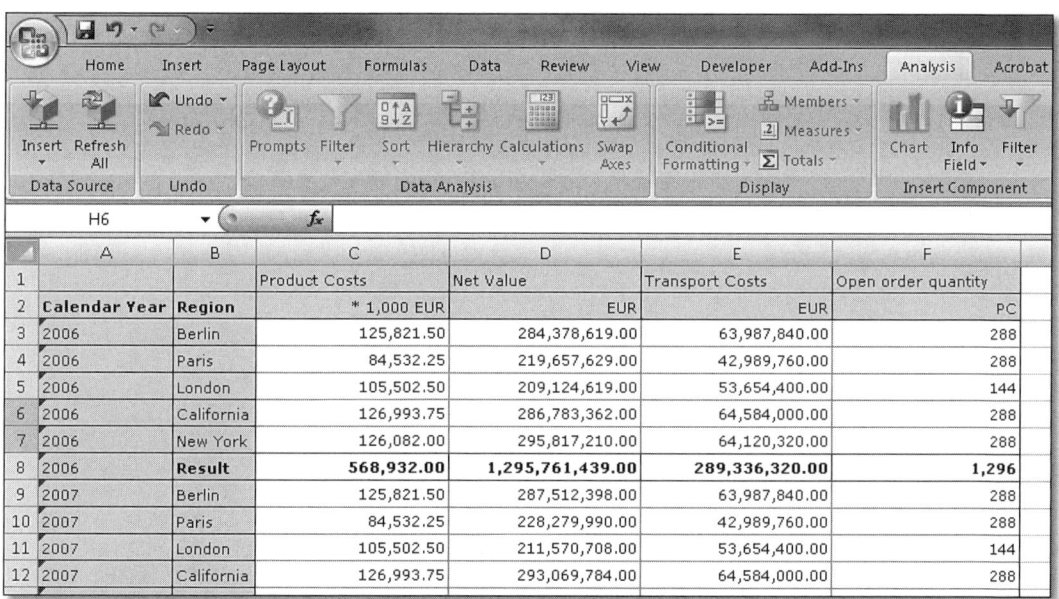

Figure 10.42 Scaling Factor

10 | Using SAP BusinessObjects Live Office

You can disable the scaling factor in the MEASURE FORMAT option in SAP BusinessObjects Analysis, edition for Microsoft Office.

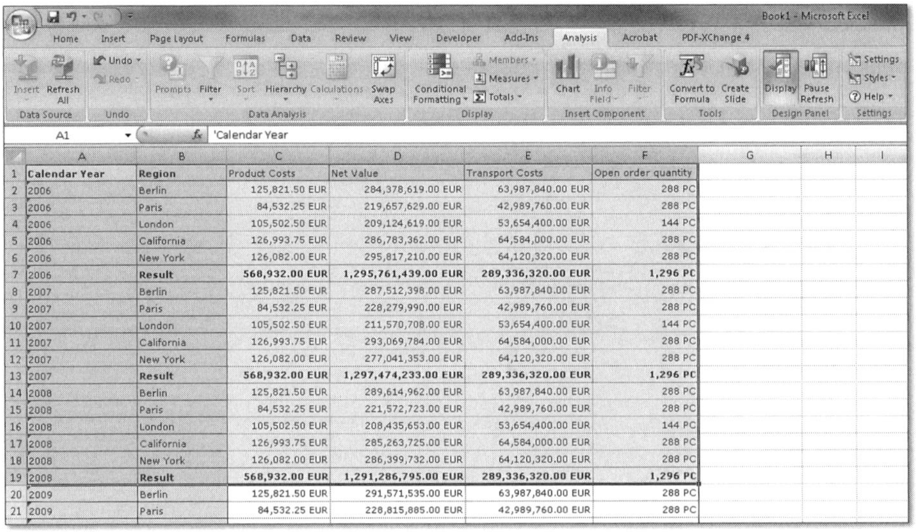

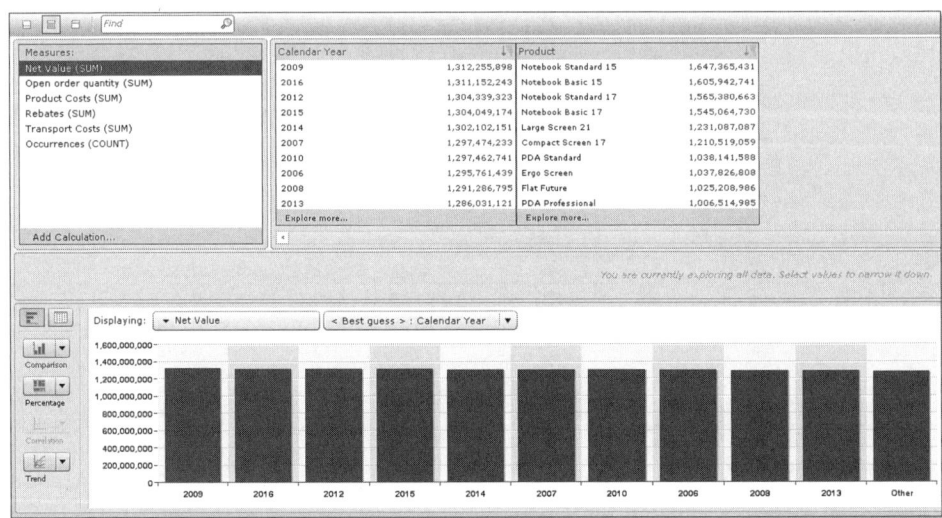

Figure 10.43 Data Selection

After those small changes, you can select the data from your workbook and explore it further using SAP BusinessObjects Explorer (see Figure 10.44).

Figure 10.44 SAP BusinessObjects Explorer

In this section you learned how you can combine SAP BusinessObjects Live Office, SAP BusinessObjects Explorer, and SAP BusinessObjects Analysis, edition for Microsoft Office.

10.4 Summary

In this chapter you learned how you can use SAP BusinessObjects Live Office to view data from your SAP BusinessObjects BI platform inside the Microsoft Office environment. This enables you to use online data that is refreshable and secure while still providing your end users with a familiar Microsoft Office environment.

SAP BusinessObjects BI workspaces allow you to combine content from your SAP BusinessObjects BI platform and define interactivity.

11   Using SAP BusinessObjects BI Workspaces

In this chapter you will learn more about the functionality and capabilities of SAP BusinessObjects BI workspaces as part of your SAP BusinessObjects BI platform. SAP BusinessObjects BI workspaces are the successor to what was known as Dashboard Manager in the XI 3.1 release.

11.1   Overview

In this section we take a quick look at SAP BusinessObjects BI workspaces before we create some content for our first BI workspace and then combine the content. SAP BusinessObjects BI workspaces are fully web-based environments that allow you to display content from your SAP BusinessObjects BI platform to your end users. You have full control over the layout and structure in terms of how all the different content objects are presented to your users. You are able to organize the content into a set of categories and in that way to align your content; for example, along an organizational structure.

SAP BusinessObjects BI workspaces can use the following content types:

- Modules
- SAP BusinessObjects Web Intelligence
- SAP BusinessObjects Dashboards
- SAP BusinessObjects Analysis, edition for OLAP
- SAP Crystal Reports
- PDF documents
- Microsoft Excel

- Microsoft Word
- Microsoft PowerPoint
- Text files
- Hyperlinks

To open a SAP BusinessObjects BI workspace, follow the steps below:

1. Start the BI launch pad by following the menu START • PROGRAMS • SAP BUSINESS-OBJECTS BI PLATFORM 4 • SAP BUSINESSOBJECTS BI PLATFORM • SAP BUSINESSOBJECTS BI PLATFORM JAVA BI LAUNCH PAD.
2. Log on using your SAP credentials.
3. Select the menu APPLICATION • BI WORKSPACE (SEE Figure 11.1).

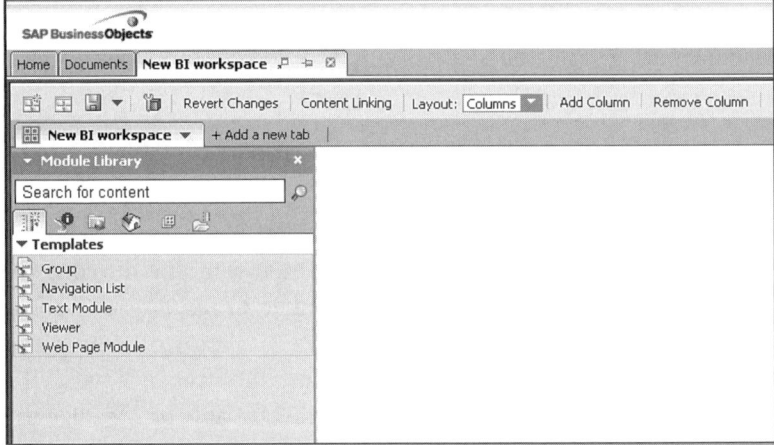

Figure 11.1 New BI Workspace

You are presented with a new BI workspace, and you can start to define the layout and the content. The SAVE menu (see Figure 11.2) allows you to save your changes or to save an existing BI workspace with a new name, which can be helpful, as there is no option to copy an existing BI workspace.

The menu option SHOW MODULE LIBRARY (see Figure 11.3) allows you to enable or disable the display of the MODULE LIBRARY.

The MODULE LIBRARY offers a set of components in a set of categories. The first category (see Figure 11.3) is a set of TEMPLATES, which you can include in your workspace.

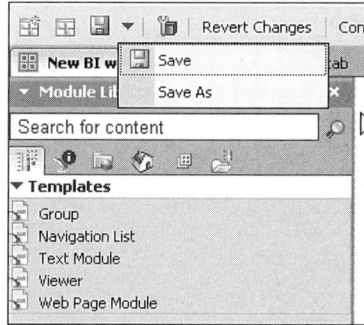

Figure 11.2 Save

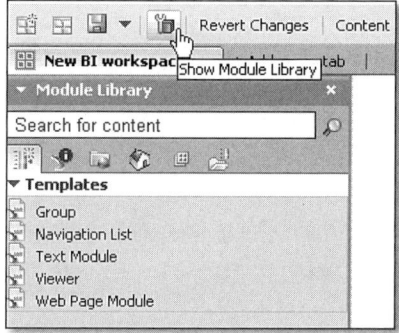

Figure 11.3 Module Library

As part of the TEMPLATES, you have the following components available:

- GROUP
- NAVIGATION LIST
  The navigation list allows you to create a custom folder structure with a list of selected content objects. In combination with the viewer template (discussed below), the navigation list can act as a selection list for the viewer.
- TEXT MODULE
  The text module allows you to display text or HTML.
- VIEWER
  The viewer allows you to display content selected from a navigation list. In the previous release, you were able to have only one viewer per workspace, but now you can have multiple viewers in a single workspace.

▶ WEB PAGE MODULE
You can use the web page module to display web pages based on a URL or a relative path.

The second category in the MODULE LIBRARY is the BI LAUNCH PAD MODULES (see Figure 11.4). These components are identical to those shown on the starting page of the BI launch pad, as also shown in Chapter 2, Section 12.2.

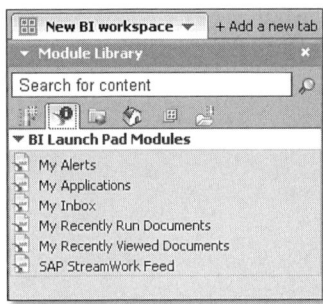

Figure 11.4 BI Launch Pad Modules

The PUBLIC MODULES category (see Figure 11.5) allows you to browse the complete repository of your SAP BusinessObjects BI platform. You can include the content from the repository in your workspace.

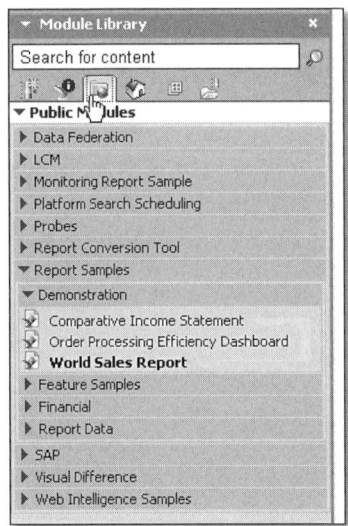

Figure 11.5 Public Modules

The Private Modules category provides access to components stored in the user's Favorite folder (see Figure 11.6).

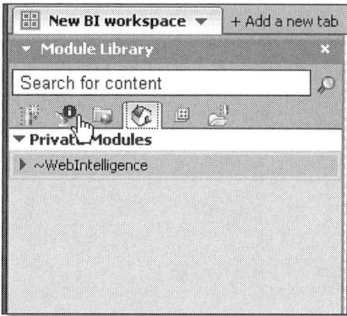

Figure 11.6 Private Modules

The Document Explorer provides you access to the documents in the SAP BusinessObjects BI platform and the Inbox for the logged on user (see Figure 11.7).

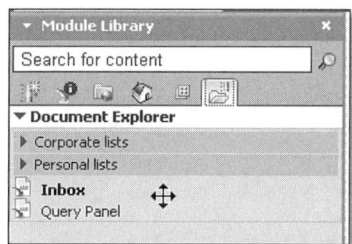

Figure 11.7 Document Explorer

The Layout option (see Figure 11.8) allows you to define the type of layout for the workspace. You can choose from Freeform, Template, and Columns. The Freeform option allows you to position and place the components of the workspace without any restrictions.

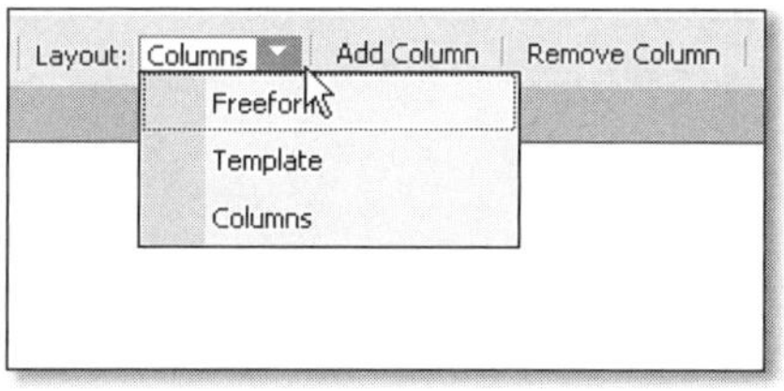

Figure 11.8 Layout Options

The TEMPLATE option allows you to select from a list of pre-configured templates (see Figure 11.9); the COLUMNS option organizes your workspace in columns, and you can add or remove columns as needed.

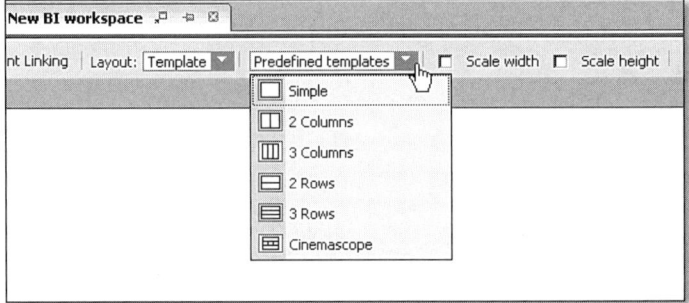

Figure 11.9 Templates

You can configure the PROPERTIES for each workspace by using the CONTEXT menu for each tab (see Figure 11.10).

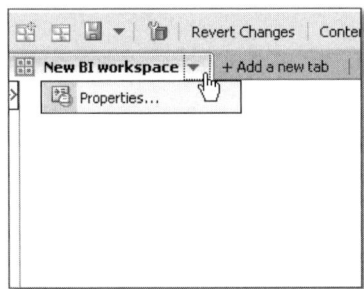

Figure 11.10 Properties

As part of PROPERTIES, you can also configure the style of your workspace (see Figure 11.11).

In the next section we create the content our first BI workspace.

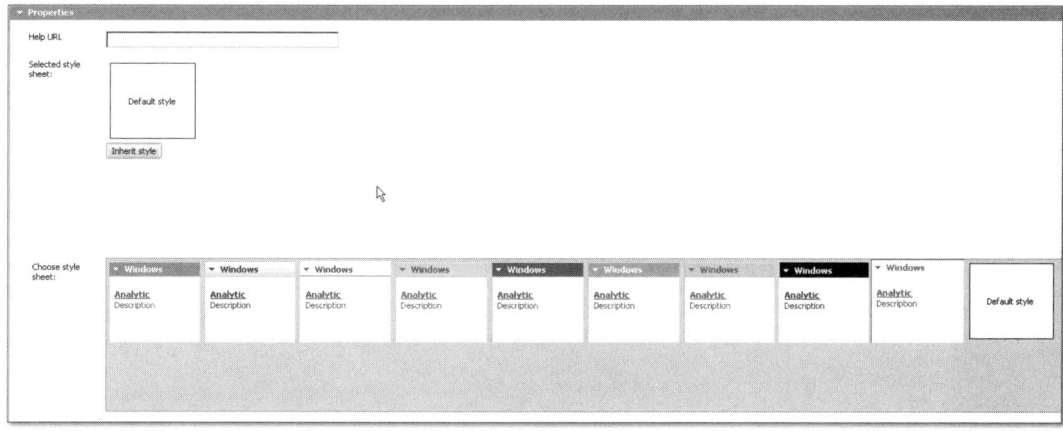

Figure 11.11 Style

11.2 Creating Content for Your First SAP BusinessObjects BI Workspace

In this section we focus on setting up the content, which you will then use as part of your first BI workspace. Your BI workspace will contain a report created with SAP Crystal Reports for Enterprise, a report created with SAP BusinessObjects Web Intelligence, and an object created with SAP BusinessObjects Dashboards. In the current release, the linking of objects supports only SAP Crystal Reports, SAP BusinessObjects Web Intelligence, and SAP BusinessObjects Dashboards. Linking in the BI workspaces is based on the use of the external interface in SAP BusinessObjects Dashboards and the use of parameters in SAP Crystal Reports for Enterprise and SAP BusinessObjects Web Intelligence.

In our example, we create an object with SAP BusinessObjects Dashboards showing revenue by country and reports with SAP BusinessObjects Web Intelligence and SAP Crystal Reports for Enterprise showing the revenue by region based on the selected country. The source for our reports will be a BEx query (see Figure 11.12) on the cube 0D_NW_M01 from the SAP NetWeaver demo model.

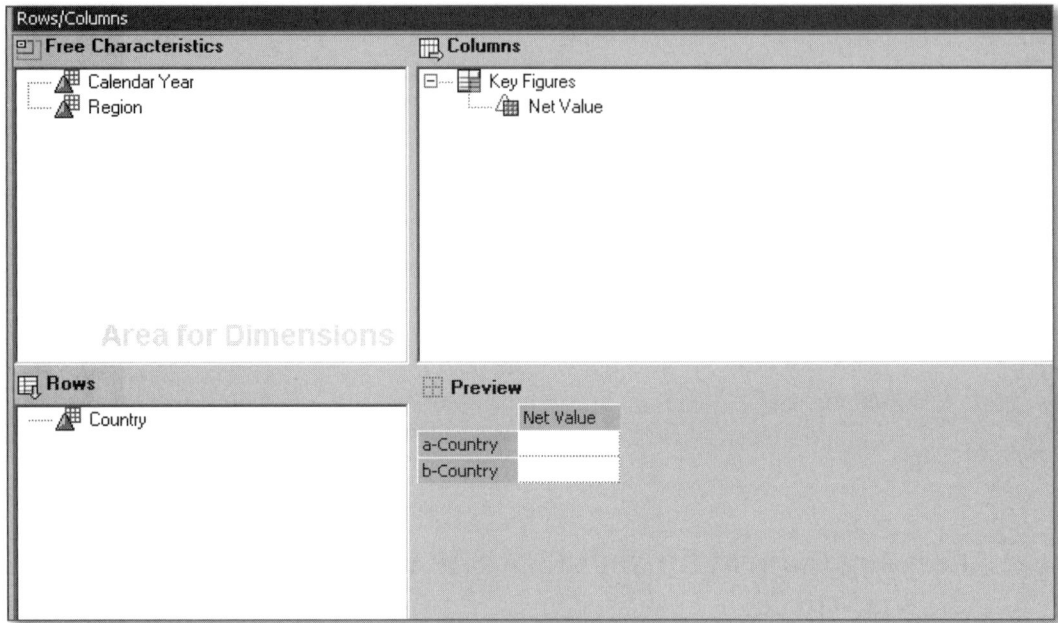

Figure 11.12 BEx Query

As a first step, set up the OLAP connection:

1. To start the configuration of a data connection, log on to the Central Management Console (CMC). Open the URL *http://localhost:8080/BOE/CMC* in your browser.
2. Log on with an administrative account.
3. Navigate to OLAP CONNECTIONS.
4. Use the icon to create a new OLAP CONNECTION.
5. Enter the necessary details for the OLAP CONNECTION.
6. Click on CONNECT.
7. You are asked to enter your SAP credentials to log on to the SAP NetWeaver BW system. After doing so you are presented with the list of InfoProviders and BEx queries.
8. Open the NETWEAVER DEMO InfoArea.
9. Open the list of BEx queries for the InfoProvider ACTUALS AND PLAN MULTIPROVIDER (0D_NW_M01).

10. Select the BEx query you created previously and click on SELECT.
11. Set the AUTHENTICATION to the value SSO.
12. Click on SAVE.

After we configure the connection, we can set up our SAP BusinessObjects Dashboards object.

1. Start the SAP BusinessObjects Dashboards Designer via the START • PROGRAMS • DASHBOARDS • DASHBOARDS menu path.
2. Select the menu FILE • NEW • NEW to create an empty model.
3. Use the menu VIEW • QUERY BROWSER to ensure that the query browser is shown as part of the design environment.
4. In the query browser, click on ADD QUERY.
5. You are asked to authenticate your SAP BusinessObjects BI platform system. Log on to the system using your SAP credentials and SAP authentication.
6. You are presented with the first step in adding a new query to your dashboard. Select the BEx option.
7. Click on NEXT.
8. You are presented with the list of available connections. Select the connection you set up for the BEx query.
9. Click on NEXT.
10. You are presented with a list of BEx queries, from which you can select the BEx query you need for your dashboard. Select the BEx query and click on OK. The query panel appears and you can start creating the first query you will use for your dashboard (see Figure 11.13).
11. Add COUNTRY to RESULT OBJECTS.
12. Add NET VALUE to RESULT OBJECTS.
13. Click on NEXT.
14. Click NEXT.
15. Click on OK.
16. Use the menu VIEW • COMPONENTS to ensure that the components list is shown as part of the design environment.
17. Drag and drop a pie chart from the CHART area in the list of components to the dashboard.

11   Using SAP BusinessObjects BI Workspaces

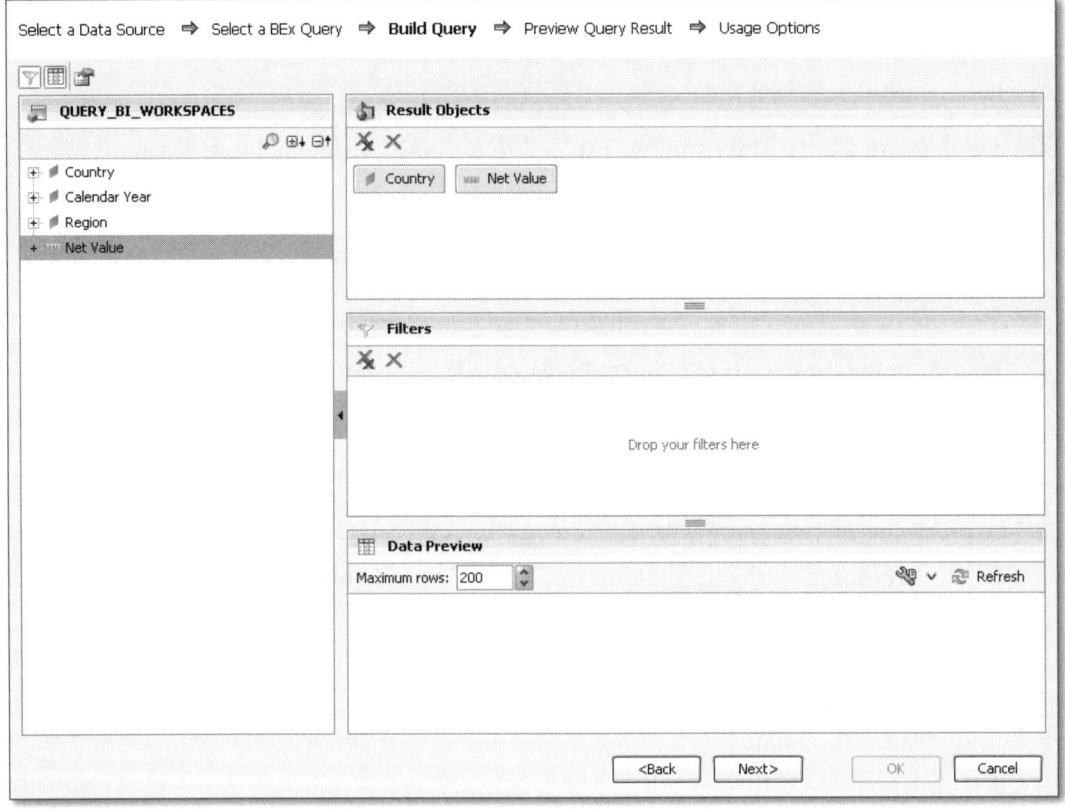

Figure 11.13 Query Panel

18. Right-click on the CHART and select the menu PROPERTIES.
19. Enter "Revenue by Country" as the title and remove the subtitle.
20. Open the menu next to the VALUES option (see Figure 11.14).
21. Select the QUERY DATA option (see Figure 11.15).
22. Select NET VALUES.
23. Click on OK.
24. Open the menu next to the LABELS option.
25. Select the option QUERY DATA.
26. Select COUNTRY.
27. Click on OK.

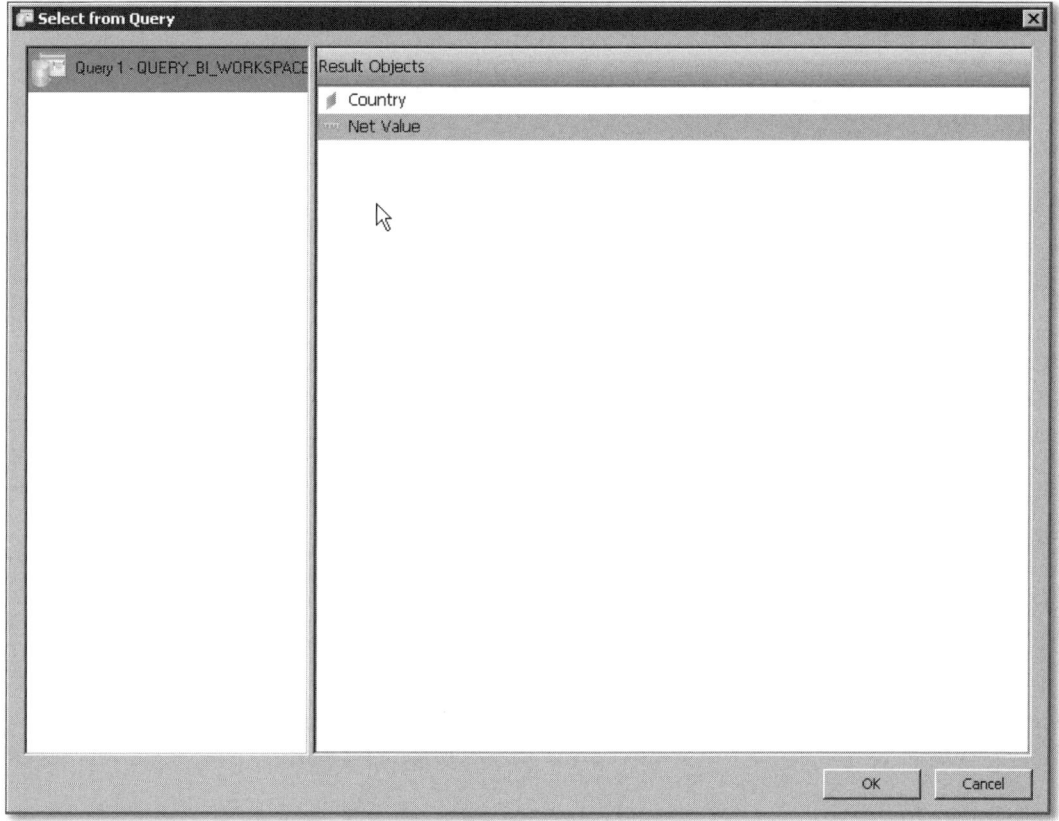

Figure 11.14 Values

Figure 11.15 Select Data

28. Select the menu DATA • CONNECTIONS.
29. Click on ADD.
30. Select the entry EXTERNAL INTERFACE CONNECTION.
31. Use the ADD icon ([+]) to create a new entry for the EXTERNAL INTERFACE CONNECTION (see Figure 11.16).
32. Enter "Country" in the RANGE NAME field.
33. Set the RANGE TYPE to CELL.
34. Set the ACCESS to READ/WRTE.
35. Use the SELECT THE RANGE icon ([icon]) next to RANGE.
36. Select cell A1 in the spreadsheet.
37. Click on OK.

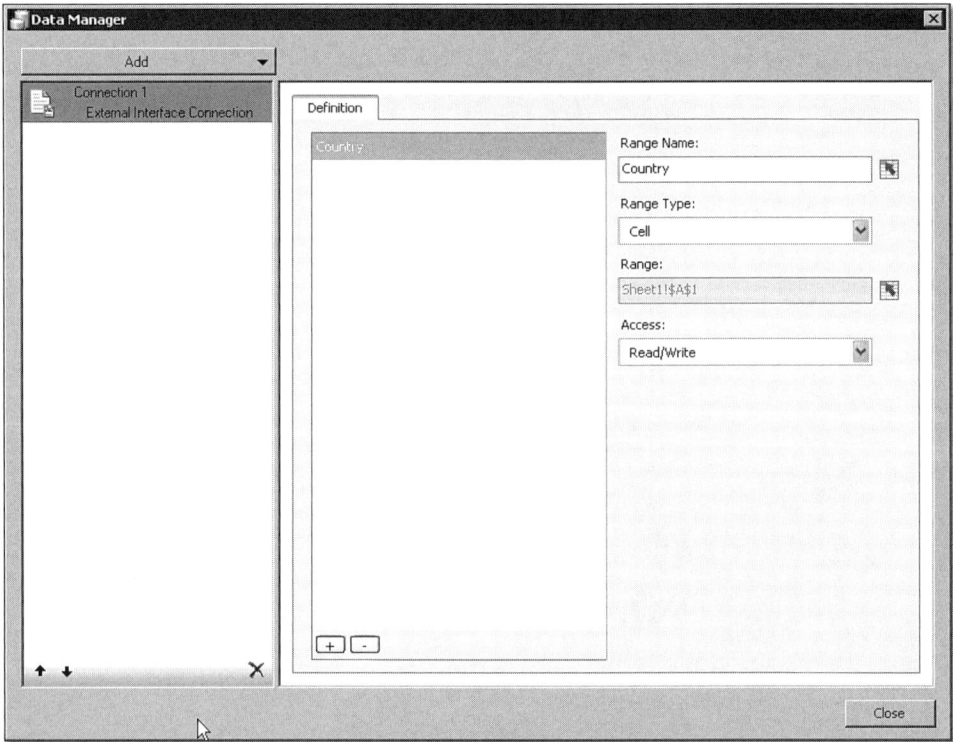

Figure 11.16 Data Manager

38. Click on CLOSE.

Without doing anything further, the chart would not send the selected value, so you need to configure the chart to send the value to the spreadsheet each time a user clicks on the chart values.

1. Right-click on the CHART and select the menu PROPERTIES.
2. Navigate to the INSERTION area.
3. Activate the ENABLE DATA INSERTION option (see Figure 11.17)

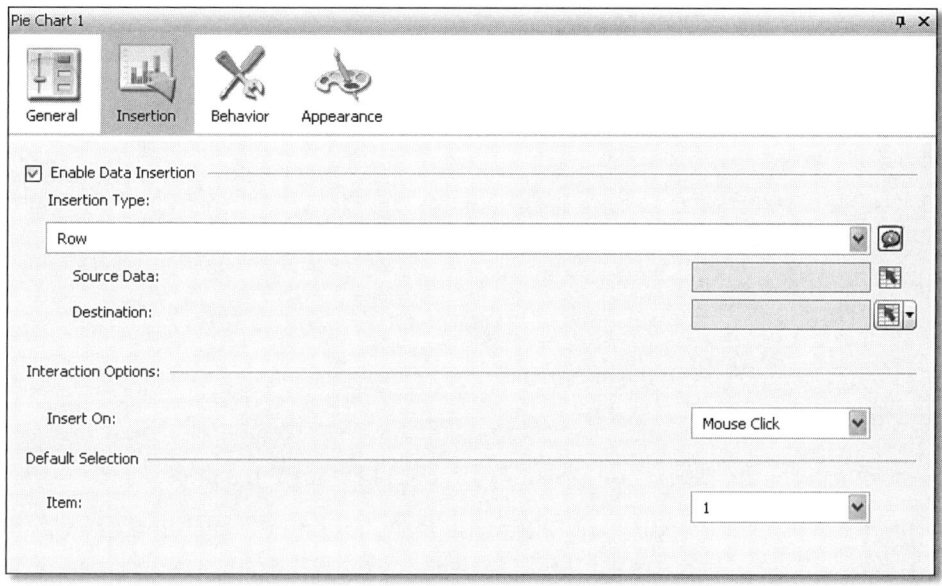

Figure 11.17 Insertion

You will notice that the INSERTION TYPE does not have the option LABEL, which means you can't just send the label from the selected country. The closest option is INSERTION TYPE ROW. For the INSERTION TYPE ROW you will notice that the SOURCE DATA field does not provide the option to point to the query data, which means that you will have to point your query data to the spreadsheet to enable your drill down.

4. Select the menu VIEW • QUERY BROWSER to ensure that the query browser is visible.
5. Select the query you created previously.
6. Select the dimension COUNTRY in the query.

433

7. Click on INSERT IN SPREADSHEET.
8. Click on the SELECT A RANGE icon (▨) next to INSERT IN SPREADSHEET and select the range from cell C1 to cell C50 in the embedded spreadsheet.
9. Click on OK.
10. Navigate back to the chart. Right-click on chart and select the menu PROPERTIES.
11. Navigate to the INSERTION area.
12. Set the INSERTION TYPE to ROW.
13. Click on the SELECT A RANGE icon (▨) next to SOURCE DATA. From your embedded spreadsheet; select the range from cell C1 to cell C50.
14. Click on OK.
15. Use the SELECT A RANGE icon (▨) next to DESTINATION to open the list and select cell A1 in your embedded spreadsheet.
16. Click on OK.
17. Select the menu FILE • SAVE TO PLATFORM.
18. Enter a name for the dashboard.
19. Click on SAVE.

Now let's build the report using SAP Crystal Reports for Enterprise.

1. Start SAP Crystal Reports for Enterprise by following the menu: START • PROGRAMS • CRYSTAL REPORTS FOR ENTERPRISE 4 • CRYSTAL REPORTS FOR ENTERPRISE 4.
2. Select the menu FILE • NEW • FROM DATA SOURCE.
3. Select the menu option BROWSE REPOSITORY from SAP BUSINESSOBJECTS BUSINESS INTELLIGENCE PLATFORM.
4. Log on to your SAP BusinessObjects BI platform with your SAP credentials.
5. Click on OK. You are presented with a list of available connections.
6. Select the previously established connection.
7. Click on NEXT. You are presented with the list of BEx queries.
8. Select the BEx query and click on OK.
9. You are presented with the query panel, and you can select the objects and add them to the RESULT OBJECTS.

10. Add the following items to the RESULT OBJECTS (see Figure 11.18):
    - REGION
    - NET VALUE

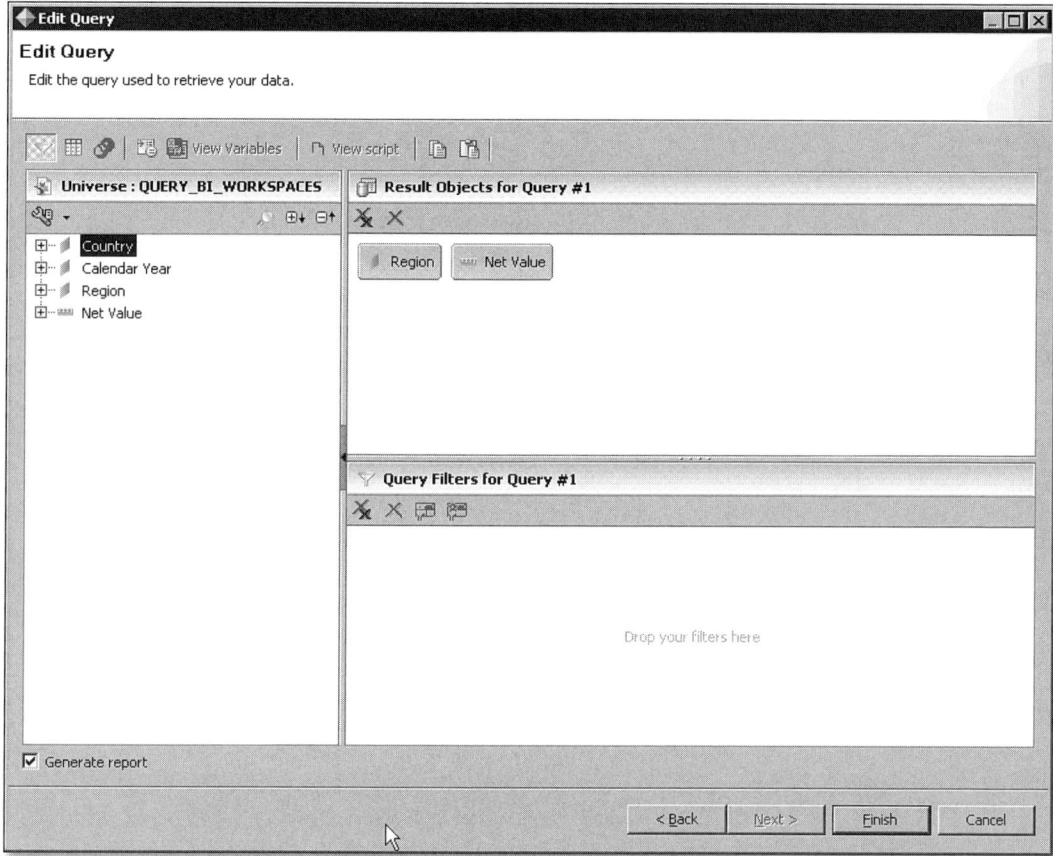

Figure 11.18 Query Panel

11. Drag and drop the dimension COUNTRY to the QUERY FILTERS (see Figure 11.19).
12. Select the PROMPT option for the filter (see Figure 11.20).
13. You are presented with a separate dialog to configure the details for the prompt (see Figure 11.21).

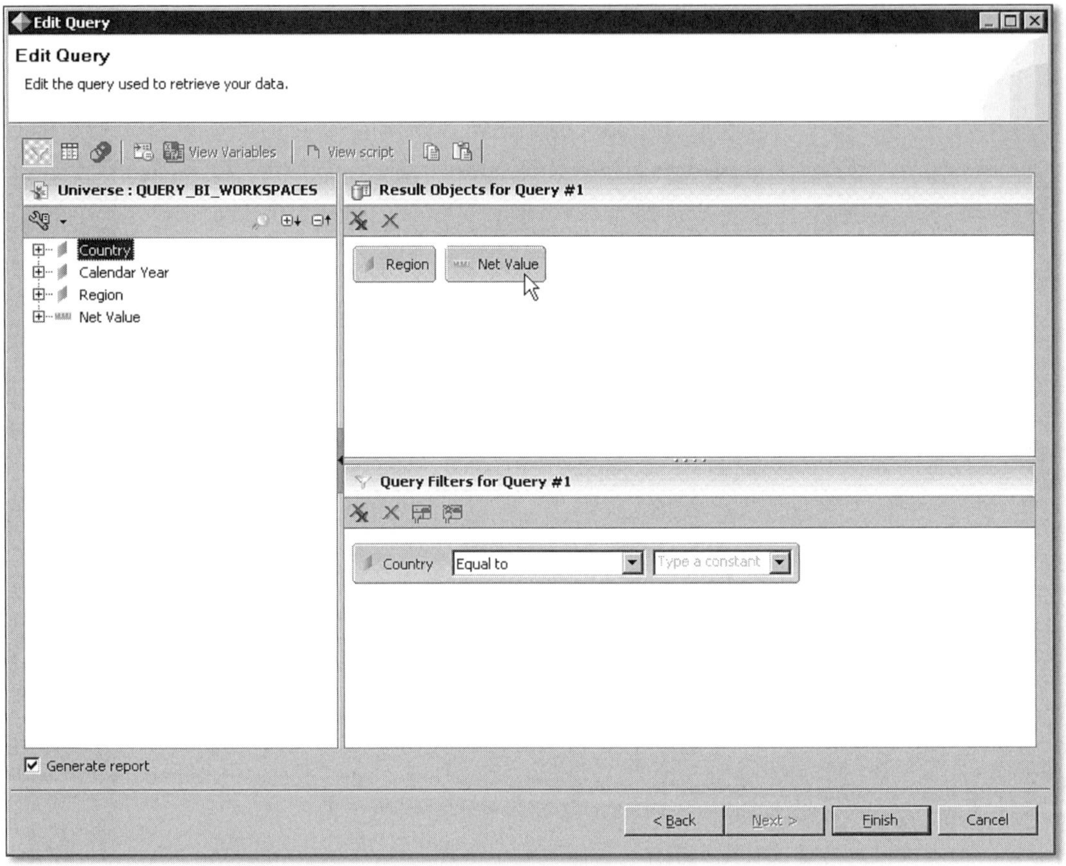

11 | Using SAP BusinessObjects BI Workspaces

Figure 11.19 Query Filters

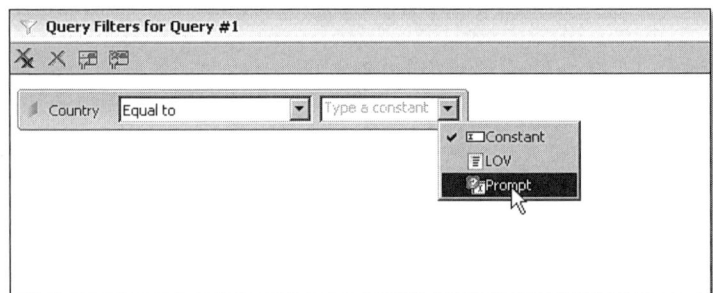

Figure 11.20 Prompt

14. Activate the OPTIONAL PROMPT option (see Figure 11.21).

Creating Content for Your First SAP BusinessObjects BI Workspace | 11.2

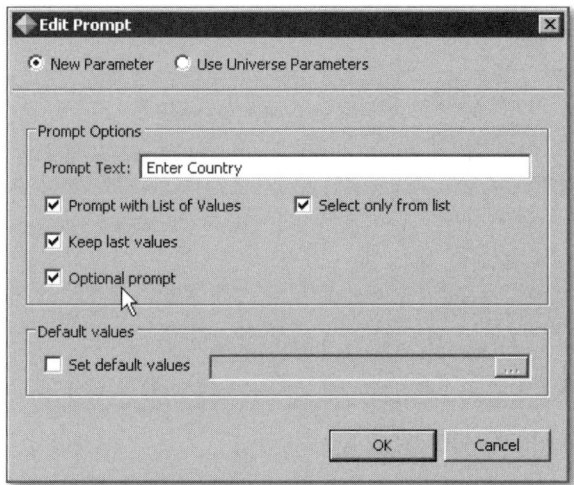

Figure 11.21 Prompt Details

15. Disable the SELECT ONLY FROM LIST option.
16. Click on OK.
17. Uncheck the GENERATE REPORT option.
18. Click on FINISH. You are prompted for a COUNTRY value but, because the prompt is optional, you do not have to provide a value right now.
19. Leave the list of values empty and click on OK.
20. Navigate to the INSERT tab.
21. Select the menu CHART • SIDE-BY-SIDE COLUMN (SEE Figure 11.22).

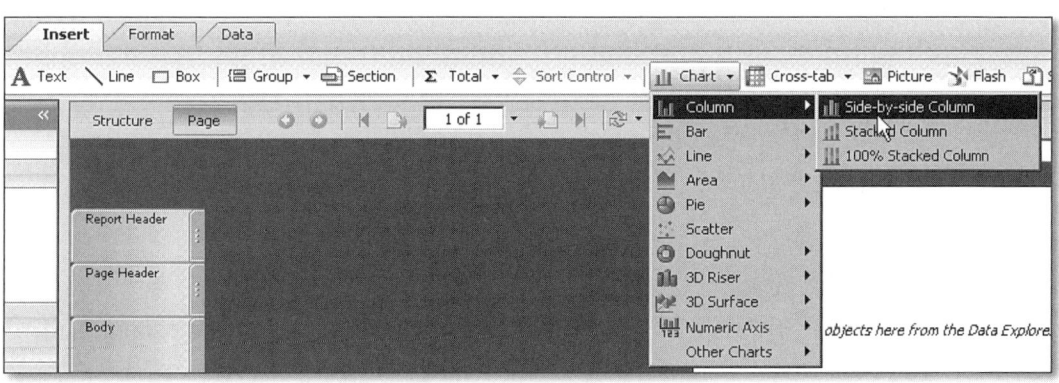

Figure 11.22 Charts

437

22. Insert the chart into the REPORT HEADER (see Figure 11.23).

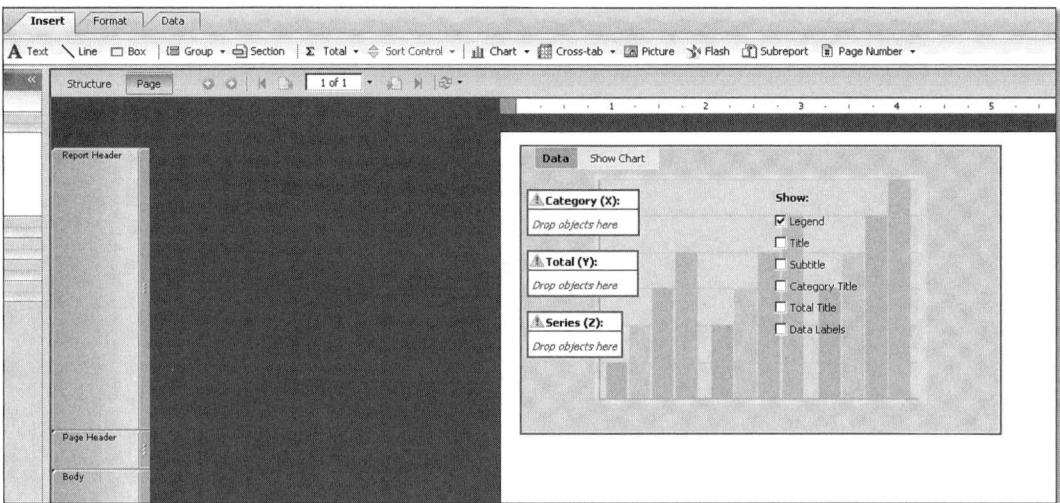

Figure 11.23 Charts

23. Drag REGION from the Data Explorer to CATEGORY (X) from the chart.
24. Drag NET VALUE from the Data Explorer to TOTAL (Y) from the chart.
25. Click on SHOW CHART.
26. Right-click on the PAGE HEADER section.
27. Select the menu option HIDE.
28. Right-click on the BODY section.
29. Select the menu option HIDE.
30. Right-click on the REPORT FOOTER section.
31. Select the menu option HIDE.
32. Select the menu FILE • SAVE AS.
33. Select a folder for the report.
34. Enter a name for the report.
35. Click on SAVE.

Now we will build the report using SAP BusinessObjects Web Intelligence.

1. Start the BI launch pad by following the menu START • PROGRAMS • SAP BUSINESSOBJECTS BI PLATFORM 4 • SAP BUSINESSOBJECTS BI PLATFORM • SAP BUSINESSOBJECTS BI PLATFORM JAVA BI LAUNCH PAD.
2. Log on using your SAP credentials.
3. Select the menu APPLICATION • WEB INTELLIGENCE APPLICATION.
4. Click on the NEW icon ( ) to start the process of creating a new report.
5. You will be asked which type of data source you would like to use for your report. Select the option BEX.
6. Click on OK.
7. You are presented with a list of available connections. As soon as you select one of the available connections, you are shown the available BEx queries on the right side of the dialog.
8. Select the connection and BEx query you created previously and click on OK.
9. You are presented with the SAP BusinessObjects Web Intelligence query panel.
10. Add the following items to the RESULT OBJECTS panel:
    - REGION
    - NET VALUE
11. Drag and drop COUNTRY to the QUERY FILTERS.
12. Set the operator for the filter to EQUAL TO (see Figure 11.24).

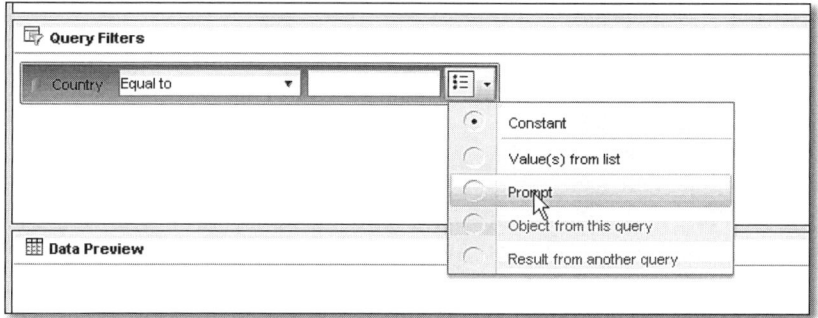

Figure 11.24 Query Filters

13. Select the PROMPT option for the filter.
14. Click on the PROPERTIES ICON ( ) to configure the prompt (see Figure 11.25)

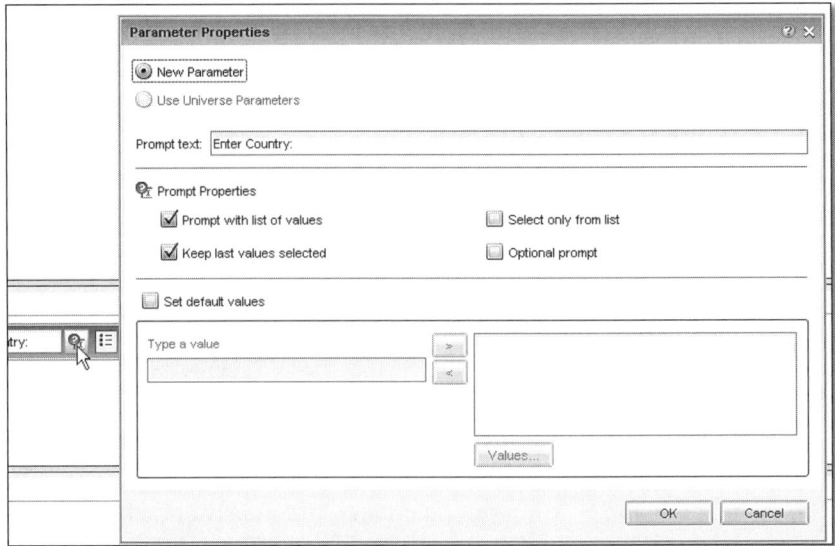

Figure 11.25 Prompt Details

15. Activate the OPTIONAL PROMPT option.
16. Click on OK.
17. Click on RUN QUERY.
18. You can leave the prompt empty, as you configured the prompt to be optional.
19. Click on OK.
20. Select the [💾] SAVE menu.
21. Select a folder for the report.
22. Enter a name for the report.
23. Click on SAVE.

You now have all the necessary content so that you can set up content linking. In this section we prepared the content for linking.

11.3 Creating Your First BI Workspace

So far we created the necessary content for the BI workspace. We will now use the content to create our first BI workspace and set up content linking.

1. Start the BI launch pad by following the menu START • PROGRAMS • SAP BUSINESS-OBJECTS BI PLATFORM 4 • SAP BUSINESSOBJECTS BI PLATFORM • SAP BUSINESS-OBJECTS BI PLATFORM JAVA BI LAUNCH PAD.
2. Log on using your SAP credentials.
3. Select the menu APPLICATION • BI WORKSPACE.
4. In the LAYOUT option select TEMPLATE.
5. From the list of PREDEFINED TEMPLATES, select option 3, COLUMNS (see Figure 11.26).

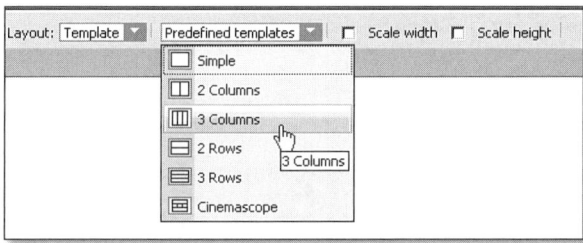

Figure 11.26 Layout

6. Activate the SCALE WIDTH and SCALE HEIGHT options.
7. Open the MODULE LIBRARY.
8. Navigate to the category PUBLIC MODULES (see Figure 11.27).

Figure 11.27 Public Modules

11 | Using SAP BusinessObjects BI Workspaces

9. Select the SAP BusinessObjects Dashboards content that you created and place it into the first column.
10. Select the SAP Crystal Reports for Enterprise content that you created and place it into the second column.
11. Select the SAP BusinessObjects Web Intelligence content that you created and place it into the third column (see Figure 11.28).

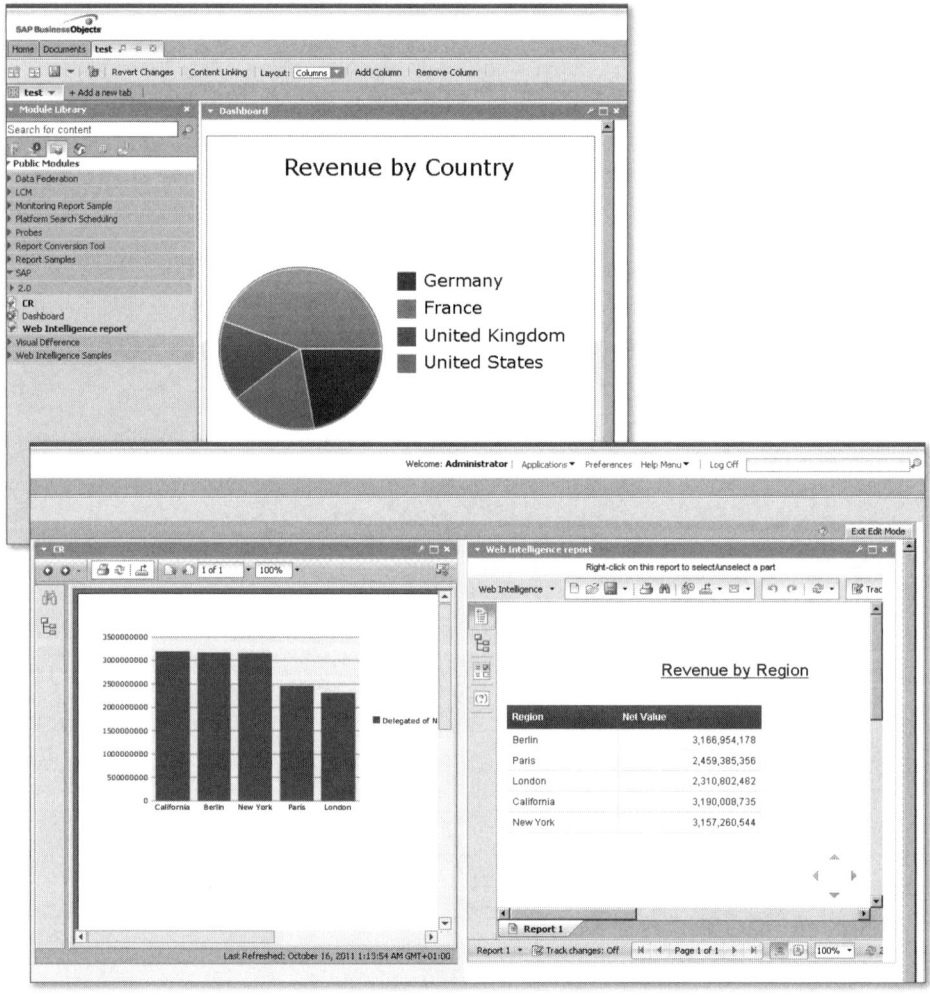

Figure 11.28 BI Workspace

12. You can now use the EDIT icon ( ) for each content object to configure further details (see Figure 11.29).

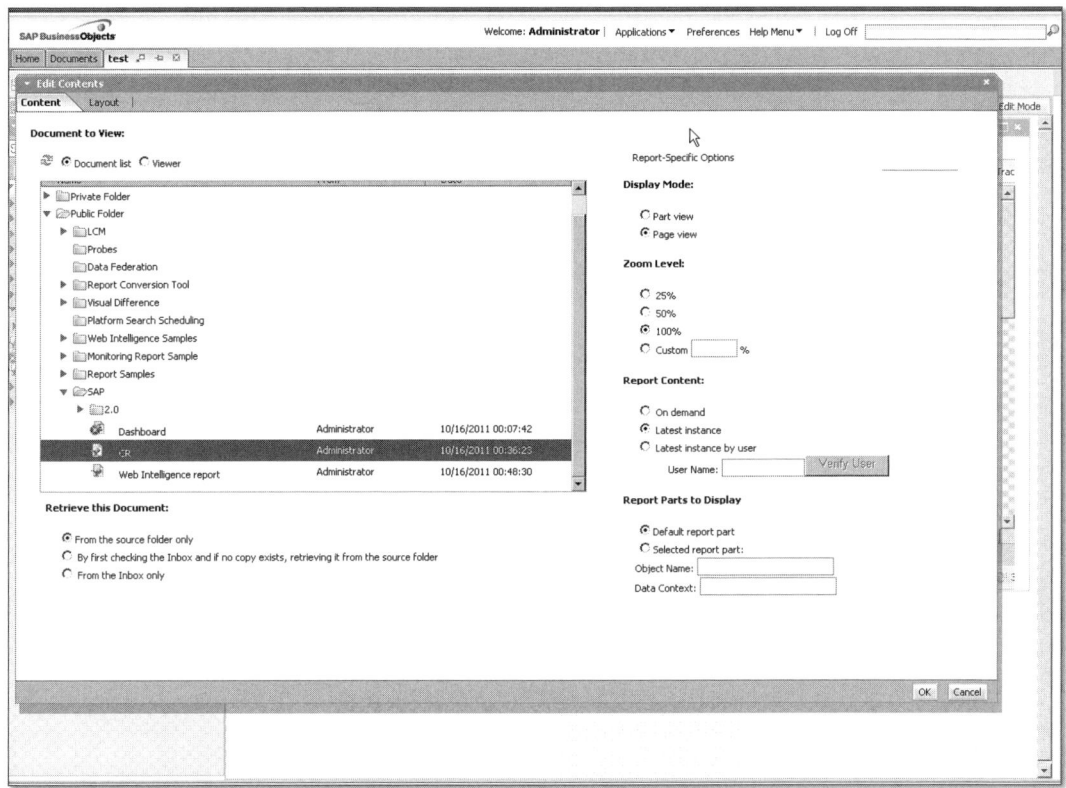

Figure 11.29 Options for SAP Crystal Reports

As part of these options, you can configure default behavior, such as the zoom level, if the report should be derived from an instance or if only a specific part of the report, such as a chart, should be shown. Now, let's save the workspace and perform content linking.

1. Use the SAVE option in the toolbar to save your BI workspace.
2. Select a folder and enter a name.
3. Click on SAVE.
4. Click on EDIT BI WORKSPACE to return to the EDIT mode.

5. Click on CONTENT LINKING (see Figure 11.30). You are presented with the content linking screen (see Figure 11.31) and any content from your BI workspace that can be used as a target or a source is shown.

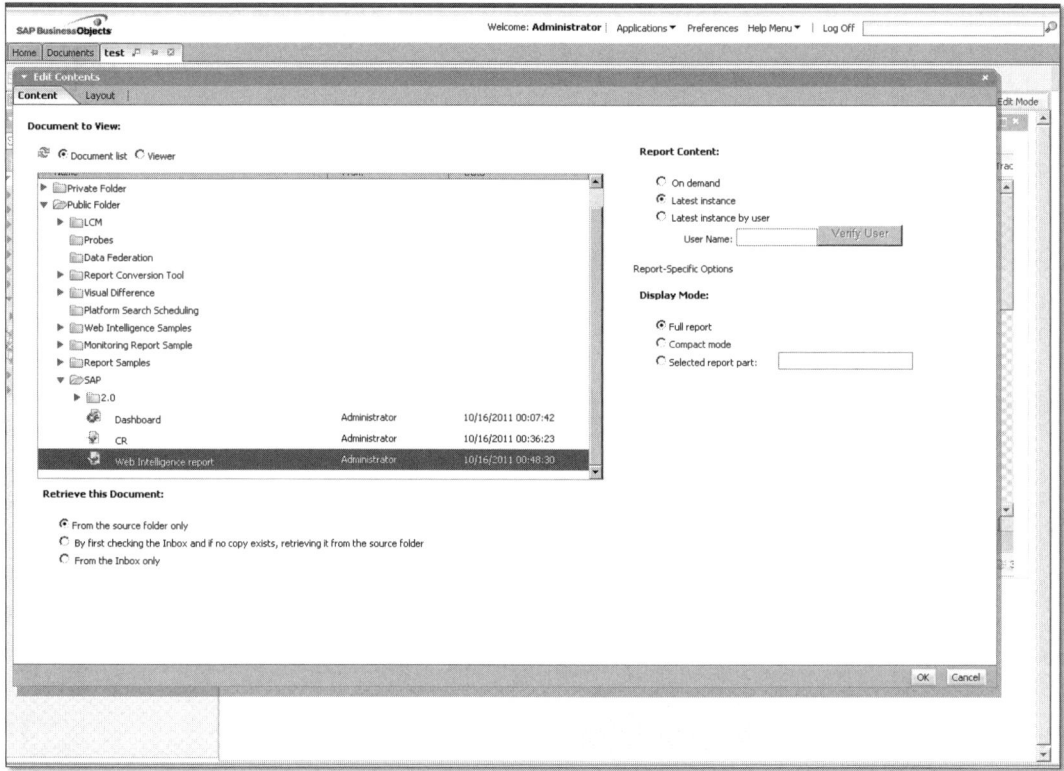

Figure 11.30 Options for SAP BusinessObjects Web Intelligence

6. Drag and drop a link from the SAP BusinessObjects Dashboards object OUT option (green) to the SAP Crystal Reports for Enterprise INPUT PROMPT (blue) (see Figure 11.32).

7. You now need to define which values are matched up between these two content objects. In the PARAMETER MAPPING table, the value from the SAP BusinessObjects Dashboard object is shown and you can select the parameter that you created from the SAP Crystal Reports for Enterprise content.

8. Click on CLICK HERE TO SELECT THE TARGET PARAMETER.

Creating Your First BI Workspace | **11.3**

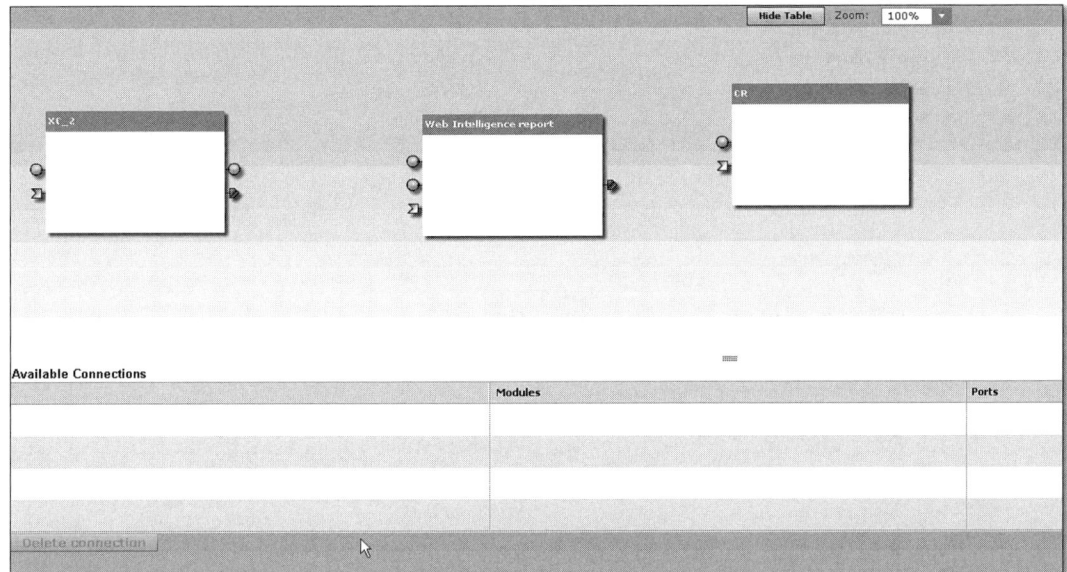

Figure 11.31 Content Linking

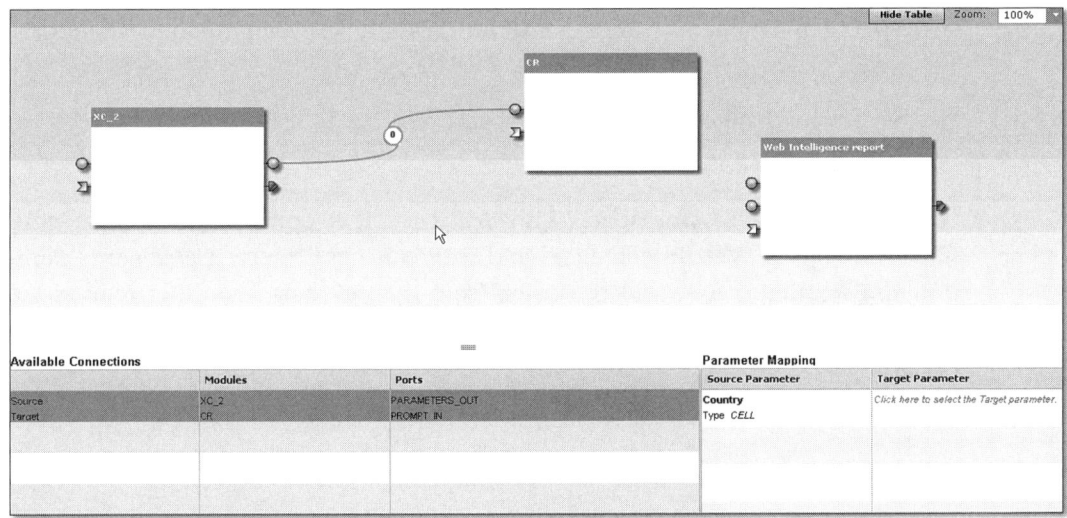

Figure 11.32 Linked Values

9. Select the parameter from the SAP Crystal Reports for Enterprise report (see Figure 11.33).

445

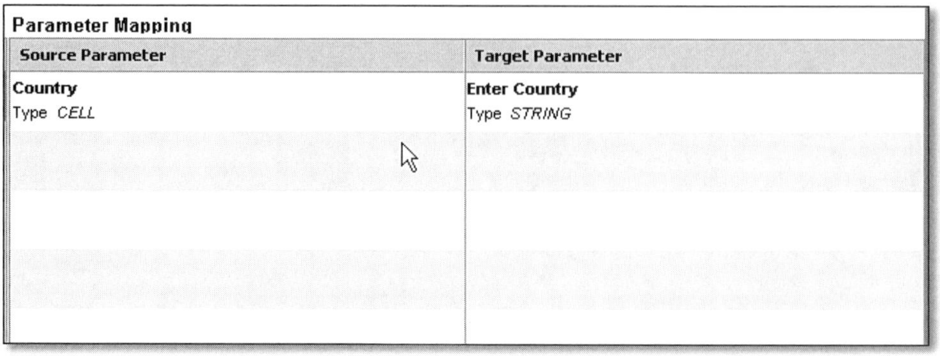

Parameter Mapping	
Source Parameter	Target Parameter
Country Type CELL	Enter Country Type STRING

Figure 11.33 Parameter Mapping

10. Drag and drop a link from the SAP BusinessObjects Dashboards object Out option (green) to the SAP BusinessObjects Web Intelligence Input prompt (blue).

11. You now need to define which values are matched up between these two content objects. Click on the text Click here to select the Target Parameter in the Parameter Mapping table.

12. Select the parameter from the SAP BusinessObjects Web Intelligence report.

13. Click on Close.

14. Save your changes to the BI workspace.

15. Click on Exit Edit Mode.

You now have a BI workspace with SAP Crystal Reports for Enterprise, SAP BusinessObjects Web Intelligence, and SAP BusinessObjects Dashboards combined. Each time a user selects a value from the pie chart, the other reports are updated and the data are filtered according to the selected value (see Figure 11.34).

Summary | **11.4**

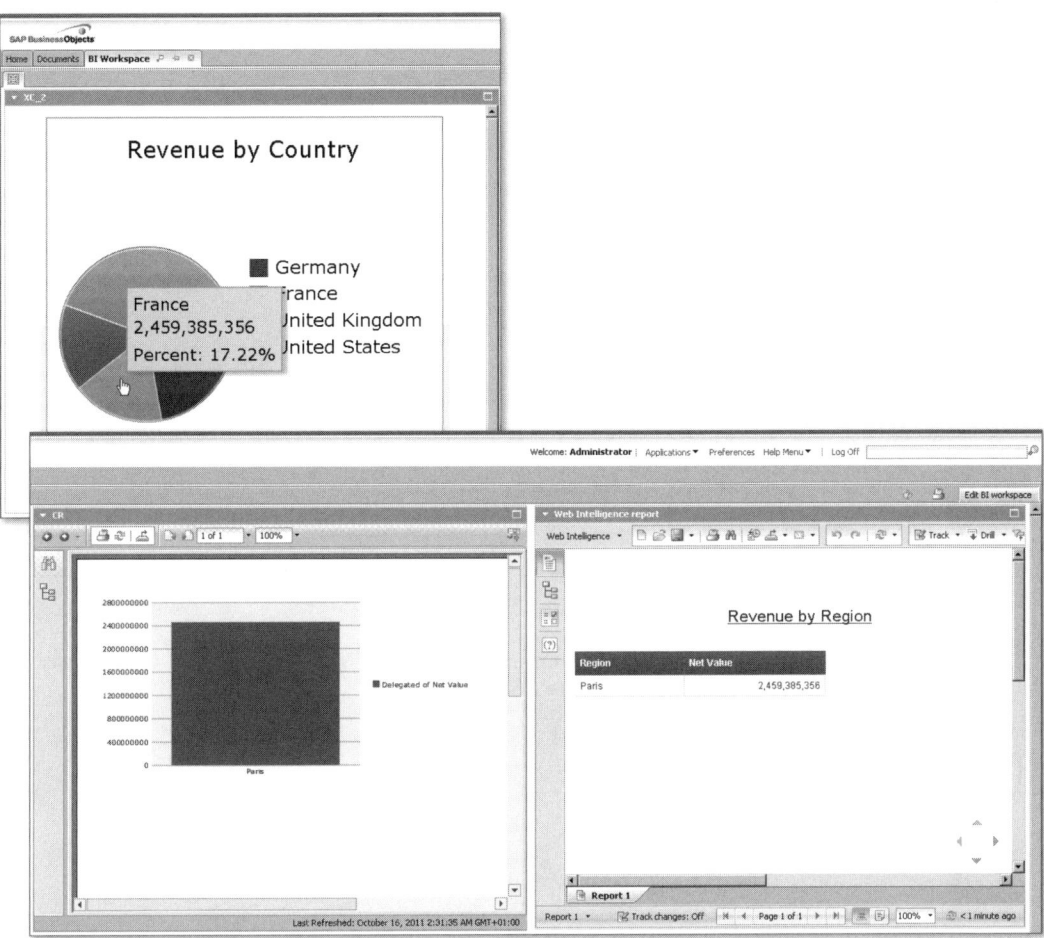

Figure 11.34 BI Workspace

11.4 Summary

In this chapter you learned how to use SAP BusinessObjects BI workspaces to combine content from the SAP BusinessObjects BI platform and include interactivity. In the next chapter we show you how to navigate the BI launch pad.

In this chapter we show you how to navigate in the BI launch pad and provide you with an overview of its functionality.

12 Navigating the BI Launch Pad

The BI launch pad is a web-based environment that allows you as the end user to perform common tasks, such as viewing a report or scheduling a report, without the need to deploy any software on your client computer. The BI launch pad provides you with all end-user functionality out-of-the-box, and allows you to provide your end users access to the complete functionality in your SAP BusinessObjects BI platform system.

In the following sections we provide a step-by-step approach of the most common tasks related to using the BI launch pad.

12.1 User Authentication

In this section we review the topic of user authentication in the context of the BI launch pad.

1. Start the BI launch pad via the menu START • PROGRAMS • SAP BUSINESSOBJECTS BI PLATFORM 4 • SAP BUSINESSOBJECTS BI PLATFORM • SAP BUSINESSOBJECTS BI PLATFORM JAVA BI LAUNCH PAD.
2. You are presented with the initial screen (see Figure 12.1).
3. As shown in Figure 12.1 you can see the name of your SAP BusinessObjects BI system, and you can also see the list of available authentication methods.
4. Select SAP as the authentication method and the logon dialog changes (see Figure 12.2).

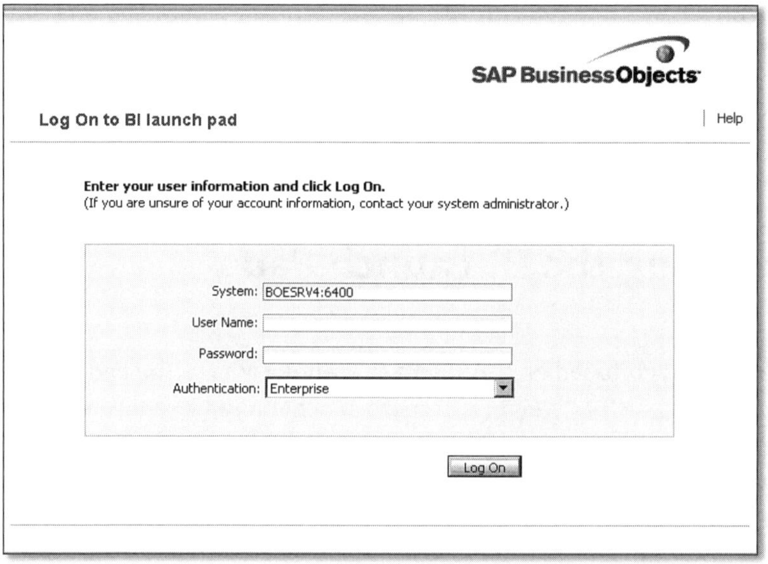

Figure 12.1 BI Launch Pad Start Screen

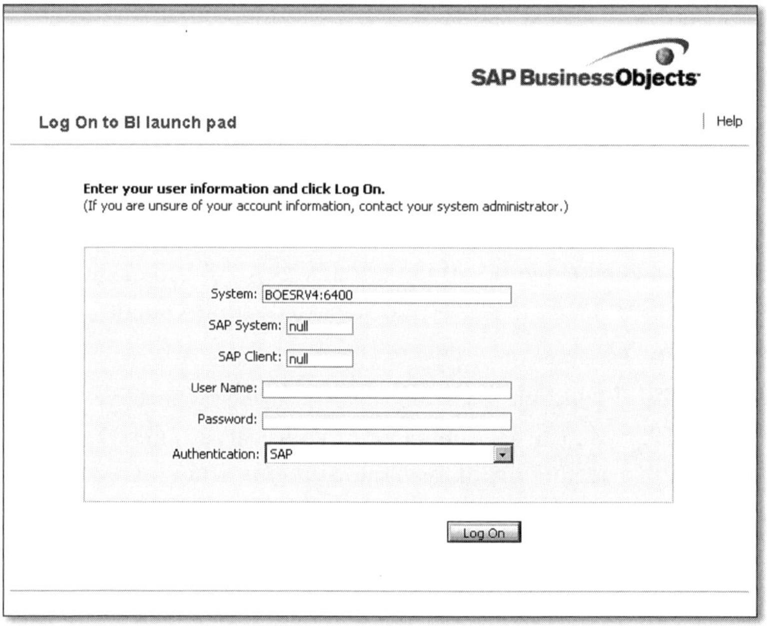

Figure 12.2 BI Launch Pad with SAP Authentication

You can use the SAP system and SAP client entries to specify the system ID and the client number from your SAP system. The option to leverage your SAP credentials for logon requires SAP authentication to be configured as part of your SAP BusinessObjects BI platform.

You can configure the behavior of the logon mask for the BI launch pad by using a configuration file. For the following steps we assume installation on a Windows operating system using Tomcat as the application server.

1. Navigate to the folder *<Install Directory>\SAP BusinessObjects\Tomcat6\webapps\BOE\WEB-INF\config\default*.
2. Open the file *BILaunchpad.properties* with an editor.
3. Set the values according to Table 12.1.

Parameter Name	Value
authentication.default	secSAPR3
authentication.visible	True
cms.default	<CMS Server Name>:<port>
cms.visible	True
logontoken.enabled	True

Table 12.1 Configuration Values for BILaunchpad.properties

4. Save your changes.
5. Close the file.
6. Restart the application server from your SAP BusinessObjects system.

With these changes, your BI launch pad will use SAP authentication as the default entry, and the CMS Server and the authentication list are visible to the end user.

In the next section we uncover the different areas of the BI launch pad user interface.

12.2 User Interface (UI) Overview

In this section we look at the different areas of the BI launch pad. After a successful user authentication, the user is presented with the start screen of the BI launch pad, as shown in Figure 12.3.

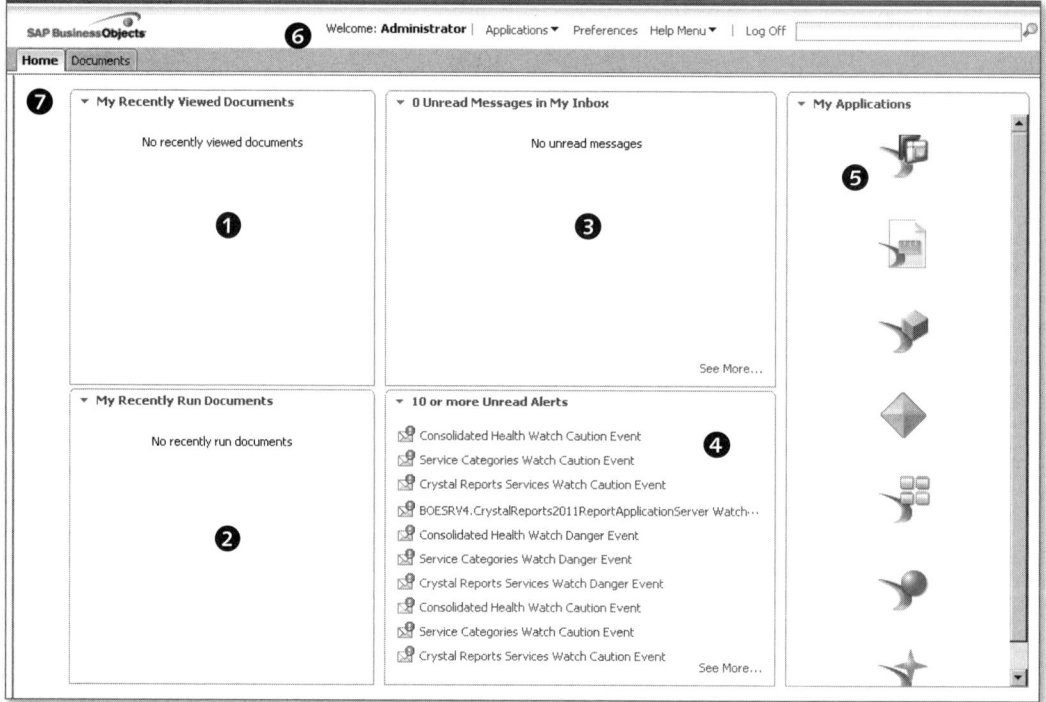

Figure 12.3 BI Launch Pad Start Screen

The following is a brief overview of each area:

1. The MY RECENTLY VIEWED DOCUMENTS (❶) area provides you access to the last viewed reports and analytics.

2. The MY RECENTLY RUN DOCUMENTS (❷) area lists those documents that you scheduled and where the scheduling job has been successfully finished.

3. The third area (❸) lists any new reports or messages that were sent to your personal Inbox.

4. The fourth area (**4**) shows any alerts. These could be alerts based on reports and analytics or alerts based on watches or issues from your SAP BusinessObjects system.
5. The fifth area, called MY APPLICATIONS (**5**), is a listing of the icons of all applications the user has access to. The list of applications also matches the APPLICATIONS menu in the toolbar.
6. At the top of the BI launch pad (**6**), you can find the different menus allowing the user to call the available applications, configure the user preferences, and calling the documentation via the Help menu. In addition, the toolbar also offers the search dialog.
7. In the top left corner (**7**), the user can navigate between the HOME screen (see Figure 12.3) and the DOCUMENTS screen (see Figure 12.4).

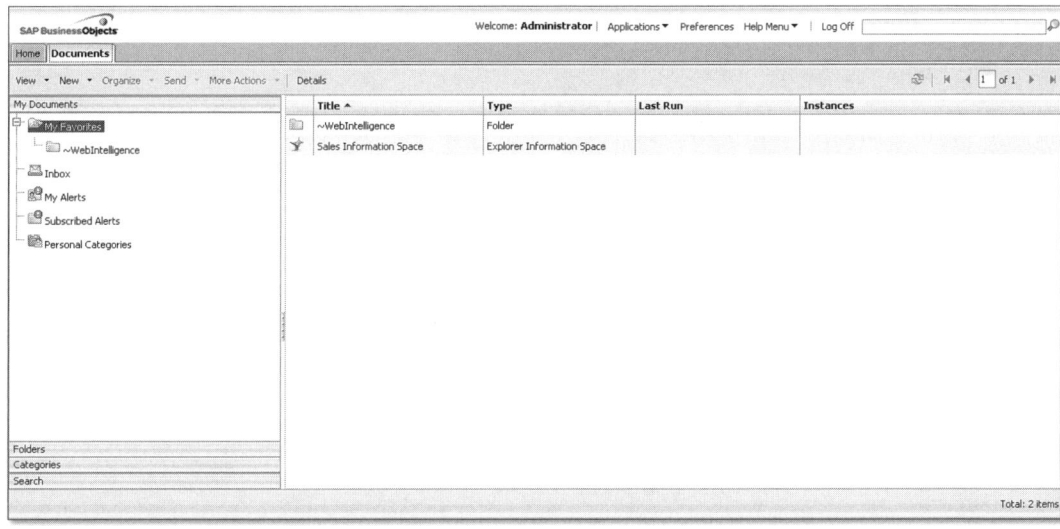

Figure 12.4 BI Launch Pad—Documents

As part of the DOCUMENTS area, you can open the following panels on the left side:

▶ MY DOCUMENTS
  Here you have access to your own reports managed in your Favorites folder.
▶ FOLDERS
  Here you have access to all folders of the SAP BusinessObjects BI platform, which you are allowed to see based on security settings.

▶ CATEGORIES

Here you can see the reports organized by categories instead of organized by folders.

▶ SEARCH

Here you can use the search dialog and search for reports or matching data.

In addition to the menus and areas outlined so far, you also have access to a set of menus (see Figure 12.5).

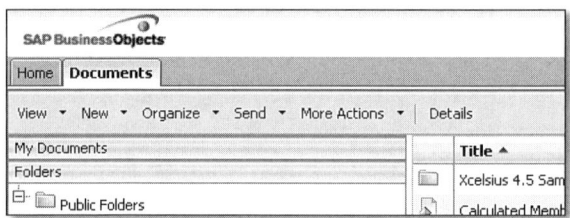

Figure 12.5 Menu Toolbar

These menus allow the user—depending on the selected object—to view, copy, schedule, delete, and assign properties to the object. The DETAILS option in the toolbar allows the user to see the configured description of the report (see Figure 12.6).

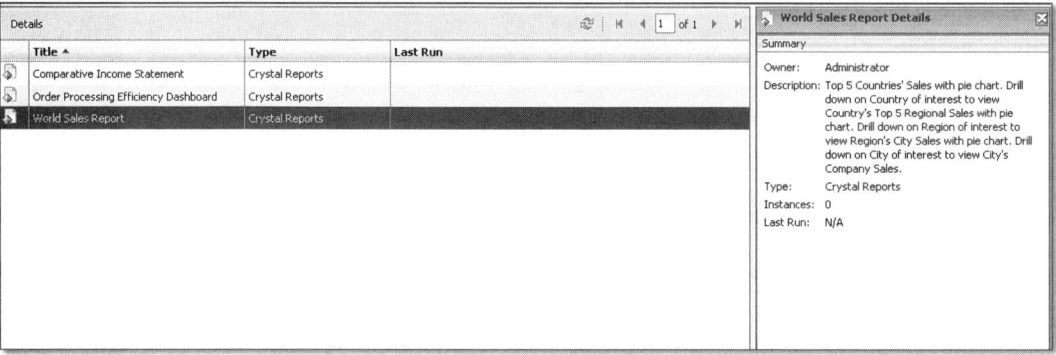

Figure 12.6 Details

In the next section we review the option to assign a folder and a category to each report.

12.3 Folders and Categories

As part of your SAP BusinessObjects BI platform, reports and analytical content can be assigned to a folder and to a category. The BI launch pad organizes objects by folders and categories. You can switch between the view along the folder structure or along the categories using the menu in the BI launch pad in the left panel. Only SAP BusinessObjects Web Intelligence offers the option to assign a category as part of the saving workflow; therefore, you need to assign categories for the other content types as part of the BI launch pad.

To assign a category for a report object, follow these steps:

1. Start the BI launch pad via the menu START • PROGRAMS • SAP BUSINESSOBJECTS BI PLATFORM 4 • SAP BUSINESSOBJECTS BI PLATFORM • SAP BUSINESSOBJECTS BI PLATFORM JAVA BI LAUNCHPAD.
2. Log on to the BI launch pad with your credentials.
3. Select the FOLDERS option in the panel (see Figure 12.7).

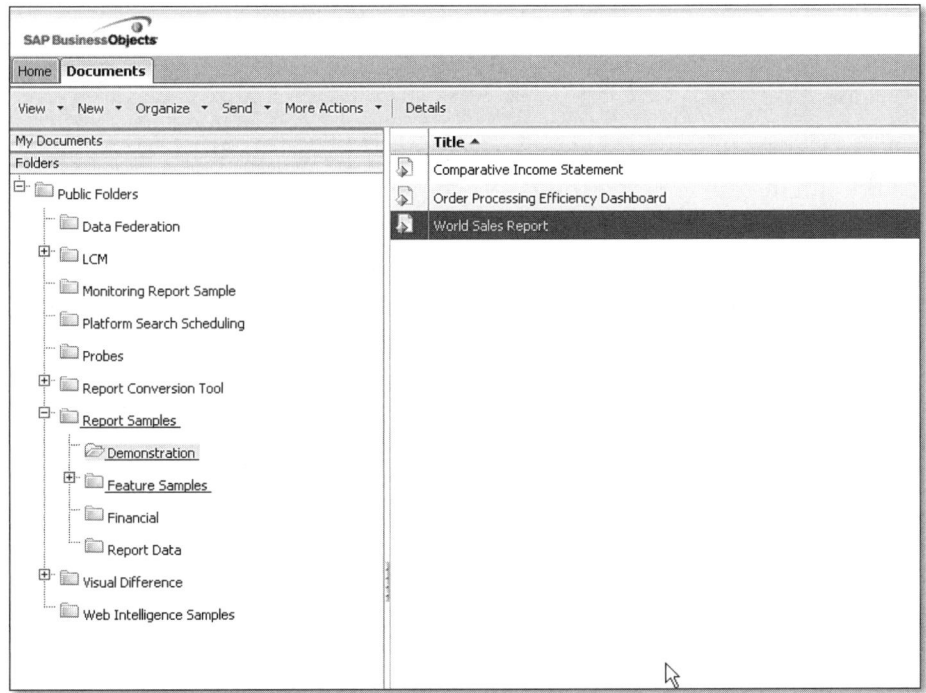

Figure 12.7 Folders

4. Navigate to the folder for the objects you created so far in the previous chapters.
5. Right-click on the SAP CRYSTAL REPORTS FOR ENTERPRISE object and select the menu item MORE ACTIONS • CATEGORIES (see Figure 12.8).

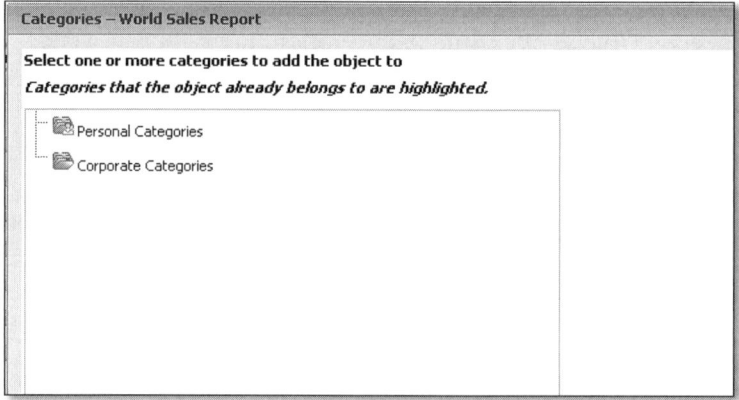

Figure 12.8 Categories

6. You can now assign the report to a category.
7. Click on OK.

After you assign the report to the category, the report is available in the folder structure and the category structure.

12.4 Using Search in the BI Launch Pad

As part of your SAP BusinessObjects BI platform 4.x, you can enable search capabilities, allowing you to search in the BI launch pad. This enables you to search content within the SAP BusinessObjects BI platform repository. It refines the search results by grouping them into categories and ranking them in order of their relevance.

You can search for SAP BusinessObjects BI platform content and SAP BusinessObjects Explorer content. In addition, you will receive a suggestion to create a new document if the search cannot find an existing document.

To configure the search application properties, complete the following steps:

1. Start the CMC via the menu START • PROGRAMS • SAP BUSINESSOBJECTS BI PLATFORM 4 • SAP BUSINESSOBJECTS BI PLATFORM • SAP BUSINESSOBJECTS BI PLATFORM CENTRAL MANAGEMENT CONSOLE.
2. Log on to the CMC with a set of administrative credentials.
3. Navigate to the APPLICATIONS area (see Figure 12.9).

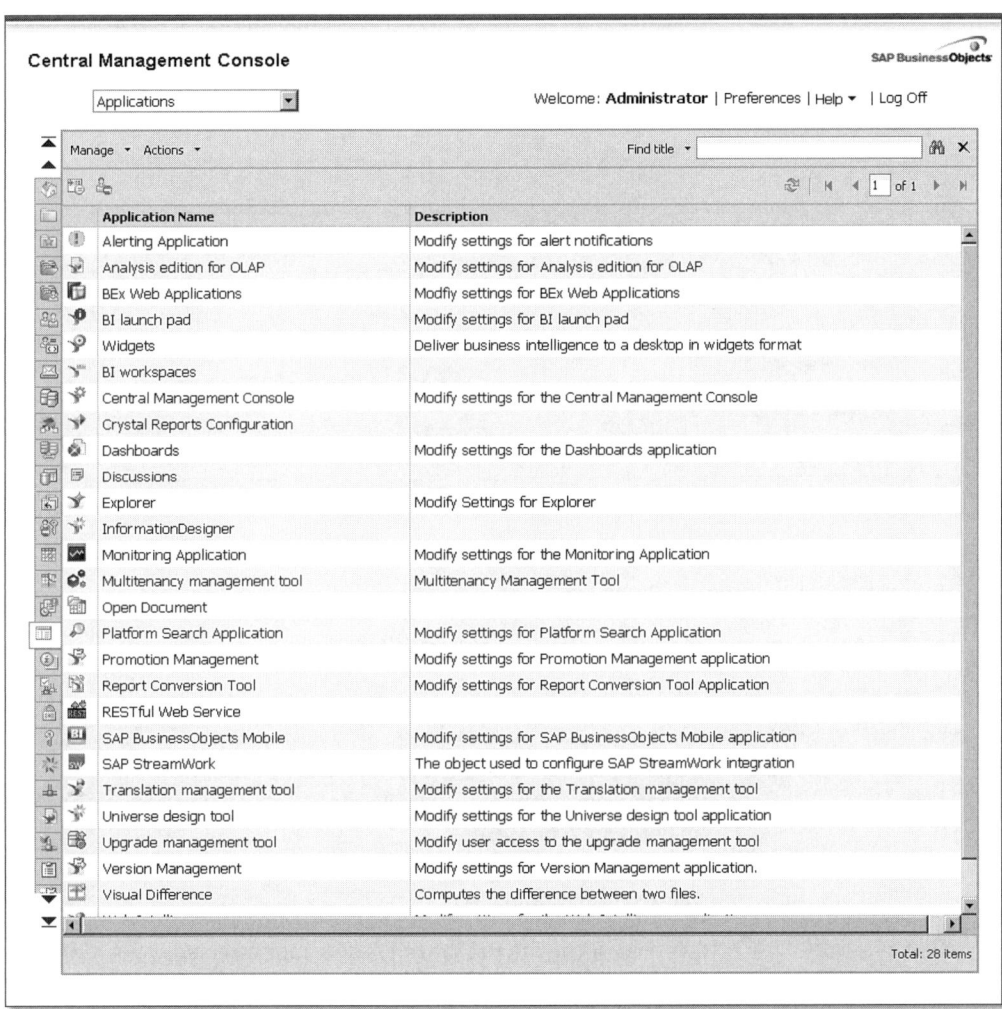

Figure 12.9 Applications

4. Double-click on the PLATFORM SEARCH APPLICATION entry (see Figure 12.10).

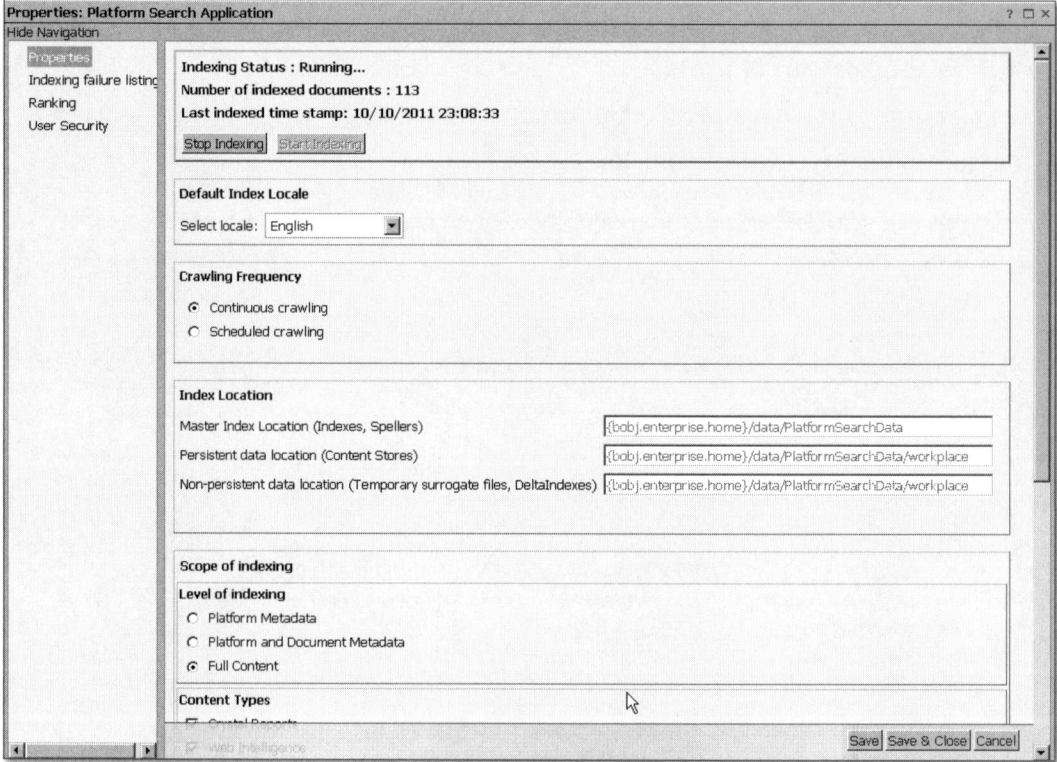

Figure 12.10 Platform Search Properties

5. Configure the settings according to Table 12.2:

Option	Description
Stop/start indexing	You can start or stop the indexing process when you want to switch from continuous crawling to schedule crawling, or for maintenance purposes. To stop indexing, click on STOP INDEXING and then click on OK in the confirmation dialog box.
Index locale	When you change the index locale to another language, PLATFORM SEARCH re-indexes the documents in the selected language.

Table 12.2 Indexing Properties

Option	Description
Index locale (Cont.)	Set the index locale to one of the following languages: Brazilian, Chinese, Czech, Danish, Dutch, English, Finnish, French, German, Italian, Japanese, Korean, Norwegian Bokmal, Polish, Portuguese, Russian, Spanish, Swedish, or Thai. By default, English is selected as the index locale.
Crawling frequency	You can index the entire SAP BusinessObjects BI platform repository by using the following options: ▶ CONTINUOUS CRAWLING: With this option, indexing is continuous where the repository is indexed whenever an object is added, modified, or deleted. It allows you to view or work with the most up-to-date content. Set by default, the continuous crawling updates the SAP BusinessObjects BI platform repository continuously with the actions that you perform. Continuous crawling works without a user's intervention and reduces the time spent indexing a document. ▶ SCHEDULED CRAWLING: With this option, indexing is based on the schedule set by the schedule options.
Index location	When the documents are indexed, they are stored in shared folders in the following locations: ▶ MASTER INDEX LOCATION: The master and speller indexes stored in this location. During a search workflow, initial hits are retrieved using the master index, and the speller indexes are used to retrieve suggestions. In a clustered deployment, this location should be on a shared file system that is accessible from all nodes in the cluster. ▶ PERSISTENT DATA LOCATION: The content store is placed in this location. It is created from the master index location and remains in sync with it. The content store is used to generate facets and process the initial hits generated from the master index location. In a clustered deployment, content stores are generated at every node.
Level of indexing	You can tune the search content by setting the level of indexing in the following ways: ▶ PLATFORM METADATA: An index is created only for the platform metadata information such as titles, keywords, and descriptions of the documents.

Table 12.2 Indexing Properties (Cont.)

Option	Description
Level of indexing (Cont.)	▶ PLATFORM AND DOCUMENT METADATA: This index includes the platform metadata as well as the document metadata. The document metadata include the creation date, modification date, and name of the author. ▶ FULL CONTENT: This index includes the platform metadata, document metadata, and other content such as: – The actual content in the document – The content of prompts and LOVs – Charts, graphs, and labels
Content types	You can select the following content types for indexing: ▶ Microsoft Word ▶ Microsoft Excel ▶ Microsoft PowerPoint ▶ Text ▶ Adobe Acrobat ▶ Rich Text ▶ SAP Crystal Reports ▶ Universe ▶ Interactive Analysis

Table 12.2 Indexing Properties (Cont.)

6. After you configured the details, click on SAVE AND CLOSE.
7. Start the BI launch pad via the menu START • PROGRAMS • SAP BUSINESSOBJECTS BI PLATFORM 4 • SAP BUSINESSOBJECTS BI PLATFORM • SAP BUSINESSOBJECTS BI PLATFORM JAVA BI LAUNCH PAD.
8. Log on with your credentials.
9. Navigate to the SEARCH panel (see Figure 12.11).
10. Enter a search term.
11. Press [Enter] on the keyboard (see Figure 12.12).

The search result is displayed along several categories, such as content type, content location, content author, and content data source. You can now navigate in the search result and display the reports.

Using Search in the BI Launch Pad | **12.4**

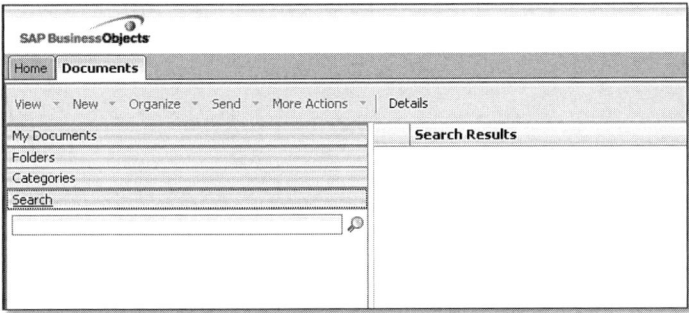

Figure 12.11 Search Panel

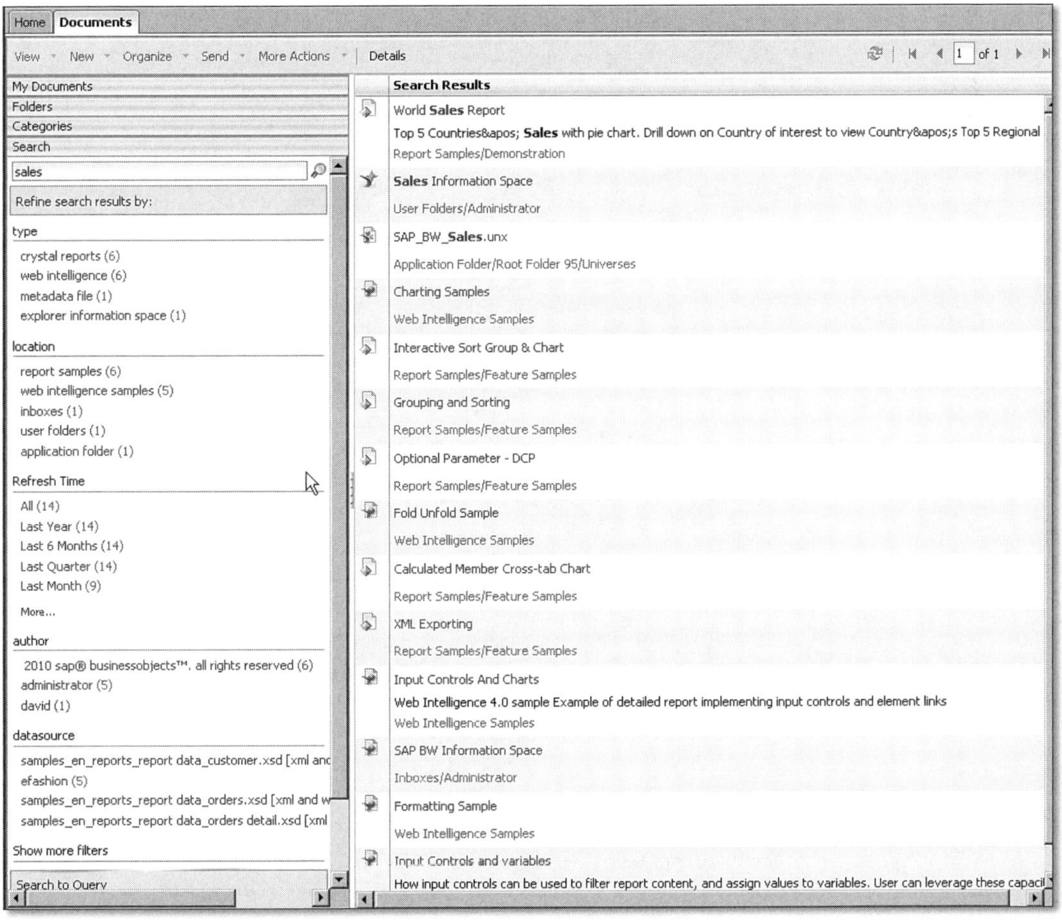

Figure 12.12 Search Result

In the next section we configure a set of preferences as part of our profile for the SAP BusinessObjects BI platform.

12.5 Configuring User Preferences

Each user has a set of preferences as part of the SAP BusinessObjects BI platform. These preferences are stored as part of the user profile and can be access and changes from the BI launch pad.

1. Start the BI LaunchPad via the menu START • PROGRAMS • SAP BUSINESSOBJECTS BI PLATFORM 4 • SAP BUSINESSOBJECTS BI PLATFORM • SAP BUSINESSOBJECTS BI PLATFORM JAVA BI LAUNCHPAD.
2. Log on with your credentials.
3. Click on PREFERENCES in the toolbar (see Figure 12.13).

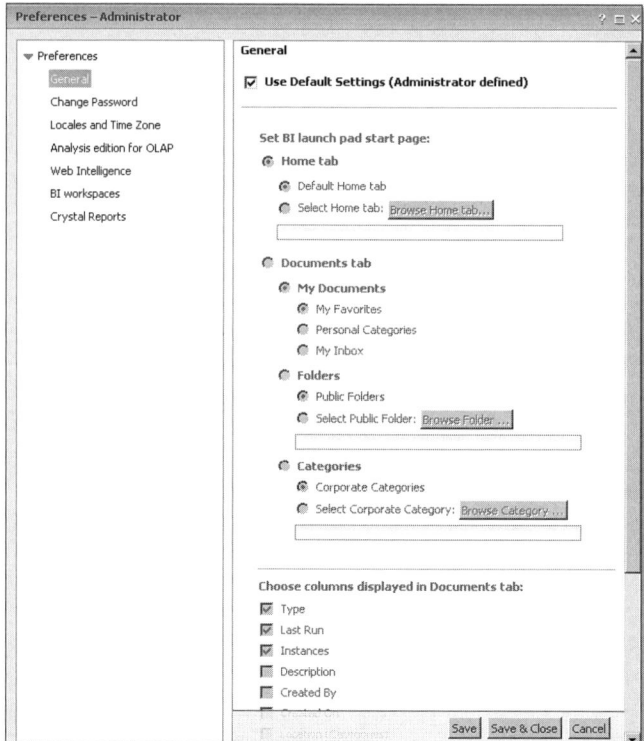

Figure 12.13 User Preferences

In the GENERAL area, you can define the initial view and content of the HOME tab, or you can configure the DOCUMENTS area to be displayed after logon. In addition, the user can specify the details that are presented for each document and whether the document will be opened as a tab or as separate window.

In the CHANGE PASSWORD (see Figure 12.14) area, the user is able to change his password. Please note that this password change is only valid for true SAP BusinessObjects BI platform accounts, not for user credentials such as SAP credentials imported via SAP authentication.

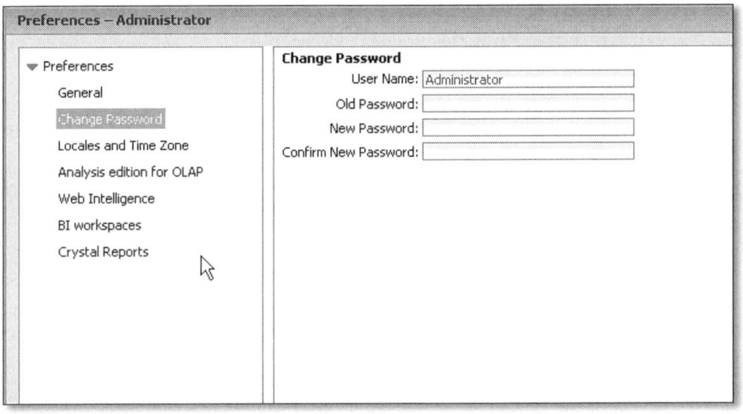

Figure 12.14 Change Password

In the area LOCALES AND TIME ZONE (see Figure 12.15), the user can configure the PRODUCT LOCALE, the PREFERRED VIEWING LOCALE, and the TIME ZONE.

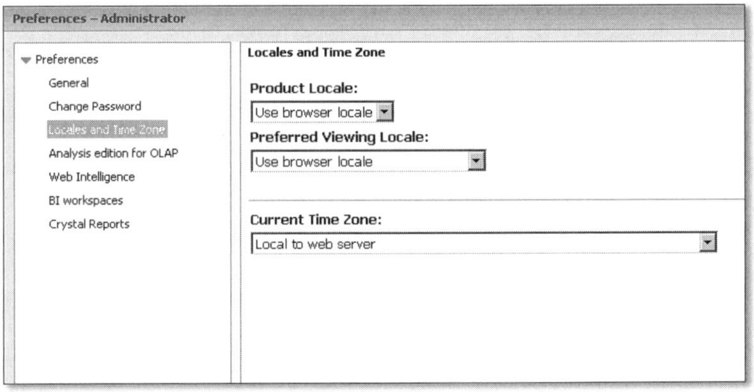

Figure 12.15 Locales and Time Zone

The PRODUCT LOCALE decides the language that is used by the BI launch pad.

The PREFERRED VIEWING LOCALE (PVL) configures how dates, times, and numbers are formatted. For multilingual objects, the PVL also sets the language used to display the object's name and description. In regard to your SAP data connection, the PVL acts as a logon language for the SAP system, and, in that way, decides the language for any multi-lingual object that is part of the result set.

The CURRENT TIME ZONE is by default configured to use the time zone from the web server. However, users log on to the Central Management Server, which might use a different time zone. It is important to set the correct time zone so that any scheduling job reflects the correct time.

If you would like to use a screen reader, you can activate the ACCESSIBILITY MODE for SAP BusinessObjects Analysis, edition for OLAP (see Figure 12.16).

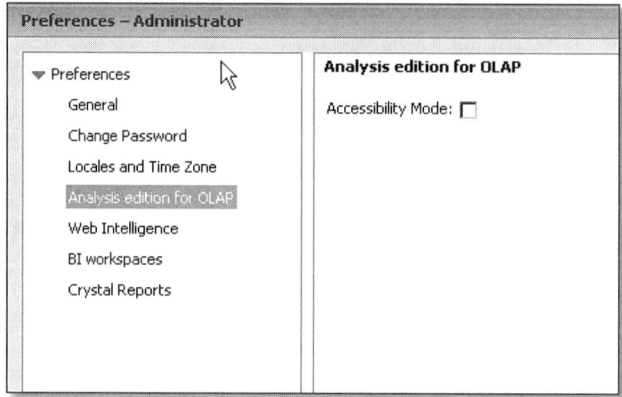

Figure 12.16 SAP BusinessObjects Analysis, Edition for OLAP—Preferences

As part of the SAP BusinessObjects Web Intelligence PREFERENCES (see Figure 12.17), you can choose the interface that is used for viewing an SAP BusinessObjects Web Intelligence report (see Table 12.3) and modifying an SAP BusinessObjects Web Intelligence report (see Table 12.4).

12.5 Configuring User Preferences

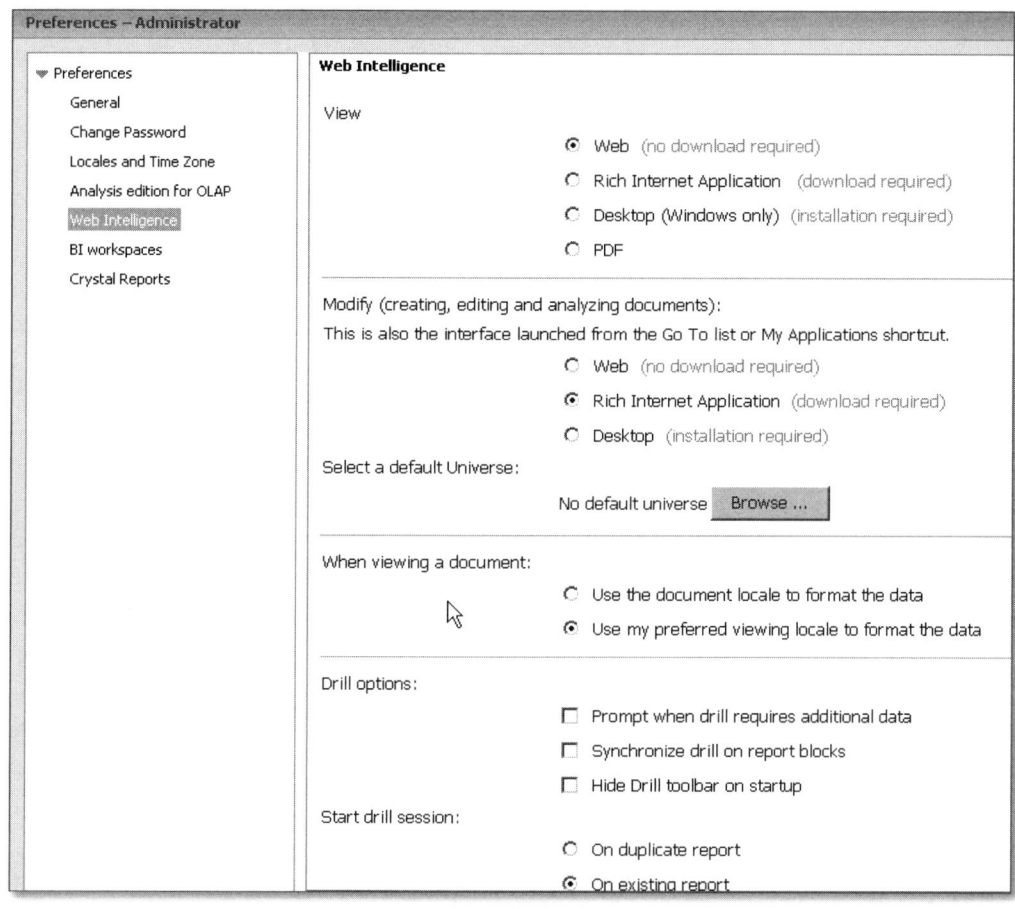

Figure 12.17 SAP BusinessObjects Web Intelligence Preferences

Interface	Description
Web	Lets you view documents online without downloading any components.
Rich Internet application	Installs and runs a Java applet that lets you view documents.
Desktop	Requires you to install the SAP BusinessObjects Web Intelligence rich client on your desktop.
PDF	Lets you view the document as a PDF.

Table 12.3 SAP BusinessObjects Web Intelligence Viewing Interfaces

465

Interface	Description
Web	Lets you create and modify documents without downloading any components.
Rich Internet application	Installs and runs a Java applet that lets you view documents.
Desktop	Requires you to install the SAP BusinessObjects Web Intelligence rich client on your desktop.

Table 12.4 SAP BusinessObjects Web Intelligence Modifying Interfaces

In addition, you can define a default universe and specify which local setting will be used to format SAP BusinessObjects Web Intelligence reports. You can also configure the behavior of SAP BusinessObjects Web Intelligence for the drill mode. You can configure the option to be prompted each time a drill operation requires an additional query for data. You can also configure the option to synchronize all blocks of your SAP BusinessObjects Web Intelligence report as part of the drill. If the SYNCHRONIZE DRILL ON REPORT BLOCKS is not activated, only the report component that you used to drill will show the detailed information. All other blocks will show the original data. For example, you could drill in a table, but the chart will not show the drilled down information. You can also decide whether the drill operation should start a new report or you would like to modify an existing report.

For BI workspaces, you can select a default style (see Figure 12.18) for newly created pages.

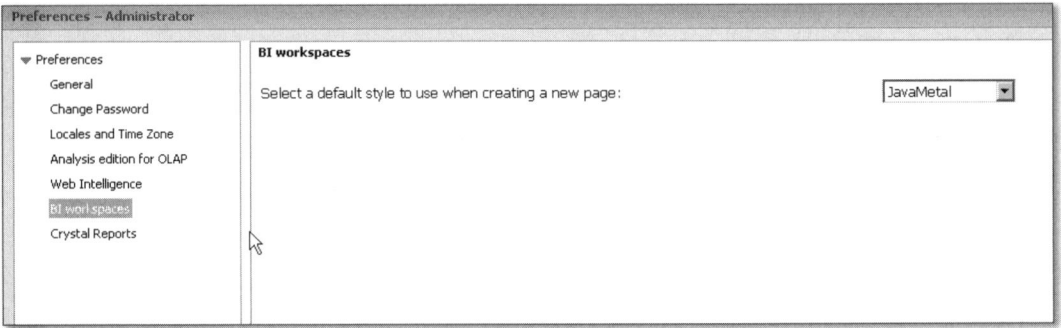

Figure 12.18 BI Workspaces Preferences

For SAP Crystal Reports, you can configure the default viewing format and the default printing control (see Figure 12.19). In addition, a default resolution and the default measuring unit can be set. Note that Web ActiveX and Web Java viewers cannot be used to view reports created in SAP Crystal Reports for Enterprise; for this, you need to configure the web viewer.

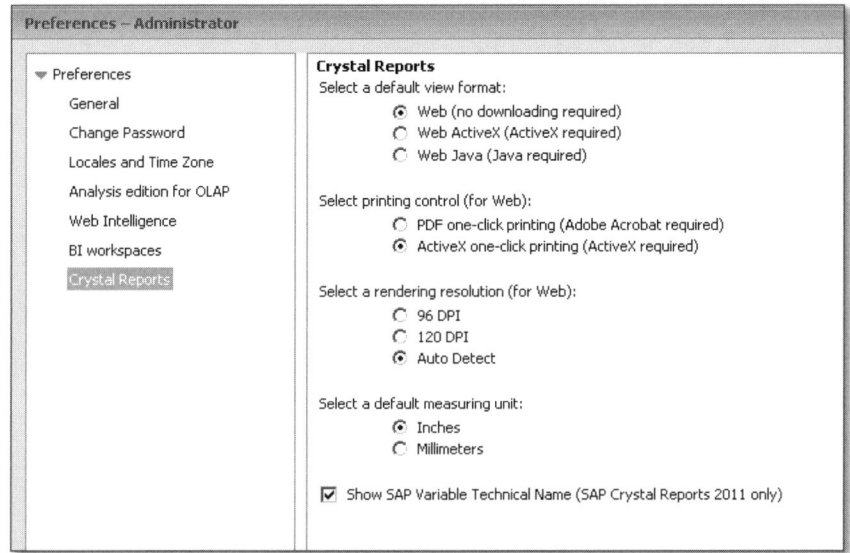

Figure 12.19 SAP Crystal Report—Preferences

In this section we reviewed the preferences as part of your user profile in the SAP BusinessObjects BI platform.

12.6 Summary

In this chapter you learned about the basic workflows in the BI launch pad, the different areas available in the BI launch pad, and how you can configure personal preferences. In the next chapter we review a set of best practices for integrating SAP BusinessObjects BI with SAP systems.

In this chapter we look at a set of best practices and tips and tricks for using SAP BusinessObjects BI tools in combination with SAP NetWeaver.

13   Best Practices and Tips and Tricks for SAP BusinessObjects BI Tools

This chapter discusses best practices, tips and tricks, and known limitations for areas such as data connectivity, BEx query design, security, performance, and several other topics. These best practices will help you use the SAP BusinessObjects BI tools as efficiently as possible and avoid some common pitfalls. Please note that any of the statements about the SAP BusinessObjects BI products in this chapter are made based on SAP BusinessObjects 4.0 FP3, and that some of the limitations will be addressed in future versions of the product. Recommendations on BEx query design and tracing are generic and are also applicable to future releases.

13.1   Selection of the Right Tool

Before we go into the details of the best practice approach, we should highlight that the most important part of your overall project approach is proper selection of tools. You should take the time to understand the consumers' requirements, their needs, and also their skill levels, and you should select the right tool based on that information. Gathering and fully understanding the requirements is very crucial for your project. Try to speak directly to the consumers of the information as much as possible and let them describe their needs, their day-to-day workflows, and how they plan to use the information. Understanding these things is essential to the success of the project.

For example, if a financial controller describes the information he needs every day, you could easily provide this information with SAP Crystal Reports or SAP BusinessObjects Web Intelligence. However, if the financial controller then continues to explain that he needs the information as part of his monthly planning and that he always exports the data from the report to a Microsoft Excel spreadsheet, your solution could now become SAP BusinessObjects Analysis, edition for Microsoft Office, which offers the consumer a Microsoft Excel-based experience with the capability to analyze data and to conduct actual planning sessions.

You can apply as much of a technical best practice approach as possible in the project, but if the initial step—gathering and understanding the consumer requirements—and the second important step—mapping those requirements to the BI products—are not done thoroughly, the project is likely to fail because end-user expectations will not be met.

Please keep this in mind when applying these best practices and refer back to Chapter 2, where we provided a detailed discussion of customer requirements and how to map the tools to these requirements.

13.2 SAP NetWeaver BEx Query Design

In this section we focus on topics concerning the SAP NetWeaver BEx query and how the properties and settings in the BEx query will influence the behavior in SAP BusinessObjects BI tools.

13.2.1 Relationship: BEx Query and Report

In the past, most customers had a one-to-one relationship (or close to it) between a BEx query and a report. In this case, a one-to-one relationship means that you are using a BEx query for a single BEx Analyzer workbook or BEx Web Analyzer report. Such situations lead to lot of administrative overhead, but given the SAP BusinessObjects BI solution, you can now improve this situation dramatically.

The BI tools are able to explicitly select only those elements from the BEx query that are required for the individual report; therefore, there is no need for a one-to-one relationship between a BEx query and a report created with the SAP BusinessObjects BI tools.

On the other hand, this does not mean that you should now create a single BEx query on top of each InfoProvider and use this single BEx query for all your reporting needs. The impact of such a large BEx query in terms of performance has been improved, but you'll still recognize a difference in performance between such a large BEx query that surfaces all the characteristics from the underlying InfoProvider and a more dedicated BEx query. Therefore, it is recommended that you create BEx queries that represent the common denominator for a certain departmental or business area. You should try to break down the requirements of your SAP NetWeaver BW environment into groups of characteristics and key figures having a high degree of commonality but also representing a manageable number of BEx queries. If you're not sure whether the BEx queries that you create are becoming too large in terms of number of elements, you can easily use the available tools to trace the runtime of your BEx queries and then take the necessary steps to make the required changes.

> **SAP NetWeaver BW 7.3**
>
> As part of SAP NetWeaver BW 7.3, the above behavior inside SAP NetWeaver BW has changed and the impact of such a very large BEx query with a large number of free characteristics has been addressed. Overall performance has been improved for such scenarios for all of the SAP BusinessObjects BI client tools.

13.2.2 Elements of an SAP NetWeaver BEx Query

A BEx query can contain elements in the following sections (see Figure 13.1):

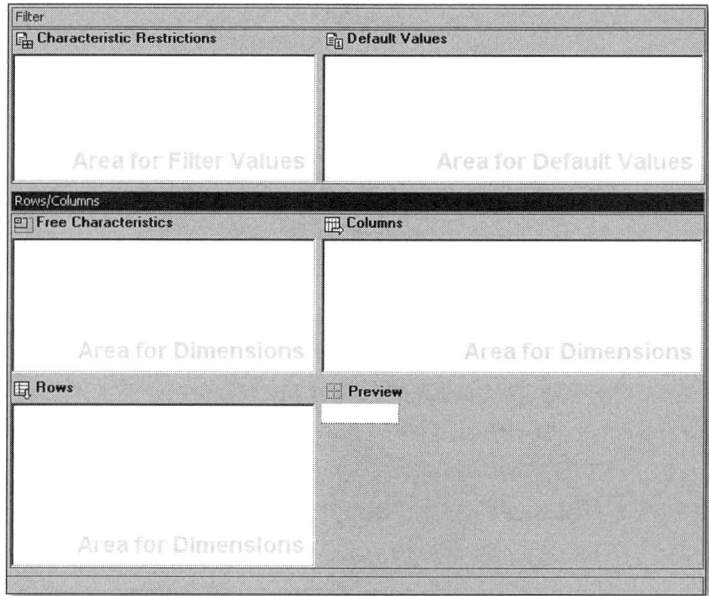

Figure 13.1 SAP NetWeaver BEx Query Designer

- Rows
- Columns
- Free characteristics
- Filter/characteristic restrictions
- Default values

When you use a SAP NetWeaver BEx query in combination with the SAP BusinessObjects BI tools, you can apply the following generic rules (unless we mentioned exceptions in previous chapters):

- All elements in the rows and columns will be available for reporting in the SAP BusinessObjects BI tools.
- All elements in the free characteristics will be available for reporting in the SAP BusinessObjects BI tools.
- Filters configured in the filter/characteristic restrictions area using a fixed list of values will get applied to the data retrieval but the actual filter values are not available for the report designer or the consumer (exception: SAP BusinessObjects Analysis, edition for Microsoft Office).
- Elements specified in the default values area will only be used by SAP BusinessObjects Analysis, edition for Microsoft Office and SAP BusinessObjects Analysis, edition for OLAP. If you are using any of the other BI clients, the values from the defaults area will be ignored. Please note that default values specified for variables are available and will be shown to the consumer.
- Custom structures defined in the BEx query are available to the report designer and consumer, and the report designer or consumer is able to retrieve a complete list of members for the structure and to select all or a subset of the elements for the reporting.
- Conditions defined in the SAP NetWeaver BEx query are only supported by SAP BusinessObjects Analysis, edition for OLAP and SAP BusinessObjects Analysis, edition for Microsoft; all other SAP BusinessObjects BI client tools will remove the condition from the BEx query at runtime and, as a consequence, receive all data from the BEx query.
- Exceptions defined in the SAP NetWeaver BEx query are transferred only to the SAP BusinessObjects Analysis, edition for Microsoft Office.
- BEx queries need to be configured with the property ALLOW EXTERNAL ACCESS in the BEx query designer, so that the SAP BusinessObjects tools can leverage it.

13.2.3 Using Variables in a BE Query

In regard to the use of variables in the SAP NetWeaver BEx query, you should consider the following:

- Variables need to be configured with the property READY FOR INPUT to be considered by any SAP BusinessObjects BI tool as a prompt.
- The selection option variable type—which provides the user with the functionality to select an operator and the functionality to decide whether to include or to exclude the values—is supported fully only by SAP BusinessObjects Analysis, edition for Microsoft Office and SAP BusienssObjects Analysis, edition for OLAP. The other SAP BusinessObjects BI tools will try to map it as closely as possible. For example, SAP Crystal Reports for Enterprise and SAP BusinessObjects Web Intelligence will provide a range value prompt in such a case.
- Text variables in a BEx query influence the description of the elements in the BEx query and therefore influence the metadata that are important for the SAP BusinessObjects BI tools. In the SAP BusinessObjects 4.0 FP3 release, text variables are supported by all BI clients.
- EXIT variables and authorization variables are fully supported by the SAP BusinessObjects BI tools.
- Especially the functionality of EXIT variables and the functionality to filter the data in the BEx query based on the system date—for example, showing the last 12 months—is something that you will only be able to do via EXIT variables in the BEx query.

13.2.4 Display Relevant Settings

The SAP NetWeaver BEx query offers several display relevant settings in the BEx query designer. In Figure 13.2, you can see the display settings for a characteristic; in Figure 13.3, you can see the display settings for a key figure.

These settings are relevant for the display of the object, and are mostly used by the SAP BusinessObjects BI 4.x tools. The most important exception for the display settings, which is not supported, is the local calculation. In a local calculation, you are able to configure how the result of a key figure is calculated; for example, instead of showing the actual numeric value, you are able to show the overall ranking of the value as part of the result.

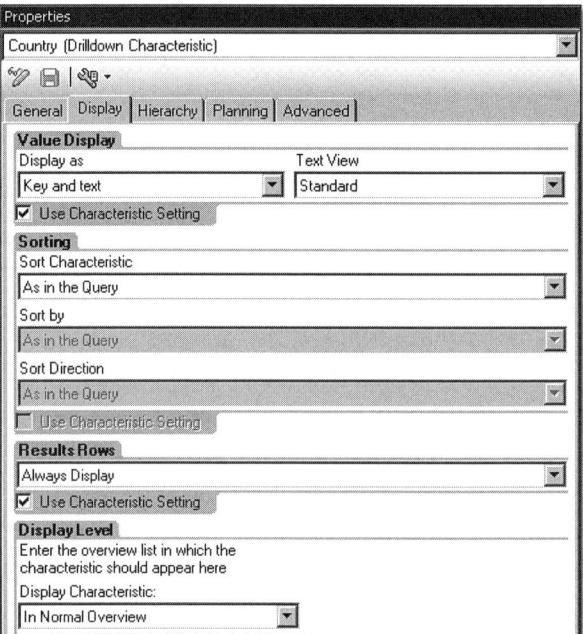

Figure 13.2 Display Settings for Characteristic

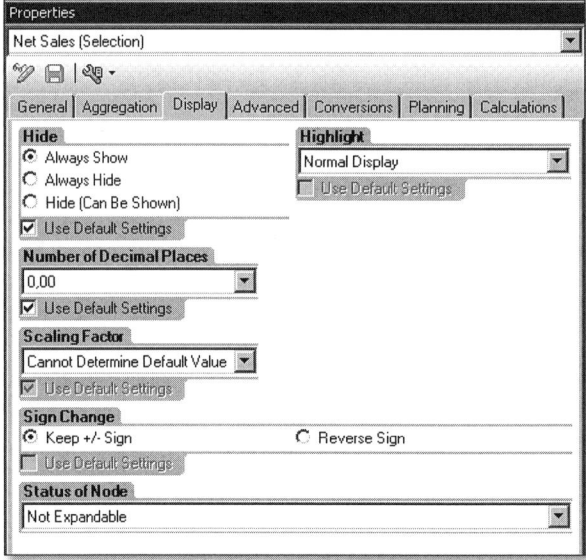

Figure 13.3 Display Settings for a Key Figure

This configuration as part of the BEx query is, as of October 2011, supported only by SAP BusinessObjects Analysis, edition for Microsoft Office and SAP BusinessObjects Analysis, edition for OLAP.

Overall, the below points outline the support for display settings:

- SAP Crystal Reports for Enterprise; SAP BusinessObjects Web Intelligence; SAP BusinessObjects Analysis, edition for OLAP; and SAP BusinessObjects Dashboards (formerly Xcelsius) use the configured scaling factor in release 4.0 but do not show the scaling factor to the report developer. This issue is addressed in the first major update (4.0 feature pack 03) of the release.
- SAP Crystal Reports for Enterprise, SAP BusinessObjects Web Intelligence, and SAP BusinessObjects Dashboards do not use the setting for the number of decimals.
- SAP Crystal Reports for Enterprise, SAP BusinessObjects Web Intelligence, and SAP BusinessObjects Dashboards do not use the setting DISPLAY AS HIERARCHY from the BEx query. This setting is used by SAP BusinessObjects Analysis, edition for Microsoft Office and SAP BusinessObjects Analysis, edition for OLAP.
- SAP Crystal Reports for Enterprise, SAP BusinessObjects Web Intelligence, and SAP BusinessObjects Dashboards will not list key figures that have been configured with a local calculation. There is no need to change the BEx query itself, as the key figure is simply removed from the list of available objects. SAP BusinessObjects Analysis, edition for Microsoft Office and SAP BusinessObjects Analysis, edition for OLAP do fully support key figures with a local calculation configured.

In this section we reviewed several areas that are important as part of the BEx query design when using SAP BusinessObjects BI in combination with SAP NetWeaver BW. In the next section we review the options for establishing connections to your SAP NetWeaver system.

13.3 Data Connectivity

In this section we look at some best practices regarding the management of the connections to your SAP system. In general, the recommendation is to use the BEx query as the entry point to the SAP NetWeaver BW system for data connectivity. The points listed below show the advantages and disadvantages of this direct access to the BEx queries.

Advantages of direct access to SAP NetWeaver BW:

- Re-use of existing BEx queries.
- Shared connectivity across all BI client tools.
- Provides true hierarchical metadata and data.
- Allows for a single connection to point to multiple BEx queries.
- Supports advanced BEx query elements, such as restricted and calculated key figures, formulas, and custom structures.

Compared to the previous available option in the XI 3.1 release, where you were able to create an OLAP universe on top of a BEx query, here are some of the disadvantages for the direct connectivity to SAP NetWeaver BW:

- Does not allow for customizations of the metadata.
- Does not allow for the creation of custom objects.
- Does not allow for administrative limits such as a connection timeout on the SAP BusinessObjects stack.
- Does not allow for the creation of universe-based parameters. All parameters need either to be based on variables in the BEx query or to be created as parameters on a report level.

Even though direct connectivity does have the limitations as outlined above, the recommendation is to use the BEx query as the entry point to your SAP NetWeaver BW system, as it provides the richest metadata.

In SAP BusinessObjects 4.x, you are able to configure OLAP connections pointing to your SAP NetWeaver BW system in the Central Management Console (CMC). You are able to define OLAP connections pointing to your SAP NetWeaver BW system, to a specific InfoProvider, or to a specific BEx query. Depending on the level at which you define the OLAP connection, the user will always have the option to select a BEx query for reporting purposes, so you simply define the entry level for the selection that the user will see.

So if you are setting up the connection pointing to your SAP NetWeaver BW system only, without selecting an InfoProvider or BEx query, the user will receive a list of all InfoProviders and can select a BEx query from any of the available InfoProviders. If you configure the connection to point to an InfoProvider, the user will retrieve only the queries for the preconfigured InfoProvider. If you select a

BEx query as part of the connection, the user will see only the configured BEx query.

In addition to these options, you want to make sure that all your connections toward your SAP system are configured to use single sign-on as authentication option so that all authorizations configured also apply.

As an alternative to direct access to the BEx Query, you can create a relational universe on top of the SAP NetWeaver BW InfoProvider, but this connectivity option also has some advantages and disadvantages.

In addition to direct access to the SAP NetWeaver BW system, the semantic layer also provides you with the option to create a relational or multisource universe on top of SAP NetWeaver BW. The relational interface on top of SAP NetWeaver BW provides you with the option to create a universe on top of the SAP NetWeaver BW system and also to combine data coming from SAP NetWeaver BW with other data source using a multisource universe.

Some of the advantages of the relational access to SAP NetWeaver BW are:

- Direct access to InfoProvider level.
- Allows the combination of multiple data sources into a single logical view.
- Allows for customization of metadata.
- Allows for creation of custom objects.

Some of the disadvantages of the relational access to SAP NetWeaver BW are:

- No support for external SAP NetWeaver BW hierarchies.
- No support for restricted and calculated key figures.
- No support for custom structures.
- No support for SAP variables.

As you can see, the relational data connectivity to SAP NetWeaver BW provides you with the pure star schema and does have several major limitations.

Overall, SAP BusinessObjects 4.x provides you with the necessary flexibility to decide how many connections you would like to set up toward your SAP NetWeaver BW system. Technically speaking, it could just be one connection, but that would lead to a situation where report developers will have to select the BEx query from a possibly long list of InfoProviders and BEx queries.

13.4 User Security

In regard to data-level security for SAP BusinessObjects BI tools when using SAP NetWeaver BW as a data source, the recommendations are very simple. In such a scenario, the recommendation is to use the SAP NetWeaver BI authorizations simply because the level of complexity that you are able to configure as part of the BI authorizations cannot be achieved in the SAP BusinessObjects BI environment. In addition, remember that as part of the SAP BusinessObjects BI 4.x recommended data connectivity—connecting directly to the BEx queries—there is no universe layer involved and therefore the only central place to set up data-level security is your SAP NetWeaver BW system using BI authorizations.

For data-level security when connecting to the SAP ERP system, you can leverage the Security Definition Editor as part of the integration with SAP Crystal Reports 2011, which allows you to define row and column level security on top of the tables in your ERP system. If you are considering leveraging the semantic layer in the form of universes on top of your SAP ERP system, you can then set up the data-level security in the universe.

For connectivity toward classic InfoSets in the ERP system, the recommendation is to set up the security in the ERP system already as part of the InfoSet and to leverage the security by using SSO for the SAP BusinessObjects tools.

For cases where it is required that you broadcast a report to a larger audience but still keep the security intact, or in a situation where you would like to pre-calculate the report and create an offline version of the report while keeping the security intact, it is recommended that you use the publications functionality on the SAP BusinessObjects BI platform backend. You can establish server-side-based trust between your SAP BusinessObjects BI platform and your SAP system (for example, based on the SAP Cryptographic Library). In this way, you can set up a password-less publication process that is able to create an instance of the report per user (multi-pass bursting).

> **Integrating SAP BusinessObjects 4.x with SAP NetWeaver**
> A complete discussion of the installation and deployment of the SAP BusinessObjects 4.x release in combination with your SAP landscape can be found in *Integrating SAP BusinessObjects BI Platform 4.x with SAP NetWeaver* (SAP PRESS, 2012).

13.5 Performance Considerations

The following is a list of recommendations regarding performance:

- Several significant performance enhancements have been made since the acquisition of SAP BusinessObjects by SAP. These performance enhancements have been incorporated into the following release: SAP NetWeaver BW 7.0 enhancement package 01 (7.01) SP05 and higher. In order to take advantage of these performance improvements, it is strongly recommended that you move to at least this release for your reporting and analysis landscape.
- As part of SAP NetWeaver BW 7.3, enhancements have been made that reduce the impact of having a huge number of free characteristics in the BEx query to provide greater flexibility for reporting and analysis. If this is an important requirement for you, you might consider upgrading to SAP NetWeaver BW 7.3.
- All SAP NetWeaver BW performance-tuning topics are still valid and relevant for integration with the SAP BusinessObjects BI tools. Topics such as setting up aggregates and creating database indexes are all still important for your performance.
- Use your SAP NetWeaver BW statistics to identify the most used but also the slowest-performing SAP NetWeaver BW queries and to identify the reasons for the performance results.
- Use Transaction ST03 to evaluate the need for aggregation of the BEx queries that you use for reporting. Pay particular attention to the overall time spent on the database and the ratio between the database selected records and the transferred records. An indicator of missing aggregates would be a ratio higher than 10 for the records and a 30% or higher database time compared to the overall time.
- In regard to setting up aggregates on the SAP NetWeaver BW side, you need to ensure that you match the aggregates to the data request from the reporting tool, which is different for each tool:
  - In SAP Crystal Reports for Enterprise, the request will include elements specified as part of the query panel used for selecting the objects from the BEx query.
  - In SAP BusinessObjects Web Intelligence, the request can be based on the elements that have been included in the SAP BusinessObjects Web Intelligence

query panel or elements that have been used in the report. If you activated query stripping, then the objects used in the report will be used; otherwise, the objects in the query panel will be used.

- In SAP BusinessObjects Dashboards using the direct connectivity toward BEx queries hosted by the SAP BusinessObjects BI platform, the objects used in the query panel are used for data retrieval.

▶ In regard to the BEx query, you should enable the setting USE SELECTION OF STRUCTURE MEMBERS, which can be enabled with Transaction RSRT as part of the query properties (see Figure 13.4).

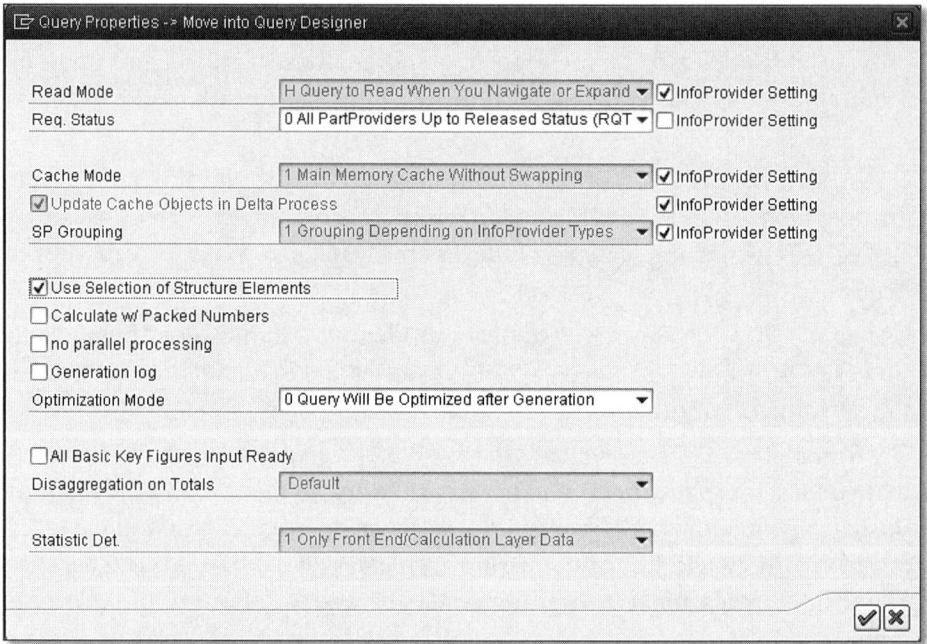

Figure 13.4 Query Properties

▶ When offering filtering of the data retrieval for the consumer, it is strongly recommended that you leverage variables in the BEx query as much as possible. This will ensure an online retrieved list of values and server side filtering.

▶ When defining selections or filters in the BEx query, make sure you use the option to include values instead of excluding values as much as possible. This is because the exclusion of values is not able to access the database indices, which will result in a lower performance.

- Restricted key figures and calculated key figures should be, as much as possible, built as part of the BEx query and not as part of the report itself to ensure the best possible processing and performance.
- In cases where it is required to provide several hierarchies as options for the consumer of the report, you should consider using a hierarchy variable. A hierarchy variable allows the user to select one of the available hierarchies. If designed as an optional variable, the consumer of the report is even able to view a non-hierarchical report by not selecting a value from the list of hierarchies.
- In cases where you require detailed information in combination with highly aggregated data, you might want to consider the functionality to link from one report to another report (for example, SAP BusinessObjects Dashboards to SAP BusinessObjects Web Intelligence) and pass the context between these reports.
- You should also pay attention to the SAP system and the number of connections being leveraged at the same time. If you offer the reporting and analysis tools to a large audience, you need to ensure that the number of possible dialog users is configured appropriately.

In regard to the overall sizing of your SAP NetWeaver BW system or your SAP BusinessObjects landscape, we strongly recommend that you engage with the field services organization from SAP and consider a sizing workshop where you can receive detailed information on the important factors for sizing your landscape. A complete sizing guideline would go far beyond the scope of this book. In addition, we recommend that you consider a staged approach and that you use all available monitoring tools, such as the SAP NetWeaver BW statistics and auditing functionality on the SAP BusinessObjects system, to gain as much information as possible and to ensure a properly sized landscape.

13.6 Known Limitations

In this section, we list all known limitations based on the SAP BusinessObjects BI 4.0 service pack 02 and SAP BusinessObjects BI 4.0 feature pack 03. The list of limitations has been created at the point of writing this book (November 2011); thus, some of these limitations may already have been addressed in subsequent releases.

- **SAP Crystal Reports 2011**
    - The BW MDX driver is not capable of passing values from manually created filters or manually created parameters in SAP Crystal Reports 2011 as actual WHERE clauses to the underlying SAP NetWeaver BW system. This means that those situations will result in client-side filtering. Therefore, it is recommended that, in such situations, you use variables in the BEx.
    - When using the menu FILE • NEW TO create a new report using the SAP NetWeaver BW MDX Driver, any list of values for a parameter will be empty and will need to be manually uploaded with values. This is only true in the SAP Crystal Reports 2011 Designer; the list of values will be retrieved online from the SAP NetWeaver BW system in BI launch pad after the report has been published to the SAP BusinessObjects system.
    - An online list of values is available only for the SAP NetWeaver BW MDX Driver and not for any of the ERP connectivity for SAP Crystal Reports 2011.
    - A hierarchy node variable is shown as a flat list in the SAP Crystal Reports 2011 Designer, but it is shown as a hierarchical tree in the BI launch pad after the report has been published to SAP BusinessObjects.
    - SAP Crystal Reports 2011 does not support a hierarchy version variable.
    - A selection option variable is turned into a complex parameter in SAP Crystal Reports 2011, offering single, multi-single, and range values as input options, but not the option to set an operator or the option to select between include or exclude.
    - A custom structure is represented in SAP Crystal Reports 2011 as a single field, and each element of the structure is delivered as a row in the data set. The report designer does not have access to the technical names of each structure element.
    - Only a single key date variable is supported. In cases where the BEx query contains more than one key date variable, SAP Crystal Reports 2011 leverages only one key date variable and ignores the additional variables. It is recommended that you use one key date variable defined as part of the global BEx query properties.
    - In cases of a hierarchy and hierarchy node variable combination, the list of available hierarchy nodes in the SAP Crystal Reports 2011 Designer is retrieved only for the first hierarchy. After the report has been published

to the SAP BusinessObjects system, the list of available hierarchy nodes and leaves will be retrieved online after the hierarchy has been selected.

- SAP Crystal Reports 2011 is not able to support conditions defined in the BEx query.

▶ **SAP Crystal Reports for Enterprise**

- SAP Crystal Reports for Enterprise is unable to support conditions defined in the BEx query.

- SAP Crystal Reports for Enterprise does not leverage defined exceptions in the BEx query. You can use the highlighting functionalities of SAP Crystal Reports for Enterprise to achieve the same result.

- If your BEx query contains compounded characteristics, SAP Crystal Reports for Enterprise will show the key values of the characteristics in a combined way. For example a key value for the Region characteristic compounded with the Country characteristic will be displayed as US/CA, indicating that the country is the US and the region is CA. In addition, SAP Crystal Reports for Enterprise is not able to support the cascading nature of compounded characteristics when used for prompting.

- SAP Crystal Reports for Enterprise does not leverage defaults defined in the defaults area of the BEx query.

- SAP Crystal Reports for Enterprise is not able to use key figures configured with a local calculation. If the BEx query contains a key figure with a local calculation configured, this key figure will not be shown as part of the complete list of available objects.

- SAP Crystal Reports for Enterprise supports NUMC characteristics as a string.

- SAP Crystal Reports for Enterprise supports DATS characteristics as a date for the value description and as a string for the key value.

- SAP Crystal Reports for Enterprise supports TIMS characteristics as a string value.

- In SAP BusinessObjects 4.0, SAP Crystal Reports for Enterprise supports the scaling factor of a BEx query by showing the correct scaled numeric value but does not show any information about the actual scaling factor. This issue has been addressed in release 4.0 feature pack 03.

- SAP Crystal Reports for Enterprise in release 4.0 does not provide any SAP ERP connectivity. This issue has been addressed by providing an integration of the semantic layer with SAP ERP in release 4.0 FP3.
- A selection option variable created in the BEx query will result in a range prompt in SAP Crystal Reports for Enterprise without the option to use operators or the option to include or exclude the selected values.
- SAP Crystal Reports for Enterprise is not able to filter data based on display attributes.
- SAP Crystal Reports for Enterprise does not provide access to the information available with the typical BEx text elements, such as the date and time of the last data upload to the InfoProvider.
- SAP Crystal Reports for Enterprise does not support the report-report interface with release 4.0. In 4.0 FP3, Crystal Reports for Enterprise supports the report-report interface as sender and receiver.

- **SAP BusinessObjects Web Intelligence**
  - SAP BusinessObjects Web Intelligence is unable to support conditions defined in the BEx query.
  - SAP BusinessObjects Web Intelligence does not leverage exceptions defined in the BEx query. You can use the highlighting functionalities of SAP BusinessObjects Web Intelligence to achieve the same result.
  - If your BEx query contains compounded characteristics, SAP BusinessObjects Web Intelligence will show the key values of the characteristics in a combined way. For example, a key value for the Region characteristic compounded with the Country characteristic will show as US/CA to indicate that the country is US and the region is CA. In addition, SAP BusinessObjects Web Intelligence is not able to support the cascading nature of compounded characteristics when used for prompting.
  - SAP BusinessObjects Web Intelligence does not leverage defaults defined in the defaults area of the BEx query.
  - SAP BusinessObjects Web Intelligence is not able to use key figures configured with a local calculation. If the BEx query contains a key figure with a local calculation configured, this key figure will not be shown as part of the complete list of available objects.

- SAP BusinessObjects Web Intelligence supports NUMC characteristics as a string.
- SAP BusinessObjects Web Intelligence supports DATS characteristics as a date for the value description and as a string for the key value.
- SAP BusinessObjects Web Intelligence supports TIMS characteristics as a string value.
- In SAP BusinessObjects 4.0, SAP BusinessObjects Web Intelligence supports the scaling factor of a BEx query by showing the correct scaled numeric value but does not show any information about the actual scaling factor. This issue has been addressed in release 4.0 FP3.
- In release 4.0, SAP BusinessObjects Web Intelligence does not provide any SAP ERP connectivity. This issue has been addressed by providing an integration of the semantic layer with SAP ERP in release 4.0 FP3.
- A selection option variable created in the BEx query will result in a range prompt in SAP BusinessObjects Web Intelligence without the option to leverage operators or the option to include or exclude the selected values.
- SAP BusinessObjects Web Intelligence is not able to filter data based on display attributes.
- SAP BusinessObjects Web Intelligence does not provide access to the information available with the typical BEx text elements, such as the date and time of the last data upload to the InfoProvider. SAP BusinessObjects Web Intelligence does not support the report-report interface.

▶ **SAP BusinessObjects Dashboards (formerly Xcelsius)**

The following limitations are based on direct connectivity hosted as part of the SAP BusinessObjects BI platform (not as part of the SAP NetWeaver BW system).

- SAP BusinessObjects Dashboards is unable to support conditions defined in the BEx Query.
- SAP BusinessObjects Dashboards does not leverage defined exceptions in the BEx query. You can use the alerting functionalities of SAP BusinessObjects Dashboards to achieve the same result.
- If your BEx query contains compounded characteristics, SAP BusinessObjects Dashboards shows the key values of the characteristics in a combined way.

- SAP BusinessObjects Dashboards does not leverage defaults defined in the defaults area of the BEx query.
- SAP BusinessObjects Dashboards is not able to use key figures configured with a local calculation. If the BEx query contains a key figure with a local calculation configured, this key figure will not be shown as part of the complete list of available objects.
- SAP BusinessObjects Dashboards only supports single and multi-single value variables. All other variable types, like interval or selection option variables, are turned into single variables.
- A selection option variable created in the BEx query will result in a range prompt in SAP BusinessObjects Web Intelligence.
- SAP BusinessObjects Dashboards has only limited visualization capabilities for hierarchies at this point in time (November 2011).
- SAP BusinessObjects Dashboards is not able to provide a cascading integration between a hierarchy and hierarchy node variable.
- SAP BusinessObjects Dashboards is not able to filter data based on display attributes. SAP BusinessObjects Dashboards does not provide access to the information available with the typical BEx text elements, such as the date and time of the last data upload to the InfoProvider.

▶ **SAP BusinessObjects Analysis, edition for Microsoft Office**
- SAP BusinessObjects Analysis, edition for Microsoft Office supports a multi-single value variable from a BEx query, but users need to select and confirm each value individually.
- SAP BusinessObjects Analysis, edition for Microsoft Office does not support the contains pattern operator as part of a selection option variable.
- SAP BusinessObjects Analysis, edition for Microsoft Office is not able to filter data based on display attributes.
- SAP BusinessObjects Analysis, edition for Microsoft Office is not able to use the scheduling or publication functionality from the SAP BusinessObjects BI platform.

▶ **SAP BusinessObjects Analysis, edition for OLAP**
- SAP BusinessObjects Analysis, edition for OLAP does not support the contains pattern operator as part of a selection option variable.

- SAP BusinessObjects Analysis, edition for OLAP is not able to filter data based on display attributes.
- SAP BusinessObjects Analysis, edition for OLAP is not able to leverage the scheduling or publication functionality from the SAP BusinessObjects BI platform.
- SAP BusinessObjects Analysis, edition for OLAP does not reuse already defined exceptions from the BEx query.
- SAP BusinessObjects Analysis, edition for OLAP does not provide access to the information available with the typical BEx text elements, such as the date and time of the last data upload to the InfoProvider. In SAP BusinessObjects 4.0, SAP BusinessObjects Analysis, edition for OLAP supports the scaling factor of a BEx query by showing the correct scaled numeric value but does not show any information about the actual scaling factor. This issue has been addressed in release 4.0 FP3.
- SAP BusinessObjects Analysis, edition for OLAP does not support the report-report interface.

▶ **SAP BusinessObjects Explorer**

- SAP BusinessObjects Explorer supports SAP HANA, SAP BW Accelerator (BWA), Microsoft Excel spreadsheets, and universes as possible data sources. In the context of SAP landscapes, this means that your connectivity without SAP HANA or SAP BWA is limited to the functionality of creating a relational universe on top of SAP BW. The limitations of such connectivity can be reviewed in Section 13.3.

▶ **Common limitations**

The following is a list of items that are relevant for all BI client tools:

- None of the SAP BusinessObjects BI client tools delivers support for variants as part of your SAP landscape.
- None of the SAP BusinessObjects BI client tools delivers support for variable personalization as part of your SAP landscape.

In this section we reviewed the known limitations of the SAP BusinessObjects BI client tools. In the next sections, you will receive a list of report design tips and tricks.

13.7 Report Design Topics

In this section we look at some tips and tricks for report design. The topics are kept on a generic level and are applicable to most of the SAP BusinessObjects tools.

- Most of the SAP BusinessObjects BI tools in release 4.x do not offer a multi-currency functionality, which consumers might be familiar with based on their experience with BEx Analyzer or BEx web reporting. In particular, the functionality to summarize totals based on a set of different currencies is not available; therefore, it is strongly recommended that you use a single currency in the underlying BEx query. An alternative approach is to use a variable as part of the BEx query, which provides the consumer with the option to select a target currency for the report or to have multiple versions of a single key figure—one per needed currency—created in the BEx query layer.

- Hierarchies and hierarchical navigation in a report is often the reason for misunderstandings and unmet user expectations. In the previous chapters you have seen the capabilities of each tool and how each tool is able to leverage a hierarchy and the type of navigation that is possible. It is important to ensure that the consumer understands the different options for using a hierarchy and navigating along a hierarchy to make sure that you select the right tool for the reports. You can revisit Chapter 2 to review the selection of the right BI tool.

- Number formatting and date formatting is based on the preferred viewing locale for each user (unless specified differently in the previous chapters). This preferred viewing locale is available as part of the user preferences in the BI launch pad on a user-by-user base. If you are using the formatted value for a key figure, which is available as a string value in the BI tools, the formatting is based on the settings in Transaction SU3 per user. In addition, you also have the currency and unit information available as a separate field; this is the recommended approach, as the unit and currency stored in SAP NetWeaver BW can be different from your regional settings.

13.8 Tracing and Troubleshooting

The following represents a list of tools that you can leverage to trace and troubleshoot most parts of the integration between SAP NetWeaver and SAP BusinessObjects:

- You can use Transaction RSRT (Query Monitor) to execute a single BEx query, to change the properties of the BEx query, and to execute the BEx query in debug mode, including the retrieval of BW statistic values, SQL statements, and information on the usage of aggregates.
- You can use the SAP NetWeaver BW trace tool, RSTT, to create a very detailed trace for a dedicated user and to analyze this trace to the complete details on BW statistics and time spent on the BW backend.
- You can use Transaction MDXTEST to manually execute MDX statements without the involvement of any SAP BusinessObjects BI tools to either ensure that the MDX statement is correct and does retrieve data or to see the performance of the retrieved MDX statement.

13.9 Summary

In this chapter you learned about best practices and steps you should consider to ensure the best possible solutions, stability, and performance for your BI solution. We also reviewed the current known limitations of the BI tools and some report design considerations. In the next chapter we will take a glimpse at the future of the BI roadmap.

In this chapter we offer a sneak peak at some of the upcoming integration options between SAP BusinessObjects BI, SAP NetWeaver BW, and SAP ERP.

14 Integration Outlook

At the time of finishing this book (November 2011), SAP BusinessObjects 4.0 had just been released to our customers, and the next major update to the SAP BusinessObjects 4.0 release was still being worked on. In addition to the first major update for the 4.0 release, which is planned for the first half of 2012, the teams are also already working on a mid-term update for the 4.0 release. The following paragraphs outline some of the ideas that are currently being evaluated for the second major update of the 4.0 release.

> **Product Roadmap Disclaimer**
> The above descriptions of future functionality are the author's interpretation of the publically available product integration roadmap. These items are subject to change at any time without any notice, and the author does not provide any warranty with regard to these statements.

14.1 SAP Crystal Reports for Enterprise

SAP Crystal Reports for Enterprise is positioned as the new SAP Crystal Reports design environment and as a successor to SAP Crystal Reports 2008. Especially for SAP-based solutions, SAP Crystal Reports for Enterprise is the right choice for enterprise reporting. In regard to the future release, the plans include functionality that would allow the report designer to create common styles and templates. In addition, integration with the SAP BusinessObjects BI platform will be strengthened to increase the high volume printing capabilities of SAP Crystal Reports for Enterprise.

14.2 SAP BusinessObjects Dashboards

For SAP BusinessObjects Dashboards, the team is looking to improve the capabilities around alerting, scorecarding, and exception highlighting, including functionalities such as sending alerts based on defined thresholds. In addition, topics such as being able to generate offline dashboards and integrate geo-spatial information into the dashboards are part of the planning. Last but not least, the team is also looking into improving integration with SAP Solution Manager in the areas of tracing and root cause analysis.

14.3 SAP BusinessObjects Web Intelligence

For SAP BusinessObjects Web Intelligence, the focus is on even further enhancing the user experience as part of the on-premise deployment and also on enhancing the new integration of SAP BusinessObjects Web Intelligence for mobile devices. In addition, integration with SAP HANA and the capability to fully take advantage of the functionality of the underlying in-memory engine are on the roadmap.

14.4 SAP BusinessObjects Analysis Suite

The SAP BusinessObjects Analysis Suite includes SAP BusinessObjects Analysis, edition for Microsoft Office; SAP BusinessObjects Analysis, edition for OLAP; and SAP BusinessObjects Analysis, edition for Application Design. Here the teams are especially working on the first release of SAP BusinessObjects Analysis, edition for Application Design as a successor to the Web Application Designer. Topics such as support for report-report interface, support for variable variants, and variable personalization are part of the planning as well. In addition to these functional enhancements, the teams are working on enhancing integration with SAP HANA and extending the available data connectivity to other sources beyond SAP HANA and SAP NetWeaver BW.

14.5 SAP BusinessObjects Explorer

The team for SAP BusinessObjects Explorer is planning to deliver an extensive set of APIs allowing management of information spaces via SDK. In addition, the capability to integrate maps as part of visualizations, the option to add a second dimension to visualizations, and the availability of SAP BusinessObjects Explorer on all type of mobile devices are other topics of the current planning.

14.6 Semantic Layer

With SAP BusinessObjects 4.0, the team delivered the first version of the semantic layer, which allows customers to combine multiple sources into a single logical view. As part of the planning for the future version, the team is seeking to enhance these capabilities and allow a combination of relational data with multidimensional data as well as to combine data from an on-premise source with data from an on-demand source. In addition, the team is looking to increase the SDK so that the semantic layer can be embedded into any application. The team is also looking into opportunities to provide capabilities such as changing object names or setting up your own class and subclass structure on top of the direct connectivity to SAP NetWeaver BW.

14.7 Summary

This chapter provided you with a brief overview of the key products and the areas in which the teams are planning to invest for future versions of the SAP BusinessObjects BI platform.

The Author

Ingo Hilgefort started with Crystal Decisions in Frankfurt, Germany, in 1999 as a trainer and consultant for Crystal Reports and Crystal Enterprise. In 2001, he became the program manager of a small team working in Walldorf at SAP's headquarters for Crystal Decisions. During this time, Ingo worked closely with the SAP NetWeaver BW development group and helped to design and shape the first integration of Crystal Reports with SAP NetWeaver BW, which then became an original equipment manufacturer (OEM) relationship between SAP and Crystal Decisions. With the acquisition of Crystal Decisions by BusinessObjects, he then moved into product management for the integration between BusinessObjects and SAP.

In addition to his experience in product management and engineering, Ingo has been involved in building and delivering BusinessObjects with SAP software for a number of worldwide customers. He has also been recognized by the SDN and BusinessObjects communities as an SAP Mentor for BusinessObjects and SAP integration-related topics. Recently, Ingo has been working on BI end-to-end solution architecture, focusing on the SAP BusinessObjects BI portfolio and helping customers and partners successfully deploy this as part of their overall SAP landscape.

He is also the author of several additional SAP PRESS books: *Integrating SAP BusinessObjects BI Platform 4.x with SAP NetWeaver*, *Inside SAP BusinessObjects Explorer*, and *Inside SAP BusinessObjects Advanced Analysis*.

Index

A

Aggregate, 479
Aggregation, 479
Alerting, 492
Alerts, 44
Analysis, 41, 301, 302, 492
Analytics, 45
Appearance, 248, 249
Application, 355, 376
Attribute
  display, 59, 61, 121, 124, 184, 187, 188, 253, 255, 299, 302, 341, 343
  navigational, 59, 62, 121, 124, 184, 187, 188, 253, 255, 299, 302, 341
Auditing, 481
Authentication, 72, 73, 90, 355, 376, 429
  method, 449
  mode, 350
  type, 76
authentication.default, 451
authentication.visible, 451
Authorization, 60, 122, 185, 254, 300, 342
  BI, 478
  variable, 473

B

Behavior, 216, 222, 245, 247, 248, 249
Best practices, 469
BEx Analyzer, 251, 297, 488
BEx query, 52, 61, 120, 123, 183, 186, 187, 252, 255, 298, 299, 301, 340, 341, 343, 476
BI, 19, 26
BI Consumer Services → BICS
BI launch pad, 449, 455
  documents, 453
  folders and categories, 455
  SAP authentication, 450
  search, 456
  user interface, 452
  user preferences, 462
BI Launchpad.properties, 451

BI Web Services, 182
BICS, 52, 58, 120, 186, 187, 251, 255, 301, 343
Break, 151
Business analyst, 46
Business intelligence → BI
Business layer, 353, 370
Business requirement, 31, 33, 35, 36, 37, 42, 46, 63, 64, 65, 189, 256, 258, 344, 345, 346, 469, 470
BW MDX, 482
BW query, 58, 120, 183, 252, 298, 340

C

Calculation, 34, 63, 189, 345
  local, 184, 253, 299, 341
Can Grow, 89
Canvas, 194, 195
Category, 194, 455, 456
Central Management Console → CMC
Characteristic, 52, 58, 61, 120, 121, 123, 183, 186, 187, 252, 255, 298, 301, 341, 471, 472, 473
  compounded, 59, 121, 184, 253, 299, 341
  free, 58, 121, 183, 252, 299, 341, 472
  value, 52
Charts, 212
Client, 72
CMC, 71, 457
Common, 246, 247
Component, 194, 211, 248
Condition, 52, 59, 121, 184, 253, 299, 341, 343, 472
Conditional formatting, 52, 81
Connectivity, 251, 297
Constant selection, 59, 121, 184, 253, 299, 341
Content type, 460
Crawling frequency, 459
Crosstab, 88
Currency, 58, 488
Custom exit, 60, 122, 185, 254, 300, 342

Index

D

Dashboard, 200, 492
Dashboard Manager, 421
Dashboarding, 39, 181
Data
   connectivity, 181, 256, 302, 339
   exploration, 339
   foundation, 351, 353, 369, 370
   panel, 138
   retrieval, 480
   source, relational, 353, 370
   type, 59, 122, 184, 253, 300, 342
Database field, 69
Date formatting, 488
Default theme, 195
Default value, 60, 122, 185, 254, 300, 342, 472
Desktop, 131
Destination, 212, 229
Detail object, 137
Dimension, 52
Direct access, 251
Display setting, 473
Distribution, 35, 190, 257, 303
Document Explorer, 425
Document preferences, 195
Drill down, 154, 216, 217, 218, 221, 433, 434
DSO objects, 339
Dynamic visibility, 216, 222

E

Embedded spreadsheet, 198
Enterprise reporting, 20, 57
ERP, 181
Excel options, 196
Exception, 52, 59, 121, 184, 253, 299, 341, 472
Exit, 60, 122, 254, 300
EXIT variable, 473
Exploration, 27
Explorer, 492

F

Field Explorer, 69
Filter, 59, 61, 121, 141, 154, 166, 184, 253, 299, 341, 472, 480, 482
Filter by Measure, 52
Financial reporting, 87
Fixed label size, 246, 247, 248
Fold, 166
Folders, 455
Format, 176
Formatted layout, 37
Formatted value, 488
Formula, 34, 58, 63, 121, 184, 189, 253, 299, 341, 345
   field, 69
   workshop, 85
Formula Editor, 165
Free form layout, 39

G

General, 223, 229, 234, 245, 246, 247
Grid preferences, 195
Group, 78
   footer, 81
Grouping, 78
Guided navigation, 26, 40

H

Hierarchical awareness, 39
Hierarchy, 34, 39, 58, 61, 121, 123, 125, 183, 186, 187, 189, 252, 255, 299, 301, 341, 343, 345, 477, 481, 488
   node variable, 39, 482
   variable, 39, 481
   version variable, 482
Highlighting, 86
Horizontal slider, 248

I

Increment, 248, 249
Index, 479
InfoCube, 58, 120, 183, 252, 298, 340

InfoProvider, 350, 352, 369, 470, 477
  transient, 62
Information Design Tool, 51, 52, 101
Information space, 355, 357, 375, 376
InfoSets, 478
InfoView, 128, 157, 172
Input control, 138
Insertion type, 218, 221, 229, 434
Interactive, 131
Interoperability, 39

K

Key date, 60, 122, 179, 185, 254, 300, 342
  variable, 482
Key figure, 52, 61, 122, 123, 186, 187, 255, 301, 471, 473
  calculated, 58, 61, 121, 123, 184, 186, 188, 253, 255, 299, 301, 341, 343, 476, 477, 481
  restricted, 58, 61, 121, 123, 184, 186, 188, 253, 255, 299, 301, 341, 476, 477, 481
Key performance indicator (KPI), 36, 37, 45, 65, 127, 258, 304, 347

L

Label, 229
Language, 72
Limitation, 469, 481
Local calculation, 121
logontoken.enabled, 451

M

Manage Spaces, 355, 376
Map, 138
MDXTEST, 489
Measure, 52
Member, 52
Metadata, 476
Metrics, 45
Microsoft Excel, 28, 385, 403, 421
Microsoft Office, 34, 345
Microsoft Outlook, 28
Microsoft PowerPoint, 28, 422
Microsoft Word, 28, 422
Module Library, 422, 441
Multiple structures, 58, 121, 184, 253, 299, 341
MultiProvider, 58, 120, 183, 252, 298, 340, 368
Multisource, 477
Multi-source enabled, 351, 370

N

Number format, 248, 249
Number formatting, 488

O

Object, 357, 376
Object browser, 194, 214, 216, 217, 218, 221
Offline, 35, 190, 257, 303, 346, 478
Offline dashboards, 492
OLAP, 26
  connection, 71, 76, 90, 428
  universe, 128

P

Page footer, 67
Page header, 67
Parameter, 100, 482
  field, 69
Parameter mapping, 444
Parameterized layout, 38
Performance, 469, 479
Personalization, 60, 122, 185, 254, 300, 342
Pioneer → SAP BusinessObjects Advanced Analysis
Precalculated value set, 60, 122, 185
Preferences, 129, 195
Preferred viewing locale (PVL), 464, 488
Prompt, 52
Properties, 194
Provider, 72
Publication, 478

Q

Query, 52, 470
 filter, 136
 panel, 403

R

Relational access, 182
Relative position, 165
Replacement path, 60, 122, 185, 254, 300, 342
Report design, 488
Report footer, 67
Report header, 67
Reporting, 41
Requirement, 302, 304
Restriction, 472
Result object, 135, 138, 158, 172
RSRT, 489
RSTT, 489
Run query, 138, 159
Running total field, 69

S

SAP authentication, 129, 157, 172
SAP BusinessObjects, 74, 186, 251
SAP BusinessObjects Advanced Analysis, 26, 42, 64, 65, 256, 473
SAP BusinessObjects Analysis, 251, 255, 256, 257, 297
SAP BusinessObjects Analysis, edition for Microsoft Office, 255, 256, 302
SAP BusinessObjects Analysis, edition for OLAP, 421, 464
SAP BusinessObjects Dashboards, 22, 64, 65, 126, 181, 186, 187, 224, 257, 344, 421, 442, 481, 485
 color schemes, 200
 data connectivity, 181, 201
 embedded spreadsheet, 198
 Live office compatibility, 196
 templates, 199
 themes, 200
SAP BusinessObjects Dashboards SDK, 22

SAP BusinessObjects Explorer, 27, 39, 46, 339, 340, 344, 347, 368
SAP BusinessObjects Live Office, 24, 28, 182, 196, 345, 385, 387, 389, 404, 470
 add/remove fields, 395
 appearance, 390
 authentication, 387
 choose Excel data range, 401
 column Heading, 390
 conceal data, 402
 copy and pace with connectivity, 389
 default Cell Values, 390
 filter Settings, 395
 modify objects, 395
 new query, 403
 prompt values, 401
 prompts, 399
 properties, 395
 properties for all objects, 402
 publish to SAP BusinessObjects, 398
 refresh, 389, 399, 402
 SAP authentication, 391, 410
 SAP BusinessObjects Web Intelligence content, 398
 switch to fields, 393, 412
 use specific logon criteria, 386
SAP BusinessObjects Live Office Live Office compatibility, 196
SAP BusinessObjects Web Intelligence, 24, 25, 27, 39, 42, 46, 119, 124, 129, 132, 154, 157, 172, 182, 190, 257, 344, 387, 421, 438, 442, 464, 469, 473, 479, 481, 484, 492
 query panel, 135, 141
SAP BusinessObjects Web intelligence, 64, 65
SAP Crystal Reports, 20, 24, 42, 57, 64, 101, 124, 127, 190, 192, 344, 387, 391, 411, 421, 456, 469, 473, 479, 482
 data connectivity, 57
SAP Crystal Reports 2011, 183
SAP Crystal Reports for Enterprise, 61, 442, 456, 491
SAP ERP, 57, 102
SAP exit, 60, 122, 185, 254, 300, 342
SAP HANA, 27, 251, 252, 297, 298, 339, 340, 344, 487, 492

SAP NetWeaver BW, 57, 182, 340, 343, 351, 355, 370, 375
SAP NetWeaver BW Accelerator, 347
SAP NetWeaver demo model, 202
Save Language, 72
Scaling, 59, 121, 184, 253, 299, 341
Scenarios, 44
Scorecarding, 492
Searching, 339
Section, 151, 166
Section Expert, 80, 83
Security, 469, 478
Security Definition Editor, 478
Selection, 58, 121, 184, 253, 299, 341, 480
Selector, 211
Self-service, 24, 39
Semantic layer, 51, 52, 124, 477, 493
Server, 72
    context, 75
    name, 75
    port number, 75
    type, 72
Show object name, 164
Sizing, 481
Skill level, 469
Source data, 212, 229
SSO, 73, 76, 90, 129, 157, 172, 429
Structure, 34, 58, 62, 121, 124, 184, 187, 188, 253, 256, 299, 302, 341, 345, 472, 476, 477, 482
Summary, 151
System, 72
    display name, 75
    number, 72

T

Tab set, 228, 229
Text variables, 473
Time dependency, 345
Time dependent, 34, 36, 101

Tracing, 488
Tracking, 178
Transient provider, 251
Trend, 379
Troubleshooting, 488

U

Unfold, 166
Unit, 58
Universe, 51, 119, 124, 182, 339, 340, 355, 375, 376, 387, 403, 404, 460, 477
    dimensional, 51
    multisource, 52
    relational, 51, 58, 120, 339, 343
Universe Designer, 51
User
    input, 60, 122, 185, 254, 300, 342
    name, 76
    type, 42, 46

V

Value set
    precalculated, 254, 300, 342
Variable, 52, 60, 62, 122, 124, 185, 187, 188, 254, 256, 300, 302, 342, 343, 473, 477, 482, 484, 485, 486, 488
Variable editor, 159
Visualization, 39, 65, 181, 193

W

Web ActiveX, 467
Web Application Designer, 492
What-if analysis, 35, 64, 126, 257, 303, 346
Workspace, 421, 427, 440, 446

X

Xcelsius → SAP BusinessObjects Dashboards

www.sap-press.com

Provides step-by-step content for using the SAP Query Tool

Covers relevant content for all ERP components (SD, MM, PP, FI, CO, etc.)

Includes 100 ready-to-use Queries

Stephan Kaleske

SAP Query Reporting–Practical Guide

If you need to know how to deploy the SAP Query tool to create reports and extend the standard reporting capabilities of an ERP system, this book is for you. Through the use of many concrete, practical examples and solutions, you learn the main features of the SAP Query tool, including drill-down functionality, rankings, statistics, traffic symbols, calculated fields of information, and MS Office integration.

402 pp., 2011, 69,95 Euro / US$ 69.95
ISBN 978-1-59229-365-0

>> www.sap-press.com

www.sap-press.com

Learn how to create effective reports for specific enterprise reporting needs using NetWeaver BW 7

Build composite reports using multiple BEx tools with ease including report designer, Web analyzer, Excel analyzer, and Web application designer

Discover a plethora of hidden reporting functionality not available anywhere else

Jason Kraft

SAP NetWeaver BW 7.x Reporting–Practical Guide

This book provides a detailed, how-to guide for anyone using NetWeaver BW and the BEx tools to generate reports. It will teach how to design effective, good looking reports that meet business objectives and provide an up-to-date resource covering the latest version of NetWeaver BW 7.0.

359 pp., 2011, 79,95 Euro / US$ 79.95
ISBN 978-1-59229-357-5

>> www.sap-press.com

www.sap-press.com

Explains how to use all of the features in Xcelsius

Teaches you how to build and customize interactive dashboards to effectively visualize your key business data

Provides guidance on using Xcelsius in an SAP environment

Ray Li, Evan DeLodder

Creating Dashboards with Xcelsius–Practical Guide

Learn how to build your own Xcelsius dashboards, with this practical book. It explains how to use Xcelsius in an end-to-end, linear "common usage" manner, while highlighting typical scenarios where each feature can be used to solve business problems. It also gives you detailed, step-by-step guidance and best-practices for each feature, along with hands-on exercises that will help you begin creating dashboards and visualizations quickly. And if you're more advanced, you'll learn how to customize the Xcelsius components, themes, and data connections so you can use Xcelsius to the fullest extent.

587 pp., 2010, 49,95 Euro / US$ 49.95
ISBN 978-1-59229-335-3

>> www.sap-press.com

www.sap-press.com

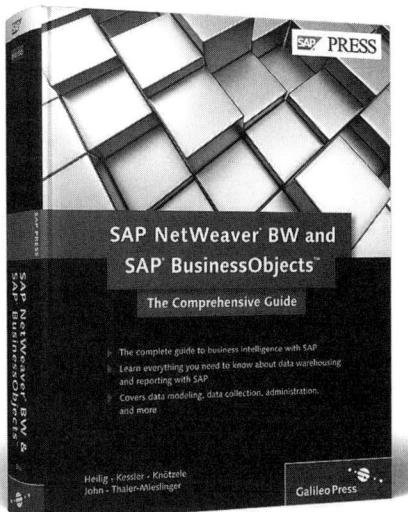

The complete guide to business intelligence with SAP

Learn everything you need to know about data warehousing and reporting with SAP

Covers data modeling, data collection, administration, and more

Loren Heilig, Torsten Kessler, Peter John, Thilo Knötzele, Karin Thaler-Mieslinger

SAP NetWeaver BW and SAP BusinessObjects

The Comprehensive Guide

Finally—the entire SAP BI world comes in one volume! This comprehensive guide provides essential knowledge for a full staff of data warehousing/business intelligence SAP consultants, IT teams, DB managers, and end-users to efficiently work together. You will learn everything you need to know about SAP NetWeaver BW and BI, backend BW issues, end user intelligence tools, planning and consolidation tools from SAP, and more.

795 pp., 2012, 79,95 Euro / US$ 79.95
ISBN 978-1-59229-384-1

>> www.sap-press.com

www.sap-press.com

Learn to easily navigate the SAP system

Work with SAP modules step-by-step

Includes many examples and detailed SAP illustrations

Olaf Schulz

Using SAP:
A Guide for Beginners and End Users

This book helps end users and beginners get started in SAP ERP and provides readers with the basic knowledge they need for their daily work. Readers will get to know the essentials of working with the SAP system, learn about the SAP systems' structures and functions, and discover how SAP connects to critical business processes. Whether this book is used as an exercise book or as a reference book, readers will find what they need to help them become more comfortable with SAP ERP.

388 pp., 39,95 Euro / US$ 39.95
ISBN 978-1-59229-408-4

>> www.sap-press.com

Interested in reading more?

Please visit our website for all
new book releases from SAP PRESS.

www.sap-press.com